Celebrating the Seasons

ROBERT ATWELL is an Anglican priest working in the Diocese of London. After six years as Chaplain of Trinity College, Cambridge, where he taught Patristics, he became a monk, spending the next ten years in a Benedictine monastery in the Cotswolds.

This selection of readings of ancient, medieval and reformed (and occasionally, contemporary) spirituality reflects both his scholarly background and many years of prayerful reflection on the Christian tradition.

He is currently Vicar of St Mary's, Primrose Hill, in north London.

Celebrating the Seasons

Daily
Spiritual Readings
for the
Christian Year

compiled and introduced by
Robert Atwell

MOREHOUSE PUBLISHING
Harrisburg, Pennsylvania

Morehouse Publishing
P.O. Box 1321
Harrisburg, PA 17105

Morehouse Publishing is a division of The Morehouse Group.

First published in 1999 by The Canterbury Press Norwich (a publishing imprint of Hymns ancient & Modern Limited, a registered charity), St. Mary's Works, St. Mary's Plain, Norwich, Norfolk, NR3 3BH U.K.

Robert Atwell has asserted his right under the Copyright, Designs, and Patents Act, 1988 (U.K.), to be identified as the Author of this Work.

Cover design by Corey Kent.

Library of Congress Cataloging-in-Publication Data
Celebrating the seasons : daily spiritual readings for the Christian year / compiled and introduced by Robert Atwell.
    p. cm.
Includes bibliographical references and indexes.
ISBN 0-8192-1847-2
      1. Church year meditations. 2. Devotional calendars—Church of England. I. Atwell, Robert

BV30. C44 2001
242'.3-dc21

00-046468

Printed in the United States
01 02 03 04 05   10 9 8 7 6 5 4 3 2 1

CONTENTS

Author's Notes

Sources of extracts, translations and notes are listed at the end of the book, together with biographical sketches of authors. To keep extracts within reasonable limits whilst maintaining their sense, sentences or paragraphs have sometimes been omitted or transposed. Occasionally these omissions are noted by dots, but normally the text has been left free of marks so as not to distract the reader. Any abridgement, paraphrase or alteration of a text is recorded in the notes.

Important days in the Calendar are supplied with a choice of readings, usually chosen to reflect the spectrum of Patristic, Medieval, Reformation (and occasionally contemporary) spirituality.

The vast majority of extracts do not exceed 500 words. Where a longer extract is reproduced, square brackets indicate sections which may be omitted if, for example, reading in church necessitates shortening the extract.

INTRODUCTION

Human life, like the dawning of each new day, is rhythmic. Our bodies have their own cycles and rhythms, oscillating between activity and sleep, in concert with the alternation between light and darkness in the world about us. In relation to these changes we construct the patterns of our personal and corporate existence, our days and our weeks, our terms and our vacations, our times of work and our periods of relaxation and rest. Women in particular are sensitive to these movements because of the biological rhythms and changes that govern their bodies. Much of contemporary living, however, at least in the West, has tended to obscure the fundamental patterns of our existence. Electric light mitigates our dependence on daylight. Urban living masks the seasonal fluctuations which so dominate the outlook and priorities of those whose lives depend on an agricultural economy. The abundance of produce on our supermarket shelves throughout the twelve months of the year testifies to our immunity from the vicissitudes of seedtime and harvest.

But the high standards of living we take for granted are paid for at a price – and not simply in the potential exploitation of poorer nations to supply and maintain our affluence. In the shadow of our material security we are in danger of becoming desensitized to the changes and rhythms of the environment that sustains us. And in the wake of our insatiable need for material security we can find ourselves out of touch with ourselves, driven by psychological forces that, if unchecked, do violence to our bodies and their legitimate needs. In short we become ill, both as persons and nations. We talk casually about the 'absence of God' in our lives, but God is God, and therefore, by definition, always present. It is we who are not sufficiently at home in our bodies to receive him.

Attending to ourselves as created beings and our place in creation is part of what it means to be human: it is fundamental to what it means to be Christian. Abundant living is both God's will and his gift to us. But abundance goes hand in hand with *ascesis*: the vine must be pruned if it is to fruit productively. Personal discipline is not an optional extra for the pious few, but integral to the Christian enterprise, and if it is not to degenerate into negative self-punishment, must accord with the natural movements and rhythms of our souls and bodies and world, implanted as they are by God.

Celebrating the Seasons

It is against this backcloth that the Church's liturgical year with its various seasons and festivals finds its place. Beginning afresh each year on Advent Sunday, the Church has crafted a rhythm of prayer and worship that continues to shape much of Christian life and thought. In the Book of Proverbs is the grave warning: 'Cursed be he who removes the ancient landmark which your ancestors set up' (Proverbs 22:28). To some the Church's festivals and fast-days are anachronisms, echoes of an antique drum we no longer follow; but to others they constitute ancient and trusted landmarks on a spiritual landscape by which Christians have plotted their course and focused their prayerful attention, and which – like other rhythms in our lives – we do well to heed.

Over the centuries, the Church's seasons (*temporale*) have coalesced into two liturgical cycles celebrating respectively the incarnation (Advent to Candlemas), and the crucifixion and resurrection (Ash Wednesday to Pentecost). This seasonal framework is peppered throughout with saints' days (*sanctorale*) which provide opportunities to reflect upon the faithful discipleship of fellow Christians down the ages, giving names and faces to the otherwise faceless 'cloud of witnesses' that surrounds us. Historically, with the exception of Easter, this latter form of personal commemoration antedated the development of the Christian Year as we know it today. But taken together, the two liturgical forms create a counterpoint which excites the Christian imagination, enabling people to meditate systematically and profoundly upon the truth at the heart of the gospel that 'God was in Christ reconciling the world to himself'.

Non-Scriptural Readings

Like its companion volume *Celebrating the Saints,* this anthology of non-Scriptural readings from the Christian Tradition is geared to the movement of the Christian Year. The custom of including non-Scriptural readings in the public worship of the Church has become increasingly common in recent years. Funerals, memorial services, weddings, eucharists on saints' days, family services and State occasions have all witnessed the change. Some Christians find this development problematic, either because it appears to threaten the supremacy of Scripture, or because it fits uncomfortably with received norms about the shape and context of the liturgy. Certainly, readings which incline to the banal or sentimental should be eschewed as unworthy of Chritian worship. But as this anthology of readings seeks to demonstrate the Christian Tradition can yield a wealth and depth of spirituality which is both profound *and* accessible.

Ironically, the custom of reading non-Scriptural texts in the worship of the Church is not the innovation it appears, and is probably monastic in origin. The monastic day was oriented to the praise of God. Life was ordered around the celebration of the Word of God, principally through the recitation of the psalms. It was a way of sanctifying the natural rhythm of the day, and above all, of fulfilling St Paul's admonition to 'pray without ceasing'. The Divine Office (or to give it its proper title 'The Liturgy of the Hours') punctuated the day with prayer, impregnating the mind and heart with the Word of God.

Unlike the offices celebrated during the daytime when short Biblical readings were preferred (ideally so that they could be readily committed to memory) the office of Vigils, which was celebrated normally just before dawn, provided for whole books of the Bible to be read consecutively over a period of time, the so-called *lectio continuans*. It was this custom that Cranmer adopted for his offices of Morning and Evening Prayer in *The Book of Common Prayer*. Reclaiming the centrality of the Scriptures in the life and worship of the Church was of prime importance to the Reformers. In monastic custom, however, the Scriptural reading at Vigils was supplemented by a non-Biblical lection. In the words of St Benedict's *Rule*: 'In addition to the inspired books of the Old and New Testaments, the works read at Vigils should include explanations of Scripture by reputable and orthodox writers.' The reading of commentaries (presumably on what had just been read) enabled the monk not only to engage with Scripture more intelligently, but also to place his personal meditation within the context of those of other Christians from different ages and traditions. It was this broader perspective, this sense of conversation, that was lost at the Reformation, but which in recent liturgical change is once again being explored right across the Christian spectrum.

Reading and Interpreting Scripture

We tend to assume (rather naively) that although our world-view may be different, fundamentally our Christian forebears approached and interpreted the Scriptures in the same way that we do. As this anthology of readings reveals, this is not the case. In the early Church, for example, it was assumed that sacred Scripture, far from being transparently clear, had different layers of meaning. There was the literal, obvious meaning, but there was also a hidden meaning. The invitation of God was to go deeper, to search for this hidden treasure. The task of the exegete was to unlock these hidden meanings. In this quest, our forbears were fascinated by the mystical significance of numbers, by typology and symbolism, by the use of allegory. These were tools with which to uncover the truth. Indeed, the Greek word for truth (*alitheia*) means literally that which is no longer hidden, that which is uncovered, exposed to view. Truth, for them, was not exclusively or even primarily an intellectual exercise: it was an event which liberated the heart. In the words of the Psalmist: 'You that desire truth in the inward parts: O teach me truth in the secret places of the heart' (Psalm 51:6).

Since all parts of Scripture were deemed to be uniformly authoritative, ancient commentators did not hesitate to lift verses and phrases out of their literary and historical contexts, and apply them elsewhere as a means of illuminating a difficult text – sometimes with bizarre results. Such critical procedures may be alien to the modern mind, but within their own terms of reference, these were valid theological enterprises. Indeed, they challenge some of our own exegetical methods which may be 'accurate' but which do not exactly lead to the liberation of the heart.

Listening with the ear of the heart

Probably the most significant change in the way Christians have approached the Scriptures occurred during the fifteenth and sixteenth centuries. Promoted by the explosion of cheaply available literature following the invention of printing, and reflecting the new taste for privacy (seen typically, for example, in the introduction of bedrooms and corridors in English country houses) there evolved the custom of silent reading. When earlier generations talked about 'reading' the Bible what they really meant was *listening*. All literature (as far as we know) was read aloud –

not necessarily loudly, but nevertheless declaimed. Reading as we know it – the silent scanning of the printed page – appears to have been unknown.

This explains, for example, the somewhat cryptic remark of St Benedict to his monks that during their siesta, when resting on their beds in the dormitory, they could read 'provided they did not disturb the others'. It also explains why patristic and medieval commentators on Scripture display such interest in the sounds of words, and in the literary devices of rhythm, rhyme, alliteration and assonance. Their interpretation of Scripture honoured the dignity of the spoken word more than our generation does. They related to its performative value, what it actually felt like as it was articulated in the mouth, spoken with the tongue, and heard with the ear. They would repeat the words of the sacred text with their lips again and again so that the body and not just the mind entered into the process. They sought to cultivate their capacity to listen to the Word of God at ever deeper levels of inward attention. They borrowed from the vocabulary of digestion to describe this process of ingesting Scripture, using such expressive terms as *ruminatio* and *mundicare,* the verb to chew the cud. This ancient language still survives today in the collect for Bible Sunday, the Last Sunday after Trinity:

> Blessed Lord, who caused all holy Scriptures
>   to be written for our learning:
> help us so to hear them,
> to read, mark, learn and inwardly digest them
> that, through patience, and the comfort of your holy word,
> we may embrace and for ever hold fast
>   the hope of everlasting life,
> which you have given us in our Saviour Jesus Christ.

Our forebears' belief that the slow digestive process of cows was well-suited to describe the process of engaging with Scripture, stands in marked contrast to the language and expectations of a fast-food generation. Their wisdom calls us to a more gentle rhythm of prayerful reading in which patience, silence and receptivity are vital ingredients. In a world of sound-bites we need to learn again the art of listening with the ear of the heart. To this end when we are praying by ourselves, reading the Bible or saying the Office alone, perhaps we should experiment with the custom of earlier generations and speak the words out loud? Whatever personal *ascesis* we evolve it should be one that engages all of us:

mind, heart, imagination and body. This assembly of non-Scriptural readings is offered to that end. As well as making accessible valued and contrasting commentaries on the Christian Way, it also reaches towards the recovery of a more balanced and integrated pattern of personal and corporate devotion.

Using this volume

In constructing this anthology of 'reputable and orthodox writers' it has not been possible (sadly) to pursue the monastic ideal of matching a reading from Scripture with an appropriate commentary from the Christian Tradition. The plethora of lectionaries and three-yearly cycles of readings makes this project unfeasible. Instead this selection has been organised thematically in close association with the movement of the Church's Year beginning with Advent Sunday. Each liturgical section also includes a brief note about the season and the material that follows. A comprehensive index is provided at the back of the book. Like *Celebrating the Saints,* its companion volume, the literature included in this anthology spans two thousand years. It contains extracts from sermons, hymns, theological treatises, Biblical commentaries, letters, prayers and poems. It constitutes a rich treasury worthy of study and reflection.

Not being tied to any one Scriptural text has the advantage that the readings chosen here may be read in conjunction with either Morning or Evening Prayer, or with the eucharistic lectionary. They may be read publicly in church or used privately for personal devotion. Although drawn from various centuries and across the spectrum of Eastern and Western spirituality, the writings of the early Fathers will be found to enjoy a special prominence, partly because translations of their works are not as available to the general public as contemporary Christian writers and they deserve a wider public, and partly because they antedate the various schisms that have dismembered the Body of Christ, and therefore occupy an honoured place in the mind of the Church.

Our Christian forebears emerge from this assembly of texts as a vibrant company of voices which both affirm and challenge us. Recognizing resonances in their voices, coming as they do from different traditions, cultures and ages, is exciting. They root our discipleship, and give us fresh hope and energy in our current cultural and ecclesiastical fragmentation.

Robert Atwell

We begin our ecclesiastical year with the glorious annunciation of his birth by angelical embassage. There being hereunto added his blessed nativity itself, the mystery of his legal circumcision, the testification of his true incarnation by the purification of her which brought him into the world, his resurrection, his ascension into heaven, the admirable sending down of his Spirit upon his chosen, and (which consequently ensued) the notice of that incomprehensible Trinity thereby given to the Church of God; again forasmuch as we know that Christ hath not only been manifested great in himself, but great in other of his saints also, the days of whose departure out of the world are to the Church of Christ as the birth and coronation days of kings and emperors, therefore especial choice being made of the very flower of all occasions in this kind, there are annual selected times to meditate of Christ glorified in them which had the honour to suffer for his sake, before they had age and ability to know him; glorified in them which knowing him as Stephen had the sight of that before death whereinto so acceptable death did lead; glorified in those sages of the East that came from far to adore him and were conducted by strange light; glorified in the second Elias of the world sent before him to prepare his way; glorified in every of those apostles whom it pleased him to use as founders of his kingdom here; glorified in the angels as in Michael; glorified in all those happy souls that are already possessed of heaven.

Richard Hooker
The Laws of Ecclesiastical Polity

ADVENT

If we wish to escape the punishment of hell and reach
eternal life, then while there is still time, while we are in
this body and can accomplish these things by the light of
life, let us hasten to do now what will profit us for eternity.

Benedict of Nursia

The season of **Advent** is above all a time of watching and waiting for the coming of the kingdom of God in power. It shares with Lent a certain spirit of restraint, preparation and penitence, but it is one shot through with confident joy as Christmas approaches. The readings reflect this dual aspect. In the early part of Advent they focus upon the coming of Christ as Judge at the Last Day. As the season progresses, the readings in company with the lectionary look towards the birth of the promised Messiah, and reflect upon the unique roles played by John the Baptist, the Lord's forerunner, and of Mary, the Mother of Jesus, in the plan of salvation.

This change in gear is most obvious around 17 December. By ancient custom the **eight days before Christmas** are observed as a time of special preparation and vigil. Proper readings for these days are provided. With the exception of the reading set for the **Fourth Sunday of Advent** which should always be preferred, these readings take precedence over those provided for the third week of Advent.

The cryptic phrase *O Sapientia* which appears in the calendar of *The Book of Common Prayer* underscores this liturgical shift. The phrase refers to the custom at Evensong during the final days of Advent, for the *Magnificat* (The Song of Mary) to have a special antiphon or refrain attached to it, the so-called 'Great O' Antiphons. These proclaim the ascriptions or 'names' given to God in the Old Testament. Each name develops into a prophecy of the forthcoming and eagerly anticipated Messiah, Jesus, the Son of God. The Biblical readings both at the Eucharist and at the Office, and those offered here, resonate with these ancient refrains which have therefore been printed here in full as a further stimulus to reflection.

Note In the old Sarum rite, the 'Great O' Antiphons were sung one day earlier beginning on 16 December, requiring an additional ascription for 23 December, this being *O Virgin of Virgins.* However, since this was clearly apposite to the Blessed Virgin Mary and not a title of God, this liturgical custom was not adopted much beyond Sarum and, with the revision of the Calendar, the Church of England has adopted the more widely-used formulae and dating.

Advent Sunday

A Reading from the *Catechetical Lectures*
of Cyril of Jerusalem

We do not preach only one coming of Christ, but a second as well, much more glorious than the first. The first coming was marked by patience; the second will bring the crown of a divine kingdom.

In general, what relates to our Lord Jesus Christ has two aspects. There is a birth from God before the ages, and a birth from a virgin at the fullness of time. There is a hidden coming, like that of rain on fleece, and a coming before all eyes, still in the future.

At the first coming he was wrapped in swaddling clothes in a manger. At his second coming he will be clothed in light as in a garment. In the first coming he endured the cross, despising the shame; in the second coming he will be in glory, escorted by an army of angels. We look then beyond the first coming and await the second. At the first coming we said: 'Blessed is he who comes in the name of the Lord.' At the second we shall say it again; we shall go out with the angels to meet the Lord and cry out in adoration: 'Blessed is he who comes in the name of the Lord.'

The Saviour will not come to be judged again, but to judge those by whom he was judged. At his own judgement he was silent; then he will address those who committed the outrages against him when they crucified him and will remind them: 'You did these things, and I was silent.'

His first coming was to fulfil his plan of love, to teach us by gentle persuasion. This time, whether we like it or not, we will be subjects of his kingdom by necessity. Malachi the prophet speaks of the two comings. 'And the Lord whom you seek will come suddenly to his temple': that is one coming.

Again he says of another coming: 'Look, the Lord almighty will come, and who can endure the day of his coming, or who will stand in his sight? Because he comes like a refiner's fire, a fuller's soap, and he will sit refining and cleansing.'

These two comings are also referred to by Paul in writing to Titus: 'The grace of God the Saviour has appeared to all humanity, instructing us to put aside impiety and worldly desires and live temperately, uprightly, and religiously in this present age, waiting for the joyful hope, the appearance of the glory of our great God and Saviour, Jesus Christ.' Notice how he speaks of a first coming for which he gives thanks, and a second, the one we still await.

That is why the faith we profess has been handed on to you in these words: 'He ascended into heaven, and is seated at the right hand of the Father, and he will come again in glory to judge the living and the dead, and his kingdom will have no end.'

Our Lord Jesus Christ will therefore come from heaven. He will come at the end of the world, in glory, at the last day. For there will be an end to this world, and the created world will be made new.

alternative reading

A Reading from a sermon of Bernard of Clairvaux

We have come to understand a threefold coming of the Lord. The third coming lies between the other two. Two of the comings are clearly visible, but the third is not. In the first coming the Lord was seen on earth, dwelling among us; and as he himself testified, they saw him and hated him. In his final coming 'all flesh shall see the salvation of our God,' and 'they will look on him whom they pierced.' The intermediate coming is hidden, in which only his chosen recognise his presence within themselves and their souls are saved. In his first coming our Lord came in our flesh and in our weakness; in the intermediate coming he comes in spirit and in power; in his final coming, he will be seen in glory and majesty.

This intermediate coming is like a road on which we travel from his first coming to his last. In the first, Christ was our redemption; in the last, he will appear as our life; in his intermediate coming, he is our comfort and our rest.

Lest anyone should think that what we are saying about this intermediate coming is our own fancy, listen to what our Lord himself says in the gospel: 'If any love me, they will keep my word, and my Father will love them, and we will come to them and make our home with them.' There is also another passage in Scripture which reads: 'Those who fear the Lord will do good.' But something more is said about those who love God, and that is that they will keep God's word. And where are his words to be kept if not in our heart? As the prophet says: 'I have kept your words in my heart lest I sin against you.'

Think of the word of God in the way you think of your food. When bread is kept in a bin, a thief can steal it, or a mouse can find its way in and gnaw it, and eventually, of course, it goes mouldy. Once you have eaten your bread, you have nothing to fear from thieves, mice or mould! In the same way, treasure the word of God, for those who keep it are blessed. Feed on it, digest it, allow its goodness to pass into your body so that your affections and whole way of behaviour is nourished and transformed. Do not forget to eat your bread and your heart will not wither. Fill your soul with God's richness and strength.

If you keep the word of God in this way, without doubt it will keep you also. The Son with the Father will come to you. The great prophet who will restore Jerusalem will come to you and make all things new. The effect of his coming will be that just as we have borne the likeness of the earthly, so we shall also bear the likeness of the heavenly. Just as the old Adam used to possess our being and control us, so now let Christ, the second Adam, who created us and redeemed us, take possession of us whole and entire.

alternative reading

A Reading from a poem by Joseph Addison

When rising from the bed of death

When rising from the bed of death,
    O'erwhelmed with guilt and fear,
I see my Maker face to face,
    O how shall I appear?

If yet, while pardon may be found,
    And mercy may be sought,
My heart with inward horror shrinks,
    And trembles at the thought;

When thou, O Lord, shalt stand disclosed
    In majesty severe,
And sit in judgement on my soul,
    O how shall I appear?

But thou hast told the troubled mind,
    Who does her sins lament,
The timely tribute of her tears
    Shall endless woe prevent.

Then see the sorrows of my heart
  Ere yet it be too late;
And hear my Saviour's dying groans,
  To give those sorrows weight.

For never shall my soul despair
  Her pardon to procure,
Who knows thine only Son has died
  To make her pardon sure.

alternative reading

A Reading from a poem by Rowan Williams

Advent Calendar

He will come like last leaf's fall.
One night when the November wind
has flayed the trees to bone, and earth
wakes choking on the mould,
the soft shroud's folding.

He will come like the frost.
One morning when the shrinking earth
opens on mist, to find itself
arrested in the net
of alien, sword-set beauty.

He will come like dark.
One evening when the bursting red
December sun draws up the sheet
and penny-masks its eye to yield
the star-snowed fields of sky.

He will come, will come,
will come like crying in the night,
like blood, like breaking,
as the earth writhes to toss him free.
He will come like child.

Monday after Advent 1

A Reading from *Le Milieu Divin*
by Pierre Teilhard de Chardin

We are sometimes inclined to think that the same things are monotonously repeated over and over again in the history of creation. That is because the season is too long by comparison with the brevity of our individual lives, and the transformation too vast and too inward by comparison with our superficial and restricted outlook, for us to see the progress of what is tirelessly taking place in and through all matter and all spirit. Let us believe in revelation, once again our faithful support in our most human forebodings. Under the commonplace envelope of things and of all our purified and salvaged efforts, a new earth is being slowly engendered.

One day, the gospel tells us, the tension gradually accumulating between humanity and God will touch the limits prescribed by the possibilities of the world. And then will come the end. Then the presence of Christ which has been silently accruing in things, will suddenly be revealed – like a flash of light from pole to pole. Breaking through all the barriers within which the veil of matter and the water-tightness of souls have seemingly kept it confined, it will invade the face of the earth. And, under the finally-liberated action of the true affinities of being, the spiritual atoms of the world will be borne along by a force generated by the powers of cohesion proper to the universe itself, and will occupy, whether within Christ or without Christ (but always under the influence of Christ), the place of happiness or pain designated for them by the living structure of the Pleroma. 'As lightning comes from the East and shines as far as the West ... as the flood came and swept them all away... so will be the coming of the Son of Man.' Like lightning, like a conflagration, like a flood, the attraction exerted by the Son of Man will lay hold of all the whirling elements in the universe so as to reunite them or subject them to his body. 'Wherever the body is, there will the eagles be gathered together.'

Such will be the consummation of the divine *milieu.*

As the gospel warns us, it would be vain to speculate as to the hour and the modalities of this formidable event. But we have to *expect* it.

Expectation – anxious, collective and operative expectation of an end of the world, that is to say of an issue for the world – that is perhaps the supreme Christian function and the most distinctive characteristic of our religion.

Tuesday after Advent 1

A Reading from a sermon of John Henry Newman

Year passes after year, silently; Christ's coming is ever nearer than it was. O that, as he comes nearer earth, we may approach nearer heaven!

O my brethren, pray him to give you the heart to seek him in sincerity. Pray him to make you in earnest. You have one work only, to bear your cross after him. Resolve in his strength to do so. Resolve to be no longer beguiled by 'shadows of religion', by words, or by disputings, or by notions, or by high professions, or by excuses, or by the world's promises or threats. Pray him to give you what Scripture calls 'an honest and good heart', or 'a perfect heart', and, without waiting, begin at once to obey him with the best heart you have. Any obedience is better than none, – any profession which is disjoined from obedience, is a mere pretence and deceit. Any religion which does not bring you nearer to God is of the world. You have to seek his face; obedience is the only way of seeking him. All your duties are obediences.

If you are to believe the truths he has revealed, to regulate yourselves by his precepts, to be frequent in his ordinances, to adhere to his Church and people, why is it, except because *he* has bid you? And to do what he bids is to obey him, and to obey him is to approach him. Every act of obedience is an approach, an approach to him who is not far off; though he seems so, but close behind this visible screen of things which hides him from us. He is behind this material framework; earth and sky are but a veil going between him and us; the day will come when he will rend that veil, and show himself to us. And then, according as we have waited for him, will he recompense us. If we have forgotten him, he will not know us; but 'Blessed are those servants whom the Lord, when he cometh, shall find watching. He shall gird himself, and make them sit down to meat, and will come forth and serve them. And if he shall come in the second watch, or come in the third watch, and find them so, blessed are those servants.' May this be the portion of every one of us! It is hard to attain but it is woeful to fail.

Life is short; death is certain; and the world to come is everlasting.

Wednesday after Advent 1

A Reading from the Letter of Clement of Rome
to the Church in Corinth

We should entreat the Creator of the universe with heartfelt prayer and supplication that the full sum of his elect, as it has been numbered throughout the world, may be preserved intact through his beloved child Jesus Christ. For through him he has called us out of darkness into light, from ignorance into the full knowledge of the glory of his name. .

Teach us, Lord, to hope in that name which is the source and fount of all creation. Open the eyes of our hearts to know you, who alone are highest among the highest, forever holy among the holy. You bring to nothing the schemings of the proud, and frustrate the devices of the nations. You raise up the humble on high, and the lofty you cast down. Riches and poverty, death and life, are all in your hand; you alone are the discerner of every spirit, and the God of all flesh. Your eyes survey the depths and scrutinise our human achievements; you are the aid of those in danger, the Saviour of those that despair, the Creator and guardian of everything that has breath. By you the nations of the earth are increased; and from them you have chosen out such as love you through your dear child Jesus Christ, by whom you have taught us, made us holy and brought us to honour.

Grant us, Lord, we beseech you, your help and protection. Deliver the afflicted, pity the humble, raise up the fallen, reveal yourself to the needy, heal the sick, bring home your wandering people, feed the hungry, ransom the prisoners, support the weak, comfort the faint-hearted. Let all the nations of the earth know that you alone are God, that Jesus Christ is your child, and that we are your people and the sheep of your pasture.

Lord, you brought to light the eternal fabric of the universe, and created the world. From generation to generation you are faithful, righteous in judgement, glorious in might and majesty, wise in what you have created, prudent in what you have established. To look around us is to see your goodness everywhere; to trust in you is to know your loving kindness.

O merciful, O most compassionate, forgive us our sins and offences, our mistakes and our shortcomings. Do not dwell upon the sins of the sons and daughters who serve you, but rather make us clean with the cleansing of your truth. Direct our paths until we walk before you in holiness of heart, and our works are good and pleasing in your sight and in the sight of those who govern us. Yes, Lord, may your face shine upon us for our good; and so shall we be sheltered by your mighty hand, and saved from all wrongdoing by your out-stretched arm. Deliver us from all who hate us without reason; and to us and to all people grant peace and concord, as you did to our forebears when they called devoutly upon you in faith and truth.

Thursday after Advent 1

A Reading from *The Spirit of Love*
by William Law

Nothing wills or works with God but the spirit of love, because nothing else works in God himself. The almighty brought forth all nature for this end only, that boundless love might have its infinity of height and depth to dwell and work in, and all the striving and working properties of nature are only to give essence and substance, life and strength, to the invisible hidden spirit of love, that it may come forth into outward activity and manifest its blessed powers, that creatures born in the strength, and out of the powers of nature, might communicate the spirit of love and goodness, give and receive mutual delight and joy to and from one another.

All below this state of love is a fall from the one life of God, and the only life in which the God of love can dwell. Partiality, self, mine, thine, etc., are tempers that can only belong to creatures that have lost the power, presence, and spirit of the universal Good. They can have no place in heaven, nor can be anywhere, but because heaven is lost. Think not, therefore, that the spirit of pure, universal love which is the one purity and perfection of heaven and all heavenly natures has been or can be carried too high or its absolute necessity too much asserted. For it admits of no degrees of higher or lower, and is not in being till it is absolutely pure and unmixed, no more than a line can be straight till it is absolutely free from all crookedness.

All the design of Christian redemption is to remove everything that is unheavenly, gross, dark, wrathful, and disordered from every part of this fallen world. And when you see earth and stones, storms and tempests, and every kind of evil, misery, and wickedness, you see that which Christ came into the world to remove, and not only to give a new birth to fallen man, but so to deliver all outward nature from its present vanity and evil and set it again in its first heavenly state. Now if you ask how came all things into this evil and vanity, it is because they have lost the blessed spirit of love which alone makes the happiness and perfection of every power of nature.

Friday after Advent 1

A Reading from a commentary on the psalms
by Augustine

'All the trees of the forest will exult before the face of the Lord, for he has come, he has come to judge the earth.' The Lord has come the first time, and he will come again. At his first coming, his own voice declared in the gospel: 'Hereafter you shall see the Son of Man coming upon the clouds.' What does he mean by 'hereafter'? Does he not mean that the Lord will come at a future time when all the nations of the earth will be striking their breasts in grief'? Previously he came through his preachers, and he filled the whole world. Let us not resist his first coming, so that we may not dread the second.

What then should Christians do? We ought to use the world, not become its slaves. And what does this mean? It means having, as though not having. So says the Apostle: 'Beloved, the appointed time is short: from now on let those who have wives live as though they had none; and those who mourn as though they were not mourning; and those who rejoice as though they were not rejoicing; and those who buy as though they had no goods, and those who deal with this world as though they had no dealings with it. For the form of this world is passing away. But I wish you to be without anxiety.' The one who is without anxiety waits without fear until the Lord comes. For what sort of love of Christ is it to fear his coming? Do we not have to blush for shame? We love him, yet we fear his coming. Are we really certain that we love him? Or do we love our sins more? Therefore let us hate our sins and love him who will exact punishment for them. He will come whether we wish it or not. Do not think that because he is not coming just now, he will not come at all. He will come, you know not when; and provided he finds you prepared, your ignorance of the time of his coming will not be held against you.

'He will judge the world with equity and the peoples in his truth.' What are equity and truth? He will gather together with him for the judgement his chosen ones, but the others he will set apart; for he will place some on his right, others on his left. What is more equitable, what more true than that they should not themselves expect mercy from the judge, who themselves were unwilling to show mercy before the judge's coming. Those, however, who were willing to show mercy will be judged with mercy. For it will be said to those placed on his right: 'Come, blessed of my Father, take possession of the kingdom which has been prepared for you from the beginning of the world.' And he reckons to their account their works of mercy: 'I was hungry and you gave me food; I was thirsty and you gave me drink.'

What is imputed to those placed on his left side? That they refused to show mercy. And where will they go? 'Depart into the everlasting fire.' The hearing of this condemnation will cause much wailing. But what has another psalm said? 'The just will be held in everlasting remembrance.'

Do you, because you are unjust, expect the judge not to be just? Or because you are a liar, will the truthful One not be true? Rather, if you wish to receive mercy, be merciful before he comes; forgive whatever has been done against you; give of your abundance. Of whose possessions do you give, if not from his? If you were to give of your own, it would be largess but since you give of his, it is restitution. 'For what have you that you have not received?' These are the sacrifices most pleasing to God: mercy, humility, praise, peace, charity. Such as these, then, let us bring and, free from fear, we shall await the coming of the judge 'who will judge the world in equity and the peoples in his truth'.

Saturday after Advent 1

A Reading from the *Instructions* of Columbanus

How blessed, how fortunate, are 'those servants whom the Lord will find watchful when he comes'. Blessed is the time of waiting when we stay awake for the Lord, the Creator of the universe, who fills all things and transcends all things.

How I wish he would awaken me, his humble servant, from the sleep of slothfulness, even though I am of little worth. How I wish he would enkindle me with that fire of divine love. The flames of his love burn beyond the stars; the longing for his overwhelming delights and the divine fire ever burn within me!

How I wish I might deserve to have my lantern always burning at night in the temple of my Lord, to give light to all who enter the house of my God. Give me, I pray you, Lord, in the name of Jesus Christ, your Son and my God, that love that does not fail so that my lantern, burning within me and giving light to others, may be always lighted and never extinguished.

Jesus, our most loving Saviour, be pleased to light our lanterns, that they may burn for ever in your temple, receiving eternal light from you, the eternal light, to lighten our darkness and to ward off from us the darkness of the world.

Give your light to my lantern, I beg you, my Jesus, so that by its light I may see that holy of holies which receives you as the eternal priest entering among the columns of your great temple. May I ever see you only, look on you, long for you; may I gaze with love on you alone, and have my lantern shining and burning always in your presence.

Loving Saviour, be pleased to show yourself to us who knock, so that in knowing you we may love only you, love you alone, desire you alone, contemplate only you day and night, and always think of you. Inspire in us the depth of love that is fitting for you to receive as God. So may your love pervade our whole being, possess us completely, and fill all our senses, that we may know no other love but love for you who are everlasting. May our love be so great that the many waters of sky, land and sea cannot extinguish it in us: for 'many waters cannot quench love.'

May this saying be fulfilled in us also, at least in part, by your gift, Jesus Christ our Lord, to whom be glory for ever and ever.

The Second Sunday of Advent

A Reading from the *Letter to Diognetus*

With goodness and kindness, like a king who sends his son, who is also a king, God sent God, the Word, among us. He sent him to save us through persuasion rather than violence, for there is no violence in God. He sent him to call us rather than to accuse us; he sent him to love us rather than to judge us.

No one has either seen God or made him known; it is God himself who has revealed himself. And he has manifested himself through faith, to which alone it is given to behold God. For God, the Lord and Creator of the universe, who made all things and arranged them in orderly fashion, has shown himself to be not only filled with love for us but also to be long-suffering in his dealings with us. Yes, he has always been, is, and will remain the same: kind, good, free from wrath, true, and the only one who is good; and he formed in his mind a great and ineffable plan which he communicated to his Son alone.

As long as he held and preserved his own wise counsel in concealment, he appeared to neglect us and to have no concern for us. But after he revealed through his beloved Son and manifested what things he had prepared from the beginning, he conferred every blessing all at once upon us, so that we should both share in his benefits and see and be active in his service. Who of us would ever have expected these things? God had thus disposed everything on his part with his Son, but until these last times he has permitted us to be borne along by unruly impulses, drawn away by the desire of pleasure and various lusts. This does not mean that God took the slightest delight in our sins but that he simply endured them; nor did he approve this time of iniquity, but rather in no way consented to it. Instead he was preparing for the present time of righteousness so that, convinced of our unworthiness to obtain life during that time on account of our faults, we might now become worthy of it through the effect of the divine goodness; and so that, after we had been shown incapable of entering into the kingdom of God by our own efforts we might become capable of doing so by the divine power.

He took on himself the burden of our iniquities, and he gave his own Son as a ransom for us, the holy one for transgressors, the blameless one for the wicked, the just one for the unjust, the incorruptible one for the corruptible, the immortal one for the mortal. Where except in the justice of God could we find that with which to cover our sins? By whom could we be justified – we who are wicked and ungodly – except by the only Son of God? What a wondrous exchange, operation, and unexpected benefits! The crime of so large number is covered over by the justice of a single just one.

In the past, God first needed to convince our nature of its inability to obtain life for itself. Now God has shown us the Saviour capable of saving even what was impossible to save. In these two ways, he willed to lead us to trust in his goodness, to esteem him as our nourisher, Father, teacher, counsellor, healer, and our wisdom, light, honour, glory, power and life.

Monday after Advent 2

A Reading from a homily of Origen

We read these words in the prophet Isaiah: 'A voice cries out: In the desert prepare the way of the Lord! Make straight in the wilderness a highway for our God.' The Lord wishes to find a way by which he might enter your hearts and walk therein. Prepare this way for him of whom it is said: 'Make straight in the wilderness a highway for our God.' The voice cries out in the desert: 'Prepare the way.' This voice first reaches our ears; and then following it, or rather with it, the Word penetrates our understanding. It is in this sense that Christ was announced by John.

Let us see, therefore, what the voice announces concerning the Word. 'Prepare,' says the voice, 'the way of the Lord.' What way are we to prepare for the Lord? Is it a material way? Can the Word of God take such a way? Ought we not rather to prepare an inner way for the Lord by making the paths of our heart straight and smooth? Indeed, this is the way by which the Word of God enters in order to take up his abode in the human heart made ready to receive him.

How great is the human heart! What width and capacity it possesses, provided it is pure! Do you wish to know its greatness and width? Look at the extent of the divine knowledge that it embraces. It tells us itself: 'God gave me sound knowledge of existing things that I might know the organisation of the universe and the force of its elements, the beginning and the end and the mid-point of times, the changes in the sun's course and the variations of the seasons. Cycles of years, positions of the stars, natures of animals, tempers of beasts, powers of the winds and thoughts of people, uses of plants and virtues of roots.'

Thus, you see that the human heart knows so many things and is of no small compass. But notice that its greatness is not one of size but of the power of thought by which it is capable of knowing so many truths.

In order to make everyone realise how great the human heart is, let us look at a few examples taken from everyday life. We still retain in our minds all the towns which we have ever visited. Their features, the location of their squares, walls, and buildings remain in our hearts. We keep the road which we have travelled painted and engraved in our memories; and the sea over which we have sailed is harboured in our silent thought. As I have just said, the human heart knows so many things and is of no small compass.

Now, if it is not small, and if it can grasp so much, we can prepare the way of the Lord there and make straight the way where the Word, the Wisdom of God, will walk. Let each of you, then, prepare the way of the Lord by a good conscience; make straight the way so that the Word of God may walk within you without stumbling and may give you knowledge of his mysteries and of his coming.

Tuesday after Advent 2

A Reading from a sermon of Bernard of Clairvaux

'Behold, the name of the Lord comes from afar.' Who could doubt these words of the Prophet? Something superlative was needed in the beginning if the majesty of God was to deign to come down from such a height, for a dwelling so unworthy of it.

And there was, indeed, something superlative about it; great mercy, immense compassion, and abundant charity. Why did Christ come to earth? We shall find the answer without difficulty, since his words and actions clearly reveal to us the reason for his coming.

It is to search for the hundredth lost sheep that came down hurriedly from the hillside. He came because of us, so that the mercies of the Lord might be revealed with greater clarity, and his wonderful works for humankind. What amazing condescension on the part of God, who searches for us, and what great dignity bestowed on the one thus sought!

If we want to glory in it, we can quite reasonably do so, not because we can be anything in ourselves, but because the God who created us has made us of such great worth. Indeed, all the riches and glory of this world, and all that one could wish for in it, is a very small thing and even nothing, in comparison with this glory. 'What are we that you make much of us, or pay us any heed?'

But then again, I should like to know why Christ determined to come among us himself and why it was not, rather, we who went to him. Surely, it was for our benefit. What is more, it is not the custom of the rich to go to the poor, even if it is their intention to do something for them.

It was, therefore, really our responsibility to go to Jesus: but a double obstacle prevented it. For our eyes were blind, and he dwells in inaccessible Light. We were lying paralysed on our pallet, incapable of reaching the greatness of God.

That is why, in his immense goodness, our Saviour, the doctor of our souls, came down from his great height and tempered for our sick eyes the dazzling brightness of his glory. He clothed himself, as it were, with a lantern, with that luminous body, I mean, free from every stain, which he put on.

Wednesday after Advent 2

A Reading from a commentary on the psalms
by Augustine

God established a time for his promises and a time for their fulfilment. The time for promises was in the time of the prophets, until John the Baptist; from John until the end is the time of fulfilment.

God, who is faithful, put himself in our debt, not by receiving anything but by promising so much. A promise was not sufficient for him; he chose to commit himself in writing as well, as it were making a contract of his promises. He wanted us to be able to see the way in which his promises were redeemed when he began to discharge them. And so the time of the prophets was the foretelling of the promises.

He promised eternal salvation, everlasting happiness with the angels, an immortal inheritance, endless glory, the joyful vision of his face, his holy dwelling in heaven, and after resurrection from the dead, no fear of dying. This is as it were his final promise, the goal of all striving. When we reach it, we shall ask for nothing more. But as to the way in which we are to arrive at our final goal, he has revealed this also, by promise and prophecy.

He has promised humankind divinity, mortals immortality, sinners justification, the poor a rising to glory. But because God's promises seemed impossible to human beings – equality with the angels in exchange for mortality, corruption, poverty, weakness, dust and ashes – God not only made a written contract with them to win their belief but also established a mediator of his good faith, not a prince or angel or archangel, but his only Son. He wanted, through his Son, to show us and give us the way he would lead us to the goal he has promised.

It was not enough for God to make his Son our guide to the way; he made him the way itself that we might travel with him as leader, and by him as the way.

Therefore, the only Son of God was to come among us, to take our human nature, and in this nature to be born as a man. He was to die, to rise again, to ascend into heaven, to sit at the right hand of the Father, and to fulfil his promises among the nations, and after that to come again, to exact now what he had asked for before, to separate those deserving anger from those deserving his mercy, to execute his threats against the wicked, and to reward the just as he had promised.

All this had therefore to be prophesied, foretold, and impressed on us as an event in the future, in order that we might wait for it in faith, and not find it in a sudden and dreadful reality.

Thursday after Advent 2

A Reading from a treatise *On the Value of Patience*
by Cyprian of Carthage

Patience is a precept for salvation given us by our Lord and teacher: 'Whoever endures to the end will be saved.' And again, 'If you persevere in my word, you will truly be my disciples; you will know the truth, and the truth will set you free.'

We must, therefore, endure and persevere if we are to attain the truth and freedom we have been allowed to hope for; faith and hope are the very meaning of our being Christians, but if faith and hope are to bear their fruit, patience is necessary.

We do not seek glory now, in the present, but we look for future glory, as St Paul instructs us when he says: 'By hope we were saved. Now hope which is seen is not hope: how can we hope for what is seen? But if we hope for what we do not see, we wait for it in patience.' Patient waiting is necessary if we are to be perfected in what we have begun to be, and if we are to receive from God what we hope for and believe.

In another place the same apostle instructs and teaches the righteous, and those active in good works, and those who store up for themselves treasures in heaven through the reward God gives them. They are to be patient also, for he says: 'Therefore while we have time, let us do good to all, but especially to those who are of the household of the faith. But let us not grow weary in doing good, for we shall reap our reward in due season.'

Paul warns us not to grow weary in good works through impatience, not to be distracted or overcome by temptations and so give up in the midst of our pilgrimage of praise and glory, and allow our past good deeds to count for nothing because what was begun falls short of completion.

Finally the apostle Paul, speaking of charity, unites it with endurance and patience. 'Charity,' he says, 'is always patient and kind; it is not jealous, is not boastful, is not given to anger, does not think evil, loves all things, believes all things, hopes all things, endures all things.' He shows that charity can be steadfast and persevering because it has learned how to endure all things.

And in another place he says: 'Bear with one another lovingly, striving to keep the unity of the Spirit in the bond of peace.' He shows that neither unity nor peace can be maintained unless we cherish each other with mutual forbearance and preserve the bond of harmony by means of patience.

Friday after Advent 2

A Reading from the *Proslogion*
of Anselm of Canterbury

O Lord my God,
　　teach my heart where and how to seek you,
　　where and how to find you.
Lord, if you are not here but absent,
　　where shall I seek you?
　　but you are everywhere, so you must be here,
　　why then do I not seek you?
Surely you dwell in light inaccessible –
　　where is it?
　　and how can I have access to light which is inaccessible?
　　Who will lead me and take me into it
　　so that I may see you there?
By what signs, under what forms, shall I seek you?
I have never seen you, O Lord my God,
I have never seen your face.

Most High Lord,
　　what shall an exile do
　　who is as far away from you as this?
　　What shall your servant do,
　　eager for your love, cast off far from your face?
He longs to see you,
　　but your countenance is too far away.

He wants to have access to you,
    but your dwelling is inaccessible.
He longs to find you,
    but he does not know where you are.
He loves to seek you,
    but he does not know your face.

Lord, you are my Lord and my God,
    and I have never seen you.
    You have created and re-created me,
    all the good I have comes from you,
    and still I do not know you.
    I was created to see you,
    and I have not yet accomplished that for which I was made.

How wretched is the fate of man
    when he has lost that for which he was created.
    How hard and cruel was our Fall.
    What has man lost, and what has he found?
    What has he left, and what is left to him?

O Lord, how long shall this be?
    How long, Lord, will you forget us?
    How long will you turn your face away from us?
    When will you look upon us and hear us?
    When will you enlighten our eyes and show us your face?
    When will you give yourself back to us?

Look upon us, Lord,
    hear and enlighten us.
    Show us your very self.
    Take pity on our efforts and strivings toward you,
    for we have no strength without you.

Teach me to seek you,
    and when I seek you show yourself to me,
    for I cannot seek you unless you teach me,
    nor can I find you unless you show yourself to me.
Let me seek you in desiring you
    and desire you in seeking you,
    let me find you by loving you,
    and love you in finding you.

Saturday after Advent 2

A Reading from a commentary on the prophecy of Isaiah
by Eusebius of Caesarea

'The voice of one crying in the wilderness: Prepare the way of the Lord, make straight the paths of our God.' The prophecy makes clear that it is to be fulfilled, not in Jerusalem but in the wilderness: it is there that the glory of the Lord is to appear, and God's salvation is to be made known to all the world.

This prophecy was fulfilled historically and literally when in the wilderness by the river Jordan John the Baptist proclaimed God's saving presence, and there God's salvation was indeed seen. The words of the prophecy were fulfilled when Christ and his glory were made manifest: after his baptism the heavens opened, and the Holy Spirit in the form of a dove rested on him, and the Father's voice was heard, bearing witness to the Son: 'This is my beloved Son, listen to him.'

The prophecy meant that God was to come to a deserted place, inaccessible from the beginning. None of the pagans had any knowledge of God, since his holy servants and prophets were kept from approaching them. The voice commands that a way be prepared for the Word of God: the rough and trackless ground is to be made level, so that our God may find a highway when he comes. 'Prepare the way of the Lord': the way is the preaching of the gospel, the new message of consolation, ready to bring to all humanity the knowledge of God's saving power.

'Climb on a high mountain, O bearer of good news to Zion. Lift up your voice in strength, O bearer of good news to Jerusalem.' These words of Isaiah harmonise very well with the meaning of what has gone before. They refer opportunely to the evangelists and proclaim the coming of God among us, after speaking of the voice crying in the wilderness. Mention of the evangelists suitably follows the prophecy on John the Baptist.

What does Zion mean if not the city previously called Jerusalem? This is the mountain referred to in that passage from Scripture: 'Here is Mount Zion where you dwelt.' Elsewhere the Apostle says: 'You have come to Mount Zion.' Does not he refer to the company of the apostles, chosen from the former people of the circumcision?

This indeed is the Zion, the Jerusalem, that received God's salvation. It stands aloft on the mountain of God, that is, it is raised high on the only-begotten Word of God. It is commanded to climb the high mountain and announce the word of salvation. Who is the bearer of the good news but the company of the evangelists? And what does it mean to bear the good news but to preach to all nations, but first of all to the cities of Judah, the coming of Christ on earth?

The Third Sunday of Advent

A Reading from a sermon of Augustine

John is the voice, but the Lord 'is the Word who was in the beginning'. John is the voice that lasts for a time; from the beginning Christ is the Word who lives for ever.

Take away the word, the meaning, and what is the voice? Where there is no understanding, there is only a meaningless sound. The voice without the word strikes the ear but does not build up the heart. However, let us observe what happens when we first seek to build up our hearts. When I think about what I am going to say, the word or message is already in my heart. When I want to speak to you, I look for a way to share with your heart what is already in mine. In my search for a way to let this message reach you, so that the word already in my heart may find a place also in yours, I use my voice to speak to you. The sound of my voice brings the meaning of the word to you and then passes away. The word which the sound has brought to you is now in your heart, and yet it is still also in mine.

When the word has been conveyed to you, does not the sound seem to say: 'The word ought to grow, and I should diminish?' The sound of the voice has made itself heard in the service of the word, and has gone away, as though it were saying: 'My joy is complete.' Let us hold on to the word; we must not lose the word conceived inwardly in our hearts.

Do you need proof that the voice passes away but the divine Word remains? Where is John's baptism today? It served its purpose, and it went away. Now it is Christ's baptism that we celebrate. It is in Christ that we all believe; we hope for salvation in him. This is the message the voice cried out.

Because it is hard to distinguish word from voice, even John himself was thought to be the Christ. The voice was thought to be the word. But the voice acknowledged what it was, anxious not to give offence to the word. 'I am not the Christ,' he said, 'nor Elijah nor the prophet.' And the question came: 'Who are you, then?' He replied: 'I am the voice of one crying in the wilderness: Prepare the way for the Lord.'

'The voice of one crying in the wilderness' is the voice of one breaking the silence. 'Prepare the way for the Lord,' the voice says, as though it were saying: 'I speak out in order to lead him into your hearts, but he does not choose to come where I lead him unless you prepare the way for him.'

'To prepare the way' means to pray well; it means thinking humbly of oneself. We should take our lesson from John the Baptist. He is thought to be the Christ; he declares he is not what they think. He does not take advantage of their mistake to further his own glory. If he had said, 'I am the Christ,' you can imagine how readily he would have been believed, since they believed he was the Christ even before he spoke. But he did not say it; he acknowledged what he was. He pointed out clearly who he was; he humbled himself. He saw where his salvation lay. He understood that he was a lamp, and his fear was that it might be blown out by the wind of pride.

Monday after Advent 3

A Reading from a treatise *Against Heresies*
by Irenaeus

God is the glory of humankind. We are the vessels which receive God's action, his wisdom and power.

Just as the skill of a doctor is revealed in the care of his patients, so the nature of God is revealed through the way he relates to us. This is the background behind Paul's statement: 'God has made the whole world prisoner of unbelief that he may have mercy on all.' Paul was speaking of the entire human race who were disobedient to God, cast off from immortality, but who then found mercy, receiving through the Son of God their adoption as God's children.

If we, without being puffed up or boastful, come to a true evaluation of created things and their divine Creator who, having brought them into being, sustains them through his power; and if we persevere in God's love, in obedience and gratitude to him, then we will receive greater glory from him. Moreover, it will be a glory which will grow ever brighter as we gradually assume the likeness of him who died for us.

He it was who took on the likeness of our sinful flesh to condemn sin and purge the flesh of its errors. He came to invite us to become like himself, commissioning us to be imitators of God, and establishing us in a way of life, grounded in obedience to the Father, that would lead to the vision of God, endowing us with power to receive the Father. He is the Word of God who dwelt among us and became the Son of Man to open the way for us to receive God, for God to dwell with us according to the will of the Father.

That is why the Lord himself gave as the sign of our salvation the one who was born of the Virgin, Emmanuel. It was 'the Lord himself who saved them', for of ourselves we had no power to be saved. For this reason Paul regularly refers to the weakness of human nature, and says: 'I know that no good dwells in my flesh.' By this he means that the blessing of salvation comes not from us but from God. Again, he says: 'O wretched man that I am! Who will save me from this body doomed to die?' And then, in answer to his own question, he speaks of a liberator, 'the grace of our Lord Jesus Christ'.

Isaiah says the same: 'Hands that are feeble, grow strong! Knees that are weak, be firm! Hearts that are faint, take courage! Fear not – behold, our God is coming in judgement and he will repay. He himself will come and save us.' We cannot save ourselves: it is only with the help of God that we are saved.

Tuesday after Advent 3

A Reading from a commentary on St John's Gospel
by Augustine

Behold, even lamps bear witness to the day because of our weakness, for we cannot bear to look at the brightness of the day. Indeed, in comparison with unbelievers, we Christians are even now light; as the Apostle says: 'There was a time when you were darkness, but now you are light in the Lord. Well, then, live as children of light.' And elsewhere he says: 'The night is far spent; the day is at hand. Let us cast off deeds of darkness and put on the armour of light. Let us live honourably as in daylight.'

Yet, in comparison with the light of that day which is to come, even the day in which we now find ourselves is still night. 'We possess,' says the Apostle, 'the prophetic message as something altogether reliable. Keep your attention closely fixed on it, as you would on a lamp shining in a dark place until the first streaks of dawn appear and the morning star rises in your hearts.'

Therefore, when our Lord Jesus Christ comes, he will as the apostle Paul also says, 'bring to light what is hidden in darkness and manifest the intention of our hearts', that everyone may receive praise from God. Then, in the presence of such a day, lamps will not be needed. No prophet shall then be read to us; no book of an apostle shall be opened. We shall not require the witness of John; we shall have no need of the gospel itself. Accordingly, when all these are taken away, all the Scriptures – which in the night of the world were as lamps kindled for us that we might not remain in darkness – shall also be taken out of the way, that they may not shine as if we needed them. Then the messengers of God by whom these were ministered to us shall themselves, together with us, behold that true and clear light. You shall see that very light, from which a ray was sent aslant and through many windings into your dark heart, in its purity, for the seeing and bearing of which you are being purified. John himself says: 'Dearly beloved, we are God's children now; what we shall later be has not yet been revealed. We know that when it is revealed we shall be like him, for we shall see him as he is.'

Wednesday after Advent 3

A Reading from *The Coming of God*
by Maria Boulding

The New Testament hope that Christ will come again is in some way earthed in our own expectations, fears and desires. If modern men and women are to be more than simply agnostic about the long-term prospects for our race, their most fundamental hope must be that it will not end in meaningless destruction. If we are going to blow ourselves out of existence as though we had never been, or make our planet uninhabitable without finding alternative accommodation, there is little point in hoping for anything else. To believe that the human race will eventually reach the end of its earthly pilgrimage is one thing; to equate the end with total, blind destruction is another. It is sad that the latter prospect is what many moderns term 'apocalyptic', if they use the word at all.

The hope that we are travelling towards a destiny, rather than a mere collapse, is linked with the faith that our origins were already purposeful. If we think that our existence is a mere fluke, the result of some wildly improbable mix in some primal soup that threw up the conditions required to sustain life, then our whole human story is a chance bubble; it has no purpose and can be pricked as meaninglessly as it was formed. But if there is a Creator who stands outside the whole cosmic evolutionary process, and yet works his will within it by a wisdom and love that are present in its every tiniest movement, then human life has a purpose. It begins from God and is on its way to a goal which, however unimaginable, will give meaning to the whole adventure.

We cannot comfort ourselves with wishful thinking. We instinctively admire the courage of those who squarely face the possibility that human life is simply absurd, that there is no future at all, and that the only honourable option is to live with dignity and kindness as we wait for our meaningless extinction. Courageous as it is, however, this view is not convincing, for it leaves too much unexplained. Deeply rooted in our experience is an obstinate certainty that our best intuitions will prove to have been the truest, and no mockery. We also want justice, however we may fear it or fall short in practising it ourselves. Our hearts demand that the very rough and uneven scheme of distribution in this life shall be redeemed within a larger justice.

No *deus ex machina* solution will satisfy our deepest desires; we could not rest content with an end which was mere comforting, the awakening from a bad dream to find that all the evil has been unreal after all. We know that if our instinct for truth is to be trusted, the whole sin of the world in which we are all accomplices must be taken with absolute, ultimate seriousness, and shown up for what it is in the light of God's holiness. Only so will our own responsibility and freedom be respected.

Thursday after Advent 3

A Reading from *The Throne of David*
by Gabriel Hebert

The Epistle to the Hebrews begins at once with the statement that God, who of old spoke to the fathers through the prophets in many fragmentary ways, has at the close of the pre-Messianic age spoken to us in his Son. We notice first that it is one and the same God who spoke both in the Old Covenant and in the New; when we join with the Church to confess the truth of the gospel concerning Jesus the Messiah, we are thereby confessing that the messianic hope of the Old Testament was a true hope. It is quite insufficient to say that the prophecies which express that hope are religiously valuable. It is necessary to affirm that God was preparing a messianic kingdom, and that the prophets were right in looking for such a kingdom, to be established by his act.

We notice secondly that he is said to have spoken by the prophets, in many fragments and in many modes. It was not only that different prophets had different styles, and that God also spoke through laws and rites and liturgical poems; but that the visions conveyed by these various modes were fragmentary and incomplete. Thus Isaiah saw one vision, and Ezekiel another, and there was the testimony both of the sacrificial rituals and of the prophets' criticisms of sacrifice. It is only in the Son of God that there is an integral embodiment of the messianic idea, so that it can be seen as a whole; he who fulfils the messianic expectation gathers up all the strands in one. From a survey of the Old Testament alone it would be impossible to produce a satisfactory statement of the messianic idea, since it would be impossible to know certainly which elements in it were primary and which secondary, and it is not till the fulfilment has come that the various elements fall into place.

Thus the Old Testament is at once the word of God and not the final word of God. It is an imperfect, provisional, preparatory covenant, needing to be made complete in the Messiah. It represents a stage in the education of the people of God.

Friday after Advent 3

A Reading from the *Meditations*
of Richard Challoner

In the office appointed for this holy time, the Church frequently puts us in mind of the mission and preaching of St John the Baptist, and of the manner in which he endeavoured to prepare the people for Christ; to the end that we may learn from the doctrine of this great forerunner of our Lord, in what dispositions we ought also to be if we would duly prepare the way for him. Now what the Baptist continually preached to the people was: that they should turn from their evil ways, and do penance, because the kingdom of heaven was at hand; that they should bring forth fruits worthy of penance, if they would escape the wrath to come–and this without delay – for that now the axe was laid at the root of the tree, and that every tree that did not bring forth good fruit should be cut up and cast into the fire. That they should not flatter themselves with the expectation of impunity or security, because they had Abraham for their father; for that God was able to raise up from the very stones children to Abraham; and therefore without a thorough conversion from their sins, they were to expect that the kingdom of God, and the grace and dignity of being children of Abraham (the father of all the faithful) should be taken away from them and given to the Gentiles. He added, that he baptized them indeed with water unto penance; but that another should come after him that should 'baptize them with the Holy Ghost and with fire; that his fan was in his hand, and that he should thoroughly cleanse his floor, and gather his wheat into the barn; but the chaff he would burn with unquenchable fire'. This was the way St John prepared the people for Christ; and it is by conforming ourselves in practice to these his lessons at this holy time, that we must also prepare the way of the Lord, and be prepared for him.

Christians, this is our great business at this holy time, if we hope to prepare ourselves for Christ; this is the proper exercise for it – to pass over in our mind in the bitterness of our soul, all our years that have been spent in sin; to bewail and lament every day of this holy season, all our past treasons against the divine majesty; to turn now to God with our whole heart; to offer our whole souls to him; to exercise ourselves in his love, and to enter into new articles with him of an eternal allegiance, with a full determination of rather dying than being any more disloyal to him; and letting not one day pass without offering him some penitential satisfaction for our past guilt, to be united to and sanctified by the passion and death of our Lord Jesus Christ. O how happy are they that employ the time of Advent in this manner! O how willingly will our Lord, at the approaching Christmas, communicate himself to such souls as these!

Saturday after Advent 3

A Reading from the treatise *The City of God*
by Augustine

After recalling the great promise of God to David and the assurances by which he so strongly confirmed it, the psalmist feared that people might think this promise was fulfilled in Solomon. To counter this hope and the disillusion that it would give rise to, he continues: 'Yet you, O Lord, have rejected and spurned your Anointed.'

What is being referred to here is what happened to Solomon's kingdom in his successors, down to the devastation of the earthly Jerusalem which was the capital of his kingdom, and especially down to the destruction of the very temple that Solomon had built. But lest anyone might think that God had been unfaithful to his promises, the psalmist immediately adds: 'You have postponed the coming of your Anointed.' If the coming of the Anointed of the Lord has been postponed, he cannot therefore be identified with Solomon or even with David himself.

It is indeed true that all the kings of the Jews, who were anointed with the mystic chrism, were called the anointed of the Lord. Not only David and his successors were thus described, but Saul also who was the first to be anointed as king of the people of the Jews and whom David himself called the Lord's anointed.

There was, however, but one true Christ or 'Anointed', of whom David and his successors were but types by virtue of their prophetic anointing. In saying that his coming was postponed, the psalmist is merely speaking from the viewpoint of those who had identified him in their thoughts with David or Solomon, whereas according to the plan and preparations of God he was to come at his own proper time.

The psalm here continues with a narrative of what happened during the interval of this delay to the kingdom of the earthly Jerusalem where hope in the eventual reign of the Anointed One, promised by the Lord, was kept alive and strong: 'You have renounced the covenant with your servant, and defiled his crown in the dust. You have broken down all his walls; you have laid his strongholds desolate. All who pass by the way have plundered him; he is made the reproach of his neighbours. You have exalted the right hands of his foes, you have gladdened all his enemies. You have turned back his sharp sword and have not sustained him in battle. You have deprived him of his lustre and hurled his throne to the ground. You have shortened the days of his youth; you have covered him with shame.'

All these misfortunes were visited upon the enslaved Jerusalem, though some of her kings reigned as heirs of the free Jerusalem from on high; they regarded their office as a role in a divine dispensation that was temporary and preparatory; they believed with a true faith that God would eventually establish the kingdom of the heavenly Jerusalem, of which they were heirs; and they placed all their hope in the one true Christ, who was to come.

Fourth Sunday of Advent

A Reading from a treatise *Against Heresies*
by Irenaeus

The Lord came into his own creation in a visible way: his own creation sustained him who sustains everything in being. His obedience on the tree of the cross reversed the disobedience at the tree in Eden; the good news of the truth announced by an angel to Mary, a virgin who was shortly to be married, undid the evil lie that had seduced Eve, a virgin also espoused to a husband.

Just as Eve was seduced by the word of an angel and fled from God after disobeying his word, so Mary in her turn welcomed the good news by the word of an angel that she should sustain God in obedience to his word. As Eve was seduced into disobeying God, so Mary was persuaded into obeying God; thus the Virgin Mary became the advocate of the virgin Eve. Just as the human race fell into bondage to death by means of a virgin, so now it is rescued by a virgin. The disobedience of one has been counter-balanced by the obedience of the other.

Christ gathered all things into one by gathering them into himself. He declared war against our enemy, crushed and trampled on the head of the one who at the beginning had taken us captive in Adam, in accordance with God's words to the serpent in Genesis: 'I will put enmity between you and the woman, and between your seed and her seed; he shall watch for your head, and you shall watch for his heel.'

The one who is described as watching for the serpent's head is the one who was born in the likeness of Adam from the Virgin. This is the seed spoken of by Paul in the Letter to the Galatians: 'The Law of works was in force until the seed should come to whom the promise was made.' This fact is stated even more clearly in the same letter when he says: 'When the fullness of time had come, God sent his Son, born of a woman.' Indeed, the enemy would not have been defeated fairly if the vanquisher had not been born of a woman, because it was through a woman that the enemy had gained mastery over humanity in the beginning, setting himself up as our adversary.

That is why the Lord proclaims himself to be the Son of Man, the one who renews in himself that first man from whom the race born of woman has derived. As by one man's defeat our race fell into the bondage of death, so by another's victory we were to rise again to life.

The Eight Days of Prayer
before Christmas

A Reading from *The Experience of Prayer* by
Sebastian Moore and Kevin Maguire

In the time of the year's darkness,
At the Winter Solstice,
We embraced the darkness
And we chose the madness
Of chaos and oblivion;
Because we chose to shut our eyes
To the darkness that was there,
And saw in the fantastic lights
That swam in our fevered eyes
A glimmer of daylight in the distance;
And this we chose, and called it Light;
Called it Light and the Will of God,
Because we had learned, living in the dark,
To identify God with the unseen light;
And in extremity we comforted ourselves
With the hope of a light we did not see.
We hoped for a light and called it God;
And so, with screwed-up eyes and heated mind,
We said we saw a glimmer and we called it God.
Yet we were in the darkness all the time,
And our fevered crazy choosing
Chose the one thing that it would not see:
That which strikes terror to the marrow of the heart;
The dark, the dark, the awful total night.
And so, for all our crazy games and blundering,
Wrapped in the darkness, we have stumbled on
The one thing that we feared and fled so long.
In the darkness we have found the centre of darkness,
And we are overwhelmed by a strange, dark, power.
This is a knowledge we have lived in constantly,
And yet had kept it hidden from our minds.
But this is now the ending of our day.
That regal splendour of our lighted world.
Now can our eyes spring free to see the night,
And the darkness that is vibrant with our God.

17 December

O Sapientia

O Wisdom, coming forth from the mouth of the Most High,
and reaching mightily from one end of the earth to the other,
ordering all things well:
Come and teach us the way of prudence.

A Reading from a letter of Leo the Great

There is no point in asserting that our Lord, the son of the Virgin Mary, was truly and completely human if he is not believed to be of that stock from which the gospel informs us that he came.

Matthew says: 'An account of the genealogy of Jesus Christ, the son of David, the son of Abraham.' He then charts Christ's human origin, tracing his lineage down to Joseph to whom the Lord's mother was betrothed. Luke, on the other hand, works backwards step by step, tracing his succession from the origins of the human race, in order to show that the first Adam and the last Adam were of the same nature.

The almighty Son of God could have come to teach and justify humankind with only the outward appearance of our humanity, just as he appeared to the patriarchs and prophets. As, for example, when he wrestled with Jacob, or when he conversed with the patriarchs, or when he did not refuse their hospitality to the point of even sharing the food they set before him. Such outward appearances pointed to this man Jesus. They had a hidden meaning which proclaimed that his reality would be taken from the stock of his forebears.

Thus God's plan for our reconciliation, formed before all eternity, was not realised by any of these prefigurations. As yet, the Holy Spirit had not come upon the Virgin nor had the power of the Most High overshadowed her. Only then, would the Word become flesh within her inviolate womb, in which Wisdom would build for herself a house. Then, too, the Creator of ages would be born in time and the nature of God would join with the nature of the slave in the unity of one person. He through whom the world was created would himself be brought forth in the midst of all creation.

If this new humanity, made in the likeness of sinful flesh, had not assumed our old nature; if he, who is one in being with the

Father, had not accepted to be one in being with the mother; if he who is alone free from sin had not united our nature to himself, then we would still be held captive under the power of the devil. We would have gained nothing from the victor's triumph if the battle had been fought outside the arena of our nature.

But, by means of this marvellous sharing, the mystery of our rebirth has shone upon us. We are reborn in newness of spirit through the same Spirit through whom Christ was conceived and born. This is why John the evangelist speaks of those who believe as those 'who were born, not of blood or of the will of the flesh or of the will of man, but of God'.

18 December

O Adonaï

O Adonaï, and leader of the House of Israel,
who appeared to Moses in the fire of the burning bush
and gave him the law on Sinai:
Come and redeem us with an outstretched arm.

A Reading from the treatise *The Refutation of all Heresies*
attributed to Hippolytus of Rome

As Christians we do not put our faith in empty phrases; we are not carried off by sudden floods of emotion; we are not seduced by smooth and eloquent speeches. On the contrary, we put our faith in words spoken by the power of God, spoken by the Word himself at God's command. It was God's purpose to turn us away from disobedience, not by using force so that we end up reduced to the status of slaves, but rather by addressing to our free will a call to liberty.

The Word spoke first of all through the prophets. But because the message was announced obscurely in language that was often misconstrued, in these last days the Father sent the Word in person. He was to be manifested visibly, so that the world could see him and be saved.

We know that the Word assumed a body from the Virgin and, through this new creation refashioned our fallen nature. We know that he was fully human, formed from the same clay as ourselves. If it were not so, then his command to imitate him as our teacher would be a futile exercise. If he were of a different substance from me, then why does he command me, weak as I am, to do as he did? The call to goodness would be undermined by the claims of justice.

But to show that he was no different from us, he undertook hard work, he went hungry and thirsty, he rested and slept. He did not shirk suffering, he submitted to death and revealed the resurrection. In all this he was offering us his own self, so that when suffering is our lot in life we do not lose heart, but will rather recognise that because we share with him a common humanity, we can expect to receive from God an identical reward.

When we have come to know the true God, both our bodies and our souls will be immortal and incorruptible. We will gain the kingdom of heaven because while on earth we knew the king of heaven. Freed from evil inclinations, from suffering whether of body or soul, we will discover ourselves companions of God and co-heirs with Christ. Indeed we will have become divine. All that we suffer in this mortal life, God permits as part of our human condition. All that belongs to God, he has promised to give us when we have been deified and have been made immortal.

This, then, is what it means to know yourself: to recognise and acknowledge in ourselves the God who made us in his image. If we do this, we know that we in turn will be recognised and acknowledged by our Creator.

19 December

O Radix Jesse

O Root of Jesse, standing as a sign to the people,
before whom kings shall shut their mouths
and nations shall seek:
Come and deliver us and do not delay.

A Reading from the Letter of Clement of Rome
to the Church in Corinth

It stands written in Scripture: 'Behold, the Lord is taking a people for himself from out of the midst of the nations, gathering the first-fruits from his threshing-floor; for from that nation shall come forth the Holy of Holies.' Let any commendation of us come from

God, and not from ourselves because self-praise is repugnant to God. Testimony to our good deeds is for other people to give, as it was once given to those righteous people whom we number as our forebears in the faith. Self-assertion, self-conceit, and arrogance are characteristics of those alienated from God; it is those who display consideration to others, who are unassuming and peaceful who win God's blessing.

Let us focus our efforts, then, on receiving his blessing, and identify which roads lead to it. Examine the early pages of history; what was it that caused our father Abraham to be blessed? Was it not his faith which prompted him to acts of righteousness and truth? Isaac's confident faith in the future gave him courage to stretch himself out upon the altar. As for Jacob, who meekly left his own country on account of his brother, and went to serve Laban, to him God gave leadership of the twelve tribes of Israel.

Now anyone who honestly examines any of these instances will recognise the magnitude of the gifts which God bestows. It is from Jacob that all the priests and Levites who serve the altar of God have descended. And from him also, according to the flesh, has descended the Lord Jesus. From Jacob have come kings and princes and governors in a line of descent that may be traced back to Judah; while the leaders of the other tribes which also sprang from him, have no small claim to fame of their own. Indeed, God promised this when he said: 'Your posterity will be like the stars of heaven.'

On all the patriarchs great honour and fame were bestowed; but not for their own sakes, or because of their own achievements, or even because of the good works they did, but by the will of God. In the same way we too, who have been called in Christ Jesus by God's will, are not justified by ourselves or our wisdom or our intelligence or godliness, or even by any good deeds we may have done in holiness of heart, but solely by that faith through which almighty God has justified his children since the beginning of time. Glory be to him for ever and ever. Amen.

What must we do, then, my brothers and sisters? Should we relax our efforts at doing good, or give up trying to exercise Christian love? God forbid! On the contrary, let us be sincerely, even passionately, eager for every opportunity to do good. Even the architect and Lord of the universe himself rejoices in his works. Good works not only embellished the lives of the upright, they are an adornment which God himself delights in. With such examples, we too should be sparing no effort to obey the will of God, and putting all our energies into living the Christian life.

20 December

O Clavis David

O Key of David, and sceptre of the House of Israel,
who opens and no one can shut,
who shuts and no one can open:
Come and bring the prisoners from the prison house,
those who dwell in darkness and the shadow of death.

A Reading from a sermon of Bernard of Clairvaux

You have heard, O Virgin, the announcement of a great mystery, and you have heard how it will happen. You have double reason for astonishment and rejoicing. 'Rejoice,' therefore, 'O Daughter of Zion, and be exceedingly glad, O Daughter of Jerusalem.' And since to you have been given tidings of joy and gladness, let us hear that joyous reply we long for, so that the bones that have been broken may rejoice. You have heard what is to happen, I say, and you have believed. Believe also the way you have heard it is to happen. You have heard that you will conceive and bear a son. You have heard that it will be not by a man, but by the Holy Spirit.

The angel is waiting for your answer: it is time for him to return to the One who sent him. And we too are waiting, O Lady, for this word of mercy, we who are overwhelmed by misery under sentence of condemnation. The price of our salvation is being offered to you. If you consent, we shall be set free straight away. In the eternal Word of God we have all been made, and look, we are dying. By one small word of yours in answer we shall be restored and brought back to life.

Adam asks this of you, O loving Virgin, poor Adam, exiled from paradise with all his poor children. Abraham begs this of you; David begs this of you; all the holy patriarchs, your very own fathers, beg this of you, as do those who dwell in the valley of the shadow of death. The whole world is waiting, kneeling at your feet. And rightly so, for on your lips hangs the comfort of the afflicted, the redemption of captives, the deliverance of the damned; in a word, the salvation of all the sons and daughters of Adam, your entire race.

Give your answer quickly, my Virgin. My Lady, speak the word which earth and hell, and heaven itself are waiting for. The very king and Lord of all, 'he who desires your beauty', is eager for your answer and assent, by which he proposes to save the world. You have pleased him by your silence: you will please him even more by your word.

If you let him hear your voice, then he will let you see our salvation. Is not this what you have been waiting for, what you have been weeping for and sighing after day and night in your prayers? Answer, O Virgin, answer the angel quickly; or rather, through the angel answer God. Speak the word and receive the Word. Offer what is yours and conceive what is God's. Breathe one fleeting word and embrace the eternal Word.

Why delay? Why be afraid? Believe, speak, receive! Let your humility be clothed with courage, and your reserve with trust. In such circumstances, O prudent Virgin, do not fear presumption, for although the reserve which makes you silent is attractive, how more important at this juncture is it for your goodness to speak.

O Blessed Virgin, open your heart to faith, your lips to speak, your womb to your Creator. Behold, the long-desired of the nations is standing at the door and knocking. Oh, what if he should pass by because of your delay and again in sorrow you should have to begin to seek for him whom your soul loves? Rise up, then, run and open! Arise by faith, run by the devotion of your heart, open by consent.

And Mary said, 'Behold, I am the handmaid of the Lord. Let it be done unto me according to your word.'

21 December

O Oriens

O Dayspring, splendour of light eternal and Sun of Righteousness:
Come and enlighten those who dwell in darkness
and the shadow of death.

A Reading from a commentary on St Luke's Gospel
by Ambrose of Milan

The angel revealed the message to the Virgin Mary, giving her a sign to win her trust. The angel told her of the motherhood of an old and barren woman to show that God is able to do all that he wills When she hears this Mary sets out for the hill country. She does not disbelieve God's word: she feels no uncertainty over the message or doubt about the sign. She goes eager in purpose, dutiful in conscience, hastening for joy.

Filled with God, where would she hasten but to the heights? The Holy Spirit does not proceed by slow, laborious efforts. Quickly, too, the blessings of her coming and the Lord's presence are made clear: as soon as 'Elizabeth heard Mary's greeting, the child leapt in her womb, and she was filled with the Holy Spirit'.

Notice the contrast and the choice of words. Elizabeth is the first to hear Mary's voice, but John is the first to be aware of grace. Elizabeth hears with the ears of the body, but John leaps for joy at the meaning of the mystery. She is aware of Mary's presence, but he is aware of the Lord's: a woman aware of a woman's presence, the forerunner aware of the pledge of our salvation. The women speak of the grace they have received while the children are active in secret, unfolding the mystery of love with the help of their mothers, who prophesy by the spirit of their sons.

The child leaps in the womb; the mother is filled with the Holy Spirit, but not before her son. Once the son has been filled with the Holy Spirit, he fills his mother with the same Spirit. John leaps for joy, and the spirit of Mary rejoices in her turn. When John leaps for joy Elizabeth is filled with the Holy Spirit, but we know that though Mary's spirit rejoices she does not need to be filled with the Holy Spirit. Her son, who is beyond our understanding, is active in his mother in a way beyond our understanding. Elizabeth is filled with the Holy Spirit after conceiving John, while Mary is filled with the Holy Spirit before conceiving the Lord. Elizabeth says: 'Blessed are you because you have believed.'

You also are blessed because you have heard and believed. A believing soul both conceives and brings forth the Word of God and acknowledges his works.

Let Mary's soul be in each of you to proclaim the greatness of the Lord. Let her spirit be in each to rejoice in the Lord. Christ has only one mother in the flesh, but we all bring forth Christ in faith. Every soul receives the Word of God if only it keeps chaste, remaining pure and free from sin, its modesty undefiled. The soul that succeeds in this proclaims the greatness of the Lord, just as Mary's soul magnified the Lord and her spirit rejoiced in God her Saviour. In another place we read: 'Magnify the Lord with me.' The Lord is magnified, not because the human voice can add anything to God but because he is magnified within us. Christ is the image of God, and if the soul does what is right and holy, it magnifies that image of God in whose likeness it was created and, in magnifying the image of God, the soul has a share in its greatness and is exalted.

22 December

O Rex Gentium

O King of the Nations, and their desire,
the cornerstone making both one:
Come and save us, whom you formed from the dust.

A Reading from a commentary on St Luke's Gospel by the Venerable Bede

Mary said: 'My soul proclaims the greatness of the Lord, my spirit rejoices in God my Saviour.'

The Lord has exalted me by a gift so great, so unheard of, that language is useless to describe it; and the depths of love in my heart can scarcely grasp it. I offer then all the powers of my soul in praise and thanksgiving. As I contemplate his greatness, which knows no limits, I joyfully surrender my whole life, my senses, my judgement, for my spirit rejoices in the eternal Godhead of that Jesus, that Saviour, whom I have conceived in this world of time.

'The Almighty has done great things for me, and holy is his name.'

Mary looks back to the beginning of her song, where she said: 'My soul proclaims the greatness of the Lord.' Only the soul for whom the Lord in his love does great things can proclaim his greatness with fitting praise and encourage those who share her desire and purpose, saying: 'Join with me in proclaiming the greatness of the Lord; let us magnify his name together.'

Those who know the Lord, yet refuse to proclaim his greatness and sanctify his name to the limit of their power, 'will be called least in the kingdom of heaven'. His name is called holy because in the sublimity of his unique power he surpasses every creature and is far removed from all that he has made.

'He has come to the help of his servant Israel for he has remembered his promise of mercy.'

In a beautiful phrase Mary calls Israel the servant of the Lord. The Lord came to his aid to save him. Israel is an obedient and humble servant, in the words of Hosea: 'Israel was a servant, and I loved him.'

Those who refuse to be humble cannot be saved. They cannot say with the prophet: 'See, God comes to my aid; the Lord is the helper of my soul.' But 'anyone who makes himself humble like a little child is greater in the kingdom of heaven.'

'The promise he made to our forebears, to Abraham and his children for ever.' This does not refer to the physical descendants of Abraham, but to his spiritual children. These are his descendants, sprung not from the flesh only, but who, whether circumcised or not, have followed him in faith. Circumcised as he was, Abraham believed, and this was credited to him as an act of righteousness.

The coming of the Saviour was promised to Abraham and to his descendants for ever. These are the children of promise, to whom it is said: 'If you belong to Christ, then you are descendants of Abraham, heirs in accordance with the promise.'

23 December

O Emmanuel

O Emmanuel, our king and lawgiver,
the desire of all nations and their Saviour:
Come and save us, O Lord our God.

A reading from *Said or Sung* by Austin Farrer

The universal misuse of human power has the sad effect that power, however lovingly used, is hated. To confer benefits is surely more godlike than to ask them; yet our hearts go out more easily to begging children than they do to generous masters. We have so mishandled the sceptre of God which we have usurped, we have played providence so tyrannically to one another, that we are made incapable of loving the government of God himself or feeling the caress of an almighty kindness. Are not his making hands always upon us, do we draw a single breath but by his mercy, has not he given us one another and the world to delight us, and kindled our eyes with a divine intelligence? Yet all his dear and infinite kindness is lost behind the mask of power. Over-whelmed by omnipotence, we miss the heart of love. How can

I matter to him? we say. It makes no sense; he has the world, and even that he does not need. It is folly even to imagine him like myself, to credit him with eyes into which I could ever look, a heart that could ever beat for my sorrows or joys, a hand he could hold out to me. For even if the childish picture be allowed, that hand must be cupped to hold the universe, and I am a speck of dust on the star-dust of the world.

Yet Mary holds her finger out, and a divine hand closes on it. The maker of the world is born a begging child; he begs for milk, and does not know that it is milk for which he begs. We will not lift our hands to pull the love of God down to us, but he lifts his hands to pull human compassion down upon his cradle. So the weakness of God proves stronger than men, and the folly of God proves wiser than men. Love is the strongest instrument of omnipotence, for accomplishing those tasks he cares most dearly to perform; and this is how he brings his love to bear on human pride; by weakness not by strength, by need and not by bounty.

24 December

Christmas Eve

A Reading from a sermon of Augustine

Awake! For your sake God was made man! 'Awake, O sleeper, and arise from the dead, and Christ shall give you light.' For your sake, I say, God was made man.

Eternal death awaited you had he not been born in time. Never would you have been freed from sinful flesh, had he not taken on himself the likeness of sinful flesh. Everlasting would have been your misery, had he not acted in mercy. You would never have returned to life, had he not shared your death. You would have been lost, had he not hastened to your aid. You would have perished, had he not come.

Let us then joyfully celebrate the coming of our salvation and redemption. Let us celebrate the hallowed day on which he who is the great and eternal day came from the great and endless day of eternity into our own short span of time. 'He has become our righteousness, our sanctification, our redemption, and so, as it is written: Let those who glory, glory in the Lord.'

'Truth,' then, 'has sprung up from the earth.' Christ who said, 'I am the truth,' is born of a virgin. 'And righteousness has looked down from heaven' : because believing in this new-born child, we are justified not by ourselves but by God. 'Truth has sprung up from the earth' because the Word was made flesh. 'And righteousness has looked down from heaven' because 'every good gift and every perfect gift is from above.' 'Truth has sprung up from the earth' – flesh born of Mary. 'And righteousness has looked down from heaven' for 'you can receive nothing unless it has been given you from heaven.'

'Being justified by faith, let us be at peace with God' for indeed 'righteousness and peace have kissed each other' through our Lord Jesus Christ, for 'truth has sprung up from the earth.' Through him we have access to that grace in which we stand, and our boast is in our hope of sharing the glory of God. St Paul does not say at this point 'our glory' but 'the glory of God'; because righteousness has not proceeded from us but has 'looked down from heaven'. Therefore let those who glory, glory not in themselves, but in the Lord.

For this reason, when our Lord was born of the Virgin, the message of the angels was: 'Glory to God in the highest, and peace to his people on earth.' For how could there be peace on earth unless 'truth has sprung up from the earth', that is, unless Christ were born of our flesh? And 'he is our peace who made the two into one' that we might be people of good will, bound together by the bond of unity.

Beloved, let us then rejoice in this grace, so that our glorying may bear witness to a good conscience, and may we glory, not in ourselves, but in the Lord. That is why Scripture says: 'He is my glory, the one who lifts up my head.' For what greater grace could God have made to dawn upon us than to make his only Son become the Son of Man, so that we might in our turn become children and heirs of God? Ask yourselves if this were merited; ask for its reason, for its justification, and see whether you find anything but sheer grace.

CHRISTMAS

God so loved us that for our sakes he,
through whom time was made, was made in time;
older by eternity than the world itself,
he became younger in age than many of his servants in the world;
God, who made man, was made man;
he was given existence by a mother
whom he brought into existence;
he was carried in hands which he formed;
he was nursed at breasts which he filled;
he cried like a baby in the manger in speechless infancy–
this Word
without which human eloquence is speechless.

Augustine

At this feast of the nativity
let each person wreathe the door of his heart
so that the Holy Spirit may delight in that door,
enter in and take up residence there;
then by the Spirit we will be made holy.

Ephrem of Syria

The readings for the **Twelve Days of Christmas** focus upon the mystery of the incarnation. The various authors chosen, both Eastern and Western, meditate not only upon the wonder of Christ's birth, but the scandal of its particularity. The significance of Bethlehem, the crib, the roles of Mary and Joseph, the sheer poverty and vulnerability of the Holy Family, are themes that recur throughout Christian literature.

Proper readings for the Feasts of **St Stephen**, **St John the Evangelist** and **The Holy Innocents** which, depending on where Christmas Day falls in the week, may or may not have to be transferred, are provided separately in the companion volume *Celebrating the Saints,* pp. 477–83.

At the end of the section, readings are provided for the **Sundays** of Christmastide. If for pastoral reasons the **Feast of the Holy Family** is observed on another date, the reading provided for First Sunday of Christmas should be used.

Christmas Day

at night:

A Reading from a sermon for the Nativity of Christ
by Julian of Vezelay

'While gentle silence enveloped the whole earth, and night was halfway through its course, your all-powerful Word, O Lord, leaped down from your royal throne in the heavens.' In this ancient text of Scripture, the most sacred moment of time is made known to us, the moment when God's all-powerful Word would leave the tender embrace of the Father and come down into his mother's womb, bringing us the news of salvation. For, as it says elsewhere in Scripture, 'God spoke to our ancestors in many and various ways by the prophets, but in these last days he has spoken to us by a Son,' declaring: 'This is my beloved Son in whom I am well pleased.' And so from his royal throne the Word of God has come to us, humbling himself in order to raise us on high, becoming poor himself in order to make us rich, becoming human in order to make us divine.

So lost and so profoundly unhappy was the human race, that it could only trust in a word that was all-powerful. Anything less would have inspired in us nothing more than the feeblest of hopes in being set free from sin and its power. Therefore, to give poor lost humanity a categorical assurance of being saved, the Word that came to save us was called all-powerful. And see how truly all-powerful that Word was! When neither heaven nor anything under the heavens as yet had existence, the Word spoke, and they came into being, created out of nothing. He spoke the command, 'Let there be earth,' and the earth came into being, and when he decreed, 'Let there be human beings,' human beings were created.

But the Word of God did not remake his creatures as easily as he had made them. He had made them by issuing a command; he remade them by dying. He made them by commanding; he remade them by suffering. 'You have burdened me,' he told them, 'with your sinning. To direct and govern the whole fabric of the world is no effort for me, for I have power to reach from one end of the world to the other, and to order all things as I please. It is only humanity, with its obstinate disregard for the law I have given, which has caused me distress by their sins. That is why I have come down from my royal throne; that is why I have not shrunk from enclosing myself in the Virgin's womb nor from entering into a personal union with poor lost humanity. See, I lie in a manger, a newly born baby wrapped in swaddling bands, since the Creator of the world could find no room in the inn.'

And so there came a deep silence and the whole earth was still. The voices of prophets and apostles were hushed, for the prophets had delivered their message, whereas the time for the apostles' preaching was yet to come. Between these two proclamations a period of silence intervened, and in the midst of this silence the Father's all-powerful Word leaped down from his royal throne. In this movement is great beauty: in the ensuing silence the mediator between God and man intervened, coming as a human being among human beings, as a mortal among mortals, to save the dead from death.

I pray that the Word of the Lord may come again this night to those who wait in silence, and that we may hear what the Lord God is saying to us in our hearts. Let us, therefore, still the desires and cravings of the flesh, the roving fantasies of our imaginations, so that we can attend to what the Spirit is saying.

during the day:

A Reading from an oration of Gregory of Nazianzus

Christ is born: let us glorify him. Christ comes down from heaven: let us go out to meet him. Christ descends to earth: let us be raised on high. Let all the world sing to the Lord: let the heavens rejoice and let the earth be glad, for his sake who was first in heaven and then on earth. Christ is here in the flesh: let us exult with fear and joy – with fear, because of our sins; with joy, because of the hope that he brings us.

Once more the darkness is dispersed; once more the light is created. Let the people that sat in the darkness of ignorance now look upon the light of knowledge. The things of old have passed away; behold, all things are made new. He who has no mother in heaven is now born without a father on earth. The laws of nature are overthrown, for the upper world must be filled with citizens. He who is without flesh becomes incarnate; the Word puts on a body; the invisible makes itself seen; the intangible can be touched; the timeless has a beginning; the Son of God becomes the Son of Man, Jesus Christ, the same yesterday, today and for ever.

Light from light, the Word of the Father comes to his own image in the human race. For the sake of my flesh he takes flesh;

for the sake of my soul he is united to a rational soul, purifying like by like. In every way he becomes human, except for sin. O strange conjunction! The self-existent comes into being; the uncreated is created. He shares in the poverty of my flesh that I may share in the riches of his Godhead.

This is the solemnity we are celebrating today: the arrival of God among us, so that we might go to God – or more precisely, return to God. So that stripping off our old humanity we might put on the new; for as in Adam we were dead, so in Christ we become alive: we are born with him, and we rise again with him.

A miracle, not of creation, but of re-creation. For this is the feast of my being made whole, my returning to the condition God designed for me, to the original Adam. So let us revere the nativity which releases us from the chains of evil. Let us honour this tiny Bethlehem which restores us to paradise. Let us reverence this crib because from it we, who were deprived of self-understanding, are fed by the divine understanding, the Word of God himself.

alternative reading

A Reading from a treatise *Against Heresies*
by Irenaeus

Just as it is possible for a mother to give her infant strong food but chooses not to do so because her child is not able yet to receive such bodily nourishment; so it was possible for God on his part to have given human beings the fullness of perfection right from the beginning, but we were not capable of receiving so great a gift being mere children. In these last days, however, when our Lord summed up all things in himself, he came to us, not as he could have done, but as we were capable of beholding him. He could, indeed, have come to us in the radiance of his glory, but we were not capable of bearing it. So, as to infants, the perfect Bread of the Father gave himself to us under the form of milk – he came to us as a human being – in order that we might be fed, so to speak, at the breast by his incarnation, and by this diet of milk become accustomed to eating and drinking the Word of God. In this way we might be enabled to keep within us the Bread of Immortality which is the Spirit of the Father.

A Reading from a sermon of Leo the Great

Dearly beloved, today our Saviour was born; let us rejoice! This is no season for sadness – it is the birthday of Life! It is a life that annihilates the fear of death; a life that brings us joy with the promise of eternal happiness.

Nobody is an outsider to this happiness; we all have common cause for rejoicing. Our Lord, the victor over sin and death, finding no one free from guilt, has come to free us all. Let the saint exult for the palm of victory is at hand. Let the sinner be glad in receiving the offer of forgiveness. Let the gentile take courage on being summoned to life.

In the fullness of time, chosen in the unfathomable depths of God's wisdom, the Son of God took on himself our human nature in order to reconcile us with our Creator. He came to overthrow the devil, the origin of death, in that very nature by which the devil had overthrown humankind. In this conflict undertaken for us, a war has been waged on the mighty and highest principles of justice. The almighty Lord has gone into battle against our cruel enemy clothed not in his own majesty, but in our weakness. In Christ majesty has taken on humility, strength has taken on weakness, eternity has taken on mortality, and all in order to settle the debt we owe for our condition.

That is why at the birth of our Lord the angels sang for joy: 'Glory to God in the highest,' and proclaimed the message 'peace to his people on earth'. For they see the heavenly Jerusalem being constructed out of all the nations of the world. How greatly then should we mere mortals rejoice when the angels on high are so exultant at this mysterious undertaking of divine love!

Let us, then, dearly beloved, give thanks to God the Father, through his Son, in the Holy Spirit, because in his great love for us he has taken pity on us, 'and when we were dead in our sins he brought us to life with Christ,' so that in him we might be a new creation, a new work of his hands. Let us throw off our old nature and all its habits and, as we have come to birth in Christ, let us renounce the works of the flesh.

Christian, acknowledge your own dignity; and now that you share in God's own nature, do not return by sin to your former base condition. Bear in mind who is your head and of whose body you are a member. Remember that 'you have been rescued from the power of darkness and brought into the light of God's kingdom.'

Through the sacrament of baptism you have become a temple of the Holy Spirit. Do not drive away so great a guest by evil conduct and become again a slave to the devil, for your liberty was bought at the price of Christ's blood.

alternative reading

A Reading from a poem by Robert Southwell

The Nativity of Christ

Behold the father is his daughter's son,
The bird that built the nest is hatched therein,
The old of years an hour hath not outrun,
Eternal life to live doth now begin,
The Word is dumb, the mirth of heaven doth weep,
Might feeble is, and force doth faintly creep.

O dying souls, behold your living spring;
O dazzled eyes, behold your sun of grace;
Dull ears, attend what word this Word doth bring;
Up, heavy hearts, with joy your joy embrace.
From death, from dark, from deafness, from despairs,
This life, this light, this Word, this joy repairs.

Gift better than himself God doth not know;
Gift better than his God no man can see.
This gift doth here the giver given bestow;
Gift to this gift let each receiver be.
God is my gift, himself he freely gave me;
God's gift am I, and none but God shall have me.

Man altered was by sin from man to beast;
Beast's food is hay, hay is all mortal flesh.
Now God is flesh and lies in manger pressed
As hay, the brutest sinner to refresh.
O happy field wherein this fodder grew,
Whose taste doth us from beasts to men renew.

26 December

A Reading from a treatise *On the Trinity*
by Hilary of Poitiers

How can we make a fitting recompense to God for stooping down to us so graciously? The one only-begotten God, born of God in a way that cannot be described, is enclosed in the shape of a tiny human embryo in the womb of the Virgin and grows in size. He who upholds the universe, in whom and through whom everything came into existence, is brought forth according to the law of human birth; he at whose voice the angels and archangels tremble, and the heavens, the earth and all the elements of the world melt, is heard in the cries of a baby. He who is invisible and incomprehensible, who cannot be judged by the reckonings of sight, sense and touch, lies wrapped in a cradle. If any consider these conditions unfitting for a God, they will have to admit that their indebtedness to such generosity is all the greater, the less they are suited to the majesty of God.

God, through whom humanity came into being, was under no compulsion to become human himself. However, it was necessary for humanity that he should be made flesh and dwell among us. He made our flesh his home by assuming our body of flesh. We have been raised up because he has stooped down to us: his abasement is our glory. He, being God, made our flesh his residence, that we in turn might be restored to God.

27 December

A Reading from a *Hymn on the Nativity*
by Ephrem of Syria

Your mother is a cause for wonder: the Lord entered her
and became a servant; he who is the Word entered
and became silent within her; thunder entered her
and made no sound; there entered the Shepherd of all,
and in her he became the Lamb, bleating as he came forth.

Your mother's womb has reversed the roles:
the Establisher of all entered in his richness,
but came forth poor; the Exalted One entered her,
but came forth meek; the Splendrous One entered her,
but came forth having put on a lowly hue.

The Mighty One entered, and put on insecurity
from her womb; the Provisioner of all entered
and experienced hunger; he who gives drink to all entered
and experienced thirst: naked and stripped
there came forth from her he who clothes all.

28 December

A Reading from a sermon of Mark Frank

Christ comes as soon to the low cottage as to the loftiest palace, to
the handmaid as to the mistress, to the poor as to the rich; nay,
prefers them here, honours a poor humble maid above all the
gallant ladies of the world. You will see his humility most if you
consider his wrapping up. He that measures the heavens with his
span, the waters in the hollow of his hand, who involves all things,
all the treasures of wisdom and knowledge, in whom all our beings
and well-beings are wrapped from all eternity; comes now to be
wrapped and made up like a new-born child – who can unwind or
unfold his humility?
    The clothes his dear mother wrapped him in are the very
badges of humility; a rag, or torn and tattered clothes: such were
the clothes she wrapped him in – such, he is so humble, he will be
content with, even with rags. What make we then such ado for
clothes? Our blessed Lord here is content with what comes next.
But Lord! to see what ado have we about our apparel! this lace,
and that trimming; this fashion, and that colour; these jewels, and
those accoutrements; this cloth, and that stuff; this silk, and that
velvet; this silver, and that gold; this way of wearing, and that garb
in them; as if our whole life were raiment, our clothes heaven,
and our salvation the handsome wearing them. We forget, we
forget our sweet Saviour's rags, his poor ragged swaddling-clothes
and our garments witness against us to our faces, our pride, our
follies, our vanities at the best.

Well, but though he was content to be wrapped in swaddling-clothes, and those none of the handsomest, neither, may we not look for a cradle at least to lay him in? No matter what we may look for, we are like to find no better than a manger for that purpose, and a lock of hay for his bed, and for his pillow, and for his mantle too. A poor condition, and an humble one indeed, for him whose chariot is the clouds, whose palace is in heaven, whose throne is with the Most High. What place can we hereafter think too mean for any of us? Stand thou here, sit thou there, under my foot-stool – places of exceeding honour compared to this. What, not a room among men, not among the meanest, in some smoky cottage, or ragged cell; but among beasts! Whither hath thy humility driven thee, O Saviour of mankind? Why, mere pity of a woman in thy mother's case, O Lord, would have made the most obdurate have removed her from the horses' feet, the asses' heels, the company of unruly beasts, from the ordure and nastiness of a stable.

And what of us? Though there be no room for him in the inn, I hope there is in our houses for him. It is Christmas time, and let us keep open house for him; let his rags be our Christmas raiment, his manger our Christmas cheer, his stable our Christmas great chamber, hall, dining-room.

[O thou that refusedst not the manger, refuse not the manger of my unworthy heart to lie in, but accept a room in thy servant's soul. Turn and abide with me. Thy poverty, O sweet Jesu, shall be my patrimony, thy weakness my strength, thy rags my riches, thy manger my kingdom; all the dainties of the world, but chaff to me in comparison of thee; and all the room in the world, no room to that, wheresoever it is, that thou vouchsafest to be. Heaven it is wheresoever thou stayest or abidest; and I will change all the house and wealth I have for thy rags and manger.]

29 December

A Reading from a sermon of John Henry Newman
preached before the University of Oxford in 1843

Little is told to us in Scripture concerning the Blessed Virgin, but there is one grace of which the evangelists, in a few simple sentences, make her the pattern of faith. Zechariah questioned the angel's message, but Mary said, 'Behold, the handmaid of the Lord; be it unto me according to thy word.' Accordingly Elizabeth, speaking with an apparent allusion to the contrast thus exhibited between her own highly-favoured husband, righteous Zechariah, and the still more highly-favoured Mary, said, on receiving her salutation, 'Blessed art thou among women, and blessed is the fruit of thy womb. Blessed is she that believed for there shall be a performance of those things which were told her from the Lord.'

But Mary's faith did not end in a mere acquiescence in divine providence and revelations: as the text informs us, she 'pondered' them. When the shepherds came, and told of the vision of angels which they had seen at the time of the nativity, and how one of them announced that the infant in her arms was the 'Saviour, which is Christ the Lord,' while others did but wonder, 'Mary kept all these things, and pondered them in her heart.' Again, when her son and Saviour had come to the age of twelve years, and had left her for awhile for his Father's service, and had been found, to her surprise, in the temple amid the doctors, both hearing them and asking them questions, and had, on her addressing him, vouchsafed to justify his conduct, we are told, 'His mother kept all these sayings in her heart.' And accordingly, at the marriage feast in Cana, her faith anticipated his first miracle, and she said to the servants, 'Whatsoever he saith unto you, do it.'

Thus St Mary is our pattern of faith, both in the reception and in the study of divine truth. She does not think it enough to accept, she dwells upon it; not enough to possess, she uses it; not enough to assent, she develops it; not enough to submit the reason, she reasons upon it; not indeed reasoning first, and believing afterwards, with Zechariah, yet first believing without reasoning, next from love and reverence, reasoning after believing. And thus she symbolises to us, not only the faith of the unlearned, but of the doctors of the Church also, who have to investigate, and weigh, and define, as well as to profess the gospel; to draw the line between truth and heresy; to anticipate or remedy the various aberrations of wrong reason; to combat pride and recklessness with their own arms; and thus to triumph over the sophist and the innovator.

30 December

A Reading from a homily of Basil the Great

God on earth, God among us! No longer the God who gives his law amid flashes of lightning, to the sound of the trumpet on the smoking mountain, within the darkness of a terrifying storm, but the God who speaks gently and with kindness in a human body to his kindred. God in the flesh! It is no longer the God who acts only at particular instants, as in the prophets, but one who completely assumes our human nature and through his flesh, which is that of our race, lifts all humanity up to him.

How, then, you will say, did the light come everywhere, through one sole person? In what manner is the Godhead in the flesh? Like fire in iron: not by moving about, but by spreading itself. The fire, indeed, does not thrust itself toward the iron, but, remaining where it is, it distributes its own strength to it. In doing so, the fire is in no way diminished, but it completely fills the iron to which it spreads. In the same manner, God the Word who 'dwelt among us' did not go outside himself; the Word which was 'made flesh' underwent no change; heaven was not deprived of him who controlled it and the earth received within itself him who is in heaven.

Look deeply into this mystery. God comes in the flesh in order to destroy the death concealed in flesh. In the same way as remedies and medicines triumph over the factors of corruption when they are assimilated into the body, and in the same way as the darkness which reigns in a house is dispelled by the entry of light, so death, which held human nature in its power, was annihilated by the coming of the Godhead. In the same way as ice, when in water, prevails over the liquid element as long as it is night, and darkness covers everything, but is dissolved when the sun comes up through the warmth of its rays: so death reigned till the coming of Christ; but when the saving grace of God appeared and the sun of justice rose, death was swallowed up in this victory, being unable to endure the dwelling of the true life among us. O the depth of the goodness of God and of his love for all of us!

Let us give glory to God with the shepherds, let us dance in choir with the angels, for 'this day a Saviour has been born to us, the Messiah and Lord.' He is the Lord who has appeared to us, not in his divine form in order not to terrify us in our weakness, but in the form of a servant, that he might set free what had been reduced to servitude. Who could be so faint-hearted and so ungrateful as not to rejoice and exult in gladness for what is taking place? This is a festival of all creation.

31 December

A Reading from an oration by Proclus,
Patriarch of Constantinople

What we celebrate today is the pride and glory of womankind, wrought in one who was both mother and virgin. Behold, earth and sea are the Virgin's escorts: the sea spreads out her waves in calm beneath the ships; the earth conducts the steps of travellers on their way unhindered. So let nature leap for joy; women are honoured! Let all the world dance; virgins receive praise! For where 'sin increased, grace has abounded yet more'.

Holy Mary has gathered us together in celebration, Mary – the untarnished vessel of virginity, the spiritual paradise of the second Adam, the workshop in which the union of human and divine natures is to be forged, the bridal chamber in which the Word is to be married to human flesh. Behold a living human bush which the fire of divine childbirth did not consume. In Mary we see both handmaid and mother, maiden and heaven, the bridge to humankind. She has become the loom of our salvation and the Holy Spirit is the weaver, a powerful worker who overshadows her from on high. The wool the weaver takes is drawn from the ancient fleece of Adam, the warp the unsullied body of the Virgin, the shuttle the immeasurable grace of him who wove it, and the weft the Word who enters her through her ear.

Who ever saw, who ever heard of the infinite God dwelling in a human womb? Heaven cannot contain God, and yet a womb did not constrict him. He was born of woman, God but not solely God, and man but not solely man. Through this birth what was once the door of sin has been transformed into the gate of salvation. Through ears that disobeyed, the serpent once poured his deadly poison; now through ears that obeyed, the Word has entered to form a living temple. In the former case, Cain emerged as its fruit, the first pupil of sin; but with Mary, it was Christ the redeemer of our race, who has sprouted unsown into life. The merciful God was not repulsed by the labour pains of a woman; for the business in hand was life.

1 January

The Naming and Circumcision of Jesus

A Reading from a treatise *On Contemplating God*
by William of St Thierry

O God, you alone are the Lord. To be ruled by you is for us salvation. For us to serve you is nothing else but to be saved by you!

But how is it that we are saved by you, O Lord, from whom salvation comes and whose blessing is upon your people, if it is not in receiving from you the gift of loving you and being loved by you? That, Lord, is why you willed that the Son of your right hand, the 'man whom you made so strong for yourself', should be called Jesus, that is to say, Saviour, 'for he will save his people from their sins'. There is no other in whom is salvation except him who taught us to love himself when he first loved us, even to death on the cross. By loving us and holding us so dear he stirred us up to love himself, who first had loved us to the end.

You who first loved us did this, precisely this. You first loved us so that we might love you. And that was not because you needed to be loved by us, but because we could not be what you created us to be, except by loving you. Having then 'in many ways and on various occasions spoken to our fathers by the prophets, now in these last days you have spoken to us in the Son', your Word, by whom the heavens were established, and all the power of them by the breath of his mouth. For you to speak thus in your Son was an open declaration, a 'setting in the sun' as it were, of how much and in what sort of way you loved us, in that you spared not your own Son, but delivered him up for us all. Yes, and he himself loved us and gave himself for us.

This, Lord, is your word to us; this is your all-powerful message: he who, 'while all things kept silence' (that is, were in the depths of error), 'came from the royal throne', the stern opponent of error and the gentle apostle of love. And everything he did and everything he said on earth, even the insults, the spitting, the buffeting, the cross and the grave, all that was nothing but yourself speaking to us in the Son, appealing to us by your love, and stirring up our love for you.

alternative reading

A Reading from a sermon of Mark Frank

This name 'which is above every name' has all things in it, and brings all things with it. It speaks more in five letters than we can do in five thousand words. It speaks more in it than we can speak today: and yet we intend today to speak of nothing else, nothing but Jesus, nothing but Jesus.

Before his birth the angel announced that this child, born of Mary, would be great: 'he shall be called Son of the Highest, and the Lord God shall give him the throne of his father David.' The angel thus intimates that this was a name of the highest majesty and glory. And what can we say upon it, less than burst out with the psalmist into a holy exclamation, 'O Lord our Governor, O Lord our Jesus, how excellent is thy name in all the world!' It is all 'clothed with majesty and honour'; it is 'decked with light'; it comes riding to us 'upon the wings of the wind'; the Holy Spirit breathes it full upon us, covering heaven and earth with its glory.

But it is a name of grace and mercy, as well as majesty and glory. For 'there is no other name under heaven given by which we can be saved,' but the name of Jesus. In his name we live, and in that name we die. As St Ambrose has written: 'Jesus is all things to us if we will.' Therefore I will have nothing else but him; and I have all if I have him.

The 'looking unto Jesus' which the apostle advises, will keep us from being weary or fainting under our crosses; for this name was set upon the cross over our Saviour's head. This same Jesus at the end fixes and fastens all. The love of God in Jesus will never leave us, never forsake us; come what can, it sweetens all.

Is there any one sad? – let him take Jesus into his heart, and he will take heart presently, and his joy will return upon him. Is any one fallen into a sin? – let him call heartily upon this name, and it will raise him up. Is any one troubled with hardness of heart, or dullness of spirit, or dejection of mind, or drowsiness in doing well? – in the meditation of this name, Jesus, all vanish and fly away. Our days would look dark and heavy, which were not lightened with the name of the 'Sun of Righteousness'; our nights but sad and dolesome, which we entered not with this sweet name, when we lay down without commending ourselves to God in it.

So then let us remember to begin and end all in Jesus. The New Testament, the covenant of our salvation, begins so, 'the generation of Jesus'; and 'Come Lord Jesus', so it ends. May we all

Christmas   *57*

end so too, and when we are going hence, commend our spirits into his hands; and when he comes, may he receive them to sing praises and alleluias to his blessed name amidst the saints and angels in his glorious kingdom for ever.

2 January

A Reading from a sermon of Augustine

Who can know all the treasures of wisdom and knowledge hidden in Christ and concealed in the poverty of his human flesh? 'Though he was rich, yet for our sake he became poor, so that by his poverty we might become rich.' When he made this mortal flesh his own and abolished death, he appeared among us in poverty; but he promised riches, riches that were only deferred – he did not lose riches that were taken from him.

How great is the abundance of his goodness which is stored up for those who fear him, which he brings to perfection in those who hope in him! Our knowledge now is partial until what is perfect is revealed. To make us fit to receive this gift, he who is equal to the Father in the form of God was made like us in the form of a slave, in order that we might be transformed into the likeness of God. The only Son of God was made Son of Man, and so the children of earth became the children of God. We were slaves, entranced by this visible form of a slave, and have now been set free and raised to the status of children so that we might see the form of God.

As Scripture says: 'We are God's children; it has not yet been revealed what we shall be, but we know that when he appears we shall be like him, for we shall see him as he is.' What are those treasures of wisdom and knowledge? What are those divine riches except that which will truly satisfy us? What is that abundance of goodness except that which fills us?

In the gospel, Philip says: 'Show us the Father and we shall be satisfied.' And in one of the psalms it is written: 'I shall be filled when your glory is revealed.' The Son and the Father are one: whoever sees the Son is seeing the Father also. So then, the Lord of hosts, the king of glory, will bring us home, and will show us his face. We shall be saved, we shall be filled, and we shall be satisfied.

Until this happens, until God shows us what will ultimately satisfy us, until we drink of him as the fountain of life and are filled – until then, we are exiles, walking by faith. Until then, we hunger and thirst for justice, longing with a passion beyond words for the beauty of the form of God. Until then, let us celebrate his birth in the form of a slave with humble devotion.

3 January

A Reading from a letter of Athanasius of Alexandria

The Scriptures record that the Word 'took to himself descent from Abraham' and that therefore it was essential that 'he should become completely like his brothers and sisters', and have a body similar to our own. This explains the role of Mary in the plan of God: she was to provide the Word with a human body so that he might offer it up as something that is his own. Scripture records her giving birth, and tell us that she 'wrapped him in swaddling-clothes'. The breasts that suckled him were called blessed. Sacrifice was offered because this child was her firstborn. The angel Gabriel announced the good news of his birth in careful and prudent language. He did not speak of 'what will be born in you', to avoid the impression that a body had been introduced into her womb from the outside. Rather, he said: 'what will be born from you', so that we might know that her child originated within her entirely naturally.

The Word adopted this pattern so that by assuming our human nature and offering it in sacrifice, he might both abolish it and invest it with his own nature. As the apostle Paul was inspired to write: 'This corruptible body must put on incorruption; this mortal body must put on immortality.'

His birth was no pretence, as some have suggested. Far from it! Our Saviour really did become human, and from this has followed the salvation of humankind. Our salvation is no pretence, nor is it the salvation of the body only. The salvation which the Word has secured is of the whole person, body and soul.

What was born of Mary, according to Scripture, was human by nature. The Lord's body was real – real because it was the same as ours. Mary, you see, is our sister, for we are all descended from Adam.

This is the meaning of the words of St John: 'The Word was made flesh.' His words have the same import as others of St Paul: 'Christ was made a curse for our sake.' The human body has acquired something wonderful through its communion and union with the Word. From being mortal it has become immortal; though physical, it has become spiritual; though made from the earth, it has passed through the gates of heaven.

4 January

A Reading from a sermon of Bernard of Clairvaux

When God emptied himself and took the form of a servant, he emptied himself only of majesty and power, not of goodness and mercy. For what does the Apostle say? 'The goodness and humanity of God our Saviour have appeared in our midst.' God's power had appeared already in creation, and his wisdom in the ordering of creation; but his goodness and mercy have appeared now in his humanity.

So what are you frightened of? Why are you trembling before the face of the Lord when he comes? God has come not to judge the world, but to save it! Do not run away; do not be afraid. God comes unarmed; he wants to save you, not to punish you. And lest you should say 'I heard your voice and I hid myself,' look – he is here, an infant with no voice. The cry of a baby is something to be pitied, not to be frightened of. He is made a little child, the Virgin Mother has wrapped his tender limbs in swaddling bands; so why are you still quaking with fear? This tells you that God has come to save you, not to lose you; to rescue you, not to imprison you.

God is already fighting your two enemies, sin and death – the death of both body and soul. He has come to conquer both of them; so do not fear, he will save you from them. He has already conquered sin in his own person, in that he took our human nature upon himself without spot of sin. From this moment on he pursues your enemies and overtakes them, and will not return until he has overcome them both. He fights sin with his life, he attacks it with his word and example; and in his passion he binds it, yes, binds 'the strong man and carries off his goods'. In the same way it is in his own person that he first conquers death when he rises as 'the firstfruits of those who sleep, the firstborn from the dead'. From now on he will conquer it in all of us as he raises up our mortal bodies, and death, the last enemy, will be destroyed.

In his rising he is clothed with honour, no longer wrapped in swaddling bands as at his birth. At his birth, in the wide embrace of his mercy, he judged no one; but at his resurrection he ties around his waist the girdle of righteousness which in some sense must define the embrace of his mercy. Henceforth we must be ready for judgement which will take place when we ourselves are raised. Today he has come to us as a little child, that before all else he might offer all people mercy; but in his resurrection he anticipates the final judgement when mercy must needs be balanced by the claims of righteousness.

5 January

A Reading from the *Catechetical Orations*
of Gregory of Nyssa

That God should have clothed himself with our nature is a fact that should not seem strange or extravagant to minds that do not form too paltry an idea of reality. Who, looking at the universe, would be so feeble-minded as not to believe that God is all in all; that he clothes himself with the universe, and at the same time contains it and dwells in it? What exists depends on the One who is, and nothing can exist except in the bosom of the One who is.

If then all is in God and God is in all, why be embarrassed about a faith that teaches us that one day God was born in the human condition, a God who still today exists in humanity?

Indeed, if the presence of God in us does not take the same form now as it did then, we can at least agree in recognising that he is in us today no less than he was then. Today, he is involved with us in as much as he maintains creation in existence. In Christ he mingled himself with our being to deify it by contact with him, after he had snatched it from death. For his resurrection becomes for mortals the promise of their ultimate return to immortal life.

The First Sunday of Christmas

The Holy Family

A Reading from *The Light of Christ* by Evelyn Underhill

The new life grows in secret. Nothing very startling happens. We see the child in the carpenter's workshop. He does not go outside the frontiers within which he appeared. It did quite well for him and will do quite well for us. There is no need for peculiar conditions in the spiritual life. Our environment itself, our home and job, are part of the moulding action of God. Have we fully realised all that is unfolded in this ? How unchristian it is to try to get out of our frame, to separate our daily life from our prayer? That third-rate little village in the hills with its limited social contacts and monotonous manual work reproves us, when we begin to fuss about opportunities and scope. And that quality of quietness and ordinariness, that simplicity with which he entered into his great vocation, endured from the beginning to the end.

The child Jesus grows as other children, the lad works as other lads. Total abandonment to the vast divine purpose working at its own pace in and through ordinary life and often, to us, in mysterious ways. I love to think that much in Christ's own destiny was mysterious to him. It was part of his perfect manhood that he shared our human situation in this too.

We often feel we ought to get on quickly to a new stage like spiritual mayflies. Christ takes thirty years to grow and two and a half to act. Only the strange dreams Joseph and Mary had, warned a workman and his young wife that they lay in the direct line of God's action, that the growth committed to them mattered supremely to the world. And when his growth reached the right stage, there is the revelation of God's call and after it, stress, discipline and choice. Those things came together as signs of maturity and they were not spectacular things. It is much the same with us in our life of prayer: the Spirit fills us as we grow, develop and make room.

We get notions sometimes that we ought to spring up quickly like seed on stony ground, we ought to show some startling sign of spiritual growth. But perhaps we are only asked to go on quietly, to be a child, a nice stocky seedling, not shooting up in a hurry, but making root, being docile to the great slow rhythm of life. When you don't see any startling marks of your own religious condition or your usefulness to God, think of the baby in the stable and the little boy in the streets of Nazareth. The very life was there which was to change the whole history of the human race. There was not much to show for it. But there is entire continuity between the stable and the Easter garden and the thread that unites them is the will of God. The childlike simple prayer of Nazareth was the right preparation for the awful privilege of the cross. Just so the light of the Spirit is to unfold gently and steadily within us, till at last our final stature, all God designed for us, is attained.

The Second Sunday of Christmas

A Reading from a sermon of Augustine

Beloved, our Lord Jesus Christ, the eternal Creator of all things, today became our Saviour by being born of a mother. Of his own will he was born for us in time, so that he could lead us to his Father's eternity. God became human like us so that we might become God. The Lord of the angels became one of us today so that we could eat the bread of angels.

Today, the prophecy is fulfilled that said: 'Pour down, heavens, from above, and let the clouds rain down righteousness: let the earth be opened and bring forth a Saviour.' The Lord who had created all things is himself now created, so that he who was lost would be found. Thus humanity, in the words of the psalmist, confesses: 'Before I was humbled, I sinned.' We sinned and became guilty; God is born as one of us to free us from our guilt. We fell, but God descended; we fell miserably, but God descended mercifully; we fell through pride, God descended with his grace.

What miracles! What wonders! The laws of nature are changed in the case of humankind. God is born. A virgin becomes pregnant. The Word of God marries the woman who knows no man. She is now at the same time both mother and virgin. She becomes a mother, yet she remains a virgin. The virgin bears a son, yet she does not know a man; she remains untouched, yet she is not barren.

EPIPHANY

God never imparts himself as he is to those
who contemplate him while still in this mortal life,
but he shows forth his brightness scantily
to the blinking eyes of our mind.

Gregory the Great

Reconciling Peace, sent to the people,
Gladdening Flash, who came to the gloomy,
Powerful Leaven, conquering all in silence,
Patient One, who has captured the creation little by little.

Blessed is he who became small without limit
to make us great without limit.

Ephrem of Syria

The date of the **Feast of the Epiphany** relates to the custom of celebrating the Feast of the Nativity of Christ in the winter solstice. The north European pre-Christian tradition of celebrating the birth of the Sun on 25 December differed from the Mediterranean and Eastern tradition of observing 6 January as the solstice. As often happens, the two dates merged into a beginning and an end of the same celebration. The Western Church adopted 'the twelve days of Christmas' climaxing on the eve of Epiphany, or 'Twelfth Night'. The implication by the fifth century was that this was the night on which the Magi arrived. The complications of dating became even more confused with the change from the Julian to the Gregorian Calendar in the West, the Eastern Church refusing to participate in the change. So the Feast of the Epiphany remains the chief day of celebrating the incarnation in Orthodox Churches.

Proper readings focusing on the traditional themes of the feast, namely, the arrival of the Magi and the mystical significance of their gifts, the Baptism of Christ in the Jordan, and the miracle at Cana of Galilee – 'the first of the signs that revealed his glory' – are provided for **The Epiphany** and for the days that follow until the Sunday after the feast which is observed as **The Baptism of Christ**. If, for pastoral reasons, the celebration of the Epiphany is transferred to the Sunday between 2 and 8 January, then the provision of readings will need to be supplemented with unused material from the Christmastide section.

The subtitle of the Feast of the Epiphany in *The Book of Common Prayer* – 'The Manifestation of Christ to the Gentiles' – reminds us that, from the moment of the incarnation, the good news of Jesus Christ is for all: Jew and Gentile, the wise and the simple, male and female. The readings throughout the season resonate with this truth, celebrating the universality of God's love, particularly as exemplified in the call of the disciples and in the public ministry of Jesus; and in the mission of the Church to embody it.

The season culminates on 2 February with **The Presentation of Christ in the Temple**, commonly known as Candlemas. According to St Luke, the occasion of Mary's ritual purification was made memorable by Simeon the High Priest acclaiming the Christ-child as 'the light of the Gentiles and the glory of his people Israel'. Recent liturgical revision has restored the feast to its pivotal place in the calendar. It now forms the finale of the incarnational cycle and turns our attention towards the forthcoming passion.

The Epiphany

A Reading from a sermon of Peter Chrysologos,
Bishop of Ravenna

In the mystery of our Lord's incarnation there were clear indications of his eternal Godhead. Yet the great events we celebrate today disclose and reveal in different ways the fact that God himself took a human body. Mortals, enshrouded always in darkness, must not be left in ignorance, and so be deprived of what they can understand and retain only by grace.

In choosing to be born for us, God chose to be known by us. He therefore reveals himself in this way, in order that this great sacrament of his love may not be an occasion for us of great misunderstanding.

Today the Magi find, crying in a manger, the one they have followed as he shone in the sky. Today the Magi see clearly, in swaddling clothes, the one they have long awaited as he lay hidden among the stars. Today the Magi gaze in deep wonder at what they see: heaven on earth, earth in heaven, humankind in God, God in human flesh, one whom the whole universe cannot contain now enclosed in a tiny body. As they look, they believe and do not question, as their symbolic gifts bear witness: incense for God, gold for a king, myrrh for one who is to die.

So the Gentiles, who were the last, become the first: the faith of the Magi is the firstfruits of the belief of the Gentiles.

Today Christ enters the Jordan to wash away the sin of the world. John himself testifies that this is why he has come: 'Behold the Lamb of God, behold him who takes away the sins of the world.' Today a servant lays his hand on the Lord, a man lays his hand on God. John lays his hand on Christ, not to forgive but to receive forgiveness.

Today, as the psalmist prophesied: 'The voice of the Lord is heard – above the waters.' What does the voice say? 'This is my beloved Son, in whom I am well pleased.'

Today the Holy Spirit hovers over the waters in the likeness of a dove. A dove announced to Noah that the flood had disappeared from the earth; so now a dove is to reveal that the world's shipwreck is at an end for ever. The sign is no longer an olive-shoot of the old stock: instead, the Spirit pours out on Christ's head the full richness of a new anointing by the Father, to fulfil what the psalmist had prophesied: 'Therefore God, your God, has anointed you with the oil of gladness above your fellows.'

Today Christ works the first of his signs from heaven by turning water into wine. But water has still to be changed into the sacrament of his blood, so that Christ may offer spiritual drink from the chalice of his body.

alternative reading

A Reading from a hymn of Ephrem of Syria

Who, being a mortal, can tell about the Reviver of all,
Who left the height of his majesty and came down to smallness?
You, who magnify all by being born, magnify my weak mind
    that I may tell about your birth,
    not to investigate your majesty,
    but to proclaim your grace.
Blessed is he who is both hidden and revealed in his actions!

It is a great wonder that the Son, who dwelt entirely in a body,
    inhabited it entirely, and it sufficed for him.
Although limitless, he dwelt in it.
His will was entirely in him; but his totality was not in him.
Who is sufficient to proclaim that
    although he dwelt entirely in a body,
    still he dwelt entirely in the universe?
Blessed is the Unlimited who was limited!

Your majesty is hidden from us; your grace is revealed before us.
I will be silent, my Lord, about your majesty,
    but I will speak about your grace.
Your grace made you a babe;
    your grace made you a human being.
Your majesty contracted and stretched out.
Blessed is the power that became small and became great!

The Magi rejoiced from afar; the scribes proclaimed from nearby.
The prophet showed his erudition, and Herod his fury.
The scribes showed interpretations; the Magi showed offerings.
It is a wonder that to one babe the kinspeople rushed
    with their swords,
    but strangers with their offerings.
Blessed is your birth that stirred up the universe!

alternative reading

A Reading from a sermon of Lancelot Andrewes preached
before King James I at Whitehall in 1620

What place more proper for him who is 'the living bread that came
down from heaven', to give life to the world, than Bethlehem, the
least and lowest of all the houses of Judah. This natural birth-place
of his sheweth his spiritual nature. Christ's birth fell in the sharpest
season, in the deep of winter. As humility his place, so affliction
his time. The time and place fit well.

And there came from the East wise men, Gentiles; and that
concerns us, for so are we. Christ's birth is made manifest to them
by the star of heaven. It is the Gentiles' star, and so ours too. We
may set our course by it, to seek and find, and worship him as well
as they. So we come in, for 'God hath also to the Gentiles set open
a door of faith,' and that he would do this, and call us in, there was
some small star-light from the beginning. This he promised by the
patriarchs, shadowed forth in the figures of the law and the temple
and the tabernacle, and foresung in the psalms, and it is this day
fulfilled.

These wise men are come and we with them. Not only in their
own names, but in ours did they make their entry; came and sought
after, and found and worshipped, their Saviour and ours, the
Saviour of the whole world. A little wicket there was left open,
whereat divers Gentiles did come in, but only one or two. But now
the great gate set wide opens this day for all – for these here with
their camels and dromedaries to enter, and all their carriage. Christ
is not only for russet cloaks, shepherds and such; but even
grandees, great states such as these came too; and when they came
were welcome to him. For they were sent for and invited by this
star, their star properly.

They came a long journey, and they came an uneasy journey.
They came now, at the worst season of the year. And all but to do
worship at Christ's birth. They stayed not their coming till the
opening of the year, till they might have better weather and way,
and have longer days, and so more seasonable and fit to travel in.
So desirous were they to come with the first, and to be there as
soon as possibly they might; broke through all these difficulties,
and behold, they did come.

And we, what excuse shall we have if we come not? If so short
and easy a way we come not, as from our chambers hither? And
these wise men were never a whit less wise for so coming; nay, to

come to Christ is one of the wisest parts that ever these wise men did. And if we believe this, that this was their wisdom, if they and we be wise in one Spirit, by the same principles, we will follow the same star, tread the same way, and so come at last whither they are happily gone before us.

[In the old ritual of the Church we find that on the cover of the canister wherein was the sacrament of his body, there was a star engraven, to shew us that now the star leads us thither, to his body there. So what shall I say now, but according as St John saith, and the star, and the wise men say 'Come'. And he whose star it is, and to whom the wise men came, saith 'Come'. And let them that are disposed 'Come'. And let whosoever will, take of the 'Bread of Life which came down from heaven' this day into Bethlehem, the house of bread. Of which bread the Church is this day the house, the true Bethlehem, and all the Bethlehem we have now left to come to for the Bread of Life – of that life which we hope for in heaven. And this our nearest coming that here we can come, till we shall by another coming 'Come' unto him in his heavenly kingdom.]

7 January

A Reading from a sermon of Bernard of Clairvaux

'The goodness and humanity of God our Saviour have appeared in our midst.' We thank God for the many consolations he has given us during this sad exile of our pilgrimage here on earth. Before the Son of God became human his goodness was hidden, for God's mercy is eternal, but how could such goodness be recognised? It was promised, but it was not experienced, and as a result few believed in it. 'Often and in various ways the Lord used to speak through the prophets.' Among other things, God said: 'I think thoughts of peace and not of affliction.' But what did we humans respond, thinking thoughts of affliction and knowing nothing of peace? They said: 'Peace, peace, there is no peace.' This response made the 'angels of peace weep bitterly', saying: 'Lord, who has believed our message?' But now they believe because they see with their own eyes, and because 'God's testimony has now become even more credible.' He has gone so far as to 'pitch his tent in the sun' so even the dimmest eyes see him.

Notice that peace is not promised but sent to us; it is no longer deferred, it is given; peace is not prophesied but achieved. It is as if God the Father sent upon the earth a purse full of his mercy.

This purse was burst open during the Lord's passion to pour forth its hidden contents – the price of our redemption. It was only a small purse, but it was very full. As the Scriptures tell us: 'A little child has been given to us, but in him dwells all the fullness of the divine nature.' The fullness of time brought with it the fullness of divinity. God's Son came in the flesh so that mortals could see and recognise God's kindness. When God reveals his humanity, his goodness cannot possibly remain hidden. To show his kindness what more could he do beyond taking my human form? My humanity, I say, not Adam's – that is, not such as he had before his fall.

How could he have shown his mercy more clearly than by taking on himself our condition? For our sake the Word of God became as grass. What better proof could he have given of his love! Scripture says: 'Lord, what are we that you are mindful of us; why does your heart go out to us?' The incarnation teaches us how much God cares for us and what he thinks and feels about us. We should stop thinking of our own sufferings and remember what he has suffered. Let us think of all the Lord has done for us, and then we shall realise how his goodness appears through his humanity. The lesser he became through his human nature, the greater was his goodness; the more he lowered himself for me, the dearer he is to me. 'The goodness and humanity of God our Saviour have appeared,' says the Apostle.

Truly great and manifest are the goodness and humanity of God. He has given us a most wonderful proof of his goodness by adding humanity to his own divine nature.

8 January

A Reading from a sermon of Leo the Great

The day on which Christ, the Saviour of the world, first appeared to the Gentiles is a great day of celebration for us all. In our hearts we should be experiencing those same joys which the three Magi first felt when, urged on by the sign and leading of a new star, they fell down in worship before the visible presence of the king of heaven and earth, in whose promise they had believed. Although this feast celebrates an event which took place many years ago, we are not simply commemorating an episode which has been handed down to us from the past. Our bounteous God is giving us the same gift now.

The gospel records the circumstances in which these three men who had no previous knowledge of the Jewish prophets or law, came from the remotest regions in the East to acknowledge the true God. But we see the same thing occurring before our eyes in the way in which people from far and wide who have been called by God, are receiving the light of faith. The prophecy of Isaiah is being fulfilled among us: 'The Lord has bared his holy arm in the sight of the nations, and all the nations of the earth have seen the salvation of our God.' And again: 'Those who were not told of him shall see, and those who had not heard will understand.' We are seeing people who have only a worldly kind of knowledge and who are far from belief in Jesus Christ, being led out of the darkness of ignorance to acknowledge the true light. There can be no doubt that the splendour of God's grace is at work among us; and whatever new light that shines in their darkened hearts is coming from rays of that same star which leads us all to the worship of God.

The gifts the Magi first brought to Bethlehem are still being offered by all who come to Christ in faith. When we acclaim Christ as King of the universe we bring him gold from the treasury of our hearts; when we believe that the only-begotten of God has become one with our human nature, we are offering myrrh for his embalming; and when we declare him to be equal in majesty to the Father, we are burning the incense of our worship before him.

9 January

A Reading from a treatise *On the Incarnation*
by Athanasius of Alexandria

The Word of God did not abandon the human race, his creatures, who are hurtling to their own ruin. By the offering of his body, the Word of God destroyed death which had united itself to them; by his teaching, he corrected their negligences; and by his power, he restored the human race.

Why was it necessary for the Word of God to become incarnate and not some other? Scripture indicates the reason in these words: 'It was fitting that in bringing many children to glory, God, for whom and through whom all things exist, should make their leader in the work of salvation perfect through suffering.' This signifies that the work of raising men and women from the ruin into which they had fallen pertained to none other than the Word of God, who had made them in the beginning.

By the sacrifice of his body, he put an end to the law which weighed upon them, and he renewed in us the principle of life by giving us the hope of the resurrection. For if it is through ourselves that death attained dominance over us, conversely, it is through the incarnation of the Word of God that death has been destroyed and that life has been resurrected, as indicated by the Apostle filled with Christ: 'As death came through one man, so the resurrection of the dead comes through another also. For as in Adam all die, so in Christ all will come to life.' It is no longer as condemned that we die. Rather, we die with the hope of rising again from the dead, awaiting the universal resurrection which God will manifest to us in his own time, since he is both the author of it and gives us the grace for it.

When the figure of someone has been painted on wood, but then effaced by external elements, we need the presence of the person whose portrait it was if we are to restore their image on the same material. And if this material is not discarded, it is because of the image painted on it which we value and wish to restore. In like manner, the most holy Son of the Father, being the image of the Father, has come into our land to renew us who had been made similar to him, and to seek us out when we had been lost, pardoning our sins, as Scripture says: 'I have come to search out and save that which was lost.'

Thus, when Jesus says, 'Unless you are born again', he does not allude to birth from a woman, but to the rebirth and recreation of humanity in his image.

10 January

A Reading from a treatise *Against Heresies*
by Irenaeus

No one can know the Father apart from God's Word, that is, unless the Son reveals him, and no one can know the Son unless the Father so wills. Now the Son fulfils the Father's good pleasure: the Father sends, the Son is sent, and he comes. The Father is beyond our sight and comprehension; but he is known by his Word, who tells us of him who surpasses all telling. In turn, the Father alone has knowledge of his Word. And the Lord has revealed both truths. Therefore, the Son reveals the knowledge of the Father by his revelation of himself. Knowledge of the Father consists in the self-revelation of the Son, for all is revealed through the Word.

The Father's purpose in revealing the Son was to make himself known to us all and so to welcome into eternal rest those who believe in him, establishing them in justice, preserving them from death. To believe in him means to do his will.

Through creation itself the Word reveals God the Creator. Through the world he reveals the Lord who made the world. Through all that is fashioned he reveals the artist who crafted it all. Through the Son the Word reveals the Father who begot him as Son. All speak of these things in the same language, but they do not believe them in the same way. Through the law and the prophets the Word revealed himself and his Father in the same way, but though all the people equally heard the message not all believed it. Through the Word, made visible and palpable, the Father was revealed, though not all believed in him. But all saw the Father in the Son, for the Father of the Son cannot be seen, but the Son of the Father can be seen.

The Son performs everything as a ministry to the Father, from beginning to end, and without the Son no one can know God. The way to know the Father is the Son. Knowledge of the Son is in the Father, and is revealed through the Son. For this reason the Lord said: 'No one knows the Son except the Father; and no one knows the Father except the Son, and those to whom the Son has revealed him.' The word 'revealed' refers not only to the future as though the Word began to reveal the Father only when he was born of Mary; it refers equally to all time. From the beginning the Son is present to creation, reveals the Father to all, to those the Father chooses, when the Father chooses, and as the Father chooses. So, there is in all and through all one God the Father, one Word and Son, and one Spirit, and one salvation for all who believe in him.

11 January

A Reading from *The Ascent of Mount Carmel*
by John of the Cross

The chief reason why it was permissible under the old Law to ask God questions and quite in order for the prophets and priests to seek revelations and visions from him was that, in those times, the faith was not yet firmly founded, nor was the law of the gospel inaugurated. Hence, it was necessary for them to question God and for God to reply. This he did sometimes in words, sometimes by visions and revelations, sometimes in figures and types, and then again by many other ways that expressed his meaning. Everything he replied and spoke and revealed was about the mysteries of our faith or matters touching upon or leading up to it.

But now that the faith is founded in Christ and the law of the gospel has been made known in this age of grace, there is no longer any reason to question God in that way. Nor need God speak and answer as he did then. When he gave us, as he did, his Son, who is his one Word, he spoke everything to us, once and for all in that one Word. There is nothing further for him to say.

This is the meaning of that passage where St Paul tries to persuade the Hebrews to abandon the primitive ways and means of communicating with God which are in the law of Moses, and instead fix their eyes on Christ alone. He says: 'In many and various ways God spoke of old to our fathers by the prophets; but in these last days he has spoken to us by a Son.' The Apostle gives us to understand that God has become as if dumb, with nothing more to say, because what he spoke before in fragments to the prophets he has now said all at once by giving us the All who is his Son.

Consequently, anyone who today would want to ask God questions or desire some further vision or revelation, would not only be acting foolishly but would be offending God by not fixing his eyes entirely on Christ, without wanting something new or something in addition to Christ.

God might give this answer: 'This is my beloved Son, with whom I am well pleased; listen to him.' I have already told you all things in my Word. Fix your eyes on him alone, because in him I have spoken and revealed all. Moreover, in him you will find more than you ask or desire.

12 January

A Reading from a sermon of Leo the Great

The loving providence of God, having determined in these last days to save the world, set as it was on its course to destruction, decreed that all nations should be saved in the person of Christ.

A promise had already been made to the holy patriarch Abraham that he was to have a countless progeny, born not from his body, but from the seed of faith. His descendants were therefore to be compared with the multitude of the stars. The father of all nations was to hope not for an earthly progeny but for a progeny from heaven. For the creation of this promised progeny, the heirs designated under the sign of the stars are awakened by the rising of a new star. The heavens themselves perform their service and bear witness: a star more brilliant than all others startles wise men from the East who, not unskilled in the observation of such things, recognise in its rising the presence of a sign.

So let the full number of the nations now come and take their place in the family of the patriarchs. Yes, let the children of the promise enter and receive their blessing in the seed of Abraham, which his children according to the flesh have spurned. In the persons of the Magi let all people adore the Creator of the universe; let God be known, not in Judea only, but throughout the whole world, so that 'his name may be great in all Israel'.

Dear friends, now that we have received instruction in this revelation of God's grace, let us celebrate with joy the day of our first harvesting, of the calling of the Gentiles. Let us give thanks to the merciful God who has counted us worthy, in the words of the Apostle, 'to share the inheritance of the saints in light; and who has rescued us from the power of darkness, and brought us into the kingdom of his beloved Son'. For as Isaiah prophesied: 'The people of the Gentiles, who sat in darkness, have seen a great light, and on those who dwelt in the region of the shadow of death has a light dawned.' He spoke of them to the Lord: 'The Gentiles, who do not know you, will invoke you, and the peoples, who knew you not, will take refuge in you.'

This is 'the day that Abraham saw, and was glad', when he knew that the children born of his faith would be blessed in his seed, that is, in Christ. Believing that he would be the father of the nations, he looked into the future, 'giving glory to God, in full awareness that God is able to do what he has promised'. This is the day that David prophesied in the psalms, when he said: 'All the nations that you have brought into being will come and fall down in adoration in your presence, Lord, and glorify your name'; and again, 'The Lord has made known his salvation; in the sight of the nations he has revealed his justice.'

This came to be fulfilled, as we know, from the time when the star beckoned the Magi out of their distant country and led them to recognise and adore the King of heaven and earth. Their worship bids us imitate their humble service, and to be servants, as best we can, of the grace that invites all people to seek Christ.

The First Sunday of Epiphany

The Baptism of Christ

A Reading from an oration of Gregory of Nazianzus

Christ is bathed in light; let us also be bathed in light. Christ is baptized; let us also go down with him, and rise with him.

John is baptizing when Jesus draws near. Perhaps he comes to sanctify his baptizer; certainly he comes to bury sinful humanity in the waters. He comes to sanctify the Jordan for our sake and in readiness for us; he who is spirit and flesh comes to begin a new creation through the Spirit and water.

The Baptist protests; Jesus insists. Then John says: 'I ought to be baptized by you.' He is the lamp in the presence of the sun, the voice in the presence of the Word, the friend in the presence of the Bridegroom, the greatest of all born of woman in the presence of the firstborn of all creation, the one who leapt in his mother's womb in the presence of him who was adored in the womb, the forerunner and future forerunner in the presence of him who has already come and is to come again. 'I ought to be baptized by you'; we should also add: 'and for you', for John is to be baptized in blood, washed clean like Peter, not only by the washing of his feet.

Jesus rises from the waters; and a drowned world rises with him. The heavens like paradise with its flaming sword, closed by Adam for himself and his descendants, are rent open. The Spirit comes to him as to an equal, bearing witness to his Godhead. A voice bears witness to him from heaven, his place of origin. The Spirit descends in bodily form like the dove that once long ago announced the ending of the flood and so gives honour to the body that is one with God.

Today let us honour Christ's baptism and celebrate this feast in holiness. Be cleansed entirely and continue to be cleansed. Nothing gives such pleasure to God as the conversion and salvation of human beings, for whom his every word and every revelation exist. He wants you to become a living force for all humanity, lights shining in the world. You are to be radiant lights as you stand beside Christ, the great light, bathed in the glory of him who is the light of heaven. You are to enjoy more and more the pure and dazzling light of the Trinity, as now you have received – though not in its fullness – a ray of its splendour, proceeding from the one God, in Christ Jesus our Lord, to whom be glory and power for ever and ever.

alternative reading

A Reading from an oration of Proclus, Patriarch of Constantinople

Christ has been revealed to the world, and has brought order to our disordered world, making it resplendent with his glory. He has taken upon himself the sin of the world, and cast down our ancient enemy. He has sanctified the flowing waters, and enlightened our souls. He has enfolded miracles with yet greater ones.

For today both earth and sea share in the grace of the Saviour, and joy has spread over the face of the whole world. Today's feast is even more miraculous than the one we have just celebrated. On the feast of our Saviour's birth, earth joined in the celebrations because she bore the Lord in a crib; but today on the Theophany, the sea leaped with exultant joy and danced with delight, delighting that it had received the blessing of sanctification in the midst of the Jordan. In the former celebration an immature infant was revealed to our gaze, witnessing to our own incompleteness; but today a full-grown man is to be seen, in obscure fashion pointing us to him who being perfect proceeds from the perfect God. At his birth the King put on the purple robe of a human body; today the deep swells round him like a river as if to clothe him.

Come then and see new and overwhelming miracles: the Sun of Righteousness bathing in the Jordan, the fire immersed in water, and God being sanctified by human ministry. Today all creation resounds with hymns, crying out: 'Blessed is he who comes in the name of the Lord.' Blessed is he who comes at all times, for this is not the first time that he has come.

So who is this? Speak more clearly, I pray, blessed David. 'God is the Lord, and he has given us light.' David the prophet does not speak alone in this; in fact the apostle Paul supports his statement with his own testimony when he says: 'The grace of God has appeared with healing for all the world.' Not just to some people, but to all – that is, both Jews and Greeks equally, God has poured forth our salvation through baptism, offering to all people everywhere a common blessing in baptism.

Come then, and see this strange and new flood, greater and more powerful than that which occurred in the days of Noah. There the water of the flood destroyed the human race; but here the water of the baptism, by the power of him who is baptized in it, has called back the dead to life. There the dove carried an olive branch in its beak, denoting the fragrance of the sweet-smelling savour of the Lord Christ, but here the Holy Spirit, descending in the form of a dove, reveals to us the presence of our merciful God.

Monday after Epiphany 1

A Reading from the *Instructions* of Columbanus

Moses wrote in the law: 'God made humankind in his image and likeness.' Consider, I ask you, the dignity of these words. God is all-powerful. We cannot see or understand him, describe or assess him. Yet he fashioned us from clay and endowed us with the nobility of his own image. What have we in common with God? Or earth with spirit? – for 'God is a spirit.' It is a glorious privilege that God should grant us his eternal image and the likeness of his character. Our likeness to God, if we preserve it, imparts high dignity.

If we apply the virtues planted in our souls to the right purpose, we will be like God. God's commands have taught us to give him back the virtues he sowed in us in our first innocence. The first command is 'to love our Lord with our whole heart because he loved us first' from the beginning, before our existence. Loving God renews his image in us. Anyone who loves God keeps his commandments, for he said: 'If you love me, keep my commandments.' His command is that we love one another. In his own words: 'This is my command, that you love one another as I also have loved you.'

True love is shown not merely 'in word, but in deed and in truth', so we must turn back our image undefiled and holy to our God and Father, for he is holy; in the words of Scripture: 'Be holy, for I am holy.' We must restore his image with love, for he is love; in John's words: 'God is love.' We must restore it with loyalty and truth, for God is loyal and truthful. The image we depict must not be that of one who is unlike God; for one who is harsh and irascible and proud would display the image of a despot.

Let us not imprint on ourselves the image of a despot, but let Christ paint his image in us with his words: 'My peace I give you, my peace I leave with you.' But the knowledge that peace is good is of no benefit to us if we do not practise it. The most valuable objects are usually the most fragile; costly things require the most careful handling. Particularly fragile is that which is lost by wanton talk and destroyed with the slightest injury of a brother or sister. People like nothing better than discussing and minding the business of others, passing superfluous comments at random and criticising people behind their backs. So those who cannot say: 'The Lord has given me a discerning tongue, that I may with a word support those who are weary' should keep silent, or if they do say anything it should promote peace.

Tuesday after Epiphany 1

A Reading from an oration 'On the Love of the Poor' by Gregory of Nazianzus

Recognise to whom you owe the fact that you exist, that you breathe, that you understand, that you are wise, and, above all, that you know God and hope for the kingdom of heaven and the vision of glory, now darkly and as in a mirror but then with greater fullness and purity. You have been made a child of God, a co-heir with Christ. Where did you get all this, and from whom?

Now let me turn to what is of less importance: the visible world around us. What benefactor has enabled you to look out upon the beauty of the sky, the sun in its course, the circle of the moon, the countless number of stars, with the harmony and order that are theirs, like the music of a harp? Who has blessed you with rain, with the art of husbandry, with different kinds of food, with the arts, with houses, with laws, with states, with a life of human-ity and culture, with friendship and the easy familiarity of kinship?

Who has given you dominion over animals, both those that are tame and those that provide you with food? Who has made you master of everything on earth? In short, who has endowed you with all that makes humankind superior to all other living creatures? Is it not God who asks you now in your turn to show yourself generous above all other creatures and for the sake of all other creatures? Because we have received from God so many wonderful gifts, will we not be ashamed to refuse him this one thing only, our generosity? Though he is God and Lord he is not afraid to be known as our Father. Shall we for our part repudiate those who are our kith and kin?

Friends, let us never allow ourselves to misuse what has been given us by God's gift. If we do, we shall hear St Peter say: 'Be ashamed of yourselves for holding on to what belongs to someone else. Resolve to imitate God's justice, and no one will be poor.' Let us not labour to heap up and hoard riches while others remain in need. If we do, the prophet Amos will speak out against us with sharp and threatening words: 'Come now, you that say: When will the new moon be over, so that we may start selling? When will sabbath be over, so that we may start opening our treasures?'

Let us put into practice the supreme and primary law of God. He sends down rain on the righteous and sinful alike, and causes the sun to rise on all without distinction. To all earth's creatures he has given the broad earth, the springs, the rivers and the forests. He has given the air to the birds, and the waters to those who live in water. He has given abundantly to all the basic needs of life, not as a private possession, not restricted by law, not divided by boundaries, but as common to all, amply and in rich measure. His gifts are not deficient in any way, because he wanted to give equality of blessing to equality of worth, and to show the abundance of his generosity.

Wednesday after Epiphany 1

A Reading from a treatise *Against the Pagans*
by Athanasius of Alexandria

'In the beginning was the Word, and the Word was with God, and the Word was God. All things were made through him, and without him nothing was made.' In these words John the theologian teaches that nothing exists or remains in being except in and through the Word.

Think of a musician tuning a lyre. By skill the musician adjusts high notes to low, and intermediate notes to the rest, and produces a series of harmonies. So too the wisdom of God holds the world like a lyre and joins things in the air to those on earth, and things in heaven to those in the air, and brings each part into harmony with the whole. By his decree and will he regulates them all to produce the beauty and harmony of a single, well-ordered universe. While remaining unchanged with his Father, he moves all creation by his unchanging nature, according to the Father's will. To everything he gives existence and life in accordance with its nature, and so creates a wonderful and truly divine harmony.

To illustrate this profound mystery, let us take the example of a choir of many singers. A choir is composed of a variety of men, women and children, of both old and young. Under the direction of one conductor, each sings in the way that is natural: men with men's voices, boys with boys' voices, old people with old voices, young people with young voices. Yet all of them produce a single harmony. Or consider the example of our soul. It moves our senses according to their several functions so that in the presence of a single object they all act simultaneously: the eye sees, the ear hears, the hand touches, the nose smells, the tongue tastes, and often the other parts of the body act as well – as, for example, the feet may walk.

Although this is only a poor comparison, it gives some idea of how the whole universe is governed. The Word of God has but to give a gesture of command and everything falls into place; each creature performs its own proper function, and all together constitute one single harmonious order.

Thursday after Epiphany 1

A Reading from a treatise *On the Lord's Prayer*
by Cyprian of Carthage

The gospel precepts are none other than instructions of God, foundations on which hope is built, firm bases for faith, fuel to rekindle the heart, guides to point out the way, and aids to the attainment of salvation. They instruct the minds of the faithful on earth in order to lead them to the kingdom of heaven. The words which God willed to let us hear from the prophets are many, but of much greater value are the words uttered by the Son, those which the Word of God who dwelled within the prophets attests with his own voice. He no longer asks that the way be prepared for the One who comes, but he comes himself to show us the way and to open it for us. Thus, we who were once blind and lacking foresight, wandering in the shadow of death, can now be enlightened by the light of grace and walk along the paths of life under the Lord's leadership and direction.

Among other saving instructions and divine teachings intended for the salvation of his people, the Lord gave us the form of prayer and urged us to pray as he has instructed us. He who gave us life also taught us how to pray with that same graciousness by which he has given and bestowed on us everything else. Thus, when we speak to the Father in the prayer that his Son has taught us, we are more readily heard.

Jesus had already announced that the hour would come when true worshippers would worship the Father in spirit and in truth and he accomplished what he promised. Having received the Spirit and the truth by his sanctifying action, we can now worship in spirit and in truth through the transmission of his teaching. Indeed, could there be a more spiritual prayer than the one left us by Christ who has also sent us his Spirit? Is there a truer way of praying to the Father than the one which has come from the lips of Christ who is Truth?

Let us pray, then, as God our Master has taught us. Affectionate and familiar is the prayer with which we implore God in the words of God, and reach his ear through the words of his Son. Let the Father recognise his Son's words in us when we offer up our prayer; and let him who dwells in our heart be always on our lips.

Friday after Epiphany 1

A Reading from a commentary on St Paul's Letter to the Romans by Cyril of Alexandria

Though many, we are one body, and members one of another, united by Christ in the bonds of love. 'Christ has made Jews and Gentiles one by breaking down the barrier that divided us, and abolishing the law with its precepts and decrees.' This is why we should all be of one mind, and if one member suffers some misfortune, all should suffer alongside; and if one member is honoured, all should be glad.

Paul says: 'Accept one another as Christ accepted you, for the glory of God.' Now accepting one another means being willing to share one another's thoughts and feelings, bearing one another's burdens, and preserving the unity of the Spirit in the bond of peace. This is how God accepted us in Christ, for John's testimony is true and he said that God the Father 'loved the world so much that he gave his own Son for us'. God's Son was given as a ransom for the lives of us all. He has delivered us from death, redeemed us from death and from sin.

Paul throws light on the purpose of God's plan when he says that Christ became the servant of the circumcised to show God's fidelity. God had promised the Jewish patriarchs that he would bless their offspring and make it as numerous as the stars of heaven. This is why the divine Word himself, who as God holds all creation in being and is the source of its well-being, appeared in the flesh and became human. He came into this world in human flesh not to be served, but, as he himself said, to serve and to give his life as a ransom for many.

Christ declared that his coming in visible form was to fulfil the promise made to Israel. 'I was sent only to the lost sheep of the house of Israel,' he said. Paul was perfectly correct, then, in saying that Christ became a servant of the circumcised in order to fulfil the promise made to the patriarchs and that God the Father had charged him with this task, as also with the task of bringing salvation to the Gentiles, so that they too might praise their Saviour and Redeemer as the Creator of the universe. In this way God's mercy has been extended to all, including the Gentiles, and it can be seen that the mystery of the divine wisdom contained in Christ has not failed in its benevolent purpose. In the place of those who fell away the whole world has been saved.

Saturday after Epiphany 1

A Reading from a commentary on the psalms by Augustine

God could give no greater gift to us than to make his Word, through whom he created all things, our head and to join us to him as his members, so that the Word might be both Son of God and Son of Man, one God with the Father, and one human being with all humankind. The result is that when we speak with God in prayer we do not separate the Son from him, and when the body of the Son prays it does not separate its head from itself: it is the one Saviour of his body, our Lord Jesus Christ, the Son of God, who prays for us and in us and is himself the object of our prayers.

He prays for us as our priest, he prays in us as our head, he is the object of our prayers as our God. Let us then recognise both our voice in his, and his voice in ours. When something is said, especially in prophecy, about the Lord Jesus Christ that seems to belong to a condition of lowliness unworthy of God, we must not hesitate to ascribe this condition to one who did not hesitate to unite himself with us. Every creature is his servant, for it was through him that every creature came to be.

We contemplate his glory and divinity when we listen to these words: 'In the beginning was the Word, and the Word was with God, and the Word was God. He was in the beginning with God.

All things were made through him, and without him nothing was made.' Here we gaze on the divinity of the Son of God, something supremely great and surpassing all the greatness of his creatures. Yet in other parts of Scripture we hear him as one sighing, praying, giving praise and thanks.

We hesitate to attribute these words to him because our minds are slow to come down to his humble level when we have just been contemplating him in his divinity. It is as though we were doing him an injustice in acknowledging in a human being the words of one with whom we spoke when we prayed to God; we are usually at a loss and try to change the meaning. Yet our minds find nothing in Scripture that does not go back to him, nothing that will allow us to stray from him.

Our thoughts must then be awakened to keep their vigil of faith. We must realise that the one whom we were contemplating a short time before in his nature as God took to himself the nature of a servant; he was made in the likeness of our flesh and found to be a man like others; he humbled himself by being obedient even to accepting death; as he hung on the cross he made the psalmist's words his own: 'My God, my God, why have you forsaken me?'

We pray to him as God, he prays for us as a servant. In the first case he is the Creator, in the second a creature. Himself unchanged, he took to himself our created nature in order to change it, and made us one with himself, head and body. We pray then to him, through him, in him, and we speak along with him and he along with us.

The Second Sunday of Epiphany

A Reading from *The Cost of Discipleship*
by Dietrich Bonhoeffer

The call of Jesus goes forth, and is at once followed by the response of obedience. The response of the disciples is an act of obedience, not a confession of faith in Jesus. But how could the call immediately evoke obedience?

The story of the call of the first disciples is a stumbling-block for the natural reason, and it is no wonder that frantic attempts have been made to separate the two events. By hook or by crook a bridge must be found between them. Something must have happened in between, some psychological or historical event. Thus we get the stupid question: Surely they must have known Jesus before, and that previous acquaintance explains their readiness to hear the Master's call. Unfortunately Scripture is ruthlessly silent on this point, and in fact it regards the immediate sequence of call and response as a matter of crucial importance. It displays not the slightest interest in the psychological reasons for a person's religious decisions. And why? For the simple reason that the cause behind the immediate following of call by response is Jesus Christ himself. It is Jesus who calls, and because it is Jesus, they follow at once.

This encounter is a testimony to the absolute, direct, and unaccountable authority of Jesus. There is no need of any preliminaries, and no other consequence but obedience to the call. Because Jesus is the Christ, he has the authority to call and to demand obedience to his word. Jesus summons us to follow him not as a teacher or a pattern of the good life, but as the Christ, the Son of God. In this short episode Jesus Christ and his claim are proclaimed to the world. Not a word of praise is given to the disciple for his decision for Christ. We are not expected to contemplate the disciple, but only him who calls, and his absolute authority. There is no road to faith or discipleship, no other road – only obedience to the call of Jesus.

And what does Scripture inform us about the content of discipleship? Follow me, run along behind me! That is all. To follow in his steps is something which is void of all content. It gives us no intelligible programme for a way of life, no goal or ideal to strive after. It is not a cause which human calculation might deem worthy of devotion, even the devotion of ourselves. At the call the disciples leave everything that they have – but not because they think that they might be doing something worthwhile, but simply for the sake of the call. Otherwise they cannot follow in the steps of Jesus. The disciples burn their boats and go ahead. They are dragged out of their relative security into a life of absolute insecurity.

When we are called to follow Christ, we are summoned to an exclusive attachment to his person. The grace of his call bursts all the bonds of legalism. It is a gracious call, a gracious commandment. Christ calls; we are to follow.

A Reading from a hymn of Ephrem of Syria

I have invited you, Lord, to a wedding feast of song,
but the wine – the utterance of praise – at our feast has failed.
You are the guest who filled the jars with good wine,
fill my mouth with your praise.

The wine that was in the jars was akin and related to
this eloquent Wine that gives birth to praise,
seeing that wine too gave birth to praise
from those who drank it and beheld the wonder.

You who are so just, if at a wedding feast not your own
you filled six jars with good wine,
do you at this wedding feast fill, not the jars,
but the ten thousand ears with its sweetness.

Jesus, you were invited to a wedding feast of others,
here is your own pure and fair wedding feast:
    gladden your rejuvenated people,
for your guests too, O Lord, need your songs:
    let your harp utter.

The soul is your bride, the body your bridal chamber,
your guests are the senses and the thoughts.
And if a single body is a wedding feast for you,
how great is your banquet for the whole Church!

Monday after Epiphany 2

A Reading from *The Light of Christ*
by Evelyn Underhill

The mystics keep telling us that the goal of prayer and the goal of
our hidden life which should itself become more and more of a
prayer, is union with God. We use that phrase often, much too
often, to preserve the wholesome sense of its awe-fulness. For
what does union with God mean? It is not a nice feeling we get in

devout moments. That may or may not be a bi-product of union – probably not. It can never be its substance. Union with God means every bit of our human nature transfigured in Christ, woven up into his creative life and activity, absorbed into his redeeming purpose, heart, soul, mind and strength. Each time it happens it means that one of God's creatures has achieved its destiny.

And if men and women want to know what this means in terms of human nature, what it costs and what it becomes, there is only one way – contemplation of the life of Christ. Then we see that we grow in wisdom and stature not just for our own sakes – just to become spiritual – but that his teaching, healing, life-giving power may possess us and work through us; that we may lose our own lives and find his life, be conformed to the pattern shown in him, conformed to the cross. Those are the rich and costly demands and experiences that lie before us as we stand and look at the Christ-child setting up a standard for both simple and learned, teaching the secrets of life; and what they ask from us on our side and from our prayer is a very great simplicity, self-oblivion, dependence and suppleness, a willingness and readiness to respond to life where it finds us and to wait, to grow and change, not according to our preconceived notions and ideas of pace, but according to the overruling will and pace of God.

Tuesday after Epiphany 2

A Reading from the Letter of Clement of Rome
to the Church in Corinth

The blessing of God and the roads that lead to it must be our objective. Search the records of ancient times. Why was our father Abraham blessed? Was it not because of his faith which inspired his life of righteousness and truth? As for Isaac's faith, it was so strong that, assured of the outcome, he willingly allowed himself to be offered in sacrifice. Jacob had the humility to leave his native land on account of his brother, and went and served Laban, and as a reward was given the headship of the twelve tribes of Israel.

Honest reflection upon each of these examples will make us realise the magnitude of God's gifts. All the priests and levites who served the altar of God were descended from Jacob. The humanity of the Lord Jesus derived from him. Through the tribe of Judah have issued kings, princes and rulers; while the other tribes are not without their own claim to fame. As God promised Abraham: 'Your descendants shall be as the stars of heaven.'

It should be clear that none of these owed their honour and renown because of any inherent right, or in virtue of their achievements or deeds of virtue. No; they owed everything to God's will. So likewise with us, who by his will have been called in Christ Jesus. We are not justified by our wisdom, intelligence, piety, or by any action of ours, however holy, but by faith, the one means by which almighty God has justified us from the beginning. To him be glory for ever and ever.

What must we do then? Give up good works? Stop practising Christian love? God forbid! We must be ready and eager for every opportunity to do good, and put our whole heart into it. Even the architect and Lord of the universe rejoices in his works. By his supreme power he set the heavens in their place; by his infinite wisdom he gave them their order. He separated the land from the waters surrounding it and made his own will its firm foundation. By his command he brought to life the beasts that roam the earth. He created the sea and all its living creatures, and then by his power set bounds to it. Finally, with his own holy and undefiled hands, he formed humankind, the highest and most intelligent of his creatures, the copy of his own image. 'Let us make man,' God said, 'in our image and likeness. So God made human beings, male and female he made them.' Then, when he had finished making all his creatures, God gave them his approval and blessing: 'increase and multiply,' he charged them.

We must recognise, therefore, that all the righteous have been graced by good works, and that even the Lord himself took delight in the glory his works gave him. With such examples before us, we should feel inspired to obey God's will, and to put all our energies into the business of living a Christian life.

Wednesday after Epiphany 2

A Reading from a treatise *On the Lord's Prayer*
by Cyprian of Carthage

The teacher of peace and the master of unity does not wish us to pray individualistically or selfishly as if we are concerned only about ourselves. We do not say: '*My* Father in heaven', or 'Give *me* today *my* daily bread.' Nor does anyone pray simply for their own sins to be forgiven, or request that he or she alone be not led into temptation or be delivered from evil. Christian prayer is public and offered for all. When we pray it is not as an individual but as a united people, for we are indeed all one. God, who is the teacher of prayer and peace, taught us peace. He wishes each of us to pray for all, just as he carries us all in himself.

What profound mysteries, my dear brothers and sisters, are contained in the Lord's Prayer! How many and how great they are! They are expressed in few words but overflow in an abundance of virtue. Nothing is left out; everything is comprehended in these few petitions. It is a compendium of spiritual teaching. 'This is how you must pray,' says the Lord, 'Our Father in heaven.' The new man or woman who has been born again and restored to God through grace, says 'Father' at the beginning of all prayer because they are already beginning to be his son or daughter. As Scripture says: 'He came among his own and his own people did not accept him. But to all who received him, who believed in his name, he gave power to become children of God.' Thus whoever has believed in his name and has been made a child of God should give thanks and acknowledge their adoption, and learn to call God their heavenly Father.

None of us would presume to call God our Father had not Christ himself taught us to pray in this way. We should realise then, dearest brothers and sisters, that if we are to call God 'Father', we ought to behave like sons and daughters of God, so that just as we are delighted to have God as our Father, so equally he can take delight in us his children.

Thursday after Epiphany 2

A Reading from *Centuries of Meditations*
by Thomas Traherne

Knowing the greatness and sweetness of love, I can never be poor in any estate. How sweet a thing is it as we go or ride, or eat or drink, or converse abroad to remember that one is the heir of the whole world and the friend of God! That one has so great a friend as God is, and that one is exalted infinitely by all his laws! That all the riches and honours in the world are ours in the divine image to be enjoyed! That a man is tenderly beloved of God and always walking in his father's kingdom under his wing, and as the apple of his eye! Verily that God hath done so much for one in his works and laws, and expressed so much love in his word and ways, being as he is divine and infinite, it should make a man to walk above the stars, and seat him in the bosom of men and angels. It should always fill him with joy and triumph, and lift him up above crowns and empires.

That a man is beloved of God, should melt him all into esteem and holy veneration. It should make him so courageous as an angel of God. It should make him delight in calamities and distresses for God's sake. By giving me all things else, he hath made even afflictions themselves my treasures. The sharpest trials are the finest furbishing. The most tempestuous weather is the best seed-time. A Christian is an oak flourishing in winter. God hath so magnified and glorified his servant, and exalted him so highly in his eternal bosom, that no other joy should be able to move us but that alone. All sorrows should appear but shadows, beside that of his absence, and all the greatness of riches and estates swallowed up in the light of his favour. Incredible goodness lies in his love. And it should be joy enough to us to contemplate and possess it. He is poor whom God hates: 'tis a true proverb. And besides that, we should so love him that the joy alone of approving ourselves to him, and making ourselves amiable and beautiful before him should be a continual feast, were we starving. A beloved cannot feel hunger in the presence of his beloved. Where martyrdom is pleasant, what can be distasteful. To fight, to famish, to die for one's beloved, especially with one's beloved, and in his excellent company, unless it be for his trouble, is truly delightful. God is always present, and always seeth us.

Friday after Epiphany 2

A Reading from a treatise *On Contemplating God*
by William of St Thierry

I who long for you, O Lord adorable and loveable, am at once confronted with the qualities that make you loveable; for from heaven and earth alike and by means of all your creatures these present themselves to me and urge me to attend to them. And the more clearly and truly these things declare you and affirm that you are worthy to be loved, the more ardently desirable do they make you appear to me.

But alas! This experience is not one to be enjoyed with unmitigated pleasure and delight; rather, it is one of yearnings, strivings, and frustration, though not a torment without some sweetness. For just as the offerings I make to you do not suffice to please you perfectly unless I offer you myself along with them, so the contemplation of your manifold perfections, though it does give us a measure of refreshment, does not satisfy us unless we have yourself along with it. Into this contemplation my soul puts all its energies; in the course of it I push my spirit around like a rasping broom. And, using those qualities of yours that make you loveable like hands and feet on which to lift my weight, with all my powers I reach up to you, to you who are Love supreme and sovereign Good. But the more I reach up, the more relentlessly am I thrust back, and down into myself, below myself.

So I look at myself, and size myself up, and pass judgement on myself. And there I am, facing myself, a very troublesome and trying business.

And yet, O Lord, when all is said and done, I am quite positive that, by your grace, I do have in me the desire to desire you and the love of loving you with all my heart and soul.

So, when my inward eyes grow blurred like this, and become dim and blind, I pray you with all speed to open them, not as Adam's fleshly eyes were opened to the beholding of his shame, but that I, Lord, may so see your glory that, forgetting all about my poverty and littleness, my whole self may stand erect and run into your love's embrace, seeing you whom I have loved and loving you whom I have yet to see. In this way, dying to myself, I shall begin to live in you.

Saturday after Epiphany 2

A Reading from a homily of Gregory of Nyssa

We shall be blessed with clear vision if we keep our eyes fixed on Christ, for he, as Paul teaches, is our head, and there is in him no shadow of evil. St Paul himself and all who have reached the same heights of sanctity had their eyes fixed on Christ, and so have all who live and move and have their being in him.

As no darkness can be seen by anyone surrounded by light, so no trivialities can capture the attention of anyone who has eyes on Christ. The one who keeps his eyes upon the head and origin of the whole universe has them on virtue in all its perfection; on truth, on justice, on immortality, and on everything else that is good, for Christ is goodness itself.

'The wise then, turn their eyes toward the One who is their head, but fools grope in darkness.' No one who puts a lamp under a bed instead of on a lampstand will receive any light from it. People are often considered blind and useless when they make the supreme Good their aim and give themselves up to the contemplation of God, but Paul made a boast of this and proclaimed himself a fool for Christ's sake. The reason he said, 'We are fools for Christ's sake,' was that his mind was free from all earthly preoccupations. It was as though he said, 'We are blind to the life here below because our eyes are raised toward the One who is our head.'

And so, without board or lodging, he travelled from place to place, destitute, naked, exhausted by hunger and thirst. When people saw him in captivity, flogged, shipwrecked, led about in chains, they could scarcely help thinking him a pitiable sight. Nevertheless, even while he suffered all this at the hands of others, he always looked toward the One who is his head and he asked: 'What can separate us from the love of Christ which is in Jesus? Can affliction or distress? Can persecution, hunger, nakedness, danger or death?' In other words: What can force me to take my eyes from him who is my head and to turn them toward things that are contemptible?

Paul bids us follow his example: 'Seek the things that are above,' he says, which is really only another way of saying: 'Keep your eyes on Christ.'

The Third Sunday of Epiphany

A Reading from *The Vision of God* by Kenneth Kirk

Our Lord has promised the vision of God as a guerdon to the pure in heart. It is extraordinary – especially in view of the prominence which the thought had attained in contemporary religion, and the high relief into which New Testament theology was about to throw it – that the sentence 'Blessed are the pure in heart' seems to stand without even an echo in the Synoptic tradition. But this judgement is at best superficial. In actual fact the idea of the vision dominates our Lord's teaching. Ideas are not conveyed by words alone: emphasis often serves to express them even better than direct enunciation. And the moment we seek to discover the emphasis of the Lord's teaching, as the Synoptists record it, the truth becomes evident. It was specifically and above all a teaching about God.

Jesus 'came preaching the good news of God'. That he spoke also of the kingdom of God makes no difference to this fact: for if anything is certain as the result of modern research, it is that the kingdom, in Jesus' thought, whether it means 'realm' or 'kingship', is wholly bound up with the character of God. It is something in which he is to come – not a state of things prepared for his coming by human effort. It is true, of course, that Jesus also spoke, and that constantly, of the character and behaviour necessary for those who would 'inherit', 'enter into', or 'possess' the kingdom; and that in so doing he purified, simplified, and breathed new life into the ethical code of Judaism. This is no more than to say that, like all great teachers, he spoke both of God and of man, or preached both doctrine and ethics. But whereas contemporary Judaism laid all the stress on man – that is to say on ethics, on what man has to do to fulfil the will of God – it is surely true to say that by contrast the emphasis of Jesus' teaching is upon God, rather than upon man – upon what God has done, is doing, and shall do for his people.

So he tells of the divine Fatherhood which watches over the lilies, the ravens, and the sparrows; which sends rain upon the just and the unjust alike; which understands our needs and gives to us liberally; which is patient and long-suffering. He tells of a God always ready to welcome the prodigal, to search for the lost sheep, or to give in his pleasure the kingdom to his flock; and of a heaven where there is infinite joy over the sinner that repents. God sees in secret and shall reward openly; God sows his seed far and wide with a lavish hand, and reveals his innermost truths to babes and sucklings. There is another side to the picture; but it is still a picture of God, though it represents him – whenever the time shall come that there is no more space for repentance – as a judge before whom there is no excuse.

For all the ethical teaching in the gospel, it seems impossible to deny that Jesus' primary thought and message was about God, and that human conduct in his mind came in a second and derivative place.

Note: If a reading about Cana of Galilee is required, see either alternative reading for Epiphany 2 or Tuesday after Trinity 9.

Monday after Epiphany 3

A Reading from a commentary on the psalms
by Ambrose of Milan

Let your door stand open to receive Christ, unlock your soul to him, offer him a welcome in your mind, and then you will see the riches of simplicity, the treasures of peace, and the joy of grace. Throw wide the gate of your heart, stand before the sun of the everlasting light that shines on every one. This true light shines on all, but if any close their windows they will deprive themselves of eternal light. If you shut the door of your mind, you shut out Christ. Though he can enter, he does not want to force his way in rudely, or compel us to admit him against our will.

Born of a virgin, he came forth from the womb as the light of the whole world in order to shine on all. His light is received by those who long for the splendour of perpetual light that night can never destroy. The sun of our daily experience is succeeded by the darkness of night, but the sun of holiness never sets, because wisdom cannot give place to evil.

Blessed then is the person at whose door Christ stands and knocks. Our door is faith; if it is strong enough, the whole house is safe. This is the door by which Christ enters. So the Church says in the Song of Songs: 'The voice of my brother is at the door.' Hear his knock, listen to him asking to enter: 'Open to me, my sister, my betrothed, my dove, my perfect one, for my head is covered with dew, and my hair with the moisture of the night.'

When does God the Word most often knock at your door? When his 'head is covered with the dew of night'. He visits in love those in trouble and temptation, to save them from being overwhelmed by their trials. His head is covered with dew or moisture when those who are his body are in distress. That is the time when you must keep watch so that when the bridegroom comes he may not find himself shut out, and make his departure. If you were to sleep, if your heart were not wide awake, he would not knock and go away; but if your heart is watchful, he knocks and asks you to open the door to him.

Our soul has a door; it has gates. 'Lift up your heads, O gates, and be lifted up, eternal gates, and the King of glory will enter.' If you open the gates of your faith, the King of glory will enter your house in the triumphal procession in honour of his passion. Holiness too has its gates. We read in Scripture what the Lord Jesus said through his prophet: 'Open for me the gates of holiness.'

It is the soul that has its door, its gates. Christ comes to this door and knocks; he knocks at the gates. Open to him; he wants to enter, to find his bride waiting and watching.

Tuesday after Epiphany 3

A Reading from *The Scale of Perfection*
by Walter Hilton

You can grow in knowledge if you take pains to set your heart most upon one thing. That thing is nothing other than a spiritual desire toward God – to please him, love him, know him, see him and have him, here by grace in a little feeling, and in the glory of heaven with a full being. If you nourish this desire, it will teach you well which is sin and which is not, and which is good, and which is the better good. And if you are willing to fasten your thought to it, it will teach you all you need and get you all that you lack. And therefore, when you arise against the ground of sin in general, or else against any special sin, hang fast on to this desire and set the point of your thought more upon God whom you desire than on the sin which you reject, for if you do so, then God fights for you and he shall destroy sin in you. You shall much sooner come to your purpose if you do this than if you leave the humble desire that looks principally to God and resolve to set your heart only against the stirring of sin, as if you wanted to destroy it by your own strength: in that way you shall never bring it about.

Do as I have said, and better if you can, and by the grace of Jesus I think you will make the devil ashamed, and so break away these wicked stirrings that they shall not do you much harm; and in this manner that image of sin can be broken down in you and destroyed, by which you are deformed from the natural shape of the image of Christ. You shall be formed again to the image of the man Jesus by humility and charity, and then you shall be fully shaped to the image of Jesus God, living here in a shadow by contemplation, and in the glory of heaven by the fullness of truth. St Paul speaks thus of this shaping to the likeness of Christ: 'My little children, whom I bear as a woman bears a child until Christ is again shaped in you.' You have conceived Christ through faith, and he has life in you in as much as you have a good will and a desire to serve and please him; but he is not yet fully formed in you, nor you in him, by the fullness of charity. And therefore St Paul bore you and me and others in the same way with travail, as a woman bears a child, until the time that Christ has his full shape in us, and we in him.

For Christ is the door, and he is the porter; and without his leave and his livery, no one can come to God. As he says: 'No one comes to the Father but by me.' That is to say, Nobody can come to the contemplation of the Deity unless by the fullness of humility and charity he is first reformed to the likeness of Jesus in his humanity.

Wednesday after Epiphany 3

A Reading from a treatise entitled *The Teacher*
by Clement of Alexandria

When a dispute arose among the apostles as to which of them was the greatest, we are told that Jesus stood a little child in their midst and said: 'Whoever would be humble, becoming like this little child, is of the greatest importance in the kingdom of heaven.'

By 'child' Jesus did not mean someone who has not yet reached the use of reason because of immaturity, as some like to suggest. Similarly, when Jesus says: 'Unless you become like little children you shall not enter the kingdom of God,' his words should not be taken literally to mean without learning. We are not 'little children' in the sense that we roll on the ground or crawl on the earth like snakes as we did in our infancy. On the contrary, we are 'little children' only in the sense that we stretch our minds to contemplate the things of heaven, and in so doing are set loose from the world and our sins. We touch the earth only with the tips of our toes and so appear to be in the world, but inwardly we are pursuing holy wisdom, even though such a quest is deemed folly to those whose souls delight in wrong-doing.

Hence, in the gospel by 'children' is really meant those who know God alone as their Father, who are simple, little ones, without guile. To these, surely, who have made progress Jesus proclaimed this utterance, bidding them to dismiss anxiety about the things of this world and exhorting them to devote themselves to the Father alone in imitation of children. That is why he goes on to tell them: 'Do not worry about tomorrow. Today has troubles enough of its own.'

He enjoins them to lay aside the cares of this life and depend on the Father alone. Whoever fulfils this command is in reality a child and an heir both to God and to the world – to the world, in the sense of one who appears to have lost his wits; to God, in the sense of one dearly beloved.

Indeed, if the detractors of spiritual childhood ridicule us, you should understand that they are really speaking evil of the Lord. They are implying that those who seek the protection of God are somehow lacking in intelligence. But if they were to understand the designation 'children' in its true and spiritual sense of innocent ones, we glory in that name. Such children are indeed new spirits who were infants in the folly of old misguided ways, but have newly become wise and have sprung into being according to the new covenant. Only recently, in fact, has God become known by the coming of Christ: 'No one knows the Father but the Son – and anyone to whom the Son wishes to reveal him.'

Therefore, in contrast to the older people, the newer people are called young, for they have learned the new blessings. We possess the exuberance of life's morning, the prime of a spiritual youth which knows no age; indeed, we are ever growing to maturity in wisdom, ever young, ever responsive, ever new. For those who have become partakers of the Word will necessarily be renewed in themselves. And whoever partakes of eternity assumes the qualities of the incorruptible. Thus, the name childhood designates for us a life-long springtime of the heart, since the truth which is in us, as well as our way of life, being saturated with the truth, cannot be touched by old age. Surely, wisdom is ever-blooming, ever fixed on the same truth, and never changing.

Thursday after Epiphany 3

A Reading from *A Serious Call to a Devout and Holy Life*
by William Law

There is no principle of the heart that is more acceptable to God than a universal fervent love to all mankind, wishing and praying for their happiness, because there is no principle of the heart that makes us more like God, who is love and goodness itself and created all beings for their enjoyment of happiness.

The greatest idea that we can frame of God is when we conceive him to be a Being of infinite love and goodness, using an infinite wisdom and power for the common good and happiness of all his creatures. The highest notion, therefore, that we can form of man is when we conceive him as like to God in this respect as he can be, using all his finite faculties, whether of wisdom, power, or prayers, for the common good of all his fellow creatures, heartily desiring they may have all the happiness they are capable of and as many benefits and assistances from him as his state and condition in the world will permit him to give them.

And on the other hand, what a baseness and iniquity is there in all instances of hatred, envy, spite, and ill will, if we consider that every instance of them is so far acting in opposition to God and intending mischief and harm to those creatures which God favours, and protects, and preserves, in order to their happiness. An ill-natured man amongst God's creatures is the most perverse creature in the world, acting contrary to that love by which himself subsists and which alone gives subsistence to all that variety of beings that enjoy life in any part of the creation.

'Whatsoever ye would that men should do unto you, even so do unto them.'

Now though this is a doctrine of strict justice, yet it is only a universal love that can comply with it. For as love is the measure of our acting toward ourselves, so we can never act in the same manner toward other people till we look upon them with that love with which we look upon ourselves.

Friday after Epiphany 3

A Reading from *The Go-Between God*
by John V. Taylor

What was Jesus Christ's role and relationship to the world? He came to be true Man, the last Adam, living the life of the new age in the midst of the world's life. His deliverance of men and women from various kinds of bondage, his existence for others, the laying down of his life, were not a task which he undertook but a function of the life of the new Man, just as breathing or eating is a function of physical life. What made his preaching of the kingdom of God distinct from that of John the Baptist was that he not only promised but lived the kingdom life. That is why he said that the least of those in the kingdom was greater than John. And kingdom life is not primarily religious but human.

Jesus's parables make it clear that life in the kingdom is the normal life that is open to humanity where men and women are found in his true relation to God as son – the Abba-relationship. So the thirty years of hidden toil at Nazareth were to him not a mere passing of the time but were the very life of Man he had come to live. There he learned to say 'My Father has never yet ceased his work and I am working too,' and by virtue of his absolute, glad obedience-in-co-operation, Jesus as Man was able to be the vehicle of God's existence for others, as all people were potentially made to be. 'If it is by the finger of God that I drive out the devils, then be sure that the kingdom of God has already come upon you.'

But the 'you' upon whom the kingdom has come are not people in the Church but people in the world. To say 'Jesus is Lord' pledges us to find the effects of his cross and resurrection in the world, not just in our inner lives, nor in the Church.

The way in which Jesus both declared the kingdom and lived in the freedom of the kingdom provides the model of what the Church is created to be. The Church is not the kingdom but, through the Spirit indwelling their fellowship, Christians live the kingdom life as men and women of the world.

The mission of the Church, therefore, is to live the ordinary life of human beings in that extraordinary awareness of the other and self-sacrifice for the other which the Spirit gives. Christian activity will be very largely the same as the world's activity – earning a living, bringing up a family, making friends, having fun, celebrating occasions, farming, manufacturing, trading, building cities, healing sickness, alleviating distress, mourning, studying, exploring, making music, and so on. Christians will try to do these things to the glory of God, which is to say that they will try to perceive what God is up to in each of these manifold activities and will seek to do it with him by bearing responsibility for the selves of others.

Saturday after Epiphany 3

A Reading from a sermon of Peter Chrysologus,
Bishop of Ravenna

God, seeing the world falling into ruin through fear, never stops working to bring it back into being through love, inviting it back by grace, holding it firm by charity, and embracing it with affection.

God washes the earth, steeped in evil, with the avenging flood. He calls Noah the father of a new world, speaks gently to him and encourages him. He gives him fatherly instruction about the present and consoles him with good hope about the future. He did not give orders, but instead shared in the work of enclosing together in the ark all living creatures on the earth. In this way the love of being together would drive out the fear born of slavery. What had been saved by a shared enterprise was now to be preserved by a community of love.

This is the reason, too, why God calls Abraham from among the nations and makes his name great. He makes him the father of those who believe, accompanies him on his journeys, and takes care of him amid foreigners. He enriches him with possessions, honours him with triumphs, and binds himself to Abraham with promises. He snatches him from harm, is hospitable to him, and astonishes him with the gift of a son he had given up hope of ever having. All this God does so that, filled with many good things, and drawn by the sweetness of divine love, Abraham might learn to love God and not to be afraid of him, to worship him in love rather than in trembling fear.

This is the reason, too, why God comforts the fugitive Jacob as he sleeps. On his way back he calls him to the contest and wrestles with him in his arms. Again, this was to teach him to love and not to fear the father of the contest.

This is why God invites Moses to be the liberator of his people, calling him with a fatherly voice and speaking to him with a fatherly voice.

All the events we are recalling reveal the human heart fired with the flame of the love of God, senses flooded to the point of intoxication with that love, leading people on, until wounded by love they begin to want to look upon the face of God with their bodily eyes.

How could the narrowness of human vision ever enclose God whom the entire world cannot contain? The law of love has no thought about what might be, what ought to be or what can be. Love knows nothing of judgement, reaches beyond reason, and laughs at moderation. Love takes no relief from the fact that the object of its desire is beyond possibility, nor is it dissuaded by difficulties. If love does not attain what it desires it kills the lover, with the result that it will go where it is led, not where it ought to go. Love breeds a desire so strong as to make its way into forbidden territory. Love cannot bear not to catch sight of what it longs for. That is why the saints thought that they merited nothing if they could not see the Lord. It is why love that longs to see God has a spirit of devotion, even if it lacks judgement. It is why Moses dares to say to God: 'If I have found favour in your sight, show me your face.'

It is also why God, aware that people were suffering pain and weariness from their longing to see him, chose as a means to make himself visible, something which was to be great to the dwellers on earth, and by no means insignificant to the dwellers in heaven. He chose to come to humankind as a human being, assuming our nature, in order to be seen by us.

The Fourth Sunday of Epiphany

A Reading from a sermon of Leo the Great

Our Lord Jesus Christ, born truly human without ever ceasing to be true God, was in his own person the prelude of a new creation, and by the manner of his birth he gave humanity a spiritual origin. What mind can grasp this? What tongue can do justice to this gift of love? Guilt becomes innocence, what was old becomes new, strangers are adopted into the family and outsiders are made heirs.

Rouse yourself, therefore, and recognise the dignity of your nature. Remember that you were made in God's image; and though defaced in Adam, that image has now been restored in Christ. Use this visible creation as it should be used: the earth, the sea, the sky, the air, the springs and rivers. Give praise and glory to their Creator for all that you find beautiful and wonderful in them. See with your bodily eyes the sunlight shining upon the earth, but embrace with your whole soul and all your affections 'the true light which enlightens everyone who comes into this world'. Speaking of this light the prophet David in the psalms says: 'Look on him and be radiant; and your face shall never be ashamed.' If we are indeed the temple of God and if the Spirit of God lives in us, then what every believer has within is of greater worth than what we can admire in the skies.

My friends, in saying this it is not my intention to make you undervalue God's works or think there is anything contrary to your faith in creation, for the good God has himself made all things good. What I do mean is that you use reasonably and in a balanced way the rich variety of creation which makes this world beautiful; for as the Apostle says: 'the things that are seen are transient but the things that are unseen are eternal.'

For we are born in the present only to be reborn in the future. Our attachment, therefore, should not be to the transitory; instead, we must be intent upon the eternal. Let us constantly reflect on how divine grace has transformed our earthly natures so that we may contemplate more closely our heavenly hope. And let us attend to the words of the apostle Paul: 'You have died and your life is hidden with Christ in God. But when Christ your life appears, then you also will appear with him in glory.'

Note: If a reading about Cana of Galilee is required, see either alternative reading for Epiphany 2 or Tuesday after Trinity 9.

Monday after Epiphany 4

A Reading from *The Revelations of Mechtild of Magdeburg*
also known as
The Flowing Light of the Godhead

GOD

You are hunting desperately for your love.
What do you bring me, O my Queen?

SOUL

Lord, I bring you my treasure;
It is greater than the mountains,
Wider than the world,
Deeper than the ocean,
Higher than the clouds,
More glorious than the sun,
More numerous than the stars,
And it outweighs the entire earth!

GOD

O image of my Godhead,
Ennobled by my own humanity,
Adorned by my Holy Spirit,
What is your treasure called?

Lord, it is called my heart's desire.
I have withdrawn it from the world,
Denied it to myself or any creature.
Now I can bear it no longer,
Where, O Lord, shall I lay it?

GOD

Your heart's desire shall you lay nowhere
But in my own Sacred Heart
And on my human breast.
There alone will you find comfort
And be embraced by my Spirit.

Tuesday after Epiphany 4

A Reading from *Abandonment to Divine Providence*
by Jean-Pierre de Caussade

'Jesus Christ,' says the Apostle, 'is the same yesterday, today and for ever.' From the origins of the world he was, as God, the principle of the life of the righteous; from the first instant of his incarnation his humanity participated in this prerogative of his divinity. He works in us all through our life; the time which will elapse before the end of the world is but a day, and this day is filled with him. Jesus Christ has lived in the past and still lives in the present; he began in himself and continues in his saints a life that will never finish.

If the world is so incapable of understanding all that could be written of the individual life of Jesus, of his words and actions when he was on earth, if the gospel gives us only the rough sketch of a few little details of it, if that first hour of his life is so unknown and so fertile, how many gospels would have to be written to recount the history of all the moments of this mystical life of Jesus Christ which multiplies wonder infinitely and eternally, since all the aeons of time are, properly speaking, but the history of the divine action?

The Holy Spirit has set out for us in infallible and incontestable characters certain moments of this vast space of time.

He has collected in the Scriptures certain drops, as it were, of this ocean. We see there the secret and unknown ways by which he caused Jesus Christ to appear in the world. We can follow the channels and veins of communication which in the midst of our confusion distinguishes the origin, the race, the genealogy of this first-born child. Of all this ocean of divine action he reveals to us but a tiny stream of water which, having reached Jesus, loses itself in the apostles and disappears in the Apocalypse, so that the history of the divine operations, in which consists the life of Jesus in holy souls until the consummation of the ages, can only be divined by our faith.

To the manifestation of the truth of God by word has succeeded the manifestation of his charity by action. The Holy Spirit carries on the work of the Saviour. While he assists the Church in the preaching of the gospel of Jesus Christ, he writes his own gospel, and he writes it in the hearts of the faithful. All the actions, all the moments of the saints make up the gospel of the Holy Spirit. Their holy souls are the paper, their sufferings and their actions are the ink. The Holy Spirit, with his own action for pen, writes a living gospel, but it will not be readable until the day of glory when it will be taken out of the printing press of this life and published.

Wednesday after Epiphany 4

A Reading from *The Mirror of Charity*
by Aelred of Rievaulx

It was pride that distorted the image of God in us and led us away from God, not by means of our feet but by the desires of our hearts. Thus we return to God by following the same path, but in the opposite direction, by the exercise of these same desires; and humility renews us in the same image in which God created us. This is why St Paul calls on us to be mentally and spiritually remade, and to be clothed in the new self made in God's image. This renewal can only come about by fulfilling the new commandment of charity given us by our Saviour, and if the mind clothes itself in charity, our distorted memory and knowledge will be given new life and new form.

How simple it is to state the new commandment, but how much it implies – the stopping of our old habits, the renewal of our inner life, the reshaping of the divine image within us. Our power to love was poisoned by the selfishness of our desires, and stifled by lust, so that it has tended always to seek the very depths of deviousness. But when charity floods the soul and warms away the numbness, love strives towards higher and more worthy objects. It puts aside the old ways and takes up a new life, and on flashing wings it dies to the highest and purest Goodness which is the source of its being.

This is what St Paul was trying to show the Athenians when he established from the books of their philosophers the existence of one God, in whom we live and move and have our being. Paul then quoted one of their own poets who said that we are God's offspring, and in the next sentence went on to enlarge on this saying. The Apostle was not using this quotation to prove that we are of the same nature or substance as God, and therefore unchangeable, incorruptible and eternally blessed like God the Son who was born of the Father from all eternity and is equal to the Father in all things. No, St Paul uses this passage from the poet Aratus to assert that we are the offspring of God because the human soul, created in the image of God, can share in his wisdom and blessedness. It is charity which raises our soul towards its destiny, but it is self-centred desire which drags it down to the things towards which, without God's help, it would not certainly be drawn.

Thursday after Epiphany 4

A reading from *The Power and Meaning of Love*
by Thomas Merton

Those of us today who seek to be Christians, and who have not yet risen to the level of full maturity in Christ, tend unfortunately to take one or other of the debased forms of love for the action of the Spirit of God and the love of Christ. It is this failure to attain to full maturity in love which keeps divisions alive in the world.

There is a 'romantic' tendency in some Christians – a tendency which seeks Christ not in love of those flesh-and-blood brothers and sisters with whom we live and work, but in some as yet unrealised ideal of 'brotherhood'. It is always a romantic evasion to turn from the love of people to the love of love itself: to love people in general more than individual persons, to love 'brotherhood' and 'unity' more than one's brothers, sisters, neighbours, and associates.

This corruption of love can be romantic also in its love of God. It is no longer Christ himself that is loved and sought, but perhaps an objectivised 'experience' of Christ, a degree of prayer, a mystical state. What is loved then ceases to be Christ, but the subjective reactions which are aroused in me by the supposed presence of Christ in thought or love or prayer.

The romantic tendency leads to a substitution of aestheticism, or false mysticism, or quietism, for genuine faith and love, and what it seeks in the Church is not so much reality as a protection against responsibility. Failing to establish a true dialogue with our brother or sister in Christ, this fallacy thwarts all efforts at real unity and cooperation among Christians.

Friday after Epiphany 4

A Reading from a homily of Gregory the Great

Let us attend to what our Lord requires of his preachers in the gospel, when he sends them out: 'Go and preach,' he says, 'and say that the kingdom of heaven has come near.' Even if the gospel were silent, the world itself would proclaim it. Its chaotic state has become a statement. On all sides we are seeing the disintegration of our society: glory has come to an end. The state of the world is revealing to us the proximity of another kingdom, another kingdom which will overtake it; and the very people who once loved the world are now revolted by it.

The world's chaos proclaims that we should not love it. If someone's house became unstable and threatened to collapse, would they not flee? Surely, those who cherished it when it stood would be the first to run away if it began to collapse. If the world is collapsing, and yet we persist in loving it, then we are effectively preferring to be overwhelmed by it than to live in it. When love blinds us to our bondage, the ruin of the world will become inseparable from our own self-destruction.

It is easier for us to distance ourselves from the world around us when we see everything in such chaos. But in our Lord's day, the situation was very different. The disciples were sent to preach the reality of an unseen kingdom at a time when everybody could see the kingdoms of this world flourishing. It was for this reason that the preachers of his word were given the gift of performing miracles. The power they displayed lent credence to their words. Those who preached something new were performing something new, as the gospel records, when the disciples were told to 'cure the sick, raise the dead, cleanse lepers, and cast out demons.'

With the world flourishing and progressing, people living longer and longer, wealth multiplying, who was going to believe in another reality? Who would ever prefer an unseen world to the tangible things in front of them? But as soon as the sick recovered their health, the dead were raised, lepers cleansed, the demoniacs cured of their demonic possession, then who would not believe in the reality of the unseen world? Such amazing miracles were performed in order to draw the human heart to believe in what it cannot see, and to explore that far greater world within us.

Saturday after Epiphany 4

A Reading from *The Longer Rules for Monks*
by Basil the Great

What words can adequately describe the gifts of God? They are so many as to be innumerable, and so wonderful that any one of them demands our total gratitude of praise. I have no time to speak of the richness and diversity of God's gifts. We will have to pass over in silence the rising of the sun, the circuits of the moon, the variation in air temperature, the patterns of the seasons, the descent of the rain, the gushing of springs, the sea itself, the whole earth and its flora, the life of the oceans, the creatures of the air, the animals in their various species – in fact everything that exists for the service of our life. But there is one gift which no thoughtful person can pass over in silence; and yet to speak of it worthily is impossible.

God made us in his image and likeness; he deemed us worthy of knowledge of himself, equipped us with reason beyond the capacity of other creatures, allowed us to revel in the unimaginable beauty of paradise, and gave us dominion over creation. When we were deceived by the serpent and fell into sin, and through sin into death and all that followed in its wake, God did not abandon us. In the first place, God gave us a law to help us; he ordained angels to guard and care for us. He sent prophets to rebuke vice and to teach us virtue. He frustrated the impact of vice by dire warnings. He stirred up in us a zeal for goodness by his promises, and confronted us with examples of the end result of both virtue and vice in the lives of various individuals. To crown these and his other mercies, God was not estranged from the human race by our continuing disobedience. Indeed, in the goodness of our Master, we have never been neglected: our callous indifference towards our Benefactor for his gifts has never diminished his love for us. On the contrary, our Lord Jesus Christ recalled us from death and restored us to life.

In Christ the generosity of God is resplendent; for as Scripture says: 'being in the form of God, he did not cling to equality with God, but emptied himself, assuming the form of a servant.' What is more, he assumed our frailty and bore our infirmities; he was wounded on our behalf that 'by his wounds we might be healed'. He set us free from the curse, having become a curse on our behalf himself, and underwent the most ignominious death that he might lead us to the life of glory. Not content with restoring us to life when we were dead, he has graced us with the dignity of divinity and prepared for us eternal mansions, the delight of which exceeds all that we can conceive.

'What then shall we render to the Lord for all his benefits to us?' God is so good that he asks of us nothing. he is content merely with being loved in return for his gifts. When I consider this I am overcome with awe and fear lest through carelessness or preoccupation with trivia, I should fall away from the love of God and become a reproach to Christ.

The Presentation of Christ in the Temple

A Reading from a sermon of Sophronius of Jerusalem

Let us all hasten to meet Christ, we who honour and venerate the divine mystery we celebrate today. Everyone should be eager to join the procession to share in this meeting. Let no one refuse to carry a light. Our bright shining candles are a sign of the divine splendour of the one who comes to expel the dark shadows of evil and to make the whole universe radiant with the brilliance of his eternal light. Our candles also show how bright our souls should be when we go to meet Christ.

The God-bearer, the most pure Virgin, carried the true Light in her arms and brought him to help those who lay in darkness. In the same way, we too should carry a light for all to see and reflect the radiance of the true light as we hasten to meet him.

Indeed, this is the mystery we celebrate today, that the Light has come and has shone upon a world enveloped in shadow; the Dayspring from on high has visited us and given light to those who were sitting in darkness. This is our feast, and we join in procession with lighted candles to show both that the Light has shone upon us and to signify the glory that is yet to come to us through him. So let us hasten all together to meet our God.

The true Light has come, 'the light that enlightens every person who is born into this world'. Let all of us, beloved, be enlightened and be radiant with its light. Let none of us remain a stranger to this brightness; let no one who is filled remain in the darkness. Let us be shining ourselves as we go together to meet and to receive with the aged Simeon the light whose brilliance is eternal. Rejoicing with Simeon, let us sing a hymn of thanksgiving to God, the Origin and Father of the Light, who sent the true Light to dispel the darkness and to give us all a share in his splendour.

Through Simeon's eyes we too have seen the salvation of God which he has prepared for all the nations, and has revealed the glory of us who are the new Israel. As Simeon was released from the bonds of this life when he had seen Christ, so we too were at once freed from our old state of sinfulness. By faith we too embraced Christ, the salvation of God the Father, as he came to us from Bethlehem. Gentiles before, we have now become the people of God. Our eyes have seen God made flesh, and because we have seen him present among us and have cradled him in our minds, we are called the new Israel. Never let us forget this presence; every year let us keep this feast in his honour.

alternative reading

A Reading from a hymn of Ephrem of Syria

Praise to you, Son of the Most High, who has put on our body!

Into the holy temple Simeon carried the Christ-child
and sang a lullaby to him:
'You have come, Compassionate One,
having pity on my old age, making my bones enter
into Sheol in peace. By you I will be raised
out of the grave into paradise.'

Anna embraced the child; she placed her mouth
upon his lips, and then the Spirit rested
upon her lips, like Isaiah
whose mouth was silent until a coal drew near
to his lips and opened his mouth.
Anna was aglow with the spirit of his mouth.
She sang him a lullaby:
'Royal Son,
despised son, being silent, you hear;
hidden, you see; concealed, you know;
God-man, glory to your name.'

Even the barren heard and came running with their provisions.
The Magi are coming with their treasures.
The barren are coming with their provisions.
Provisions and treasures were heaped up suddenly among the
poor.

The barren woman Elizabeth cried out as she was accustomed,
'Who has granted to me, blessed woman,
to see your Babe by whom heaven and earth are filled?
Blessed is your fruit
that brought forth the cluster on a barren vine.'

Praise to you, Son of the Most High, who has put on our body!

A Reading from a sermon of Guerric of Igny

Today as we bear in our hands lighted candles, how can we not fail to remember that venerable old man Simeon who on this day held the child Jesus in his arms – the Word who was latent in a body, as light is latent in a wax candle – and declared him to be 'the light to enlighten the nations'? Indeed, Simeon was himself a bright and shining lamp bearing witness to the Light. Under the guidance of the Spirit which filled him, he came into the temple precisely in order that, 'receiving your loving kindness, O God, in the midst of your temple', he might proclaim Jesus to be that loving kindness and the light of your people.

Behold then, the candle alight in Simeon's hands. You must light your own candles by enkindling them at his, those lamps which the Lord commanded you to bear in your hands. So come to him and be enlightened that you do not so much bear lamps as become them, shining within yourselves and radiating light to your neighbours. May there be a lamp in your heart, in your hand and in your mouth: let the lamp in your heart shine for yourself, the lamp in your hand and mouth shine for your neighbours. The lamp in your heart is a reverence for God inspired by faith; the lamp in your hand is the example of a good life; and the lamp in your mouth are the words of consolation you speak.

We have to shine not only before others by our good works and by what we say, but also before the angels in our prayer, and before God by the intentions of our hearts. In the presence of the angels our lamps will shine with unsullied reverence when we sing the psalms attentively in their sight or pray fervently; before God our lamp is single-minded resolve to please him alone to whom we have entrusted ourselves.

My friends, in order to light all these lamps for yourselves, I beg you to approach the source of light and become enlightened – I mean Jesus himself who shines in Simeon's hands to enlighten your faith, who shines on your works, who inspires your speech, who makes your prayer fervent and purifies the intentions of your heart. Then, when the lamp of this mortal life is extinguished, there will appear for you who had so many lamps shining within you the light of unquenchable life, and it will shine for you at the evening of your life like the brightness of the noonday sun.

Though you may think your light is quenched in death, you will rise like the daystar and your darkness be made bright as noon. As Scripture says, 'No longer will you need the light of sun to shine upon you by day, or the light of the moon by night; but the Lord will be an everlasting light for you.' For the light of the new Jerusalem is the Lamb.

To him be glory and praise for ever!

ORDINARY TIME
BEFORE LENT

O Paradise,
share in the sorrow of Adam who is brought to poverty,
and with the sound of your leaves pray to the Creator
that we may not find your gates closed for ever.
We are fallen;
in your compassion have mercy on us.

Hymn for the Sunday before Lent
in the Orthodox Church

Depending on the date of Easter, the period of **Ordinary Time** between Candlemas and Ash Wednesday will be of variable length, and in any given year many of the readings provided in this section will be surplus to requirements.

The Book of Common Prayer follows medieval custom in naming the three Sundays before Lent respectively *Septuagesima, Sexagesima* and *Quinquagesima.* This designation reflected the monastic custom of maintaining a longer, more rigorous fast in preparation for Easter. In the revision of the Calendar, the Church of England has dispensed with the medieval nomenclature whilst retaining something of a penitential flavour to this time of the year.

In the Eastern Churches the Sunday immediately before Lent is known as the 'Sunday of Forgiveness'. Before renewing our relationship with Christ through the Lenten fast and Paschal mystery, there must be a renewal of relationships within the Body of Christ through the offering and receiving of forgiveness which alone leads to a restoration of trust. The readings chosen for this period of Ordinary Time reflect these themes.

The Fifth Sunday before Lent

A Reading from a homily of John Chrysostom

'You are the salt of the earth.' It is not for your own sake, Christ says to his disciples, but for the world's sake that the word is entrusted to you. I am not sending you to a couple of cities, to ten or twenty cities, not even to a single nation, as I sent the prophets of old, but across land and sea, to the whole world. And that world is in a pitiful state. For when Jesus says: 'You are the salt of the earth,' he is indicating that all humanity had lost its savour and been corrupted by sin.

What else do his words imply? For example, were the disciples to restore what had already turned rotten? Not at all. Salt cannot help what has already become corrupted. That is not what they did. Rather what had first been renewed and freed from corruption by Christ, and then turned over to them, they salted and preserved in the newness the Lord had bestowed. It took the power of Christ to free humanity from the corruption caused by sin; it was the task of the apostles through hard work to prevent that corruption from returning.

Have you noticed how, little by little, Christ demonstrates the apostles to be superior to the prophets of old? He says they are to be teachers not simply for Palestine but for the whole world. Do not be surprised, then, he says, that I address you apart from the others and involve you in such a dangerous enterprise. Consider the numerous and extensive cities, peoples and nations I will be sending you to. This is why I would have you make others prudent, as well as being prudent yourselves. For unless you can do that, you will not be able to sustain your own lives.

If others lose their savour, then your ministry will help them regain it. But if you yourselves suffer that loss, you will drag others down with you. Therefore, the greater the undertaking put into your hands, the more zealous you must be. This is why Jesus says: 'But if salt becomes tasteless, how can its flavour be restored? It is good for nothing now, but to be thrown out and trampled under foot.'

Then Jesus passes on to a yet more exalted comparison: 'You are the light of the world.' Once again, note that he says 'of the world': not of one nation or twenty cities, but of the whole world. The light of which he speaks is an interior light, something far superior to the rays of the sun we see, just as the salt of which he speaks is a spiritual salt. First salt, then light, so that you may learn how profitable sharp words may be and how important clear doctrine is. Such teaching brings coherence and prevents dissipation; it leads a person to the practice of virtue and sharpens the mind's eye. 'A city set on a hill cannot be hidden; nor do you light a lamp and put it under a basket.' Once again Jesus urges his disciples to a careful manner of life and teaches them to be watchful, for they live under the scrutiny of others and have the whole world for the arena of their struggles.

Monday after 5 before Lent

A Reading from *Revelations of Divine Love*
by Julian of Norwich

Sin is the sharpest scourge that any elect soul can be flogged with. It is the scourge which so reduces a man or woman and makes him loathsome in his own sight that it is not long before he thinks himself fit only to sinkdown to hell until the touch of the Holy Spirit forces him to contrition, and turns his bitterness to the hope of God's mercy. Then he begins to heal his wounds, and to rouse his soul as it turns to the life of Holy Church. The Holy Spirit leads him on to confession, so that he deliberately reveals his sins in all their nakedness and reality, and admits with great sorrow and shame that he has befouled the fair image of God. Then for all his sins he performs penance imposed by his confession according to the doctrine of Holy Church, and by the teaching of the Holy Spirit. This is one of the humble things that greatly pleases God. Physical illness that is sent by him is another. Others are those humiliations and griefs caused by outside influences, or by the rejection and contempt of the world, by the various kinds of difficulty and temptation a person may find himself in, whether they be physical or spiritual.

Dearly, indeed, does our Lord hold on to us when it seems to us that we are nearly forsaken and cast away because of our sin – and deservedly so. Because of the humility we acquire this way we are exalted in the sight of God by his grace, and know a very deep contrition and compassion and a genuine longing for God. Then suddenly we are delivered from sin and pain, and raised to blessedness and even made great saints!

Our courteous Lord does not want his servants to despair even if they fall frequently and grievously. Our falling does not stop his loving us. Peace and love are always at work in us, but we are not always in peace and love. But he wants us in this way to realise that he is the foundation of the whole of our life in love, and furthermore that he is our eternal protector, and mighty defender against our enemies who are so very fierce and wicked. And, alas, our need is all the greater since we give them every opportunity by our failures.

Tuesday after 5 before Lent

A Reading from a homily of Basil the Great

'Where your treasure is, there will your heart be also.' This is why the commandments of our Lord trouble the rich, demanding of them a life that is impossible to live unless they dispense with useless goods.

Your heart will be weighed in the balance and found to be inclined either toward true life or toward present pleasures. It is in stewardship and not in pleasure that one ought to use riches: such ought to be the conviction of those who reason wisely. In giving up wealth they ought to rejoice, convinced that this will be beneficial for others, instead of being tormented by the loss of their own fortune. Why this chagrin? Why this mourning at the injunction to 'Sell what you have'? It is these same goods which will follow you into eternity. Overshadowed by the glory of heaven, they are not worth eagerly retaining in this life. Since you must leave them here, why not sell them and bring the profits with you to heaven? After all, when you spend gold to buy a horse, you experience no suffering. But at the idea of exchanging corruptible goods for the kingdom of heaven, you cry and repel the offer, refuse to proceed, inventing the pretext of a thousand expenses.

What are you going to tell the judge, you who cover your walls but do not cover the human being? You who adorn your horses and then loudly mock your brother in rags? You who are able to leave alone both your wheat and those who are starving? You who bury your gold and scorn those who are strangled?

Wednesday after 5 before Lent

A Reading from an *Introduction to the Devout Life*
by Francis de Sales

Before we can receive the grace of God into our hearts they must be thoroughly emptied of self-glory. Humility repulses Satan and preserves in us the gifts and graces of the Holy Spirit.

If you would know whether a person is truly wise, learned and generous, observe whether his gifts make him humble, modest and open. If so, the gifts are genuine. If they swim on the surface, however, always seeking attention, then they are less than true.

If we stand upon our dignity about places, or precedence, or how we should be addressed, besides exposing ourselves and our gifts to scrutiny and possible contradiction, we render those same gifts unattractive and contemptible. Honour is beautiful when it is freely bestowed: it becomes ugly when it is exacted or sought after.

The pursuit and love of virtue begins a process by which we become virtuous; but the pursuit and love of honour will make us contemptible and open to ridicule. Generous minds do not need the amusement of such petty toys as rank, honour and obsequious greetings; they have better things to do. Such baubles are only important to degenerate spirits.

It is said that the surest way of attaining to the love of God is to dwell on his mercies; the more we value them, the more we shall love God. Certainly, nothing can so humble us before the compassion of God as the contemplation of the abundance of his mercies; and nothing so humble us before his justice as the abundance of our misdeeds. Let us, then, reflect upon all that God has done for us, and all that we have done against him. And as we enumerate our sins, let us also count his mercies.

Thursday after 5 before Lent

A Reading from *The Laws of Ecclesiastical Polity*
by Richard Hooker

God is himself the teacher of the truth, whereby is made known the supernatural way of salvation and law for them to live in that shall be saved.

This supernatural way had God in himself prepared before all worlds. The way of supernatural duty which to us God hath prescribed, our Saviour in the Gospel of St John doth note, terming it by an excellency, the work of God: 'This is the work of God, that ye believe in him whom he hath sent.' Not that God doth require nothing unto happiness at the hands of men saving only a naked belief (for hope and charity we may not exclude) but that without belief all other things are as nothing, and it is the ground of those other divine virtues.

Concerning faith, the principal object whereof is that eternal verity which hath discovered the treasures of hidden wisdom in Christ; concerning hope, the highest object whereof is that everlasting goodness which in Christ doth quicken the dead; concerning charity, the final object whereof is that incomprehensible beauty which shineth in the countenance of Christ the Son of the living God. Concerning these virtues, the first of which beginning here with a weak apprehension of things not seen, endeth with the intuitive vision of God in the world to come; the second beginning here with trembling expectation of things far removed and as yet but only heard of, endeth with real and actual fruition of that which no tongue can express; the third beginning here with a weak inclination of heart towards him unto whom we are not able to approach, endeth with endless union, the mystery whereof is higher than the reach of the thoughts of men; concerning that faith, hope, and charity, without which there can be no salvation, was there ever any mention made saving only in that law which God himself hath from heaven revealed? There is not in the world a syllable muttered with certain truth concerning any of these three, more than hath been supernaturally received from the mouth of the eternal God.

Friday after 5 before Lent

A Reading from a treatise entitled *The Teacher*
by Clement of Alexandria

Our Teacher is the holy God Jesus, the Word, who is the guide of all humanity: God himself, who loves us, is our Teacher.

In a song in Scripture the Holy Spirit says of him: 'He provided for the people in the wilderness. He led them through the desert in the thirst of the summer heat, and instructed them. He guarded them as the apple of his eye. As an eagle hovers over her nest, and protects her young, spreading out her wings, rising up, and bearing them on her back, so the Lord alone was their leader. No strange god was with them.' In my opinion, Scripture is offering us here a picture of Christ the Teacher of children, and is describing the sort of guidance he imparts. Indeed, when he speaks in his own person, he confesses himself to be the Teacher: 'I, the Lord, am your God, who brought you up out of the land of Egypt.' Who has the power to lead us if not our Teacher?

He is the one who appeared to Abraham and said to him: 'I am your God; be pleasing before me.' He formed him by a gradual process into a faithful child, as any good teacher would, saying: 'Be blameless; and I will establish my covenant between me and you, and your descendants.' What is being offered is a share in the Teacher's friendship. Who, then, could train us more lovingly than Christ? Formerly, God's ancient people had an old covenant; the law disciplined the people with fear, and the word was an angel. But the new and young people of God have received a new and young covenant: the Word has become flesh, fear has been turned into love, and the mystic angel has been born – Jesus.

Formerly, this same Teacher said: 'Fear the Lord your God.' But now he says to us: 'Love the Lord your God.' That is why he tells us: 'Cease from your own works, from your old sins'; 'Learn to do good; love justice and hate iniquity.' This is my new covenant written in the old letter. Thus, the newness of the word must not be made ground for reproach. For the Lord says through Jeremiah: 'Say not, "I am too young." Before I formed you in the womb I knew you, before you were born I dedicated you.' Perhaps this prophetic word refers to us: before the foundation of the world we were known by God as those destined for the faith, but we are still only infants. The will of God has only recently been fulfilled; we are only newly born in the scheme of our calling and salvation.

Saturday after 5 before Lent

A Reading from *Holy Living* by Jeremy Taylor

God is especially present in the consciences of all persons, good and bad, by way of testimony and judgement: He is a remembrancer to call our actions to mind, a witness to bring them to judgement, and judge to acquit or to condemn. And although this manner of presence is, in this life, after the manner of this life, that is, imperfect, and we forget many actions of our lives; yet the greatest changes of our state of grace or sin, our most considerable actions, are always present like capital letters to an aged and dim eye. Because we covered them with dust and negligence, they were not then discerned. But when we are risen from our dust and imperfection, they all appear plain and legible.

Now the consideration of this great truth is of a very universal use in the whole course of the life of a Christian. He that remembers that God stands a witness and a judge, beholding every secrecy, besides his impiety, must have put on impudence, if he be not much restrained in his temptation to sin. He is to be feared in public, he is to be feared in private. Be sure, that while you are in his sight, you behave yourself as becomes so holy a presence. But if you will sin, retire yourself wisely, and go where God cannot see for nowhere else can you be safe. And certainly, if men would always actually consider and really esteem this truth, that God is the great eye of the world, alway watching over our actions, and an ever-open ear to hear all our words, it would be the readiest way in the world to make sin to cease from amongst the children of men, and for men to approach to the blessed estate of the saints in heaven, who cannot sin, for they always walk in the presence, and behold the face of God.

The Fourth Sunday before Lent

A Reading from the *Confessions* of Augustine

Where in my consciousness, Lord, do you dwell? Where in it do you make your home? What resting-place have you made for yourself? You are the Lord God of the mind. All things are liable to change. But you remain unchangeable over all things; and yet you have deigned to dwell in my memory since the time that I learnt about you. Why do I ask in which area of my memory you dwell, as if there really are places there? Surely my memory is where you dwell, because I remember you since first I learnt of you, and I find you there when I think about you.

Where then did I find you to be able to learn of you? For you were not in my memory before I learnt of you. Where then did I find you so that I could learn of you if not in the fact that you transcend me? There is no place, whether we go this way or that; the concept of place has no meaning. O truth, everywhere you preside over all who ask counsel of you. You respond at one and the same time to all, even though they are consulting you on different subjects. You reply clearly, but not all hear you clearly. All ask your counsel on what they desire, but do not always hear what they would wish. Your best servant is the person who does not attend so much to hearing what he himself wants, as to willing what he hears from you.

Late have I loved you, O beauty so ancient and so new; late have I loved you! For you were within me and I was in the external world and sought you there, and in my unlovely state I plunged into those lovely created things which you made. You were with me, and I was not with you. The lovely things kept me from you, though if they did not have their existence in you, they would have had no existence at all. You called and cried out loud to me and shattered my deafness. You were radiant and resplendent, you put to flight my blindness. You were fragrant, and I drew in my breath and now I pant after you. I tasted you and now I feel nothing but hunger and thirst for you. You touched me, and now I burn for your peace.

When I shall be united to you with my whole being, I shall never experience pain and toil again, and my entire life will be full of you. You lift up the person whom you fill. But for the present, because I am not full of you, I am a burden to myself. There is a struggle between my regrets at my evil past and my memories of good joys, and I do not know which side has secured the victory. Alas, Lord, have mercy upon me, wretch that I am. See, I do not hide my wounds. You are the physician, I am the patient. You are merciful, and I need your mercy.

Monday after 4 before Lent

A Reading from *An Exposition of the Church Catechism*
by Thomas Ken

O my God, when in any of thy commands a duty is enjoined, love tells me the contrary evil is forbidden; when any evil is forbidden, love tells me the contrary duty is enjoined; O do thou daily increase my love to good, and my antipathy to evil.

Though thy commands and prohibitions, O Lord, are in general terms, yet let thy love direct my particular practice, and teach me, that in one general are implied all the kinds and degrees and occasions and incitements and approaches and allowances, relating to that good or evil which are also commanded or forbidden, and give me grace to pursue or to fly them.

O my God, keep my love always watchful and on its guard that in thy negative precepts I may continually resist evil; keep my love warm with an habitual zeal that in all thy affirmative precepts I may lay hold on all seasons and opportunities of doing good.

Let thy love, O thou that only art worthy to be beloved, make me careful to persuade and engage others to love thee, and to keep thy commandments as well as myself.

None can love thee, and endeavour to keep thy holy commands, but his daily failings in his duty, his frequent involuntary and unavoidable slips, and surreptitions and wanderings, afflict and humble him; the infirmities of lapsed nature create in him a kind of perpetual martyrdom because he can love thee no more, because he can so little serve thee.

But thou, O most compassionate Father, in thy covenant of grace dost require sincerity, not perfection; and therefore I praise and love thee.

O my God, though I cannot love and obey thee as much as I desire, I will do it as much as I am able: I will to the utmost of my power, keep all thy commandments with my whole heart and to the end. O accept of my imperfect duty, and supply all the defects of it by the merits and love and obedience of Jesus, thy beloved.

Tuesday after 4 before Lent

A Reading from *The Cloud of Unknowing*

We must pray in the height, depth, length, and breadth of our spirits. Not in many words, but in a little word of one syllable. What shall this word be? Surely such a word as is suited to the nature of prayer itself. And what word is that? First let us see what prayer is in itself, and then we shall know more clearly what word will best suit its nature.

In itself prayer is nothing else than a devout setting of our will in the direction of God in order to get good, and remove evil. Since all evil is summed up in sin, considered casually or essentially, when we pray with intention for the removing of evil, we should neither say, think, nor mean any more than this little word 'sin'. And if we pray with intention for the acquiring of goodness, let us pray, in word or thought or desire, no other word than 'God'. For in God is all good, for he is its beginning and its being. Do not be surprised then that I set these words before all others. If I could find any shorter words which would sum up fully the thought of good or evil as these words do, or if I had been led by God to take some other words, then I would have used those and left these. And that is my advice for you too.

But don't study these words, for you will never achieve your object so, or come to contemplation; it is never attained by study, but only by grace. Take no other words for your prayer than those that God leads you to use. Yet if God does lead you to these, my advice is not to let them go, that is, if you are using words at all in your prayer: not otherwise. They are very short words. But though shortness of prayer is greatly to be recommended here, it does not mean that the frequency of prayer is to be lessened. For as I have said, it is prayed in the length of one's spirit, so that it never stops until such time as it has fully attained what it longs for. We can turn to a terrified man or woman, suddenly frightened by fire, or death, for an example. They never stop crying their little words, 'Help!' or 'Fire!' till such time as they have got all the help they need in their trouble.

Wednesday after 4 before Lent

A Reading from *The Life of Moses* by Gregory of Nyssa

The divine law leads us along a royal highway, and the person who has been purified of all desires and passions, will deviate neither to the left nor to the right. And yet how easy it is for a traveller to turn aside from the way. Imagine two precipices forming a high narrow pass; from its centre the person crossing it is in great danger if he veers in either direction because of the chasm on either side that waits to engulf those that stray. In the same way, the divine law requires those who follow its paths not to stray either to left or right from the way which, as the Lord says, is 'narrow and hard'.

This teaching declares that virtue is to be discerned in the mean: evil operates in either a deficiency or in an excess. For example, in the case of courage, cowardice is the product of a lack of virtue, and impetuosity the product of its excess. What is pure and to be identified as virtue is to be discovered in the mean between two contrasting evils. Similarly, those things in life which reach after the good also in some strange way follow this middle course between neighbouring evils.

Wisdom clings to the mean between shrewdness and innocence. Neither the wisdom of the serpent nor the innocence of the dove is to be praised if a person opts for one to the neglect of the other. Rather it is the frame of mind that seeks to unite these two attitudes by their mean that constitutes virtue. One person, for example, who lacks moderation becomes self-indulgent; another person whose demands exceed what moderation dictates has his 'conscience seared', as the apostle Paul says. For one has abandoned all restraint in the pursuit of pleasure, and the other ridicules marriage as if it were adultery; whereas the frame of mind formed by the mean of these two attitudes is moderation.

Since, as our Lord says, 'this world is ensnared in wickedness', and everything that is wicked (and therefore opposed to virtue) is alien to those who obey the divine law, it follows that those in this life who pick their way through this world will only reach the destination of their journey in safety if they faithfully keep to that highway which is hardened and smoothed by virtue, and who under no circumstances, veer aside to explore the byways of evil.

Thursday after 4 before Lent

A Reading from *Life Together*
by Dietrich Bonhoeffer

'Confess your faults one to another.' He who is alone with his sin is utterly alone. It may be that Christians, notwithstanding corporate worship, common prayer, and all their fellowship in service, may still be left to their loneliness. The final breakthrough to fellowship does not occur, because, though they have fellowship with one another as believers and as devout people, they do not have fellowship as the undevout, as sinners. The pious fellowship permits no one to be a sinner. So everybody must conceal their sin from themselves and from each other. We dare not be sinners. Many Christians are unthinkably horrified when a real sinner is suddenly discovered among the righteous. So we remain alone with our sin, living in lies and hypocrisy. The fact is that we are sinners!

But it is the grace of the gospel, which is so hard for the pious to understand, that it confronts us with the truth and says: You are a sinner, a great, desperate sinner; now come as the sinner that you are, to God who loves you. He wants you as you are: he does not want anything from you, a sacrifice, a work: he wants you alone. As Scripture says: 'My child, give me your heart.' God has come to you to save the sinner. Be glad! This message is liberation through truth. You can hide nothing from God. The mask you wear before others will do you no good before him. He wants to see you as you are, he wants to be gracious to you. You do not have to go on lying to yourself and your brothers and sisters, as if you were without sin; you can dare to be a sinner. Thank God for that: he loves the sinner but he hates sin.

In confession the breakthrough to community takes place. Sin demands to have a person by himself. It withdraws us from the community. The more isolated a person is, the more destructive will be the power of sin over him, and the more deeply he becomes involved in it, the more disastrous is his isolation. Sin wants to remain unknown. It shuns the light. In the darkness of the unexpressed it poisons the whole being of a person. In confession the light of the gospel breaks into the darkness and seclusion of the heart.

Since the confession of sin is made in the presence of a Christian sister or brother, the last stronghold of self-justification is abandoned. The sinner surrenders: he gives up all his evil. He gives his heart to God, and he finds the forgiveness of all his sin in the fellowship of Jesus Christ and his sister and brother. The expressed, acknowledged sin has lost all its power. The sin confessed has helped the person find true fellowship with his brothers and sisters in Christ. If a Christian is in the fellowship of confession with a sister or brother, he will never be alone again, anywhere.

Friday after 4 before Lent

A Reading from *The Enchiridion* by Augustine

Every lie constitutes a sin. It is a sin, not only when we know the truth and blatantly lie, but also when we are mistaken and deceived in what we say. It remains our duty to speak what we think in our heart, whether it be true, or we just think that it's true. A liar says the opposite of what he thinks in his heart, because his purpose is to deceive.

We have been given the gift of speech not to deceive one another, but to communicate truly with each other. To use speech for the purpose of deception is to pervert its purpose and is sinful. Nor should we kid ourselves that there are lies that are not sinful, because (we suppose) in telling a lie we are doing someone a service. One could say the same thing about stealing: it is alright to steal from a rich person because they will never feel the loss if it is in order to help the poor. Or you could make an argument for committing adultery: if I don't sleep with this woman she will die of love for me. Your action is no less sinful. We value marital fidelity, refusing to countenance anything that will violate a marriage; but are quite happy to violate a relationship by lying. It cannot be denied that they have attained a very high standard of goodness who never lie, except perhaps to protect a person from injury; but even in such cases, it is not the deceit that is praiseworthy, but the good intention. Such deception is pardonable, but not laudable, particularly among Christians.

So let us be true heirs of the new covenant, to whom our Lord said: 'Let your Yes be Yes, and your No, No; for whatever else comes from the evil One.' And it is on account of our many failures in this regard, failures which never cease to creep into our living, that we co-heirs of Christ cry out: 'Lord, forgive us our sins.'

Saturday after 4 before Lent

A Reading from the treatise *Pastoral Care*
by Gregory the Great

Let every Christian leader be both alongside each person under their pastoral care in compassion, and lifted above all in contemplation, so that he may both transfer to himself the weaknesses of others through the inner depths of his mercy, and at the same time, transcend himself seeking the unseen through the heights of contemplation. This balance is important lest in seeking to scale the heights a leader despise the weakness of his neighbour, or in attending to the weakness of his neighbour, he lose his desire for the sublime.

Thus it was that Paul was led into paradise and searched the secrets of the third heaven, and yet, though raised aloft in the contemplation of the unseen, was still able to give his mind to the needs of ordinary people, and even lay out norms governing the conduct of Christian marriage.

Note that Paul had already been introduced into the secrets of heaven, yet by a graciousness of love was still able to give advice to ordinary men and women. He can raise his heart to the contemplation of the unseen, and being so lifted up, can turn in compassion to the secrets of those who are weak. He reaches the heavens in contemplation, yet in his care for others does not ignore the marriage-bed. United by a bond of charity to the highest and lowest alike, a leader is readily caught up in the contemplation of heaven, but equally content to be 'weak with those who are weak'.

In a similar vein, we find Paul declaring that: 'To the Jews, I became a Jew.' Paul did this, not by abandoning his faith, but by expanding his loving-kindness. Thus, by transfiguring the person of the unbeliever into his own person, he learnt at first hand how he ought to be compassionate to others.

The Third Sunday before Lent

A Reading from a treatise *On the Lord's Prayer*
by Cyprian of Carthage

When we pray 'Your will be done on earth as in heaven' we are not praying that God may accomplish what he wills, but that we may be able to do what God wills. For who can prevent God from doing what he wills? The reality is that it is we who are prevented from completely obeying God in our thoughts and deeds because of the activity of the devil. That is why we pray that we may will what God wills. If this is to happen we need God's goodwill, by which is meant his help and protection. Nobody is sufficiently strong, whatever their inner resources: it is only by the grace and mercy of God that we are saved.

Indeed, our Lord himself revealed the fragility of his own humanity when he prayed: 'Father, if it is possible, let this cup pass me by.' And then he gave his disciples an example that they should do God's will and not their own when he went on to say: 'Nevertheless, not what I will but what you will.' If the Son was obedient to the Father's will, how much more should we servants be concerned to do the will of our Master!

It was the will of God, then, that Christ exemplified both in his deeds and in his teaching. It requires humility in behaviour, constancy in faith, modesty in conversation, justice in deeds, mercy in judgements, discipline in morals. We should be incapable of doing wrong to anyone but, at the same time, able to bear patiently wrongs done to us. It requires that we live at peace with our neighbours, loving God with our whole heart: loving him as our Father, fearing him as our God. It means preferring nothing whatever to Christ who preferred nothing to us. It means holding fast to his love and never letting go; standing by his cross bravely and fearlessly when his name and honour are challenged; exhibiting in our speech a conviction that will confess our faith. It also means that even under torture we sustain a confidence that will not surrender; and that in the face of death we allow our patience to be our crown. This is what is entailed in being a co-heir with Christ. This is what it means to accomplish the commandment of God, to fulfil the will of the Father.

Monday after 3 before Lent

A Reading from the discourses of Dorotheus of Gaza

In the Book of Proverbs it says: 'Those who have no guidance fall like leaves, but there is safety in much counsel.' Take a good look at this saying, brothers. Look at what Scripture is teaching us. It assures us that we should not set ourselves up as guide-posts, that we should not consider ourselves sagacious, that we should not believe we can direct ourselves. We need assistance, we need guidance in addition to God's grace. No one is more wretched, no one is more easily caught unawares, than someone who has no one to guide them along the road to God. Scripture says: 'Those who have no guidance fall like leaves.' Leaves are always green in the beginning, they grow vigorously and are pleasing to look at. Then after a short time they dry up and fall off the tree, and in the end they are blown about by the wind and trodden under foot. So is the person who refuses guidance. At first he has great fervour about fasting, keeping vigil, keeping silence, and obedience and other good customs. Then, after a short time, the fire is extinguished and, not having anyone to guide him and strengthen him and kindle his fire again, he shrivels up and so, becoming disobedient, he falls and finally becomes a tool in the hand of his enemies, who do what they like with him.

Concerning those who make a report about what concerns their interior life and do everything with counsel, Scripture says: 'There is safety in much counsel.' When it says 'much counsel' it does not mean taking counsel from all and sundry, but clearly from someone in whom one has full confidence. And we should not be silent about some things and speak about others, but we should report everything and take counsel about everything. To those doing this consistently there is indeed safety in much counsel. But if someone does not bring to light everything about himself, especially if he has turned away from evil habits and a bad upbringing, and if the devil finds in him one bit of self-will or self-righteousness, he will cast him down through that. For when the devil looks at a person who sincerely desires not to sin, he is not so unintelligent as to suggest to him (as he would to a hardened sinner) that he go and commit fornication or go and steal. He knows we do not want that, and he does not set out to tell us something we do not want to hear; instead he finds out that little bit of self-will or self-righteousness and through that, with the appearance of well doing, he will do us harm. For when we are masters of our own affairs and we stand in our own righteousness as if we were doing great things, we are giving ourselves counsel – and we do not know how it is we are destroyed. For how can we know the will of God or seek it completely if we believe only in ourselves and hold on to our own will?

May God shelter us from this danger of being our own guides that we may be worthy to take the road our fathers took and pleased God.

Tuesday after 3 before Lent

A Reading from *The Revelations of Mechtild of Magdeburg*
also known as
The Flowing Light of the Godhead

Lord, my sin because of which I have lost you,
Stands before my eyes like a huge mountain,
Creating between us
Darkness and distance.
O Love, above all love
Draw me to yourself again.

But Lord, the prospect of future falls
Plague my mind:
They beckon to me like the mouth of a fiery dragon
Eager to swallow me whole.
O my only Good, help me now
That I may flow sinless towards you.

Lord, my earthly being lies before me
As an acre of dust
On which little good has grown.
O sweet Jesus Christ,
Send me now the fruitful rain of your humanity,

And the gentle dew of the Holy Spirit
That I may plead my heart's sorrow.

Your everlasting kingdom
Lies open before my eyes
Like a wedding feast,
Inviting me to your everlasting banquet.
O true lover
Never cease to draw to your side this lovesick bride.
All the gifts I have ever received from you
Stand before me as a heavy reproach
For this your highest gift humbles me to the dust.

Then God who gives us everything answered thus:
'Your mountain of darkness shall be melted away by my love,
Your enemies shall win no victory over you,
Your acre has been scorched by the rays of the hot sun
Yet its fruit has not been destroyed.
In my kingdom you will live as a new bride,
There I will greet you with the kiss of love
And all my Godhead shall sweep through your soul;
My three-fold being shall play ceaselessly
In your two-fold heart.
What place then has mourning?
If you were to pray for a thousand years
I would never give you cause
For a single sigh.'

Wednesday after 3 before Lent

A Reading from *The Scale of Perfection*
by Walter Hilton

Jesus is knitted and fastened to a person's soul by a good will and a
great desire for him, to have him alone and to see him in his
spiritual glory. The greater this desire, the more firmly is Jesus
knitted to the soul; the less the desire, the more loosely is he
joined. Thus whatever spirit or feeling it is that lessens this desire
and wants to draw it down from its natural ascent toward Jesus in
order to set it upon itself, this spirit will unknit and undo Jesus
from the soul; and therefore it is not from God but from the

working of the enemy. Nevertheless, if a spirit, a feeling or a revelation by an angel increases this desire, knits firmer the knot of love and devotion to Jesus, opens the sight of your soul more clearly to spiritual knowledge, and makes it humbler in itself, this spirit is from God.

Here you can partly see that you must not willingly allow your heart to rest or find all its delight in any such feelings of comfort or sweetness in the body even if they are good, but you shall hold them in your own view as little or nothing compared with spiritual desire; and you shall not fix your heart in them in thought, but forget them if you can and always seek to come to the spiritual feeling of God: and that is to know and experience the wisdom of God, his infinite might and his great goodness, both in himself and in his creatures. For this is contemplation, and the other is not.

Be rooted and grounded in charity, that you may know, as St Paul says, not a sound in the ear, or sweet taste in the mouth, or any such bodily thing, but that with the saints you may know and feel what is the length of the infinite being of God, the breadth of the wonderful charity and goodness of God, the height of his almighty majesty, and the bottomless depth of his wisdom.

Thursday after 3 before Lent

A Reading from a letter of Basil the Great

The best guide for discovering the way to conduct our life is the thorough study of Scripture. Here are to be found not only instructions about conduct appropriate for a Christian, but also, in the stories of holy men and women, vital images of godly living which invite our imitation. In whatever respect any of us may feel deficient, by devoting ourselves to this process, we will discover as if from a pharmacy, appropriate medicine for our sickness.

Those who seek temperance will discover the story of Joseph. From him they will learn the virtue of chaste conduct, finding him not only steadfast in the face of seduction, but habitually virtuous. Those who seek courage will learn from Job, who remained faithful, his nobility of soul unimpaired, when the circumstances of life conspired against him. Once rich, suddenly one day he finds himself destitute, and instead of being surrounded by his devoted children, he becomes childless. He was even provoked by his friends who in theory had come to console him, but actually interrogated him and undermined him. Or again, suppose someone needs to know how to combine gentleness and passion in life, so as to be passionate against sin but gentle towards others. For such a seeker there is David, noble in exploits of war, gentle and calm in the treatment of his enemies. Moses was the same. He rose in great passion against those who had sinned against God, but was able to endure with a gentle spirit the accusations that his own people brought against him. Those who want to become perfect in every kind of virtue should become like a painter who, in making a picture, will keep referring to his model in his determination to transfer its character into his painting. Thus we should study intensely the lives of holy people, as if they were living and moving statues, and make their goodness our own through imitation.

Prayer after such reading of Scripture will leave us refreshed and our love for God invigorated. Ideally, such prayer should imprint upon our minds a clear idea of God, and with God established in our memory, we will experience his indwelling. We become the temple of God when our continuous meditation is no longer fragmented by anxiety and our mind no longer assailed by unexpected emotions. So let us flee from materialism and hold fast to God. Let us repudiate all feelings that encourage us to self-indulgence, and instead give our energy to the pursuit of virtue.

Friday after 3 before Lent

A Reading from a treatise *On Spiritual Friendship*
by Aelred of Rievaulx

Love is the source of friendship – not love of any sort whatever, but that which proceeds from reason and affection simultaneously, which, indeed, is pure because of reason and sweet because of affection. A foundation of friendship should be laid in the love of God, to which all things which are proposed would be referred, and these ought to be examined as to whether they conform to the foundation or are at variance with it.

One should pay attention to the four steps which lead up to the heights of perfect friendship; for a friend ought first to be selected, next tested, then finally admitted, and from then on treated as a friend deserves. And speaking of selection, we exclude the quarrelsome, the irascible, the fickle, the suspicious, and the talkative; and yet not all, but only those who are unable or unwilling to regulate or restrain these passions. For many are affected by these disturbances in such a manner that their perfection is not only in no way injured, but their virtue is even more laudably increased by the restraint of these passions. As though we were unbridled horses, we tend to be carried away headlong under the impulse of these passions, and inevitably slip and fall into those vices by which friendship, as Scripture testifies, is wounded and dissolved; namely, insults, reproaches, betrayal of secrets, pride, and the stroke of treachery.

If, nevertheless, you suffer all these evils from him whom you once received into friendship, your friendship should not be broken off immediately, but dissolved little by little, and that such reverence should be maintained for the former friendship, that, although you withdraw your confidence from him, yet you never withdraw your love, refuse your aid, or deny him your advice. But if his frenzy breaks out even to blasphemies and calumny, do you, nevertheless, yield to the bonds of friendship, yield to charity, so that the blame will reside with him who inflicts, not with him who bears, the injury.

Saturday after 3 before Lent

A Reading from a commentary on the psalms by Augustine

Some people's strength is based not on wealth, or in their physical well-being, or even in the power that their position in society gives them, but in a sense of their own righteousness. Above all others, it is these people whom we should guard ourselves against. They should be feared and repulsed, and in no way imitated. The individuals who most worry me are not those who rely on their physical prowess, their private means, their class or status – things which are temporal, fleeting, unreliable and ephemeral – but rather those with an in-built confidence in their own righteousness.

It was precisely this kind of strength that prevented the Jewish leaders from passing through the eye of the needle. They took their righteousness for granted, and in their own eyes considered themselves healthy. They had no need of medicine, and the physician himself they slew. They were strong; they were not weak! And that is why they did not respond to the call of the One who said, 'It is not the healthy who need a doctor but the sick. I have come to call not the righteous, but sinners to repentance.' The people who ridiculed Christ's disciples because their master visited the homes of the sick and dared to eat with them were the strong ones. 'Why,' they said, 'does your master eat with tax collectors and sinners?' O strong ones who boast that you have no need of a doctor! This strength of yours is not healthy; it is born of madness! Nothing is stronger than a madman; a madman can intimidate even the strongest person. So although these people may appear strong to the rest of us, in fact they are teetering on the edge of their own destruction. God grant that we may never imitate such strength.

The teacher of humility, who shared our weakness and deigned to give us a share in his divinity, came to teach us the way; indeed, to be the Way himself. It was his own humility that he impressed upon us. He even willingly submitted to be baptized by one of his own servants, so that we might learn to confess our sins and know our own weakness, because only in so doing can we become truly strong. As Paul the apostle wrote: 'When I am weak, then I am strong.'

Christ rejected the path of strength. But these people, who crave to be strong, who end up relying on their own virtue as their self-justification, will end up tripping over the stumbling block. In their eyes, the Lamb was a goat, and because they did not recognise him as such, they killed him. They were not worthy to be redeemed by the Lamb. In their strength they attacked Christ, priding themselves in their sense of justice.

They put themselves a cut above the sick multitude who were not ashamed to run to the doctor. Why did they exalt themselves? Because they thought of themselves as strong. They even managed to entice others into their camp, and ended up killing the physician who had power to heal them all. But the murdered physician, by his very death, has compounded a medicine out of his own blood to heal the sick.

The Second Sunday before Lent

A Reading from *Revelations of Divine Love*
by Julian of Norwich

It was at this time that our Lord showed me spiritually how intimately he loves us. I saw that he is everything that we know to be good and helpful. In his love he clothes us, enfolds and embraces us; that tender love completely surrounds us, never to leave us. As I saw it God is everything that is good.

And he showed me more, a little thing, the size of a hazelnut, on the palm of my hand, round like a ball. I looked at it thoughtfully and wondered, 'What is this?' And the answer came, 'It is all that is made.' I marvelled that it continued to exist and did not suddenly disintegrate; it was so small. And again my mind supplied the answer, 'It exists, both now and for ever, because God loves it.' In short, everything owes its existence to the love of God.

In this 'little thing' I saw three truths. The first is that God made it; the second is that God loves it; and the third is that God sustains it. But what he is who is in truth Maker, Keeper, and Lover I cannot tell, for until I am essentially united with him I can never have full rest or real happiness; in other words, until I am so joined to him that there is absolutely nothing between my God and me.

We have got to realise the littleness of creation and to see it for the nothing that it is before we can love and possess God who is uncreated. This is the reason why we have no ease of heart or soul, for we are seeking our rest in trivial things which cannot satisfy, and not seeking to know God, almighty, all-wise, all-good. He is true rest. And it is his will that we should know him, and his pleasure that we should rest in him.

Monday after 2 before Lent

A Reading from *Abandonment to Divine Providence*
by Jean-Pierre de Caussade

Once we are able to grasp that each moment of our lives contains some sign of the will of God, we shall find in it all that our heart can desire. For what can there be more reasonable, more perfect, more divine than the will of God? Can its infinite value increase through differences of time, place and circumstance? If you are given the secret of finding it at every moment, in every event, you possess all that is most precious and worthy in your desiring. What more do you want, you who seek perfection? Do not hold back then, allow your desires to transport you beyond all measures and limits; dilate your hearts to an infinite extent, I have enough to fill them: there is no moment at which I cannot make you find all that you can desire.

The present moment is always full of infinite treasures, it contains far more than you have the capacity to hold. Faith is the measure; what you find in the present moment will be according to the measure of your faith. Love also is the measure: the more your heart loves, the more it desires, and the more it desires the more it finds. The will of God presents itself to us at each instant like an immense ocean which the desire of our hearts can never empty, but we can receive something of that ocean as our hearts expand by faith, trust and love. The whole of the created universe cannot fill or satisfy the human heart because it has a greater capacity except that of God himself. The mountains which overawe us are but tiny atoms to the heart. The will of God is an abyss, the opening of which is always the present moment. Plunge into this abyss and you will find it deeper than your desires.

Pay court to no one, do not worship illusions, they can neither enrich you nor rob you of anything. Only the will of God will wholly fill you and satisfy you; adore that will, go straight towards it, pierce through and expose all its disguises. The stripping, death and destruction of the senses will establish the reign of faith: the senses adore creatures, faith adores the divine will. Deprive the senses of their idols and they will weep like children in despair; but faith will triumph, for faith cannot be deprived of the will of God. When the present moment terrifies us, starves, strips and attacks the senses, it is just at that moment that God nourishes, enriches and vitalises faith, which laughs at the losses of the senses as the governor of an impregnable town laughs at useless attacks.

When the will of God has been revealed to us and we in our turn, make it plain that we are only too glad to abandon ourselves to it, we will be given very powerful help. We shall know the joy of the coming of God, and will savour it more intensely the more completely we abandon ourselves to God's adorable will.

Tuesday after 2 before Lent

A Reading from a sermon of Caesarius of Arles

Strive by your thinking, as well as by your praying, to fulfil in your daily life what you sing with your lips in church; and make the Holy Spirit who speaks through your lips be glad to dwell in your heart. It is indeed good and entirely pleasing to God when a person sings the psalms devoutly; but is better still when their life is in harmony with the words on their tongue. Our words and our lives should be in agreement. Never let the words we sing be contradicted by our evil habits, lest our tongue witness against us. If one thing is being uttered by our mouth, but something completely different by our actions, then what is being built up by our tongue is being dismantled by our actions.

For your part, my brothers and sisters, make sure you savour the sense of a passage in the psalms and not merely the sound of the music. The sound of the words in your ears may be pleasant; but the meaning of the text should be equally pleasing to your heart. Remember the words of the psalm: 'How sweet are your words to my tongue, O Lord!' And again, 'The words of the Lord are more to be desired than gold and many precious stones; they are sweeter than honey, the honey that drips from the honeycomb.' If a person when singing the psalms is attending only to the music and the arrangement of the words, but is not heeding the meaning of the words, his ears may be nourished for a moment, but the word of God will never permeate his heart. It is as if he were chewing the wax of the honeycomb, but never discerning the sweetness of the honey it contains.

So, dear brothers and sisters, let us be sure to take note of the inner meaning of the psalms. Whenever we sing them, consider carefully what is being communicated in their words and practise it interiorly. In so doing, while your tongue praises the Lord, the blessing of God will come upon your souls.

Wednesday after 2 before Lent

A Reading from *The Cost of Discipleship*
by Dietrich Bonhoeffer

Cheap grace is the deadly enemy of our Church. We are fighting today for costly grace.

Cheap grace means grace sold on the market like cheapjack's wares. The sacraments, the forgiveness of sin, and the consolations of religion are thrown away at cut prices. Grace is represented as the Church's inexhaustible treasury, from which she showers blessings with generous hands, without asking questions or fixing limits. Grace without price; grace without cost! The essence of grace, we suppose, is that the account has been paid in advance; and, because it has been paid, everything can be had for nothing. Since the cost was infinite, the possibilities of using and spending it are infinite. What would grace be if it were not cheap?

Cheap grace means grace as a doctrine, a principle, a system. It means forgiveness of sins proclaimed as a general truth, the love of God taught as the Christian 'conception' of God. An intellectual assent to that idea is held to be of itself sufficient to secure remission of sins. The Church which holds the correct doctrine of grace has, it is supposed, a part in that grace. In such a Church the world finds a cheap covering for its sins; no contrition is required, still less any real desire to be delivered from sin.

Cheap grace is the preaching of forgiveness without requiring repentance, baptism without church discipline, communion without confession, absolution without personal confession. Cheap grace is grace without discipleship, grace without the cross, grace without Jesus Christ, living and incarnate.

Costly grace is the treasure hidden in the field; for the sake of it a person will gladly go and sell all that he has. It is the pearl of great price to buy which the merchant will sell all his goods. It is the kingly rule of Christ, for whose sake a man will pluck out the eye which causes him to stumble. It is the call of Jesus Christ at which the disciple leaves his nets and follows him.

Thursday after 2 before Lent

A Reading from *The Dark Night of the Soul*
by John of the Cross

There are two vices which beginners on their spiritual journey are specially prone to: spiritual envy and sloth.

With regard to envy, many people feel sad about the spiritual good of others, and actually experience grief when they perceive their neighbour ahead on the road to perfection. They dislike hearing others praised. Hearing of the virtues of others depresses them; they cannot bear to listen while another person is praised without contradicting what is being said or interjecting some criticism intent on unravelling the compliments being paid. They are angry because they are not receiving the praise themselves and because they long to be the centre of attention.

All this is quite contrary to the spirit of charity which St Paul says 'rejoices in goodness'. If any envy accompanies charity, let it be a 'holy envy' which is saddened at not having the virtues of others, which rejoices that others do have them, happy that others are further ahead in their service of God, conscious of one's own inadequacy in relation to God.

With regard to spiritual sloth, beginners usually become weary of the spiritual exercises that confront them and run away from the challenge. They are so used to finding delight in the practice of their religion that they become bored when suddenly they do not find it any longer. If they do not experience the instant satisfaction in their prayer for which they crave – for after all, it is entirely fitting that God should withdraw this in order to test them – they at once give up or else return to prayer very grudgingly. Because of their sloth, they subordinate the way of perfection (which entails denial of self-will and of self-satisfaction for the sake of God) to the pursuit of pleasure and delight in their own will.

When we begin our spiritual journey we often want God to desire what we want, and become dejected if we have instead to learn to desire what God wants. We measure God by ourselves and not ourselves by God, which is quite contrary to the gospel. For our Lord says that those who lose their lives for his sake will gain it, but that they who desire to gain their life will lose it.

Friday after 2 before Lent

A Reading from *Revelations of Divine Love*
by Julian of Norwich

God is nearer to us than our own soul, for he is the ground in which it stands, and he is the means by which substance and sensuality are so held together that they can never separate. Our soul reposes in God its true rest, and stands in God, its true strength, and is fundamentally rooted in God, its eternal love. So if we want to come to know our soul, and enjoy its fellowship as it were, it is necessary to seek it in our Lord God in whom it is enclosed.

Our substance and our sensuality together are rightly named our soul, because they are united by God. That wonderful city, the seat of our Lord Jesus, is our sensuality in which he is enclosed, just as the substance of our nature is enclosed in him as with his blessed soul he sits at rest in the Godhead.

I saw quite clearly that with our longing should go penitence, until such time as we are led so deeply into God that we do in very truth know our own soul. It is our Lord himself who leads us into these lofty deeps with the self-same love that created us, and redeemed us through the mercy and grace of his blessed passion. All the same, we can never attain to the full knowledge of God until we have first known our own soul thoroughly. Until our soul reaches its full development we can never be completely holy; in other words, not until our sensuality has been raised to the level of our substance through the virtue of Christ's passion and enriched by all the trials laid upon us by our Lord in his mercy and grace.

These are the foundation for our development and perfection. We have our life and our being in nature: we develop and reach fulfilment through mercy and grace.

Saturday after 2 before Lent

A Reading from *New Seeds of Contemplation*
by Thomas Merton

We do not go into the desert to escape people but to learn how to find them; we do not leave them in order to have nothing more to do with them, but to find out the way to do them the most good. But this is only a secondary end.

The one end that includes all others is the love of God.

The truest solitude is not something outside you, not an absence of people or of sound around you; it is an abyss opening up in the centre of your own soul.

And this abyss of interior solitude is a hunger that will never be satisfied with any created thing. The only way to find solitude is by hunger and thirst and sorrow and poverty and desire, and the one who has found solitude is empty, as if he had been emptied by death.

He has advanced beyond all horizons. There are no directions left in which he can travel. This is a country whose centre is everywhere and whose circumference is nowhere. You do not find it by travelling but by standing still.

Yet it is in this loneliness that the deepest activities begin. It is here that you discover act without motion, labour that is profound repose, vision in obscurity, and beyond all desire, a fulfilment whose limits extend to infinity.

The Sunday next before Lent

A Reading from a homily of Origen

Christ is the 'light of the world' and he enlightens the Church with his light. And as the moon receives its light from the sun so as in turn to enlighten the night, so does the Church, receiving her light from Christ, enlighten all who dwell in the night of ignorance. It is

Christ, therefore, who is 'the true light which gives light to every one coming into the world'; and the Church, receiving his light, becomes herself the light of the world, enlightening those in darkness, in accord with Christ's word to his disciples: 'You are the light of the world.' This goes to show that Christ is the light of the apostles, and the apostles in their turn are the light of the world.

The sun and the moon shed light on our bodies; in the same way Christ and the Church shed light on our minds. At least they enlighten them if we are not spiritually blind people. Just as the sun and the moon do not fail to shed their light on the blind who are unable to benefit by the light, so does Christ send his light into our minds; but we shall not receive any enlightenment if we meet it with blindness. If that is so, let the blind begin by first following Christ and crying out: 'Son of David, have pity on us.' Then once they have recovered their sight, thanks to his favour, they will be able to benefit by the radiation of the splendour of the light.

Again, all who see are not equally illumined by Christ, but each is enlightened according to his or her capacity to receive the light. The eyes of our body are not equally enlightened by the sun. Also, the higher we climb in high places, and the higher the spot from which we contemplate the sunrise, the better we also perceive the sun's splendour and its warmth. The same is true of our mind.

The more we go up and rise Christward and expose ourselves to the splendour of his light, the more wonderfully and brilliantly we too shall be flooded with his brightness, as he said himself through the Prophet: 'Come near to me and I shall come near to you, says the Lord.' And elsewhere: 'Am I a God near at hand only, says the Lord, and not a God far off?'

It is not by the same road, however, that all of us travel to God, but 'according to each one's abilities'. We might go to him with the crowds and he would feed us with parables lest we faint in the way because we are fasting; or we might remain constantly at his feet intently listening to his words, without being anxious about diverse matters, 'having chosen the better portion' and we 'shall not be deprived of it'. By coming closer to Christ we also receive more light from him. And if, like the apostles, we do not separate ourselves in the least from him and faithfully remain with him in all his tribulations, he then explains to us secretly what he had said to the crowds, and greater is the brightness with which he enlightens us.

Finally, if we can ascend with him to the top of the mountain, like Peter, James, and John, not only will we receive the enlightenment from Christ, but we hear the very voice of the Father.

alternative reading

A Reading from the hymn for the Sunday of Forgiveness,
being the Sunday next before Lent
in the Orthodox Church

Banished from the joys of paradise,
Adam sat outside and wept,
and beating his hands upon his face, he said:
'I am fallen, in your compassion have mercy on me.'

When Adam saw the angel drive him out
and shut the door of the divine garden,
he groaned aloud and said:
'I am fallen, in your compassion have mercy on me.'

O Paradise, share in the sorrow of your master
who is brought to poverty,
and with the sound of your leaves pray to the Creator
that he may not keep your gate closed for ever.
'I am fallen, in your compassion have mercy on me.'

O Paradise, perfect, all-holy and blessed,
planted for Adam's sake and shut because of Eve,
pray to God for the fallen.
'I am fallen, in your compassion have mercy on me.'

Monday before Ash Wednesday

A Reading from the *Meditations* of William of St Thierry

Have mercy on us, Lord, have mercy! You are our potter and we are the clay. Somehow or other, we have held together until now; we are still carried by your mighty hand, and we are still clinging to your three fingers, faith, hope and charity, with which you support the whole great bulk of earth – that is to say, the whole weight of your holy Church. Cleanse our reins and our hearts by the fire of your Holy Spirit, and establish the work that you have wrought in us, lest we be loosed asunder and return again to clay or nothingness. We were created for you by yourself, and towards you our face is set. We acknowledge you our maker and Creator; we adore your wisdom and pray that it may order all our life. We adore your goodness and mercy, and beg them ever to sustain and help us.

O God, you who have made us, bring us to perfection; perfect in us the image and likeness of yourself for which you made us.

Shrove Tuesday

A reading from a homily of John Chrysostom

Would you like me to list also the paths of repentance? They are numerous and quite varied, and all lead to heaven.

A first path of repentance is the condemnation of your own sins: 'Be the first to admit your sins and you will be justified.' For this reason, too, the prophet wrote: 'I said: I will accuse myself of my sins to the Lord, and you forgave the wickedness of my heart.' Therefore, you too should acknowledge your own sins; that will be enough reason for the Lord to forgive you, for if you acknowledge your own sins you are slower to commit them again. Rouse your conscience to accuse you within your own house, lest it become your accuser before the judgement seat of the Lord.

That, then, is one very good path of repentance. Another and no less valuable one is to put out of our minds the harm done us by our enemies, in order to master our anger, and to forgive our fellow servants' sins against us. Then our own sins against the Lord will be forgiven us. Thus you have another way to atone for sin: 'For if you forgive your debtors, your heavenly Father will forgive you.'

Do you want to know of a third path? It consists of prayer that is fervent, careful and comes from the heart.

If you want to hear of a fourth, I will mention almsgiving whose power is great and far-reaching.

If, moreover, one lives a modest, humble life, that no less than the other things I have mentioned takes sin away. Proof of this is the tax-collector who had no good deeds to mention, but offered humility instead and was relieved of a heavy burden of sins.

Thus I have shown you five paths of repentance: acknowledgement of your own sins, forgiveness of our neighbour's sins against us, prayer, almsgiving and humility.

Do not be idle, then, but walk daily in all these paths; they are easy, and you cannot plead your poverty. For, though you live out your life amid great need, you can always set aside your wrath, be humble, pray diligently and acknowledge your own sins. Poverty is no hindrance to our carrying out the Lord's bidding, even when it comes to that path of repentance which involves giving money. The widow proved that when she put her two mites into the box!

Now that we have learned how to heal our wounds, let us apply the cures. Then, when we have regained genuine health, we can approach the holy table with confidence, go gloriously to meet Christ the king of glory, and attain the eternal blessings through the grace, mercy and kindness of Jesus Christ our Lord.

LENT

Sorrow for sin is indeed necessary, but it should not
involve endless self-preoccupation. You should dwell also
on the glad remembrance of the loving kindness of God.

Bernard of Clairvaux

My turning, my conversion, is to the crucified.
His cross is my glory; with it my brow is signed,
in it my mind rejoices, by it my life is directed,
and my death is made dear.

William of St Thierry

The English word 'Lenten' derives from the lengthening of days, and it underscores an understanding of Lent as a time of spiritual growth and renewal. The observance of **Lent** as an ecclesiastical season has its origins in the preparation of candidates for baptism in the ancient Church when Easter was the only time in the year when baptisms were regularly administered. Not surprisingly, the days running up to Easter held a particular significance for catechumens. It represented the final stage in their long preparation of Christian initiation, with baptism occurring in the context of the Easter liturgy.

Lent was also a time of preparation for those who had been excommunicated for grave and public sin. The lapsed were reconciled and the excommunicate readmitted to the Church's sacramental life in time for Easter after the completion of a period of penance.

It was not long before the Church came to realize the benefit to all Christian people of such a period of preparation for the celebration of the death and resurrection of Christ at Easter. Typically, such preparation came to be marked by penitence, fasting, almsgiving and prayer. In antiquity, fasting was not only about negation and denial. Like anointing with oil, it was thought to be a purifying and strengthening practice – a preparation for some challenge yet to come. Significantly, the popular idea of 'giving things up for Lent' was always balanced in the ancient Church by the requirement to give to the poor: you cannot claim to love the God whom you have not seen if you do not love the poor at your door whom you do see. The tradition of Lent as a conscious re-enactment of our Lord's time in the wilderness was a later, if distinctive, theological development. This, together with other Lenten themes, all find a place in the readings that follow.

Passiontide marks a shift in the feeling of Lent as attention moves to Good Friday and Easter. Beginning on Lent 5 the readings increasingly focus on the cross, meditating on the suffering of Christ and the victory of the cross.

A reading for **Mothering Sunday** is provided at Lent 4 on p.183 should this be required.

Ash Wednesday

A Reading from the Letter of Clement of Rome
to the Church in Corinth

Let us fix our thoughts on the blood of Christ and reflect how precious it is in the eyes of God, since it was poured out for our salvation and has brought the grace of repentance to all the world. If we were to survey the various ages of history, we would see that in every generation the Lord has offered the chance of repentance to any who were willing to turn to him. For example, when Noah preached God's call to repentance, those who gave heed to him were saved. When, after Jonah had proclaimed destruction to the citizens of Nineveh, they repented and made fitting atonement to God with prayers and supplications, they were saved – though they were not members of God's chosen people.

Under the inspiration of the Holy Spirit, all those who were ministers of God's grace have spoken of repentance. Indeed, the very Master of the universe has spoken of it with an oath: 'As I live, says the Lord, I do not desire the death of sinners, but their repentance.' He adds this gracious pronouncement: 'Repent, O house of Israel, and turn from your wickedness. Tell my people: If their sins should reach from earth to heaven, if they are brighter than scarlet and blacker than sackcloth, you need only turn to me with your whole heart and say, "Father," and I will listen to you as to a holy people.'

In other words, God wanted all his beloved ones to have the opportunity to repent and he confirmed this desire by his own almighty will. Let us obey, then, his sovereign and glorious will. Let us prayerfully entreat his mercy and goodness, casting ourselves upon his compassion, rejecting empty works and quarrelling and jealousy which only lead to death.

My friends, let us have a little humility, and put aside all self-assertion, arrogance and foolish anger. Rather, we should act in accordance with the Scriptures, as the Holy Spirit says: 'The wise must not glory in wisdom nor the strong in strength nor the rich in riches. Rather, let the one who glories glory in the Lord, by seeking him and doing what is right and just.' Recall especially what the Lord Jesus said when he taught gentleness and forbearance. 'Be merciful,' he said, 'so that you may have mercy shown to you. Forgive, so that you may be forgiven. As you treat others, so you will be treated. As you give, so you will receive. As you judge, so you will be judged. As you are kind to others, so you will be treated kindly. The measure of your giving will be the measure of your receiving.'

Let these commandments and precepts strengthen us to live in humble obedience to his sacred words. As Scripture asks: 'Whom shall I look upon with favour except the humble and peaceful who tremble at my words?'

Sharing then in the heritage of so many vast and glorious achievements, let us hasten toward the goal of peace which has been set before us from the outset. Let us keep our eyes firmly fixed on the Father and Creator of the whole universe, and hold fast to his glorious and transcendent gifts of peace, rejoicing in all his blessings.

alternative reading

A Reading from a sermon of John Donne
preached before King James I
on the First Sunday of Lent

Forgive me O Lord; O Lord, forgive my sins, the sins of my youth, and my present sins, the sin that my parents thrust upon me, original sin, and the sins that I cast upon my children, in an ill example; actual sins, sins which are manifest to all the world, and sins which I have so laboured to hide from the world, and that now they are hid from mine own conscience, and mine own memory.

Forgive me my crying sins, and my whispering sins, the sins of uncharitable hate, and sins of unchaste love, sins against thee and thee, against thy power, O Almighty Father, against thy wisdom, O glorious Son, against thy goodness, O blessed Spirit of God. Forgive me my sins against him and him, against superiors and equals, and inferiors; and sins against me and me, against mine own soul, and against my body, which I have loved better than my soul.

Forgive me O Lord, O Lord in the merits of thy Christ and my Jesus, thine anointed, and my Saviour; forgive me my sins, all my sins, and I will put Christ to no more cost, nor thee to more trouble, for any reprobation or malediction that lay upon me, otherwise than as a sinner. I ask but an application, not an extension of that benediction: 'Blessed are they whose sins are forgiven.' Let me be but so blessed, that I shall envy no man's blessedness. Say thou to my sad soul: 'Son, be of good comfort, thy sins are forgiven thee.' Let me be so blessed, that I shall envy no man's blessedness. O say thou to my sad soul: 'Son, be of good comfort, thy sins are forgiven thee.'

alternative reading

A Reading from a poem by Robert Herrick

To keep a true Lent

Is this a Fast, to keep
    The Larder lean?
    And clean
From fat of Veals and Sheep?

Is it to quit the dish
    Of Flesh, yet still
    To fill
The platter high with Fish?

Is it to fast an hour
    Or rag'd to go,
    Or show
A downcast look, and sour?

No; 'tis a Fast, to dole
    Thy sheaf of wheat
    And meat
Unto the hungry soul.

It is to fast from strife,
    From old debate
    And hate;
To circumcise thy life.

To show a heart grief-rent;
    To starve thy sin,
    Not Bin;
And that's to keep thy Lent.

A Reading from *A Season for the Spirit*
by Martin Smith

Lent is the season for the Spirit of truth, who drove Jesus into the wilderness to initiate him into the truth which sets free. Mark's harsh word 'drove' was softened by Matthew and Luke to the milder expression 'led'. But this word 'drove' is very precious. I know that inertia, illusion and fear hold me back from answering God's invitation to enter into the truth and gain freedom. Yet even Jesus, free as he was from inertia like mine, needed the full force of the Wind of God (Spirit, Breath, Wind are all equally valid translations of the Greek word *pneuma*) to make him enter the testing-ground of the wilderness. If I am going to go forward into that truth for which God knows I am ready at this point in my life, I am going to need the Spirit to drive me.

Perhaps then the word 'surrender' should be enough for our prayer on this Ash Wednesday. Not the surrender of submission to an enemy, but the opposite, the laying down of resistance to the One who loves me infinitely more than I can guess, the One who is more on my side than I am myself. Dwelling on this thought of letting go, and handing myself over to the Spirit will bring me much closer to the experience of Jesus than the word 'discipline' which so many of us have been trained to invoke at the beginning of Lent. It should help us smile at our anxious attempts to bring our life under control, the belt-tightening resolutions about giving up this or taking on that. What we are called to give up in Lent is control itself! Deliberate efforts to impose discipline on our lives often serve only to lead us further away from the freedom which Jesus attained through surrender to the Spirit, and promised to give. 'Where the Spirit of the Lord is, there is freedom.'

Lent is about freedom which is gained only through exposure to the truth. And 'What is truth?' Pilate's question is partially answered by unpacking the Greek word *aletheia* which we translate as truth. The word literally means 'unhiddenness'. Truth is not a thing, it is rather an event. Truth happens to us when the coverings of illusion are stripped away and what is real emerges into the open. 'When the Spirit of truth comes, he will guide you into all the truth.' The truth we are promised if we live the demands of this season of Lent consists not in new furniture for the mind, but in exposure to the reality of God's presence in ourselves and the world. The Spirit promises to bring us into truth by stripping away some more of the insulation and barriers which have separated us from living contact with reality, the reality of God, of God's world, and our true selves.

Thursday after Ash Wednesday

A Reading from a commentary on the prophecy of Joel
by Jerome

'Return to me with all your heart' and prove that your repentance is genuine by fasting and weeping and mourning. Fast now so that you may feast hereafter; weep now and you will laugh hereafter. Present mourning will give way to future joy. It is customary for those in sorrow or adversity to tear their garments. Indeed, the gospel records that the high priest did this to exaggerate the charge against our Lord and Saviour at his trial; and we read that Paul and Barnabas did so when they heard words of blasphemy. I bid you not to tear your garments but rather to 'rend your hearts' which are laden with sin and which like wine-skins will burst of their own accord unless they are cut open. When you have done this, return to the Lord your God, from whom you had been alienated by your sins. Never despair of his mercy, no matter how great your sins, for his great mercy can take away great sins.

For the Lord is 'gracious and merciful' and prefers the conversion of a sinner rather than the sinner's death. 'Slow to anger and generous in his mercy', God does not become impatient like us, but is prepared to wait a whole lifetime for our return to him. So extraordinary is the Lord's mercy in the face of evil, that if we repent of our sins, he repents of his own threats and does not carry out against us the evil sanctions he had formerly threatened. With the changing of our attitude, God's heart is softened. But in this passage of Joel we should interpret 'evil' to mean, not the opposite of virtue, but simply affliction, in the sense in which our Lord said in another place: 'Sufficient for the day are its own evils.' Or as in another quotation: 'If there is evil in the city, God did not create it.'

In like manner, Joel speaks of God as 'gracious and merciful, slow to anger and generous in mercy, above all evil and repenting of evil'. Lest the magnitude of his clemency make us lax and negligent, God adds this word through his prophet: 'Who knows whether he will not turn and repent and leave behind him a blessing?' In other words, Joel is saying, for my part I exhort you to repentance, because it is my duty, and I assure you that God's mercy exceeds our wildest expectations. As David says in the psalms: 'Have mercy on me, O God, according to your great mercy, and in the fullness of your compassion, blot out all my iniquities.'

Friday after Ash Wednesday

A Reading from a sermon of Peter Chrysologus,
Bishop of Ravenna

There are three things by which faith stands firm, devotion remains constant, and virtue endures. They are prayer, fasting and mercy. Prayer knocks at the door, fasting obtains, mercy receives. Prayer, mercy and fasting: these three are one, and they give life to each other.

Fasting is the soul of prayer, mercy is the lifeblood of fasting. Let no one try to separate them; they cannot be separated. If you have only one of them or not all together, you have nothing. So if you pray, fast; if you fast, show mercy; if you want your petition to be heard, then hear the petition of others. If you do not close your ear to others you open God's ear to yourself.

When you eat, see the fasting of others. If you want God to know that you are hungry, know that another is hungry. If you hope for mercy, show mercy yourself. If you look for kindness, show kindness yourself. If you want to receive, give. If you ask for yourself what you deny to others, your asking is a mockery.

Let this be the pattern for all when they practise mercy: show mercy to others in the same way, with the same generosity, with the same promptness, as you want others to show mercy to you.

Therefore, let prayer, mercy and fasting be one single plea to God on our behalf, one speech in our defence, a threefold united prayer in our favour.

Let us use fasting to make up for what we have lost by despising others. Let us offer our souls in sacrifice by means of fasting. There is nothing more pleasing that we can offer to God, as the psalmist said in prophecy: 'The sacrifice of God is a broken spirit; God does not despise a bruised and humbled heart.'

Offer your soul to God, make him an oblation of your fasting, so that your soul may be a pure offering, a holy sacrifice, a living victim, remaining your own and at the same time made over to God. Whoever fails to give this to God will not be excused, for if you are to give him yourself you are never without the means of giving.

To make these acceptable, mercy must be added. Fasting bears no fruit unless it is watered by mercy. Fasting dries up when mercy dries up. Mercy is to fasting as rain is to the earth. However much you may cultivate your heart, clear the soil of your nature, root out vices, sow virtues: if you do not release the springs of mercy, your fasting will bear no fruit.

When you fast, if your mercy is thin your harvest will be thin; when you fast, what you pour out in mercy overflows into your barn. Therefore, do not lose by saving, but gather in by scattering: give to the poor, and you give to yourself. You will not be allowed to keep what you have refused to give to others.

Saturday after Ash Wednesday

A Reading from a homily of John Chrysostom

Let each of us, with an informed conscience, enter into a review of our actions, and bring our whole life before our minds for assessment, and try to discern whether we are deserving of correction or punishment. When we are indignant that somebody whom we reckon guilty of various crimes escapes with impunity, let us first reflect upon our own faults, and perhaps our indignation will cease. Certain crimes appear great because they usually involve great or notorious matters; but once we inquire into our own actions, we will perhaps find numerous other matters for concern.

For example, to steal or to defraud a person is the same thing: the gravity of the offence is not lessened by whether it is gold or silver that is at stake. In either case it is the attitude of mind that is the root cause. A person who steals a small object will not balk at the chance of stealing something bigger. If he does not steal, it is probably because he lacks the opportunity. A poor man who robs a poorer person would not hesitate to rob the rich given half the chance. His forbearance issues simply from weakness, not from choice.

So when you say, 'That ruler is robbing his subjects,' tell me, do you not steal from others yourself? It is no use you objecting that he is stealing vast sums of money whereas you are taking only a little. Remember the widow gave two copper coins to charity and in so doing acquired as much merit as the rich man who offered gold. Why was that? It was because God sees the intentions of the heart and is not interested in mere quantity.

The First Sunday of Lent

A Reading from a sermon of Leo the Great

None of us, dear friends, is so perfect and holy as to make reflection and improvement unnecessary. All of us, regardless of rank or dignity, should be concerned to embark on the race that is set before us with fresh determination this Lent, making an effort over and above the norm.

How apposite are the words of the apostle Paul: 'Behold, now is the accepted hour; behold, now is the day of salvation.' Indeed, what is more acceptable than this season of Lent, what more suitable to our salvation than these days in which war is declared against vice, and progress is made in virtue?

Certainly, we need to be on our guard all the year round against the enemy of our salvation, never leaving any vulnerable spot exposed to the tempter's art; but during Lent greater wariness and keener prudence are called for, because Satan is raging against us with fiercer hatred. The reason why vigilance is necessary is because our enemy's ancient power is being actively broken: countless numbers of people are being removed from his clutches. People of all nations and languages are breaking away from his tyranny. Literally thousands of thousands are being prepared for baptism, to be reborn in Christ at Easter; and always, as the birth of a new creature draws near, so we can expect the power of evil to raise its head. Against whom would not Satan compete, given that he did not balk at trying to overthrow our Lord Jesus Christ himself when he was in the wilderness?

When we reflect on the temptations which assailed our Lord, we should ponder in particular our Redeemer's precept: 'Man does not live by bread alone, but by every word that proceeds from the mouth of God.' Whatever degree of personal abstinence we observe this Lent, it is vital that all of us should desire above all to feast upon the word of God, entering upon this solemn fast not with a barren abstinence of food which we may impose upon our recalcitrant body or in an attempt to treat the disease of greed, but instead with a spirit of generous self-giving. In truth, let the Truth speak to us, saying: 'Blessed are they who hunger and thirst after righteousness, for they shall be satisfied.' Let works of justice, therefore, be our delight. Let us fill ourselves with the kinds of food that will feed us for eternity. Let us rejoice in the feeding of the poor and the clothing of the destitute. Let our humanity receive outward expression in tenderness toward the sick, the house-bound, refugees, orphans and widows. Let no Christian say he does not have the resources to help such needy folk. No one's income is small whose heart is big. The measure of mercy and goodness does not depend on the size of our means. Wealth of goodwill should never be lacking in a Christian, even in those whose purses are modest.

This season, therefore, let faults be forgiven, let bonds be loosed, let offences be wiped clean, let plans for vengeance fall through, that through the divine and human grace of Christ, the holy festival of Easter may find us all happy and innocent.

alternative reading

A Reading from *True Wilderness* by Harry Williams

Lent is supposed to be the time when we think of Jesus in the wilderness. And the wilderness belongs to us. It is always lurking somewhere as part of our experience, and there are times when it seems pretty near the whole of it. Most people's wilderness is inside them, not outside. Our wilderness is an inner isolation. It's an absence of contact. It's a sense of being alone – boringly alone, or saddeningly alone, or terrifying alone.

This Lent, unlike the ecclesiastical charade, this sense of being isolated and therefore unequipped, is a necessary part, or a necessary stage, of our experience as human beings. It therefore found a place in the life of the Son of Man. Because he is us, he too did time in the wilderness. And what happened to him there shows us what is happening to ourselves. Here, as always, we see in his life the meaning of our own.

Notice first that it is by the Spirit that Jesus is driven, thrown out is the actual word used by St Mark, into the wilderness, the same Spirit which had brought him the conviction of being called to do great things. The Spirit is ourselves in the depths of what we are. It is me at the profoundest level of my being, the level at which I can no longer distinguish between what is myself and what is greater than me. So, theologically, the Spirit is called God in me. And it is from this place where God and me mingle indistinguishably that I am thrown out into the wilderness. The story of Jesus reminds us that being thrown out in this way must be an inevitable concomitant of our call to God's service. To feel isolated, to be incapable for the time being of establishing communion, is part of our training. That is because so far our communion has been shallow, mere pirouetting on the surface. We've come to see its superficiality, its unrealness. Hence the feeling of loss. The training doesn't last for ever. In fact, new powers of communion with our world are being built up within us. We are being made the sort of people of whom it can be said, 'All things are yours.' But it belongs to the training to feel it will last for ever.

And so, we are tempted of Satan. Tempted to give up, to despair. Tempted to cynicism. Tempted sometimes to cruelty. Tempted not to help others when we know we can, because, we think, what's the use. Tempted to banish from our life all that we really hold most dear, and that is love, tempted to lock ourselves up, so that when we pass by people feel, 'There goes a dead man.' And behind each and all of these temptations is the temptation to disbelieve in what we are, the temptation to distrust ourselves, to deny that it is the Spirit himself which beareth witness with our spirit. God in us.

And this self-distrust conjures up the wild beasts. Sometimes they're sheer terror, panic, which makes us feel about the most ordinary undangerous things, 'I can't do it.' Or the wild beasts are the violent rages roaring inside us triggered off by something ridiculously insignificant – a word, a glance, a failure to show interest in some petty concern. Or the beasts prowl around snarling as envy, hatred, malice, and all uncharitableness.

This then is our Lent, our going with Jesus into the wilderness to be tempted. And we might apply to it some words from the First Epistle of St Peter: 'Beloved, do not be surprised at the fiery ordeal which comes upon you to prove you, as though something strange were happening to you. But rejoice, in so far as you share Christ's sufferings, that you may also rejoice and be glad when his glory is revealed.'

Christ's glory is his full and satisfying communion with all that is. It is the opposite of being isolated. You don't have to wait for this until you die or the world comes to an end. It can be yours now. Accept your wilderness. From the story of the Son of Man realise what your Lent really means, and then angels will minister to you as they did to him.

Monday after Lent 1

A Reading from *The Sayings of the Desert Fathers*

A brother said to an old man, 'I do not see any warfare in my heart.' The old man said to him, 'Then you are a building open on all four sides; whoever wishes to, goes in and out of you, but you do not notice it. But if you had a door and shut it and did not let the evil thoughts come in through it, then you would see them standing outside warring against you.'

It was said of an old man that when his thoughts said to him, 'Relax today, and tomorrow repent,' he retorted, 'No, I am going to repent today, and may the will of God be done tomorrow.'

An old man said, 'He who loses gold or silver can find more to replace it, but he who loses time cannot find more.'

Another old man used to say, 'If the inner man is not vigilant, it is not possible to guard the outer man.'

An old man was asked, 'How can I find God?' He said, 'In fasting, in watching, in labours, in devotion, and above all, in discernment. I tell you, many have injured their bodies without discernment and have gone away from us having achieved nothing. Our mouths smell bad through fasting, we know the Scriptures by heart, we can recite all the psalms of David, but we have not that which God seeks: charity and humility.'

Tuesday after Lent 1

A Reading from a sermon of Augustine

We cannot just assume that we are living good lives, free from sin. Let a person's life be praised only insofar as that person asks for pardon. But we are hopeless creatures, and the less attentive we are to our own sins, the more we tend to pry into those of other people. We seek not what we can correct, but what we can criticise. And since we are not able to excuse ourselves, we are ready to accuse others.

This was not the way that David showed us how to pray and make amends to God. In the psalms he says, 'I acknowledge my transgressions, and my sin is ever before me.' David was not interested in other people's sins. He turned his mind to himself, not in self-flattery, but went down deep inside himself. He did not spare himself, and thus it was not presumptuous of him to pray that he might be spared.

Do you want to be reconciled to God? Then learn how to act towards yourself so that God may be reconciled with you. Reflect on what you read in the same psalm: 'If you wanted sacrifice, I would give it; but you take no pleasure in burnt offerings.' Do you think you have no sacrifice at all? Do you feel you have nothing to offer, nothing to appease God? Go on with the psalm, listen and say: 'The sacrifice of God is a broken spirit: a broken and contrite heart, O God, you will not despise.' You have that to offer. Do not examine the flock. Do not prepare ships and journey to the most distant provinces to bring back exotic incense. Seek rather in your heart what is acceptable to God: you must rend your heart. Why do you fear that it may perish if it is broken? Attend to the words of Scripture again. 'Create in me a clean heart, O God.' So then, that a pure heart may be created, let the impure one be broken.

Wednesday after Lent 1

A Reading from a treatise *On the Lord's Prayer*
by Cyprian of Carthage

When we pray 'And lead us not into temptation' we should know that the Lord is teaching us inwardly. The words are there to reassure us that the adversary can do nothing against us because all is ultimately within the control of God. All power is from God. So in the temptations that assail us we should consciously give our fear, our devotion and our obedience to God alone.

When we pray in these words we are put in touch with our vulnerability and inner weakness. We ask for help lest any should insolently exalt themselves, or become proud and conceited, or even hug to themselves the glory either of confessing their faith or of suffering for Christ, as if it were all their own doing. The Lord himself has taught us to be humble when he said: 'Watch and pray that you enter not into temptation. The spirit is indeed willing, but the flesh is weak.' When, however, we confess our need of God humbly and quietly, and surrender to God the glory that is properly his, then the prayer that is offered in the fear of God and to his honour will be met by his loving kindness.

At the end of various petitions, the Lord's Prayer concludes with a brief clause which neatly sums up all that has gone before. We conclude: 'And deliver us from evil,' – an expression that includes everything that the enemy can devise against us in this world. We pray this in the conviction that God is a faithful and dependable protector who will give his help readily to all who ask and beg for it. Consequently, when we pray 'Deliver us from evil,' there is nothing left to ask for. When once we have asked for God's protection in the face of evil and secured it, then we stand secure and safe against any kind of machination of the devil and the evils of this world. For what is there in life to be afraid of when the Lord God is our protector?

Thursday after Lent 1

A Reading from *Revelations of Divine Love*
by Julian of Norwich

Our courteous Lord does not want his servants to despair even if they fall frequently and grievously. Our falling does not stop his loving us. Peace and love are always at work in us, but we are not always in peace and love. But he wants us in this way to realise that he is the foundation of the whole of our life in love, and furthermore that he is our eternal protector, and mighty defender against our enemies who are so very fierce and wicked. And alas, our need is all the greater since we give them every opportunity by our failures.

It is an expression of royal friendship on the part of our courteous Lord that he holds on to us so tenderly when we are in sin, and that, moreover, his touch is so delicate when he shows us our sin by the gentle light of mercy and grace. When we see ourselves to be so foul, we know that God is angry with us for our sin. In turn we also are moved by the Holy Spirit to pray contritely, desiring to amend our life to the best of our ability, that we may quench the anger of God and find rest of soul, and an easy conscience. Then we hope that God has forgiven us our sins. And so he has! It is then that our Lord in his courtesy shows himself to the soul, gaily and with cheerful countenance, giving it a friendly welcome as though it had been suffering in prison. 'My beloved,' he says, 'I am glad that you have come to me. In all your trouble I have been with you. Now you can see how I love you. We are made one in blessedness.' So sins are forgiven through merciful grace, and our soul is honourably and joyfully received (just as it will be when it gets to heaven!) whenever it experiences the gracious work of the Holy Spirit, and the virtue of Christ's passion.

Friday after Lent 1

A Reading from *The Coming of God* by Maria Boulding

The desert in our lives is the place where in our poverty, our sin and our need we come to know the Lord. For us, like the Israelites before us, it is the place of the essential confrontations, where the irrelevancies are stripped away and the elemental things become all-important, where the truth in our hearts is revealed.

Our desert place is any place where we confront God. It is the place of truth, but also of tenderness; the place of loneliness but also of God's closeness and care. The journey is precarious, but God is faithful, even though our own fidelity is shaky. In the place of hunger and poverty of spirit we are fed by the word of God, as Jesus himself was in the desert.

Part of our poverty may be that we are not even aware of our longing for God, only aware of the suffocating burden of our own sinfulness, of the slum within. But the desert is the place of confrontation not just with our sins, but with the power of God's redemption. You come to see it as the place where there can be springing water, manna to keep you going, the strength you never knew you had, the surprise of the quail that plops down at your feet, a tenderness that cares for you and a knowing Lord. These things are not the promised land, but they are tokens of love and may be sacraments of glory. Your life, your prayer, can be the wilderness to which you must look steadfastly if you would see the glory of God.

Saturday after Lent 1

A Reading from *The Vision of God* by Kenneth Kirk

If life is to be disciplined at all, of what fashion shall the discipline be? Amongst all the variations of ethics which have sheltered under the name of 'Christian', two in particular stand out in marked contrast.

On the one hand, there have been teachers and sects who have prescribed for their adherents, and individuals who have prescribed for themselves, a life of rigorous self-denial, self-mortification and other-worldliness. Not that such a life is always regardless of the active duties of society, nor that it must lead, in every case, to the extreme of eremitic solitude; but that it tends to test the worth of every action by its cost to the giver, and the degree to which it requires him to mortify his own affections and exercise constraint upon his natural instincts, rather than by its value to the receiver. Puritanism, asceticism, rigorism – whatever we choose to call it – here is a well-marked type of thought and practice, which in all ages has appealed to the self-abnegation and cross of our Redeemer as its final example and justification. Perhaps it finds fewer sponsors and adherents at the present day than it has done at other epochs; but that fact alone would not justify us in eliminating it from the Christian scheme. It claims, or has often claimed, to represent the sole ideal of life worthy of the name of Christian; and even if it be non-suited in that plea it may still retain a claim to stand for something without which – even if only in combination with other elements – no Christian life can be complete.

Against this rigorist other-worldliness must be arrayed a 'this-worldly' code of ethics, which also appeals for its sanctions to the gospel. This humanist code, if we may so call it, bids us enjoy life in due moderation, and realise the highest possibilities of every instinct and factor in the complex organism of personality. It prescribes positive social virtues as the ideal, and seeks to set up a new Jerusalem by steady evolution out of the existing world-order. It finds goodness in embracing the world and its joys, not in flight from them; it looks for God in his creation, instead of seeking him by spurning what he has made. This reading of the Christian message is familiar to the modern mind; it is engrained, we might almost say, in the modern temperament.

Within the womb of the Christian Church these two children – rigorism and humanism – have striven for the mastery from the moment of their conception; and to the fortunes of that fierce battle no student of Christian ethics can be indifferent. Here are two tendencies pointing towards codes of very different types. Which of them is Christian and which non-Christian; or better still, if both are Christian, how are they to be harmonised in a single code of conduct?

The Church has had a vast experience of both traditions; and it has known the danger of leaving the tensions unsolved, and the disasters of solving them amiss. Theologians have reviewed the problems in the light of the vision of God which they have accepted as the keynote and the test of all the principles of Christian life. The solutions they have offered have varied in different generations, as their conceptions of the beatific vision and all that it implies have varied too. It is only by noticing the most apparent of these variations, examining their causes and recording their results that Christians today can in their turn take up the task transmitted to them. And the starting-point is the same for all – 'Blessed are the pure in heart, for they shall see God.'

The Second Sunday of Lent

A Reading from a sermon of Leo the Great

The Lord has said in the gospel: 'I have come to call, not the righteous, but sinners to repentance.' In other words no one can be saved except through the forgiveness of their sins, and we can never know the extent to which the grace of the Spirit can enrich those whom the wisdom of the world despises.

Therefore, let the people of God be holy and let them be good: holy, in order to turn away from what is prohibited; good, in order to act according to the commandments. It is a noble thing, no doubt, to have the right faith and possess sound doctrine; and sobriety, meekness, and purity are virtues that deserve high praise; but all these things remain empty if they are not accompanied by charity. Furthermore, no behaviour should be deemed excellent and fruitful if it does not proceed from love.

In the Gospel of John the Lord says: 'By this will all know that you are my disciples, if you have love for one another.' In a letter of the same apostle we read: 'Beloved, let us love one another, for love is from God, and everyone who loves is born of God and knows God; whoever does not love does not know God, for God is love.'

During this season, therefore, the faithful should enter into themselves and make a true discernment of the attitudes of their mind and heart. If they discover some store of love's fruit in their hearts, they must not doubt that God is within them. And if they would increase their capacity to receive so great a guest, then they should practise greater generosity in doing good and persevere in charity. If God is love, charity should know no bounds, for God cannot be confined.

Any time is the right time for works of charity, but these days of Lent provide a special opportunity. Those who want to be present at the Lord's Passover in holiness of mind and body should seek above all to win this grace, for charity contains all other virtues and as Scripture says, 'covers a multitude of sins'.

As we begin our preparations to celebrate the greatest of all the mysteries, namely, that of the blood of Jesus Christ which washes away our iniquities, let us prepare ourselves principally by the sacrifice of mercy. In so doing we will render to those who have offended us that which God has given us. May insults be cast into oblivion, may mistakes be freed from tortured remembrance, and may all offences be set free from the fear of vengeance. May the prisons have no one in them, and may the sad groans of the condemned be no longer heard echoing through gloomy dungeons.

If any detain such prisoners for some misdemeanour or other, let them know well that they themselves are sinners. And, that they may obtain pardon themselves, let them rejoice to have found someone to whom they can give pardon. And so, when we say, following the Lord's teaching: 'forgive us the wrong we have done as we forgive those who wrong us,' let us not doubt that, when we express our prayer, we will indeed obtain the pardon of God.

We must also show more generosity to the poor and to those who suffer from various handicaps, that more numerous voices may render thanks to God. Our fasts should contribute to the relief of those who are in need. No act of devotion on the part of the faithful gives God more pleasure than that which is lavished on his poor. Where God finds charity with its loving concern, there he recognises the reflection of his own fatherly care.

In these acts of giving do not fear a lack of means. A generous spirit is itself great wealth. There can be no shortage of material for generosity where it is Christ who feeds and Christ who is fed. In all these actions there is present the hand of him who multiplies the bread by breaking it, and increases it by giving it away. Givers of alms should be free from anxiety and full of joy. Their gain will be greatest when they keep back least for themselves.

A Reading from a poem by George Herbert

Discipline

Throw away thy rod,
Throw away thy wrath:
  O my God,
Take the gentle path.

For my heart's desire
Unto thine is bent:
  I aspire
To a full consent.

Not a word or look
I affect to own,
  But by book,
And thy book alone.

Though I fail, I weep;
Though I halt in pace,
  Yet I creep
To the throne of grace.

Then let wrath remove;
Love will do the deed;
  For with love
Stony hearts will bleed.

Love is swift of foot,
Love's a man of war,
  And can shoot,
And can hit from afar.

Who can 'scape his bow?
That which wrought on thee,
  Brought thee low,
Needs must work on me.

Throw away thy rod:
Though man frailties hath,
Thou art God:
Throw away thy wrath.

Monday after Lent 2

A Reading from *A Serious Call to a Devout and Holy Life*
by William Law

Prayer is the nearest approach to God and the highest enjoyment of
him that we are capable of in this life. No one will pretend to say
that he knows and feels the true happiness of prayer who does not
think it worth his while to be early at it. It is not possible in nature
for an epicure to be truly devout; he must renounce this habit of
sensuality before he can relish the happiness of devotion.

Now he that turns sleep into an idle indulgence does as much
to corrupt and disorder his soul, to make it a slave to bodily
appetites and keep it incapable of all devout and heavenly tempers,
as he that turns the necessities of eating into a course of
indulgence.

A person that eats and drinks too much does not feel such
effects from it as those do who live in notorious instances of
gluttony and intemperance; but yet his course of indulgence,
though it be not scandalous in the eyes of the world nor such as
torments his own conscience, is a great and constant hindrance to
his improvement in virtue; it gives him eyes that see not and ears
that hear not; it creates a sensuality in the soul, increases the power
of bodily passions, and makes him incapable of entering into the
true spirit of religion.

Now this is the case of those who waste their time in sleep; it
does not disorder their lives or wound their consciences as
notorious acts of intemperance do; but like any other more
moderate course of indulgence, it silently and by smaller degrees
wears away the spirit of religion and sinks the soul into a state of
dullness and sensuality.

If you consider devotion only as a time of so much prayer, you
may perhaps perform it though you live in this daily indulgence.
But if you consider it as a state of the heart, as a lively fervour of
the soul that is deeply affected with a sense of its own misery and
infirmities and desiring the Spirit of God more than all things in

the world, you will find that the spirit of indulgence and the spirit of prayer cannot subsist together. Mortification of all kinds is the very life and soul of piety, but he that has not so small a degree of it as to be able to be early at his prayers can have no reason to think that he has taken up his cross and is following Christ.

Tuesday after Lent 2

A Reading from the *Catechetical Lectures*
of Cyril of Jerusalem

If there are any slaves of sin here present, they should at once prepare themselves through faith for the rebirth into freedom that makes us God's adopted children. They should lay aside the wretchedness of slavery to sin, and put on the joyful slavery of the Lord, so as to be counted worthy to inherit the kingdom of heaven. By acknowledging your sins you strip away your former self, seduced as it is by destructive desires, and put on the new self, renewed in the likeness of its Creator. Through faith you receive the pledge of the Holy Spirit, so that you may be welcomed into the everlasting dwelling places. Draw near to be marked with the supernatural seal, so that you may be easily recognised by your Master. Become a member of Christ's holy and spiritual flock, so that one day you may be set apart on his right hand, and so gain the life prepared as your inheritance.

Those whose sins still cling to them like goatskin will stand on his left hand because they did not approach Christ's fountain of rebirth to receive God's grace. By rebirth I mean, not rebirth of the body, but the spiritual rebirth of the soul. Our bodies are brought into being by parents who can be seen, but our souls are reborn through faith: 'the Spirit breathes where he wills.' At the end, if you are made worthy, you may hear the words: 'Well done good and faithful servant,' when, that is, you are found with no stain of hypocrisy on your conscience.

If any here present are thinking of putting God's grace to the test, they are deceiving themselves, and they do not understand the nature of things. You are but human; there is One who searches out human thoughts and hearts. You must keep your soul innocent and free from deceit.

The present is a time for the acknowledgement of sins. Acknowledge what you have done, in word or deed, by night or day. Acknowledge your sins at a time of God's favour, and on the day of salvation you will receive the treasures of heaven.

Wash yourself clean, so that you may hold a richer store of grace. Sins are forgiven equally for all, but communion in the Holy Spirit is given in the measure of each person's faith. If you have done little work, you will receive little; if you have achieved a great deal, great will be your reward. The race in which you are running is for your own advantage; so look after your own interests.

If you have a grudge against anyone, forgive that person. You are drawing near to receive forgiveness for your own sins; you must yourself forgive those who have sinned against you.

Wednesday after Lent 2

A Reading from a sermon of Baldwin,
Archbishop of Canterbury

The Lord knows the thoughts and intentions of our hearts. Without a doubt, every one of them is known to him, while we know only those which he lets us read by the grace of discernment. Our spirit does not know all that is in us, nor all of the thoughts which we have, willingly or unwillingly. We do not always perceive our thoughts as they really are. Having clouded vision, we do not discern them clearly with our mind's eye.

Often under the guise of devotion, a suggestion occurs to our mind – coming from our own thoughts or from another person or from the tempter – and in God's eyes we do not deserve any reward for our virtue. For there are certain imitations of true virtues as also of vices which play tricks with the heart and bedazzle the mind's vision. As a result, the appearance of goodness often seems to be in something which is evil, and equally the appearance of evil seems to be in something good. This is part of our wretchedness and ignorance, causing us anguish and anxiety.

It has been written: 'There are paths which seem to be right, but which in the end lead to hell.' To avoid this peril, St John gives us these words of advice: 'Test the spirits to see if they are from God.' Now no one can test the spirits to see if they are from God unless God has given us discernment of spirits to enable us to investigate spiritual thoughts, inclinations and intentions with honest and true judgement. Discernment is the mother of all the virtues; everyone needs it either to guide the lives of others or to direct and reform their own lives.

In the sphere of action, a right thought is one ruled by the will of God, and intentions are holy when directed single-mindedly toward God. True discernment is a combination of right thinking and good intention. Therefore, we must do all our actions in the light of discernment as if in God and in his presence.

Thursday after Lent 2

A Reading from a sermon of Maximus of Turin

My friends, what is the use of us observing this Lenten fast of forty days without reflecting upon the meaning of what we are doing? What, for example, is the use of denying ourselves banquets, but then spending time in endless litigation? What is the use of not eating the bread we possess, if we persist in stealing that which belongs to the poor?

A Christian's fast ought to be fostering peace, not quarrels. What advantage is there in making one's stomach holy with fasting while defiling one's lips with lies? My brothers and sisters in Christ, you will be able to come to church with integrity only if your feet are not entangled in the snares of usury. You will have the right to pray only if envy is not eating your heart within you. The money you give away to the poor will be given in all righteousness only if first you have not extorted what you are giving away from somebody else who is poor.

So, let us imitate, as far as is possible, the fasting of Christ by practising the virtues. In so doing, grace may come upon us through the twofold fasting of body and spirit.

Friday after Lent 2

A Reading from the *Conferences* of John Cassian

To keep yourself continually mindful of the presence of God, you should set this formula before your eyes: 'O God, come to my aid; O Lord, make haste to help me.'

Our prayer for rescue in bad times and for protection against pride in good times should be founded on this verse of Scripture. The thought of this verse should be turning unceasingly in your heart. Never cease to recite it in whatever task or service or journey you find yourself. Think upon it as you sleep, as you eat, in the various occupations of your daily life. This heartfelt thought will prove to be a formula of salvation for you. Not only will it protect you against the assaults of the devil, but it will purify you from the stain of all earthly sin, and lead you on to the contemplation of the unseen and the heavenly, and to that burning urgency of prayer which is indescribable and which is experienced by very few. Let sleep close your eyes as you meditate on its words until as a result of good habit you find yourself repeating them in your sleep.

This verse should be the first thing to occur to you when you wake up. It should precede all your thoughts as you keep vigil. It should overwhelm you as you rise from your bed and as you kneel in prayer. Afterwards it should accompany you in all your work and duties during the day. It should be at your side at all times. Meditate on its meaning according to the precept of Moses, 'as you sit at home or walk along your way', when you lie down at night and when you rise in the morning. Write it upon the threshold and gateway of your mouth. Place it on the walls of your house and in the inner sanctum of your heart. Let it form a continuous prayer, an endless refrain when you bow down in worship and when you rise up to do all the necessary things of life.

Saturday after Lent 2

A Reading from a sermon of Lancelot Andrewes,
preached before King James I at Whitehall,
Ash Wednesday 1609

'Therefore now, saith the Lord, Turn you unto me with all your heart, and with fasting, and with weeping, and with mourning.'

The Church carrying to her children the tender heart of a mother, if there were a more easy or gentle repentance than this of the prophet Joel, she would have chosen that rather for this season of Lent. For she takes no pleasure to make us sad, or to put upon us more than needs she must. Which in that she hath not, we may well presume this of Joel is it she would have us hold ourselves to, and that this is to be the mould of our repentance.

Repentance is nothing else but a kind of circling, to return to God by repentance from whom by sin we have turned away. And much after a circle is this text of Joel. He begins with the word 'turn', and returns about to the same word again. Twice he repeats the word, which two must needs be two different motions.

First, a 'turn' wherein we look forward to God, and with our whole heart resolve to turn to him. Then a turn again, wherein we look backward to our sins wherein we have turned from God, and with beholding them our very heart breaketh. These two are distinct, both in nature and names: one, conversion from sin; the other, contrition for sin. One resolving to amend that which is to come, the other reflecting and sorrowing for that which is past. One declining from evil to be done hereafter, the other sentencing itself for evil done heretofore. These two between them make up a complete repentance, or to keep to our text, a perfect revolution.

The Third Sunday of Lent

A Reading from a sermon of Augustine

Let us sing 'Alleluia' here and now in this life, even though we are oppressed by various worries, so that we may sing it one day in the world to come when we are set free from all anxiety. Why is it that we worry so much in this life? I suppose it is hardly surprising that we worry when we read in the Scriptures: 'Are not the days of our life full of trouble?' Are you surprised that I am worried when I hear the words: 'Watch and pray that you enter not into temptation'? Are you surprised that I am worried when in the face of so many temptations and troubles the Lord's Prayer orders us to pray: 'Forgive us our debts as we also forgive our debtors'?

Every day we pray and every day we sin. Do you think that I can be free from anxiety when every day I need to seek pardon for my sins and help in the face of difficulties? When I have said for my past sins: 'Forgive us our debts as we also forgive our debtors,' I immediately go on to add, because of the difficulties that lie ahead: 'Lead us not into temptation.' How can the congregation be in security when it cries out with me: 'Deliver us from evil'? And yet, my brothers and sisters, in this evil plight of ours we must nevertheless sing 'Alleluia' to the good God who delivers us from evil.

In the middle of the dangers and trials that beset us we and all people must sing 'Alleluia', for as Paul says, 'God is faithful and God will not let you be tempted beyond your strength.' So then, we must sing 'Alleluia'. We may be sinners, but God is faithful. And note, Scripture does not say, 'God will not let you be tempted,' but rather 'God will not let you be tempted beyond your strength, but with the temptation God will also provide a means of escape that you may be able to endure it.' If you enter temptation God will also provide a means of escape so that you do not perish. Just as a potter forms a vase, so you are to be moulded by preaching; you are to be fired in the kiln of tribulation. Thus when you enter temptation, think of a means of escape; for God is faithful. As it says in one of the psalms: 'The Lord will preserve your coming in and your going out.'

Monday after Lent 3

A Reading from a treatise *On the Six Days of Creation*
by Ambrose of Milan

No wise person will deny the existence of evil in the world. Not least, we are all familiar with the evil of death. But from what I have been arguing, I hope it is evident that evil is not a living substance. I believe it to be a perversion of mind and spirit, swerving away from the way of true virtue, which frequently overtakes us when we are unwary.

It should be apparent that the greatest danger does not lie outside us. It comes from our very selves: the enemy is within. Within us is the 'father of lies'; within us, I say, dwells our adversary. Hence, we must examine our aims, explore our patterns of thought, and generally be vigilant over our thoughts and the desires of our heart.

You yourself are the cause of your wickedness. You yourself are the commander of your shameful acts, and the instigator of your crimes. Why blame another agent as an excuse for your own faults? If only you would not incite yourself, that you would not rush heedlessly on, that you would not entangle yourself in ludicrous projects, or foster indignation and passionate desires, for all these things will hold you captive as in a net.

Most certainly these tendencies belong to us. We are perfectly able to moderate our endeavours, to restrain our anger, to curb our desires. On the other hand, we can also give in to self-indulgence, foster evil passions, nurse anger, give a ready ear to those who incite trouble, become puffed up with pride, or give in to fits of anger, instead of growing in humility and lovingly practising gentleness.

Hence, why should we blame 'nature'? Admittedly, there are impediments in our nature; for example, there is old age and infirmity. But both states also have their advantages: old age brings more friendly manners, distils more useful counsels, inspires a deeper acceptance of the finality of death, and curbs evil passions more easily. The weakness of the body too has its counterpart in a certain sobriety of mind. Hence, the Apostle says: 'When I am powerless, it is then that I am strong.' Accordingly, Paul gloried in his infirmities, and not in his powers. And there came to him the luminous and salutary answer that 'in weakness power is made perfect.'

Let us, therefore, stop seeking for causes outside ourselves or blaming others for what goes wrong. Instead let us own our failings. For we should willingly attribute to ourselves, not to others, whatever evil we can avoid doing when we so choose.

Tuesday after Lent 3

A Reading from a sermon of Caesarius of Arles

If anyone is in conflict with another, end the quarrel lest you yourself end badly. Do not consider this unimportant, my beloved. Let us call to mind that our life here is mortal and frail, that it is endangered by many and great temptations, and this makes us pray that we may not be overcome.

And so, we realise that a righteous person is not without some sins. But there is one remedy which enables us to keep alive. For God, our Master, told us to say in our prayers: 'Forgive us the wrong we have done as we forgive those who wrong us.' We have made a contract with God and taken a resolution, adding for safety's sake the condition that the wrong must be forgiven. This makes us ask with complete confidence to be forgiven provided we too forgive.

If, on the contrary, we do not forgive, how can we in good conscience hope that our sins will be forgiven? Let no one deceive themselves: God deceived no one. It is human to be angry, but I wish it were impossible. It is human to become angry, but let us not water the small plant born of anger with various suspicions. Let us not permit it to develop into a tree of hatred. It happens also frequently that a parent is angry with a child, but the parent does not hate the child. The parent is angry because of wishing to correct the child. If this is the purpose, the anger is animated by love.

We read in Scripture: 'Why look at the speck in another's eye when you miss the plank in your own?' You find fault with another person for being angry, and you keep hatred in yourself. Anger in comparison with hatred is only a speck, but if the speck is fostered, it becomes a plank. If, on the contrary, you pluck out the speck and cast it away, it will amount to nothing.

Jesus says in another place: 'Anyone who hates his brother is a murderer.' Someone who hates another, walks around, goes out, comes in, marches on, is not burdened by any chains and is not shut up in any prison, but is bound by guilt. So do not think of such a person as not being imprisoned. The heart is that person's prison. When you hear: 'One who hates another is in darkness all the while,' lest you might despise that darkness, the evangelist adds: 'Anyone who hates his brother is a murderer.'

You have hated others and walk safely around and refuse to be reconciled with them, and God has given you time and opportunity. You are a murderer and are still alive. If you felt God's wrath you would be suddenly snatched away with your hatred toward others. But God spares you; so spare others likewise; make up and seek reconciliation with them.

But suppose you want reconciliation and the other person does not want it. That is enough for you; you have something to grieve for, you have freed yourself. If you want agreement and that person refuses, then say confidently: 'Lord, forgive us the wrong we have done as we forgive those who wrong us.'

Wednesday after Lent 3

A Reading from the book addressed to Autolycus by
Theophilus of Antioch

If you say: 'Show me your God,' I will say to you: 'Show me what kind of person you are, and I will show you my God.' Show me whether the eyes of your mind can see, and the ears of your heart can hear.

It is like this. Those who can see with the eyes of their bodies are aware of what is happening in this life. They get to know things that are different from each other. They distinguish light and darkness, ugliness and beauty, elegance and ugliness, proportion and lack of proportion, excess and defect. The same is true of the sounds we hear: high or low or pleasant. So it is with the ears of our heart and the eyes of our mind in their capacity to hear or see God.

God is seen by those who have the capacity to see him, provided that they keep the eyes of their mind open. All have eyes, but some have eyes that are shrouded in darkness, unable to see the light of the sun. Because the blind cannot see it, it does not follow that the sun does not shine. The blind must trace the cause back to themselves and their eyes. In the same way, you have eyes in your mind that are shrouded in darkness because of your sins and evil deeds. A person's soul should be clean, like a mirror reflecting light. If there is rust on the mirror a person's face cannot be seen in it. In the same way no one who has sin within can see God.

But if you will you can be healed. Entrust yourself to the doctor, to the One who will be able to open the eyes of your mind and heart. Who is this doctor? It is God, who heals and gives life through his Word and wisdom. Through his Word and wisdom he created the universe, for 'by his Word the heavens were established, and by his Spirit all their array.' His wisdom is supreme. God 'by wisdom founded the earth, by understanding he arranged the heavens, by his knowledge the depths broke forth and the clouds poured out their dew'.

If you understand this, and live in purity and holiness and justice, you may see God. But, before all, faith and the fear of God must take the first place in your heart, and then you will understand all this. When you have laid aside mortality and been clothed in immortality, then you will see God according to your merits. God raises up your flesh to immortality along with your soul, and then, once made immortal, you will see the immortal One, if you believe in him now.

Thursday after Lent 3

A Reading from *Modern Man in Search of a Soul*
by Carl Gustav Jung

The truly religious person knows that God has brought all sorts of strange and inconceivable things to pass, and seeks in the most curious ways to enter the human heart. Such a person senses in everything the unseen presence of the divine will. This is what I mean by 'unprejudiced objectivity'. We cannot change anything unless we accept it. Condemnation does not liberate, it oppresses. I am the oppressor of the person I condemn, not his friend and fellow-sufferer. I do not in the least mean to say that we must never pass judgement in the cases of persons whom we desire to help and improve. But if we wish to help a human being we must be able to accept them as they are. And we can do this in reality only when we have already seen and accepted ourselves as we are.

In life it requires the greatest discipline to be simple, and the acceptance of oneself is the essence of the moral problem and the epitome of a whole outlook upon life. That I feed the hungry, that I forgive an insult, that I love my enemy in the name of Christ – all these are undoubtedly great virtues. What I do unto the least of my brethren, that I do unto Christ. But what if I should discover that the least amongst them all, the poorest of all beggars, the most impudent of all the offenders, the very enemy himself – that these are within me, and that I myself stand in need of the alms of my own kindness – that I myself am the enemy who must be loved – what then? As a rule, the Christian's attitude is then reversed; there is no longer any question of love or long-suffering; we say to the brother within us *'Raca'* and condemn and rage against ourselves. We hide it from the world; we refuse to admit ever having met this least among the lowly in ourselves. Had it been God himself who drew near to us in this despicable form, we should have denied him a thousand times before a single cock had crowed.

To accept ourselves in all our wretchedness is the hardest of tasks, and one which it is almost impossible to fulfil. The very thought can make us livid with fear. We therefore do not hesitate, but light-heartedly choose the complicated course of remaining in ignorance about ourselves while busying ourselves with other people and their troubles and sins. This activity lends us an air of virtue, and we thus deceive ourselves and those around us. In this way, thank God, we can escape from ourselves. There are countless people who can do this with impunity, but not everyone can, and these few break down on the road to Damascus. But how can I help such people if I am myself a fugitive? Only the person who has fully accepted himself will have 'unprejudiced objectivity'.

Friday after Lent 3

A Reading from an oration by Proclus,
Patriarch of Constantinople

Humankind was deep in debt and incapable of paying what it owed. By the hand of Adam we had all signed a bond to sin. The devil held us in slavery. He kept producing our bills which he wrote on our poor suffering bodies. There he stood, the wicked forger, threatening us with our debts and demanding payment.

One of two things had to happen: either the penalty of death had to be exacted on all, since indeed, 'all had sinned'; or else a substitute had to be found who was fully entitled to plead on our behalf. No human being could be found who could save us; the debt was a common liability. No angel could buy us out; such a ransom was beyond their powers. One who was sinless had to die for those who had sinned; that was the only way left by which to break the bonds of evil.

What happened then? The very one who had brought every creature into existence and whose bounty never fails, he it was who won life for the condemned and secured our freedom from the bands of death. He became man. How this happened God alone knows, for to explain this miracle is beyond the power of human language. By what he became he died; by what he was, he set us free. As Paul says: 'In him we have redemption through his blood, the forgiveness of our sins.'

What a transaction! It was for others that he procured immortality, since he himself was immortal. No one either before or since or ever in the future, no one other than he who was born of a virgin, God and man, could do this for us. His dignity was such as not only to outweigh the multitude of condemned, but also to cancel the sentences spoken against us. For he was the Son, maintaining his unchangeable likeness to the Father; the Creator, possessed of unfailing power; the merciful, revealing his endless compassion; the high priest, who was worthy to plead on our behalf. None of these qualities could ever be found in another, whether in the same or similar degree.

Behold his love! Freely accepting condemnation himself, he destroyed the death that was due to those who crucified him; and the sins of those who killed him, he turned into the salvation of sinners.

Saturday after Lent 3

A Reading from an oration of Gregory of Nazianzus

'Blessed are the merciful, for they shall obtain mercy,' says the Scripture. Mercy is not least in importance among the beatitudes. Again it is written: 'Blessed are they who are considerate to the needy and the poor.' And yet again: 'It goes well with those who act generously and lend.' In another place it is written: 'The righteous always give and lend.' My brothers and sisters, let us lay hold of this blessing, let us earn the name of being considerate, let us be generous.

Not even the night should interrupt you in your duty of mercy. Do not ever say: 'Go away and come back later and I will give you something tomorrow.' There should be no delay between your intention and carrying out your good deed. Generosity is the one thing that cannot admit of delay.

'Share your bread with the hungry, and bring the needy and the homeless into your home,' with a joyful and eager heart. 'Whoever does acts of mercy should do so with cheerfulness.' The grace of a good deed is doubled when it is done with promptness and speed. What is given with bad grace or against one's will is distasteful and far from praiseworthy.

When we perform an act of kindness we should rejoice and not be glum about it. 'If you undo the shackles and the irons of injustice,' says the prophet Isaiah, that is, if you do away with meanness and counting the cost, with prevarication and grumbling, what will be the result? Something great and wonderful! What a marvellous reward there will be: 'Your light will break forth like the dawn, and your healing will rise up quickly.' Who would not aspire to light and healing?

If you think that I have something to say, servants of Christ, his co-heirs, let us visit Christ whenever we may; let us care for him, feed him, clothe him, welcome him, honour him, not only at our table, as some have done; or by anointing him, as Mary did; or only by lending him a tomb, like Joseph of Arimathaea; or by arranging for his burial, like Nicodemus, who loved Christ half-heartedly; or by giving him gold, frankincense and myrrh, like the Magi who came before all the others. The Lord of all asks for mercy, not sacrifice, and mercy is greater than myriads of fattened lambs. Let us then show him mercy in the persons of the poor and those who today are lying on the ground, so that when we come to leave this world, they in their turn may receive us into everlasting dwelling places, in Christ our Lord himself to whom be glory for ever and ever.

The Fourth Sunday of Lent

A Reading from the *Pastoral Prayer*
of Aelred of Rievaulx

Lord, look at my soul's wounds.
Your living and effective eye sees everything.
It pierces like a sword, even to part asunder soul and spirit.
Assuredly, my Lord, you see in my soul
the traces of my former sins,
my present sins,
my present perils,
and also motives and occasions for others yet to be.
You see these things, Lord,
and I would have you see them.
You know well, O searcher of my heart,
that there is nothing in my soul that I would hide from you,
even had I the power to escape your eyes.
Woe to the souls that want to hide themselves from you.
They cannot make themselves not to be seen by you,
but only miss your healing and incur punishment.

So see me, sweet Lord, see me.
My hope, most merciful, is in your loving kindness;
for you will see me, either as a good physician sees,
intent upon my healing,
or else as a kind master, anxious to correct,
or a forbearing father, longing to forgive.

This, then, is what I ask, O font of pity,
trusting in your mighty mercy and merciful might:
I ask you, by the power of your most sweet name,
and by the mystery of your holy humanity,
to put away my sins and heal the languors of my soul,
mindful only of your goodness,
not of my ingratitude.

Mothering Sunday

A Reading from a sermon of Augustine

Stretching out his hand over his disciples, the Lord Christ declared: 'Here are my mother and my brothers; anyone who does the will of my Father who sent me is my brother and my sister and my mother.' I would urge you to ponder these words. Did the Virgin Mary, who believed by faith and conceived by faith, who was the chosen one from whom our Saviour was born among us, who was created by Christ before Christ was created in her – did she not do the will of the Father? Indeed the blessed Mary certainly did the Father's will, and so it was for her a greater thing to have been Christ's disciple than to have been his mother, and she was more blessed in her discipleship than in her motherhood. Hers was the happiness of first bearing in her womb him whom she would obey as her master.

Now listen and see if the words of Scripture do not agree with what I have said. The Lord was passing by and crowds were following him. His miracles gave proof of divine power and a woman cried out: 'Happy is the womb that bore you, blessed is that womb!' But the Lord, not wishing people to seek happiness in a purely physical relationship, replied: 'More blessed are those who hear the word of God and keep it.' Mary heard God's word and kept it, and so she is blessed. She kept God's truth in her mind, a nobler thing than carrying his body in her womb. The truth and the body were both Christ: he was kept in Mary's mind insofar as he is truth, he was carried in her womb insofar as he is human; but what is kept in the mind is of a higher order than what is carried in the womb.

The Virgin Mary is both holy and blessed, and yet the Church is greater than she. Mary is a part of the Church, a member of the Church, a holy, an eminent – the most eminent – member, but still only a member of the entire body. The body undoubtedly is greater than she, one of its members. This body has the Lord for its head, and head and body together make up the whole Christ. In other words, the head is divine – our head is God.

Now, beloved, give me your whole attention, for you also are members of Christ; you also are the body of Christ. Consider how you yourselves can be among those of whom the Lord said: 'Here are my mother and my brothers.' Do you wonder how you can be the mother of Christ? He himself said: 'Whoever hears and fulfils the will of my Father in heaven is my brother and my sister and my mother.' As for our being the brothers and sisters of Christ, we can understand this because although there is only one inheritance and Christ is the only Son, his mercy would not allow him to remain alone. It was his wish that we too should be heirs of the Father, and co-heirs with himself.

Now having said that all of you are brothers and sisters of Christ, shall I not dare to call you his mother? Much less would I dare to deny his own words. Tell me how Mary became the mother of Christ, if it was not by giving birth to the members of Christ? You, to whom I am speaking, are the members of Christ. Of whom were you born? 'Of Mother Church,' I hear the reply of your hearts. You became children of this mother at your baptism, you came to birth then as members of Christ. Now you in your turn must draw to the font of baptism as many as you possibly can. You became children when you were born there yourselves, and now by bringing others to birth in the same way, you have it in your power to become the mothers of Christ.

Monday after Lent 4

A Reading from *Revelations of Divine Love*
by Julian of Norwich

I understood more what our blessed Lord meant when he showed me that I should sin. I had taken this simply to refer to me as an individual, nor was the contrary shown me at the time. But by our Lord's very gracious enlightenment that came subsequently I saw that he meant humankind in general: that is to say, Everyone, who is and will be sinful to the very end. I am included in that, I hope, by the mercy of God. The blessed comfort that I saw is large enough to embrace us all. This taught me to look at my own sin and not at others', unless it was going to be a comfort and help to my fellow Christians. In the same revelation about my sinning I learned to be afraid because of my instability. For I do not know in what way I shall fall, nor the extent or greatness of my sin. I would have liked to have known that – with due fear, of course. But I got no answer.

At the same time our courteous Lord showed very clearly and convincingly the eternal and unchanging nature of his love, and that, through the keeping power of his great goodness and grace, there will be no separation between his love and our souls. So in this fear I have good reason for a humility which will save me from presuming, and in that blessed revelation of love good reason too for real and joyful comfort which will keep me from despairing.

This revelation, so intimate and homely, teaches a lovely lesson, and one that is gracious and sweet. It is a comfort for our soul, and comes from our courteous Lord himself. Through his delightful and intimate love he intends us to know that all the experience contrary to this, whether it be within us, or without, is from the enemy and not from God. For example, if we are inclined to get careless about the way we are living or are guarding our hearts because we know this abundant love, there is all the more need for us to beware. This inclination, should it come, is false, and we ought to abominate it. It bears no resemblance to God's will.

When we fall through our weakness or blindness our Lord in his courtesy puts his hand on us, encourages us, and holds on to us. Only then does he will that we should see our wretchedness, and humbly acknowledge it. It is not his intention for us to remain like this, nor that we should go to great lengths in our self-accusation, nor that we should feel too wretched about ourselves. He means us to look at once to him. For he stands there apart, waiting for us to come in sorrow and grief. He is quick to receive us, for we are his delight and joy, and he our salvation and our life.

Tuesday after Lent 4

A Reading from a sermon of Augustine

'If any would come after me, let them deny themselves, take up their cross and follow me.' The Lord's command seems hard and difficult. And yet it is not hard and difficult given that it is the command of him who helps us in carrying out what he commands.

What was spoken to him in the voice of the psalmist is true: 'Because of your command I have followed the hard road.' But true, also, are Christ's own words: 'My yoke is easy and my burden is light.' Or to put it another way, whatever is hard in the precept is made easy by love.

But what is the meaning of the words: 'take up the cross'? It means we should bear whatever is troublesome: on that understanding alone can a person follow Christ. For when we begin to follow Christ in his character and teaching, we will encounter many who will contradict us, many who will try to forbid us, many who will seek actively to dissuade us from following Christ – this can even occur among those who are companions of Christ. Remember, the people who tried to prevent the blind man from calling out to Jesus were the same people who walked at Christ's side. Whether, therefore, it is a matter of threats or flattery or prohibitions, if you wish to follow Christ, turn to the cross, endure, bear up, and refuse to give in.

It is in this world which is holy, good, reconciled, saved, – or rather in the process of being saved, at the moment only saved in hope, as Scripture says: 'in this hope were we saved' – in this world in which the Church tries to follow Christ in totality, Jesus calls out to people everywhere: 'If any would come after me, let them deny themselves.'

Wednesday after Lent 4

A Reading from a homily of Origen

'Abraham took the wood for the burnt offering and placed it upon his son Isaac, and he took the fire and a knife in his hands, and they went on together.' Isaac himself carries the wood for his own burnt offering: this is a figure of Christ. For he bore the burden of the cross, and yet to carry the wood for the burnt offering is really the duty of the priest. He is then both victim and priest. This is the meaning of the expression: 'they went on together.' For when Abraham, who has to perform the sacrifice, carried the fire and the knife, Isaac did not walk behind him, but with him. In this way he showed that he exercised the priesthood equally with Abraham.

What happens after this? Isaac said to Abraham his father: 'Father.' This plea from the son was at that instant the voice of temptation. For do you not think the voice of the child who was about to be sacrificed struck a responsive chord in the heart of the father? Although Abraham did not waver because of his faith, he responded with a voice full of affection and asked: 'What is it, my son?' Isaac answered him: 'Here are the fire and the wood, but where is the sheep for the burnt offering?' And Abraham replied: 'God will provide for himself a sheep for the burnt offering, my son.'

The careful yet loving response of Abraham moves me greatly. I do not know what he saw in spirit, because he did not speak of the present but of the future: 'God will provide for himself a sheep.' His reply concerns the future, yet his son inquires about the present. Indeed, the Lord himself provided a sheep for himself in Christ.

'Abraham extended his hand to take the knife and slay his son, and the angel of the Lord called to him from heaven and said: "Abraham, Abraham." And he responded: "Here I am." And the angel said: "Do not lay your hand upon the boy or do anything to him, for now I know that you fear God." ' Compare these words to those of the Apostle when he speaks of God: 'He did not spare his own Son but gave him up for us all.' God emulates humanity with magnificent generosity. Abraham offered to God his mortal son who did not die, and God gave up his immortal Son who died for all of us.

'And Abraham, looking about him, saw a ram caught by the horns in a thicket.' We said before that Isaac is a type of Christ. Yet this also seems true of the ram. To understand how both are figures of Christ – Isaac who was not slain and the ram who was – is well worth our inquiry.

Christ is the Word of God, but 'the Word became flesh.' Christ therefore suffered and died, but in the flesh. In this respect, the ram is the type, just as John said in his Gospel: 'Behold the lamb of God, behold him who takes away the sins of the world.' The Word, however, remained incorruptible. This is Christ according to the spirit, and Isaac is the type. Therefore, Christ himself is both victim and priest according to the spirit. For he offers the victim to the Father according to the flesh, and he is himself offered on the altar of the cross.

Thursday after Lent 4

A Reading from the *Moral Reflections on the Book of Job*
by Gregory the Great

Blessed Job is a type of the Church. At one moment we find him speaking for the body, and the next for the head. Indeed, while he is speaking of the members of the body he is suddenly caught up to speak in the name of their head. And so it is in the case of the text where he says: 'I have suffered this without sin on my hands, for my prayer to God was pure.'

Christ suffered without sin on his hands, for 'he committed no sin and no deceit was found on his lips.' Yet he suffered the pain of the cross for our redemption. His prayer to God was pure, his alone out of all humanity, for in the midst of his suffering he prayed for his persecutors: 'Father, forgive them, for they do not know what they are doing.'

Is it possible to offer, or even to imagine, a purer kind of prayer than that which shows mercy to one's torturers by making intercession for them? It was thanks to this kind of prayer that the frenzied persecutors who shed the blood of our Redeemer drank it afterward in faith and proclaimed him to be the Son of God.

Job's next words speak aptly of Christ's blood: 'Earth, do not cover over my blood, do not let my cry find a hiding place in you.' When humankind sinned, God addressed them saying: 'Earth you are, and to earth you shall return.' Earth does not cover over the blood of our Redeemer, for all sinners, as they drink the blood that is the price of their redemption, offer praise and thanksgiving, and to the best of their ability make the worth of that blood known to all around them. Earth has not hidden away Christ's blood, for the Church has preached in every corner of the world the mystery of its redemption.

Notice what follows in the text: 'Do not let my cry find a hiding place in you.' The blood that is drunk, the blood of redemption, is itself the cry of our Redeemer. Paul speaks of 'the sprinkled blood that calls out more eloquently than Abel's'. Of Abel's blood we find it written in Scripture that: 'The voice of your brother's blood cries out to me from the earth.' The blood of Jesus calls out more eloquently than Abel's, for the blood of Abel sought the death of his brother Cain who had murdered him, whereas the blood of the Lord has sought and obtained life for his persecutors.

Therefore, if the sacrament of the Lord's passion is to work its effect in us, we must imitate what we receive and proclaim to others what we revere. The cry of the Lord finds a hiding place in us if our lips fail to speak of this, though our hearts believe in it. So that his cry may not lie concealed in us, it is incumbent upon us all, to the best of our ability, to make known to those around us the mystery of our new life in Christ.

Friday after Lent 4

A Reading from *The Ascetical Treatises*
of Isaac of Nineveh

Lord Jesus Christ our God, who wept for Lazarus and shed tears for him of grief and compassion, accept the tears I shed this day.
By your sufferings soothe my suffering.
By your wounds heal my wounds.
By your blood purify my blood, and mingle with my body the fragrance of your life-giving body.
May the gall, which enemies gave you to drink, sweeten my soul of the bitterness that I have drunk at the hands of the adversary.
May your body, outstretched upon the wood of the cross, give wings to my mind which is dragged down by the demons, and make it rise up to you.
May your head, which you bowed on the cross, lift up my head which the enemies strike at.
May your most holy hands, nailed by unbelievers to the cross, lift me out of the pit of destruction and raise me up to you, as you have promised.
May your face, struck and spat upon by men, enlighten my face which is disfigured by wrongdoing.
May your soul, which on the cross you surrendered to the Father, lead me to you by your grace.
I have no heart full of anguish with which to search you out. I have no contrition which brings back children to their inheritance. O Master, I do not even have tears to intercede for myself.
My spirit is in darkness and my heart is cold. I do not know how to make it warm again by my tears of love for you.
O Lord Jesus Christ, my God, grant me complete repentance: break my heart, that with my whole soul I may start out on my search for you. Without you, nothing is real.
May the Father, who in his womb begot you timelessly and eternally, renew in me the marks of your image.
I have forsaken you: do not forsake me.
I have wandered far from you. Come and seek me out: lead me back to your fold and number me among the sheep of your chosen flock. Make me feed with them on the green pasture of your divine mysteries, where the pure in heart find their rest.
And may we all be worthy of such splendour through your grace and by your love for the world, O Jesus Christ our Saviour, for ever and ever. Amen.

Saturday after Lent 4

A Reading from *Resurrection* by Rowan Williams

The crucified is God's chosen: it is with the victim, the condemned, that God identifies, and it is in the company of the victim, so to speak, that God is to be found, and nowhere else. We are, insistently and relentlessly, in Jerusalem, confronted with a victim who is *our* victim. When we make victims, when we embark on condemnation, exclusion, violence, the diminution or oppression of anyone, when we set ourselves up as judges, we are exposed to judgement, and we turn away from salvation. To hear the good news of salvation, to be converted, is to turn back to the condemned and rejected, acknowledging that there is hope nowhere else. Salvation does not bypass the history and memory of guilt, but rather builds upon and from it.

To judge is to be exposed to judgement. Conversion is the realisation that this equation shows us where we look for our vindication: the relationship we have set up, of judge to victim, is first of all to be reversed and then transcended.

The problem is that in ordinary human relationships, boundaries are very fluid indeed. Even in a single relationship, I may be *both* oppressor and victim, and I can become involved in all manner of subtle collusions with both my oppressors and my victims. The human world is not one of clearly distinguishable bodies of oppressors and victims, those who inflict damage and those who bear it. Where is a 'pure' victim to be found?

What Christian preaching asserts is that conversion, return to the victim in hope, is possible because Jesus embodies the condition of a pure victim. Judgement here is also mercy and hope because of the quality of this particular victim. The tradition made it clear that Jesus offered no 'violence' to any who turned to him in hope: he accepts, he does not condemn, resist or exclude. His life is defined as embodying an unconditional and universal acceptance, untrammelled by social, ritual or racial exclusiveness. The tradition also recorded Jesus' silent resignation at his trial.

Jesus, as a man perfectly obedient to the Father, consistently refuses the role of oppressor: he does no violence, he utters no condemnation, he has no will to exclude or diminish. He emerges as the pure victim, the lamb who bears the sins of the world, who can only suffer 'violence', never inflict it; a man who is essentially and archetypally victim.

The exaltation of Jesus to be judge, to share the ultimate authority of God, is thus God's proclamation to all earthly judges, to the condemning court and the hostile city, that it is the pure victim who alone can 'carry' the divine love, the divine opposition to violence, oppression and exclusion. And so far from being passive, it is the pure victim alone who is capable of creative action, the transforming of the human world, the release from the pendulum swing of attack and revenge. The victim as 'pure' victim is more than victim: when God receives and approves the condemned Jesus and returns him to his judges through the preaching of the Church, he transcends the world of oppressor–oppressed relations to create a new humanity, capable of other kinds of relation – between human beings, and between humanity and God.

The Fifth Sunday of Lent

A Reading from the *Catechetical Lectures*
of Cyril of Jerusalem

The Catholic Church glories in every deed of Christ. Her supreme glory, however, is the cross. Well aware of this, Paul says: 'God forbid that I should glory in anything but the cross of our Lord Jesus Christ!'

At the Pool of Siloam, there was a sense of wonder, and rightly so. A man born blind recovered his sight. But of what importance is this, when there are so many blind people in the world? Lazarus rose from the dead, but even this only affected Lazarus. What of those countless numbers who have died because of their sins? Those five miraculous loaves fed five thousand people. Yet this is a small number compared to those all over the world who were starved by ignorance. After eighteen years a woman was freed from the bondage of Satan. But are we not all shackled by the chains of our sins?

For us all, however, the cross is the crown of victory! It has brought light to those blinded by ignorance. It has released those enslaved by sin. Indeed, it has redeemed the whole of the human race! Do not, then, be ashamed of the cross of Christ; rather, glory in it. Although it is a stumbling block to the Jews and folly to the Gentiles, the message of the cross is our salvation. Of course, it is folly to those who are perishing, but to us who are being saved it is the power of God. For it was not a mere human being who died for us, but the Son of God, God incarnate.

In the Mosaic law a sacrificial lamb banished the destroyer. But now 'it is the Lamb of God who takes away the sin of the world.' Will he not free us from our sins even more? The blood of an animal, a sheep, brought salvation. Will not the blood of the only-begotten Son bring us greater salvation?

He was not killed by violence, he was not forced to give up his life. His was a willing sacrifice. Listen to his own words: 'I have the power to lay down my life and to take it up again.' Yes, he willingly submitted to his own passion. He took joy in his achievement; in his crown of victory he was glad and in the salvation of humanity he rejoiced. He did not blush at the cross for by it he was to save the world. No, it was not a mere man who suffered, but God incarnate. He entered the contest for the reward he would win by his patient endurance.

Certainly in times of tranquillity the cross should give you joy. But maintain the same faith in times of persecution. Otherwise you run the risk of being a friend of Jesus in times of peace and his enemy during war. Now you are receiving the forgiveness of your sins and the generous gift of grace from your king. So when war comes, fight courageously for him.

Jesus never sinned; yet he was crucified for you. Will you refuse to be crucified for him, who for your sake was nailed to the cross? You are not the one who is bestowing a favour; you have received one first. For your sake he was crucified on Golgotha. Now you are to return his favour; you are fulfilling your debt to him.

Monday after Lent 5

A Reading from a homily of John Chrysostom

Have you considered the nature of the wonderful victory that is ours? Have you considered the glorious deeds of the cross? Let me tell you how the victory was won and you will be even more amazed. Christ conquered the devil using the very means by which the devil conquered us: Christ took up the weapons with which the devil had fought, and defeated him. Listen now to how it was achieved.

If you reflect upon the Scriptures and the story of our redemption, you will recall that a virgin, a tree and a death were the symbols of our defeat. The virgin's name was Eve: she knew not a man. The tree was the tree of the knowledge of good and evil. The death was Adam's penalty. But now those very symbols of our defeat – a virgin, a tree and a death – have become symbols of Christ's victory. In place of Eve there is Mary; in place of the tree of the knowledge of good and evil, there is the tree of the cross; and in place of the death of Adam, there is the death of Christ.

Can you now see how the very circumstances in which the devil conquered us have become the pattern of his own defeat? At the foot of the tree the devil overcame Adam; at the foot of the tree Christ vanquished the devil. As a result of the first tree humankind were consigned to Hades; now a second Adam calls back to life even those who had already descended there. The first tree hid a man who knew himself to have been undermined and stripped bare; the second tree displays the naked victor for all the world to see. The first death condemned those who were born after it; but this second death gives life even to those who were born before it. Who can describe sufficiently the mighty deeds of the Lord? For by his death we have become immortal. Such are the glorious deeds of the cross.

Have you now understood the victory? Have you grasped how it was achieved? Remember, the victory was gained without any effort or work on our part. No weapons of ours were stained with blood. We were not in the front line of battle, nor were we wounded or the object of aggression. And yet we have obtained the victory. The battle was the Lord's, but the crown is ours. Since then the victory is ours, let us imitate victorious soldiers and sing a song of victory with great joy. Let us praise the Lord and say: 'Death is swallowed up in victory! O death, where is your victory? O death where is your sting?'

My dear people, the cross has achieved all these wonderful things for us. The cross is a war memorial erected against the demons, a sword raised against sin, the sword with which Christ slew the serpent. The cross is the Father's will, the glory of the only-begotten, and the Spirit's exaltation. It is the beauty of angels and the guardian of the Church. Paul gloried in the cross of Christ, for it is indeed the rampart of the saints and the light of the whole world.

Tuesday after Lent 5

A Reading from *A Serious Call to a Devout and Holy Life*
by William Law

Deep is the foundation of humility laid in the deplorable circumstances of the human condition, which show that it is as great an offence against truth and the reason of things for a man in this state of things to lay claim to any degrees of glory as to pretend to the honour of creating himself. If man will boast of anything as his own, he must boast of his misery and sin, for there is nothing else but this that is his own property. Turn your eyes toward heaven and fancy that you saw what is doing there, that you saw cherubims and seraphims and all the glorious inhabitants of that place all united in one work, not seeking glory from one another, not labouring their own advancement, not contemplating their own perfections, not singing their own praises, not valuing themselves and despising others, but all employed in one and the same work, all happy in one and the same joy, 'casting down their crowns before the throne of God, giving glory, and honour, and power to him alone'.

Then turn your eyes to the fallen world and consider how unreasonable and odious it must be for such poor worms, such miserable sinners to take delight in their own fancied glories whilst the highest and most glorious sons of heaven seek for no other greatness and honour but that of ascribing all honour and greatness and glory to God alone.

Pride is only the disorder of the fallen world, it has no place amongst other beings; it can only subsist where ignorance and sensuality, lies and falsehood, lusts and impurity, reign. Let a man, when he is most delighted with his own figure, look upon a crucifix and contemplate our blessed Lord stretched out and nailed upon a cross, and then let him consider how absurd it must be for a heart full of pride and vanity to pray to God through the sufferings of such a meek and crucified Saviour.

These are the reflections that you are often to meditate upon, that you may thereby be disposed to walk before God and man in such a spirit of humility as becomes the weak, miserable, sinful state of all that are descended from fallen Adam.

Wednesday after Lent 5

A Reading from a treatise *On the Incarnation of the Lord*
by Theodoret of Cyr

Of his own free will, Jesus hastened to meet the suffering which, according to Scripture, was his destiny. He had often warned his disciples that he would suffer, and when Peter protested against this, Jesus rebuked him. At the end he also taught his disciples that the salvation of the world depended on his suffering. This is why he gave himself up to those who came to arrest him, saying: 'I am the one whom you seek.'

Jesus wept over Jerusalem, for he realised it was moving inexorably towards its own destruction through its lack of faith. He warned that the once famous temple would be destroyed. He endured being hit on the face at his trial from a man who both in reality and in spirit was a slave. Beaten, spat upon, ridiculed, tormented, scourged and finally nailed to the cross, Jesus accepted as his companions in punishment two thieves, one on his right hand, the other on his left. He was numbered among murderers and criminals, given gall and vinegar from the evil vine to drink, and instead of being crowned with a wreath of palm leaves and clusters of grapes was given a crown of thorns. He was dressed in purple, mocked, struck with a reed, pierced in the side by a spear, and finally laid in a tomb.

All these things Jesus suffered in the cause of our salvation. For us who were slaves to sin, he who was without sin accepted the penalties due to sin. He who had lived a life of complete holiness, now took upon himself the punishment of sinners, wiping out by the cross the curse that had been decreed long ago.

We are healed through the sufferings of our Saviour. This is what the prophet Isaiah taught when he said: 'Surely he has borne our griefs and carried our sorrows; yet we esteemed him stricken, abandoned by God and afflicted. But he was wounded for our iniquities; his suffering has made us whole, and by his wounds we are healed. All we like sheep have gone astray; like a lamb he has been led to the slaughter and like a sheep before its shearers, he was dumb.'

When a shepherd sees that his sheep have scattered, he takes hold of one of them and leads it to the pastures he has chosen, and the others instinctively follow this one sheep. In the same way the Word of God saw humankind wandering aimlessly, and took upon himself our full humanity, assuming the form of a slave. Then he

led us to the pastures of God, we who beforehand had been under-
nourished and prey to wolves.

This is why our Saviour assumed our human nature. This is
why Christ our Lord submitted to his saving passion.

Thursday after Lent 5

A Reading from an oration 'In Adoration of the Cross'
by Theodore of Studios

How precious is the gift of the cross, how splendid to contemplate!
In the cross there is no mingling of good and evil, as in the tree of
paradise: it is wholly beautiful to behold and good to taste. The
fruit of this tree is not death but life, not darkness but light. This
tree does not cast us out of paradise, but opens the way for our
return.

This was the tree on which Christ, like a king on a chariot,
destroyed the devil, the lord of death, and freed the human race
from tyranny. This was the tree upon which the Lord, like a brave
warrior wounded in hands, feet and side, healed the wounds of sin
that the evil serpent had inflicted on our nature. A tree once caused
our death, but now a tree brings life. Once deceived by a tree, we
have now repelled the cunning serpent by a tree. What an
astonishing transformation! That death should become life, that
decay should become immortality, that shame should become
glory! Well might the holy Apostle exclaim: 'Far be it from me to
glory except in the cross of our Lord Jesus Christ, by which the
world has been crucified to me, and I to the world!' The supreme
wisdom that flowered on the cross has shown the folly of worldly
wisdom's pride. The knowledge of all good, which is the fruit of
the cross, cut away the shoots of wickedness.

The wonders accomplished through this tree were fore-
shadowed clearly even by the mere types and figures that existed
in the past. Meditate on these, if you are eager to learn. Was it not
the wood of a tree that enabled Noah, at God's command, to escape
the destruction of the flood together with his sons, his wfe, his
sons' wives and every kind of animal? And surely the rod of Moses
prefigured the cross when it changed water into blood, swallowed
up the false serpents of Pharaoh's magicians, divided the Red Sea
at one stroke and then restored the waters to their normal course,
drowning the enemy and saving God's own people? Aaron's rod,
which blossomed in one day in proof of his true priesthood, was

another figure of the cross; and did not Abraham foreshadow the cross when he bound his son Isaac and placed him on the pile of wood?

By the cross death was slain and Adam was restored to life. The cross is the glory of the apostles, the crown of the martyrs, the sanctification of the saints. By the cross we put on Christ and cast aside our former self. By the cross we, the sheep of Christ, have been gathered into one flock, destined for the sheepfolds of heaven.

Friday after Lent 5

A Reading from *The Dialogue* by Catherine of Siena

Open your mind's eye and look at the bridge of my only-begotten Son, and notice its greatness. Look! It stretches from heaven to earth, joining the earth of your humanity with the greatness of the Godhead. This is what I mean when I say it stretches from heaven to earth – through my union with humanity.

This was necessary if I wanted to remake the road that had been broken up, so that you might pass over the bitterness of the world and reach life. From earth alone I could not have made it great enough to cross the river and bring you to eternal life. The earth of human nature by itself was incapable of atoning for sin and draining off the poison from Adam's sin, for that poison has infected the whole human race. Your nature had to be joined with the height of mine, the eternal Godhead, before it could make atonement for all of humanity. Then human nature could endure the suffering, and the divine nature, joined with that humanity, would accept my Son's sacrifice on your behalf to release you from death and give you life.

So the height stooped to the earth of your humanity, bridging the chasm between us and rebuilding the road. And why should he have made of himself a roadway? So that you might in truth come to the same joy as the angels. But although my Son has made of himself a bridge for you, he cannot bring you to life unless you make your way along that bridge.

O immeasurably tender love! Who would not be set afire with such love? What heart could keep from breaking! You, deep well of charity, it seems you are so madly in love with your creatures that you could not live without us! Yet you are our God, and have no need of us. Your greatness is no greater for our well-being, nor are you harmed by any harm that comes to us, for you are supreme eternal Goodness. What could move you to such mercy! Neither duty nor any need you have of us (we are sinful and wicked debtors) – but only love!

If I see clearly at all, supreme eternal Truth, it is I who am the thief, and you have been executed in my place. For I see the Word, your Son, nailed to a cross. And you have made him a bridge for me, as you have shown me, wretched servant that I am! My heart is breaking and yet cannot break for the hungry longing it has conceived for you!

Saturday after Lent 5

A Reading from an oration of Gregory of Nazianzus

We are soon going to share in the Passover, and although we still do so only in a symbolic way, the symbolism already has more clarity than it possessed in former times because, under the law, the Passover was, if I may dare to say so, only a symbol of a symbol. Before long, however, when the Word drinks the new wine with us in the kingdom of his Father, we shall be keeping the Passover in a yet more perfect way, and with deeper understanding. He will then reveal to us and make clear what he has so far only partially disclosed. For this wine, so familiar to us now, is eternally new.

It is for us to learn what this drinking is, and for him to teach us. He has to communicate this knowledge to his disciples, because teaching is food, even for the teacher.

So let us take our part in the Passover prescribed by the law, not in a literal way, but according to the teaching of the gospel; not in an imperfect way, but perfectly; not only for a time, but eternally. Let us regard as our home the heavenly Jerusalem, not the earthly one; the city glorified by angels, not the one laid waste by armies. We are not required to sacrifice young bulls or rams, beasts with horns and hoofs that are more dead than alive and devoid of feeling; but instead, let us join the choirs of angels in offering God upon his heavenly altar a sacrifice of praise. We must now pass through the first veil and approach the second, turning our eyes toward the Holy of Holies. I will say more: we must sacrifice ourselves to God, each day and in everything we do, accepting all that happens to us for the sake of the Word, imitating his passion by our sufferings, and honouring his blood by shedding our own. We must be ready to be crucified.

If you are a Simon of Cyrene, take up your cross and follow Christ. If you are crucified beside him like one of the thieves, now, like the good thief, acknowledge your God. For your sake, and because of your sin, Christ himself was regarded as a sinner; for his sake, therefore, you must cease to sin. Worship him who was hung on the cross because of you, even if you are hanging there yourself. Derive some benefit from the very shame; purchase salvation with your death. Enter paradise with Jesus, and discover how far you have fallen. Contemplate the glories there, and leave the other scoffing thief to die outside in blasphemy.

If you are a Joseph of Arimathea, go to the one who ordered his crucifixion, and ask for Christ's body. Make your own the expiation for the sins of the whole world. If you are a Nicodemus, like the one who worshipped God by night, bring spices and prepare Christ's body for burial. If you are one of the Marys, or Salome, or Joanna, weep in the early morning. Be the first to see the stone rolled back, and even the angels perhaps, and Jesus himself.

HOLY WEEK

Nails were not enough to hold God-and-man nailed and
fastened to the cross, had not love held him there.

Catherine of Siena

We are celebrating the feast of the cross
which drove away darkness and brought in the light.
As we keep this feast, we are lifted up with the crucified
Christ, leaving behind us earth and sin so that we may gain
the things above. So great and outstanding a possession is
the cross that whoever wins it has won a treasure.
Rightly could I call this treasure the fairest of all fair things
and the costliest, in fact as well as in name, for on it and
through it, and for its sake, the riches of salvation
that had been lost were restored to us.

Andrew of Crete

The readings selected for **Holy Week** mirror the liturgical movement of the week, beginning with the solemn commemoration of Christ's triumphant entry into Jerusalem on **Palm Sunday**, and concluding with the crucifixion, deposition and burial. The readings are closely allied to the theological themes of the lectionary, focusing predominantly on the suffering of Christ and the victory of the cross.

The provision for **Maundy Thursday** offers a variety of readings appropriate to the different themes of the day: the Last Supper, the institution of the Eucharist, and the foot-washing.

The readings for Holy Week conclude on **Holy Saturday** with readings from the Syriac Church which meditate upon Christ's descent into hell. This remains a distinctive feature of Eastern theology.

Palm Sunday

A Reading from an oration of Andrew of Crete

Let us go together to meet Christ on the Mount of Olives. Today he returns from Bethany and proceeds of his own free will toward his holy and blessed passion, to consummate the mystery of our salvation. He who came down from heaven to raise us from the depths of sin, to raise us with himself, we are told in Scripture: 'above every sovereignty, authority and power, and every other name that can be named', now comes of his own free will to make his journey to Jerusalem. He comes without pomp or ostentation. As the psalmist says: 'He will not dispute or raise his voice to make it heard in the streets.' He will be meek and humble, and he will make his entry in simplicity.

Let us run to accompany him as he hastens toward his passion, and imitate those who met him then, not by covering his path with garments, olive branches or palms, but by doing all we can to prostrate ourselves before him by being humble and by trying to live as he would wish. Then we shall be able to receive the Word at his coming, and God, whom no limits can contain, will be within us.

In his humility Christ entered the dark regions of our fallen world and he is glad that he became so humble for our sake, glad that he came and lived among us and shared in our nature in order to raise us up again to himself. And even though we are told that he has now ascended above – his love for us will never rest until he has raised our earthbound nature from glory to glory, and made it one with his own in heaven.

So let us spread before his feet, not garments or soulless olive branches, which delight the eye for a few hours and then wither, but ourselves, clothed in his grace, or rather, clothed completely in him. We who have been baptized into Christ must ourselves be the garments that we spread before him. Now that the crimson stains of our sins have been washed away in the saving waters of baptism and we have become white as pure wool, let us present the conqueror of death, not with mere branches of palms but with the real rewards of his victory. Let our souls take the place of the welcoming branches as we join today in the children's holy song: 'Blessed is he who comes in the name of the Lord. Blessed is the king of Israel.'

A Reading from an oration by Gregory of Nazianzus

Why was the blood that was shed for us, God's most precious and glorious blood, this blood of the One who carried out the sacrifice and of the One who was himself the sacrifice? Why was it poured out, and to whom was it offered? These are questions that echo within my mind.

If the death of Christ was a ransom paid to the Father, the question that arises is for what reason? We were not held captive by the Father. And anyway, why should the blood of his only Son be pleasing to the Father who once refused to accept Isaac when Abraham his father offered him as a burnt offering, and instead was pleased to accept the sacrifice of a ram?

Surely it is evident that the Father accepts the sacrifice of Christ, not because he demands it, still less because he feels some need of it, but in order to carry forward his own purposes for the world. Humanity had to be brought back to life by the humanity of God. We had to be summoned to life by his Son.

Let the rest be adored in silence.

Nothing can equal the miracle of my salvation. A few drops of blood have set free the entire universe.

alternative reading

A Reading from the hymns for Palm Sunday
in the Orthodox Church

Let the mountains and all the hills
Break out into great rejoicing at the mercy of God,
And let the trees of the forest clap their hands.
Give praise to Christ, all nations,
Magnify him, all peoples, crying:
'Glory to thy power, O Lord!'

Seated in heaven upon thy throne
And on earth upon a foal, O Christ our God,
Thou hast accepted the praise of the angels
And the songs of the children who cried out to thee:
'Blessed art thou that comest to call back Adam!'

alternative reading

A Reading from a poem by R. S. Thomas

The Coming

And God held in his hand
A small globe. Look, he said.
The son looked.
Far off,
As through water, he saw
A scorched land of fierce
Colour. The light burned
There; crusted buildings
Cast their shadows; a bright
Serpent, a river
Uncoiled itself, radiant
With slime.

On a bare
Hill a bare tree saddened
The sky. Many people
Held out their thin arms
To it, as though waiting
For a vanished April
To return to its crossed
Boughs. The son watched
Them. Let me go there, he said.

Monday in Holy Week

A Reading from a homily of John Chrysostom

The cross used to denote punishment but it has now become a focus of glory. It was formerly a symbol of condemnation but it is now seen as a principle of salvation. For it has now become the source of innumerable blessings: it has delivered us from error, enlightened our darkness, and reconciled us to God; we had become God's enemies and were foreigners afar off, and it has given us his friendship and brought us close to him. For us it has become the destruction of enmity, the token of peace, the treasury of a thousand blessings.

Thanks to the cross we are no longer wandering in the wilderness, because we know the right road; we are no longer outside the royal palace because we have found the way in; we are not afraid of the devil's fiery darts because we have discovered the fountain. Thanks to the cross we are no longer in a state of widowhood for we are reunited to the Bridegroom; we are not afraid of the wolf because we have the Good Shepherd. Thanks to the cross we dread no usurper, since we are sitting beside the King.

That is why we keep festival as we celebrate the memory of the cross. St Paul himself invites us to this festival in honour of the cross: 'Let us celebrate the feast not with the old leaven, that of corruption and wickedness, but with the unleavened bread of sincerity and truth.' And he tells us why, saying: 'Christ our Passover has been sacrificed for us.'

Now do you see why he appoints a festival in honour of the cross? It is because Christ was immolated on the cross. And where he was sacrificed, there is found abolition of sins and reconciliation with the Lord; and there, too, festivity and happiness are found: 'Christ our Passover has been sacrificed for us.'

Where was he sacrificed? On a gibbet. The altar of this sacrifice is a new one because the sacrifice himself is new and extraordinary. For he is at one and the same time both victim and priest: victim according to the flesh and priest according to the spirit.

This sacrifice was offered outside the camp to teach us that it is a universal sacrifice, for the offering was made for the whole world; and to teach us that it effected a general purification and not just that of the Jews. God commanded the Jews to leave the rest of the world and to offer their prayers and sacrifices in one particular place; because all the rest of the world was soiled by the smoke and smell of all the impurities of pagan sacrifices. But for us, since Christ has now come and purified the whole world, every place has become an oratory.

Tuesday in Holy Week

A Reading from a treatise *On the Holy Spirit*
by Basil the Great

When humankind was estranged by disobedience, God our Saviour made a plan for raising us from our fall and restoring us to friendship with himself. According to this plan Christ came in the flesh, he showed us the gospel way of life, he suffered, died on the cross, was buried and rose from the dead. He did this so that we could be saved by imitation of him, and recover our original status as children of God by adoption.

To attain holiness, then, we must not only pattern our lives on that of Christ by being gentle, humble and patient, but we must also imitate him in his death. Taking Christ for his model, Paul said that he wanted to become like him in his death in the hope that he too would be raised from death to life.

We imitate Christ's death by being buried with him in baptism. If we ask what this kind of burial means and what benefit we may hope to derive from it, it means first of all making a complete break with our former way of life, and our Lord himself said that this cannot be done unless we are born again. In other words, we have to begin a new life, and we cannot do so until our previous life has been brought to an end. When runners reach the turning point on a racecourse, they have to pause briefly before they can go back in the opposite direction. So also when we wish to reverse the direction of our lives there must be a pause, or a death, to mark the end of one life and the beginning of another.

Our descent into hell takes place when we imitate the burial of Christ by our baptism. The bodies of the baptized are in a sense buried in the water as a symbol of their renunciation of the sins of their unregenerate nature. As the Apostle says: 'The circumcision you have undergone is not an operation performed by human hands, but the complete stripping away of your unregenerate nature. This is the circumcision that Christ gave us, and it is accomplished by our burial with him in baptism.' Baptism cleanses the soul from the pollution of worldly thoughts and inclinations: 'You will wash me,' says the psalmist, 'and I shall be whiter than snow.' We receive this saving baptism only once because there was only one death and one resurrection for the salvation of the world, and baptism is its symbol.

Wednesday in Holy Week

A Reading from *Revelations of Divine Love*
by Julian of Norwich

Our good Lord Jesus Christ said, 'Are you well satisfied with my suffering for you?' 'Yes, thank you, good Lord,' I replied. 'Yes, good Lord, bless you.' And the kind Lord Jesus said, 'If you are satisfied, I am satisfied too. It gives me greater happiness and joy and, indeed, eternal delight ever to have suffered for you. If I could possibly have suffered more, I would have done so.'

In his word 'If I could possibly have suffered more, I would have done so,' I saw that he would have died again and again, for his love would have given him no rest until he had done so. I was most attentive to discover how often he might have died. The number, indeed, was so far beyond my comprehension and knowledge that I was unable to count it. Yet all this potential dying he would count as nothing for love of us. In comparison with this it seemed a small matter.

For though the dear humanity of Christ could only suffer once, his goodness would always make him willing to do so – every day if need be. If he were to say that for love of me he would make a new heaven and a new earth, this would be a comparatively simple matter; something he could do every day if he wanted, with no great effort. But for love of me to be willing to die times without number – beyond human capacity to compute – is, to my mind, the greatest gesture our Lord God could make to the human soul. This is his meaning: 'How could I not, out of love for you, do all I can for you? This would not be difficult, since for love of you I am ready to die often, regardless of the suffering.'

And here I saw that the love which made him suffer is as much greater than his pain as heaven is greater than earth. For his suffering was a noble and most worthy deed worked out by love in time – and his love has no beginning, but is now, and ever shall be. It was because of this love he said, 'If I could possibly have suffered more, I would have done so.' I saw Christ's complete happiness; his happiness would not have been complete if it were at all possible to have done it better.

Maundy Thursday

A Reading from the instructions of Cyril of Jerusalem
to the newly baptized

Our Lord Jesus Christ, on the same night in which he was betrayed, took bread, and when he had given thanks he broke it, and said: 'Take, eat; this is my body'; and having taken the cup and given thanks, he said: 'Take, drink, this is my blood.' Since he himself has declared and said of the bread: 'This is my body,' who can dare doubt the truth of his words? And since he has affirmed and said: 'This is my blood,' who need ever hesitate, saying that it is not his blood?

Therefore with complete confidence let us all partake of the body and blood of Christ: for in the figure of bread is given to you his body, and in the figure of wine his blood; for in so partaking of the body and blood of Christ, you will be made of the same body and the same blood with him. This is how we as Christians come to bear Christ in us, because his body and blood are diffused through our members; as the blessed Peter himself said: 'we become partakers of the divine nature.'

Once, when discoursing with the Jews, Christ said: 'Except you eat my flesh and drink my blood, you have no life in you.' The Jews did not grasp the spiritual significance of what he was saying, and were offended at his words: they went backwards, supposing that he was inviting them to eat flesh.

Even under the Old Testament there was shewbread; but this, as it belonged to the Old Testament, came to an end; but in the New Testament there is the bread of heaven, and the cup of salvation, sanctifying soul and body; for as the bread has respect to our body, so is the Word appropriate to our soul.

Contemplate, therefore, the bread and wine not as bare elements, for they are, according to the Lord's declaration, the body and blood of Christ. Though sense suggests otherwise, let faith steady you. Judge not this matter from taste, but from faith be fully assured without misgiving, that you have been promised the body and blood of Christ.

Having learned these things, let us be fully persuaded that what appears to be bread is not so, that although bread by taste it is nothing less than the body of Christ; and that what seems to be wine is not wine, that although its taste suggests so, it is in fact the blood of Christ. Concerning this David sang of old: 'Bread which strengthens our heart, and oil which gives us a shining countenance.' So I bid you, strengthen your heart, partaking of these things spiritually, and so make the countenance of your soul shine. And thus having the mystery unveiled by a pure conscience, may you 'behold as in a mirror the glory of the Lord', and proceed from 'glory to glory', in Christ Jesus our Lord.

alternative reading

A Reading from a commentary on St John's Gospel
by Augustine

'A new commandment I give you, that you love one another.' This commandment that the Lord Jesus is giving the disciples is a new one. Yet was it not contained in the old law, where it is written: 'You shall love your neighbour as yourself'? Why does the Lord, then, call it new when it is clearly so old? Or is the commandment new because it divests us of our former selves and clothes us with the new person? Love does indeed renew the one who hears, or rather obeys, its command; but only that love which Jesus distinguished from a natural love by the qualification: 'as I have loved you'.

This is the kind of love that renews us. When we love as Jesus loved us we become new people, heirs of the new covenant and singers of the new song. My beloved, this was the love that even in bygone days renewed the holy ones, the patriarchs and prophets of old. In later times it renewed the blessed apostles, and now it is the turn of the Gentiles. From the entire human race throughout the world this love gathers together into one body a new people, to be the bride of God's only Son. She is the bride of whom it is asked in the Song of Songs: 'Who is this who comes clothed in white?' White indeed are her garments, for she has been made new; and the source of her renewal is none other than this new commandment.

And so all her members make each other's welfare their common care. When one member suffers, all the members suffer too, and if one member is glorified all the rest rejoice. They hear and obey the Lord's words: 'A new commandment I give you, that you love one another,' not as people love one another for their own selfish ends, nor merely on account of their common humanity, but because they are all gods and children of the Most High. They love one another as God loves them so that they may be brothers and sisters of his only Son. He will lead them to the goal that alone will satisfy them, where all their desires will be fulfilled. For when God is all in all, there will be nothing left to desire.

This love is the gift of the Lord who said: 'As I have loved you, so you also must love one another.' His object in loving us, then, was to enable us to love each other. By loving us himself, our mighty head has linked us all together as members of his own body, bound to one another by the tender bond of love.

alternative reading

A Reading from a hymn on the crucifixion
by Ephrem of Syria

Blessed are you, O Upper Room, so small
    in comparison to the entirety of creation,
yet what took place in you
    now fills all creation – which is even too small for it.
Blessed is your abode, for in it was broken
    that Bread which issues from the blessed Wheat Sheaf,
and in you was trodden out
    the Cluster of Grapes that came from Mary
to become the Cup of Salvation.

Blessed are you, O Upper Room,
    no one has ever seen
nor ever shall see, what you beheld;
    Our Lord became at once
True Altar, Priest, Bread, and Cup of Salvation.
    In his own person he could fulfil all these roles,
none other was capable of this:
    Whole Offering and Lamb, Sacrifice and Sacrificer,
Priest and the One destined to be consumed.

A Reading from *A Rule of Life for a Recluse*
by Aelred of Rievaulx

Now then go up with our Lord into the large upper room, furnished for supper, and rejoice to share the delights of the meal which brings us salvation. Let love overcome shyness, affection drive out fear, so that he may at least give you an alms from the crumbs of that table when you beg for something. Or stand at a distance and, like a poor man looking to a rich man, stretch out your hand to receive something. Let your tears declare your hunger.

But when he rises from table, girds himself with the towel and pours water into the basin, consider what majesty it is that is washing and drying the feet of mere mortals, what graciousness it is that touches with his sacred hands the feet of the traitor. Look and wait and, last of all, give him your own feet to wash, because those whom he does not wash will have no part with him.

Why are you in such a hurry to go out now? Wait a little while. Do you see? Who is that, I ask, who is reclining on his breast and bends back his head to lay it in his bosom? Happy is he, whoever he may be. O, I see: his name is John. O John, tell us what sweetness, what grace and tenderness, what light and devotion you are imbibing from that fountain.

There indeed are all the treasures of wisdom and knowledge, the fountain of mercy, the abode of loving kindness, the honeycomb of eternal sweetness.

Good Friday

A Reading from a sermon of Leo the Great

Those who have a true devotion to the passion of the Lord must so contemplate Jesus on the cross with the eyes of their heart that they identify themselves with his flesh. Let the earth tremble when its Redeemer is put to death; let the rocks of faithless hearts be split open; and let those who are imprisoned in the sepulchres of their mortality push off the tombstones that imprison them, and leap forth. May signs of our future resurrection appear today in the holy city, that is, the Church of God, and hearts experience that which our bodies will one day undergo.

The victory of the cross is denied to none of the weak: there is no one on earth who cannot be helped by the prayer of Christ. For if his prayer aided those who insisted on raging against him, how much more will it aid those who turn to him in love? Ignorance has been banished, difficulties have been eased, and the sacred blood of Christ has extinguished the flaming sword of the cherubim which has blocked our path to life. The gloom of the old night has given way to the true light. Christian people everywhere are invited to share the riches of paradise. The road home to that lost country from which we have been in exile is now made plain to all who have been reborn. The way lies open before us all: it was opened even to a thief, and can only be closed through our own fault.

So my dear people, as we celebrate this profound mystery of our redemption, let us acknowledge in the teaching of God's Spirit, the glory we are called to share, and the hope into which we have entered. We must not allow the activities of our life to fill us either with anxiety or pride, so that we are unable to strive with our whole being to be conformed to the pattern of our Redeemer, and to walk in his way. He has achieved and suffered everything necessary for our salvation, so that the power which was in the Head might also be found in us, his body.

alternative reading

A Reading from a sermon of Augustine

The passion of our Lord and Saviour Jesus Christ gives us the confidence of glory and a lesson in the endurance of suffering. Is there anything which the hearts of the faithful may not look forward to through the grace of God? It was not enough that the only Son of God, co-eternal with the Father, should be born among us as one of us, he even died at the hands of those whom he had himself created.

What God promises us for the future is great, but what God has already done for us in Christ is greater still. Who can doubt that he will give us his life, since he has already given us his death? Why is human weakness so slow to believe that we will one day live with God? After all, a much more incredible thing has already happened: God died for us.

For who is this Christ unless that which 'in the beginning was the Word, and the Word was with God, and the Word was God'? This Word of God 'became flesh and dwelt among us'; for in himself he was incapable of dying for us, unless he had assumed mortal flesh from us. In this way the immortal one was able to die; in this way he was able to give his life for mere mortals. Later, he would make them sharers in his divinity, he who had already shared in their humanity. Of ourselves we did not have the ability to live, just as of himself he did not have the ability to die.

In this way Christ secured a wonderful transaction, a transaction of mutual sharing. He died from what was ours; we will live from what is his. Thus, far from being ashamed of the death of the Lord our God, we should have the fullest trust in it; indeed, it should be our greatest boast. For by assuming death from us, death which he found in us, he promised most faithfully to give us life from what is his.

Christ loved us so much that what we deserved because of sin, he who was without sin, suffered on our behalf. Surely then, he who justifies sinners will give us what justice demands. He whose promise is faithful will give us the rewards of his saints, since though without wickedness himself he bore the punishment of the wicked.

So my brothers and sisters, let us acknowledge without fear, indeed, let us announce publicly that Christ was crucified for us. Let us proclaim it not trembling, but rejoicing; not shamefacedly, but boasting. As the apostle Paul said: 'Far be it from me to glory except in the cross of our Lord Jesus Christ.'

A Reading from the treatise *The Tree of Life*
by Bonaventure

What tongue can tell,
what intellect can grasp
the heavy weight of your desolation,
Blessed Virgin?
You were present at all these events,
standing close by and participating in them
in every way.

This blessed and most holy flesh –
which you so chastely conceived,
so sweetly nourished
and fed with your milk,
which you so often held on your lap,
and kissed with your lips –
you actually gazed upon
with your bodily eyes
now torn by the blows of the scourges,
now pierced by the points of the thorns,
now struck by the reed,
now beaten by hands and fists,
now pierced by nails and fixed to the wood of the cross,
and torn by its own weight as it hung there,
now mocked in every way,
finally made to drink gall and vinegar.

But with the eye of your mind
you saw that divine soul
filled with gall of every form of bitterness,
now groaning in spirit,
now quaking with fear,
now wearied,
now in agony,
now in anxiety,
now in confusion,
now oppressed by sadness and sorrow
partly because of his most sensitive response
to bodily pain,

partly because of his most fervent zeal
for the divine honour taken away by sin,
partly because of his pity poured out upon wretched men,
partly because of his compassion for you,
his most sweet mother,
as the sword pierced the depths of your heart,
when with devoted eyes
he looked upon you standing before him
and spoke to you these loving words:
'Woman, behold your son,'
in order to console in its trial your soul,
which he knew had been more deeply pierced
by a sword of compassion
than if you had suffered
in your own body.

alternative reading

A Reading from a sermon of Lancelot Andrewes preached
before King James I on Good Friday 1605

In pain we know the only comfort if we be in it, is to be quickly out of it. This the cross hath not, but is, 'a death of dimensions, a death long in dying'. And it was therefore purposely chosen by them. Blasphemy they condemned him of: then was he to be stoned; that death would have despatched him too soon. They indicted him anew of sedition, not as of a worse fault, but only because crucifying belonged to it; for then he must be whipped first, and that liked them well, and then he must die by inch-meal, not swallow his death at once but taste it, and take it down by little and little. And then he must have his legs and arms broken, and so was their meaning his should have been. Else, I would gladly know to what purpose provided they to have a vessel of vinegar ready in the place, but only that he might not faint with loss of blood, but be kept alive till they might hear his bones crash under the breaking, and so feed their eyes with the spectacle also. The providence of God indeed prevented this last act of cruelty; their will was good though.

And yet all this is but half, and the lesser half by far of the pain of the cross. All this his body endured. Was his soul free the while? No; but suffered as much. As much? nay more, infinitely much more on the spiritual, than his body did on the material cross. For a spiritual cross there was too: all grant a cross beside that which Simon of Cyrene did help him to bear. Great were those pains, and this time too little to show how great; but so great that in all the former he never shrunk, nor once complained, but was as if he scarce felt them. But when these came, they made him complain and cry aloud, 'a strong crying'.

In all those no blood came, but where passages were made for it to come out by, but in this it strained out all over, even at all places at once. This was the pain of 'the press' – so the prophet calleth it, wherewith as if he had been in the wine-press, all his garments were stained and gored with blood. Certainly the blood of Gethsemane was another manner of blood than that of Gabbatha, or that of Golgotha either; and that was the blood of his internal cross. Of the three passions that was the hardest to endure, yet that did he endure too. It is that which belief itself doth wonder how it doth believe, save that it knoweth as well the love as the power of God to be without bounds; and his wisdom as able to find, how through love it might be humbled, as exalted through power, beyond the uttermost that man's wit can comprehend.

alternative reading

A Reading from a poem by George Herbert

The Agony

Philosophers have measur'd mountains,
Fathom'd the depths of seas, of states, and kings,
Walk'd with a staff to heav'n, and traced fountains:
But there are two vast, spacious things,
The which to measure it doth more behove:
Yet few there are that sound them: Sin and Love.

Who would know Sin, let him repair
Unto Mount Olivet; there shall he see
A man so wrung with pains, that all his hair,
His skin, his garments bloody be.
Sin is that press and vice, which forceth pain
To hunt his cruel food through ev'ry vein.

Who knows not Love, let him assay
And taste that juice, which on the cross a pike
Did set again abroach; then let him say
If ever he did taste the like.
Love is that liquor sweet and most divine,
Which my God feels as blood; but I, as wine.

alternative reading

A Reading from *Peter Abelard* by Helen Waddell

From somewhere near them in the woods a cry rose, a thin cry, of
such intolerable anguish that Abelard turned dizzy on his feet, and
caught at the wall of the hut. 'It's a child's voice,' he said.

Thibault had gone outside. The cry came again. 'A rabbit,' said
Thibault. He listened. 'It'll be in a trap. Hugh told me he was
putting them down.'

'O God,' Abelard muttered. 'Let it die quickly.'

But the cry came yet again. He plunged through a thicket of
hornbeam. 'Watch out,' said Thibault, thrusting past him. 'The trap
might take the hand off you.'

The rabbit stopped shrieking when they stooped over it, either
from exhaustion, or in some last extremity of fear. Thibault held
the teeth of the trap apart, and Abelard gathered up the little
creature in his hands. It lay for a moment breathing quickly, then
in some blind recognition of the kindness that had met it at the
last, the small head thrust and nestled against his arm, and it died.

It was that last confiding thrust that broke Abelard's heart. He
looked down at the little draggled body, his mouth shaking.
'Thibault,' he said, 'do you think there is a God at all? Whatever
has come to me, I earned it. But what did this one do?'

Thibault nodded.

'I know,' he said. 'Only, I think God is in it too.'

Abelard looked up sharply.

'In it? Do you mean that it makes him suffer, the way it does
us?'

Again Thibault nodded.

'Then why doesn't he stop it?'

'I don't know,' said Thibault. 'Unless it's like the prodigal son. I
suppose the father could have kept him at home against his will.
But what would have been the use? All this,' he stroked the limp

body, 'is because of us. But all the time God suffers. More than we do.'

Abelard looked at him, perplexed. 'Thibault, do you mean Calvary?'

Thibault shook his head. 'That was only a piece of it – the piece that we saw – in time. Like that.' He pointed to a fallen tree beside them, sawn through the middle. 'That dark ring there, it goes up and down the whole length of the tree. But you only see it where it is cut across. That is what Christ's life was; the bit of God that we saw. And we think God is like that, because Christ was like that, kind, and forgiving sins and healing people. We think God is like that for ever, because it happened once, with Christ. But not the pain. Not the agony at the last. We think that stopped.'

Abelard looked at him, the blunt nose and the wide mouth, the honest troubled eyes. He could have knelt before him.

'Then, Thibault,' he said slowly, 'you think that all this,' he looked down at the little quiet body in his arms, 'all the pain of the world, was Christ's cross?'

'God's cross,' said Thibault. 'And it goes on.'

Easter Eve

A Reading from a homily of Ephrem of Syria

Death trampled our Lord underfoot, but he in his turn treated death as a highroad for his own feet. He submitted to it, enduring it willingly, because by this means he would be able to destroy death in spite of itself. Death had its own way when our Lord went out from Jerusalem carrying his cross: but when by a loud cry from that cross he summoned the dead from the underworld, death was powerless to prevent it.

Death slew him by means of the body which he had assumed, but that same body proved to be the weapon with which he conquered death. In slaying our Lord, death itself was slain. It was able to kill natural human life, but was itself killed by the life that is above the nature of mortals. Death could not devour our Lord unless he possessed a body, neither could hell swallow him up unless he bore our flesh; and so he came in search of a chariot in which to ride to the underworld. This chariot was the body which he received from the Virgin; in it he invaded death's fortress, broke open its strongroom and scattered all its treasure.

At length he came upon Eve the mother of all the living. She was that vineyard whose enclosure her own hands had enabled death to violate, so that she could taste its fruit; thus the mother of all the living became the source of death for every living creature. But in her stead Mary grew up a new vine in place of the old. Christ, the new life, dwelt within her. When death, with its customary impudence, came foraging for her mortal fruit, it encountered its own destruction in the hidden life that fruit contained. All unsuspecting, it swallowed him up, and in so doing released life itself and set free a multitude.

He who was also the carpenter's glorious son set up his cross above death's all-consuming jaws, and led the human race into the dwelling place of life. Since a tree had brought about the downfall of humankind, it was upon a tree that humankind crossed over to the realm of life. Bitter was the branch that had once been grafted upon that ancient tree, but sweet the young shoot that has now been grafted in, the shoot in which we are meant to recognise the Lord whom no creature can resist.

We give glory to you, Lord, who raised up your cross to span the jaws of death like a bridge by which souls might pass from the region of the dead to the land of the living. We give glory to you who put on the body of a single mortal and made it the source of life for every other mortal. You are incontestably alive. Your murderers sowed your living body in the earth as farmers sow grain, but it sprang up and yielded an abundant harvest of people raised from the dead.

Come then, my brothers and sisters, let us offer our Lord the great and all-embracing sacrifice of our love, pouring out our treasury of hymns and prayers before him who offered his cross in sacrifice to God for the enrichment of us all.

alternative reading

A Reading from an ancient hymn of the Syriac Church
commemorating Christ's descent into hell

I stretched out my hands and offered myself to the Lord.
The stretching out of my hands is the sign of my offering,
The stretching out on the wood
Where the Just One was hanged, there by the roadside.

Hell saw me and was vanquished.
Death let me depart, and many with me.
I was gall and vinegar to it.
I descended with it to the depths of hell.

Death could not bear my face.
I made of the dead an assembly of the living.
I spoke to them with living lips
So that my word should not be in vain.

They ran towards me, the dead.
They cried out, 'Take pity on us, O Son of God!
Deliver us out of the darkness that fetters us.
Open the gate for us that we may go out with you.
We see that death has no hold on you.
Deliver us also, for you are our Saviour!'

And I heard their voices and I traced my name on their heads.
So they are free and they belong to me.
Alleluia!

EASTER

Yesterday I was crucified with Christ;
  today I am glorified with him.
Yesterday I was dead with Christ;
  today I am sharing in his resurrection.
Yesterday I was buried with him;
  today I am waking with him from the sleep of death.

Gregory of Nazianzus

Easter Day is the Sunday of Sundays, the first day of a new creation: 'This is the day that the Lord has made: let us rejoice and be glad in it.' In the early Church catechumens were baptized at the Easter liturgy. New converts entered sacramentally into Christ's redeeming death and resurrection at the same time as the whole Church celebrated its memorial of those events. By ancient custom, therefore, the readings during Eastertide meditate not only upon the victory and resurrection of Christ, but also upon the reality of the Church as the baptized community. Prominent among the readings will be found various addresses to the newly baptized.

Recent liturgical reform has sought to recover and strengthen the unity of the season – the **Great Fifty Days** which runs from Easter Day until and including Pentecost. Within Eastertide the feast of the **Ascension** enjoys a special status as a celebration of Christ's triumphant exaltation. The nine days that follow it are observed as a time of preparation and waiting upon the outpouring of the Holy Spirit.

Pentecost, the Jewish Feast of Weeks, falls on the fiftieth day after Passover. It marked the completion of the barley harvest. From at least the inter-testamental period, Pentecost was also seen as the anniversary of the giving of the law on Mount Sinai. It was in commemoration of this that the disciples had assembled in Jerusalem. As the Fathers pointed out, whereas the giving of the law was accompanied by thunder and lightning, the birth of the Church was accomplished when the new law of love was written with the fire of the Holy Ghost upon the pages of the human heart.

'We are an Easter people and alleluia is our song.'

Easter Day

The Easter Sermon, ascribed to John Chrysostom,
which is traditionally read in the Orthodox Church
at the climax of the Easter Liturgy

If any be lovers of God, let them rejoice in this beautiful and radiant feast.

If any be faithful servants, let them gladly enter into the joy of their Lord.

If any are wearied with fasting, let them now reap their reward.

If any have laboured from the first hour, let them receive today their just wages.

If any have come after the third hour, let them celebrate the feast with thankfulness.

If any have arrived after the sixth hour, let them not doubt, for they will sustain no loss.

If any have delayed until the ninth hour, let them not hesitate but draw near.

If any have arrived only at the eleventh hour, let them not be ashamed because they have arrived so late. For the Master is gracious and welcomes the last no less than the first. He gives rest to those who come at the eleventh hour just as kindly as those who have laboured since dawn. The first he fills to overflowing: on the last he has compassion. To the one he grants his favour, to the other pardon. He does not look only at the work: he looks into the intention of the heart.

Enter then, all of you, into the joy of your Master. First and last, receive alike your reward. Rich and poor, dance together. You who have fasted and you who have not, rejoice today. The table is fully laden: let all enjoy it. The fatted calf is served: let no one go away hungry. Come, all of you, share in the banquet of faith: draw on the wealth of his mercy.

Let no one lament their poverty; for the universal kingdom has been revealed. Let no one weep for their sins; for the light of forgiveness has risen from the grave. Let no one fear death; for the death of the Saviour has set us free.

He has destroyed death by undergoing death.

He has despoiled hell by descending into hell.

Hell was filled with bitterness when it tasted his flesh, as Isaiah foretold: 'Hell was filled with bitterness when it met you face to face below' –

filled with bitterness, for it was brought to nothing;

filled with bitterness, for it was mocked;
filled with bitterness, for it was overthrown;
filled with bitterness, for it was destroyed;
filled with bitterness, for it was put in chains.
It received a body, and encountered God. It received earth, and confronted heaven. It received what it saw, and was overpowered by what it did not see.

O death, where is your sting?
O hell, where is your victory?
Christ is risen, and you are cast down.
Christ is risen, and the demons are fallen.
Christ is risen, and the angels rejoice.
Christ is risen, and life reigns in freedom.
Christ is risen, and the grave is emptied of the dead.

For Christ, being raised from the dead, has become the first-fruits of those who sleep. To him be the glory and dominion to the ages of ages. Amen.

alternative reading

A Reading from a sermon of Lancelot Andrewes,
preached before King James I at Whitehall
on Easter Day 1620

The risen Christ comes unknown, stands by Mary Magdalene, and she little thought it had been he. Not only not knew him, but mis-knew him, took him for the gardener. Tears will dim the sight, and it was not yet scarce day, and she seeing one, and not knowing what any one should make in the ground so early but he that dressed it, she might well mistake. But it was more than so; her eyes were not holden only that she did not know him, but over and beside he did appear in some such shape as might resemble the gardener whom she took him for.
 Proper enough it was, it fitted well the time and place, this person. The time, it was the spring; the place, it was the garden: that place is most in request at that time, for that place and time a gardener doth well.
 Yet Mary did not mistake in taking him for a gardener; though she might seem to err in some sense, yet in some other she was in

Easter

the right. For in a sense, and a good sense, Christ may well be said to be a gardener, and indeed is one.

A gardener he is. The first, the fairest garden that ever was, paradise, he was the gardener, for it was of his planting. And ever since it is he as God makes all our gardens green, sends us yearly the spring, and all the herbs and flowers we then gather; and neither Paul with his planting, nor Apollos with his watering, could do any good without him. So he is a gardener in that sense.

But not in that alone. He it is that gardens our 'souls' too, and makes them, as the prophet Jeremiah saith, 'like a well-watered garden'; weeds out of them whatsoever is noisome or unsavoury, sows and plants them with true roots and seeds of righteousness, waters them with the dew of his grace, and makes them bring forth fruit to eternal life.

Christ rising was indeed a gardener, and that a strange one, who made such an herb grow out of the ground this day as the like was never seen before, a dead body to shoot forth alive out of the grave.

But I ask, was he so this day alone? No, but this profession of his, this day begun, he will follow to the end. For he it is that by virtue of this morning's act shall garden our bodies too, turn all our graves into garden plots; yea, shall one day turn land and sea and all into a great garden, and so husband them as they shall in due time bring forth live bodies, even all our bodies alive again.

Mary Magdalene standing by the grave's side, and there weeping, is brought to represent unto us the state of all mankind before this day, the day of Christ's rising again, weeping over the dead. But Christ quickened her, and her spirits that were good as dead. You thought you should have come to Christ's resurrection today, and so you do. But not to his alone, but even to Mary Magdalene's resurrection too. For in very deed a kind of resurrection it was was wrought in her; revived as it were, and raised from a dead and drooping, to a lively and cheerful estate. The gardener had done his part, made her all green on the sudden.

A Reading from a poem by Edmund Spenser

Easter

Most glorious Lord of life, that on this day,
Didst make thy triumph over death and sin:
And having harrowed hell, didst bring away
Captivity thence captive us to win:
This joyous day, dear Lord, with joy begin,
And grant that we, for whom thou diddest die,
Being with thy dear blood clean washed from sin,
May live for ever in felicity.
And that thy love we weighing worthily,
May likewise love thee for the same again:
And for thy sake that all like dear didst buy,
With love may one another entertain.
So let us love, dear love, like as we ought,
Love is the lesson which the Lord us taught.

alternative reading

A Reading from a poem by George Herbert

Easter

Rise heart; thy Lord is risen. Sing his praise
Without delays,
Who takes thee by the hand, that thou likewise
With him mayst rise:
That, as his death calcined thee to dust,
His life may make thee gold, and much more, just.

Awake, my lute, and struggle for thy part
With all thy art.
The cross taught all wood to resound his name,
Who bore the same.
His stretched sinews taught all strings, what key
Is best to celebrate this most high day.

Consort both heart and lute, and twist a song
Pleasant and long:
Or, since all music is but three parts vied
And multiplied,
O let thy blessed Spirit bear a part,
And make up our defects with his sweet art.

Monday of Easter Week

A Reading from a paschal homily of Melito of Sardis

Beloved, you must understand that the paschal mystery we
celebrate is both ancient and new, transient and eternal, corruptible
and incorruptible, mortal and immortal. In terms of the law it is
ancient, but in terms of the Word it is new. It is transient as a
passing figure, eternal in the grace it signifies. It is corruptible in
the slaughter of the lamb, but incorruptible in the eternal life of the
Lord. It is mortal because of his burial in the earth, but immortal
because of his resurrection from the dead.

Christ was slain as a lamb; he rose again as God. As Scripture
says: 'He was led like a sheep to the slaughter,' and yet, of course,
he was not a sheep. He was silent as a lamb, yet he was not a lamb.
The figure has passed away; the reality has come. God has come in
the place of the lamb; a human being has come in place of a sheep;
and that person is Christ, who fills all creation.

The sacrifice of the lamb, the celebration of the Passover, and
the regulations of the law have been fulfilled in Jesus Christ.
Under the ancient law, and still more under the new dispensation,
everything pointed towards Christ. Both the law and the Word
came forth from Zion and Jerusalem, but now the law has given
place to the Word, the ancient to the new. The commandment has
become grace, the figure a reality. The lamb has become a Son, the
sheep a human being, and humanity has become divine.

He who suspended the earth is suspended; he who fastened the
heavens is himself fastened; he who fixed the universe is now
fixed on wood: God has been murdered.

God has clothed himself in humanity. For me a sufferer he has
suffered; for one who was in prison, he was made captive; for one
who was condemned, he has been judged; for one who was buried

in the grave, he has been buried. But now he is risen from the dead. He cries out:

'Who will contend with me? Let them confront me.
I have freed those who were condemned;
I have given life to those who were dead;
I have raised up the dead from their graves.
Who will dispute my cause?
I am the Christ.
I have abolished death;
I have triumphed over the enemy;
I have trampled hell underfoot;
I have bound the strong one, and I have raised humanity up to
    the heights of heaven: Yes, I am the Christ.

Come, then, all you nations, receive forgiveness for the sins that
    defile you. For I am your forgiveness.
I am the Passover that brings salvation.
I am the lamb who was slain for you.
I am your ransom, your life, your resurrection, your light.
I am your salvation and your king.
I will raise you to the heights of heaven.
With my own right hand I will raise you up, and I will show you
    the eternal Father.'

Tuesday of Easter Week

A Reading from a commentary on the psalms by
Augustine

Our thoughts in this present life should turn on the praise of God, because it is in praising God that we shall rejoice for ever in the life to come; and one cannot be ready for the next life unless trained for it now. So we praise God during our earthly life, and at the same time we make our petitions to him. Our praise is expressed with joy, our petitions with yearning. We have been promised something because the promise was made by one who keeps his word, we trust him and are glad; but insofar as possession is delayed, we can only long and yearn for it. It is good for us to persevere in longing until we receive what was promised, and yearning is over; then praise alone will remain.

Because there are these two periods of time – the one that now is, beset with the trials and troubles of this life, and the other yet to come, a life of everlasting serenity and joy – we are given two liturgical seasons, one before Easter and the other after. The season before Easter signifies the troubles in which we live here and now, while the time after Easter which we are celebrating at present signifies the happiness that will be ours in the future. What we commemorate before Easter is what we experience in this life; what we celebrate after Easter points to something we do not yet possess. This is why we keep the first season with fasting and prayer; but now the fast is over and we devote the present season to praise. Such is the meaning of the 'Alleluia' we sing.

Both these periods are represented and demonstrated for us in Christ our head. The Lord's passion depicts for us our present life of trial. It shows how we must suffer and be afflicted and finally die. The Lord's resurrection and glorification show us the life that will be given to us in the future.

Now, therefore, we urge you to praise God. That is what we are all telling each other when we sing 'Alleluia'. You say to your neighbour: 'Praise the Lord!' and your neighbour says the same to you. We are all urging one another to praise the Lord, and all thereby doing what each of us urges the other to do. But see that your praise comes from your whole being; in other words, see that you praise God not with your lips and voices alone, but with your minds, your lives and all your actions.

We are praising God now, assembled as we are here in church; but when we go our separate ways again, it seems as if we cease to praise God. But provided we do not cease to live a good life, we shall always be praising God. You cease to praise God only when you swerve from justice and from what is pleasing to God. If you never turn aside from the good life, your tongue may be silent but your actions will cry aloud, and God will perceive your intentions; for as our ears hear each other's voices, so do God's ears hear our thoughts.

Wednesday of Easter Week

A Reading from *Resurrection* by Rowan Williams

When we read the Gospels it is hard to dismiss the consistent echo of disorientation and surprise concerning the resurrection. A chronicle of Easter Day would be a hopeless enterprise. Perhaps all we can recover across the centuries is the piercing note of shock; and that says a great deal.

Even in the Gospels, one thing is never described. There is a central silence, not broken until the second century, about the *event* of resurrection. Even Matthew, with his elaborate mythological scenery, leaves us with the strange impression that the stone is rolled away from a tomb that is empty. Jesus is not released by an angel (like Luke's Peter in Acts), but raised by the Father. It is an event which is not describable, because it is precisely there that there occurs the transfiguring expansion of Jesus' humanity which is the heart of the resurrection encounters. It is an event on the frontier of any possible language, because it is the moment in which our speech is both left behind and opened to new possibilities. It is as indescribable as the process of imaginative fusion which produces any metaphor; and the evangelists withdraw, as well they might.

Jesus' life is historical, describable; the encounters with Jesus risen are historical and (after a fashion) describable, with whatever ambiguities and unclarities. But there is a sense in which the *raising* of Jesus, the hinge between these two histories, the act which brings the latter out of the former, does not and cannot belong to history: it is not an event, with a before and after, occupying a determinate bit of time between Friday and Sunday. God's act in uniting Jesus' life with his eludes us: we can speak of it only as the necessary condition for our living as we live. And as a divine act it cannot be tied to place and time in any simple way. It is, indeed, an 'eternal' act: it is an aspect of the eternal will by which God determines how he shall be, his will to be the Father of the Son. These are abstract words, they describe nothing. They can only point to the truth that God's being and will are always and necessarily *prior* to ours. The event of resurrection, then, cannot but be hidden in God's eternal act, his eternal being himself; however early we run to the tomb, God has been there ahead of us. Once again, he decisively evades our grasp, our definition and our projection.

Thursday of Easter Week

A Reading from the instructions of Cyril of Jerusalem
to the newly baptized

You were led to the holy pool of divine baptism, as Christ was carried from the cross to the sepulchre which is before our eyes. And each of you was asked whether you believed in the name of the Father, and of the Son, and of the Holy Spirit, and you made that saving confession, and descended three times into the water, and ascended again; in so doing covertly pointing by a figure at the three-days burial of Christ. For as our Saviour passed three days and three nights in the heart of the earth, so you also in your first ascent out of the water represented the first day of Christ in the earth, and by your descent, the night; for as he who is in the night sees no more, but he who is in the day remains in the light, so in descending you saw nothing as in the night, but in ascending again you were as in the day. And at the self-same moment, you died and were born; and that water of salvation was at once your grave and your mother. And what Solomon spoke of others will suit you also: for he said: 'There is a time to be born and a time to die'; but to you, on the contrary, the time to die is also the time to be born; and one and the same season brings about both of these, and your birth went hand in hand with your death.

O strange and inconceivable thing! We did not really die, we were not really buried, we were not really crucified and raised again, but our imitation was merely in a figure, while our salvation is in reality. Christ was actually crucified, and actually buried, and truly rose again; and all these things have been vouchsafed to us, that we, by imitation communicating in his sufferings, might gain salvation in reality. O surpassing loving-kindness! Christ received the nails in his undefiled hands and feet and endured anguish; while to me without suffering or toil, by fellowship of his pain he vouchsafes salvation.

Let no one then suppose that baptism is merely the grace of remission of sins, or that of adoption, as John's baptism bestowed only the remission of sins. Indeed we know full well that as it purges our sins, and conveys to us the gift of the Holy Spirit, so also it is the counterpart of Christ's sufferings. For this reason Paul cried aloud and says: 'Know you not that as many of us as were baptized into Christ Jesus were baptized into his death? Therefore we are buried with him by baptism into death.'

Friday of Easter Week

A Reading from a treatise *On Flight from the World*
by Ambrose of Milan

Where your heart is, there will your treasure be also. God is not accustomed to refusing a good gift to those who ask for one. Since he is good, and especially to those who are faithful to him, let us hold fast to him with all our soul, our heart, our strength, and so enjoy his light and see his glory and possess the grace of supernatural joy. Let us reach out with our hearts to possess that good, let us exist in it and live in it, let us hold fast to it, that good which is beyond all we can know or see and is marked by perpetual peace and tranquillity, a peace which is beyond all we can know or understand.

This is the good that permeates creation. In it we all live; on it we all depend. It has nothing above it; it is divine. No one is good but God alone. What is good is therefore divine, and what is divine is therefore good. Scripture says: 'When you open your hand all things will be filled with goodness.' It is through God's goodness that all that is truly good is given us, and in it there is no admixture of evil. These good things are promised by Scripture to those who are faithful: 'The good things of the land will be your food.'

We have died with Christ. We carry about in our bodies the sign of his death, so that the living Christ may also be revealed in us. The life we live is not now our ordinary life but the life of Christ: a life of sinlessness, of chastity, of simplicity and every other virtue. We have risen with Christ. Let us live in Christ, let us ascend in Christ, so that the serpent may not have the power here below to wound us in the heel.

Let us take refuge from this world. You can do this in spirit, even if you are kept here in the body. You can at the same time be here and present to the Lord. Your soul must hold fast to him, you must follow after him in your thoughts, you must tread his ways by faith, not in outward show. You must take refuge in him. He is your refuge and your strength. David addresses him in these words in one of the psalms: 'I fled to you for refuge, and I was not disappointed.'

Since God is our refuge, God who is in heaven and above the heavens, we must take refuge from this world in that place where there is peace, where there is rest from toil, where we can celebrate the great sabbath, as Moses said: 'The sabbaths of the land will provide you with food.' To rest in the Lord and to see his joy is like a banquet, and full of gladness and tranquillity.

Let us take refuge like deer beside the fountain of waters. Let our soul thirst, as David thirsted, for the fountain. And what is that fountain? Listen to David again: 'With you is the fountain of life.' Let my soul say to this fountain: 'When shall I come and see you face to face?' For the fountain is God himself.

Saturday of Easter Week

A Reading from *True Resurrection* by Harry Williams

If we have been aware of resurrection in this life, then, and only then, shall we be able or ready to receive the hopes of final resurrection after physical death. Resurrection as our final and ultimate future can be known only by those who perceive resurrection with us now encompassing all we are and do. For only then will it be recognised as a country we have already entered and in whose light and warmth we have already lived.

The possibility of the body's resurrection now in the present is thus of no mere theoretical interest. It is a matter of urgent concern to us all. What does it mean?

It means my body being raised up to its own life. It means mind and body no longer making war on each other in a bid for domination, but recognising that they are both equally me. When I can feel that I am my body, and that this does not in any way contradict the fact that I am my mind, then I shall have had experience of resurrection. For it is death which separates and life which unites. To be raised to life, therefore, is to discover that I am one person. In the experience of resurrection body and mind are no longer felt to be distinct. They function as a single entity. When I feel that my body is me, and that this is the same as my mind being me, then what I am feeling is that I am me. It is an experience which has come to most of us at some time or other. But it is generally a temporary experience which is quickly forgotten, for the bias of our basic assumptions is against it and our fear soon once again takes control. The battle for domination reasserts itself. Body and mind fall apart and compete with each other for the prize of being me. And in their falling apart the disintegration of death has set in.

Yet the experience of resurrection returns and I know myself again as one person for whom to be body is to be mind and to be mind is to be body. And this experience of oneness within myself invariably brings with it the experience of oneness with the external world. I no longer feel separated from the people and things I live among. While remaining fully themselves and preserving their own inalienable identity, they also become part of what I am. The separation between me and them is overcome so that I share an identity with them. My own resurrection is also the resurrection of the world.

The Second Sunday of Easter

A Reading from a sermon of Augustine
for the Octave of Easter

I speak to you who have just been reborn in baptism, my little children in Christ, you who are the new offspring of the Church, gift of the Father, proof of Mother Church's fruitfulness. All of you who stand fast in the Lord are a holy seed, a new colony of bees, the very flower of our ministry and fruit of our toil, my joy and my crown. The words of the Apostle I address to you: 'Put on the Lord Jesus Christ, and make no provision for the flesh and its desires,' so that you may be clothed with the life of him whom you have put on in this sacrament. 'You have all been clothed with Christ by your baptism in him. There is neither Jew nor Greek; there is neither slave nor free; there is neither male nor female; you are all one in Christ Jesus.'

Such is the power of this sacrament: it is a sacrament of new life which begins here and now with the forgiveness of all past sins, and will be brought to completion in the resurrection of the dead. 'You have been buried with Christ by baptism into death in order that, as Christ has risen from the dead, you also may walk in newness of life.'

You are walking now by faith, still on pilgrimage in a mortal body away from the Lord; but he to whom your steps are directed is himself the sure and certain way for you: Jesus Christ, who for our sake became human. For all who fear him he has stored up abundant happiness, which he will reveal to those who hope in him, bringing it to completion when we have attained the reality which even now we possess in hope.

This is the octave day of your new birth. Today is fulfilled in you the sign of faith that was prefigured in the Old Testament by the circumcision of the flesh on the eighth day after birth. When the Lord rose from the dead, he put off the mortality of the flesh; his risen body was still the same body but it was no longer subject to death. By his resurrection he consecrated Sunday, or the Lord's day. Though the third after his passion, this day is the eighth after the Sabbath, and thus also the first day of the week.

And so your own hope of resurrection, though not yet realised, is sure and certain, because you have received the sacrament or sign of this reality, and have been given the pledge of the Spirit. 'If, then, you have risen with Christ, seek the things that are above, where Christ is seated at the right hand of God. Set your hearts on heavenly things, not the things that are on earth. For you have died and your life is hidden with Christ in God. When Christ, your life, appears, then you too will appear with him in glory.'

alternative reading

A Reading from a homily of Gregory the Great

'Thomas, called the Twin, who was one of the twelve, was not with them when Jesus came.' Thomas was the only disciple missing. When he returned and heard what had happened, he refused to believe what he heard. The Lord came again and offered his side to his sceptical disciple to touch. He showed his hands; and by showing the scars of his wounds he healed the wound of Thomas' unbelief.

What conclusion, dear sisters and brothers, do you draw from this? Do you think it was by chance that this chosen disciple was absent? Or that on his return he heard, that hearing he doubted, that doubting he touched, and touching he believed? This did not happen by chance, but by the providence of God. Divine mercy brought it about most wonderfully, so that when that doubting disciple touched his Master's wounded flesh he healed the wound of our unbelief as well as his own. Thomas' scepticism was more advantageous to us than was the faith of the other disciples who believed. When he was led to faith by actually touching Jesus, our hearts were relieved of all doubt, for our faith is made whole.

After his resurrection Jesus allowed this disciple to doubt, and he did not desert him in his doubt. He became a witness to the reality of the resurrection. Thomas touched him and cried out: 'My Lord and my God.' Jesus said to him: 'Because you have seen me, Thomas, you have believed.' When the apostle Paul says that 'faith is the guarantee of the blessings that we hope for, the proof of the realities that are unseen,' it is clear that faith provides the proof of those things that are not evident; visible things do not require faith, they command recognition. Why, when Thomas saw and touched him, did Jesus say: 'Because you have seen me, you have believed'? What Thomas saw was one thing; what he believed, was another. A mortal could not have seen God. Thomas saw a human being, but by his words, 'My Lord and my God', he acknowledged his divinity. It was by seeing that he believed. He recognised the reality of the man and testified that he was the invisible God.

Let us rejoice at what follows: 'Blessed are they who have not seen and have believed.' This expression makes special reference to us for we have not seen him in the flesh but know him in the mind. The reference is for us, but only if we follow up our faith with good works. Those who give expression to their faith are the genuine believers.

Monday after Easter 2

A Reading from the Letter of Clement of Rome
to the Church in Corinth

Reflect, my dear friends, how the Lord keeps reminding us of the resurrection that is to come, of which he has made the Lord Jesus Christ the firstfruits by raising him from the dead. My friends, look at the processes of resurrection that are occurring at this very time. Day and night show us an example of it; the night lies in sleep, day rises again; the day departs, night comes again. Or think about the harvest; how does a crop come into existence, and in what way? The sower goes out and casts each seed onto the ground. Dry and bare, they fall into the earth and decay. Then the greatness of the Lord's providence raises them up again from decay, and out of one grain many are produced and yield their fruit.

In this hope then, let our hearts be bound fast to him who is faithful in his promises and just in his judgements. He forbade us to tell lies; still less will he tell a lie himself. Nothing is impossible for God except to lie. So let our faith in him be rekindled; let us reflect that everything that exists is close to him.

By the word of his power he established all things, and by his word he can reduce them to ruin. 'Who shall say to him: What have you done? Or who can withstand the power of his might?' He will accomplish everything when he wills and as he wills, and nothing that he has decreed shall pass away. All things stand in his presence, and nothing lies hidden from his counsel. 'The heavens tell forth the glory of God, and the firmament reveals the work of his hands: day speaks to day, and night to night proclaims knowledge; yet there are no words, no speeches, and their voices are not heard.'

Since all things lie open to his eyes and ears, let us hold God in awe and rid ourselves of our hateful fondness for making mischief, so that we may find shelter in his mercy from the judgement that is to come. Which of us can escape his mighty hand? And what sort of world would ever give asylum to one who runs away from God? As it says in the psalms: 'Where can I go, where can I hide from his face? If I go up to heaven, you are there; if I go to the ends of the earth, your right hand is there; if I lie down in the grave, your spirit is there.' Where, then, can one go, where can one escape from the presence of God whose hands embrace the entire universe?

Let us then approach him in holiness of soul, raising up to him hands pure and undefiled, out of love for our good and merciful Father who has chosen us to be his own.

Tuesday after Easter 2

A Reading from a commentary on St John's Gospel
by Augustine

The Lord has marked out for us the fullness of love that we ought to have for each other. He tells us: 'No one has greater love than those who lay down their lives for their friends.' In these words, the Lord tells us what the perfect love we should have for one another involves. John, the evangelist who recorded them, draws this conclusion in one of his letters: 'As Christ laid down his life for us, so we too ought to lay down our lives for our sisters and brothers. We should indeed love one another as he loved us, he who laid down his life for us.'

This is surely what is meant when we read in the Proverbs of Solomon: 'If you sit down to eat at the table of a ruler, observe carefully what is set before you; then stretch out your hand, knowing that you must provide the same kind of meal yourself.' What is this ruler's table if not the one at which we receive the body and blood of him who laid down his life for us? What does it mean to sit at this table if not to approach it with humility? What does it mean to observe carefully what is set before you if not to meditate devoutly on so great a gift? What does it mean to stretch out one's hand, knowing that one must provide the same kind of meal oneself, if not what I have just said, namely, that as Christ laid down his life for us, so we in our turn ought to lay down our lives for our sisters and brothers? This is what the apostle Peter said: 'Christ suffered for us, leaving us an example, that we should follow in his footsteps.'

This must not be understood as saying that we can be the Lord's equals by bearing witness to him even to the extent of shedding our blood. He had the power of laying down his life; we by contrast cannot choose the length of our lives, and we die even if it is against our will. He, by dying, destroyed death in himself; we are freed from death only in his death. His body did not see corruption; our body will see corruption and only then be clothed through him in incorruption at the end of the world. He needed no help from us in saving us; without him we can do nothing. He gave himself to us as the vine to the branches; apart from him we cannot have life.

Finally, even if kindred die for kindred, yet no martyr by shedding blood brings forgiveness for the sins of others, as Christ brought forgiveness to us. In this he gave us, not an example to imitate but a reason for rejoicing. Let us then love one another as Christ also loved us and gave himself up for us.

Wednesday after Easter 2

A Reading from an ancient paschal homily
by an unknown author

Jesus has shown in his own person all the fullness of life offered on the tree of the cross.

For me this tree is a plant of eternal health. I feed on it; by its roots I find stability; by its branches I reach out to others. I rejoice in its dew; I am invigorated by the rustling of its leaves. I freely enjoy its fruits as if they were meant just for me from the beginning of the world. It is my food when I am hungry; it is my fountain when I am thirsty; it is my very clothing, for its leaves are the spirit of life.

The tree of which I speak has celestial dimensions, reaching from earth to heaven, a plant of eternity which is planted in both heaven and earth, the foundation of the universe, gathering under its canopy all the diverse peoples of the world, fastened by invisible nails of the Spirit, so that its link with divine power may never be broken.

O divine crucifixion! Your reach extends everywhere and embraces all things. O unique event, whose singularity gathers all things into unity!

Even Hades knew the divine coming. Christ gave himself up completely to death, so that the devouring beast might be secretly poisoned. It searched everywhere in his sinless body for food, but when it found nothing in him that it could eat, it was imprisoned in itself: it was starved to death, it was its own death.

O heavenly Easter! By you, O Christ, the darkness of death has been destroyed and life poured out on every creature. The gates of heaven stand open: God himself has revealed himself in human form and humanity has ascended and become God!

Thanks to you the gates of hell have been shattered. Thanks to you the great banqueting hall is full for the marriage feast, the guests are dressed in their wedding attire, and no one will be cast out into the darkness. Thanks to you the fire of love is burning in all, in spirit and body, fuelled by the very oil of the risen Christ.

Thursday after Easter 2

A Reading from *The Resurrection of Christ*
by Michael Ramsey

The good news that Jesus proclaimed was the coming of the reign of God. The reign had come. Both the teaching and the mighty works of the messiah bore witness to it. The teaching unfolded the righteousness of the kingdom, and summoned men and women to receive it. The mighty works asserted the claims of the kingdom over the whole range of human life. The healing of the sick; the exorcism of devils; the restoration of the maimed, the deaf, the dumb, and the blind; the feeding of the hungry; the forgiveness of sinners; all these had their place among the works of the kingdom. But though the kingdom was indeed here in the midst of them, neither the teaching nor the mighty works could enable its coming in all its fullness. For the classic enemies – sin and death – could be dealt with only by a mightier blow, a blow which the death of the messiah himself alone could strike. And the righteousness of the kingdom could not be perfected by a teaching and an example for others to follow; it involved a personal union of man with Christ himself, a sharing in his own death and risen life. Thus he has a baptism to be baptized with, and he was straitened until it was accomplished. But when it was accomplished there was not only a gospel in words preached by Jesus, but a gospel in deeds embodied in Jesus himself, living, dying, conquering death. There is a hint at the identity between the gospel of Jesus and the person of Jesus in the arresting words 'for my sake and the gospel's'.

Thus it was that the gospel preached by Jesus became merged into the gospel that is Jesus. This is the gospel which the apostles preach. It is still the gospel of God. It is still the gospel of the kingdom. But its content is Jesus. The striking phrase 'to gospel Jesus' appears in the Acts of the Apostles. The apostles preach his life, death, resurrection and gift of the Spirit; for all this constitutes the drama of the mighty acts of God who came to deliver and to reign.

Friday after Easter 2

A Reading from a sermon of Mark Frank

The angel answered and said unto the women: 'Fear not; for I know that ye seek Jesus which was crucified. He is not here: for he is risen, as he said. Come, see the place where the Lord lay.'

But is he not here? What do we, then, here today? 'Come, see the place where the Lord lay.' – why, it is not worth the seeing now; it is but a sad place now he is gone.

Our Lord, indeed, is gone, but risen and gone away himself. Had we found him here in the grave, it had been sad indeed. He had been lost, and we had been lost, and both lost for ever.

The pious women came early to the sepulchre to embalm their master's body; whilst they yet stood without for fear, this angel that sat before the stone spoke to them. Scripture tells us that the 'angels are all ministering spirits sent forth to minister to them who shall be heirs of salvation'. They stand by us when we think not of them. They speak to us often when we do not mind them.

I find men think commonly that strict devotion is but women's work – they themselves may live with greater freedom – but so it is not; it is only this seeking Jesus which can really arm us against the grave, or fit us for the resurrection. The word of the angel was timely, for though it was a good work the women came about, he would not have them in error. Too often we do that which is good upon a wrong ground.

Sometimes, we seek Christ in the grave; that is, in fading, dying things, in earthly comforts; but he is not there.

Sometimes, we seek him in the graves of sins and lusts, and continue in them; but his body is not in the graves of lust. He is not there.

Sometimes we seek him in a melancholy fit, in a humour sad as the grave, in a mood of discontent, all godly of a sudden. We have buried a friend or son or wife or brother; we are disappointed of a preferment; we have missed out on an estate; lost an expectation; and now, forsooth, are seeking Christ; but he is not here.

Sometimes we seek him in outward elements, in mere ceremonies and formalities, and mind no further; think if we hear a sermon or come to prayers, make a formal show of piety and religion, all will be well. But if we bring not somewhat also within, he is not here either.

You see why it is when we seek Christ we so often miss him. We seek him where he is not found – amidst graves and sepulchres – whilst we are dead in our trespasses and sins. Learn there how to lie down in death, and learn there also how to rise again; to die with Christ and to rise with him. It is the principal moral of our text and the whole business of this day. In other words, die to sin and live to righteousness, that when we must lie down ourselves, we may lie down in peace and rise in glory.

Saturday after Easter 2

A Reading from a commentary on St John's Gospel
by Augustine

The Church recognises two kinds of life as having been commended to her by God. One is a life of faith, the other a life of vision; one is a life of pilgrimage in time, the other a dwelling place in eternity; one is a life of toil, the other of repose; one is spent on the road, the other in our homeland; one is active, involving labour, the other contemplative, the reward of labour.

The first kind of life is symbolised by the apostle Peter, the second by the apostle John. All of the first life is lived in this world, and it will come to an end with this world. The second life will be imperfect till the end of this world, but it will have no end in the next world. And so Christ says to Peter: 'Follow me'; but of John he says: 'If I wish him to remain until I come, what is that to you? Your duty is to follow me.'

You are to follow me by imitating my endurance of transient evils; John is to remain until my coming, when I will bring eternal blessings. A way of saying this more clearly might be: Your active life will be perfect if you follow the example of my passion, but to attain its full perfection John's life of contemplation must wait until I come.

Perfect patience is to follow Christ faithfully, even to death, but for perfect knowledge we must await his coming. Here, in the land of the dying, the sufferings of the world must be endured; there, in the land of the living, shall be seen the good things of the Lord.

Christ's words, 'I wish him to remain until I come,' should not be taken to imply that John was to remain on earth until Christ's coming, but rather that he was to wait because it is not now but only when Christ comes that the life he symbolises will find fulfilment. On the other hand, Christ says to Peter: 'Your duty is to follow me,' because the life Peter symbolises can attain its goal only by action here and now.

Yet we should make no mental separation between these great apostles. Both lived the life symbolised by Peter; both were to attain the life symbolised by John. Symbolically, one followed, the other remained, but living by faith they both endured the sufferings of this present life of sorrow and they both longed for the joys of the future life of happiness.

Nor were they alone in this. They were one with the whole Church, the bride of Christ, which will in time be delivered from the trials of this life and live for ever in the joy of the next. These two kinds of life were represented respectively by Peter and John, yet both apostles lived by faith in this present, passing life, and in eternal life both now have the joy of vision.

The Third Sunday of Easter

A Reading from a sermon of Gregory the Great

Two disciples were walking together. They did not believe, yet they were talking about Jesus. Suddenly, he appeared, but under characteristics which they could not recognise. To their bodily eyes the Lord thus manifested externally what was taking place in their innermost depths, in the thoughts of their heart. The disciples were inwardly divided between love and doubt. The Lord was really present at their side, but he did not let himself be recognised. He offered his presence to these disciples who spoke of him, but because they doubted him he hid his true visage from them. He spoke to them and reproached them for their little sense. He interpreted for them every passage of Scripture which referred to him, but since he was still a stranger to the faith of their heart he acted as if he were going further.

In acting in such a manner, the Truth who is sincere was not being deceitful: he was showing himself to the eyes of his disciples as he appeared in their minds. And the Lord wished to see whether these disciples, who did not yet love him as God, would at least be friendly to him under the guise of a stranger. But those with whom Truth walked could not have been far from charity; they invited him to share their lodging, as one does with a traveller. Can we say simply that they invited him? The Scripture says that 'they pressed him.' It shows us by this example that when we invite strangers under our roof, our invitation must be a pressing one.

They thus set the table, serve the food, and in the breaking of bread discover the God whom they had failed to come to know in the explanation of the Scriptures. It was not in hearing the precepts of God that they were enlightened, but in carrying them out: 'It is not those who hear the law who are justified in the sight of God; it is those who keep it who will be declared just.' If anyone wishes to understand what you have heard, hasten to put into practice whatever you have grasped. The Lord was not recognised while he was speaking; he was pleased to make himself known while he was offered something to eat. Let us then, beloved, love to practise charity. It is of this that Paul speaks to us: 'Love your fellow Christians always. Do not neglect to show hospitality, for by that means some have entertained angels without knowing it.' Peter also says: 'Be mutually hospitable without complaining.' And Truth himself speaks to us of it: 'I was a stranger and you welcomed me.' 'As often as you did it for one of my least brothers or sisters,' the Lord will declare on the day of judgement, 'you did it for me.'

Despite this, we are so slothful in the face of the grace of hospitality! Let us appreciate the greatness of this virtue. Let us receive Christ at our table so as to be welcomed at his eternal supper. Let us show hospitality to Christ present in the stranger now so that at the judgement he will not ignore us as strangers, but will welcome us as brothers and sisters into his kingdom.

alternative reading

A Reading from *Resurrection* by Rowan Williams

Easter means coming to the memory of Jesus, looking for consolation, and finding a memory that hurts and judges, that sets a distance, even an alienation between me and my hope, my Saviour. Easter occurs, again and again, in this opening-up of a void, the sense of absence which questions our egocentric aspirations and our longing for 'tidy drama'; it occurs when we find in Jesus not a dead friend but a living stranger.

'We had hoped that he was the one to redeem Israel,' says Cleopas. The memory of a man who had given flesh to the hope of Israel's redemption would be worth treasuring, even if this hope had never been fully realised, had indeed been violently cut off. But the elegiac, the wistful retrospect of the tragic hero, is not to be the key in which Jesus' disciples speak of him: Cleopas is not the definitive theological voice of the first believers. Cleopas *possesses* a memory of Jesus; yet he is aware of the disturbing and disorienting absence of a corpse, a tangible memorial; and he addresses his remarks to a questioning stranger. The empty tomb at least prevents him closing off his story as an elegiac memory; but it remains problematic – 'him they did not see.' It still remains for him to lose that conventional martyr's tale as he recognises the stranger for who he is. He, and the other disciples, *will* 'see'. In Cleopas' little speech, Luke takes us into the very middle of that reconstruction and redirection of understanding that is the Easter experience, the process in which we are forcibly parted from the consoling recollection assimilated with ourselves and confronted with one who is still and forever *other*.

One of the strangest features of the resurrection narratives is precisely this theme of the otherness, the unrecognizability, of the risen Jesus. Three major stories (Luke's Emmaus episode, John's account of Mary Magdalene at the tomb, and the 'Galilean fantasia' which concludes his Gospel) underline the point. Whatever the experiences of the disciples at Easter were, it is hard to deny that this element must have played a part – that for some at least, the encounter with the risen Jesus began as an encounter with a stranger. And this is one of the most important pieces of evidence counting against the suggestion that the risen Christ is to be seen as a projection of the community's own belief, its sense of continuity with the identity of Jesus. In the Emmaus story, Jesus sharply rebukes Cleopas for his failure not only to grasp the foreordained character of Messiah's sufferings but to make the connection between suffering and 'glory', between the cross and creative freedom and power. Jesus condemns the inadequacy of their earlier understanding: he is not what they have thought him to be, and thus they must 'learn' him afresh, as if from the beginning. Once again, John crystallises this most powerfully by presenting the disciples in their fishing boats, as if they had never known Jesus: they must begin again.

So the void of the tomb and the unrecognisable face of the risen Lord both speak of the challenge of Easter to a God who is primarily 'the God of our condition'. The Lordship of Jesus is not constructed from a recollection but experienced in the encounter with one who evades our surface desires and surface needs, and will not subserve the requirements of our private dramas.

Monday after Easter 3

A Reading from a sermon of Lancelot Andrewes preached before King James I at Whitehall on Easter Day 1622

The risen Christ gave Mary Magdalene a commission. 'Go' is her mission, and 'tell my brethren' is her commission. A commission, to publish the first news of his rising, and as it falls out, of his ascending too.

The Fathers say that by this word she was by Christ made an apostle, nay 'an apostle to the apostles themselves'. An apostle; for what lacks she? Sent first, immediately from Christ himself; and what is an apostle but so? Secondly, sent to declare and make known. And last, what was she to make known? Christ's rising and ascending. And what are they but 'the gospel', yea the very gospel of the gospel?

This day, with Christ's rising, begins the gospel; not before. Crucified, dead and buried, no good news, no gospel in themselves. And them the Jews believe as well as we. The first gospel of all is the gospel of this day, and the gospel of this day is this Mary Magdalene's gospel, the prime gospel of all, before any of the other four. That Christ is risen and upon his ascending, and she the first that ever brought these glad tidings. At her hands the apostles themselves received it first, and from them we all.

Which, as it was a special honour, and 'wheresoever this gospel is preached, shall be told for a memorial of her', so was it withal, not without some kind of reproaching to them, to the apostles, for sitting at home so drooping in a corner, that Christ not finding any of them is fain to seek him a new apostle. And finding her where he should have found them and did not, to send by the hand of her that he first found at the sepulchre's side, and to make himself a new apostle. And send her to them, to enter them as it were, and catechise them in two articles of the Christian Faith, the resurrection and the ascension of Christ. To Mary Magdalene, they and we both owe them, the first notice of them.

Tuesday after Easter 3

A Reading from a treatise of Baldwin,
Archbishop of Canterbury

'The word of God is living and active, sharper than any two-edged sword.' The word of God is plainly shown in all its strength and wisdom to those who seek out Christ, who is the word, the power and the wisdom of God. This word was with the Father in the beginning, and in its own time was revealed to the apostles, then preached by them and humbly received in faith by believers. So, the word is in the Father, as well as on our lips and in our hearts.

This word of God is living; the Father gave it life in itself, just as he has life in himself. For this reason it not only is alive, but it is life, as he says of himself: 'I am the way, the truth and the life.' Since he is life he is both living and life-giving. For, 'as the Father raises up the dead and gives them life, so also the Son gives life to those whom he chooses.' He is life-giving when he calls the dead from the grave and says: 'Lazarus, come forth.'

When this word is preached, in the very act of preaching, it gives to its own voice which is heard outwardly a certain power which is perceived inwardly, so much so that the dead are brought back to life, and by these praises the children of Abraham are raised from the dead. This word then is alive in the heart of the Father, on the lips of the preacher, and in the hearts of those who believe and love him. Since this word is so truly alive, undoubtedly it is full of power.

It is powerful in creation, powerful in the government of the universe, powerful in the redemption of the world. For what is more powerful, more effective? Who shall speak of its power; who shall make all its praises heard? It is powerful in what it accomplishes, powerful when preached. It does not come back empty; it bears fruit in all to whom it is sent.

It is powerful and 'sharper than any two-edged sword' when it is believed and loved. For what is impossible to the believer? What is difficult for a lover? When this word is spoken, its message pierces the heart like the sharp arrows of a strong archer, like nails driven deep; it enters so deeply that it penetrates to the innermost recess. This word is much sharper than any two-edged sword, inasmuch as it is stronger than any courage or power, sharper than any shrewdness of human ingenuity, keener than all human wisdom, or the subtlety of learned argument.

Wednesday after Easter 3

A Reading from *The Cost of Discipleship*
by Dietrich Bonhoeffer

Baptism is essentially passive – *being baptized, suffering* the call of Christ. In baptism we become Christ's own possession. When the name of Christ is spoken over the candidate, he or she becomes a partaker in this name, and is baptized '*into* Jesus Christ'. From that moment they belong to Jesus Christ. They are wrested from the dominion of the world, and pass into the ownership of Christ.

Baptism therefore betokens a *breach*. Christ invades the realm of Satan, lays hold on his own, and creates for himself his Church. The breach with the world is complete. It demands and produces the death of our old nature. In baptism a person dies together with his old world. This death, no less than baptism itself, is a passive event. It is not as though a person must achieve his own death through various kinds of renunciation and mortification. That would never be the death of the old nature which Christ demands. The old Adam cannot will his own death or kill himself. He can only die in, through and with Christ. Christ is his death. For the sake of fellowship with Christ, and in that fellowship alone a person dies. In fellowship with Christ and through the grace of baptism we receive his death as a gift. This death is a gift of grace: we can never accomplish it by ourselves.

The old Adam and his sin are judged and condemned, but out of this judgement a new person arises, who has died to the world and to sin. Thus this death is not the act of an angry Creator finally rejecting his creation in his wrath, but the gracious death which has been won for us by the death of Christ; the gracious assumption of the creature by his Creator. It is death in the power and fellowship of the cross of Christ. He who becomes Christ's own possession must submit to his cross, and suffer and die with him. He who is granted fellowship with Jesus must die the baptismal death which is the fountain of grace, for the sake of the cross which Christ lays upon his disciples. The cross and death of Christ were cruel and hard but the yoke of our cross is easy and light because of our fellowship with him.

Thursday after Easter 3

A Reading from the *Instructions* of Columbanus
on 'Christ the Fount of Life'

Let us follow that vocation by which we are called from life to the fountain of life. Christ is the fountain, not only of living water, but of eternal life. He is the fountain of light and spiritual illumination; for from him come all these things: wisdom, life and eternal light. The author of life is the fountain of life; the creator of light is the fountain of spiritual illumination. Therefore, let us seek the fountain of light and life and the living water by despising what we see, by leaving the world and by dwelling in the highest heavens. Let us seek these things, and like rational and shrewd fish may we drink the living water which 'wells up to eternal life.'

Merciful God, good Lord, I wish that you would unite me to that fountain that there I may drink of the living spring of the water of life with all those who thirst after you. There in that heavenly region may I ever dwell, delighted with abundant sweetness, and say: 'How sweet is the fountain of living water which never fails, the water welling up to eternal life.'

O God, you are yourself that fountain ever and again to be desired, ever and again to be consumed. Lord Christ, give us always this water to be for us the 'source of the living water which wells up to eternal life'. I ask you for your great benefits. Who does not know it? but you, King of Glory, know how to give great gifts, and you have promised great things. There is nothing greater than you, and you bestowed yourself upon us; you gave yourself for us.

Therefore, we ask that we may know what we love, since we ask nothing other than that you give us yourself. For you are our all: our life, our light, our salvation, our food and our drink, our God. Inspire our hearts, I ask you, Jesus, with that breath of your Spirit; wound our souls with your love, so that the soul of each and every one of us may be able to say in truth: 'Show me my soul's desire,' for I am wounded by your love.

These are the wounds I wish for, Lord. Blessed is the soul so wounded by love. Such a soul seeks the fountain of eternal life and drinks from it, although it continues to thirst and its thirst grows ever greater even as it drinks. Therefore, the more the soul loves, the more it desires to love, and the greater its suffering, the greater its healing. In this same way may our God and Lord Jesus Christ, the good and saving physician, wound the depths of our souls with a healing wound – the same Jesus Christ who reigns in unity with the Father and the Holy Spirit, for ever and ever.

Friday after Easter 3

A reading from an oration of Ambrose of Milan upon the death of his brother Satyrus

The Lord shows in the gospel how a person will rise again. He not only quickened Lazarus, he quickened the faith of us all. For if people believe, as they read, their dead spirits will also be quickened with that of Lazarus. For when the Lord went to the sepulchre and loudly cried out: 'Lazarus, come forth,' what other meaning is there in this act except that he wished to give visible proof of our future resurrection?

Why did Jesus cry out loudly? Was it because he was not used to working through the Spirit, or because he was not accustomed to command in silence? No, he intended rather to emphasise the Scriptural statement that 'in a moment, in the twinkling of an eye, at the last trumpet, the dead shall rise again incorruptible.' For the lifting of his voice corresponds to the peal of trumpets. He added the name of Lazarus lest the resurrection might seem to be accidental rather than something deliberate.

The dead man, therefore, heard and came forth from the tomb. He was bound and his face was covered with a cloth. But he who arose and walked, had sight. For, where the power of a divine command was operating, nature no longer followed its own course, but obeyed the divine will.

If anyone is astonished at this, inquire who gave the command and your astonishment will cease. It was Jesus Christ, the power of God, the life, the light, the resurrection of the dead. The power lifted up a man lying in the grave; the life made him walk; the light dispelled the darkness and restored his sight; the resurrection renewed the gift of life.

Perhaps you are concerned by the fact that Jesus took away the stone and loosened the bands, and you are worried that there will be no one to take away the stone from your grave. As if he who could restore life could not remove a stone, or that he who made a bound man walk could not break bonds, or that he who shed light upon covered eyes could not uncover a face, or that he who could renew nature could not split a rock!

But in order that they who had refused to believe in their hearts might at least believe with their eyes, they removed the stone, they saw the corpse, they smelled the stench, they broke the bands. No longer could they deny that this man was dead whom they saw rising again. They saw the marks of death, and now also they saw the proofs of life.

Saturday after Easter 3

A Reading from a treatise *On the Holy Spirit*
by Basil the Great

The Lord, the dispenser of our life, has inaugurated a covenant of baptism which carries with it the figure of death and the figure of life. Water is symbolic of death and the Spirit signifies the seal of life. This relates to the problem which has been raised as to why water and Spirit are associated in baptism. The reason is that baptism has two purposes: on the one hand, to destroy the body of sin and prevent us from bearing fruit in death; and on the other hand, to give us life in the Spirit with its fruit borne in holiness. The water is a symbol of death: it receives the body as if it were into a tomb. The Spirit bestows life-giving energy, recalling our souls from the death of sin to the vitality they once enjoyed. This is what is meant by being 'born again of water and the Spirit'. Death itself is killed in the water and the Spirit restores us to life.

The great mystery of baptism is accomplished with three immersions and three invocations. In this way the figure of death is represented and the baptized are enlightened by the handing on of divine knowledge. If there is any grace in the water it is not because of any inherent power the water may possess but because of the presence of the Spirit. For, as Scripture asserts, baptism is 'not the washing away of dirt but the appeal made to God from a clear conscience'. This is why the Lord, in order to prepare us for the resurrection life, lays before us the way of the gospel. We are to avoid anger, practise patience, be detached from the pursuit of pleasure and the love of money. In this way, by the exercise of our own free choice, we are anticipating the character of the coming age.

Through the Holy Spirit paradise is regained for us; we are able to ascend to the kingdom of heaven and our status as adopted children of God is restored whereby we have the confidence to call God our Father. We share in the grace of Christ and are called 'children of light' and 'sharers in the eternal glory'. To put it simply, we are filled with all the blessings not only of this age but of the age that is to come. We can observe as in a mirror, as though already present, the grace of the good things which are in store for us in the future, the enjoyment of which we receive now through faith. If the pledge is of this order, how wonderful must be its perfection! If the first fruits are so rich, how great must be the consummation!

The Fourth Sunday of Easter

A Reading from a homily of Gregory the Great

'I am the Good Shepherd. I know my sheep and my sheep know me.' In these words it is as if our Lord were saying: 'Those who love me, obey me.' Certainly, those who do not love the truth cannot yet know it.

My dear brothers and sisters, let us reflect upon how these words of our Lord imply a test of our own. Ask yourselves first if you are indeed sheep of Jesus; and secondly, if you know him and recognise the light of truth. We recognise truth not simply by faith but by love. You recognise truth not by the assent of the intellect, but by the love you express in your deeds. As the apostle John says: 'Those who say that they love God, but disobey his commandments, are liars.'

Jesus goes on to add the following words: 'My sheep hear my voice, and I know them, and they follow me, and I will give them eternal life.' A little earlier he said also: 'If any enter by me, they will be saved, and will go in and out and find pasture.' That is to say, they will go in by faith, and go out from faith to vision, from belief to contemplation, and will find pasture in the eternal banquet God has prepared.

The Lord's sheep will find the Lord's pastures. Those who follow Christ with an undivided heart will be nourished in pastures that are forever green. And what are such pastures if not the most profound joy of feeding in the everlasting fields of paradise? For the pasture of the saints is to see God face to face. When the vision of God never fades, the soul is filled with an abundance of food for eternal life.

And so dear friends, let us seek these pastures and join the throng of the citizens of heaven. Let their happiness and celebration be an invitation to us. Let our hearts grow warm; let our faith be rekindled; let our desire for the things of heaven increase; for to love in this way is indeed to be on the way.

We should allow no misfortune to distract us from this happiness and deep joy; for if you are determined to reach the destination of your spiritual journey the roughness of the road will not deter you. Nor should the delights of material prosperity in this life ever entice you astray; only the foolish traveller, spotting a pleasant field on the way, forgets that he is en route to a greater destination.

Monday after Easter 4

A Reading from the treatise *On the Soul*
by Ambrose of Milan

In the Song of Songs, the bride says: 'Set me as a seal on your heart, as a seal on your arm.' Christ is the seal on the forehead, the seal on the heart: on the forehead, that we may ever confess him; on the heart, that we may always love him; a seal on the arm that we may carry out his tasks.

Therefore, let his image radiate in our confession, let it radiate in our love, let it radiate in our works and deeds, so that all his beauty may be expressed in us if it is possible. Let him be our head, because 'the head of everyone is Christ.' Let him be our eye, that through him we may see the Father. Let him be our voice, that through him we may speak to the Father. Let him be our right hand, that through him we may bring our sacrifice to God the Father. He is also our seal, which is the sign of perfection and love, because the Father loved the Son and set his seal on him, as we read: 'It is on him that God the Father has set his seal.'

Therefore, Christ is our love. Love is good, when it has offered itself to death for transgressions; love is good, when it has remitted sins. Hence, let our soul put on love, a kind of love which is as 'strong as death'. For just as death is the end of sins, so is love as well, since those who love the Lord cease to commit sin. For 'love thinks no evil and does not rejoice in what is wrong, but endures all things.' For if you do not seek your own good, how will you seek the good of others?

Strong too is that death through the bath of baptism through which every sin is buried and every transgression pardoned. Such was the love brought forward by that woman in the gospel, about whom the Lord says: 'Her many sins are forgiven – because of her great love.'

Tuesday after Easter 4

A Reading from *Gateway to Hope* by Maria Boulding

Though God is an almighty lover, he can find himself shut out, and he longs to find an open door of vulnerability in us. It is extraordinarily hard for us to realise this, conditioned as we are by a secular ethic of success and a religious ideal of moral perfection which may owe little to the gospel. God calls us, implants his life in the deepest centre of our being at baptism, and loves us into growth. He does not propose to us some lofty, rigid ideal to which we must attain by our own unaided human resources. We are more sinful than we know, more deeply flawed than we can recognise by any human insight; but grace works in us in the deepest places of body and spirit. We must live from our weakness, from the barren places of our need, because there is the spring of grace and the source of our strength, as Paul discovered: 'When I am weak, then I am strong.' When we can stand before God in the truth of our need, acknowledging our sinfulness and bankruptcy, then we can celebrate his mercy. Then we are living by grace, and we can allow full scope to his joy.

For many of us it is difficult to live honestly from this place of failure and weakness. Even if we know with our heads we should, we may still slip back into the old attitudes and behave as though God were expecting us to succeed and making his love conditional upon our achievements. If we have become hardened in such an attitude it may take some deep experience of failure to disabuse us. When a crisis occurs I may find in myself the sheer moral impossibility of obeying God. It is not simply a matter of emotional rebellion, or of knowing that 'the spirit is willing but the flesh is weak'; the will itself is unwilling. I am rebellious to the core and do not even want to want God's will. Perhaps I can push it one stage further from me, and say with a kind of tortured effort, 'I want to want to want your will,' and then ask myself if there is even a grain of honesty or good will in that. I am helpless; and as the father of the epileptic boy cried to Jesus, 'I do believe, help my unbelief,' so I can only say to God, 'I am rebellious down to my roots, help me.'

Here, as we teeter on the edge of despair, beset by every kind of temptation and feeling as though we had already fallen, the Spirit is released. This is his own place, the deepest place of our being where he is wedded to our spirit, where he can act and give life, where he can free us from all that hampers the true thrust of our will. God himself creates our freedom; he gives us freedom as his continuing gift of love, and he alone can influence it from within, in no way violating or diminishing it. Entombed Lazarus is a sign not simply of a certain group of people who had obviously closed their hearts against Jesus, but of each one of us. In this hopeless situation, where you are nothing but stark failure, you know the miracle of grace. This tomb is the place of resurrection, and if you believe you will see the glory of God.

Wednesday after Easter 4

A Reading from the *First Apology* of Justin
in defence of the Christians

Through Christ we received new life and we consecrated ourselves to God. I wish to explain to you the way in which we did this.

Those who believe that what we Christians teach is true and who give assurance of their ability to live according to that teaching, are taught to ask God's forgiveness for their sins by prayer and fasting and we pray and fast with them. We then lead them to a place where there is water and they are reborn in the same way that we were reborn; that is to say, they are washed in the water in the name of God, the Father and Lord of the whole universe, of our Saviour Jesus Christ and of the Holy Spirit. This is done because Christ said: 'Unless you are born again you will not enter the kingdom of heaven.' It is obviously impossible for anyone, having once been born, to re-enter their mother's womb.

An explanation of how repentant sinners are to be freed from their sins is given through the prophet Isaiah in the words: 'Wash yourselves and be clean. Remove the evil from your souls; learn to do what is right. Be just to the orphan, plead for the widow. Come, let us reason together, says the Lord. If your sins are like scarlet, I will make them white as wool; if they are like crimson, I will make them white as snow. But if you do not heed me, you shall be devoured by the sword. The mouth of the Lord has spoken.'

The apostles taught us the reason for this ceremony. With regard to our first birth we each came into being without our knowledge or consent by the moist seed when our parents came together; we were born into an evil world and bad habits. So if we were not to remain children of compulsion and ignorance, we needed a new birth of which we ourselves would be conscious, and which would be the result of our own free choice. We needed, too, to have our sins forgiven. This is why the name of God, the Father and Lord of the whole universe, is pronounced in the water over anyone who chooses to be born again and who has repented of sin. The person who leads the candidate for baptism to the font calls upon God by this name alone, for God so far surpasses our powers of description that no one can really give a name to him. Any who dare to say that they can must be hopelessly insane.

This baptism is called 'illumination' because of the mental enlightenment that is experienced by those who learn these things. The person receiving this enlightenment is also baptized in the name of Jesus Christ, who was crucified under Pontius Pilate, and in the name of the Holy Spirit, who through the prophets foretold everything concerning Jesus.

Thursday after Easter 4

A Reading from a *Catechetical Oration*
of Gregory of Nyssa

To those who reflect upon the complexity of reality, the fact that God should have clothed himself with our human nature does not seem odd or extravagant. Who, studying the universe, would be so narrow in his thinking as not to believe that God is in everything, that he clothes himself with the universe, and that at one and the same time he both contains it and dwells in it? Everything that exists depends on the One who is, and nothing can exist except in the bosom of the One who is.

If then everything that exists is in God, and God is in everything, why should we be embarrassed at our faith which teaches that one day God was born into the human condition, the same God who still exists in humanity?

Indeed, if the presence of God in us does not take the same form now as it did in Christ, we can at least agree in recognising that God is in us today no less than he was then. Today, he is involved with us in as much as he maintains creation in existence. In the incarnation he mingled himself with our being in order to make us divine through contact with his nature, after he had snatched it from death. His resurrection becomes for mortals the promise of our return to immortality.

Our whole nature had to be recalled from death to life. God therefore stooped over our dead body, offering his hand (so to speak) to the poor creature lying there. He came near enough to death to make contact with our mortal remains, and by means of his own body provided human nature with the capacity for resurrection, thus by his power raising to life the whole of humanity.

Friday after Easter 4

A Reading from a treatise *On Death as a Blessing*
by Ambrose of Milan

The apostle Paul tells us: 'The world is crucified to me, and I to the world.' We are to understand from this that this death by crucifixion takes place in this life, and that this death is a blessing. So he goes on to urge us 'to bear the death of Jesus in our bodies', for whoever bears 'the death of Jesus in the body will bear also in the body the life of the Lord Jesus'.

Death must be active within us if life also is to be active within us. 'Life' is life after death, a life that is a blessing. This blessing of life comes after victory, when the contest is over, when the law of our fallen nature no longer rebels against the law of our reason, when we no longer need to struggle against the body that leads to death, for the body already shares in victory. It seems to me that this 'death' is more powerful than 'life'. I accept the authority of the Apostle when he says: 'Death is therefore active within us, but life also is active within you.' Yet the 'death' of this one was building up life for countless multitudes of peoples! He therefore teaches us to seek out this kind of death even in this life, so that the death of Christ may shine forth in our lives – that blessed death by which our outward self is destroyed and our inmost self renewed, and our earthly dwelling crumbles away and a home in heaven opens before us.

Those who cut themselves off from this fallen nature of ours and free themselves from its chains are imitating death. These are the bonds spoken of by the Lord through Isaiah: 'Loose the bonds of injustice, untie the thongs of the yoke, set free the oppressed and break every yoke of evil.'

The Lord allowed death to enter this world so that sin might come to an end. But he gave us the resurrection of the dead so that our nature might not end once more in death; death was to bring guilt to an end, and the resurrection was to enable our nature to continue for ever.

'Death' in this context is a passover to be made by everyone. You must keep facing it with perseverance. It is a passover from corruption, from mortality to immortality, from rough seas to a calm harbour. The word 'death' must not trouble us; the blessings that come from a safe journey should bring us joy. What is death but the burial of sin and the resurrection of goodness? Scripture says: 'Let my soul die among the souls of the just'; that is, let me be buried with the righteous, so that I may cast off my sins and put on the grace of the righteous, of those who bear the death of Christ with them, in their bodies and in their souls.

Saturday after Easter 4

A Reading from a sermon of Leo the Great

The days between the Lord's resurrection and his ascension, my dear friends, did not pass by without purpose: great mysteries were established in them, and great truths were revealed. During these days, the fear of the horror of death was taken away, and the immortality of the body as well as the soul was made known. During them the Lord breathed on all his apostles and filled them with the Holy Spirit; and to Peter above the others was entrusted the care of the Lord's flock, having already had entrusted to him the keys of the kingdom.

It was during this time that the Lord joined the two disciples as their companion on the road to Emmaus, and by rebuking them for their timid and fearful hesitation dispelled the darkness of uncertainty from all our minds. Their enlightened hearts received the flame of faith; lukewarm before, their hearts now burnt within them as the Lord unfolded the Scriptures to them. As they ate with him, their eyes were opened in the breaking of bread, opened much more happily to the revealed glory of our nature than were the eyes of the first members of our race who were filled with shame at their sin.

Throughout this time between the Lord's resurrection and ascension, the Lord in his providence fulfilled one purpose, taught one lesson, set one consideration before the eyes and hearts of his followers; namely, that the Lord Jesus Christ, who was truly born, truly suffered and truly died, should be recognised as truly risen. The apostles and all the disciples had been filled with fear by his death on the cross, and their faith in the resurrection had been hesitant; but now they gained such great strength from seeing the truth, that when the Lord went up to heaven, far from feeling sadness, they experienced great joy.

Indeed, they had a great and mysterious cause for rejoicing. For in the sight of a vast company of the faithful human nature was exalted above the dignity of all the creatures of heaven, passing beyond the ranks of angels, raised above the seat of the archangels, to receive an elevation that would have no limit until it was admitted into the eternal Father's dwelling, to share the glorious throne of him to whose nature it had been united in the person of the Son.

The Fifth Sunday of Easter

A Reading from a commentary on St John's Gospel
by Cyril of Alexandria

The Lord calls himself the vine and those united to him branches in order to teach us how much we shall benefit from our union with him, and how important it is for us to remain in his love. By receiving the Holy Spirit, who is the bond of union between us and Christ our Saviour, those who are joined to him, as branches are to a vine, share in his own nature.

On the part of those who come to the vine, their union with him depends upon a deliberate act of the will; on his part, the union is effected by grace. Because we had good will, we made the act of faith that brought us to Christ, and received from him the dignity of adoption that made us his own kin, according to the words of St Paul: 'Whoever is joined to the Lord is one spirit with him.'

The prophet Isaiah calls Christ the foundation, because it is upon him that we as living and spiritual stones are built into a holy priesthood to be a dwelling place for God in the Spirit. Upon no other foundation than Christ can this temple be built. Here Christ is teaching the same truth by calling himself the vine, since the vine is the parent of its branches, and provides their nourishment.

From Christ and in Christ, we have been reborn through the Spirit in order to bear the fruit of life; not the fruit of our old, sinful life but the fruit of a new life founded upon our faith in him and our love for him. Like branches growing from a vine, we now draw our life from Christ, and we cling to his holy commandment in order to preserve this life. Eager to safeguard the blessing of our noble birth, we are careful not to grieve the Holy Spirit who dwells in us, and who makes us aware of God's presence in us.

Let the wisdom of John, then, teach us how we live in Christ and Christ live in us: 'The proof that we are living in him and he is living in us is that he has given us a share in his Spirit.' Just as the trunk of the vine gives its own natural properties to each of its branches, so, by bestowing on them the Holy Spirit, the Word of God, the only-begotten Son of the Father, gives Christians a certain kinship with himself and with God the Father because they have been united to him by faith and determination to do his will in all things. He helps them to grow in love and reverence for God, and teaches them to discern right from wrong and to act with integrity.

alternative reading

A Reading from *Centuries of Meditations*
by Thomas Traherne

The world serves you as it teaches you more abundantly to prize the love of Jesus Christ. For since the inheritance is so great to which you are restored, and no less than the whole world is the benefit of your Saviour's love, how much are you to admire that person that redeemed you from the lowest hell to the fruition of it? Your forfeiture was unmeasurable and your sin infinite, your despair insupportable, and your danger eternal. How happy are you, therefore, that you have so great a Lord, whose love rescued you from the extremest misery!

This visible world is wonderfully to be delighted in and highly to be esteemed because it is the theatre of God's righteous kingdom. Who as himself was righteous because he made it freely, so he made it that we might freely be righteous too. For in the kingdom of glory it is impossible to fall. No one can sin that clearly seeth the beauty of God's face because no one can sin against his own happiness, that is, none can when he sees it clearly, willingly and wittingly forsake it, tempter, temptation, loss and danger being all seen. But here we see God's face in a glass, and more dimly behold our happiness as in a mirror; by faith therefore we are to live, and to sharpen our eye that we may see his glory. We are to be studious and intent in our desires and endeavours. For we may sin, or we may be holy. Holiness, therefore, and righteousness naturally flow out of our fruition of the world: for who can vilify and debase himself by any sin while he actually considers he is the heir of it? It exalts a man to a sublime and honourable life: it lifts him above lusts and makes him angelical.

Monday after Easter 5

A Reading from a treatise *On the Love of God*
by Bernard of Clairvaux

Christians know well their utter need of Jesus and him crucified. While they embrace and wonder at the love revealed in Christ, they are overwhelmed by a sense of shame because they do not return in response to such love and consolation, even the very little that they are. They readily love God above all things because they understand just how greatly they are loved by God; for those to whom less love is given, will respond with less love.

The passion of Jesus, in this respect, was all harvest. All time before it led towards it: the ages under the dominion of sin and death found in the cross their climax and fruition. You should see the splendours of the resurrection as flowers of the age of grace that has now been inaugurated, blossoms of a new springtime of creation which, in the general resurrection of the dead at the end of time, will bear an abundant and eternal harvest.

For, as the Bride in the Song of Songs says: 'See, the winter is past; the rains are over and gone, and the flowers have appeared in our land.' By these words she would have us understand that summer has indeed come with him who, freed from the winter of death into the springtime of the risen life, declares: 'Behold, I make all things new.' For, sown in death, his body in his resurrection has flowered anew. To greet its budding fragrance our life's parched landscape now grows green, the glaciers within us melt, and the dead return to life.

Tuesday after Easter 5

A Reading from a sermon of Augustine

In the psalms it says, 'Sing to the Lord a new song; sing his praise in the assembly of the saints.' We are urged to sing to the Lord a new song. It is a new person who knows a new song. A song is a joyful thing and if we reflect more deeply, it is also an offering of love. Thus anyone who has learned how to love a new life will also have learned how to sing a new song. For the sake of the new song, however, we need to be reminded what the nature of the new life is. Indeed a new person, a new song and the new covenant, are all manifestations of the one kingdom: a new person will both sing a new song and belong to the new covenant.

Everybody loves; the question is, what is the object of our love? In Scripture we are not urged to stop loving, but instead to choose what we love. But how can we choose unless we are first chosen? We cannot even love unless we are first loved. Listen to the words of John the apostle: 'We love because God first loved us.' If you investigate why it is that people love God, you will discover absolutely no other reason than that God loved them. God has given us himself: God is both the object of our love and the source of our love. And if you want to know what has been given us as the source of our love, you will find a clearer explanation in the words of the apostle Paul: 'The love of God has been poured into our hearts.' Where does it come from? From ourselves? No. 'Through the Holy Spirit who has been given to us.' With this assurance, then, let us love God by the gift of God. God offers himself, so there is no need to offer us more. He calls out to us: 'Love me and you will possess me, because you cannot love me unless you possess me.'

My brothers and sisters, my children, infants of the Catholic Church, holy and heavenly seed, you who have been born again in Christ, born from above, listen to me – or rather, listen to God through me: 'Sing to the Lord a new song.' 'But I do sing,' you reply. Yes, you do sing; of course you sing. I can hear you! But make sure that your life is singing the same tune as your tongue. Sing with your voices, sing with your hearts, sing with your lips, sing with your lives.

And if you were to ask me what you should sing in praise of God, and you are busy looking for songs, then know that the singer himself is the praise contained in the song. Do you want to speak the praise of God? Then be yourselves what you speak. If you lead good lives you are God's praise.

Wednesday after Easter 5

A Reading from *The Mirror of Charity*
by Aelred of Rievaulx

When you have given up the fleshpots of Egypt, the cares of this world, its ambitions and dissensions, in exchange for the poverty of Christ and a life of obedience, do not be surprised if you do not immediately receive God's manna from heaven. You have crossed the Red Sea like a true Israelite; you have chosen solitude and silence, a life of brotherly love and voluntary poverty; you have withdrawn from the tumult of this world. Do not, therefore, murmur against God if you do not immediately experience the sweetness of his love. Do not wonder if God is still with you, for Christ has said that if anyone loves God, he will keep God's commandments and God will love him, coming to him and living in his soul. Do not allow into your mind any blasphemous thought that might suggest to you that the service of God is a waste of time, and that there is no reward for those who keep his commandments.

You may be tempted to feel, along with what the psalmist felt, that you have ordered your heart in vain, that you have washed your hands among the innocent, and that you have been punished for doing so, whereas sinners appear to wallow in wealth, and even – or so it might appear – in spiritual consolation. And if, as you possibly suspect, there is more consolation from God in a life of luxury, then you might be tempted to think it better to eat and drink and enjoy the good things of this world rather than those of the life to come. Yet you need not be surprised that you do not immediately receive heavenly consolation, when you remember St Paul's reminder that we cannot enter into the kingdom of God without suffering many difficulties in this life. These trials must not make us waver, he tells us, since they are our appointed lot.

We should also remember that the children of Israel were often encouraged while in slavery in Egypt by the sight of the wonderful miracles performed on their behalf, and that there they ate of the Paschal Lamb; but after they had crossed the Red Sea they were not immediately given manna from heaven to eat. Far from it, they were led first to the bitter waters of Marah and tempted there. Only after that, when they were led by the twelve springs into the secret place of the desert, were they filled with the bread from heaven.

And so you too, who have left Egypt behind you and gone dry-shod through the Red Sea, should anticipate that you will first be led to the bitter waters, where labour and weariness will cast you down, and there you will discover for yourself how true it is that the way of life is a narrow way. God will tempt you indeed, but you must be one of those of whom Christ can say: 'You are one of those who have continued with me in my trials.'

Thursday after Easter 5

A reading from *The Power and Meaning of Love*
by Thomas Merton

The union that binds the members of Christ together is not the union of proud confidence in the power of an organisation. The Church is united by the humility as well as by the charity of her members. Hers is the union that comes from the consciousness of individual fallibility and poverty, from the humility which recognises its own limitations and accepts them, the meekness that cannot take upon itself to condemn, but can only forgive because it is conscious that it has itself been forgiven by Christ.

The union of Christians is a union of friendship and mercy, a bearing of one another's burdens in the sharing of divine forgiveness. Christian forgiveness is not confined merely to those who are members of the Church. To be a Christian one must love all people, including not only one's own enemies but even those who claim to be the 'enemies of God'. 'Whosoever is angry with his brother or sister shall be in danger of the judgement. Love your enemies, do good to them that hate you, pray for them that persecute and speak calumny of you, that you may be the children of your Father who is in heaven.'

The solidarity of the Christian community is not based on the awareness that the Church has authority to cast out and to anathematise, but on the realisation that Christ has given her the power to forgive sin in his name and to welcome the sinner to the banquet of his love in the holy Eucharist. More than this, the Church is aware of her divine mission to bring forgiveness and peace to all men and women. This means not only that the sacraments are there for all who will approach them, but that Christians themselves must bring love, mercy and justice into the lives of their neighbours, in order to reveal to them the presence of Christ in his Church. And this can only be done if all Christians strive generously to love and serve all people with whom they come into contact in their daily lives.

Friday after Easter 5

A Reading from a commentary on St John's Gospel
by Augustine

Jesus said, 'No one can come to me unless drawn by the Father who sent me.' Do not imagine that you are being drawn to God against your will, for the mind can also be drawn by love. Nor should we be afraid of being criticised by those who interpret the words of Scripture too literally and are quite incapable of grasping the divine truths they contain. Such folk might object to these words saying: 'How can I believe of my own free will if I am being drawn?' In reply to which I say this: 'You are being drawn not merely by your free will, but also by delight.'

But what does it mean to be drawn by delight? In the psalms it is written: 'Let the Lord be your delight, and he will grant you the desires of your heart.' And one of our own poets has also said: 'Everyone is drawn by his own dear delight' – note: not by necessity but by delight, not by compulsion but by pleasure. So there is all the more reason to suppose that when people delight in truth, in all that is worthwhile, in righteousness, in the prospect of eternal life, they are in fact being drawn by Christ himself, for Christ is all these things.

Must we assume that although the bodily senses have their delights the mind is not permitted any? If the soul has no delights, how is it that Scripture says: 'All nations will take refuge in the shadow of your wings. They will feast on the abundance of your house, and you will give them drink from the river of your delights. For with you is the fountain of life: in your light we see light'?

Show me a lover, for lovers understand what I am talking about. Show me someone who wants something, someone who is hungry, someone who is a pilgrim in this wilderness, thirsting and panting for the fountains of their eternal home, show me such a person, and he or she will understand what I am saying. But if I am speaking to those without feeling, then they will not know what I am talking about. Offer a handful of green grass to a sheep and you draw it toward you. Show a boy some nuts and he is enticed. The child is drawn by the things he wants to grasp, drawn because he wants them, drawn without physical coercion, drawn simply by the pull of his own appetite. If then, the things that lovers see as the delights and pleasures of the earth can draw them (because it is true that 'everyone is drawn by his own dear delight') then does not Christ draw us when he is revealed to us by the Father? What does the mind desire more strongly than truth? For what does it have an insatiable appetite, and why is it so concerned to cleanse its palate for discerning the truth, unless it is that it may eat and drink wisdom, righteousness, truth and eternity?

In this life we do indeed hunger; but our hopes are fixed on the hereafter when we shall be satisfied. In the gospel Christ speaks both of our present experience when he says: 'Blessed are those who hunger and thirst for righteousness,' and also of our future hope: 'for they shall be satisfied'. And we should also note that when he said, 'No one comes to me unless drawn by the Father who sent me,' he immediately added: 'And I shall raise them up on the last day.' I will give them the thing they love. I will give them all that they hope for. They will behold what they believe but do not yet see. They will eat what they hunger for and be filled with that for which they thirst. When? At the resurrection of the dead, for 'I will raise them up on the last day.'

Saturday after Easter 5

A Reading from *The Resurrection of Christ*
by Michael Ramsey

While traditional Christianity insists upon distinguishing the revealed doctrine of resurrection from a philosophical belief in the immortality of the soul, it regards the latter not as untrue and irrelevant so much as incomplete, distressingly dull and missing the gift of the gospel. There are grounds, both philosophical and psychological and religious, for believing that the soul survives death; though the life of a soul without the body is a conception which it is difficult to imagine. It is *incomplete*; because the self is far more than the soul, and the self without bodily expression can hardly be the complete self. It is *dull*; because it implies the prolongation of man's finite existence for everlasting years. In contrast both with the incompleteness and the dullness of the immortality of the soul Christianity teaches a future state (not as of right but as of God's gift) wherein the soul is not unclothed but clothed upon a bodily expression, and wherein the finite human life is raised so as to share, without losing its finiteness, in the infinite life of Christ himself.

The Christian gospel was not first addressed to people who had *no* belief in a future state. Greeks were familiar with a philosophical doctrine of immortality. Jews believed in the resurrection of the body. Sometimes this was thought of as a resuscitation of human relics and a reconstruction of human existence after the fashion of the present life. Sometimes it was thought of as a transformation of dead bodies into an utterly new state of glory and spiritualization. But nowhere, either for Greek or for Jew, was belief in the future life vivid, immediate, central and triumphant. Nowhere did the belief combine a conscious nearness of the world to come with a moral exalting of life in this present world. This was what Christianity brought. Its doctrine was not a flight to another world that left this world behind, nor was it a longing for another world that would come when the history of this world was ended. It was the very near certainty of another world, with which the Christians were already linked and into which the life of this world would be raised up.

For the Christian belief about the future state centred in Jesus Christ. He had been seen and loved in this life; and he had been seen and loved also as one who had conquered death. He had become vividly known as the Lord both of the living and the dead; and the conviction of his people concerning the future life rested upon their conviction about him in whose life they shared. It was an intense and triumphant conviction that where he was there also would his people be. It found utterance in ringing tones: 'He has brought life and immortality to light through the gospel.' 'Fear not; I am the first and the last, and the living one; I was dead, and behold I am alive for evermore, and I have the keys of death and of Hades.' 'Awake, O sleeper, and rise from the dead, and Christ shall shine upon you.'

The Sixth Sunday of Easter

A Reading from a sermon of Leo the Great

The whole of the mystery of Easter has been given us in the gospel narratives; the terrible betrayal of our Lord Jesus Christ, his condemnation, his cruel crucifixion, his glorious resurrection. Now you must implant in your hearts the words of the gospel.

The cross of which Christ made use to save humankind, is both a mystery, and an example: a mystery in which the fullness of the divine power is involved, an example which leads us to generosity.

When all the human race had fallen, God determined in his mercy to give aid, through his only-begotten Son Jesus Christ, to the creatures made in his own image; he wished that the restoration of their nature should not come from outside, but that it should be raised to a dignity superior to that of its origin. Happy they would have been, if they had not fallen from this first dignity in which he had placed them, but far happier still will they be, if they remain in that to which he has elevated them. It was already much to have recovered their beauty from the hands of Christ, but it is still better to be incorporated in Christ for ever.

The divine nature in him has indeed captured us; we have become his property. In himself, in the unity of his person, he has united human nature to the divine nature. Infirmity and mortality, which are not sinful, but the punishment of sin, were taken by the Redeemer of the world that he might be able to suffer and pay our ransom. Hence, that which is in others the heritage of condemnation, is in Christ the mysterious witness to his loving kindness. For he, who owed nothing, offered himself to the pitiless demands of his creditor; he abandoned his sinless flesh to be tortured by the hands of his enemies, the devil's instruments. He wished to possess a mortal body until his resurrection, so that faith in him would make persecutions bearable, and even death incapable of depressing us; sure of sharing the same nature, we are certain of receiving the same glory.

It follows then, that if we firmly believe in our heart what we profess with our lips, then in Christ we have been crucified, have died, been buried and have also been raised the third day. The Apostle says: 'Risen, then, with Christ, you must lift your thoughts above, where Christ now sits at the right hand of God. Set your minds on the things that are above, not on earth. You have died, and now your life is hid with Christ in God. When Christ is made manifest, who is your life, then you too will be made manifest with him in glory.'

And that the faithful may know how to raise their thoughts to such lofty heights and despise worldly lusts, our Lord pledges to us his presence, saying: 'And behold I am with you all through the days that are coming, until the consummation of the world.'

We must, therefore, neither lose our heads among vanities, nor tremble at adversities. Doubtless, such pleasures have their attractions and work is hard. But since 'the earth is filled with the Lord's kindness,' the victory of Christ which is ours is everywhere. It is the fulfilment of his words: 'Take courage, I have overcome the world.'

Monday after Easter 6

A Reading from a commentary on St Paul's Second Letter
to the Corinthians by Cyril of Alexandria

Those who have a sure hope, guaranteed by the Spirit, that they will rise again lay hold of what lies in the future as though it were already present. They say: Outward appearances will no longer be our standard in judging others. Our lives are all controlled by the Spirit now, and are not confined to this physical world that is subject to corruption. The light of the only-begotten has shone on us, and we have been transformed into the Word, the source of all life. While sin was still our master, the bonds of death had a firm hold on us, but now that the righteousness of Christ has found a place in our hearts we have freed ourselves from our former condition of corruptibility.

This means that none of us lives in the flesh any more, at least not insofar as living in the flesh means being subject to the weaknesses of the flesh, which include corruptibility. 'Once we thought of Christ as being in the flesh, but we do not do so any longer,' says St Paul. By this he meant that the Word became flesh and dwelt among us; he suffered death in the flesh in order to give life to all. It was in this flesh that we knew him before, but we do so no longer. Even though he remains in the flesh, since he came to life again on the third day and is now with the Father in heaven, we know that he has passed beyond the life of the flesh; for 'having died once, he will never die again, death has no power over him any more. His death was a death to sin, which he died once for all; his life is life with God.'

Since Christ has in this way become the source of life for us, we who follow in his footsteps must not think of ourselves as living in the flesh any longer, but as having passed beyond it. St Paul's saying is absolutely true that 'whoever is in Christ becomes a completely different person: their old life is over and a new life has begun.' We have been justified by our faith in Christ and the power of the curse has been broken. Christ's coming to life again for our sake has put an end to the sovereignty of death. We have come to know the true God and to worship him in spirit and in truth, through the Son, our mediator, who sends down upon the world the Father's blessings.

And so St Paul shows deep insight when he says: 'This is all God's doing: it is he who has reconciled us to himself through Christ.' For the mystery of the incarnation and the renewal it accomplished could not have taken place without the Father's will. Through Christ we have gained access to the Father, for as Christ himself says, no one comes to the Father except through him. 'This is all God's doing,' then. 'It is he who has reconciled us to himself through Christ, and who has given us the ministry of reconciliation.'

Tuesday after Easter 6

A Reading from Dietrich Bonhoeffer to Eberhard Bethge
written from Tegel prison, and dated 27 June 1944

It is said that the distinctive feature of Christianity is its proclamation of the hope of resurrection and that this means the emergence of a genuine religion of redemption, the main emphasis now being on the far side of the boundary drawn by death. But it seems to me that this is just where the mistake and the danger lie. Redemption now means redemption from cares, distress, fears, and longings, from sin and death, in a better world beyond the grave.

But is this really the essential character of the proclamation of Christ in the Gospels and by Paul? I should say it is not. The difference between the Christian hope of resurrection and a mythological hope is that the former sends a person back to his life on earth in a wholly new way, which is even more sharply defined than it is in the Old Testament. The Christian, unlike the devotees of the redemption myths, has no last line of escape available from earthly tasks and difficulties into the eternal. But, like Christ himself, he must drink the earthly cup to the dregs, and only in his doing so, is the crucified and risen Lord with him, and he crucified and risen with Christ. This world must not be prematurely written off. In this the Old and New Testaments are one. Redemption myths arise from human boundary-experiences, but Christ takes hold of a man in the centre of his life.

Wednesday after Easter 6

A Reading from an oration 'On the resurrection'
by Gregory of Nyssa

The reign of life has begun, the tyranny of death is ended. A new birth has taken place, a new life has come, a new order of existence has appeared, our very nature has been transformed! This birth is not brought about 'by human generation, by the will of man, or by the desire of the flesh, but by God'.

If you wonder how, I will explain in clear language. Faith is the womb that conceives this new life, baptism the rebirth by which it is brought forth into the light of day. The Church is its nurse, her teachings are its milk, the bread from heaven is its food. It is brought to maturity by the practice of virtue; it is wedded to wisdom; it gives birth to hope. Its home is the kingdom; its rich inheritance the joys of paradise; its end, not death but the blessed and everlasting life prepared for those who are worthy.

'This is the day that the Lord has made' – a day very different from those made when the world was first created and which are measured by the passage of time. This is the beginning of a new creation. On this day, as the prophet says, God makes a new heaven and a new earth. What is this new heaven? you may ask. It is the firmament of our faith in Christ. What is the new earth? A good heart, a heart like the earth, which drinks up the rain that falls on it and yields a rich harvest.

In this new creation, purity of life is the sun, the virtues are the stars, transparent goodness is the air, and 'the depths of the riches of wisdom and knowledge', the sea. Sound doctrine, the divine teachings are the grass and plants that feed God's flock, the people whom he shepherds, the keeping of the commandments is the fruit borne by the trees.

On this day is created a new humanity, one made in the image and likeness of God. For 'this day the Lord has made' is the beginning of this new world. Of this day the prophet says that it is not like any other day, nor is this night like other nights. But still we have not spoken of the greatest gift it has brought us. This day destroyed the pangs of death and brought to birth the firstborn of the dead.

'I am ascending to my Father and to your Father, to my God and to your God,' declares the risen Christ. O what wonderful good news! He who for our sake became like us in order to make us his brothers and sisters, now presents to his true Father his own humanity in order to draw all his brothers and sisters up after him.

Ascension Day

A Reading from a sermon of Leo the Great

At Easter, it was the Lord's resurrection which was the cause of our joy; our present rejoicing is on account of his ascension into heaven. With all due solemnity we are commemorating that day on which our poor human nature was carried up in Christ, above all the hosts of heaven, above all the ranks of angels, beyond the highest heavenly powers to the very throne of God the Father. It is upon this ordered structure of divine acts that we have been firmly established, so that the grace of God may show itself still more marvellous when, in spite of the withdrawal from our sight of everything that is rightly felt to command our reverence, faith does not fail, hope is not shaken, charity does not grow cold.

For such is the power of great minds, such the light of truly believing souls, that they put unhesitating faith in what is not seen with the bodily eye; they fix their desires on what is beyond sight. Such fidelity could never be born in our hearts, nor could anyone be justified by faith, if our salvation lay only in what was visible.

And so our Redeemer's visible presence has passed into the sacraments. Our faith is nobler and stronger because sight has been replaced by a doctrine whose authority is accepted by believing hearts, enlightened from on high. This faith was increased by the Lord's ascension and strengthened by the gift of the Spirit; it would remain unshaken by fetters and imprisonment, exile and hunger, fire and ravening beasts, and the most refined tortures ever devised by brutal persecutors. Throughout the world women no less than men, girls as well as boys, have given their life's blood in the struggle for this faith. It is a faith that has driven out devils, healed the sick and raised the dead.

Even the blessed apostles, though they had been strengthened by so many miracles and instructed by so much teaching, took fright at the cruel suffering of the Lord's passion and could not accept his resurrection without hesitation. Yet they made such progress through his ascension that they now found joy in what had terrified them before. They were able to fix their minds on Christ's divinity as he sat at the right hand of the Father, since what was presented to their bodily eyes no longer hindered them from turning all their attention to the realisation that he had not left his Father when he came down to earth, nor had he abandoned his disciples when he ascended into heaven.

The truth is that the Son of Man was revealed as Son of God in a more perfect and transcendent way once he had entered into the Father's glory; he now began to be indescribably more present in divinity to those from whom he was further removed in humanity. A more mature faith enabled their minds to stretch upward to the Son in his equality with the Father; it no longer needed contact with Christ's tangible body, in which as a human being he is inferior to the Father. For while his glorified body retained the same nature, the faith of those who believed in him was now summoned to heights where, as the Father's equal, the only-begotten Son is reached not by physical handling but by spiritual discernment.

alternative reading

A Reading from a commentary on St John's Gospel
by Cyril of Alexandria

Our Lord Jesus Christ has opened for us a new and living way into God's presence, 'not entering a sanctuary made by human hands, but by entering heaven itself to appear before God on our behalf'. For Christ has not entered heaven in order to make his own appearance before God the Father. He was, and is, and always will be in the Father, in the sight of the One from whom he receives his being, for in him is the Father's unending joy.

But today, the Word, who had never been clothed in human nature before, has ascended as a human being, revealing himself in a new and unfamiliar way. And he has done this for us and in our name, so that being like us (though with the status of the Son) and hearing the command to 'Sit at my right hand', he might transmit to fellow members of the human race the glory of being children of God. For since he became man it is as one of us that he sits at the right hand of God the Father, though in truth he is above all creation and is one in being with his Father: God from God, Light from Light.

It was, then, as a human being on our behalf that he appeared before the Father today, to enable those who had been cast out from the Father's presence because of sin to once again behold the face of God. As the Son he took his seat to enable us as sons and daughters through him to be called the children of God. That is why Paul, who claims to speak for Christ, teaches that the whole human race participates in the life of Christ, saying: 'God has raised us up with Christ and enthroned us with him in the heavenly places.'

alternative reading

A Reading from a sermon of Augustine

Today our Lord Jesus Christ ascended into heaven; let our hearts ascend with him. Listen to the words of the Apostle: 'If you have risen with Christ, set your hearts on the things that are above where Christ is, seated at the right hand of God; seek the things that are above, not the things that are on earth.' For just as he remained with us even after his ascension, so we too are already in heaven with him, even though what is promised us has not yet been fulfilled in our bodies.

Christ is now exalted above the heavens, but he still suffers on earth all the pain that we, the members of his body, have to bear. He showed this when he cried out from above: 'Saul, Saul, why are you persecuting me?' and when he said: 'I was hungry and you gave me food.'

Why do we on earth not strive to find rest with him in heaven even now, through the faith, hope and love that unites us to him! While in heaven he is also with us; and we while on earth are with him. He is here with us by his divinity, his power and his love. We cannot be in heaven, as he is on earth, by divinity; but in him, we can be there by love. He did not leave heaven when he came down to us; nor did he withdraw from us when he went up again into heaven. The fact that he was in heaven even while he was on earth is borne out by his own statement: 'No one has ever ascended into heaven except the one who descended from heaven, the Son of Man, who is in heaven.'

These words are explained by our oneness with Christ, for he is our head and we are his body. No one ascended into heaven except Christ because we also are Christ: he is the Son of Man by his union with us, and we by our union with him are children and heirs of God. So the Apostle says: 'Just as the human body, which has many members, is a unity, because all the different members make one body, so is it also with Christ.' He too has many members, but one body.

Out of compassion for us he descended from heaven, and although he ascended alone, we also ascend, because weare in him by grace. Thus, no one but Christ descended and no one but Christ ascended; not because there is no distinction between the head and the body, but because the body as a unity cannot be separated from the head.

alternative reading

A Reading from a poem by George Herbert

Praise

King of Glory, King of Peace,
 I will love thee:
And that love may never cease,
 I will move thee.
Thou hast granted my request,
 Thou hast heard me:
Thou didst note my working breast,
 Thou hast spar'd me.

Wherefore with my utmost art
 I will sing thee,
And the cream of all my heart
 I will bring thee.
Though my sins against me cried,
 Thou didst clear me;
And alone, when they replied,
 Thou didst hear me.

Sev'n whole days, not one in seven,
 I will praise thee.
In my heart, though not in heaven,
 I can raise thee.
Small it is, in this poor sort
 to enrol thee:
Ev'n eternity is too short
 To extol thee.

Friday after Ascension Day

A Reading from a commentary on St John's Gospel
by Cyril of Alexandria

After Christ had completed his mission on earth, it still remained necessary for us to become sharers in the divine nature of the Word. We had to give up our own life and be so transformed that we would begin to live an entirely new kind of life that would be pleasing to God. This was something we could do only by sharing in the Holy Spirit.

It was most fitting that the sending of the Spirit and his descent upon us should take place after the departure of Christ our Saviour. As long as Christ was with them in the flesh, it must have seemed to believers that they possessed every blessing in him; but when the time came for him to ascend to his heavenly Father, it was necessary for him to be united through his Spirit to those who worshipped him, and to dwell in our hearts through faith. Only by his own presence within us in this way could he give us confidence to cry out: 'Abba, Father,' make it easy for us to grow in holiness and, through our possession of the all-powerful Spirit, fortify us invincibly against the wiles of the devil and the assaults of men and women.

It can easily be shown from examples both in the Old Testament and the New that the Spirit changes those in whom he comes to dwell; he so transforms them that they begin to live a completely new kind of life, foretold by the prophet Samuel: 'The Spirit of the Lord will take possession of you, and you shall be changed into another person.' St Paul writes: 'As we behold the glory of the Lord with unveiled faces, that glory which comes from the Lord who is the Spirit, transforms us all into his own likeness, from one degree of glory to another.'

Does this not show that the Spirit changes those in whom he comes to dwell and alters the whole pattern of their lives? With the Spirit within them it is quite natural for people who had been absorbed by the things of this world to become entirely other-worldly in outlook, and for cowards to become people of great courage. There can be no doubt that this is what happened to the disciples. The strength they received from the Spirit enabled them to hold firmly to the love of Christ, facing the violence of their persecutors unafraid. Very true, then, was our Saviour's saying that it was to their advantage for him to return to heaven.

Saturday after Ascension Day

A reading from a treatise *On the Lord's Prayer*
by Cyprian of Carthage

We should live as temples of God that it may be plain to all that God dwells in us. It is important that our conduct should not degenerate and we become unworthy of the Spirit. Rather let us who have set out to be heavenly and spiritual, entertain only heavenly and spiritual thoughts and behaviour. For as the Lord God himself has declared: 'I will glorify those who glorify me; but those that despise me, I shall despise.' The blessed apostle Paul has also stated in one of his letters: 'You are not your own; you were bought at a price. Therefore, glorify God in your body.'

In the Lord's Prayer we go on to say: 'Hallowed be your name.' We are not envisaging that God will be made holy by our prayers: we are asking rather that his holiness should shine in us. Anyway, by whom could God be sanctified since it is God himself who sanctifies? But observe that in Scripture it is also written: 'Be holy because I am holy.' Thus it should be our earnest desire that we, who have been made holy in baptism, should continue to grow in what we have begun to be; and for this we pray every day. We certainly need to be made holy daily because every day we sin, and every day we need to have those sins washed away. In this way we are engaged in a process that makes us ever more deeply sanctified.

The Seventh Sunday of Easter

(The Sunday after the Ascension)

A Reading from a homily of Gregory of Nyssa

When love has cast out fear from our souls completely, and all fear in us has been transformed into love, then the unity which is the gift of our Saviour will be fully realised among us, because we will all be united with each other through our union with the one supreme Good.

Following his ascension, after conferring all power on his disciples by his blessing, our Lord obtained many other gifts for them by his prayer to the Father. Among these was the greatest gift of all, which was that they were no longer to be divided in their judgement about what was right and good, because they were all to be united to the one supreme Good. As the Apostle says, they were to be bound together with the bonds of peace in the unity that comes from the Holy Spirit. They were to be made one body and one spirit by the one hope to which they were all called. We shall do well, however, to quote the sacred words of the gospel itself. 'I pray', the Lord says, 'that they all may be one; that as you, Father, are in me and I am in you, so they also may be one in us.'

Now the bond that creates this unity is glory. That the Holy Spirit is called glory no one can deny if one reflects upon our Lord's words: 'The glory you gave to me, I have given to them.' In fact, he gave this glory to his disciples when he said to them: 'Receive the Holy Spirit.' Although he had always possessed it, even before the world existed, our Lord received this glory when he put on human nature. Then, when his human nature had been glorified by the Spirit, the glory of the Spirit was passed on to all his brothers and sisters, beginning with his disciples. This is why he said: 'The glory you gave to me, I have given to them, so that they may be one as we are one. With me in them and you in me, I want them to be perfectly one.'

Whoever then grows from infancy to adulthood and attains to spiritual maturity possesses the mastery of human compulsions and an inner purity that makes it possible to receive the glory of the Spirit.

Monday before Pentecost

A Reading from *The Go-Between God*
by John V. Taylor

The prayer of the first Christians was simply a reflection of the living Christ in their midst. It was prayer 'in his name'; and by this, we mean not that a formula was added at the end of every petition, but that in all their prayer they joined themselves to the prayer of Christ himself, and knew that it was his spirit which prayed in them. The best worship they could offer was simply his self-oblation in them. Praying in that Spirit, the Christian's prayer is immersed in the ocean of the Son's communion with the Father: 'Praying in the Holy Spirit, keep yourselves in the love of God.' And again, 'Keep your watch with continuous prayer and supplication, praying the whole time in the Spirit. With constant wakefulness and perseverance you will find opportunity to pray for all the Christian brethren.' 'We do not even know how we ought to pray, but through our inarticulate groans the Spirit himself is pleading for us, and God who searches our inmost being knows what the Spirit means, because he pleads for God's own people in God's own way.'

To live in prayer, therefore, is to live in the Spirit, and to live in the Spirit is to live in Christ. I am not saying that prayer is a means or a method which we have to use in order to have more of Christ in us or in order to be more fully possessed by the Spirit. I am saying something simpler and more fundamental: to live in Christ is to live in prayer. Prayer is not something you do; it is a style of living. It is living under the witness which the Spirit bears with our spirit that we are children of God. Such a witness lays upon us the aweful freedom of adult sonship. Prayer is our response to both the privilege and the responsibility whereby we cry Abba, Father! To engage in the mission of God, therefore, is to live this life of prayer; praying without ceasing, as St Paul puts it, that is to say, sustaining a style of life that is focused upon God. This is indeed to engage in the mission of the Holy Spirit by being rather than by doing. To realise that the heart of mission is communion with God in the midst of the world's life will save us from the demented activism of these days.

Tuesday before Pentecost

A Reading from a sermon of the Venerable Bede

The Holy Spirit will give to those who love God the perfect peace of eternity. But even now the Spirit gives them great peace when kindling in their hearts the celestial fire of love. In fact, the Apostle says: 'This hope will not leave us disappointed, because the love of God has been poured out in our hearts through the Holy Spirit who has been given to us.'

The true, indeed, the only peace for souls in this world consists in being filled with divine love and animated with heavenly hope to the point of setting no store on the successes and failures of this world, of stripping ourselves wholly of earthly desires, of renouncing all worldly covetousness and rejoicing in injuries and persecutions suffered for Christ's sake, so that we can say with the Apostle: 'We boast of our hope for the glory of God. But not only that – we even boast of our afflictions!' Those who expect to find peace in riches and in the enjoyment of this world's goods are only self-deceived. The frequent troubles of life here below and the fact that this world will end should convince such people that they are building their foundations on sand.

On the other hand, all those who, touched by the breath of the Holy Spirit, have taken upon themselves the excellent yoke of God's love and who, following Christ's example, have learned to be gentle and lowly in heart – these do already rejoice in a peace which even now is the image of eternal rest. In the depths of their souls they are separated from the commotion of humanity, they have the joy of remembering the presence of their Creator wherever they may be, and they thirst for the attainment of perfect contemplation, saying with St John the Apostle: 'We know that when it is revealed we shall be like him, for we shall see him as he is.'

If we want to be rewarded with this vision, we shall need to bear the gospel in mind unceasingly and to show ourselves heedless of all worldly attractions; then we shall be found worthy to receive the grace of the Holy Spirit which the world cannot receive. Let us love Christ and persevere in observing his commandments which we have begun to follow.

The more we love him, the more we shall merit to be loved by his Father, and then he himself will grant us the grace of his great love in eternity. In this life he gives us faith and hope; in the life to come we shall see him face to face and he will show himself to us in the glory which he had with his Father before the world was made.

Wednesday before Pentecost

A Reading from the treatise *The Mirror of Faith*
by William of St Thierry

When obscure mysteries are presented to your timid nature by your faith, take courage and say: 'How have these things emerged?' Do not ask in an aggressive way, but with the love of a disciple. Let your questioning become your prayer, your love, your piety, your humble desire for God; not seeking to plumb the depths of God's majesty, but looking for your salvation in the healing activity of the One who comes to save us.

And when you thus pray, the angel of counsel will reply to you: 'When the Counsellor comes, he whom I shall send to you from the Father, he will call to mind all things, and lead you into all truth.' For, as Scripture says, 'What human being knows what is truly human except the human spirit within? So also, no one comprehends what is truly God's except the Spirit of God.'

Hasten then to become a sharer in the Holy Spirit. The Spirit is present whenever called upon; nor could he be called upon were he not already present. When we pray to the Spirit, he comes to us bearing the abundance of the gifts of God. The Spirit is the ever-flowing river which gives joy to the city of God.

If, when he comes to your soul, he finds you humble and still and receptive to the words of God, he will rest upon you. He will reveal to you what God the Father withholds from the clever and prudent of this world; and those same things will begin to dawn on you which Wisdom could say to the disciples on earth, but which they were unable to bear until the Spirit came to lead them into all truth.

In the diligent seeking after these things, in the learning of these lessons, it would be idle to expect from any human teacher what can only be sought and learnt from the lips of Truth himself; for as that Truth says in the gospel: 'God is spirit.' And just as it is necessary for those who worship him to do so in spirit and in truth, so for those who wish to learn from him or know him, it is only in the Holy Spirit that the understanding of the faith, and the perception of the pure and unadorned truth can be sought.

In the darkness and ignorance of this world the Holy Spirit is life: he is the light which enlightens the poor in spirit. He is the love which draws us to God, the sweetening presence, our very approach to God in prayer, the love we experience in loving, devotion and piety. He reveals to the faithful the justice of God which issues from faith and ends in faith.

Thursday before Pentecost

A Reading from the *Catechetical Lectures*
of Cyril of Jerusalem

'The water that I shall give you will become in you a fountain of living water, welling up into eternal life.' This is a new kind of water, a living, leaping water, welling up for those who are worthy. But why did Christ call the grace of the Spirit water? Because all things are dependent on water; plants and animals have their origin in water. Water comes down from heaven as rain, and although it is always the same in itself, it produces many different effects, one in the palm tree, another in the vine, and so on throughout the whole of creation. It does not come down, now as one thing, now as another, but while remaining essentially the same, it adapts itself to the needs of every creature that receives it.

In the same way the Holy Spirit, whose nature is always the same, simple and indivisible, apportions grace to each as the Spirit wills. Like a dry tree which puts forth shoots when watered, the soul bears the fruit of holiness when repentance has made it worthy of receiving the Holy Spirit. Although the Spirit never changes, the effects of the Spirit's action, by the will of God and in the name of Christ, are both many and marvellous.

The Spirit makes one a teacher of divine truth, inspires another to prophesy, gives another the power of casting out devils, enables another to interpret Scripture. The Spirit strengthens one person's self-control, shows another how to help the poor, teaches another to fast and lead a life of asceticism, makes another oblivious to the needs of the body, trains another for martyrdom. This action is different in different people, but the Spirit is always the same. 'In each person,' Scripture says, 'the Spirit reveals his presence in a particular way for the common good.'

The Spirit comes gently and makes himself known by his fragrance. The Spirit is not felt as a burden, for the Spirit is light, very light. Rays of light and knowledge stream before him as he approaches. The Spirit comes with the tenderness of a true friend and protector to save, to heal, to teach, to counsel, to strengthen, to console. The Spirit comes to enlighten the mind first of the one who receives him, and then, through that person, the minds of others as well.

As light strikes the eyes of those who come out of darkness into the sunshine and enables them to see clearly things they could not discern before, so light floods the souls of those counted worthy of receiving the Holy Spirit and enables them to see things beyond the range of human vision, things hitherto undreamed of.

Friday before Pentecost

A Reading from a commentary on St John's Gospel
by Cyril of Alexandria

In a plan of surpassing beauty the Creator of the universe decreed the renewal of all things in Christ. In his design for restoring human nature to its original condition, he gave a promise that he would pour out on it the Holy Spirit along with his other gifts, for otherwise our nature could not enter once more into the peaceful and secure possession of those gifts.

He therefore appointed a time for the Holy Spirit to come upon us: this was the time of Christ's coming. He gave this promise when he said: 'In those days,' that is, the days of the Saviour, 'I will pour out a share of my Spirit on all humanity.'

When the time came for this great act of unforced generosity, which revealed in our midst the only-begotten Son, clothed with flesh on this earth, born of woman, in accordance with holy Scripture, God the Father gave the Spirit once again. Christ, as the first-fruits of our restored nature, was the first to receive the Spirit. John the Baptist bore witness to this when he said: 'I saw the Spirit coming down from heaven, and it rested on him.'

Christ 'received the Spirit' insofar as he was human, and insofar as a human being could receive the Spirit. He did so in such a way that, though he is the Son of God the Father, begotten of his substance, even before the incarnation, indeed before all ages, yet he was not offended at hearing the Father say to him after he had become human: 'You are my Son; today I have begotten you.'

The Father says of Christ, who was God, begotten of him before the ages, that he has been 'begotten today', for the Father is to accept us in Christ as his adopted children. The whole of our nature is present in Christ, insofar as he is human. So the Father can be said to give the Spirit again to the Son, though the Son possesses the Spirit as his own, in order that we may receive the Spirit in Christ. The Son therefore took to himself the seed of Abraham, as Scripture says, and became like us in all things.

The only-begotten Son receives the Spirit, but not for his own advantage, for the Spirit is his, and is given in him and through him, as we have already said. He receives it to renew our nature in its entirety and to make it whole again, for in becoming human he took our entire nature to himself. If we reason correctly, and use also the testimony of Scripture, we can see that Christ did not receive the Spirit for himself, but rather for us in him; for it is also through Christ that all gifts come down to us.

Saturday before Pentecost

A Reading from a treatise *On the Holy Spirit*
by Basil the Great

Is there anyone who, on hearing the various titles of the Holy Spirit, does not experience a certain exaltation as their mind contemplates that supreme nature? For it is called the 'Spirit of God', 'the Spirit of truth who proceeds from the Father', the 'right Spirit', the 'guiding Spirit'. But the chief and distinctive title is simply 'Holy Spirit', which is appropriate for that which is without material body and cannot be divided.

Our Lord when teaching the Samaritan woman at the well who thought God to be merely an object of local worship, said that 'God is Spirit'; in other words that God is without material body and unable to be comprehended. If we consider this statement, it precludes any idea of a circumscribed nature, subject to change and chance, or anything resembling a creature. On the contrary, we are compelled to push the categories of our thinking to the limit, and to conceive of the Spirit in terms of an intelligent essence, of infinite power, of unlimited greatness, traversing all times and ages.

The Spirit is generous in bestowing gifts; and in response, every creature turns to the Spirit to be made holy. Those who are concerned to live virtuously reach out to the Spirit, and by the breath of the Spirit's inspiration, are enabled to travel toward their natural and proper end. The Spirit lacks nothing because he is the source of all perfection. The Spirit needs no restoration because he is himself the supplier of life. The Spirit requires no additions because from all eternity the Spirit is abundantly full, self-established, present everywhere, the source of holiness and the light of our understanding, offering illumination to every mind that is searching for truth.

Although the Spirit is by nature inaccessible, yet through the generosity of God we can receive him. The Spirit fills all creation with his power, but this reality is only apprehended by those who are worthy. Moreover, not everyone shares in the Spirit to the same degree, but rather as Scripture says, the Spirit distributes his energy 'according to a person's faith'. Thus the Spirit is simple in essence but manifold in power. The Spirit is present to each individual in fullness, and in fullness is present everywhere. The Spirit is shared, but does not suffer division. All share in the Spirit and yet the Spirit remains entire, like a sunbeam whose gentle light falls upon a person who enjoys it as though the sun shone for her alone, whereas in reality the sun is shining over land and sea and mingles with the air. In the same way, the Spirit is present to all those who are capable of receiving him as if given to each uniquely, and sends forth grace sufficient and great enough for all, yet without loss to itself; and we profit by sharing in this, but according to our capacity, not according to the Spirit's power.

Through the Spirit's aid hearts are raised on high, the weak are led by the hand, and those who are reaching forward in life are led on to perfection. Shining on those whose hearts are purified and stainless, the Spirit makes them truly spiritual through the intimate union they have been granted. As when a ray of light touches a polished and shining surface, and the object becomes even more brilliant, so too souls that are enlightened by the Spirit become spiritual themselves and reflect their grace to others.

The grace of the Holy Spirit enables them to foresee the shape of the future, to penetrate mysteries, to discern the meaning of obscure realities, to receive spiritual blessings, to focus their minds on their heavenly citizenship, and to dance with the angels. Thus is their joy unending and their perseverance in God unfailing. Thus do they become like God, and most wonderful of all, thus do they themselves become divine.

Pentecost

(Whit Sunday)

A Reading from a treatise *Against Heresies*
by Irenaeus

When the Lord told his disciples 'to go and teach all nations' and to 'baptize them in the name of the Father and of the Son and of the Holy Spirit', he conferred on them the power of giving people new life in God.

He had promised through the prophets that in these last days he would pour out his Spirit on his servants and handmaids, and that they would prophesy. So when the Son of God became the Son of Man, the Spirit also descended upon him, becoming accustomed in this way to dwelling with the human race, to living in them and to inhabiting God's creation. The Spirit accomplished the Father's will in people who had grown old in sin, and gave them new life in Christ.

Luke says that the Spirit came down on the disciples at Pentecost, after the Lord's ascension, with power to open the gates of life to all nations and to make known to them the new covenant. So it was that people of every language joined in singing one song of praise to God, and scattered tribes, restored to unity by the Spirit, were offered to the Father as the firstfruits of all the nations.

This was why the Lord had promised to send the Advocate: he was to prepare us as an offering to God. Like dry flour, which cannot become one lump of dough, one loaf of bread, without moisture, we who are many could not become one in Christ Jesus without the water that comes down from heaven. And like parched ground, which yields no harvest unless it receives moisture, we who were once like a waterless tree could never have lived and borne fruit without this abundant rainfall from above. Through the baptism that liberates us from change and decay we have become one in body; through the Spirit we have become one in soul.

'The Spirit of wisdom and understanding, the Spirit of counsel and strength, the Spirit of knowledge and the fear of God' came down upon the Lord, and the Lord in turn gave this Spirit to his Church, sending the Advocate from heaven into all the world into which, according to his own words, the devil too had been cast down like lightning.

If we are not to be scorched and made unfruitful, we need the dew of God. Since we have our accuser, we need an Advocate as well. And so the Lord in his pity for us who had fallen into the hands of brigands, having himself bound up our wounds and left for our care two coins bearing the royal image, entrusted us to the Holy Spirit. Now, through the Spirit, the image and inscription of the Father and the Son have been given to us, and it is our duty to use the coin committed to our charge and make it yield a rich profit for the Lord.

alternative reading

A Reading from a sermon of Leo the Great

'And there appeared tongues as of fire, distributed on each of them and resting upon them. And they were all filled with the Holy Spirit, and began to speak with other tongues as the Holy Spirit gave them utterance.'

O how rapid is the discourse of wisdom, and where God is the teacher, how soon is the lesson taught! It was not necessary for the apostles to receive some sort of interpretation in order that they might hear better; they were not given time to familiarise themselves with a vocabulary in order to be more eloquent; they had no time for study; but by the Spirit of truth 'blowing where he willed' the various languages of various nations were made common speech in the mouth of the Church.

It was on this day of Pentecost that the trumpet of the preaching of the gospel sounded forth. It was on this day that showers of spiritual gifts fell from heaven, streams of blessings which watered every desert place and all dry ground, for 'the Spirit of God was moving over the face of the waters' in order to 'renew the face of the earth'. New flashes of light were beaming forth to drive out the old darkness, seeing that by the splendour of the radiant tongues was being received the lustrous Word of the Lord, a fiery utterance in which is present an energy which illuminates, a burning force which stimulates intelligence and consumes sin.

A Reading from the *Meditations* of Richard Challoner

The Israelites observed the solemnity of Pentecost as one of the three principal feasts of the year, because on that day the old law was published from Mount Sinai in thunder and lightning. How much more ought Christians religiously to observe this solemnity, because on this day the new law of grace and love was published on Mount Zion, by the coming down of the Holy Ghost in tongues of fire.

Consider also that the Holy Ghost came down upon the apostles in the shape of tongues, to signify that he came to make them fit preachers of his word, and to endow them with the gift of tongues, accompanied with the heavenly wisdom and understanding of the mysteries of God and all the gospel truths, to the end that they might be enabled to teach and publish, throughout the whole world, the faith and law of Christ! And these tongues were of fire, to signify how his divine Spirit sets those souls on fire in which he abides, inflaming them with divine love, consuming the dross of their earthly affections, putting them in a continual motion of earnest desires and endeavours to go forward from virtue to virtue as fire is always in motion, and carrying them upwards towards the God of Gods in his heavenly Zion, as the flame is always ascending upwards towards its element.

O blessed fire, when shall I partake of thy sacred flames? O come and take possession of my heart, consume all these bonds that tie it to the earth, and carry it up with thee towards the heavenly furnace from whence thou comest. Sweet Jesus thou hast said, 'I am come to cast fire on the earth, and what will I but that it be kindled?' O cast this fire into my soul, that it may be kindled there!

alternative reading

A Reading from *The Go-Betwen God*
by John V. Taylor

'The Church exists by mission as fire exists by burning.'It is not by chance that Emil Brunner chose that great biblical metaphorof the Spiritand his mission. Jewish teachers hadtakentheburning bush to be a symbol of the ideal Israel on fire with God's purpose and action in the world, yet unconsumed. The true Church also exists by being the inexhaustible fuel of the Holy Spirit's mission in the world. While they burn together the branches and twigs are the fire, yet they do not in themselves constitute the fire. The fire, rather, contains them, living around them in the interstices, and if a twig drops to the ground the fire that seemed to be in it soon vanishes. Only in their togetherness can Christians remain alight with the fire of the Spirit. That is the sole purpose of our visible fellowship – to be the fuel upon which the fire is kindled in the earth. The Church must be shaped to carry out that purpose or it will be as frustrating as a badly laid fire. The question we have continually to put to the organisation and structure of the Church is this: does it bring Christian face to face with Christian in that communion which is the sphere of the Holy Spirit's presence?

Our theology would improve if we thought more of the Church being given to the Spirit than of the Spirit being given to the Church. For if we phrase it in the second way, although it is the New Testament way, we are in danger of perpetuating the irreverence of picturing God's Spirit as a grant of superhuman power or guidance, like a fairy sword or magic mirror to equip us for our adventures. The promised power from on high is not of that kind at all. The primary effect of the pentecostal experience was to fuse the individuals of that company into a fellowship which in the same moment was caught up into the life of the risen Lord. In a new awareness of him and of one another they burst into praise, and the world came running for an explanation. In other words, the gift of the Holy Spirit in the fellowship of the Church first enables Christians to be, and only as a consequence of that sends them to do and to speak. The Holy Spirit is given to enable 'the two or three gathered together' to embody Jesus Christ in the world.

alternative reading

A Reading from a poem by Joyce Rupp

inside each of us

inside each of us
there awaits
a wonder
full
spirit of freedom

she waits
to dance
in the rooms
of our heart
that are closed
dark and cluttered

she waits
to dance
in the spaces
where negative feelings
have built barricades
and stock-piled weapons

she waits
to dance
in the corners
where we still
do not believe
in our goodness

inside each of us
there awaits
a wonder
full
spirit of freedom

she will lift light feet
and make glad songs
within us
on the day
we open the door of ego
and let the enemies
stomp out

ORDINARY TIME
AFTER PENTECOST

We are compelled to attempt what is unattainable,
to climb where we cannot reach, to speak what we cannot utter.
Instead of the bare adoration of faith we are compelled
to entrust the deep things of religion
to the perils of human expression.

Hilary of Poitiers

All occasions invite God's mercies,
and all times are his seasons.

John Donne

During **Ordinary Time,** there is no seasonal emphasis, except during the period between All Saints' Day and Advent Sunday which is observed as a time to celebrate and reflect upon the reign of Christ in earth and heaven. Readings for this period are provided separately.

At the end of this section will be found readings suitable for the **Dedication Festival** of a church. This is normally held on the anniversary of its dedication or consecration. When the date of consecration is unknown, the Dedication Festival may be observed on the first Sunday in October, or on the last Sunday after Trinity or on a suitable date chosen locally.

Monday after the Day of Pentecost

A Reading from *Ways of Imperfection* by Simon Tugwell

The Church has known many different moods in the course of history. Sometimes she appears to be very confident of herself and of the value of her message, sometimes she seems rather to be a bit confused and unsure of herself; sometimes she boldly tells everyone exactly what they ought to be doing, sometimes she gives the impression of groping in the darkness. And it is not necessarily in her 'best' moments, when she is most confident and clear, that she is most true to herself. There is a kind of unsatisfactoriness written into her very constitution, because she is only a transitional organisation, keeping people and preparing them for a new creation, in which God will be all and in all, and every tear will be wiped away. When she speaks too securely, she may obscure the fact that her essential business is with 'what no eye has seen, no ear has heard, nor has it entered the heart of man'. The blunt truth is, as St John says, that 'we have not yet been shown what we shall be'. A time of confusion like our own, when people become disillusioned with the Church and with Christianity, should be a salutary, educative time, when we face the facts.

Christianity has to be disappointing, precisely because it is not a mechanism for accomplishing all our human ambitions and aspirations: it is a mechanism for subjecting all things to the will of God. The first disciples were disappointed because Jesus turned out not to be the kind of Messiah they wanted. Even after the resurrection St Luke shows us how the apostles were still dreaming of a political restoration of the kingdom of Israel. They had to be disappointed. When people turn away from the Church, because they find more satisfaction elsewhere, it is important not to assume that we, as Christians, ought to be providing such satisfaction ourselves; it is much more urgent that we take yet another look at just what it is that we have genuinely been given in the Church. We may indeed say that Christianity does direct us towards the fulfilment of all our desires and hopes; but we shall only say this correctly if we understand it to mean that a great many of the desires and hopes we are conscious of will eventually turn out to be foolish and misconceived. It is God who knows how to make us happy, better than we know ourselves. Christianity necessarily involves a remaking of our hopes. And our disappointments are an unavoidable part of the process.

Tuesday after the Day of Pentecost

A Reading from *The Ascetical Treatises*
of Isaac of Nineveh

When the Spirit dwells within a person, from the moment that person has become prayer, the Spirit never leaves them. For the Spirit himself never ceases to pray within us. Whether we are asleep or awake, from then on prayer never departs from our soul. Whether we are eating or drinking or sleeping or whatever else we may be doing, even if we are in the deepest of sleeps, the incense of prayer is rising without effort in our heart. Prayer never again deserts us. In every moment of our life, even when it appears to have ceased, prayer is secretly at work within us continuously.

One of the Fathers, the bearers of Christ, teaches that prayer is the silence of the pure in heart; for their very thoughts are the movements of God. The movements of the heart and the intellect that have been purified become voices full of sweetness with which such people never cease to sing in secret to the hidden God.

Wednesday after the Day of Pentecost

A Reading from *Life Together* by Dietrich Bonhoeffer

Innumerable times a whole Christian community has broken down because it had sprung from a wish dream. The serious Christian, set down for the first time in a Christian community, is likely to bring with him or her a very definite idea of what Christian life together should be and try to realise it. But God's grace speedily shatters such dreams. Just as surely as God desires to lead us to a knowledge of genuine Christian fellowship, so surely must we be overwhelmed by a great general disillusionment with others, with Christians in general, and, if we are fortunate, with ourselves.

By sheer grace God will not permit us to live even for a brief period in a dream world. He does not abandon us to those rapturous experiences and lofty moods that come over us like a dream. God is not a God of the emotions but the God of truth. Only that fellowship which faces such disillusionment, with all its unhappy and ugly aspects, begins to be what it should be in God's sight, begins to grasp in faith the promise that is given to it. The sooner this shock of disillusionment comes to an individual and to a community the better for both. A community which cannot bear and cannot survive such a crisis, which insists upon keeping its illusion when it should be shattered, permanently loses in that moment the promise of Christian community. Sooner or later it will collapse. Every human wish dream that is injected into the Christian community is a hindrance to genuine community and must be banished if genuine community is to survive. He who loves his dream of a community more than the Christian community itself becomes a destroyer of the latter, even though his personal intentions may be ever so honest and earnest and sacrificial.

Because God has already laid the only foundation of our fellowship, because God has bound us together in one body with other Christians in Jesus Christ, long before we entered into common life with them, we enter into that common life not as demanders but as thankful recipients. We thank God for what he has done for us. We thank God for giving us brothers and sisters who live by his call, by his forgiveness, and his promise. We do not complain of what God does not give us; we rather thank God for what he does give us daily.

Thursday after the Day of Pentecost

A Reading from the *Meditations* of William of St Thierry

Loving as you are, O Lord, now you multiply your loving-kindness on us all, and we begin to see your mercies that are over all your works. For when, O God, instead of fleeing from us, you begin to draw near and to rejoice our spirits with your consolation, the soul's dead senses catch the fragrance of your healing presence and perceive its touch, and forthwith come to life; faith leaps up and confidence is cheered; the heart is kindled, and tears run down to fan the new-lit fire, not to quench it.

When your Spirit helps our weakness, your sweetness moves us to weep copious floods of sweet and fruitful tears; and when your loving-comfort wipes the tears away, they flow the more profusely and become our meat by day and night, a strong and pleasant food. For it is a happy thing for us who are your people and the sheep of your pasture, O Lord our God, to weep before you who are our Creator.

When first I put myself to school in your service, I seemed to see a new earth and new heavens, for of a sudden you made all things new for me. I am a countryman, Lord, who comes from the country of the world. Teach me your city's ordered ways, the courtesies and gracious manners of your court. Remove from me the likeness of the world on which I have been modelling myself, and make me like your citizens, lest in their midst I seem as one deformed. And teach me too the language that I do not know, the language that I began to hear when I came out of Egypt, but do not understand because I had grown up in an alien land. Teach me the language you speak with your children, and they with you, and make me understand those little signs by which you give understanding hearts to know what is your good, acceptable and perfect will.

Friday after the Day of Pentecost

A Reading from a sermon entitled 'On Christian Growth'
preached at St Cuthbert's, Darlington, in 1892
by Brooke Foss Westcott

My friends, let us be sure of this, that the world is for us, that life is for us, as we see it, as we make it, either an ever-widening vision of God's glory, or a narrow and pitiful spectacle of the conflicts of man's selfishness. We can see only that for which our eyes are opened, and the Holy Spirit alone can open the eyes of the soul.

Have we realised our wants and our opportunities? Have we grown with the growth of eighteen centuries? Our faith is not for the student, or the hermit, or the prelate, but for man as man; not for the cell or the council-chamber – though it is indeed for these – but for the market and for the fireside. It is the apprehension not of a thought, or a message, or a command, but of a fact which reveals what God is and what man is, a Father whose love is limited only by the uttermost need of his children, a child whose lasting joy must be to rest with the light upon him from his Father's eyes.

Have we mastered this truth in life?

The gospel of the Word incarnate has, I believe, and alone can have, the power to answer the questions and satisfy the desires of men which the circumstances of the time are shaping to a clear expression.

No doubt, the end – the divine end – will be reached. The seed of the tree of life, of which the 'leaves shall be for the healing of the nations', will grow we know not how. This confidence can never be shaken. But oh the difference for us in that great hour of revelation if we have watched over the earliest growth of the budding germ with tender foresight, if we have cleared a free space for the spreading branches of the rising plant with diligent care, if we have prepared men to seek their rest under its sheltering arms.

In Christ born, crucified, ascended is the unity, the redemption, the life of humanity. His promise cannot fail: 'I, if I be lifted up from the earth will draw all men unto me.' In the strength of that promise let us hasten his coming, each bringing his own service for the consummation of the one life. The learning of the scholar, now as in every age, needs the chastening sense of its due relation to the whole. The devotion of the saint needs the invigorating discipline of active ministry. The exercise of authority needs the sympathetic grace of sacrifice. The routine of little cares, which forms for most of us the simple record of our days of labour, needs the ennobling influence of a divine companionship. And Christ is waiting to crown each need with blessing.

The work to which we offer ourselves is not ours: it is the work of God.

Saturday after the Day of Pentecost

A Reading from a homily of John Chrysostom

Prayer, loving conversation with God, is the supreme good. It is both a relationship with God and union with him. As the eyes of the body are made sharper by the sight of light, so the soul yearning for God is illumined by his ineffable light. Prayer is not the result of an external attitude; it comes from the heart. It is not limited to set hours or minutes, but, night and day, it is a continuous activity.

It is not enough to direct one's thoughts to God when concentrating exclusively on prayer; even when absorbed in other occupations – such as, caring for the poor, or some other concern in the way of a good or useful work – it is important to combine the work with desire for and remembrance of God. For thus you will be able to offer the Lord a very pleasing food from the universe, seasoned with the salt of love for God.

Prayer is the light of the soul, true knowledge of God, a mediating activity between God and the world. Through it, the soul rises heavenward and embraces the Saviour with ineffable love. As a suckling to its mother, it cries to God, weeping, thirsting for the divine milk. It expresses its deepest desires and receives gifts greater than anything on earth. Prayer, by which we respectfully present ourselves to God, is the joy of the heart and the soul's rest.

Prayer brings the soul to the heavenly fountain, satisfies the soul with this draught, and raises up in it 'a fountain leaping up to provide eternal life'. Prayer gives a real assurance of the good things to come, in faith, and makes present blessings more recognisable. Do not imagine that prayer consists only in words. It is a leap to God, an inexpressible love that is not of our making, as the Apostle says: 'We do not know how to pray as we ought; but the Spirit himself makes intercession for us with groanings too deep for words.'

Such prayer, when the Lord grants it to anyone, is a treasure that cannot be taken away, a heavenly food that satisfies the soul. One who tastes it is filled with an eternal desire for God, such a devouring flame that it kindles the heart. Let this fire flare up in you in all its fullness, to adorn the dwelling place of the heart with kindness and humility, to make it shine with the light of righteousness, and to polish its floor with good deeds.

Hence, adorn your house and instead of mosaics decorate it with faith and magnanimity. And as a finishing touch put prayer at the top of your building. Then you will have prepared a house worthy to receive the Lord, as a royal place, and you yourself, through grace, will already be possessing him, in a certain manner, in the temple of your soul.

Trinity Sunday

A Reading from a letter of Athanasius of Alexandria
to Serapion

It will not be out of place to consider the ancient tradition, teaching and faith of the Catholic Church, which was revealed by the Lord, proclaimed by the apostles and guarded by the fathers. For upon this faith the Church is built, and if anyone were to lapse from it, they would no longer be Christian either in fact or in name.

We acknowledge the Trinity, holy and perfect, to consist of the Father, the Son and the Holy Spirit. In this Trinity there is no intrusion of any alien element or of anything from outside, nor is the Trinity a blend of creative and created being. It is a wholly creative and energising reality, self-consistent and undivided in its active power, for the Father makes all things through the Word and in the Holy Spirit, and in this way the unity of the holy Trinity is preserved. Accordingly, in the Church, one God is preached, one God who is 'above all things and through all things and in all things'. God is 'above all things' as Father, for he is principle and source; he is 'through all things' through the Word; and he is 'in all things' in the Holy Spirit.

Writing to the Corinthians about spiritual matters, Paul traces all reality back to one God, the Father, saying: 'Now there are varieties of gifts, but the same Spirit; and varieties of service, but the same Lord; and there are varieties of working, but it is the same God who inspires them all in everyone.'

Even the gifts that the Spirit dispenses to individuals are given by the Father through the Word. For all that belongs to the Father belongs also to the Son, and so the graces given by the Son in the Spirit are true gifts of the Father. Similarly, when the Spirit dwells in us, the Word who bestows the Spirit is in us too, and the Father is present in the Word. This is the meaning of the text: 'My Father and I will come to him and make our home with him.' For where the light is, there also is the radiance; and where the radiance is, there too are its power and its resplendent grace.

This is also Paul's teaching in his second Letter to the Corinthians: 'The grace of our Lord Jesus Christ and the love of God and the fellowship of the Holy Spirit be with you all.' For grace and the gift of the Trinity are given by the Father through the Son in the Holy Spirit. Just as grace is given from the Father through the Son, so there could be no communication of the gift to us except in the Holy Spirit. But when we share in the Spirit, we possess the love of the Father, the grace of the Son and the fellowship of the Spirit himself.

alternative reading

A Reading from a treatise *On the Trinity*
by Hilary of Poitiers

Our Lord commanded us to baptize in the name of the Father and of the Son and of the Holy Spirit. In baptism, then, we profess faith in the Creator, in the only-begotten Son and in the Gift which is the Spirit. For in God there is one Father from whom all things have their being; and there is one only-begotten Son, our Lord Jesus Christ, through whom all things exist; and there is one Spirit, God's gift to us who is in all. So all follow their due order, according to the proper operation of each: one power from whom all things have come into being; one Son, through whom all things come to be; and one Gift who sustains us in perfect hope. Nothing is wanting in this flawless union: in Father, Son and Holy Spirit, there is an infinity of endless being, the perfect reflection of the divine image, and mutual enjoyment of the Gift.

Christ taught us that God, being Spirit, must be worshipped in the Spirit, and he revealed to us just what freedom and knowledge, what boundless scope for adoration lies in the worship of God the Spirit when we pray in the Spirit.

He described the purpose of the Spirit's presence within us in these words: 'I have yet many things to say to you, but you cannot bear them now. It is to your advantage that I go away; if I go, I will send you the Advocate.' And also: 'I will ask the Father and he will give you another Counsellor to be with you for ever, the Spirit of truth. He will guide you into all the truth; for he will not speak on his own authority, but whatever he hears he will speak, and he will declare to you the things that are to come. He will glorify me, for he will take what is mine.'

Our Lord spoke these words to show how the multitudes might enter the kingdom of heaven, for they reveal to us the intention of the Giver, the nature of the Gift and the condition for its reception. Since our weak minds cannot comprehend the Father or the Son, we have been given the Holy Spirit as our intermediary and illuminator, to shed light on that hard doctrine of our faith, namely, the incarnation of God.

Let us therefore make full use of this benefit, and seek for personal experience of this most important Gift. We receive the Spirit of truth in order that we might know the things of God. Consider how useless the faculties of our body would become if they are denied exercise. Our eyes cannot fulfil their task without light, either natural or artificial; our ears will not function without sound vibrations, and in the absence of any smell our nostrils are ignorant of their function. Not that these senses would lose their own nature if they were not used; rather, they demand, they require external stimulus in order to function. It is the same with the human soul. Although the mind has an innate ability to know God, unless the soul absorbs the Gift of the Spirit through faith, it lacks the light necessary for that knowledge.

This unique Gift which is in Christ is offered in its fullness to every person. It is denied to none, and given to each in proportion to a person's readiness to receive it. Its presence is the richer, the greater our desire to be worthy of it. This Gift will remain with us until the end of the world, and will be our comfort in the time of waiting. By the favours it bestows, it is the pledge of our hope for the future, the light of our minds, and the splendour that irradiates our understanding.

alternative reading

A Reading from the *Instructions* of Columbanus

Who, I ask, will search out the Most High in his own being, for he is beyond words or understanding? Who will penetrate the secrets of God? Who will boast that he knows the infinite God, who fills all things, yet encompasses all things, who pervades all things, yet reaches beyond all things, who holds all things in his hand, yet escapes the grasp of all things? 'No one has ever seen God as he is.' No one must then presume to search for the unsearchable things of God: his nature, the manner of his existence, his selfhood. These are beyond telling, beyond scrutiny, beyond investigation. With simplicity, but also with fortitude, only believe that this is how God is and this is how he will be, for God is incapable of change.

Who then is God? He is Father, Son and Holy Spirit, one God. Do not look for any further answers concerning God. Those who want to understand the unfathomable depths of God must first consider the world of nature. Knowledge of the Trinity is rightly compared with the depth of the sea. Wisdom asks: 'Who will find out what is so very deep?' As the depths of the sea are invisible to human sight, so the godhead of the Trinity is found to be beyond the grasp of human understanding. If anyone, I say, wants to know what you should believe, you must not imagine that you understand better through speech than through belief; the knowledge of God that you seek will be all the further off than it was before.

Seek then the highest wisdom, not by arguments in words but by the perfection of your life, not by speech but by the faith that comes from simplicity of heart, not from the learned speculations of the unrighteous. If you search by means of discussions for the God who cannot be defined in words, he will depart further from you than he was before. If you search for him by faith, wisdom will stand where wisdom lives, 'at the gates'. Where wisdom is, wisdom will be seen, at least in part. But wisdom is also to some extent truly attained when the invisible God is the object of faith, in a way beyond our understanding, for we must believe in God, invisible as he is, though he is partially seen by a heart that is pure.

alternative reading

A Reading from *Love's Endeavour, Love's Expense*
by W. H. Vanstone

Man discovers in himself not only the need to be loved but also the need to love. When he loves, and when his love is completed and fulfilled in the response of the beloved, he finds himself the gainer. His life has a richness which was not there before. Despite the tragic possibilities which the power to love contains, we need both the power to love and the response of the other to our love: and without the satisfaction of this double need we are incomplete.

Christian theology asserts that this 'need' is met within the being of God himself, and requires, for its satisfaction, no response from the creation. In the dynamic relationship within the being of the Trinity, love is already present, already active, already completed and already triumphant: for the love of the Father meets with the perfect response of the Son. Each, one might say, endlessly enriches the Other: and this rich and dynamic interrelationship is the being and life of the Spirit. Therefore nothing beyond the being of God is necessary to the fullness or fulfilment of God. God is not like man – who must look beyond himself to an other who, by responding, will satisfy his need to love. Within the mystery of the divine being there is present both the power to love and the triumphant issue of love in the response the Beloved.

Such is the assertion of Trinitarian theology. It precludes any possibility that the creation has a claim upon the Creator – the claim of being a means to, or necessity for, the divine fulfilment. No creature may cherish the thought that, without him, without his being and his response, God himself would be reduced or unfulfilled or incomplete. No creature may place his confidence in a relationship of mutual necessity between himself and his Creator. It is not necessary to the being or the fulfilment of God that any creature, or any created thing, should be.

Trinitarian theology asserts that God's love for his creation is not the love that is born of 'emptiness'. It is not analogous to the love with which a woman, deprived of children, may love a dog or a doll. It is the love which overflows from fullness. Its analogue is the love of a family who, united in mutual love, take an orphan into the home. They do so not of need but in the pure spontaneity of their own triumphant love. Nevertheless, in the weeks that follow, the family, once complete in itself, comes to need the new-comer. Without him the circle is now incomplete: his absence now causes anxiety: his waywardness brings concern: his goodness and happiness are necessary to those who have come to love him: upon his response depends the triumph or the tragedy of the family's love. In spontaneous love, the family has surrendered its own fulfilment and placed it, precariously, in the orphan's hands. Love has surrendered its triumphant self-sufficiency and created its own need. This is the supreme illustration of love's self-giving or self-emptying – that it should surrender its fullness and create in itself the emptiness of need. Of such a nature is the *kenosis* of God – the self-emptying of him who is already in every way fulfilled.

Monday after Trinity Sunday

A Reading from the *First Apology* of Justin
in defence of the Christians

No one may share the Eucharist unless they believe that what we teach is true, unless they are washed in the regenerating waters of baptism for the remission of sins, and unless they live in accordance with the principles given us by Christ.

We do not consume the eucharistic bread and wine as if it were ordinary food and drink. We have been taught that just as Jesus Christ became a human being of flesh and blood by the power of the Word of God for our salvation, so also the food that our flesh and blood assimilate for their nourishment becomes the flesh and blood of this Jesus who became flesh by the power of his word in the prayer of thanksgiving.

The apostles, in their memoirs, which are called 'Gospels', have handed down to us what Jesus commanded them to do. They tell us that he took bread, gave thanks and said: 'Do this in memory of me. This is my body.' In the same way he took the cup, he gave thanks and said: 'This is my blood.' The Lord gave this command to them alone. Ever since then we Christians have constantly reminded one another of these things. The rich among us help the poor and we meet together regularly. For all that we receive we give thanks to the Creator of the universe through his Son Jesus Christ and through the Holy Spirit.

On Sundays we hold an assembly of all our members, whether they live in the city or in the outlying districts. The memoirs of the apostles or the writings of the prophets are read, as long as time permits. When the reader has finished, the president of the assembly speaks to us urging everyone to imitate the examples of virtue we have heard in the readings. Then we all stand up together and pray.

When we have finished praying, bread and wine and water are brought forward. The president offers prayers and gives thanks as well as possible, and the people give their assent by saying: 'Amen.' Then follows the distribution of the food over which the prayer of thanksgiving has been recited; everyone present receives some, and the deacons take some to those who are absent.

The wealthy, if they wish, may make a contribution – they themselves decide the amount. The collection is placed in the custody of the president, who uses it to help the orphans and widows and all who for any reason are in distress, whether because they are sick, in prison, or away from home. In short, the president takes care of all who are in need.

We hold our assembly on Sundays because it is the first day of the week, the day on which God put darkness and chaos to flight and created the world, and because on that same day our Saviour Jesus Christ rose from the dead. For he was crucified on Friday and on Sunday he appeared to his apostles and disciples and taught them the things that we have placed before you for your consideration.

Tuesday after Trinity Sunday

A Reading from *The Dialogue* by Catherine of Siena

O eternal God, light surpassing all other light because all light comes forth from you! O fire surpassing every fire because you alone are the fire that burns without consuming! You consume whatever sin and selfishness you find in the soul. Yet your consuming does not distress the soul but fattens her with insatiable love, for though you satisfy her she is never sated but longs for you constantly. The more she possesses you the more she seeks you, and the more she seeks and desires you the more she finds and enjoys you, high eternal fire, abyss of charity!

O supreme eternal Good! What moved you, infinite God, to enlighten me, your finite creature, with the light of your truth? You yourself, the very fire of love, you yourself are the reason. For it always has been and always is love that constrains you to create us in your own image and likeness, and to show us mercy by giving your creatures infinite and immeasurable graces.

O Goodness surpassing all goodness! You alone are supremely good, yet you gave us the Word, your only-begotten Son, to keep company with us, though we are filth and darksomeness. What was the reason for this? Love. For you loved us before we existed. O good, O eternal greatness, you made yourself lowly and small to make us great! No matter where I turn, I find nothing but your deep burning charity.

Can I, wretch that I am, repay the graces and burning charity you have shown and continue to show, such blazing special love beyond the general love and charity you show to all your creatures? No, only you, most gentle loving Father, only you can be my acknowledgement and my thanks. The affection of your very own charity will offer you thanks, for I am she who is not. And if I should claim to be anything of myself, I should be lying through my teeth! I should be a liar and a daughter of the devil, who is the father of lies. For you alone are who you are, and whatever being I have and every other gift of mine I have from you, and you have given it all to me for love, not because it was my due.

Wednesday after Trinity Sunday

A Reading from the Letter of Clement of Rome
to the Church in Corinth

My dear friends, let us fix our gaze on the Father and Creator of the whole world, and when we reflect how precious and incomparable are his gifts of peace and blessing, let us embrace them eagerly. Let us contemplate him in our thoughts and with our mind's eye reflect upon the peaceful and restrained unfolding of his plan; let us consider the care with which he provides for the whole of creation.

By his direction the heavens are set in motion, and are subject to him in peace. Day and night fulfil the course he has established without interfering with each other. The sun, the moon and the choirs of stars revolve in harmony at his command in their appointed orbits without deviation. By his will the earth blossoms in due season and produces an abundance of food for every man, beast and living creature without reluctance and without violation of what God has ordained.

Even the as yet unexplored regions of the earth and deep are subject to God's laws. The mass of the boundless sea, joined together by his ordinance into a single expanse, does not overflow its prescribed limits but flows as he commanded it. For he said: 'Thus far shall you come, and here shall your waves stop.' The ocean, impassable for humans, and the worlds that lie beyond it, are governed by the same edicts of the Lord.

The seasons, spring, summer, autumn and winter, follow one another in harmony. From the four corners of the earth the winds blow in due season without the least deviation. And the ever-flowing springs, created for our health as well as our enjoyment, unfailingly offer their breasts to sustain human life. The tiniest of living creatures meet together in harmony and peace. The great Creator and Lord of the universe commanded all these things to be established in peace and harmony, in his goodness to all, and in overflowing measure to us who seek refuge in his mercies through our Lord Jesus Christ; to him be glory and majesty for ever and ever.

Corpus Christi

A Day of Thanksgiving for the Eucharist

A Reading from a treatise *On the Trinity*
by Hilary of Poitiers

We believe that the Word became flesh and that we receive his flesh in the Lord's Supper. How then can we fail to believe that he really dwells within us? When he became human, he actually clothed himself in our flesh, uniting it to himself for ever. In the sacrament of his body he actually gives us his own flesh, which he has united to his divinity. This is why we are all one, because the Father is in Christ, and Christ is in us. He is in us through his flesh and we are in him. With him we form a unity which is in God.

The manner of our indwelling in Christ through the sacrament of his body and blood is evident from the Lord's own words: 'This world will see me no longer but you shall see me. Because I live you shall live also, for I am in my Father, you are in me, and I am in you.' If it had been a question of a mere unity of will, why should he have given us this explanation of the steps by which it is achieved? He is in the Father by reason of his divine nature, we are in him by reason of his human birth, and he is in us through the mystery of the sacraments. This, surely, is what he wished us to believe; this is how he wanted us to understand the perfect unity that is achieved through our mediator, who lives in the Father while we live in him, and who, while living in the Father, lives also in us. This is how we attain to unity with the Father. Christ is in very truth in the Father by his eternal generation; we are in very truth in Christ, and he likewise is in us.

Christ himself bore witness to the reality of this unity when he said: 'You who eat my flesh and drink my blood live in me and I in you.' No one will be in Christ unless Christ himself has been in that one: Christ will take to himself only the flesh of those who have received his flesh.

He had already explained the mystery of this perfect unity when he said: 'As the living Father sent me and I draw life from the Father, so he who eats my flesh will draw life from me.' We draw life from his flesh just as he draws life from the Father. Such comparisons aid our understanding, since we can grasp a point more easily when we have an analogy. And the point is that Christ is the wellspring of our life. Since we who are in the flesh have

Christ dwelling in us through his flesh, we shall draw life from him in the same way as he draws life from the Father.

alternative reading

A Reading from a sermon of Augustine

You see on God's altar bread and a cup. That is what the evidence of your eyes tells you but your faith requires you to believe that the bread is the body of Christ, and the cup the blood of Christ. In these few words we say perhaps all that faith requires. Yet faith does crave understanding; so you may now say to me: 'You have told us what we have to believe, but explain it so that we can understand it'.

Perhaps the following argument has arisen in someone's mind: 'We know from whom our Lord Jesus Christ took his flesh – it was from the Virgin Mary. As a baby, he was suckled at her breast, fed, developed, and grew to maturity. He was slain on the cross, he was taken down from it, he was buried, and he rose again on the third day. On the day of his own choosing, he ascended to heaven, taking his body with him; and it is from heaven that he will come to judge the living and the dead. So if he is there, seated at the right hand of the Father, how can bread be his body? And the cup, or rather what the cup contains, how can that be his blood?'

These things, my sisters and brothers, are called sacraments, because our eyes see in them one thing, and our understanding another. Our eyes see a material reality; our understanding perceives its spiritual effect. If you want to know what the body of Christ is, you must listen to what the apostle Paul tells the faithful: 'Now you are the body of Christ, and individually you are members of it.'

If that is so, it is the sacrament of yourselves that is placed on the Lord's table, and it is the sacrament of yourselves that you are receiving. You reply 'Amen' to what you are, and thereby agree that such you are. You hear the words 'The body of Christ' and you reply 'Amen.' Be, then, a member of Christ's body, so that your 'Amen' may accord with the truth.

Yes, but why all this in bread? Here let us not advance any ideas of our own, but listen again to what the Apostle says when speaking of this sacrament: 'Because there is one loaf, we, though we are many, form one body.' Let your mind assimilate that statement and be glad, for there you will find unity, truth, devotion and love. Bear in mind that bread is not made of a single grain, but of many. Be, then, what you see, and receive what you are.

So much for what Paul says about the bread. As for the cup, what we have to believe is equally clear, though Paul does not mention it expressly. Just as Scripture describes the unity of the faithful in the words: 'They were of one mind and heart in God,' so the image of the wine functions in the same way as that of the kneading of many grains into one visible loaf. Think how wine is made. Many grapes hang on the vine in clusters, but their juice flows together into an indivisible liquid once they are crushed. It was in these images that Christ our Lord signified to us that we should belong to him, when he hallowed the sacrament of our peace and unity on his table.

alternative reading

A Reading from *The Shape of the Liturgy*
by Gregory Dix

Was ever another command so obeyed? For century after century, spreading slowly to every continent and country and among every race on earth, this action has been done, in every conceivable human circumstance, for every conceivable human need from infancy and before it to extreme old age and after it, from the pinnacles of earthly greatness to the refuge of fugitives in the caves and dens of the earth. Men have found no better thing than this to do for kings at their crowning and for criminals going to the scaffold; for armies in triumph or for a bride and bridegroom in a little country church; for the proclamation of a dogma or for a good crop of wheat; for the wisdom of the Parliament of a mighty nation or for a sick old woman afraid to die; for a schoolboy sitting an examination or for Columbus setting out to discover America; for the famine of whole provinces or for the soul of a dead lover; – one could fill many pages with the reasons why men have done this, and not tell a hundredth part of them. And best of all, week by week and month by month, on a hundred thousand successive Sundays, faithfully, unfailingly, across all the parishes of Christendom, the pastors have done this just to *make* the *plebs sancta Dei* – the holy common people of God.

A Reading from a poem by Margaret Saunders

Corpus Christi

Don't give rich food to starving babies.

It chokes them

gives them belly ache.

They need

pilgrim food for journeying

manna, waybread

bread of affliction.

They need thin gruel

to sustain

the aching loneliness.

Perhaps only the bread

that holds them in that narrow place

in which the broken body

is fragmented and shared

can be food for the journey.

Friday after Trinity Sunday

A Reading from an ancient Celtic poem
commonly known as
St Patrick's Breastplate

I rise today
>   in power's strength, invoking the Trinity,
>   believing in threeness,
>   confessing the oneness,
>   of creation's Creator.

I rise today
>   in the power of Christ's birth and baptism,
>   in the power of his crucifixion and burial,
>   in the power of his rising and ascending,
>   in the power of his descending and judging.

I rise today
>   in the power of the love of cherubim,
>   in the obedience of angels
>   and service of archangels,
>   in hope of rising to receive the reward,
>   in the prayers of patriarchs,
>   in the predictions of prophets,
>   in the preaching of apostles,
>   in the faith of confessors,
>   in the innocence of holy virgins,
>   in the deeds of the righteous.

I rise today
>   in heaven's might,
>   in sun's brightness,
>   in moon's radiance,
>   in fire's glory,
>   in lightning's quickness,
>   in wind's swiftness,
>   in sea's depth,
>   in earth's stability,
>   in rock's fixity.

I rise today
> with the power of God to pilot me,
> God's strength to sustain me,
> God's wisdom to guide me,
> God's eye to look ahead for me,
> God's ear to hear me
> God's word to speak for me,
> God's hand to protect me,
> God's way before me,
> God's shield to defend me,
> God's host to deliver me:
>> from snares of devils,
>> from evil temptations,
>> from nature's failings,
>> from all who wish to harm me,
>> far or near,
>> alone and in a crowd.

May Christ protect me today
> against poison and burning,
> against drowning and wounding,
> so that I may have abundant reward;
> Christ with me, Christ before me, Christ behind me;
> Christ within me, Christ beneath me, Christ above me;
> Christ to right of me, Christ to left of me;
> Christ in my lying, Christ in my sitting,
> Christ in my rising;
> Christ in the heart of all who think of me,
> Christ on the tongue of all who speak to me,
> Christ in the eye of all who see me,
> Christ in the ear of all who hear me.

I rise today
> in power's strength, invoking the Trinity,
> believing in threeness,
> confessing the oneness,
> of creation's Creator.

For to the Lord belongs salvation,
and to the Lord belongs salvation
and to Christ belongs salvation.

May your salvation, Lord, be with us always.

Saturday after Trinity Sunday

A Reading from a homily of Gregory of Nyssa

The divine nature, as it is in itself, in its essence, transcends every attempt at comprehensive knowledge. It cannot be approached or attained by human speculation. We have never discovered a faculty to comprehend the incomprehensible; nor have we ever been able to devise an intellectual technique for grasping the inconceivable. For this reason the great apostle Paul calls God's ways 'unfathomable', teaching us by this that the way that leads to the knowledge of the divine nature is inaccessible to our reason; and hence none of those who have lived before us has given us the slightest hint of comprehension suggesting that we might eventually come to know that which in itself is above all knowledge.

Such then is God whose essence is above every nature, invisible, incomprehensible. Yet God can be seen and apprehended in another way, and the ways of this apprehension are numerous. For we can see him, who 'has made all things in wisdom', by the process of inference through the wisdom that is reflected in the ordering of the universe.

It is just as in works of art, where the mind can in a sense picture the creator of the ordered structure that it contemplates, inasmuch as the work betrays the artistry of its maker. But notice that what we are picturing here is not the essence of the artist, but merely the artistic skill which has left its imprint on the work of art. So too, when we consider the order of creation, we form an image not of the essence but of the wisdom of the One who has done all things wisely.

Or to give another example, when we consider the origin of human life, how God came to create us not out of any necessity but simply by the goodness of his free will, we say that we can contemplate God in this way, but it is his goodness and not his essence that is the object of our knowledge. And so it is with all the things which raise the mind towards the supreme good; in all of them we may speak of a certain knowledge of God, since all of these wonderful considerations are bringing an understanding of God within our finite comprehension.

Trinity 1

A Reading from *Centuries of Meditations*
by Thomas Traherne

Wants are the bands and cements between God and us. Had we not wanted we could never have been obliged. Whereas now we are infinitely obliged, because we want infinitely. From eternity it was requisite that we should want. We could never else have enjoyed anything: our own wants are treasures. And if want be a treasure, sure everything is so. Wants are the ligatures between God and us, the sinews that convey senses from him into us, whereby we live in him, and feel his enjoyments. For had we not been obliged by having our wants satisfied, we should not have been created to love him. And had we not been created to love him, we could never have enjoyed his eternal blessedness.

Love has a marvellous property of feeling in another. It can enjoy in another, as well as enjoy him. Love is an infinite treasure to its object, and its object is so to it. God is love, and you are his object. You are created to be his love, and he is yours. He is happy in you when you are happy, as parents in their children. He is afflicted in all your afflictions. And whosoever toucheth you, toucheth the apple of his eye. Will not you be happy in all his enjoyments? He feeleth in you; will not you feel in him? He hath obliged you to love him. And if you love him, you must of necessity be heir of the world, for you are happy in him. All his praises are your joys, all his enjoyments are your treasures, all his pleasures are your enjoyments. In God you are crowned, in God you are concerned. In him you live, and move, and have your being, in him you are blessed. Whatsoever therefore serveth him, serveth you and in him you inherit all things.

O the nobility of divine friendship! Are not all his treasures yours, and yours his? Is not your very soul and body his: is not his life and felicity yours: is not his desire yours? Is not his will yours? And if his will be yours, the accomplishment of it is yours, and the end of all is your perfection. You are infinitely rich as he is, being pleased in everything as he is. And if his will be yours, yours is his. For you will what he willeth, which is to be truly wise and good and holy. And when you delight in the same reasons that moved him to will, you will know it.

Monday after Trinity 1

A Reading from a treatise *Concerning Faith*
by Basil the Great

The nature and majesty of God cannot be defined in language or comprehended by human intellect. It cannot be explained or grasped in any one phrase or concept, but requires a variety of language. Inspired Scripture has instructed the pure in heart, but only with difficulty, and then 'as in a mirror, darkly'. For to see God face to face and to have our knowledge perfected is promised for the age to come, and then, only to those who are deemed worthy of it. But now in this present life, even though we be a Peter or a Paul, and though we see truly and be not deceived or subject to fantasy, yet must we always remember that we are still seeing 'as in a mirror, darkly'. So let us cherish what insights we have in this life with joy, as we wait for the perfection of hereafter.

When we study Scripture we become increasingly aware of its witness to the partiality of our present knowledge and the incomprehensibility of the divine mystery. As a person progresses in this life so horizons expand, and the prospect of achieving a satisfactory understanding diminishes. We wait for that day when the partial shall be abolished and the wholeness of perfection established. No single title is sufficient to declare the glory of God, and there is great danger in fastening upon one phrase as if it were all-sufficient. For example, one person says 'God' but that does not necessarily connote Father; and in the title 'Father', the idea of Maker is absent. And where in these titles are the others found in Scripture: goodness, wisdom, power, and so on? Again, if we apply the term 'Father' to God (in the strict sense in which we habitually use it), then are we not predicating of God passions, sexual impulses, ignorance, weakness, and various things? Similarly with the term 'Maker'; in human construct this involves time, the use of materials and various instruments and assistance. But these images are wholly inappropriate when applied to God, and as far as is humanly possible, they must be excluded from our thinking. For, as I have said, though every mind were to be united in investigating the mystery of God, though every tongue were united in its proclamation, yet no one would be found worthy of comprehending what is by definition, incomprehensible.

Tuesday after Trinity 1

A Reading from *The Imitation of Christ*
by Thomas à Kempis

Do not care much who is with you and who is against you; but make it your greatest care that God is with you in everything you do.

Have a good conscience, and God will defend you securely; no one can hurt you if God wishes to help you.

If you know how to suffer in silence, you will surely receive God's help. Since he knows best the time and the way to set you free, resign yourself to him, for God helps you and frees you from all confusion.

It is often good for us, and helps us to remain humble, if others know our weaknesses and confront us with them.

When we humble ourselves for our faults, we more easily please others and mollify those we have angered.

God protects and frees a humble person; he loves and consoles a humble person; he favours a humble person; he showers the humble with graces; then, after suffering, God raises the humble up to glory.

God reveals his secrets to a humble person and in his kindness invitingly draws that person to himself. When humble people are brought to confusion, they experience peace, because they stand firm in God and not in this world. Do not think that you have made any progress unless you feel that you are the lowest of all people.

Above all things, keep peace within yourself, then you will be able to create peace among others. It is better to be peaceful than learned.

The passionate person often thinks evil of a good person and easily believes the worst; a good and peaceful person turns all things to good.

One who lives at peace suspects no one. But one who is tense and agitated by evil is troubled with all kinds of suspicions; such a person is never at peace within, nor does such a person permit others to be at peace.

Such people often speak when one should be silent, and fail to say what would be truly useful. They are well aware of the obligations of others but neglect their own.

So be zealous first of all with yourself, and then you will be more justified in expressing zeal for your neighbour.

You are good at excusing and justifying your own deeds, and yet you will not listen to the excuses of others. It would be more just to accuse yourself and to excuse your neighbour.

If you wish others to put up with you, first put up with them.

Wednesday after Trinity 1

A reading from *The Power and Meaning of Love*
by Thomas Merton

The difference between real and unreal love is not to be sought in the *intensity* of the love, or in its subjective *sincerity*, or in its *articulateness*. These three are very valuable qualities when they exist in a love that is real. But they are very dangerous when they are associated with a love that is fictitious. In neither case are they any sure indication of the nature of the love to which they belong, though it is true that one might expect a person to feel an intense, sincere and articulate love only for a real object and not for an unreal one.

The trouble is that love is something quite other than the mere disposition of a subject confronted with an object. In fact, when love is a mere subject–object relationship, it is not real love at all. And therefore it matters little to inquire whether the object of one's love is real or not, since if our love is only our impulsion towards an 'object' or a 'thing', it is not yet fully love.

The reality of love is determined by the relationship itself which it establishes. Love is only possible between persons as persons. That is to say, if I love you, I must love you as a person and not as a thing. When we love another 'as an object', we refuse or fail to pass over into the realm of their spiritual reality, their personal identity. Our contact with them is inhibited by remoteness and by a kind of censorship which *excludes* their personality and uniqueness from our consideration. We are not interested in them as themselves but only as an another specimen of the human race.

To love another as an object is to love them as 'a thing', as a commodity which can be used, exploited, enjoyed and then cast off. But to love another as a person we must begin by granting him or her autonomy and identity as a person. We have to love them for what they are in themselves, and not for what they are to us. We have to love them for their own good, not for the good we get out of them. And this is impossible unless we are capable of a love which 'transforms' us, so to speak, into the other person, making us able to see things as they see them, love what they love, experience the deeper realities of their own life as if they were our own. Without sacrifice, such a transformation is utterly impossible. But unless we are capable of this kind of transformation 'into the other' while remaining ourselves, we are not yet capable of a fully human existence. Yet this capacity is the key to our divine sonship also.

Thursday after Trinity 1

A Reading from the *Meditations* of William of St Thierry

Where are you, Lord, where are you? And where, Lord, are you not? This much at least I know, and that most certainly, that you, 'in whom we move and have our being', are in a manner present here with me, and that from that most healthgiving presence comes the longing and fainting of my soul for your salvation. I know in very truth, I am aware most healthfully, that you are with me. I know, I feel, I worship, and I render thanks. But, if you are with me, why am I not with you? What hinders it? What is the obstacle? What gets in the way? If you are with me, working for my good, why am I not in the same way with you, enjoying you, the supreme Good of all? Is it because of my sins? But where is he who took them out of the way and nailed them to his cross? And surely it is not because I do not love him! Would I not die a hundred and a thousand times for you, Lord Jesus? If this is not enough for you, no more is it for me; for nothing satisfies my soul, nor does she seem to herself to love you at all, if she has no joy of you. But she cannot so enjoy you, until you grant her to see and know you after her own manner.

But why does she not see you? As I now love you even unto death, so would I love unto eternal life. Already, Lord, some of your nameless fragrance reaches me; if I could only sense it perfectly, henceforward I should search no more. You do indeed send me at times as it were mouthfuls of your consolation; but what is that for hunger such as mine? O you, salvation of my soul, tell her, please tell her, why you have inbreathed this longing into her; surely it is not merely to torment and rend and slay! And yet, if only it would slay!

Lord, I implore you: is this then my hell? Very well, so be it! Go on putting me to torture ceaselessly, and, in that hell, let me burn ceaselessly, knowing no respite from its pains one single day, or hour, or moment even, till I appear before your presence and behold your glory, and the eternal feast day of your face has shone upon my soul.

Friday after Trinity 1

A Reading from a treatise *On Prayer* by Origen

Anyone who prays shares in the prayer of the Word of God, who is present even among those who do not know him and is never absent from anyone's prayer. The Son prays to the Father in union with the believer whose mediator he is. The Son of God is, in fact, the high priest of our offerings and our advocate with the Father. He prays for those who pray and pleads for those who plead.

The high priest is not alone in uniting himself to those who are genuinely praying. There are the angels as well, of whom Scripture asserts that 'there will be more joy in heaven over one sinner who repents than over ninety-nine righteous persons who have no need of repentance.' Likewise, the souls of the saints who have fallen asleep before us pray for us.

Knowledge, we are told, is disclosed to those who are worthy in this present life 'as in a mirror' and 'in a riddle', but hereafter 'face to face'. It seems absurd to me not to employ this analogy of other virtues because what has been prepared for in this life will be brought to perfection in the world to come. And the chief of all the virtues, according to the divine Word, is love of neighbour. It must be, therefore, that the saints who are already dead love more than ever those who are still struggling in this life, much more indeed than those who try to come to the aid of their weaker brothers and sisters but who are themselves still subject to human weakness. It is not in this life only that the words of Scripture – 'if one member suffers, all suffer together; if one member is honoured, all rejoice together' – are operative. It is love that animates the body of Christ beyond this life.

One can equally apply the apostle Paul's words: 'my anxiety is for all the churches. Who is weak, and I am not weak? Who is made to fall, and I am not indignant?' Does not Christ himself say that he is ill with those who are ill, that he is with those who have neither clothes nor home, that he is hungry and thirsty alongside hungry and thirsty men and women? Who among those who have read the gospel does not know that Christ makes all suffering his own?

Saturday after Trinity 1

A Reading from *The Cost of Discipleship*
by Dietrich Bonhoeffer

The path of discipleship is narrow, and it is fatally easy to miss one's way and stray from the path, even after years of discipleship. And it is hard to find. On either side of the narrow path deep chasms yawn. To be called to a life of extraordinary quality, to live up to it, and yet to be unconscious of it is indeed a narrow way. To confess and testify to the truth as it is in Jesus, and at the same time to love the enemies of that truth, his enemies and ours, and to love them with the infinite love of Jesus Christ, is indeed a narrow way. To believe the promise of Jesus that his followers shall possess the earth, and at the same time to face our enemies unarmed and defenceless, preferring to incur injustice rather than to do wrong ourselves, is indeed a narrow way. To see the weakness and wrong in others, and at the same time refrain from judging them; to deliver the gospel message without casting pearls before swine, is indeed a narrow way.

The way is unutterably hard, and at every moment we are in danger of straying from it. If we regard this way as one we follow in obedience to an external command, if we are afraid of ourselves all the time, it is indeed an impossible way. But if we behold Jesus Christ going on before step by step, we shall not go astray. But if we worry about the dangers that beset us, if we gaze at the road instead of at him who goes before, we are already straying from the path. For he is himself the way, the narrow way and the strait gate. He, and he alone, is our journey's end.

When we know that, we are able to proceed along the narrow way through the strait gate of the cross, and on to eternal life, and the very narrowness of the road will increase our certainty. The way which the Son of God trod on earth, and the way which we too must tread as citizens of two worlds, on the razor edge between this world and the kingdom of heaven, could hardly be a broad way. The narrow way is bound to be right.

Trinity 2

A Reading from an oration of Gregory of Nazianzus

Although there are divers choices of lifestyle on this earth, and God has many mansions reserved for and divided among us in accord with our merits, there is only one road to salvation for all. Everyone must practise the different virtues, or all of them, if possible. And all must move forward on their human journey toward what awaits them. On foot they must follow Christ who gloriously leads the way and keeps us in step, who guides us along the narrow road, through the narrow gate to the wide expanse of celestial blessedness.

In obedience to Paul and Christ himself, we must regard charity as the first and greatest commandment, the sum of the law and the teaching of the prophets. And the chief traits of charity are love for the poor and compassion for our kin. God is worshipped more by mercy than by any other single act, for nothing is so appropriate as mercy in his regard, since 'mercy and truth go before him'. We must offer him mercy for other people rather than our condemnation of them. Furthermore, this kind of deed is repaid by nothing so much as kindliness, when one makes just recompense and places pity on the scales and in the balance.

We must open the heart of our compassion to all the poor and to those afflicted with misfortune, no matter what the cause, in obedience to the exhortation to rejoice with the joyful and weep with the sorrowful. Since we ourselves are only human, we must set before others the meal of kindness no matter why they need it – whether because they are widows, orphans, or refugees; or because they have been brutalised by masters, crushed by rulers, dehumanised by tax-collectors, assaulted by robbers, or victimised by the insatiate greed of thieves, be it through confiscation of property or ship-wreck. All such people are equally deserving of mercy, and they look to us for their needs just as we look to God for ours.

Among these unfortunate people, those who are made to suffer unjustly deserve more pity than those who lead wretched lives. We should especially feel compassion for those who are afflicted with physical suffering and betrayed by this troublesome, wretched, and deceitful body of ours.

For although we are spirit, we are flesh as well. God wants us to realise that we are at the same time most lordly and most lowly, earth dwellers and heavenward bent, transient yet immortal, heirs to the light and fire, but caught in darkness as well – according to what we ourselves decide. We are made up of this compound, and I think the reason for it is that when we are exalted by our likeness to God we may also be humbled by the earth from which we are made.

As I lament the weakness of our flesh in considering the sufferings of others, I conclude that we must tend the bodies which share such kinship and slavery with us. Though I get angry with my body as if it were an enemy because of its passions, I nevertheless embrace it as a friend because of him who united me to it. We should tend the bodies of our neighbours as we tend our own – both those that are healthy and those afflicted with the sickness that consumes our own. For we are all one in Christ, whether we be rich or poor, slave or free, healthy or sick.

Monday after Trinity 2

A Reading from an *Introduction to the Devout Life*
by Francis de Sales

Our Lord has declared: 'In patience you shall possess your souls.' There is great happiness in possessing one's soul; the more complete our patience, the more completely will we possess our souls. Remember that our Lord saved us through suffering and patience. Thus it is appropriate that we, for our part, should work out our salvation through sufferings and afflictions, bearing injuries and contradictions with great calm and serenity.

Do not put a limit on your patience in the face of various kinds of injury or affliction, but rather embrace every trial that God permits to come upon you. Be patient, not only in the face of great trials which may befall you, but also in the face of petty things and accidents. Many people do not mind encountering difficulties, provided they are not put out by them. 'I don't mind being poor,' says one person, 'were it not for the fact that it means that I cannot entertain my friends and give my children a proper education, and maintain a decent lifestyle.' 'It would not concern me,' says another, 'if I were poor, provided people did not think it was through my fault.' Another might be happy to suffer scandal patiently, provided no one believed it. Others are willing to suffer a little, but not too much: they do not mind being ill as long as they have the money to pay for a cure.

Ordinary Time

To all such I say that we must be patient, not only with the fact of illness, but with the particular circumstances in which we suffer. When you become ill, apply the remedies that are in your power, and trust to the will of God. To act otherwise is to tempt divine providence. Having done so, wait with openness to the result that God should be pleased to send. If the remedy overcomes the illness, thank God with humility; if, on the contrary, the sickness does not respond to the medication, then bless God with all patience.

Complain as little as possible when you are ill. Inevitably, those who complain end up sinning because their self-preoccupation distorts the pain they are suffering, exaggerating their condition. Above all, never complain to emotional or censorious people. If you have to complain, either to remedy an offence or to secure peace of mind for yourself, then choose someone who is humble, generous and who truly loves God. Otherwise, instead of easing your heart, they will provoke you to greater pain. Instead of extracting the thorn, they will sink it deeper in your flesh.

On the other hand, there are some who on becoming ill, upset, or hurt by others, refrain from complaining or revealing that they have been hurt lest it should appear as weakness or refusal to be open to the will of God. They much prefer others to sympathise with their lot, and find ways of encouraging them to do so. They want to appear brave *and* afflicted. By contrast, a truly patient person will neither complain nor want others to complain for him. When he speaks of his sufferings, he will speak honestly and straight-forwardly, without moaning, complaining or exaggeration. If he is pitied, he receives it with patience, unless he feels the pity is misplaced, in which case he will say so.

When you are sick, offer to Christ all your pains, your suffering and your listlessness. Beg him to unite them with those he suffered for you. Obey your doctor, take your medicine, your food and other remedies, and all for the love of God, remembering how Christ tasted gall for the love of you. Desire to recover in order to serve him, but always be prepared to suffer on in obedience to his will, and be prepared to die when he calls you, that you may be with him and praise him for ever.

Tuesday after Trinity 2

A Reading from a homily of Gregory the Great

'Many are called but few are chosen.' Many indeed are called to faith by God, but few reach the heavenly kingdom. Look how many of us are here in church today to celebrate the Eucharist. We fill it to the doors. But who knows how few among us God counts as his elect? We all acknowledge Jesus Christ with our lips, but our lives do not proclaim the same message. The greater part of us follow God with their lips, but retreat from him in our lives. This is surely what Paul meant when he wrote: 'They profess that they know God; but in their works they deny him.' And James writes in his Letter: 'Faith apart from works is dead.'

In the sheepfold of the Church goats intermingle with sheep. But as the gospel tells us, when the just judge comes, he will separate the good from the bad, just as a shepherd separates the sheep from the goats. Those who are steeped in the pleasures of the world cannot be numbered among God's flock in his kingdom. There the just judge will separate the humble from those who are puffed up with pride.

Although you see many such people in the Church, I beg you not to despair, and above all, not to imitate their lives. We see what they are today; but we do not know where they will be tomorrow. It may be that those whom we now like to think tag along behind us, will on the last day have outstripped us in good works by their industry and tenacity. It may be that tomorrow it will be we who are taking up the rear.

Thus, since many are called but few are chosen, none of us should become complacent. Although we have been called to faith, we do not know that God will find us worthy of eternal life. Furthermore, no one should ever despair of his or her neighbour because no one can plumb the depths of God's mercy.

Wednesday after Trinity 2

A Reading from a *Catechetical Oration*
of Gregory of Nyssa

God made human beings to share in his goodness. To that end he endowed our nature with great potential so that it could attain an excellence in all matters, and thus grow towards the origin of all perfection. In so doing it is inconceivable that God would have deprived humanity of the most precious form of goodness, namely, the gift of liberty and free-will. For if human existence were ruled by necessity of any kind, that would make it wholly unlike its archetype, and the image of God in us would have been falsified at that point. For how could a nature that was enslaved and subject to necessity be termed an image of the sovereign nature of God? By definition, our nature which has been endowed with a likeness to the divine at every point, must include this capacity for self-determination and liberty, so that our participation in all that is good is the reward of virtue.

How then, you may ask, did it come about that men and women who were so honourably endowed with excellence in all these ways, should have exchanged such blessings for something inferior? The answer is all too clear. The existence of evil did not have its origin in the divine will – it would not be blameworthy if it could claim God for its Creator and Father – rather it has its origin in some way within us mortals. It is the product of free choice whenever our souls withdraw from what is good.

Just as sight is an activity of nature and blindness a privation of this activity, so virtue stands in the same kind of antithesis to evil. The origin of evil can only be understood as the absence of good. If you remove light, darkness ensues; if light is present, darkness does not exist. In the same way, as long as good is present in nature, evil as such is non-existent; withdraw goodness, and you have the beginning of its opposite. Since the distinctive character of human free-will is freely to choose what it pleases, God cannot be the cause of the present lamentable state of mankind. He has provided us with a free and independent nature; it is human folly that has chosen the inferior path to what is good.

Thursday after Trinity 2

A Reading from *The Herald of Divine Love*
by Gertrude of Helfta

One day between Easter and the feast of the Ascension I went into the garden before Prime, and sitting down beside the pond, I began to consider what a pleasant place it was. I was charmed by the clear water and flowing streams, the fresh green of the surrounding trees, the birds flying so freely about, and especially the doves. But most of all, I loved the quiet, hidden peace of this secluded spot. I asked myself what more was needed to complete my happiness in a place that seemed to me so perfect, and I reflected that it was the presence of a friend, intimate, affectionate, wise, and companionable, to share my solitude.

And then you, my God, source of ineffable delights, who, as I believe, did but inspire the beginning of this meditation to lead it back to yourself, made me understand that, if I were to pour back like water the stream of graces received from you in that continual gratitude I owe you; if, like a tree, growing in the exercise of virtue, I were to cover myself with the leaves and blossoms of good works; if, like the doves, I were to spurn earth and soar heavenward; and if, with my senses set free from passions and without distractions, I were to occupy myself with you alone; then my heart would afford you a dwelling most suitably appointed from which no joys would be lacking.

I pondered these thoughts all day in my mind, and at evening, as I was kneeling in prayer before going to rest, suddenly there came into my head this passage from the gospel: 'If anyone loves me, he will keep my word. And my Father will love him; and we will come to him and make our home with him.' And inwardly, my heart of clay felt your coming and your presence.

O God, may you ever find me as attentive to yourself as you show yourself to me. Then I shall attain to that perfection to which your justice allows your mercy to raise a soul weighed down with the weight of the flesh, which always resists your love. May I breathe my last breath in the protection of your close embrace, with your all-powerful kiss! May my soul find herself without delay there where you are, whom no place can circumscribe, indivisible, living, and exulting in the full flowering of eternity.

Friday after Trinity 2

A Reading from *Abandonment to Divine Providence*
by Jean-Pierre de Caussade

Let us proceed to reflect upon our understanding of the divine action and its loving deceptions. What God seems to take away from us, he returns to us, as it were, incognito. Never does he allow us to be in want. He acts like one who at first maintains a friend by gifts of which he is openly the source, but who subsequently, in the interest of his friend, pretends no longer willing to oblige him, while continuing to help him anonymously.

If the friend did not suspect this mysterious ruse of love, he might well feel hurt. What reflections would he not make on the behaviour of his benefactor? But as soon as the mystery began to unveil itself, God knows what sentiments of tender joy, of gratitude and love, of confusion and admiration would arise in his soul. Would he not burn still more with zealous affection for his friend, and would not this trial confirm him in his attachment, fortifying him for the future against similar surprises?

The application of this parable is simple. The more we seem to lose with God, the more we gain; the more he strips us of the natural, the more he showers us with supernatural gifts. We loved him a little for his gifts; when we no longer see them, we begin to love God for himself alone. It is by the apparent subtraction of those sensible gifts that God is preparing us to receive this great gift, the vastest and most precious of all because it contains all the rest.

Saturday after Trinity 2

A Reading from a treatise *On the Love of God*
by Bernard of Clairvaux

You wish me to tell you why God should be loved, and in what way or measure we should love him. My answer is: the reason for loving God *is* God; and the measure of our love is that there should be none.

There are two reasons why God should be loved for his own sake. First, no one can be loved more justly; and secondly, no one can be loved more profitably. When it is asked why God should be loved, there are two possible ways in which to interpret the question. It may mean either, what claim does God have upon our love? or, what advantage do we gain by loving God? My answer to both questions is the same: I can see no other reason for loving God than himself.

With regards to his claim upon our love, surely he merits much from us who gave himself to us, unworthy though we were. What better gift could he have given us than himself? Hence, when seeking why God should be loved, if one asks what right he has to be loved, the answer is that the main reason for loving him is that 'he loved us first.' Surely he is worthy of being loved in return when one thinks of who loves, whom he loved, and how much he loves. Is it not he whom every spirit acknowledges, saying: 'You are my God, you have no need of my goods.'

This divine love is sincere, for it is the love of One who does not seek his own advantage. To whom is such love shown? It is written: 'When we were still his enemies, we were reconciled to God.' God has loved us and loved us freely, while we were enemies. How much has he loved us? John answers: 'God so loved the world that he gave his only-begotten Son.' And Paul adds: 'He did not spare his own Son but delivered him up for us.' And the Son himself says: 'Greater love has no one than this, that a man lay down his life for his friends.'

This is the claim that the Just One has on sinners, the Highest on the lowest, the Almighty on the weak.

Trinity 3

A Reading from *Love's Endeavour, Love's Expense*
by W. H. Vanstone

Among the circumstances which restrict the expression of love is the capacity of the other to receive. A parent knows the danger of overwhelming or imprisoning a child by expressions of love which are untimely or excessive. A friend knows that expressions of friendship too sudden or demonstrative may simply embarrass. A wife knows that, out of love for her husband, she must sometimes 'think about herself'. The external restraint which love practises is often a mark of its freedom from internal limit. Love does not lay down the condition that it must be allowed freedom to express itself, nor limit its activity to those circumstances in which it may freely act. Love accepts without limit the discipline of circumstances. Although it always aspires to enlarge its own activity, it sometimes finds its most generous enlargement in the acceptance of restraint. Love must sometimes express itself in the renunciation of not disclosing itself.

That which love withholds is withheld for the sake of the other who is loved – so that it may not harm them, so that it may be used for a more timely service or so that it may mature into a richer gift. A person who loves holds nothing for himself: he reserves nothing as of right. That which he holds, he holds either on trust or as gift. He holds on trust that which awaits its own maturity or the need or capacity of the other to receive it: he holds as gift that which is returned to him in the response of the other who is loved. The enrichment which many discover in the experience of loving is not an enlargement of rights or an increase in possession: it is the discovery as trust or gift of that which had previously been known only as possession. When a person loves, all that is in their power is invested with a sense of purpose, as available for the other, or becomes a cause or occasion of gratitude, as received by gift from the other.

The falsity of love is exposed wherever any limit is set by the will of those who profess to love: wherever, by their will something is withheld. Therefore the authenticity of love must imply a totality of giving – that which we call the giving of self or self-giving. The self is the totality of what a person has and is: and it is no less than this that is offered or made available in love. When we become aware that something less than the self is offered, we become aware of the falsity of love.

Monday after Trinity 3

A Reading from the discourses of Dorotheus of Gaza

Whatever God does to us, he does always out of goodness because he loves us, and what he does is always right. Nothing else could be right for us but the way in which he mercifully deals with us.

If someone has a friend and is absolutely certain that his friend loves him, and if that friend does something which causes him suffering and upsets him, he will be convinced that his friend acts out of love and he will never be persuaded to believe that his friend does it to hurt him. How much more ought we to be convinced about God who created us, who drew us out of nothingness to existence and life, and who became man for our sake and died for us, and who does everything out of love for us?

It is conceivable that a friend may do something because he loves me and is concerned about me which, in spite of his good intentions, does me harm; this is likely to happen because he does not have complete knowledge and understanding of what my needs and destiny are. But we cannot say the same about God, for he is the fountain of wisdom and knows everything that is to my advantage, and with this in view he arranges everything that concerns me without counting the cost. Again, about the friend who loves me and is concerned about me and conscientiously looks after my welfare, it can certainly happen in certain circumstances that he thinks I need help and yet he is powerless to help me. Even this we cannot say about God. For to him all things are possible; as Scripture says, 'With God nothing is impossible.'

God, we know, loves and takes care of what he has fashioned. He is the fountain of wisdom and he knows what to do to promote our welfare and nothing is beyond his power. Hence we must be convinced that all he does, he does for our benefit and we ought to receive it with gratitude, as we said before, as coming from a beneficent and loving Master – and this even if some things are distressing, for all things happen by God's just judgement.

Tuesday after Trinity 3

A Reading from the treatise *Pastoral Care*
by Gregory the Great

It is vital that Christian leaders when occupied with exterior matters should not lessen their solicitude for the inner life, and by the same token, when occupied with their inner life should not relax their watch on exterior concerns. Otherwise, by being engrossed in the pressing duties that assail a leader, they will experience an interior collapse; or by being preoccupied with the things that concern the inner life, they will end up neglecting their external duties to their neighbours.

It often happens in the Church that some leaders, forgetting that they have been given oversight of their brothers and sisters for the sake of their souls, end up devoting the energies of their heart to secular causes. These they gladly attend to as often as occasion demands; and when occasion is not present, find themselves bereft, hankering after engagements day and night, their minds disoriented and awry. If they discover they have some free time because they have no commitments, they suddenly feel exhausted – not through stress, but by the emotional vacuum. The reality of their situation is that they have found significance in being weighed down by external duties, and find it impossible to stop working. They rejoice in being weighed down by the many heavy demands of the world, but neglect their inner life which ought to be the well from which they teach others.

As a direct consequence of this, it is inevitable that the life of their people will languish. Although their people want to make spiritual progress, in the example of their leaders they are confronted by a stumbling-block As long as the head languishes, the members will degenerate. It is a waste of time for an army, seeking to engage the enemy in battle, to hurry behind the general if he has lost his way. No exhortation will succeed in raising the minds of people, no rebuke will succeed in amending their faults, if it issues from a spiritual guardian who prefers to be immersed in secular duties: the shepherd's care of the flock will be missing. People cannot see the light of truth, for when secular affairs take over a pastor's mind, dust, driven by the winds of temptation, blinds the eyes of the Church.

Wednesday after Trinity 3

A Reading from a homily of Basil the Great
preached 'in a time of famine and drought'

We see the sky, closed, naked and cloudless, this clear weather causing gloom and grief by its purity, while in the past we desired it, when clouds overhead made us gloomy and sunless. Now the farmland is withered dirt, unpleasant, sterile and unfruitful, cracked and pierced to the depths by the sun's heat. The rich and flowing streams have abandoned us and the torrents of the great rivers have been exhausted. The smallest children walk there, and women traverse them carrying bundles. Many of our wells have also dried up and we lack the very necessities of life. We are like new Israelites seeking a new Moses and his marvellous, effective rod in order that stones, being struck, might supply the needs of a thirsting people and clouds might drop down manna, that unaccustomed food. Let us beware. Let us not become a new tale of famine and judgement for those who come after us.

I saw the fields, and many weeping for their fruitlessness, and I too poured out lamentation because no showers were pouring out upon us. The sown seed was parched in the clods of earth which the plough turned under. That which was peeping out and sprouting was miserably withered by the heat. In fact, some people now ironically invert the gospel passage by saying, 'The labourers are many and there is little harvest.' The farmers, pressing heavily on the fields and gripping their knees with their hands (this indeed is the outward appearance of those who lament) weep over their vain toil, looking toward their young children and crying, gazing at their lamenting wives and wailing, stroking and, like a blind man, groping for their parched produce, wailing greatly like fathers losing their sons in the flower of manhood.

Starvation, the distress of the famished, is the supreme human calamity, a more miserable end than all other deaths. For when one considers other life-threatening calamities, the sword brings a quick end; fire too extinguishes life shortly; and also wild beasts, as they rend the limbs apart with their teeth inflict fatal wounds which assure that distress will not be prolonged. But famine is a slow evil, always approaching, always holding off like a beast in its den. The heat of the body cools. The form shrivels. Little by little strength diminishes. Flesh stretches across the bones like a spider's web. The skin loses its bloom, as the rosy appearance fades and blood melts away. Nor is the skin white but rather it withers into black while the livid body, suffering pitifully, manifests a dark and pale mottling. The knees no longer support but drag themselves by force, the voice is powerless, the eyes are sunken as if in a casket, like dried up nuts in their shells; the empty belly collapsed, conforming itself to the shape of the backbone without any natural elasticity of the bowels.

The person who rushes by such a body, how greatly worthy is he of chastisement? What excess of cruelty will he allow? Should he not be reckoned with the savagery of the beasts, accursed and a homicide? Whoever has it in his power to alleviate this evil, but deliberately opts instead for profit, should be condemned as a murderer.

Thursday after Trinity 3

A Reading from *Reason and Emotion*
by John Macmurray

'I am come', said Jesus, 'that they might have life, and that they might have it abundantly.' The abundance of our life depends primarily upon the abundance of our sensuous experience of the world around us. If we are to be full of life and fully alive, it is the increase in our capacity to be aware of the world through our senses which has first to be achieved.

Now, there are two distinct ways in which we can employ our senses; a thin and narrow way, and a full and complete way. The thin way comes from restricting the senses to the use we can make of them for practical purposes. We have a marvellous capacity for failing to notice what stares us in the face, if it is not immediately related to the purpose and interest that dominates our minds. If the interest is narrowly practical, what we perceive in the world will be a narrow range of utilisable facts. The fuller and wider way of using our senses is to live in them for the sake of the experience, to use them for the joy of using them.

The education of the emotions consists in this cultivation of a direct sensitiveness to the reality of the world around us. The reason why our emotional life is so undeveloped, is that we habitually suppress a great deal of our sensitiveness and train our children from their earliest years to suppress much of their own. It might seem strange that we should cripple ourselves so heavily in this way. But there is a simple reason for it: we are afraid of what would be revealed to us if we did not. In imagination we feel sure that it would be lovely to live with a full and rich awareness of the world. But in practice sensitiveness hurts. It is not possible to develop the capacity to see beauty without developing also the capacity to see ugliness, for they are the same capacity. The capacity for joy is also the capacity for pain. We soon find that any increase in our sensitiveness to what is lovely in the world increases also our capacity for being hurt. That is the dilemma in which life has placed us. We must choose between a life that is thin and narrow, uncreative and mechanical, with the assurance that even if it is not very exciting it will not be intolerably painful; and a life in which the increase in its fullness and creativeness brings a vast increase in delight, but also in pain and hurt.

If we choose to minimise pain we must damp down human sensitiveness, and so limit the sources of possible delight. If we decide to increase our joy in life we can only do it by accepting a heightened sensitiveness to pain. On the whole we seem to have chosen to seek the absence of pain, and as a result we have produced stagnation and crudity.

Friday after Trinity 3

A Reading from *The Ascent of Mount Carmel*
by John of the Cross

The road that leads us to God does not entail a multiplicity of considerations, methods, manners and experiences – though these may be our lot at the beginning of our spiritual journey – rather it demands one thing only: true self-denial, both in our daily life and in our interior world, through the surrender of ourselves to the suffering of Christ. We progress only through the imitation of Christ who is the way, the truth, and the life. No one goes to the Father except through him. As he states himself in the Gospel according to John: 'I am the door, if any enter by me they shall be saved.' Consequently, anyone who wants to go forward in sweetness and ease, but runs away from imitating Christ, cannot be taken seriously.

Since, as I have said, Christ is the way, and that this way entails dying to our natural selves both in sense and spirit, I would like to explain how this is modelled on Christ, since he is our example and our light.

First of all, there is no doubt that Christ died to his senses, spiritually during the course of his lifetime, and physically at the point of death. As he himself remarked, he had nowhere to lay even his head.

Secondly, it is certain that at the moment of his death he was also annihilated in his soul, devoid of any consolation or relief. His Father abandoned him in his innermost aridity of heart. He was compelled to cry out: 'My God, my God, why have you forsaken me?' This was the most extreme abandonment conceivable. And by suffering it, Christ achieved his greatest work, greater than anything he had done hitherto in his life, however miraculous, on earth or in heaven. He reconciled and united the human race with God through grace.

This he did, as I say, at the very moment when this Lord was most annihilated in all things: in his human reputation, since in seeing him die people mocked him instead of valuing him; in his body because he was annihilated in dying; in spiritual support and comfort because his Father had deserted him. As a result of this Christ was able to pay our debt without qualification, uniting all humanity with God.

The truly spiritual person will understand the mystery of the door and the way (which is Christ himself) and which leads to union with God. This union with God is the most noble and sublime state attainable in this life. Our spiritual journey, then, is not a leisure activity. Nor does it consist in accumulating experiences and spiritual feelings, but in the living, sensory and spiritual, outward and inward death of the cross.

Saturday after Trinity 3

A Reading from *The Country Parson* by George Herbert

The Country Parson owing a debt of charity to the poor, and of courtesy to his other parishioners, he so distinguisheth, that he keeps his money for the poor, and his table for those that are above alms. Not but that the poor are welcome also to his table, whom he sometimes purposely takes home with him, setting them close by him, and carving for them, both for his own humility, and their comfort, who are much cheered with such friendliness. But since both is to be done, the better sort invited, and meaner relieved, he chooseth rather to give the poor money, which they can better employ to their own advantage, and suitably to their needs, than so much given in meat at dinner. Having then invited some of his parish, he taketh his times to do the like to the rest; so that in the compass of the year, he hath them all with him, because country people are very observant of such things, and will not be persuaded, but being not invited, they are hated. Which persuasion the parson by all means avoids, knowing that where there are such conceits, there is no room for his doctrine to enter. Yet doth he oftenest invite those, whom he sees take best courses, that so both they may be encouraged to persevere, and others spurred to do well, that they may enjoy the like courtesy. For though he desire that all should live well and virtuously, not for any reward of his, but for virtue's sake; yet that will not be so: and therefore as God, although we should love him only for his own sake, yet out of his infinite pity hath set forth heaven for a reward to draw men to piety, and is content, if at least so, they will become good: So the country parson, who is a diligent observer, and tracker of God's ways, sets up as many encouragements to goodness as he can, both in honour and profit and fame; that he may, if not the best way, yet any way, make his parish good.

Trinity 4

A Reading from a homily of Gregory the Great

My friends, I would like to advise you to leave all earthly goods, but I do not want to sound presumptuous. So if you cannot abandon everything that the world offers, then at least hold the things of this world in such a way that you are not held by them. Earthly goods must be possessed: do not let them possess you. The things that you own must be under the control of your mind. Otherwise, if your mind is dominated by the love of earthly things, you will become possessed by your own possessions.

Let temporal possessions be what we use, eternal things what we desire. Let temporal goods be for use on the way, eternal goods be desired for when we arrive at our journey's end. As regards the business of this world, we should view it obliquely, with a detachment. Let the eyes of our minds gaze straight ahead of us, their attention focused on the destination for which we are bound. Our faults must be torn up by the roots, eradicated not simply from our behaviour, but also from the meditation of our hearts. The pleasures of the flesh, the anxieties of life, the fever of ambition must not be allowed to hold us back from the great supper of the Lord. We must even practise a holy indifference with regard to those honourable things which we do in the world, so that the earthly things which delight us may always serve our body and not distract our heart.

My brothers and sisters, I do not presume to tell you to give up everything. Instead I am suggesting that even while retaining your possessions, you can if you wish, let go of them, by so handling temporal matters that you continue to strive with the whole of your mind after eternal aims. With such an attitude, people are able to use this world as if they had no use for it, bringing to the service of their lives only that which is necessary while never allowing materialism to dominate them. All worldly concerns should be under control, serving a person externally, as it were, and never deflecting the concentration of the mind as it aspires to higher things. Those who act in this way have earthly things for their use but not as objects of their desires. They use whatever they need but the sin of avarice is not in them.

So let there be nothing to hold back the desire of your mind; and do not let the delights of this world ensnare you.

Monday after Trinity 4

A Reading from a commentary on the psalms
by Ambrose of Milan

We must always meditate on God's wisdom, keeping it in our hearts and on our lips. Your tongue must speak justice, and the law of God must be in your heart. Hence Scripture tells you: 'You shall speak of these commandments when you sit in your house, and when you walk along the way, and when you lie down, and when you get up.' Let us then speak the Lord Jesus, for he is wisdom, he is the word, the Word indeed of God.

It is also written: 'Open your lips, and let God's word be heard.' God's word is uttered by those who repeat Christ's teaching and meditate on his sayings. Let us always speak this word. When we speak about wisdom, we are speaking of Christ. When we speak about virtue, we are speaking of Christ. When we speak about justice, we are speaking of Christ. When we speak about peace, we are speaking of Christ. When we speak about truth and life and redemption, we are speaking of Christ.

'Open your lips,' says Scripture, 'and let God's word be heard.' It is for you to open, it is for him to be heard. So David said: 'I shall hear what the Lord says in me.' The very Son of God says: 'Open your lips, and I will fill them.' Not all can attain to the perfection of wisdom as Solomon or Daniel did, but the spirit of wisdom is poured out on all according to their capacity, that is, on all the faithful. If you believe, you have the spirit of wisdom.

Meditate, then, at all times on the things of God, and speak of the things of God, 'when you sit in your house'. By house we can understand the Church, or the secret place within us, so that we are to speak within ourselves. Speak with prudence, so as to avoid falling into sin, as by excess of talking. 'When you sit in your house', speak to yourself as if you were a judge. 'When you walk along the way', speak so as never to be idle. You speak 'along the way' if you speak in Christ, for Christ is the way. When you walk along the way, speak to yourself, speak to Christ. Hear him say to you: 'I desire that in every place people should pray, lifting holy hands without anger or quarrelling.' When you lie down, speak so that the sleep of death may not steal upon you. Listen and learn how you are to speak as you lie down: 'I will not give sleep to my eyes or slumber to my eyelids until I find a place for the Lord, a dwelling place for the God of Jacob.' And when you get up or rise again, speak of Christ, so as to fulfil what you are commanded.

Tuesday after Trinity 4

A Reading from *The Spirit of Prayer*
by William Law

This pearl of eternity is the Church, or temple of God within thee, the consecrated place of divine worship where alone thou canst worship God in spirit and in truth. In spirit, because thy spirit is that alone in thee which can unite and cleave unto God and receive the workings of his divine Spirit upon thee. In truth, because this adoration in spirit is that truth and reality of which all outward forms and rites, though instituted by God, are only the figure for a time, but this worship is eternal.

Accustom thyself to the holy service of this inward temple. In the midst of it is the fountain of living water, of which thou mayest drink, and live for ever. There the mysteries of thy redemption are celebrated, or rather opened in life and power. There the supper of the Lamb is kept, the bread that came down from heaven, that giveth life to the world, is thy true nourishment. All is done and known in real experience, in a living sensibility of the work of God in the soul. There the birth, the life, the sufferings, the death, the resurrection and ascension of Christ are not merely remembered but inwardly found and enjoyed as the real states of thy soul, which has followed Christ in the regeneration. When once thou art well grounded in this inward worship, thou wilt have learnt to live unto God above time and place. For every day will be Sunday to thee, and wherever thou goest, thou wilt have a priest, a church, and an altar along with thee.

For when God has all that he should have of thy heart, when renouncing the will, judgement, tempers and inclinations of the old man, thou art wholly given up to the obedience of the light and spirit of God within thee, to will only his holy will, to love only in his love, to be wise only in his wisdom, then it is that everything thou doest is as a song of praise, and the common business of thy life is a conforming to God's will on earth, as angels do in heaven.

Wednesday after Trinity 4

A Reading from a sermon of John Cosin
preached in Paris in 1651

Some men by the benefit of the light of nature have found out things profitable and useful for mankind. Others have made use of that light to search and find out all the secret corners of pleasure and gain to themselves.

All the ways both of worldly wisdom and of natural craft lay open to this light, but when they have gone all these ways and searched into all these corners, they have got no further all this while than to walk by a tempestuous sea-side, and there gathered up a few cockle-shells of vanity, or other peddling pebbles that are of no greater use than to play withal, or to do mischief with them when they have them.

But to make now our best use of this light, the light of nature and reason. If we can take this light of reason that is in us, this poor stuff of light that is almost out in us, that is, our faint and dim knowledge of the things of God which riseth out of this light of nature; if we can but find out one small coal in those embers, though it be but as a little spark of fire left among those cold ashes of our nature, yet if we will take the pains to kneel down and blow that coal with our devout and humble prayers, we shall by this means light ourselves a little candle, and by that light fall to reading that book which we call the history of the Bible, the will and the word of God. Then if with that candle we can go about and search for Christ, where he is to be found, in all the mysteries of his religion, beginning with his incarnation, and if we can find a Saviour there, we will bless God for this beginning. It will be the best sight that ever we saw in our lives and concerns us most.

By the quantity in the light of the moon we know the position and distance of the sun, how far or how near the sun is to her; so by the working of the light of nature and reason in us, we may discern how near to the other greater light, the light of faith in Christ, we stand.

Thursday after Trinity 4

A Reading from the *Dogmatic Poems*
of Gregory of Nazianzus

O God who transcends all,
How can we call you by any name?
What hymn of praise can we sing of you?
No name can describe you.
What mind can grasp you?
No intellect can conceive you.
You are beyond words;
And yet all that is spoken comes from you.
You are unknowable;
And yet all thought comes from you.
All creatures praise you,
Both those who speak and those that are dumb.
All creatures bow down before you,
Both those that can think and those that cannot.
The longing of the universe,
The groaning of creation reaches out to you.
Everything that exists prays to you,
And every creature that can read your universe
Directs to you a hymn of silence.
In you alone do all things exist.
All things find their goal in you;
You are the destiny of every creature.
You are unique.
You dwell in all but are not any.
You are not an individual creature,
Nor are you the sum of your creatures;
All names are yours; so how shall I address you,
You who alone cannot be named?

O God who transcends all, have mercy;
How can we call you by any name?

Friday after Trinity 4

A Reading from *Waiting on God* by Simone Weil

God created through love and for love. God did not create anything except love itself, and the means to love. He created love in all its forms. He created beings capable of love from all possible distances. Because no other could do it, he himself went to the greatest possible distance, the infinite distance. This infinite distance between God and God, this supreme tearing apart, this agony beyond all others, this marvel of love, is the crucifixion. Nothing can be further from God than that which has been made accursed.

This tearing apart, over which supreme love places the bond of supreme union, echoes perpetually across the universe in the midst of the silence, like two notes, separate yet melting into one, like pure and heart-rending harmony. This is the Word of God. The whole creation is nothing but its vibration. When human music in its greatest purity pierces our soul, this is what we hear through it. When we have learnt to hear the silence, this is what we grasp more distinctly through it. Those who persevere in love hear this note from the very lowest depths into which affliction has thrust them. From that moment they can no longer have any doubt.

Men struck down by affliction are at the foot of the cross, almost at the greatest possible distance from God. It must not be thought that sin is a greater distance. Sin is not a distance, it is a turning of our gaze in the wrong direction. It is true that there is a mysterious connection between this distance and an original disobedience. From the beginning, we are told, humanity turned its gaze away from God and walked in the wrong direction for as far as it could go. That was because it could walk then. As for us, we are nailed down to the spot, only free to choose which way we look, ruled by necessity. A blind mechanism, heedless of degrees of spiritual perfection, continually tosses men about and throws some of them at the very foot of the cross. It rests with them to keep or not to keep their eyes turned towards God through all the jolting. It does not mean that God's providence is lacking.

Saturday after Trinity 4

A Reading from the discourses of Dorotheus of Gaza

There are times when we not only condemn but also despise people; for it is one thing to condemn and quite another to despise. Contempt adds to condemnation the desire to set someone at nought – as if the neighbour were a bad smell which has to be got rid of as something disgusting, and this is worse than rash judgement and exceedingly destructive.

Those who want to be saved scrutinise not the shortcomings (as below) of their neighbour but always their own and they set about eliminating them. Such was the man who saw his brother doing wrong and groaned, 'Woe is me: him today – me tomorrow.' You see his caution? You see the preparedness of his mind? How he swiftly foresaw how to avoid judging his brother? When he said 'me tomorrow' he aroused his fear of sinning, and by this he increased his caution about avoiding those sins which he was likely to commit, and so he escaped judging his neighbour; and he did not stop at this, but put himself below his brother, saying. 'He has repented for his sin but I do not always repent. I am never first to ask for forgiveness and I am never completely converted.' Do you see the divine light in his soul? Not only was he able to escape making judgement but he humbled himself as well. And we miserable fellows judge rashly, we hate indiscriminately and set people at nought whether we see something, or hear something, or even only suspect something. And what is worse, we do not stop at harming ourselves, but we go and gossip and say, 'Here, listen to what has just happened!' We harm our neighbour and put sin into his heart also.

How can we put up with this behaviour unless it is because we have no true love? If we have true love, with sympathy and patient labour, we will not go about scrutinising our neighbour's shortcomings. As it is said, 'Love covers up a multitude of sins.' If we have true love, that very love should screen anything of this kind, as did the saints when they saw the shortcomings of others. Were they blind? Not at all. But they simply would not let their eyes dwell on sins. Who hated sin more than the saints? But they did not hate the sinners or condemn them, nor turn away from them, but they suffered with them, admonished them, comforted them, gave them remedies as sickly members, and did all they could to heal them.

Let us acquire tenderness towards our neighbour so that we may guard ourselves from speaking evil of our neighbour, and from judging and despising them. Let us help one another, for we are indeed members one of another.

Trinity 5

A Reading from the *Covenant Service: Directions for Renewing our Covenant with God,* published by John Wesley in 1780

Yield yourselves to the Lord, that is, as his servants, give up the dominion and government of yourselves to Christ. Pray that he put you to whatsoever work he pleaseth. Servants, as they must do their master's work, so they must be for any work their master has for them to do: they must not pick and choose, this I will do, and that I will not do; they must not say this is too hard, or this is too mean, or this may be well enough, let alone. Good servants, when they have chosen their master, will let their master choose their work, and will not dispute his will, but do it.

Christ has many services to be done, some are more easy and honourable, others more difficult and disgraceful; some are suitable to our inclinations and interests, others are contrary to both: in some we may please Christ and please ourselves, as when he requires us to feed and clothe ourselves, to provide things honest for our maintenance, yes, and there are some spiritual duties that are more pleasing than others; as to rejoice in the Lord, to be blessing and praising of God, to be feeding ourselves with the delights and comforts of religion: these are the sweet works of a Christian. But then there are other works wherein we cannot please Christ but by denying ourselves, as giving and lending, bearing and forbearing, reproving men for their sins, withdrawing from their company, witnessing against wickedness, when it will cost us shame and reproach; sailing against the wind; parting with our ease, our liberties, and accommodations for the name of our Lord Jesus.

It is necessary, beloved, to sit down and consider what it will cost you to be the servants of Christ, and to take a thorough survey of the whole business of Christianity and not engage hand over head, to you know not what.

First, see what it is that Christ expects, and then yield yourselves to his whole will: do not think of compounding, or making your own terms with Christ, that will never be allowed you.

Go to Christ, and tell him, Lord Jesus, if you will receive me into your house, if you will but own me as your servant, I will not stand upon terms; impose upon me what conditions you please, write down your own articles, command me what you will, put me to anything you see as good; let me come under your roof, let me be your servant, and spare not to command me; I will be no longer my own, but give up myself to your will in all things.

Monday after Trinity 5

A Reading from the *Conferences* of John Cassian

Nourished by the Scriptures, we should learn to penetrate so deeply into the meaning of the psalms that we sing them not as though they had been composed by the prophet, but as if we ourselves had written them, as if this psalm were our own private prayer to God, uttered amid the deepest compunction of our heart. We should think of the psalms as having been specially composed for us, and recognise that what they are expressing is real – not simply historically so in the life and person of the prophet, but now, today, they are being fulfilled in our own lives.

When we pray in this way, we will find that the Scriptures lie ever more clearly open to us. They will be exposed to our gaze, heart and sinew. Experience will not only allow us to know the psalms intimately, but will actually lead us to anticipate what they convey. The meaning of the words comes through to us not just by means of commentaries but by what we ourselves have gone through. Seized by the identical feelings in which a psalm was composed or sung we find ourselves becoming, as it were, its author. We find ourselves anticipating its ideas instead of just following them. We have a sense of the psalm even before we make out the meaning of the words. The sacred words stir memories within us, memories of the daily attacks which we have endured and are enduring, marks of our negligence or profits of our zeal, the good things of providence and the deceits of the enemy, the subtle tricks of memory, the mistakes of human frailty, the improvidence of blindness.

All these things we will find expressed in the psalms. They are the bright mirror in which we become more profoundly conscious of what is happening to us in our lives. We are made sensitive by our own experience. It is no longer a question of second-hand knowledge. We are in touch with reality. Their meaning is not like something entrusted to our memory but rather, something we give birth to in the depths of our heart through an intuition that forms part of our being. We enter into their meaning not because of what we have read but because of what we have ourselves experienced.

This method of prayer does not involve the contemplation of some image or other. It is marked by no sounds or words. It is rather an outburst of flame in the soul, an indescribable exaltation, an insatiable thrust of the soul to God. Free of what is sensed and seen, wordless in its groans and sighs, the soul pours out its prayer to God.

Tuesday after Trinity 5

A Reading from a treatise *On the Value of Patience*
by Cyprian of Carthage

Each one of us, when we are born into the inn of this world, begins our life with tears. Even though we be largely unconscious and ignorant of life, yet from the very first hours of birth, we know how to cry. It is as though our nature had foresight. From the moment of our birth, our inexperienced soul in its tears and wails testifies to the anxieties and burdens of human life, and the perils and storms that it is entering upon. For as long as this life lasts sweat and toil are part of the human condition. Nor is there any consolation for those who must endure them except patience.

While patience is helpful and necessary for everyone, it is especially appropriate for us Christians who are more aware of the onslaught of the devil. We have to fight him in the front-line of battle every day, and end up exhausted by the tactics of our inveterate and skilful enemy. In addition to the various and continuous battles of temptation, we are also having to face in this time of persecution the loss of family inheritances, the terror of imprisonment, being clamped in irons, and the loss of our lives either through the sword, or through being savaged by wild beasts, or by being burnt to death, or by being crucified. In short, every kind of torture and penalty is ours to be endured in faith and with the courage of patience.

Patience is a precept for salvation given us by our Lord and teacher: 'Whoever endures to the end will be saved.' And again, 'If you persevere in my word, you will truly be my disciples; you will know the truth, and the truth will set you free.' My dear brothers and sisters, we must endure and persevere so that having tasted the hope of truth and freedom, we may finally attain its reality. It is this dynamic that gives us our faith and hope. But if that faith and hope are to be fulfilled, then we need to be patient. We are pursuing a future glory, not the glory of this present world. We should ponder the words of the apostle Paul: 'In hope we were saved. Now hope that is seen is not hope. For who hopes for what is seen? But if we hope for what we do not see, we wait for it with patience.' Thus, waiting and patience are never wasted. They enable us to be formed more truly in what we have begun to be so that we may be ready to receive from God what we hope for and believe.

Wednesday after Trinity 5

A Reading from a commentary on St John's Gospel
by Augustine

'I am the living bread which has come down from heaven. Whoever eats this bread shall live forever; the bread that I will give is my flesh for the life of the world.'

How could flesh comprehend that the Lord was giving the name flesh to bread? He calls it 'flesh', something which flesh cannot comprehend. His hearers were horrified at this statement: they said it was too much for them; they thought it impossible. 'It is my flesh', Jesus says, 'for the life of the world.'

Believers know the body of Christ, if they do not neglect to be the body of Christ. Let them become the body of Christ, if they wish to live by the Spirit of Christ. You are a human being; you have both a spirit and a body. I call spirit that which is called the soul; that which makes you human, for you consist of soul and body. And so you have an invisible spirit and a visible body. Tell me which lives from the other; does your spirit live from the body, or your body from your spirit? Every living person can answer that question; and if any cannot answer it, I do not think they are alive. What do they answer? My body, of course, lives by my spirit within me.

If you would then live by the Spirit of Christ, be rooted in the body of Christ. My body does not live by your spirit. My body lives by my spirit, and your body by your spirit. The body of Christ can live only by the Spirit of Christ. That is why the apostle

Paul, expounding on this bread, says: 'There is one bread, but we, many though we be, are one body.'

O sacrament of goodness! O sign of unity! O bond of charity! Whoever would live knows wherein the source of life resides. Draw near, believe; be embodied, that you may be made to live. Do not flee from intimacy with your fellow Christians; do not be a rotten member that deserves to be cut off. Do not be a deformed member of which the body is ashamed. Be a just, healthy and sound member of the body of Christ; cleave to the body, and live for God by God.

Thursday after Trinity 5

A Reading from *Befriending our Desires*
by Philip Sheldrake

Delight, play and pleasure are not words that many of us instinctively associate with holiness, the search for God, or spirituality. We may admit that the word 'desire' has some kind of spiritual dimension but its passionate sexual connotations seem to lack the sober quality needed among sound and serious seekers. So the question of the relationship between desire, intimacy and sexuality needs to be addressed. It is not merely a question of asking how we can be spiritual with all the distractions of family and wage-earning. An even sharper question is: how can sexuality be spiritual experience as opposed to something that, at the very least, is spiritually confusing or, at worst, some kind of loss of innocence and of our essential energies?

Our desires imply a condition of incompleteness because they speak to us of what we are not, or do not have. Desire is also, therefore, a condition of openness to possibility and to future. Desires may ground us in the present moment but at the same time they point to the fact that this moment does not contain all the answers. Clearly, such ideas have a great deal to do with our experience of choice and change. Being people of desire implies a process of continually choosing. Here, once again, desire comes into its own as the condition for discerning what our choices are and then choosing from within the self rather than according to extrinsic demands. Discernment may be thought of as a journey through desires – a process whereby we move from a multitude of desires, or from surface desires, to our deepest desire which as it were, *contains* all that is true and vital about ourselves.

This is a process of inclusion rather than exclusion. The movement inwards is where the essential self, or 'image of God' within, may be encountered. Yet this journey also involves engaging with the ambiguities of desire. Initially we are aware of so many, sometimes contradictory desires. How are we to recognise the level of deepest desire that truly includes all that we *are*? All that is good and has meaning is part of what we mean by deepest desire because it is a centre that is a point of intersection where my deepest desire and God's desiring in me meet and are found to coincide.

Friday after Trinity 5

A Reading from *A Treatise on Death* by
Miles Coverdale, Bishop of Exeter

The body of man is a very frail thing. Sickness may consume it, wild beasts may devour it, the fire may burn it, the water may drown it, the air may infect it, a snare may choke it, the pricking of a pin may destroy it. Therefore when our temporal life shall end, we cannot tell.

The principal cause why we know not the time of death, is even the grace of God; to the intent that we by no occasion should linger the amendment of our lives until age, but alway fear God, as though we should die tomorrow.

If an old silver goblet be melted, and be new fashioned after a beautiful manner, then is it better than afore, and neither split nor destroyed. Even so have we no just cause to complain of death, whereby the body being delivered from all filthiness, shall in his due time be perfectly renewed.

The egg shell, though it be goodly and fair-fashioned, must be opened and broken, that the young chick may slip out of it. None otherwise doth death dissolve and break up our body, but to the intent that we may attain the life of heaven.

The mother's womb carrieth the child seven or nine months, and prepareth it, not for itself, but for the world wherein we are born. Even so this present time over all upon earth serveth not to this end, that we must ever be here, but that we should be brought forth and born out of the body of the world into another and everlasting life. Hereunto behold the words of Christ: 'A woman when she travaileth, hath sorrow because her hour is come: but as soon as she is delivered of the child, she remembereth no more the anguish, for joy that a man is born into the world.' Namely, like as a child out of the small habitation of his mother's womb, with danger and anguish is born into this wide world; even so goeth a man through the narrow gate of death with distress and trouble out of the earth into the heavenly life.

For this cause did the old Christians call the death of the saints a new birth. Therefore ought we to note well this comfort, that to die is not to perish, but to be first of all born aright.

Saturday after Trinity 5

A Reading from the Letter of Ignatius of Antioch
to the Church in Magnesia

Do not let us be blind to Christ's loving-kindness. If he were ever to imitate the way we ourselves behave, we would have been lost indeed. Therefore let us become his disciples and learn to live like Christians. To profess any other name but that is to be lost to God; so cast out the evil leaven, now grown stale and sour, and change to the new, which is Jesus Christ. He must be the salt of your lives, and then there will be no scent of corruption about any of you – for it is by your wholesomeness that you will be judged. To profess Jesus Christ while continuing to follow Jewish customs is an absurdity. The Christian faith does not look to Judaism, but Judaism looks to Christianity, in which every other race and tongue that confesses a belief in God has now been comprehended.

In pointing these things out to you, brothers and sisters, it is not that I know if any of you are disaffected; it is simply that I am anxious, in all humility, to warn you in good time of the pitfalls of shallow teaching. I want you to be unshakeably convinced of the birth, the passion, and the resurrection which were the true and indisputable experiences of Jesus Christ, our hope, in the days of Pontius Pilate's governorship. God grant that none of you may ever be turned away from that hope.

May you be my joy in all things, if I am worthy of it. For even though I am in chains and you have none, I am still unfit to bear comparison with any one of you. For you, as I know so well, are wholly free from pride, having Jesus Christ within you; and I am aware that any praise from me only makes you more distrustful of yourselves – even as, in the words of Scripture, 'the righteous are their own accusers.'

Do your utmost to stand firm in the teachings of the Lord and the apostles, so that you may prosper in everything that you do, both in body and in soul, in faith and in love, from beginning to end in the Son and the Father and the Spirit, together with your most reverend bishop and that beautifully woven spiritual crown, your presbyters and godly minded deacons. Be as obedient to the bishop and to one another as Jesus Christ was to his Father, and as the apostles were to Christ and the Father; so that there may be complete unity, in the flesh as well as in the spirit.

Knowing how amply filled with God you are, I have been brief in these exhortations. Remember me in your prayers, so that I may win my way to God; and remember the Church in Syria too, of which I am an unworthy member.

Trinity 6

A Reading from a commentary of Augustine
on the First Letter of John

The life of a good Christian is an experience of an ever deepening desire for God. What you desire you cannot as yet see; but the desire gives you the capacity, so that when you eventually see you are satisfied. Imagine that you are filling some sort of bag. You know the bulk of what you will be given so you stretch the opening of the sack or the skin or whatever you are using to accommodate it. You know how big the object is but you realise that the bag you have chosen is too small, so you increase its capacity by stretching it. In the same way, by deferring our hope, God is stretching our desire, and by deepening our desire he is expanding our soul and increasing its capacity.

Let us desire, my brothers and sisters, for we are to be filled. In the Scriptures we witness the apostle Paul stretching wide his heart to embrace whatever was to come. He says, 'Not that I have already achieved this or am already perfect; my friends, I do not reckon that I have made it my own as yet.' What, then, Paul are you doing in this life if you have not yet made it your own? 'But one thing I do: forgetting what lies behind me and reaching out for that which lies ahead, I press on towards the goal to win the prize which is God's call to the life above in Christ Jesus.' He describes himself as 'reaching out' and 'pressing on'. He felt himself inadequate to embrace 'what eye has not seen nor ear heard, what has not entered into the human heart'. This is the pattern of our life, an experience of being expanded by desire.

But we are expanded by our desire for God only insofar as we have severed our various yearnings of love of this world. I have already said: Empty out that which is to be filled. You are to be filled with goodness; so pour out what is bad in you. Imagine that God wants to fill you with honey. If you are already full of vinegar where is the honey to go? That is also why what was in the vessel must not only be poured out, but the container itself be washed, cleansed and scoured. The process may be hard work, but it is necessary in order to make it fit to house something else, whatever it may be. Whether we call it honey or gold or wine is immaterial because the reality we are describing cannot be named, and whatever we want to say may be summed up in one word: 'God'. And when we have said 'God', what in fact have we said? That one syllable is the distillation of all we hope for. Whatever is in our power to say must in reality be less than God.

So, let us stretch ourselves, reaching out to God so that when he comes he may indeed fill us. Remember: 'We shall be like him, for we shall see him as he is.'

Monday after Trinity 6

A Reading from a sermon of Hugh Latimer,
Bishop of Worcester, preached in 1552

Who is in this world which hath not need to say: 'Lord, forgive me'? No man living, nor never was, nor shall be, our Saviour excepted. Truly, no saint in heaven, be they as holy as ever they will, yet they have had need to say: 'Lord, forgive us our trespasses.' Now you ask, wherein standeth our righteousness? Answer: in that, that God forgiveth unto us our unrighteousness. Wherein standeth our goodness? In that, that God taketh away our illness; so that our goodness standeth on his goodness.

We desire all things necessary for our bodily life, as long as we be here in this world. 'For every man hath a certain time appointed him of God, and God hideth that same time from us.' For some die in young age, some in old age, according as it pleaseth him. God hath not manifested to us the time, because he would have us at all times ready: else if I knew the time, I would presume upon it, and so should be worse. But he would have us ready at all times, and therefore he hideth the time from us, but we may be sure, there shall not fall one hair from our head without his will; and we shall not die before the time that God hath appointed unto us which is a comfortable thing, specially in time of sickness or wars.

For there be many men which are afraid to go to war, and to do the king service, for they fear ever they shall be slain. Vicars and parsons be afraid when there cometh sickness in the town; therefore they are wont to get themselves out of the way. Ye vicars, parsons or curates, what name soever you bear, when there cometh any sickness in your town, leave not your flock without a pastor, but comfort them in their distress. Be assured in your heart that thou canst not shorten thy life with well-doing.

There is neither man nor woman that can say they have no sin; for we be all sinners. But how can we hide our sins? Marry, the blood of our Saviour Jesus Christ hideth our sins, and washeth them away. All comfort is in Christ, in his love and kindness.

Tuesday after Trinity 6

A Reading from a sermon *On the Song of Songs*
by Bernard of Clairvaux

Love is a great thing; but it has different degrees, and the love of the bride is the highest of them all.

Children love their father, but sometimes their eyes stray to the inheritance they hope to receive from him, and they end up respecting him more than they actually love him because they are frightened of being disinherited. Love which is motivated by the hope of getting something is suspect to my way of thinking. It is flawed, because it will collapse if the object of its hope is withdrawn. It is sullied, because it is seeking for something other than itself. Pure love is not mercenary, nor does it derive its strength from such hope or, indeed, experience the resultant anguish of distrust. This is the love of the bride to which I have alluded. It is itself her whole being, her hope; she is full of it and the bridegroom is glad that it should be so. He requires nothing more of her, for she has nothing to give. It is this deep love which makes them who they are: bridegroom and bride. It is the love unique to marriage, and nobody, not even a child, can share it.

Rightly then, does the bride renounce all other affections and devote herself entirely to love and love alone, since love is the one thing she can reciprocate. But when she has poured out her whole being in love, what does it amount to when set alongside the inexhaustible and ever-flowing fountain of the love of God? The river of love himself – the Word who is the bridegroom – and the river of her who loves him – the human soul who is his bride – do not flow equally. You might just as well compare a thirsty person to the spring at which he drinks.

What then are we to say? Are the hope of the bride for perfect union, her yearning and desiring, her confidence and ardour, all to perish and fail in their purpose because she cannot keep up with the Giant who runs ahead of her, or equal the Honey in its sweetness, the Lamb in his meekness, the Lily in its stunning purity, the Sun in his splendour, and Love's own self in love? No. For though she does love less than the Word because she is a creature, yet she does love with her whole being – nothing is lacking for the whole of her is there. And to love God like that is, as I have indicated, like the experience of marriage. It is not possible for a soul to love God like this and not to experience the joy of being the beloved, and it is this very reciprocity of love that constitutes their marriage.

Wednesday after Trinity 6

A Reading from *New Seeds of Contemplation*
by Thomas Merton

Souls are like wax waiting for a seal. By themselves they have no special identity. Their destiny is to be softened and prepared in this life, by God's will, to receive, at their death, the seal of their own degree of likeness to God in Christ.

And this is what it means, among other things, to be judged by Christ.

The wax that has melted in God's will can easily receive the stamp of its identity, the truth of what it was meant to be. But the wax that is hard and dry and brittle and without love will not take the seal: for the hard seal, descending upon it, grinds it to powder.

Therefore if you spend your life trying to escape from the heat of the fire that is meant to soften and prepare you to become your true self, and if you try to keep your substance from melting in the fire – as if your true identity were to be hard wax – the seal will fall upon you at last and crush you. You will not be able to take your own true name and countenance, and you will be destroyed by the event that was meant to be your fulfilment.

Thursday after Trinity 6

A Reading from an *Introduction to the Devout Life*
by Francis de Sales

One form of gentleness that we should all practise is towards ourselves. We should never get irritable with ourselves, fretting at our imperfections. It is entirely reasonable to be displeased and feel sorry when we have done something wrong, but we should refrain from being full of self-recrimination, fretful or spiteful to ourselves.

Some people make the great mistake of being angry because they have been angry, hurt because they have allowed themselves to be hurt, vexed because they have allowed themselves to be vexed. They think that they are getting rid of their anger, that the second remedies the first; but actually, they are trapped in a destructive cycle of emotion which will come to the surface in a fresh outburst of anger on a later occasion.

Besides this, irritation and anger with ourselves tends to foster pride, and springs from no other source than self-love which is always disconcerted and upset at discovering that we are not perfect after all. We should regard our faults with calm, collected and firm displeasure. Just as a judge, when sentencing a criminal, functions much better when guided by reason, conducting the proceedings with tranquillity, rather than allowing himself to have an emotional or violent response to the case; so too we will correct ourselves better by a quiet persevering repentance than by an irritated, hasty and passionate one. Repentance generated by anger proceeds not in relation to our faults, but is controlled by our inner compulsions.

When your heart has fallen, raise it up softly, gently, humbling yourself before God, acknowledging your fault, but without being surprised at your fall. Human infirmity is infirmity; human weakness is weak; and human frailty is frail. Own your fault before God, and return to the way of virtue which you had forsaken, with great courage and confidence in the mercy of God.

Friday after Trinity 6

A Reading from a commentary on the psalms
by Ambrose of Milan

Though all Scripture is fragrant with God's grace, the Book of Psalms has special attractiveness.

Moses wrote the history of Israel's ancestors in prose, but after leading the people through the Red Sea – a wonder that remained in their memory – he broke into a song of triumph in praise of God when he saw Pharaoh drowned along with his forces. His genius soared to a higher level, to match an accomplishment beyond his own powers.

Miriam too raised her timbrel and sang encouragement for the rest of the women, saying: 'Let us sing to the Lord, for he has triumphed gloriously; he has cast horse and rider into the sea.'

In the Book of Psalms there is profit for all, with healing power for our salvation. There is instruction from history, teaching from the law, prediction from prophecy, chastisement from denunciation, persuasion from moral preaching. All who read it may find the cure for their own individual failings. All with eyes to see can discover in it a complete gymnasium for the soul, a stadium for all the virtues, equipped for every kind of exercise; it is for each to choose the kind each judges best to help gain the prize.

If you wish to read and imitate the deeds of the past, you will find the whole history of the Israelites in a single psalm: in one short reading you can amass a treasure for the memory. If you want to study the power of the law, which is summed up in the bond of charity ('Whoever love their neighbours have fulfilled the law'), you may read in the psalms of the great love with which one person faced serious dangers single-handedly in order to remove the shame of the whole people. You will find the glory of charity more than a match for the parade of power.

What am I to say of the grace of prophecy? We see that what others hinted at in riddles was promised openly and clearly to the psalmist alone: the Lord Jesus was to be born of David's seed, according to the word of the Lord: 'I will place upon your throne one who is the fruit of your flesh.'

In the psalms, then, not only is Jesus born for us, he also undergoes his saving passion in his body, he lies in death, he rises again, he ascends into heaven, he sits at the right hand of the Father. What no one would have dared to say was foretold by the psalmist alone, and afterward proclaimed by the Lord himself in the gospel.

Saturday after Trinity 6

A Reading from the writings on prayer
of Theophan the Recluse

How should you order yourself inwardly so as to enjoy peace of soul? Secure for yourself inner solitude. But such solitude is not a mere vacuum nor can it be gained simply by creating complete emptiness in oneself. When you retreat into yourself, you should stand before the Lord, and remain in his presence, not letting the eyes of the mind turn away from the Lord. This is the true wilderness – to stand face to face with the Lord. This state of standing before the Lord is something that supports and maintains itself. To be with the Lord is the aim of our existence, and when we are with him we cannot fail to experience a feeling of well-being; this feeling naturally attracts our attention to itself, and through this, to the Lord from whom the feeling comes.

It is good to withdraw from distractions under the protection of four walls, but it is even better to withdraw into solitude within oneself. The first without the second is nothing, whereas the last is of the utmost value even without the first.

It is an excellent thing to go to church, but if you can accustom yourself to pray at home as if in church, such prayer at home is equally valuable.

Just as a man sees another face to face, try thus to stand before the Lord, so that your soul is face to face with him. This is something so natural that there should have been no need to mention it specially, for by its very nature the soul should strive always towards God. And the Lord is always near. There is no need to arrange an introduction between them, for they are old acquaintances.

Trinity 7

A Reading from *The Spirit of Love*
by William Law

God always was and always will be the same immutable will to all goodness. So that as certainly as he is the Creator, so certainly is he the Blesser of every created thing, and can give nothing but blessing, goodness, and happiness from himself because he has in himself nothing else to give. It is much more possible for the sun to give forth darkness than for God to do, or be, or give forth anything but blessing and goodness. Now this is the ground and original of the spirit of love in the creature; it is and must be a will to all goodness, and you have not the spirit of love till you have this will to all goodness at all times and on all occasions. You may indeed do many works of love and delight in them, especially at such times as they are not inconvenient to you, or contradictory to your state or temper or occurrences in life. But the spirit of love is not in you till it is the spirit of your life, till you live freely, willingly, and universally according to it.

For every spirit acts with freedom and universality according to what it is. It needs no command to live its own life, or be what it is, no more than it need bid wrath be wrathful. And therefore when love is the spirit of your life, it will have the freedom and universality of a spirit; it will always live and work in love, not because of this or here or there, but because the spirit of love can only love, wherever it is or goes or whatever is done to it. As the sparks have no motion but that of flying upwards, whether it be in the darkness of the night or in the light of the day, so the spirit of love is always in the same course; it knows no difference of time, or persons, but whether it gives or forgives, bears or forbears, it is equally doing its own delightful work, equally blessed from itself. For the spirit of love, wherever it is, is its own blessing and happiness because it is the truth and reality of God in the soul, and therefore is in the same joy of life and is the same good to itself, everywhere and on every occasion.

Monday after Trinity 7

A Reading from *The Dark Night of the Soul*
by John of the Cross

It should be understood that when a person turns to the service of God with real determination, God normally nurtures their spirit and warms their heart, like a loving mother with her baby. A mother protects the child at her breast, feeding it with sweet milk, and easily digestible food. She carries the child in her arms and hugs him. But as the child grows, so the mother sets him down on the ground to teach him to walk. She does this so that eventually the child can leave behind childish ways and mature, gradually taking on greater things, more real things.

It is the same with the soul. The loving mother of the grace of God brings each person to rebirth through a warmth and enthusiasm for serving God. And in return, God offers the soul sweet and satisfying food. This is part of the attraction of spirituality.

However, the conduct of beginners in the ways of God tends to gravitate towards the love of pleasure and the love of self. God desires to detach them from this way of loving and lead them to a higher degree of divine love. He is concerned to liberate them from unhealthy dependence upon the senses and formalised meditation, and instead lead them to the exercise of the spirit, in which they become capable of a communion with God which is both richer and freer. But God can do this only after they have obtained some rudiments in the way of virtue, and persevered in meditation and prayer. It is through this process that they begin to detach themselves from worldly pleasure and gain spiritual strength from God.

It is then that God darkens all this light, and closes the door and spring of sweet spiritual water they were used to imbibing as often as they wished. As long as they were weak and tender, no door was ever closed to them, as John remarks in the Apocalypse. But now God leaves them in such darkness that they do not know which way to turn. Previously, they used to know how to respond, but now their senses feel engulfed by night.

God leaves them in this dryness in order that not only should they fail to find satisfaction in their former ways of praying and meditating, but actually abandon them as distasteful. When God sees that they have grown a little, like a mother nursing the infant at her breast, he weans them so that they may grow stronger. He removes their swaddling bands, sets them down on the floor so that they can get to learn to walk by themselves. Inevitably, they find this new phase in their spiritual journey bewildering, since everything has been turned back-to-front. But God is giving the person the food of the spiritually mature. It is a food, however, that can only be received in dryness and darkness.

Tuesday after Trinity 7

A Reading from *Community and Growth* by Jean Vanier

In all ages and in many religions, people have come to live together, yearning and searching for communion with God. Some of these communities were founded on the mountain tops or in desert lands, far away from the hustle and bustle of cities. Life in these communities is frequently austere, directed essentially toward a personal relationship with God and to acts of common worship and work. Other communities – particularly those in the Christian heritage – were founded to serve the poor, the lost, the hungry and those in need, in the ghettos and the hustle and bustle of cities.

The quest for the eternal, all-beautiful, all-true and all-pure, and the quest to be close to the poor and most broken people appear to be so contradictory. And yet, in the broken heart of Christ, these two quests are united. Jesus reveals to us that he loves his Father, and is intimately linked to him; at the same time he is himself in love with each person and in a particular way with the most broken, the most suffering and the most rejected. To manifest this love, Jesus himself became broken and rejected, a man of sorrows and of anguish and of tears; he became the Crucified One.

And so, communities formed in his name will seek communion with the Father through him and in him; they will also seek to bring good news to the poor, and liberation to the oppressed and the imprisoned.

Within the Church, over the ages, one or the other aspect of this double mission has been emphasised, according to the call of God in different times and places, but both are also present. There are those who are called to the desert or the mountain top to seek greater union with God through the Crucified One; and their prayer will flow upon the broken and the crucified ones of this world. And there are those called together to give their lives for and with the crucified and broken ones in the world; and they will always seek a personal and mystical union with Jesus so that they may love as he loves.

Every community and every family are called to live both forms of mission, but in different ways: to pray and to be present in a special way to the smallest and the weakest within their own community or outside it, according to their individual call. God is the fountain from whom we are all called to drink, and this source of life is meant to flow, through each of us, upon all those who thirst.

Some people drink first of the waters flowing from God and then discover that they are called to give water to the thirsty. Others begin by giving water to the thirsty but soon find that their well is empty; they then discover the sources of water flowing from the heart of God which become in them 'a source of water welling up into eternal life'.

Seen in this way, community life is not something extraordinary or heroic, reserved only for an elite of spiritual heroes. It is for us all; it is for every family and every group of friends committed to each other. It is the most human way of living; and the way that brings the greatest fulfilment and joy to people. As people live in communion with the Father, they enter more and more into communion with one another; they open their hearts to the smallest and the weakest. Being in communion with the smallest and the weakest, their hearts are touched and the waters of compassion flow forth; in this way they enter more deeply into communion with the Father.

Wednesday after Trinity 7

A Reading from a treatise *On the Lord's Prayer*
by Cyprian of Carthage

When we pray, our words and petitions must be properly ordered, and our attitude should be receptive and modest. Our bodily posture and tone of voice should reflect the fact that we are standing in the presence of God. Loud people end up shouting noisily at God, but a more modest person will pray in a quiet manner. Moreover, in the course of his teaching on the subject, the Lord himself taught us to pray in secret, in hidden and private places, even in our very bedrooms. This way of praying is best suited to our faith in order that we may know that God is present everywhere, that he hears and sees everything, and that in the fullness of his majesty he penetrates even hidden and secret places. For it is written: 'I am a God nearby, and not a God far off. Who can hide in secret places so that I cannot see them? Do I not fill heaven and earth?' And another passage of Scripture says: 'The eyes of the Lord are in every place, keeping watch on the evil and the good.'

Hannah was faithful and obedient in these things, and as such is an image of the Church. In Scripture we are told that she prayed to God not with loud petitions, but silently and modestly in the secret places of her heart. She uttered a hidden prayer, but with obvious faith. She spoke not with her voice, but with her heart knowing that the Lord hears such prayer. She truly received because she asked in the right way. As holy Scripture records of her: 'Hannah was praying silently; only her lips moved, but her voice was not heard,' and the Lord heard her. We also read in the psalms: 'Speak in the silence of your hearts, and ponder your sins upon your bed.' The Holy Spirit, moreover, suggests and teaches the same thing in the words of Jeremiah: 'But in your heart say, "It is you, O Lord, whom we must worship." '

Finally, my friends, let no worshipper be ignorant of how the tax gatherer, as compared to the pharisee, prayed in the temple. The tax gatherer would not even raise his eyes to heaven let alone pray with his hands lifted up ostentatiously. Instead he struck his breast and admitted the sins that lay hidden within, begging the help of the divine mercy. Although the pharisee was rather pleased with himself, it was in fact the tax gatherer who was deemed holy because again, he asked God in the right way. He did not place his hope of salvation in an imagined innocence – indeed, before God no one can claim innocence. Rather he confessed his sins and prayed humbly, and the God who attends to the humble heard his prayer.

Thursday after Trinity 7

A Reading from a treatise *On Spiritual Friendship*
by Aelred of Rievaulx

There are four qualities which must be tested in a friend: loyalty, right intention, discretion and patience, that you may entrust yourself to him securely. The right intention, that he may expect nothing from your friendship except God and its natural good. Discretion, that he may understand what is to be done on behalf of a friend, what is to be sought from a friend, what sufferings are to be endured for his sake, upon what good deeds he is to be congratulated; and, since we think that a friend should sometimes be corrected, he must know for what faults this should be done, as well as the manner, the time and the place. Finally, patience, that he may not grieve when rebuked, or despise or hate the one inflicting the rebuke, and that he may not be unwilling to bear every adversity for the sake of his friend.

There is nothing more praiseworthy in friendship than loyalty, which seems to be its nurse and guardian. It proves itself a true companion in all things – adverse and prosperous, joyful and sad, pleasing and bitter – beholding with the same eye the humble and the lofty, the poor and the rich, the strong and the weak, the healthy and the infirm. A truly loyal friend sees nothing in his friend but his heart.

Embracing virtue in its proper place, and putting aside all else as if it were outside him, the faithful friend does not value them much if they are present, and does not seek them if they are absent. Moreover, loyalty is hidden in prosperity, but conspicuous in adversity. A friend is tested by necessity. A rich person's friends abound, but whether they are true friends only emerges when adversity proves their worth. Solomon says: 'He that is a friend loves at all times, and a brother is proved in distress.'

Friday after Trinity 7

A Reading from the Letter of Ignatius of Antioch
to the Church at Tralles in Asia

From Ignatius, whose other name is Theophorus, to the holy Church at Tralles in Asia; beloved of God the Father of Jesus Christ, elect and worthy of God, enjoying peace of body and soul through the passion of Jesus Christ, who is our hope through our resurrection when we rise again through him.

Your obedience to your bishop, as though he were Jesus Christ, shows me plainly enough that yours is no worldly manner of life, but that of Jesus Christ himself, who gave his life for us that faith in his death might save you from death. At the same time, however, essential as it is that you should never act independently of your bishop – as evidently you do not – you must also be no less submissive to your presbyters, and regard them as apostles of Jesus Christ our hope, in whom we shall one day be found, if our lives are lived in him. The deacons too, who serve the mysteries of Jesus Christ, must be universally approved in every way; since they are not mere dispensers of meat and drink, but servants of the Church of God, and therefore under obligation to guard themselves against any slur or imputation of wrong-doing as they would against fire.

Equally, it is for the rest of you to hold the deacons in as great respect as Jesus Christ; just as you should also look on the bishop as a type of the Father, and the presbyters as the apostolic circle forming his council; for without these three orders no Church has any right to the name.

Let obedience and unselfishness be your weapons; be born again in the faith which is the body of the Lord and in the love which is the blood of Jesus Christ. There must not be any ill-feeling between neighbours. You must not give the pagans the slightest pretext so that the great majority who serve God are not brought into disrepute through the thoughtlessness of a few.

Turn a deaf ear to anyone who preaches to you without speaking of Jesus Christ. Christ was of David's line. He was the son of Mary; he was really and truly born; he ate and drank; he was persecuted in the days of Pontius Pilate, and was really and truly crucified, and gave up his spirit in the sight of all heaven and earth and the powers of the underworld. He was also truly raised up again from the dead, for his Father raised him; and in Jesus Christ will his Father similarly raise us who believe in him, since apart from him there is no true life for us.

Avoid then those who preach otherwise; they are poisonous growths which bear a deadly fruit, and one taste of it is fatal. They are not of the Father's planting; if they were, they could at once be known for true branches of the cross, and there would be no corruption in their fruit. It is by the cross that through his passion he calls you, who are parts of his own body, to himself.

Saturday after Trinity 7

A Reading from the treatise *Pastoral Care*
by Gregory the Great

It is vital that leaders in the Church should be studiously vigilant to ensure that they are not motivated by the desire simply to please people. It is vital that they should not seek to be loved by their people more than they seek truth, lest while relying on good deeds and securing for themselves the appearance of being strangers to this world, their self-love renders them strangers to their Creator.

Christian leaders are enemies to our Redeemer if on the strength of the good works they perform, they desire to be loved by the Church more than by Christ; indeed, such servants are guilty of adulterous thinking. Although in truth it is the bridegroom who sends gifts through his servants to his bride the Church, the servants are busy trying to secure the eyes of the bride for themselves. When such self-love captures the mind, it propels a person either into inordinate laxity or into brutal irascibility. From love of self, the leader's mind becomes lax. He sees people sinning, but dares not correct them because he is frightened their love for him will be weakened; or even worse, rather than reprove them, he will actually go so far as to gloss over their faults with adulation.

Leaders tend to display such an attitude to those of whom they are frightened, those whom they think can wreck their pursuit of temporal glory. By contrast, folk who (in their estimation) cannot harm them, they constantly hound with bitter and harsh words. Incapable of admonishing such people gently, they abandon any pretence of pastoral sensitivity, and terrify them into submission by insisting on their right to govern. The divine word rebukes such leaders when the prophet says: 'You ruled over the people with force and with a high hand.' Such leaders love themselves more than their Creator, and brag of the qualities of their leadership. They have no real idea about what they should be doing, and are infatuated by power. They have no fear of the judgement that is to come. They glory arrogantly in their temporal power; it gives them a thrill to do what is wrong with no one to restrain them, made confident by the lack of opposition.

Those who act in such ways, and expect others to be silent, witness against themselves, for they want to be loved more than the truth, and expect no criticism. Of course, no one in a position of leadership can go through life without sinning; but we should always want truth to be loved rather than ourselves, and should not seek to protect others from the truth. We learn from Scripture that Peter willingly accepted the rebuke of Paul, and that David willingly accepted the reprimand of his servant Nathan. Good leaders who are not trapped by self-love, welcome free and sincere criticism as an opportunity to grow in humility. It is important, therefore, that the gift of leadership should be exercised with the great art of moderation, in order that those in their care should have freedom of speech and not feel intimidated from expressing an opinion.

Good leaders will want to please their people, but always in order to draw them to the love of truth. The love of their people should become a sort of road which leads the hearts of their hearers to the love of their Creator. It is difficult for a leader who is not loved, however well he may preach, to obtain a sympathetic hearing. But let those who lead aim at being loved in order that they may be listened to, and not for their own sake lest it become the root of an inner rebellion of the mind against the One whom publicly in their office they serve.

Trinity 8

A Reading from a treatise *On the Trinity*
by Hilary of Poitiers

I am well aware, almighty God and Father, that the over-riding duty of my life to you is that you should be the subject of my every word and thought. You have conferred on me the gift of eloquence, and it can yield no greater return than to be placed at your service, acknowledging and declaring you Father, Father of the only-begotten God; and proclaiming this truth both to those who are ignorant of you, and to those who deny you.

I recognise that so far, this is only a declaration of intent. I need also to pray for the gift of your help and your mercy if the sails of personal belief and public confession which we here unfurl before you are to be filled with the breath of your Spirit, driving us onward along the course we have plotted of proclaiming your truth. Indeed, he who said: 'Ask and it will be given you; seek and you will find; knock and it will be opened to you,' will not be unfaithful to his promise.

Of course, in our poverty we will pray for what is lacking. We will study diligently the words of your prophets and apostles, knocking on every door where hidden knowledge abides. But, Lord, it is for you to answer our prayer, to be found when we seek, to open the door on which we knock.

There is an inertia in our nature which dulls our understanding. We try to penetrate the realities of your truth only to come up against the limitations of the human mind to comprehend.

Nevertheless the desire to understand itself trains us, and by obedience of faith we are propelled beyond mere human reasoning.

We hope that you will guide our first faltering steps on this venture, that you will strengthen our path as we journey on, and will invite us to share in the spirit who guided the prophets and apostles so that we may grasp more effectively their message, discerning the authentic meaning of everything they said.

We shall declare things which they announced as a mystery: that you are the eternal God; the Father of the eternal, only-begotten God; that you are one and not born of another; and that the Lord Jesus is also one, born of you from all eternity. In saying this we do not envisage a number of gods of different natures, nor do we deny he is begotten of you who are the one God. He is to be acknowledged as nothing other than that true God who has been born of you who are true God the Father.

Give us then, O God, an insight into the meaning of the words of Scripture. Enlighten our understanding and give us felicity with language. Give us loyalty to the truth. Grant that we may be able to communicate what we believe about you, the one God and Father, and about the one Lord Jesus Christ. May we have grace, in the face of those who deny you, to honour you as God, yet not alone, and to preach Jesus Christ as true and no false God.

Monday after Trinity 8

A Reading from a treatise *On the Love of God*
by Bernard of Clairvaux

In the psalms it is written: 'It is good for me to hold fast to God. Whom have I in heaven but you, and there is no one upon earth that I desire in comparison with you. God is the strength of my heart, and my portion for ever.'

A soul would reach the highest Good at last, if it tried successively lesser goods and found them wanting. Unfortunately, it is a practical impossibility to embark upon such a trial-run before we finally turn to God. Life is too short; our strength is limited; the number of competitors seeking this world's goods are too many; the journey is too arduous; and the resultant toil would wear us out. We want all our desires to be satisfied, but find that we cannot get possession of all desirable things. We would do much better to make some choices, not by endless experiment, but by using our intelligence. This we can do easily, and it will achieve results.

The rational mind is more dependable than our unchecked bodily senses, and vastly more discerning. That is why God gave us reason in the first place, so that it may guide the senses in the choices we make, and see to it that they be not indulged except in regard to that which reason approves. Remember the counsel of the apostle Paul: 'Test all things, and hold fast to that which is good.' In other words, let reason guide your senses so that their desire may be attained only in the way that your reason wills. There will be no ascent to God for you, no standing in his holy place, the gift of reason will have been bestowed upon you to no point, if like wild animals you follow the dictates of your senses while your reason just looks on.

But the righteous tread the royal highway, turning neither to left nor right. These are the souls of whom the prophet writes: 'The way of the righteous is upright, and the path they tread is straight.' They pay heed to the timely warning and avoid the unprofitable maze. They make their choice to work efficiently, their effort focused through righteousness. They do not grasp at everything they see, but instead sell what they possess and give it away to the poor.

I will repeat what I have said from the beginning; the reason for our loving God *is* God. I spoke the truth, for God is both the prime mover of our love and its final end. God is himself the occasion of our human loves; he gives us the power to love, and brings our desire to its consummation. God is in himself loveable in his essential Being, and gives himself to us as the object of our love. He wills our love for him to result in our happiness, and not to be empty or disappointing. His love both opens up the way for us to love and is our love's reward.

Tuesday after Trinity 8

A Reading from a treatise entitled *The Teacher*
by Clement of Alexandria

Jesus our Teacher has set before us the true life and has effected the education of those who abide in Christ. The cast and character of the life he enjoins is not particularly formidable, though it is not made altogether easy by reason of his gracious kindness. He makes demands, it is true, but then gives them such a character that they can be put into practice.

In my understanding God formed us out of dust, regenerated us by water, enabled us to grow through the Spirit, educated us by the Word, and directed us by his sacred precepts towards our adoption as heirs and our salvation. He did this in order to transform an earth-born human being into a holy and heavenly being by his coming, and so fulfil to the utmost his own divine utterance: 'Let us make humankind in our image, according to our likeness.' It is Christ, in fact, who became that perfect realisation of what God spoke; the rest of humanity is conceived as being created merely in his image.

Hence, let us who are children of the good Father and infants at the breast of the good Teacher fulfil the Father's will, pay heed to the Word, and be truly fashioned by the saving life of the Saviour. Then, inasmuch as we shall already be leading a heavenly life which makes us divine, let us anoint ourselves with the unfailingly youthful oil of gladness, that incorruptible oil of sweet fragrance. This we do by regarding the Lord's life as a shining example of incorruptibility and by following in the footsteps of God.

Christ's main concern is to consider the way and the means in which our life might be rendered better. In order to give us a life that is simple and unencumbered by worry, he sets before us the life of a pilgrim, one that is easy to lead and easy to leave on our on-going journey to the attainment of eternal happiness. He teaches that each one of us must be his own storehouse. 'Do not worry about tomorrow'; in other words, we who have devoted ourselves to Christ ought to be self-sufficient and our own servants, living life from day to day.

It is not for war that we are being educated, but for peace. War requires serious preparation, and self-indulgence craves the acquisition of an endless supply of food. But peace and love, those simple and quiet sisters, require neither arms nor endless preparation, and the Word is our sustenance. This Word has received the charge to show us the way and to educate us. From him we learn to love simply and humbly, and to honour everything that relates to the pursuit of truth, the love of humanity, and the love of excellence. In short, through him we become like God through sharing in his moral excellence. So we must not slide back into carelessness and sloth, but strive unceasingly. We will then become what we dare not hope for, what we dare not imagine.

Wednesday after Trinity 8

A Reading from *The Reformed Pastor*
by Richard Baxter

Take heed to yourselves lest your example contradict your doctrine, and lest you lay such stumbling blocks before the blind as may be the occasion of their ruin: lest you unsay with your lives what you say with your tongues; and be the greatest hinderers of the success of your own labours. It much hindereth our work when other men are all the week long contradicting to poor people in private that which we have been speaking to them from the Word of God in public, because we cannot be at hand to expose their folly; but it will much more hinder if we contradict ourselves, and if our actions give our tongue the lie, and if you built up an hour or two with your mouths, and all the week after pull down with your hands! This is the way to make men think that the Word of God is but an idle tale, and to make preaching seem no better than prating. He that means as he speaks, will sure do as he speaks.

It is a palpable error in those ministers that make such a disproportion between their preaching and their living: that they will study hard to preach exactly, and study little or not at all to live exactly. They are loath to misplace a word in their sermons, or to be guilty of any notable infirmity (and I blame them not, for the matter is holy and weighty), but then make nothing of misplacing affections, words and actions in the course of their lives. O how curiously have I heard some men preach; and how carelessly have I seen them live! Certainly, brethren, we have very great cause to take heed what we do, as well as what we say: if we will be the servants of Christ indeed, we must not be tongue servants only, but must serve him with our deeds, and be 'doers of the word that we may be blessed in our deed'. As our people must be 'doers of the word and not hearers only'; so we must be doers and not speakers only, lest we 'deceive our own selves'. A practical doctrine must be practically preached. We must study as hard how to live well, as how to preach well. O brethren! it is easier to chide at sin than to overcome it.

Thursday after Trinity 8

A Reading from a letter of Augustine

If we wish to inherit the true blessed life, the Lord who is that true blessed life has taught us how to pray. We do not have use a lot of words as if being heard by God depended upon the sophistication of our language, because we are praying to the One who, as the Lord himself tells us in the gospel, 'knows what things we need before we even ask'.

Nevertheless, God who knows how to give good gifts to his children urges us to 'ask and to seek and to knock'. Why this should be necessary, given that God knows everything before we even ask might perplex us. But we should understand that our Lord and God wants us to articulate our needs before him not in order to be informed of our wishes (since to him they cannot be hidden), but rather that through the process of our asking, desire may deepen in us, and through our desire God is able to prepare us to receive the gifts he wishes to bestow.

His gifts are very great: our capacity to receive them is small and meagre. That is why it is also said to us in Scripture: 'Open wide your hearts and do not share the lot of unbelievers.' We are being prepared to receive that which is immensely great, that which eye has not seen because it is not colour, that which ear has not heard because it is not sound, that which has entered no human heart because the human heart must itself expand to enter it. We shall receive in proportion to the simplicity of our faith, the firmness of our hope, and the intensity of our desire.

Friday after Trinity 8

A Reading from a treatise *On Christian Perfection*
by Gregory of Nyssa

'Christ is our peace, for he has made both one.' Since Christ is our peace, we may call ourselves true Christians only if our lives express Christ by our own peace. As the apostle Paul has said: 'Christ has brought hostility to an end.' So it is incumbent upon us not to allow that hostility to be resuscitated in us in any way at all; we must proclaim its death absolutely. God has destroyed it in a marvellous way for our salvation. Thus it is important that we do not allow ourselves to become resentful or to nurse grudges because these things will threaten the well-being of our souls. We must not stir to life by our evil actions the very thing that is better left dead in us.

But because we bear the name of Christ who is peace, we too are called upon to secure the end of all hostility. In this way what we believe with our minds will be professed in our lives. Christ destroyed the dividing wall and brought the two sides together in himself, thus making peace. We too, then, should not only seek to be reconciled with those who attack us externally, we should also be actively seeking to reconcile the warring factions that rage within us, so that flesh and spirit are no longer in constant opposition. Then, with our minds stable and our flesh subject to the divine law, we will be refashioned into a unified creature, into men and women of peace. When the two have been made one, we shall experience peace within ourselves.

Peace may be defined as a harmony between opposing factions. When, therefore, the civil war in our nature has been brought to an end and we are at peace within ourselves, then we ourselves will become peace. Only then can we be true to the name of Christ that we bear.

Saturday after Trinity 8

A Reading from *Befriending our Desires*
by Philip Sheldrake

True desire is non-possessive. It is an openness to future, to possibility, to the other – whether a human other or God. This is true of sexual desire too if it is not simply infatuation. Desire is as much about self-giving as about wishing to receive. That is why desire is such a wonderful metaphor for prayer. As non-possessive, our deep desire has no limit (for it touches infinity) and equally does not seek to limit what it reaches out towards.

The way of true desire is a way of attentive, contemplative awareness of myself, other people and the world around – and, in all of them, God. As such, it is not just a self-indulgent journey inwards, but is simultaneously a movement outwards. Contemplative prayer and action do not oppose each other. Rather, each is the precondition of the other. The way of desire, therefore, also seeks the transformation of our relationships – from a tendency to be self-serving to being increasingly non-possessive, non-oppressive, non-hierarchical. To allow ourselves to touch deep desire is to open ourselves to being purged of thoughtless and self-centred wanting. This is profoundly challenging of all my ways of seeking to define others in terms of myself or my group. That is why truly contemplative people touch, with compassion and with pain, the heart of their own self, the edge of infinity and equally all reality around them. That is why the way of desire is also a way of conversion and transformation.

Trinity 9

A Reading from *The Mirror of Charity*
by Aelred of Rievaulx

Charity must be shown by all, to all, for it is incumbent on us all to choose the good in life and to try to achieve it. But as to enjoying goodness ourselves, then obviously not everyone we meet will bring us equal enjoyment. There are few people in this world, if any, who are truly able to love everyone, not simply with good intention, but with an overflow of affection from the heart.

It is such a great joy to have the consolation of someone's affection, someone to whom one is deeply united by the bonds of love; someone in whom our weary spirit may find rest, and to whom we may pour out our soul, someone whose conversation is as sweet as a song in the tedium of daily life. Such a friend will be a refuge to creep into when the world is too much for us; someone to whom we can confide all our thoughts. Their presence is a gift, a comforting kiss that heals the sickness of our preoccupied hearts. A friend will weep with us when we are troubled, and rejoice with us when we are happy. A friend will always be on hand to consult in times of uncertainty.

In fact, we are so deeply bound to our friends in our hearts that even when they are far away, we feel united in spirit, together and yet alone. The world may fall asleep all round you, but you will experience your soul at rest, embraced by a profound peace. Your two hearts will lie quiet together, united as if they were one, as the grace of the Holy Spirit flows over you both.

In this life we can love a few people in this way, with heart and mind in harmony, for they are more bound to us by the ties of love than any other people. Our Lord Jesus Christ is our example in this too, for we know that there was one disciple whom he loved above all the rest. If anyone should look askance at such a love they should remember how Jesus came to take pity on us, transforming our love by showing us his. He showed us that love by giving his heart as a resting place for one head in particular. This was a special sign of love for the beloved disciple, given to one alone, not to all. All were loved equally, no one doubts that, but for John Jesus had a special love as we know from the name he gives himself: 'the disciple whom Jesus loved'.

Monday after Trinity 9

A Reading from *The Sayings of the Desert Fathers*

An old man used to tell how one day someone committed a serious sin. Filled with compunction, he went to confess it to an old man; but he did not say what he had done, simply, 'If a thought of this kind comes upon someone, can he be saved?' And the old man, who was without the experience of discernment, said to him, 'He has lost his soul.'

When he heard this, the brother said to himself, 'If I am lost, I may as well return to the world.' Now as he was returning, he decided to go and manifest his thoughts to Abba Sylvain. Now this Abba Sylvain possessed great spiritual discernment. Coming up to him, the brother did not say what he had done, but proceeded in the same way, 'If thoughts of this kind come upon someone, can he be saved?' The father opened his mouth; and beginning with the Scriptures, he attempted to show him that condemnation is not the lot of those who have these thoughts. When he heard this, the brother's hope revived and he also told him what he had done. Like a good doctor, the father, with the help of Scriptures, tended his soul, showing him that repentance is possible for those who seriously turn to God.

Later on, our abba went to visit the other father, and related all this to him, and said, 'Look how he despaired of himself and was on the point of returning to the world. Has become a star in the midst of his brethren.'

I have related this story so that we may know what danger there is in manifestation, whether of thoughts or of sins, to those who do not have discernment.

Tuesday after Trinity 9

A Reading from a commentary on St John's Gospel
by Augustine

The miracle wrought by our Lord Jesus Christ at Cana in Galilee in which he turned water into wine, is not marvellous to those who know that God did it. For he who made wine that day at the marriage feast in the six stone water-jars which he had ordered to be filled to the brim with water, performs the same miracle each year in vines. Just as what the servants had put into the water-jars was changed into wine by the agency of the Lord, so what the clouds pour forth is changed into wine by the agency of the same Lord. We do not marvel at this, simply because it happens each year; familiarity has dulled our capacity for wonder. But it should demand of us a more profound consideration than something which once happened in some water-jars. Is there anyone who, contemplating the works of God by which the entire universe is governed and ordered, is not amazed and overwhelmed by a sense of the miraculous? The power and strength of a single grain of seed is itself an amazing thing, inspiring awe in its contemplation. But humanity, preoccupied with its own petty agenda, has lost the capacity to contemplate the works of God by which it should daily render praise to God as Creator.

This is why God has, as it were, reserved to himself certain extraordinary and unexpected actions, in order that by such marvels he might startle people out of their lethargy into worship. A dead man rose again; people marvelled. By contrast, numerous babies are born every day, and no one marvels. If only we would reflect upon life more carefully, we would come to see that it is a greater miracle for a child to be given existence who before did not exist, than for a man to come back to life who already existed. People hold cheap what they see every day of their lives, but suddenly, confronted by extraordinary events, they are dumb-founded, though these events are truly no more wonderful than the others. Governing the universe, for example, is a greater miracle than feeding five thousand people with loaves of bread, but no one marvels at it. People marvel at the feeding of the five thousand not because this miracle is greater, but because it is out of the ordinary. Who is even now providing nourishment for the whole world if not the God who creates a field of wheat from a few seeds?

Miracles are presented to our senses in order to stimulate our minds. They are put before our eyes in order to engage our understanding and so make us marvel at the God we do not see through his works which we do see. For then, when we have been raised to the level of faith and purified by faith, we desire to behold, though not with our eyes, the unseen God whom we have recognised through what is seen.

Wednesday after Trinity 9

A Reading from *Hymn of the Universe*
by Pierre Teilhard de Chardin

Blessed be you, harsh matter, barren soil, stubborn rock: you who yield only to violence, you who force us to work if we would eat.

Blessed be you, perilous matter, violent sea, untameable passion: you who unless we fetter you will devour us.

Blessed be you, mighty matter, irresistible march of evolution, reality ever new-born; you who, by constantly shattering our mental categories, force us to go ever further and further in our pursuit of the truth.

Blessed be you, universal matter, immeasurable time, boundless ether, triple abyss of stars and atoms and generations: you who by overflowing and dissolving our narrow standards of measurement reveal to us the dimensions of God.

Blessed be you, impenetrable matter: you who, interposed between our minds and the world of essences, cause us to languish with the desire to pierce through the seamless veil of phenomena.

Blessed be you, mortal matter: you who one day will undergo the process of dissolution within us and will thereby take us forcibly into the very heart of that which exists.

Without you, without your onslaughts, without your uprootings of us, we should remain all our lives inert, stagnant, puerile, ignorant both of ourselves and of God. You who batter us and then dress our wounds, you who resist us and yield to us, you who wreck and build, you who shackle and liberate, the sap of our souls, the hand of God, the flesh of Christ: it is you, matter, that I bless.

I bless you, matter, and you I acclaim: not as the pontiffs of science or the moralizing preachers depict you, debased, disfigured – a mass of brute forces and base appetites – but as you reveal yourself to me today, in your totality and your true nature.

Your realm comprises those serene heights where saints think to avoid you – but where your flesh is so transparent and so agile as to be no longer distinguishable from spirit.

Raise me up then, matter, to those heights, through struggle and separation and death; raise me up until at long last, it becomes possible for me in perfect chastity to embrace the universe.

Thursday after Trinity 9

A Reading from a treatise *On the Mortality Rate*
by Cyprian of Carthage,
written after a virulent outbreak of the plague in the city

There are certain people who are disturbed because this disease has attacked equally pagans and Christians. They talk as if being a Christian somehow guaranteed the enjoyment of happiness in this world and immunity from contact with illness, rather than preparing us to endure adversity in the faith that our full happiness is reserved for the future. It disturbs some of our number that death seems to have no favourites. And yet what is there in this world that is not common to us all? As long as we are subject to the same laws of generation we have a common flesh. As long as we are in this world we share an identical physicality with the rest of humankind, even if our spiritual identity singles us out. Until this corruptible form is clothed with incorruptibility, and this mortal frame receives immortality, and the Spirit leads us to God the Father, we share with the rest of humanity the burden of our flesh.

When the soil is exhausted and the harvest poor, famine makes no distinction of persons. When an army invades and a city is taken, everyone suffers a common desolation. When the skies are cloudless and the rains fail, all alike suffer from the drought. When a ship goes aground on treacherous rocks, the shipwreck affects all who sail in her without exception. Diseases of the eye, attacks of fever, weakness in limbs, are all as common to Christians as to anyone else because this is the lot of all who bear human flesh in this world.

The righteous have always displayed a capacity for endurance. The apostles maintained such a discipline in obedience to the commandment of the Lord not to murmur in adversity, but to accept bravely and patiently whatever may happen to them in the world. In the same way the fear of God and faith in God ought to prepare you for anything. If you have lost all your worldly goods, or your limbs are racked by constant pain and discomfort, or you have lost your wife, your children or friends, and you are swamped by grief, do not let these things become stumbling blocks to your faith, but rather battles. Such things should not undermine or break the faith of Christians but reveal their courage in the struggle. The pain which these current troubles can inflict on us is nothing when compared with the future blessings that are assured us.

There can be no victory without a battle: only when victory has been secured through engaging in the battle is the victor's crown bestowed. The true helmsman is recognised in the midst of a storm. The true soldier is proven only on the battlefield. There can be no authentic testing where there is no danger. When the struggle is real, then the testing is real. The tree which has sent down deep roots is not disturbed by gales, and the ship that has been made of decent timber may be buffeted by the waves but will not be broken. When corn is beaten on the threshing-floor, the solid and heavy grains rebuke the wind, whereas the empty chaff is carried away on the breeze.

To summarise: the difference between us and those who do not know God is that when misfortune occurs, others complain and murmur, but we are not distracted by adversity from the true path of virtue and faith; indeed, in the midst of suffering we are made strong.

Friday after Trinity 9

A Reading from a sermon of Peter Chrysologus,
Bishop of Ravenna

'I appeal to you by the mercy of God.' Paul makes a request, or rather God makes a request to us through Paul, because he wants to be loved rather than feared. God makes a request, because he does not want to be so much the Lord as a father. God makes a request in his mercy, rather than punish in his severity.

We hear God crying out to us in Scripture: 'O my people, what have I done to you, how have I hurt you? Answer me!' And then listen to what the Lord then says: 'If my divinity is something you cannot comprehend, then know me in my flesh. You see in me your body, your limbs, your organs, your bones, your blood. If you are afraid of my divinity, why do you not love me in your humanity? If you run away from your Lord, why do you not run back to your brother? Perhaps you are ashamed because of the greatness of the suffering you inflicted on me. Well, do not be afraid. This cross is not mine; it is the sting of death. These nails do nor pierce me with pain; they pierce me more deeply with love of you. These wounds do not draw groans from me; rather they draw you into my heart. The stretching-out of my body makes room for you in my heart; it does not increase my pain. My blood is not lost to me; it is paid in advance for your ransom. Come then, come back to me, and come to know me as a father; for see, I return good for evil, love for injuries, and for deep wounds a deeper love.'

But let us listen now to the content of the appeal St Paul makes: 'I appeal to you to present your bodies as a living sacrifice.' By this request the apostle has raised all humankind to the level of priests: 'to present your bodies as a living sacrifice'. How unique is the duty of the Christian priesthood! For there we are called to be both sacrifice and priest; we do not look for something outside ourselves to offer to God; we are to bring with ourselves and in ourselves and for ourselves a sacrifice to God. The victim is not consumed and the priest's task can never be completed; the victim is slain but lives, the sacrificing priest is unable to kill. What a wonderful sacrifice! A body is offered without a body, blood without blood. 'I appeal to you by the mercy of God to present your bodies as a living sacrifice.'

My brothers and sisters, this sacrifice follows the pattern of Christ himself, who by his life sacrificed his body for the life of the world; he truly made his body a living sacrifice because, though slain, he lives. Be, therefore, yourselves both a sacrifice to God and priests. Do not lose what the divine authority gave and conceded to you.

God seeks belief from you, not death. God thirsts for self-dedication, not blood.

Saturday after Trinity 9

A Reading from the *Proslogion* of Anselm

Lord, you hide from my soul in your light and beauty, and therefore I still live in darkness and in misery. I look all round, but I do not see your beauty. I listen, but I do not hear your harmony. I smell, but I do not gather your fragrance. I taste, but do not know your savour. I touch, but do not feel your yielding. For, Lord God, it is in your own unutterable manner that you have these things; you have given them to what you have created in a manner which can be felt, but the senses of my soul have been hardened, dulled, and blocked by the ancient sickness of sin.

I seek for joy and gladness, and once again there is confusion; sorrow and grief stand in the way. My soul was hoping to be filled, and once again it is overcome with need. I was striving to be filled, and now I hunger all the more. I tried to rise up to the light of God, and I have fallen back into the darkness of myself. Or rather I have not only fallen into it, I feel myself surrounded by it. 'Before my mother conceived me' I fell into it, I was conceived in it, and when I was born it wrapped me round. In fact we all fell once in him 'in whom all have sinned'. There was that which he held easily, and unhappily lost for us and for himself; in him we have all lost it, and when we want to seek it, we are ignorant of it; when we look for it, we do not find it; when we find it, it is not what we were looking for. Help me, 'according to your goodness', Lord. 'I have sought your face; your face, Lord, will I seek; hide not your face from me.' Raise me from myself to you.

Cleanse, heal, make keen, illuminate the eye of my inner being, so that I may see you. Let my soul gather together all its powers, and direct its whole understanding towards you, Lord.

Trinity 10

A Reading from a treatise *On Prayer*
by Tertullian

Prayer is the spiritual offering that has done away with the ancient custom of sacrifices. 'What good do I receive from the multiplicity of your sacrifices?' asks God. 'I have had enough of burnt offerings of rams, and I do not want the fat of lambs and the blood of bulls and goats. Who has asked for these from your hands?'

What God has asked for we learn from the gospel. 'The hour will come,' we are told, 'when true worshippers will worship the Father in spirit and in truth. God is a spirit,' and this is the kind of worshipper he wants.

We are true worshippers and true priests. We pray in spirit, and so offer in spirit the sacrifice of prayer. Prayer is an offering which belongs to God and is acceptable to him. It is the offering he has asked for, the offering he planned as his own. We must dedicate this offering with our whole heart, we must fatten it on faith, tend it by truth, keep it unblemished through innocence and clean through chastity, and crown it with love. We must escort it to the altar of God in a procession of good works to the sound of psalms and hymns. Then it will gain for us all that we ask of God.

What will God deny to a prayer which is offered in spirit and in truth, seeing it is he who demands it? How great is the evidence of its power, as we read and hear and believe. Of old, prayer was able to rescue from fire and beasts and hunger, even before it received its perfection from Christ. How much greater then is the power of Christian prayer. No longer does prayer bring an angel of comfort to the heart of a fiery furnace, or close up the mouths of lions, or transport to the hungry food from the fields. It has no special power to avert the experience of suffering. Instead it gives the armour of patience to those who suffer, who feel pain, who are distressed. It strengthens the power of grace, so that faith may know what it is gaining from the Lord, and understand what it is suffering for the name of God.

In the past prayer was able to bring down plagues, rout armies, withhold the blessing of rain. Now, however, the prayer of the just turns aside the whole anger of God, keeps vigil for its enemies, pleads for persecutors. Is it any wonder that it can call down water from heaven when it could obtain fire from heaven as well? Prayer is the one thing that can conquer God. But Christ has willed that it should work no evil, has given it all power over good.

Its only art is to call back the souls of the dead from the very highway of death, to give strength to the weak, to heal the sick, to exorcise the possessed, to open prison cells, to free the innocent from their chains. Prayer cleanses from sin, drives away temptations, stamps out persecutions, comforts the faint-hearted, gives new strength to the courageous, brings travellers safely home, calms the waves, confounds robbers, feeds the poor, overrules the rich, lifts up the fallen, supports those who are falling, sustains all those who stand firm.

All the angels pray. All creation prays. Cattle and wild beasts pray, and bend their knees. As they come from their barns and caves they invariably look up to heaven and call out, lifting up their spirit in their own fashion. The birds too rise and lift themselves up to heaven: instead of hands, they open out their wings in the form of a cross, and give voice to what seems to be a prayer. What more need be said on the duty of prayer? Even the Lord himself prayed: to him be honour and power for ever and ever.

Monday after Trinity 10

A Reading from a sermon *On the Song of Songs*
by Bernard of Clairvaux

Those who are to fulfil the office of preaching in the Church, and who are to prepare her for her marriage to the heavenly bridegroom, are here among us. For in the Song of Songs the bride says: 'The watchmen who guard the city found me.' And who are these watchmen? Surely those servants of whom the Saviour spoke in the gospel: 'Blessed are they whom the Lord, when he comes, finds watching.' What good watchmen they are who keep vigil while we sleep that they may give an account of our souls! What good guardians they are who are awake in spirit and spend the night in prayer, exposing the tricks of the enemy, undermining their plots, discovering their subterfuges, breaking their snares, rending their nets and foiling their evil plans! Such are the lovers of their brothers and sisters and of all Christian people, who pray for others and for the well-being of the holy city. The sheep of the Lord are committed to the charge of such people, and in their tender care for the flock, they seek early the Lord who made them, and pray to the Lord Most High. They keep watch, they pray, they are conscious of their own inadequacy and that 'unless the Lord keeps the city, the watchmen keep vigil in vain.'

The fact that the Lord himself gave us the command to watch and to pray lest we enter into temptation, shows that without this two-fold activity on the part both of the faithful and those who guard them, neither the city nor the bride nor the flock can continue in safety. Do you ask what is the difference between these three? The answer is none: they are one. The 'city' is called so because it represents a unity of souls; the 'bride' because she is the beloved; the 'flock' because of the tender care that is required.

Take note of this, you friends of the bridegroom – if such you are. It was not for nothing that the Lord, when committing his sheep to his care, three times asked Peter if he loved him. It was as if he were saying: 'Unless your conscience bears witness that you love me perfectly and entirely, more than your own interests, more than your own family, more even than your own life, you must on no account take up this charge or have any dealings whatsoever with the sheep for whom I shed my blood.'

Pay attention, then, you who have been called to the ministry. Pay attention to yourselves and to the precious charge committed to your care. It is a city; watch over it, to keep it in safety and peace. It is a bride; honour her beauty. It is a flock; lead it to rich pastures.

Tuesday after Trinity 10

A Reading from the Letter of Clement of Rome to the Church in Corinth

My dear friends, Jesus Christ is our salvation, he is the high priest through whom we present our offerings and the protector who supports us in our weakness. Through him our gaze penetrates the heights of heaven and we see, as in a mirror, the most holy face of God. Through him the eyes of our hearts are opened, and our weak and clouded understanding unfolds like a flower toward the light. Through him the Lord God willed that we should taste the wisdom of eternity. For Christ is the radiance of God's glory, and as much greater than the angels as the name God has given him is superior to theirs.

So then, let us do battle with all our might under his unerring leadership. Think of the soldiers serving under our military commanders in the field. How well disciplined they are! How readily and submissively they carry out their orders! Not everyone can be a prefect, a tribune, a centurion, or a captain; but each rank executes the orders of the emperor and their commanding officer. The great cannot exist without those of humble condition, nor can those of humble condition exist without the great.

Every organism is composed of different elements; and this ensures its own good. Take our own body as an example: the head is helpless without the feet; and the feet can do nothing without the head. Even our least important members are useful and necessary to the whole body, and all work together for its well-being in a common subordination, with the result that the body remains intact.

Let us, then, preserve the unity of the body that we form in Christ Jesus, and let all give their neighbours the respect to which their particular gifts entitle them. The strong should care for the weak and the weak respect the strong. Let the wealthy assist the poor and the poor thank God for giving them someone to supply their needs. The wise should show wisdom not by eloquence but by good works; the humble should not proclaim their own humility, but leave others to do so. Let those who are physically chaste not brag about it, but recognise that the ability to control their desires is itself a gift of God.

Think of how we first came into being, of what we were at the first moment of our existence. Think of the dark tomb out of which our Creator brought us into his world where he had his gifts prepared for us even before we were born. To God we owe everything and for everything we must give him thanks. To him be glory for ever and ever.

Wednesday after Trinity 10

A Reading from the *Admonitions* of Francis of Assisi

'I did not come to be served but to serve,' says the Lord. Those who are placed over others should glory in such an office only as much as they would were they assigned the task of washing the feet of the brothers. And the more they are upset about their office being taken from them than they would be over the loss of the office of washing feet, so much the more do they store up treasures to the peril of their souls.

Be conscious, O man, of the wondrous state in which the Lord God has placed you. For he created you and formed you in the image of his beloved Son according to the body, and to his likeness according to the spirit. And yet all the creatures under heaven, each according to its nature, serve, know, and obey their Creator better than you. And even the demons did not crucify him, but you together with them have crucified him, and crucify him even now by delighting in vices and sins.

In what then can you glory? For if you were so subtle and wise that you had all knowledge and knew how to interpret tongues, and minutely investigated the course of the heavenly bodies, in all these things you could not glory, for one demon knew more about the things of earth than all mortals together, even including if there were someone who received from the Lord a special knowledge of the highest wisdom. Likewise, even if you were more handsome and richer than everyone else in the world, and even if you performed wonders such as driving out demons, all these things would be an obstacle to you and none of them would belong to you, nor could you glory in any of these things. But in this alone can we glory: in our infirmities, and bearing daily the holy cross of our Lord Jesus Christ.

Thursday after Trinity 10

A Reading from *New Seeds of Contemplation*
by Thomas Merton

Contemplation is the highest expression of man's intellectual and spiritual life. It is that life itself, fully awake, fully active, fully aware that it is alive. It is spiritual wonder. It is spontaneous awe at the sacredness of life, of being. It is gratitude for life, for awareness and for being. It is a vivid realisation of the fact that life and being us proceed from an invisible, transcendent and infinitely abundant Source. Contemplation is, above all, awareness of the reality of that Source. It knows the Source, obscurely, inexplicably, but with a certitude that goes both beyond reason and beyond simple faith. For contemplation is a kind of spiritual vision to which both reason and faith aspire, by their very nature, because without it they must always remain incomplete. Yet contemplation is not vision because it sees 'without seeing' and knows 'without knowing'. It is a more profound depth of faith, a knowledge too deep to be grasped in images, in words or even in clear concepts. It can be suggested by words, by symbols, but in the very moment of trying to indicate what it knows the contemplative mind takes back what it has said, and denies what it has affirmed. For in contemplation we know by 'unknowing'. Or, better, we know *beyond* all knowing or 'unknowing'.

In other words, contemplation reaches out to the knowledge and even to the experience of the transcendent and inexpressible God. It knows God by seeming to touch him. Or rather it knows him as if it had been invisibly touched by him. Touched by him who has no hands, but who is pure reality and the source of all that is real! Hence contemplation is a sudden gift of awareness, an awakening to the Real within all that is real. A vivid awareness of infinite Being at the roots of our limited being. An awareness of our contingent reality as received, as a present from God, as a free gift of love. This is the existential contact of which we speak when we use the metaphor of being 'touched by God'.

Friday after Trinity 10

A Reading from a sermon of Caesarius of Arles

Some people think that while it is unlawful for women to have sexual relations before marriage, it is perfectly acceptable for men to do so. This licentiousness is wrong, made worse by the fact that many men are behaving in this way without any sense of fear of the Lord. In fact, their behaviour has become so habitual that in the eyes of many people their actions are viewed as inconsequential and trivial, nothing serious.

Now in the Catholic Faith there can be no double-standards. Whatever is unlawful for a woman is equally unlawful for a man. Men and women were redeemed together for one price, and together have been called into the assembly of the Christian Church. Together they receive the sacrament of baptism; together they approach the altar to receive the body and blood of Christ. Both sexes are bound by the same precepts. Since this is the case, with what arrogance, or with what sort of a conscience, do men think they can do with impunity things which are unlawful for men and women equally? Men who behave in this sort of way should know for certain that if they do not amend their ways quickly and make suitable reparation, if they are suddenly struck down in this life they can expect no respite from the punishment due to them in the world to come.

Let me point out another wrong. How is it that many men are quite happy to live with various women before they marry, but suddenly, when it suits them, they get rid of these poor women in order to contract a more advantageous marriage? Before God and his angels I attest and declare that God condemns such behaviour and in no way approves of such actions. It never has been and never shall be lawful for Christians to behave in this way. Men who do this may claim the authority of the market place for their behaviour, but they do not enjoy the authority of heaven. They are controlled by lust, whereas they should be ordering their lives according to justice.

Saturday after Trinity 10

A reading from a homily of Origen

Each of our souls contains a well of living water. Within it is buried the image of God. It is this same well that the hostile powers of the universe have blocked up with earth. But now that our Isaac has appeared – I mean Christ – so let us welcome his coming and dig out our wells, clearing out the earth and cleansing them of all impurities. In spite of all the accumulated pollution, we shall find in them living water, water of which the Lord says: 'Those who believe in me, out of their belly shall flow streams of living water.'

For the Word of God is present there, within us, and his work is to remove the earth from the soul of each of us, to let the springs of water within gush free. This spring is within you and does not come from outside, for 'the kingdom of God is within you.' Or to give another analogy from Scripture, the woman who had lost her silver coin found it not outside, but inside her house. She lit her lamp, swept out the house, and there she found the silver coin. For your part, if you light your 'lamp', if you make use of the illumination of the Holy Spirit, if 'you see light in his light', then you too will find the silver coin within you. For the image of our heavenly king is within us.

When God created human beings in the beginning, he made them 'in his own image and likeness'. He does not imprint this image exteriorly on us, but within us. It could not be seen in you as long as your house was dirty, full of junk and rubbish. But once you let the Word of God clear the great pile of earth that is weighing down your soul, then the image of the heavenly king will again shine out in you.

The maker of this image is the Son of God. And he is a craftsman of such surpassing skill that though his image may indeed become obscured by our neglect, it can never be destroyed by evil. The image of God always remains within you.

Trinity 11

A Reading from a homily of Gregory of Nyssa

'Blessed are the pure in heart, for they shall see God.' In trying to penetrate the meaning of this text, we should note that the Lord does not say that it is blessed to know something about God, but rather to possess God within ourselves. I do not wish to suggest that God presents himself literally face to face with those who have been purified. Rather, I interpret this marvellous saying in line with what the Word expresses in another context, namely that 'The kingdom of God is within you.' By this we should learn that if our hearts have been purified of every creature and material sentiment, then we shall see in our own beauty the image of the godhead.

In this short saying I think the Word is giving us this advice: there is a desire within us as human beings to contemplate the supreme Good. When you are told that the majesty of God is exalted far above the heavens, that the divine glory is inexpressible, that its beauty is indescribable, and its nature inaccessible, do not despair at never being able to behold what you desire. It is within your reach; you have in you the ability to see God. For the One who made you also endowed your nature with this marvellous quality. For God imprinted on you the image of his perfection, as the mark of a seal is impressed upon wax. But sin has distorted the imprint of God in you, and this good has become profitless, hidden beneath a covering of dirt. You must wash off the dirt that clings to your heart like plaster by a good life, and then the divine beauty will once again shine forth in you.

A similar thing happens with iron. If freed from rust by a whetstone what was one moment black suddenly gleams and glistens in the sunlight. So it is with our inner selves (because this is what our Lord means when he talks about the heart); once rid of the rust-like dirt that has accumulated by our degenerate behaviour, then we will rediscover our goodness, shining forth in the likeness of our model. For what resembles the Good is in itself good. Hence, when those who are pure of heart look into themselves, they will see the One whom they seeking. That is why they are termed blessed, for in gazing at their own translucency they are beholding the model in the image.

Or to give a further analogy: it is just like looking at the sun in a mirror. Even though you do not look directly at the heavens, you do see the sun in the mirror's reflection just as if you were looking directly at it. And so it is with us, says our Lord. Even though we are not strong enough to contemplate the reality of the light, yet if we rediscover the beauty of the image in which we were created at the beginning, then we will find within us what we are seeking.

Monday after Trinity 11

A Reading from *The Revelations of Mechtild of Magdeburg* also known as
The Flowing Light of the Godhead

Dear Love of God, embrace this soul of mine,
For it would grieve me bitterly
To be parted from you.
Therefore I beg you not to let my love grow cold,
For my works are dead,
If I am not conscious of your presence.

O Love, you make both pain and need sweet to me,
You give wisdom and comfort to the children of God.
O bond of Love, your hand is powerful,
Binding both young and old;
You make the heaviest burdens light,
Whereas our little sins to you are great.
You serve all your creatures gladly
For love alone.

O sweet Love of God, should I sleep too long,
Carelessly neglecting all good things,
Come and awaken me and sing to me;
For the song with which you touch my soul
Delights me better than sweet music.

O Love, fling me down under you,
Gladly would I submit to your embrace.
Should you even take my life from me
I would still find comfort,
For you, O most gentle Love of God
Are too ready to indulge me
And I weep.

O Love, your voice fills my heart with joy!
The pain your touch brings enables me to live free from sin;
Your constancy brings me much sweet sorrow.
O Divine Love, how can I be content when I lack you?
Yet, when you desert me
Your very absence
Breathes in me a strong and heavenly courage.

O wondrous Love, happy is she whom you teach
For it is a joyful humility
Which begs you to turn from the soul.
O Love, however small you find her
Who now seeks you with all her might,
Relentlessly pursuing you,
Bidding you with the eagerness of love
To flee from her unworthiness –
Yet there are many who call after you with their voices
But turn away from you in their lives–
But your going and coming, O Love,
Are equally welcome to my soul:
You have achieved what God began in us
With heartfelt love.
Your noble clarity stands as a mirror
Between God and the pure soul,
And awakens a burning love in the heart of this woman
For Jesus, her own dear love.

May your holy compassion
Confound the wiles of the enemy.
May your sweet peace
Bring us gentle feelings and purity of life.
May your holy sufficiency lead free spirits
To embrace a willing poverty.

Tuesday after Trinity 11

A Reading from *Life Together* by Dietrich Bonhoeffer

In the Christian community thankfulness is just what it is anywhere else in the Christian life. Only they who give thanks for little things receive the big things. We prevent God from giving us the great spiritual gifts he has in store for us, because we do not give thanks for daily gifts. We think we dare not be satisfied with the small measure of spiritual knowledge, experience, and love that has been given to us, and that we must constantly be looking forward eagerly for the highest good. Then we deplore the fact that we lack the deep certainty, the strong faith, and the rich experience that God has given to others, and we consider this lament to be pious. We pray for the big things and forget to give thanks for the ordinary, small (and yet really not small) gifts. How can God entrust great things to one who will not thankfully receive from him the little things? If we do not give thanks daily for the Christian fellowship in which we have been placed, even where there is no great experience, no discoverable riches, but much weakness, small faith, and difficulty; if, on the contrary, we only keep complaining to God that everything is so paltry and petty, so far from what we expected, then we hinder God from letting our fellowship grow according to the measure and riches which are there for us all in Jesus Christ.

Christian community is like the Christian's sanctification. It is a gift of God which cannot claim. Only God knows the real state of our fellowship, of our sanctification. What may appear weak and trifling to us may appear great and glorious to God. Just as Christians should not be constantly feeling their spiritual pulse, so, too, the Christian community has not been given to us by God for us to be constantly taking its temperature. The more thankfully we daily receive what is given to us, the more surely and steadily will fellowship increase and grow from day today as God pleases.

Christian brotherhood is not an ideal which we must realise: it is rather a reality created by God in Christ in which we may participate. The more clearly we learn to recognise that the ground and strength and promise of all our fellowship is in Jesus Christ alone, the more serenely shall we think of our fellowship and pray and hope for it.

Wednesday after Trinity 11

A Reading from *The Enchiridion* by Augustine

In the universe, that which we habitually label as evil, when seen in its proper perspective, only serves to enhance our admiration of what is good. We enjoy and value the good all the more when we place it alongside what is evil. For almighty God who (as the pagans admit) has supreme power over everything, being himself supremely good, would never permit the existence of anything evil among his works if he were not so omnipotent and good that he can bring good even out of evil. Thus, what is that which we label evil other than an absence of good?

In the bodies of animals, diseases and wounds indicate the absence of health. When a cure is effected, it does not mean that the evils which were present suddenly go elsewhere – they cease to exist. The wound or disease is not a substance, but a defect in the substance of the flesh which is in itself good, a symptom of the flesh's lack of health. In the same way, what are called vices in the soul are really privations of natural good.

Everything that exists, seeing that the Creator of all is supremely good, is good. However, unlike their Creator who is supremely and unchangeably good, their good is subject to both diminishment and increase. When the good diminishes we call it evil, though even then, if the creature is to continue to exist, it is necessary for some good to remain to constitute its being. However small, and of whatever kind a being may be, it cannot be destroyed without destroying the being itself. This is why an uncorrupted nature is held in esteem, and why the incorruptible nature of God is of the highest value.

In other words, there is nothing which we call evil, which does not co-exist with what is good. A good which is wholly without evil is perfection. A good, on the other hand, which contains evil is flawed: it is a good which has not reached perfection.

Although no one doubts that good and evil are opposites, not only can they co-exist, but evil cannot exist without good, or in anything that is not inherently good. Good, on the other hand, can exist without evil. From what is good, then, evils arose; and except in relation to what is good they do not exist: there is no alternative source of evil in the universe.

Thursday after Trinity 11

A Reading from *Revelations of Divine Love*
by Julian of Norwich

The purpose of God's revelation to me was to teach our soul the wisdom of cleaving to the goodness of God. And so our customary practice of prayer was brought to mind: how through our ignorance and inexperience in the ways of love we spend so much time on petition. I saw that it is indeed more worthy of God and more truly pleasing to him that through his goodness we should pray with full confidence, and by his grace cling to him with real understanding and unshakeable love, than that we should go on making as many petitions as our souls are capable of. For however numerous our petitions they still come short of being wholly worthy of him. For in his goodness is included all one can want, without exception.

As I am saying, at this time my mind was reflecting thus: we are able to pray to God because of his holy incarnation, his precious blood, his holy passion, his most dear death and wounds. The blessed consequence of all this, eternal life, springs from his goodness. When we pray for love of the sweet Mother who bore him, the help she gives is due to his goodness. And if we pray by the holy cross on which he died, the strength and the help we get through that cross is through his goodness. Similarly the help that comes from particular saints and the blessed company of heaven, the delightful love and eternal fellowship we enjoy with them, are all due to his goodness. For through his goodness God has ordained the means to help us, both glorious and many.

To know the goodness of God is the highest prayer of all, and it is a prayer that accommodates itself to our most lowly needs. It quickens our soul, and vitalises it, developing it in grace and virtue. Here is the grace most appropriate to our need, and most ready to help. Here is the grace which our soul is seeking now, and which it will ever seek until that day when we know for a fact that he has wholly united us to himself. He does not despise the work of his hands, nor does he disdain to serve us, however lowly our natural need may be. He loves the soul he has made in his own likeness.

The love of God Most High for our soul is so wonderful that it surpasses all knowledge. No created being can know the greatness, the sweetness, the tenderness of the love that our Maker has for us. By his grace and help therefore let us in spirit stand and gaze, eternally marvelling at the supreme, surpassing, single-minded, incalculable love that God, who is goodness, has for us. Then we can ask reverently of our lover whatever we will. For by nature our will wants God, and the good-will of God wants us. We shall never cease wanting until we possess him in fullness and joy. Then we shall have no further wants, Meanwhile his will is that we go on knowing and loving until we are perfected in heaven.

Friday after Trinity 11

A Reading from *The Life of Moses* by Gregory of Nyssa

Scripture says 'Moses approached the dark cloud where God was.' What does it mean when it says that Moses entered the darkness and that he saw God in it?

What is recounted here seems to be in contradiction to the first appearance of God to Moses in the burning bush, for then the divine was beheld in light but now in darkness. We should not think that these statements are mutually contradictory. Rather, they point to a sequence of spiritual movement we need to contemplate. Scripture is teaching us here that at first religious knowledge comes to those who receive it as light. Thus, what is perceived to be contrary to religion is identified as darkness, and the escape from darkness comes about when we participate in light. However, as the mind progresses and, through an ever greater and more perfect searching after God, comes to apprehend reality, as it approaches more nearly to the contemplation of God, we realise just how great is the divine nature we have yet to contemplate.

Leaving behind everything that had been observed hitherto, not only what our senses have comprehended, but also what the intelligence thinks it sees, our minds keep on penetrating deeper until by the intelligence's yearning for understanding, we gain access to the invisible and the incomprehensible, and there we see God. This is the true knowledge of what the mind has been seeking; this is the seeing that consists in not seeing, because that which is sought transcends all knowledge, being surrounded on all sides by incomprehensibility as by a kind of darkness. This is why John the Sublime, who penetrated into the luminous darkness of God, says: 'No one has ever seen God,' thus asserting that knowledge of the divine essence is unattainable not simply by us humans, but also by every intelligent creature.

When, therefore, Moses grew in knowledge, he declared that he had seen God in the darkness, that is, that he had come to know that what is divine is beyond all knowledge and comprehension, for the text says: 'Moses approached the dark cloud where God was.' What God? The God who, as the Psalmist says, 'made the darkness his hiding place'.

Saturday after Trinity 11

A Reading from an *Introduction to the Devout Life*
by Francis de Sales

The diligence and care with which we should attend to our business affairs must never be confused with anxiety and worry. Care and diligence are compatible with tranquillity and peace of mind; anxiety, scrupulosity and agitation are not.

Be careful and diligent in all your affairs, for God who has committed these things to your care would want things done well in accord with his will, but without your care and attention degenerating into nervous anxiety. Do not hurry or excite yourself because this will undermine your judgement and prevent you executing your responsibilities effectively.

Nothing is ever done well that is done with haste and impetuosity. We should take time to listen, in accordance with the advice of Solomon: 'He that is in haste is in danger of stumbling.' We will accomplish our duties in good time when we take time to do them properly. Try, then, to meet the decisions facing you quietly, one at a time. If you try to do everything at once or out of order, your spirit will be so overcharged and depressed that it will probably sink under the burden without achieving anything.

In all your undertakings rely wholly on God's providential care, through which alone comes success. Work steadily on your part, seeking always to co-operate with God's designs. Then you may be assured, that if you trust all to God, whatever happens will indeed be the best for you, whether it seems in your own judgement good or bad. Imitate little children who, while holding onto their father with one hand, like to gather strawberries or blackberries from the hedgerow with their free hand. In the same way, you too, whilst gathering and handling the affairs of this world with one hand, must always make sure that you are holding onto your heavenly Father with your other hand, looking at him from time to time to make sure your actions and decisions are pleasing to him. But above all, making sure that you never let go, or preferring to gather more things, fall flat on your face.

My meaning in all this is that amid the affairs and duties of life, we should be sure to look more to God than to them. And when our duties are of such importance that they demand our undivided attention, then we should still make sure that from time to time we cast a look towards God, rather like sailors who in setting their course for port look more at the stars of heaven than the open sea. In so doing God will work with you and in you and for you, and you will not labour in vain but will be filled with God's consolation.

Trinity 12

A Reading from a treatise *On the Lord's Prayer*
by Cyprian of Carthage

How necessary, how important and how salutary is the Lord's declaration to us that we are sinners when he compels us to pray on account of our sins! For in the process of asking for God's forgiveness we become aware of the state of our conscience. Moreover we are commanded to pray daily for the forgiveness of our sins, and by so doing we are prevented from fantasising about our supposed innocence, or exalting our egos and thereby increasing the risk of our perdition. In his epistle John warns us as follows: 'If we say we have no sin, we deceive ourselves, and the truth is not in us. If we confess our sins, the Lord is faithful and just and will forgive us our sins.' In his epistle John has combined two ideas: that we should seek pardon for our sins; and that when we ask for forgiveness, God may be trusted to grant it. This is why he states that God is faithful and true to his promise of forgiveness. He who taught us to pray on account of our sins and offences has promised that the fatherly mercy and pardon of God will be granted.

The Lord has clearly set forth the condition of such pardon; he has stated it as a law and expressed it as a covenant. We can only expect our sins to be forgiven according to the degree that we ourselves forgive those who sin against us. We are informed categorically that we will not be able to obtain what we ask for in respect of our sins unless we have acted ourselves in the same way to those who have sinned against us. Thus our Lord says in another place in Scripture: 'The measure you deal out will be dealt back to you.' Similarly, the servant who refused to cancel his fellow servant's debt, in spite of having had his own debts cancelled by his master, was thrown into prison. Because he refused to be generous to his fellow servant, he forfeited the indulgence that had been shown to him by his master.

These ideas Christ sets forth even more directly and stamps it with his own authority when he says: 'Whenever you stand praying, forgive, if you have anything against anyone; so that your

Father in heaven may also forgive you your debts. But if you do not forgive, neither will your Father in heaven forgive you your debts.' You will have no excuse on the day of judgement; you will be judged according to the sentence you have passed on others; whatever you have dealt out will be dealt back to you.

God commands us to be peacemakers, to live in harmony, and to be of one mind in his house. He warns those who have been born again to retain the character of their second birth. We who are the children of God must make the peace of God a reality in our lives; we who share in the one Spirit must also be of one heart and mind. God refuses the sacrifice of the quarrelsome, and instructs them to leave their gift before the altar, to go and be reconciled to their brother or sister. God is only pacified by prayer that is offered in a spirit of peace. So let our peace and fraternal harmony be the great sacrifice we offer God. In this way we will become a people gathered into the unity of the Father, the Son, and the Holy Spirit.

Monday after Trinity 12

A Reading from *Mens Creatrix* by William Temple

The question is not whether the God of Christianity suits us, but whether we suit him. A sane man does not say, 'The law of gravitation does not suit me, so I can ignore it and walk over the edge of this cliff in security'; nor will a sane man say, 'A God who requires me to love my very tiresome neighbour and even my most wicked enemy does not suit me, so I will pursue my selfish interests in security.' If God is love, selfishness is enmity against omnipotence – a foolish enmity. We may reject God if we like, but it makes no difference to his achievement of his purpose.

The power of God is love. To all that is selfish the love of God is infinitely terrible; to realise that love is the law of the universe, and that, whether we will or not, we are being used and used up for the good of the whole society of spirits, must be to the selfish soul an agony of torture. Love rejoices in the union with all things living wherein it finds itself. The realisation of this truth about God is heaven or hell according as love or pride is uppermost in the heart.

But the divine love cannot be content with using as puppets of its purpose the souls whom it created to be worthy of itself. The kind of power that God exerted in the world before the birth of Christ was not enough. Not only events, but hearts and wills must be ruled. So the love was made known in an intelligible form through life and death, so that omnipotence should be complete, and, by the responding love called forth, the free allegiance of hearts and wills be won. By power and by love God would deliver us from pride, which is the one poison of the soul, and bring us into union with himself.

Tuesday after Trinity 12

A Reading from a letter of Augustine

At certain times we need consciously to bring our minds back to the business of prayer, and to detach ourselves from other matters and preoccupations which cool our desire for God. We need to remind ourselves by the words we pray to focus on what we really desire. This we do to prevent what may have begun to grow lukewarm in us from becoming cold, or worse still, from being entirely extinguished. The solution is to fan our desire regularly into flame. This is why when the apostle Paul says: 'Let your requests be made known to God' his words should not be interpreted as though this is how God becomes aware of human need. God undoubtedly knows our needs before ever we utter them. Paul's words should be understood in the sense that it is in the presence of God that *we* become aware of our inner desires as we wait patiently upon him in prayer. That is why it is not appropriate that they should be paraded before other folk in ostentatious public prayer.

We should welcome all opportunities for extended periods of prayer when other duties involving good and necessary activity do not prevent us – although even in the midst of activity we can still pray without ceasing by cherishing our deepest desire. And note, praying for long is not the same thing as praying 'with much speaking' as some Christians seem to think. To be verbose is one thing; to extend prayer in the warmth of a desire for God is quite another. In the Scriptures we are told that our Lord himself spent a whole night in prayer, and that in his agony in Gethsemane he prayed even more fervently. Is he not giving us an example? In time he is the intercessor we need; in eternity he dwells with the Father and is the hearer of our prayer.

The monks in Egypt are said to offer frequent prayers, but these are very brief and are, so to speak, darted forth like arrows lest the vigilant and alert attention which is vital in prayer be weakened or blunted through being over-extended. In this way even these monastics are demonstrating that mental concentration should not be allowed to become exhausted through excess; and on the other hand, if it is sustained, should not be suddenly broken off. Far be it from us then, to use 'much speaking' in our prayer; or if concentration be sustained to curtail our prayer abruptly.

To use a lot of words when we pray is superfluous. But to long for God in prayer, if the desire and concentration persist, is good. It will necessitate beating upon the door of him to whom we are praying by long and deep stirring of the heart. Often prayer consists more in groans than in words, more in tears than in speech. But God collects our tears; our groaning is not hidden from him who created all things by his Word, and who has no need of human words.

Wednesday after Trinity 12

A Reading from a poem of John of the Cross

A Song of the soul in intimate communication and union with the love of God

Flame, alive, compelling.
yet tender past all telling,
reaching the secret centre of my soul!
Since now evasion's over,
finish your work, my Lover,
break the last thread, wound me and make me whole!

Burn that is for my healing!
Wound of delight past feeling!
Ah, gentle hand whose touch is a caress,
foretaste of heaven conveying
and every debt repaying:
slaying, you give me life for death's distress.

O lamps of fire bright-burning
with splendid brilliance, turning
deep caverns of my soul to pools of light!
Once shadowed, dim, unknowing,
now their strange new-found glowing
gives warmth and radiance for my Love's delight.

Ah! gentle and so loving
you wake within me, proving
that you are there in secret and alone;
your fragrant breathing stills me,
your grace, your glory fills me
so tenderly your love becomes my own.

Thursday after Trinity 12

A Reading from the writings on prayer
of Theophan the Recluse

There are various degrees of prayer. The first degree is bodily prayer, consisting for the most part in reading, in standing and in making prostrations. In all this there must needs be patience, labour and sweat; for the attention runs away, the heart feels nothing and has no desire to pray. Yet in spite of this, give yourself a moderate rule and keep to it. Such is active prayer.

The second degree is prayer with attention: the intellect becomes accustomed to collecting itself in the hour of prayer, and prays consciously throughout, without distraction. The intellect is focused upon the written words to the point of speaking them as if they were its own.

The third degree is prayer of feeling: the heart is warmed by concentration, so that what hitherto has only been thought now becomes feeling. Where first it was a contrite phrase now it is contrition itself; and what was once petition in words is transformed into a sensation of entire necessity. Whoever has passed through action and thought to true feeling all pray without words, for God is God of the heart.

When the feeling of prayer reaches the point where it becomes continuous, then spiritual prayer may be said to begin. This is the gift of the Holy Spirit praying for us, the last degree of prayer that our intellects can grasp.

But there is, they say, yet another kind of prayer which cannot be comprehended by the intellect, and which goes beyond the limits of consciousness.

What then is prayer? Prayer is the raising of the mind and heart to God in praise and thanksgiving to him and in supplication for the good things that we need, both spiritual and physical. The essence of prayer is, therefore, the spiritual lifting of the heart towards God. The principal thing is to stand before God with the intellect in the heart, and to go on standing before him unceasingly day and night until the end of life.

Friday after Trinity 12

A Reading from *Centuries of Meditations*
by Thomas Traherne

The cross is the abyss of wonders, the centre of desires, the school of virtues, the house of wisdom, the throne of love, the theatre of joys, and the place of sorrows. It is the root of happiness, and the gate of heaven.

Of all the things in heaven and earth it is the most peculiar. It is the most exalted of all objects. It is an ensign lifted up for all nations; to it shall the Gentiles seek. Its rest shall be glorious: the dispersed of Judah shall be gathered together to it from the four corners of the earth. If love be the weight of the soul, and its object the centre, all eyes and hearts may convert and turn unto this object, cleave unto this centre, and by it enter into rest. There we might see all nations assembled with their eyes and hearts upon it. There we may see God's goodness, wisdom, and power, yea, his mercy and anger displayed. There we may see man's sin and infinite value, his hope and fear, his misery and happiness. There we might see the rock of ages and the joys of heaven. There we may see a man loving all the world, and a God dying for mankind. There we may see all types and ceremonies, figures and prophecies, and all nations adoring a malefactor – an innocent malefactor, yet the greatest in the world. There we may see the most distant things in eternity united, all mysteries at once couched together and explained.

The only reason why this glorious object is so publicly admired by churches and kingdoms, and so little thought of by particular men, is because it is truly the most glorious. It is the root of comforts and the fountain of joys. It is the only supreme and sovereign spectacle in all worlds. It is a well of life beneath in which we may see the face of heaven above, and the only mirror wherein all things appear in their proper colours: that is, sprinkled in the blood of our Lord and Saviour.

The cross of Christ is the Jacob's ladder by which we ascend into the highest heavens. There we see joyful patriarchs, expectant saints, prophets ministering, apostles publishing, and doctors teaching, all nations concentering, and angels praising. That cross is a tree set on fire with invisible flame that illuminateth all the world. The flame is love: the love in his bosom who died on it, in the light of which we see how to possess all the things in heaven and earth after his similitude.

Saturday after Trinity 12

A Reading from a homily of Gregory of Nyssa
'On the Love of the Poor'

We have seen in these days a remarkable rise in the number of vagrants who are wandering about homeless and practically naked. For the most part they are victims of war who knock at our doors. But one also finds strangers and exiles. Their roof is the sky. For shelter they use porticoes, alleys, and the deserted corners of the town. They hide in the cracks of walls like male and female owls. Their clothing consists of wretched rags. Their harvest depends on human pity. For meals they have only the alms tossed at them by those who pass by. For drink they use the fountains, drinking with the animals. Their cup is the hollow of their hand, their storeroom their pocket, or rather whatever part of it has not been torn and cannot hold whatever has been put into it. For a dining table they use their joined knees, and their lamp is the sun. Instead of using the public baths they use the river or the pond which God gives to all. This life of theirs, which is wandering and brutal, was not that assigned to them by birth, but is a result of their tribulations and their miseries.

Assist these people, you who practise abstinence. Be generous on behalf of your unfortunate brethren. That which you withhold from your belly, give to the poor. Let a fear of God level out the differences between you and them: with self-control, carefully avoid two contrary evils: your own gorging and the hunger of your brethren. This is how the physician works: he puts some on diets, and gives supplementary food to others, in this way curing sicknesses with one or the other of these methods. So follow this salutary advice. Let good words open the doors of the rich. This counsel might thus encourage the poor to turn themselves and appeal to the wealthy. But words alone cannot enrich the poor. Let the eternal Word of God give also a house and a light and table, by means of the household of the Word. Speak to them with affection and alleviate their miseries with your own substance.

But there are still other wretched ones, those who are not only poor but sick. Let us take care of those in the neighbourhood. Don't let a stranger treat those who are in your neighbourhood. Don't let another rob you of the treasure you are depositing. Embrace the wretched as gold: care for their miseries as if treating yourself, as if saving your wife, your children, your domestics and all your house. The poor person who is sick is doubly destitute. For at least those in good health are always able to go from door to door, knocking at the homes of the rich, or setting up camp at the crossroads and from there, hailing all who pass by. But the sick, shut up in their narrow nooks, are only able, like Daniel in his cistern waiting for Habakkuk, to wait for you, for your charity, your offerings. Become a friend, then, of the prophet with your alms. Nourish those in need, immediately and without hesitation.

Trinity 13

A Reading from a homily of John Chrysostom

In my view there is nothing so frigid as a Christian who does not care about the salvation of other people. It is useless to plead poverty in this respect, for the poor widow who put two copper coins in the treasury will be your accuser. So will Peter who said, 'Silver and gold have I none,' and indeed Paul was so poor that he often went hungry and without the basic necessities of life. Nor can you plead humble birth because the apostles were of humble origin and from obscure families. You cannot claim lack of education because they too were illiterate. And do not plead sickness because Timothy suffered poor health and was often ill. Everyone can be of service to their neighbour if only we exercise our responsibilities.

Look at the trees of the forest. See how sturdy they are, how beautiful, how tall, and how smooth their bark; but they do not bear fruit. If we had a garden we would prefer to plant pomegranates or olive trees. The other trees may be delightful to look at but they are not grown for profit, or if they are, it is very small. People who are concerned only for themselves are like those trees of the forest – no, they are not even as worthwhile. At least forest timber can be used for building houses and fortifications, whereas they are good only for the bonfire. They are like the foolish virgins in the parable: chaste certainly, discreet and modest too, but useless. That is why they were rejected. Such is the fate of all who do not nourish Christ.

You should reflect on the fact that none of them is charged with specific sins such as fornication or perjury; they are charged simply with being of no service to their fellow men and women. Take the example of the man who went and buried his talent. He led a blameless life but a life that was not of service to others. How can such a person be called a Christian? If yeast when it is mixed with the flour fails to leaven the dough, how can it be called yeast? Or again, if perfume cannot be sensed by those present, how can it be called perfume in any meaningful sense? So do not say, 'I cannot encourage others to become Christians; it is impossible'; because if you were really a Christian, it would be impossible for you not to do so.

In the natural world, the way things behave is an expression of their properties. It is the same situation here: what I am describing belongs to the very nature of being a Christian. So do not insult God. To claim that the sun cannot shine or that a Christian cannot do good is insulting to God and reveals you as a liar. If we get our lives ordered the rest will follow as a natural consequence. It is impossible for the light of a Christian to be hidden; it is impossible for so resplendent a lamp to be concealed.

Monday after Trinity 13

A Reading from a sermon of John Wesley
preached in 1748

The kingdom of God comes to a particular person when he repents and believes the gospel; when he is taught of God, not only to know himself, but to know Jesus Christ and him crucified. As 'this is eternal life, to know the only true God and Jesus Christ whom he hath sent'; so it is the kingdom of God begun below, set up in a believer's heart. The Lord God Omnipotent reigns when he is known through Christ Jesus. He takes unto himself his mighty power that he may subdue all things unto himself. He goes on in the soul conquering and to conquer, till he has put all things under his feet, till every thought is brought into captivity to the obedience of Christ.

For this we pray; but we also pray for the coming of God's everlasting kingdom, the kingdom of glory in heaven which is the continuation and perfection of the kingdom of grace on earth. Consequently, our prayer is offered for the whole intelligent creation who are all interested in this grand event, the final renovation of all things, by God's putting an end to misery and sin, to infirmity and death, taking all things into his own hands and setting up the kingdom which endures throughout all ages.

We ourselves can claim nothing of right, but only of free mercy. We deserve not the air we breathe, the earth that bears, or the sun that shines upon us. All our desert, we own, is hell. But God loves us freely; therefore, we ask him to give what we can no more procure for ourselves, than we can merit it at his hands.

Not that either the goodness or the power of God is a reason for us to stand idle. It is his will that we should use all diligence in all things, that we should employ our utmost endeavours, as much as if our success were the natural effect of our wisdom and strength. And then, as though we had done nothing, we are to depend on him, the Giver of every good and perfect gift.

Thus when we pray 'Give us this day our daily bread', we are to take no thought for the morrow. For this very end has our wise Creator divided life into these little portions of time, so clearly separated from each other that we might look on every day as a fresh gift of God, another life, which we may devote to his glory; and that every evening may be as the close of life, beyond which we are to see nothing but eternity.

Tuesday after Trinity 13

A Reading from the discourses of Dorotheus of Gaza

Let us examine how it is that sometimes a person hears a disparaging remark and passes it by without being disturbed, as if he had hardly heard it, whilst at another time he hears it and is immediately disturbed. What is the reason for such a difference? Is there only one reason for this difference or are there many? I think there are several reasons for this state of affairs, but there is one thing which is the basic generating cause of them all. It results from the state of mind the person is in at the time.

For example, if it happens when a person is at prayer or spiritually at rest, and being, as one might say, in a good disposition he bears with his brother and is not disturbed. Again it may happen that he has a special affection for the person who attacks him, and out of love will suffer without difficulty anything that person does to him. Then there is the person who disdains the one who wants to cause him pain and despises what he does, regarding him as the lowest of souls and not worth even a reply.

The root cause of all these disturbances, if we are to investigate it accurately, is that we do not accuse ourselves; hence we have all these commotions and we never find rest. We reckon to achieve peace of soul and to take a straight road to it, yet we never come to the point of accusing ourselves. This is true, isn't it? If we were to discipline ourselves in a thousand ways and not take this road, we would never stop troubling others or being troubled by them, and we would waste all our labours.

Of course, someone may ask why he should accuse himself when he had been sitting in peace and quiet, minding his own business, and a brother has come up and upset him with some hurtful or insulting remark. Since he is not going to put up with that, he feels justifiably angry and upset. For, he argues, if the brother had not intruded and spoken and made trouble he would not have sinned.

This is a delusion; this is false reasoning. Surely that brother did not inject the passion of anger into him by saying what he did. Rather he has revealed the passion already latent within him, so that if he so wishes he may now repent of it. This brother is like early wheat, outwardly bright and shining, but when crushed its rottenness appears.

In other words, this man who is sitting in peace and quiet, as he thinks, in fact has this latent anger inside him and he did not know it. One hurtful word spoken by another who happens to be passing by and immediately all the poison and rottenness within gushes out. If he wishes to gain mercy let him repent and purify himself and make efforts to do better and he will see that instead of complaining, he should give thanks to that brother as the person responsible for bringing him such self-knowledge. Temptations will not trouble him so much in the future because the more he progresses the easier he will be able to handle them. For as the soul advances it becomes stronger and better able to put up with whatever hardships may come its way.

Wednesday after Trinity 13

A Reading from *The Coming of God*
by Maria Boulding

In prayer we are led into the desert, and there, away from the masks and camouflages, we have to stand in the truth. Prayer is very humbling, for you have nothing to shield you from the truth as you stand there before God day after day in your naked poverty. But to flee from this humbling experience is useless; we have to live with our own darkness, failure, temptation, confusion and weakness, because it is the only way in which these areas in us can be opened up to the Lord of the wilderness. We have to look steadfastly towards the wilderness of our own being, and it may be that there, in that unlikely place, we shall see the glory of the Lord.

Our desert is any situation of stripping, of hopelessness, of chaos; it is the place of sterility and loneliness, and there is nothing as sterile and lonely as sin. Of these desert areas also he is Lord. They can be opened up to him and become the place of new life. Sin and suffering often seem inextricably mixed in this desert experience, because when the pressure is on us and we are afraid, tempted and in pain, we know the humbling truth of our selfishness and betrayals. We never feel we have come through creditably. In mental suffering and depression it may be nearly impossible for us to know what is our own fault and what is a desert time that we have to endure, but fortunately it is not we who have to sort that out. The desert is only the real desert when it is too big for you, when you cannot see it as spiritually significant, when you do not know your way and have no reliance except God.

Our desert is any place where we confront God. It is not a change of scene, nor a place to run from our failures, nor a heroic adventure that does something for our ego. Our desert experience may be tedium, weariness, disappointment, loneliness, personal emptiness, emotional confusion, the feeling that we have nothing to give, the conviction that we constantly fail God in prayer. You just have to keep on keeping on in prayer, and you are not aware of 'progress', because there seems to be nothing by which it could be measured. There are no paths in the desert except the ones you make by walking on them.

Thursday after Trinity 13

A Reading from a commentary on St John's Gospel
by Cyril of Alexandria

In order that we ourselves may join together, and be blended into unity with God and with one another – although through the actual differences which exist among us we have a distinct individuality of soul and body – the Only-begotten has contrived means which his own due wisdom and counsel have sought out. For by one body, that is, his own, blessing through the mystery of the Eucharist those who believe in him, he makes us of the same body with himself and with one another.

Who could sunder or divide from their natural union with one another those who are knit together through his holy body, which is one in union with Christ? For if 'we all partake of the one bread' we are all made one body; for Christ cannot suffer severance. Therefore, the Church has also become Christ's body, and we are also individually his members, according to the wisdom of Paul. Since all of us are united with Christ inasmuch as we have received him who is one and indivisible in our own bodies, we owe the service of our members to him rather than to ourselves.

The fact that those who partake of his holy flesh gain this actual physical unity with Christ is further attested by Paul when he says, with reference to the mystery of godliness: 'I am speaking of the mystery of Christ, unknown to people in former ages but now revealed by the Spirit to the holy apostles and prophets. It is no less than this: in Christ Jesus the Gentiles are now co-heirs with the Jews, members of the same body and sharers of the promise.'

If all of us are members of the same body in Christ, and not only with one another but also with him who is in us through his flesh, are we not then all of us clearly one both with one another and with Christ? For Christ is the bond of union, since he is at once God and human.

With reference, then, to the unity that is by the Spirit (I mean the Holy Spirit), following in the same track of inquiry, we say once more that we all receiving one and the same Spirit (I mean the Holy Spirit) are somehow blended together with one another and with God. For though we are many, and Christ who is the Spirit of the Father and his own Spirit dwells in each of us severally, the Spirit is still one and indivisible, binding together the dissevered spirits of the individualities of one and all of us. Just as the power of his holy flesh makes those in whom it exists to be of the same body, so also the indivisible Spirit of God who abides in all, being one, binds all together into spiritual unity.

Friday after Trinity 13

A Reading from a commentary on the psalms by
Augustine

'Sing to God a new song, sing to him with joyful melody.' Each of us tries to discover how best to sing to God. We must sing to God, but we must sing well. God does not want his ears assaulted by our discordant voices. So sing well, my brothers and sisters, sing well!

If you were asked: 'Sing to please this musician,' you would not dare to do so without first having had some music lessons, because you would not want to offend such an expert in the art. An undiscerning listener does not notice the faults that an accomplished musician would point out to you. Who, then, will offer to sing well for God, the great artist whose discrimination is faultless, whose attention notices the minutest detail, whose ear nothing escapes? When will you be able to offer him a perfect performance so that you will in no way displease such a supremely discerning listener?

But see how God himself provides you with a way of singing. You do not have to search for words, as if you had to find the right lyric to please God. Sing to him rather simply 'with songs of joy'. This is singing well to God, just singing with songs of joy.

And how is this accomplished? You must first understand that words cannot express the things that are sung by the heart. Take the case of people singing while harvesting in the fields or in the vineyards or when any other strenuous work is in progress. Although they begin by giving expression to their happiness in words, yet quite quickly there is a change. It is as if they are so happy that words can no longer express what they feel, and they discard the restriction of language. They burst out into a simple shout of joy, of jubilation. Such a cry of joy is a sound signifying that the heart is bringing to birth what it cannot utter in words.

Now, who is more worthy of such a cry of jubilation than God himself, whom all the words in the world can never describe? If words will not serve, and yet you must not remain silent, what else can you do but cry out for joy? Your heart must rejoice in a song beyond words, soaring into an ocean of gladness, unrestrained by the fetters of language. So, 'sing to God with songs of joy.'

Saturday after Trinity 13

A Reading from an ancient treatise entitled
The Teaching of the Twelve Apostles

Concerning the Eucharist you should celebrate it as follows: Say
over the cup: 'We give you thanks, our Father, for the holy vine of
David, your servant, which you made known to us through Jesus
your servant. *To you be glory for ever.*'
 Over the broken bread say: 'We give you thanks, our Father,
for the life and the knowledge which you have revealed to us
through Jesus your servant. *To you be glory for ever.*
 'As this broken bread scattered on the mountains was gathered
and became one, so too, may your Church be gathered together
from the ends of the earth into your kingdom. *For the glory and
power are yours through Jesus Christ for ever.*'
 Do not let anyone eat or drink of your Eucharist except those
who have been baptized in the name of the Lord. For the statement
of the Lord applies here also: 'Do not give to dogs what is holy.'
 When you have finished the meal, offer thanks in this manner:
'We thank you, Holy Father, for your name which you enshrined in
our hearts. We thank you for the knowledge and faith and
immortality which you revealed to us through your servant Jesus.
To you be glory for ever.
 'Almighty Lord, you created all things for the sake of your
name; you gave us food and drink to enjoy so that we might give
you thanks. Now you have favoured us through Jesus your servant
with spiritual food and drink as well as with eternal life. Above all
we thank you because you are mighty. *To you be glory for ever.*
 'Remember, Lord, your Church and deliver her from all evil.
Perfect her in your love; and, once she has been sanctified, gather
her together from the four winds into the kingdom which you have
prepared for her. *For the power and glory are yours for ever.*
 'May grace come and this world pass away! *Hosanna to the
God of David!* If any are holy, let them come. If any are not, let
them repent. *Maranatha. Amen.*'
 On the Lord's day, when you have been gathered together,
break bread and celebrate the Eucharist. But first confess your sins
so that your offering may be pure. If anyone has a quarrel with a
neighbour, that person should not join you until the quarrel has
been reconciled. Your sacrifice must not be defiled. For this is the
offering of which the Lord has spoken: 'In every place and time

offer me a pure sacrifice. For I am a great king, says the Lord, and my name is great among the nations.'

Trinity 14

A Reading from a treatise *Against Heresies*
by Irenaeus

There is one God, who by his word and wisdom created all things and set them in order. His Word is our Lord Jesus Christ, who in this last age became man among us to unite the end and the beginning, that is, humanity and God.

The prophets, receiving the gift of prophecy from this same Word, foretold his coming in the flesh, which brought about the union and communion between God and humankind ordained by the Father. From the beginning the word of God prophesied that God would be seen by people and would live among them on earth; he would speak with his own creation and be present to it, bringing it salvation and being visible to it. He would 'free us from the hands of all who hate us', that is, from the universal spirit of sin, and enable us 'to serve him in holiness and righteousness all the days of our life'. We were to receive the Spirit of God and so attain to the glory of the Father.

The prophets, then, foretold that God would be seen by mere mortals. As the Lord himself says: 'Blessed are the pure in heart for they shall see God.' In his greatness and inexpressible glory 'no one can see God and live,' for the Father is beyond our comprehension. But in his love and generosity and omnipotence God allows even this to those who love him, that is, even to see God, as the prophets foretold. 'For what is impossible for human beings is possible to God.'

By our own powers we cannot see God, yet God will be seen by us because he wills it. He will be seen by those whom he chooses, at the time he chooses, and in the way he chooses, for God can do all things. He was seen of old through the Spirit in prophecy; he is seen through the Son by our adoption as his children, and he will be seen in the kingdom of heaven in his own being as the Father. The Spirit prepares us to receive the Son of God, the Son leads us to the Father, and the Father, freeing us from change and decay, bestows the eternal life that comes to everyone from seeing God.

As those who see light are in the light sharing its brilliance, so those who see God are in God sharing his glory, and that glory gives them life. To see God is to share in life.

Monday after Trinity 14

A reading from an essay entitled 'The Philosophy of Solitude' by Thomas Merton

Withdrawal from others can be a special form of love for them. It should never be a rejection of others or of society. But it may well be a quiet and humble refusal to accept the myths and fictions with which social life cannot help but be full. To despair of the illusions and facades which men and women build around themselves is certainly not to despair of mankind. On the contrary, it may be a sign of love and of hope. For when we love someone, we refuse to tolerate what destroys and maims their personality. If we love mankind, can we blind ourselves to the human predicament? You will say: we must do something about their predicament. But there are some whose vocation it is to realise that they, at least, cannot help in any overt social way. Their contribution is a mute witness, a secret and even invisible expression of love which takes the form of their own option for solitude in preference to the acceptance of social fictions. For is not our involvement in fiction, particularly in political and demagogic fiction, an implicit confession that we despair of humanity and even of God?

Christian hope in God and in the world to come is inevitably also hope in man, or at least *for* mankind. How can we despair of humanity when the Word of God was made flesh in order to save us all? But our Christian hope is, and must remain, inviolably pure. It must work and struggle in the chaos of conflicting policy which is the world of egotism: and in order to do so it must take on visible, symbolic forms by which to declare its message. But when these symbols become confused with other secular symbols, then there is danger that faith itself will be corrupted by fictions, and there is a consequent obligation, on the part of some Christians, to affirm their faith in all its intransigent purity.

At such a time, some men and women will seek clarity in isolation and silence, not because they think they know better than the rest, but because they want to see life in a different perspective. They want to withdraw from the babel of confusion in order to listen more patiently to the voice of their conscience and to the Holy Spirit. And by their prayers and their fidelity they will invisibly renew the life of the whole Church.

Tuesday after Trinity 14

A Reading from *The Ladder of Divine Ascent*
by John Climacus

The light of dawn comes before the sun, and meekness is the precursor of all humility. So let us listen to the order in which Christ, our Light, places these virtues. He says, 'Learn from me because I am meek and humble of heart.' Therefore, before gazing at the sun of humility we must let the light of meekness flow over us. If we do, we will then be able to look steadily at the sun. The true order of these virtues teaches us that we are totally unable to turn our eyes to the sun before we have first become accustomed to the light.

Meekness is a mind consistent amid honour and dishonour. Meekness prays quietly and sincerely for a neighbour, however troublesome he may be. Meekness is a rock looking out over the sea of anger which breaks the waves which come crashing on it and stays entirely unmoved. Meekness is the bulwark of patience, the door, indeed the mother of love, and the foundation of discernment. For it is said, 'The Lord will teach his ways to the meek.' And it is meekness that earns pardon for our sins, gives confidence to our prayers and makes a place for the Holy Spirit. As it stands in the prophecy of Isaiah: 'To whom shall I look if not to the meek and the peaceful?'

Meekness works alongside obedience; it guides a religious community, checks frenzy, curbs anger. It is a minister of joy, an imitation of Christ, the possession of angels, a shackle for demons, a shield against bitterness. The Lord finds rest in the hearts of the meek, while the turbulent spirit is the home of the devil, for 'the meek shall inherit the earth.'

Wednesday after Trinity 14

A Reading from *Befriending our Desires*
by Philip Sheldrake

When we think about the discernment of our desires it is important
to remember that each of us is a single, unified human being even
if we all have many dimensions. The problem is that so often in
practice we tend to distinguish between the emotional, intellectual,
physical and spiritual parts of ourselves. And so we divide up our
'passions' according to their association with one particular aspect
of our human existence. Yet these dimensions of our personality,
and the kinds of desires associated with them, exist in a continuous
interdependence. Thus the way we treat our bodies affects the
deepest longings of our spirits. And our spiritual desires find their
expression in our immediate feelings and in our bodily reactions.
We need to pay much more attention to the way that changes in
our body are indicators of spiritual well-being or spiritual
confusion.

What it is important to grasp is that our so-called 'spiritual'
desires do not exist in a separate compartment of life. The whole
of my life is spiritual. We cannot say that any desire is irrelevant
to the process of spiritual growth and discernment. Every kind of
desire is touched by the Spirit of God in some sense even if it is
capable of being misdirected.

One of the most common, and also most difficult, experiences
that I know is that of being pulled in opposite directions by
apparently contradictory desires. This is particularly true when
these desires, in the first instance, seem good and important. We
find ourselves powerfully, almost willy-nilly, drawn towards
people, objects and ideals that are not merely diverse but
sometimes incompatible. We are sometimes moved by passions
that fragment us, perhaps violently so. In this context, discernment
is the way of sifting through a confusion of desires in order that
our lives may be shaped by the best of them. The 'best of them'
does not imply that we live in a two-tier universe in which certain
types of human desires are inherently better or that 'the best' are
immediately recognisable. We are all the products, and sometimes
the victims, of our upbringing and environment. Sometimes we
have to struggle against assuming that we must always make
certain kinds of choices if we are to be 'good Christians'.

As a process, discernment enables us, in the first instance, to
be aware of and to accept the full range of desires that we

experience. From this starting point we are slowly led to understand the way in which our desires vary greatly in their quality. Certain desires, or ways of desiring, if we follow them through, will tend to push towards a dispersion of our spiritual and psychic energy or a fragmentation of our attention, experience and personalities. Other desires seem, rather, to promise a greater concentration of energy and a harmonious centredness. What is sometimes initially confusing is that the less helpful or healthy desires appear to be more strikingly attractive because they make us feel good. In other words the direction and potential of our desires is not always immediately self-evident. To come to appreciate these things demands patient reflection.

Thursday after Trinity 14

A Reading from a commentary on the psalms by
Augustine

My brothers and sisters, where does time go? The years slip and slide past us, day by day. Those things which were, no longer are; those things yet to come, are not here. The past is dead; the future is yet to come, but only to pass away in turn. Today exists only for the moment in which we speak. Its first hours are already over and behind us, the remainder do not as yet exist; they are still to come, but only to fall into nothingness.

Nothing in this world has constancy in itself. The body does not possess being; it has no permanence. It changes with age; it changes with time and place; it changes as a result of sickness or accident. The stars have as little constancy; they are always changing in hidden ways, they go whirling into outer space. They are not stable, they do not possess being.

Nor is the human heart any more constant. How often it is disturbed by various conflicting thoughts and ambitions! How many pleasures draw it, one minute this way, and the next minute, that way, tearing it apart! The human spirit, although endowed by God with reason, changes; it does not possess being. It wills and does not will; it knows and does not know; it remembers this but forgets that. No one has unity of being in himself.

After so much suffering, disease, difficulties and pain, let us return humbly to God, to that one Being. Let us enter into that heavenly Jerusalem, that city whose citizens share in Being itself.

Friday after Trinity 14

A Reading from the writings on prayer of Innocent,
Metropolitan of Moscow

The Holy Spirit confers true humility. However intelligent, sensible, and clever a person may be, if he does not possess the Holy Spirit within him, he cannot know himself properly; for without God's help we cannot see the inner state of our soul. But when the Holy Spirit enters the human heart, he shows us all our inner poverty and weakness, the corruption of our soul and heart, and our remoteness from God. The Holy Spirit shows us all the sins that coexist with our virtues and righteousness: our laziness and lack of zeal for salvation and for the good of others, the selfishness that informs what appear to be our most unselfish virtues, the crude self-love that lurks where we never suspected it. In brief, the Holy Spirit shows everything in its true aspect. Enlightened by the Holy Spirit, we begin to experience true humility, distrusting our own powers and virtues and regarding ourselves as the worst of mankind.

The Holy Spirit teaches true prayer. No one, until he receives the Spirit, can pray in a manner truly pleasing to God. This is so, because anyone who begins to pray without having the Holy Spirit in him, finds that his soul is dispersed in all directions, turning to and fro, so that he cannot fix his thoughts on one thing. Moreover he does not properly know either himself, or his own needs; he does not know how or what to ask from God; he does not even know who God is. But those in whom the Holy Spirit is dwelling know God and see that he is our Father. They know how to approach him, how to ask and what to ask for. Their thoughts in prayer are orderly, pure, and directed to one object alone – God; and by their prayer they are truly able to do everything.

Saturday after Trinity 14

A Reading from a treatise *The Steps of Humility
and Pride* by Bernard of Clairvaux

There are three stages in the perception of truth: we must look for truth within ourselves, within our neighbour, and in itself. We look for truth in ourselves when we judge ourselves: we look for truth in our neighbour when we have sympathy for them in their sufferings: we look for truth in itself when we contemplate it with a pure heart. It is important to observe the order of these stages of perception as well as their number.

First of all, Truth teaches us that we must look for it in our neighbours before we seek it in itself. In so doing, you will quickly understand why you must seek it in yourself before you seek it in your neighbours. Reflect on the list of beatitudes: the merciful are spoken of before the pure of heart. The merciful quickly grasp the truth in their neighbours when their heart goes out to them with a love that unites them so intimately that they feel their neighbours' good and ill as if it were their own. With the weak they are weak, with the down-trodden they burn with indignation. They rejoice with those who rejoice and weep with those who weep. Their hearts are made more perceptive by love, and they experience the delight of contemplating truth, not now in others but in itself, and for love of it they bear and suffer their neighbours' sorrow.

Those who do not live in harmony with their brothers and sisters, who mock at those who weep and are cynical about those who rejoice, have no sympathy with them because their feelings do not affect them, and consequently can never really see the truth in them. The proverb suits them well: 'The healthy person does not understand the pain of the sick, nor the well-fed grasp the hunger-pains of the starving.' It is only fellow sufferers who readily feel compassion for the sick and the hungry. For just as truth in its purity is seen only by those who are pure in heart, so also, the miseries of a brother or sister are truly experienced only by those who have known misery in their own lives. You will never have real mercy for the failings of others until you know and realise that the same failings exist in your own soul. Then you will be able to help them through knowledge of yourself.

When we do this we are imitating the example of our Saviour. He willed to suffer so that he might feel for our wretchedness, and to learn mercy he shared our misery. It is written: 'He learned obedience in the school of suffering.' And he learned mercy in the same way. I do not mean by this that he did not know how to be merciful before. On the contrary, his mercy is from everlasting. But what in his divine nature he knows from all eternity he learned by experience in time.

Trinity 15

A Reading from the treatise *On the Lord's Prayer*
by Cyprian of Carthage

The petition 'Give us today our daily bread' may be understood both in a spiritual sense and in a literal sense: either interpretation is a God-given help to salvation. We recognise Christ to be the bread of life; and this bread is not common property, but belongs to us in a special way. Inasmuch as we have learned to say 'Our Father' and know God to be the Father of those who understand and believe; so also we have learned to call Christ 'our bread' because he is the food of those who are members of his body. Thus when we pray that we may receive this bread daily, we are asking that we who are incorporated into Christ may receive his Eucharist daily as the food of our salvation. It is our prayer that we may not fall into some serious sin and be forced to abstain from communion because this would deprive us of the bread of heaven and separate us from the body of Christ.

But this petition may also be understood in a different way, namely, that we who have renounced the world and have forsaken its riches and pomp in an act of faith in God's grace, should only ever seek of God food and inner strength. In the gospel the Lord has stated: 'None of you can be my disciple if you do not give up your possessions.' Having renounced our possessions in obedience to the word of our Master, and begun a life of discipleship, we ought to pray for our food daily. And note, we are not to seek future needs because elsewhere the Lord also says: 'Do not worry about tomorrow, for tomorrow will bring worries of its own. Today's trouble is enough for today.' With good reason then should we, as Christ's disciples, learn to ask simply for enough for each day. We are forbidden to ask for more. Indeed it is hypocritical and a contradiction in terms to be pleading at one moment for a long life in this world, and the next moment to be asking that the kingdom of God may come quickly!

We should also recollect the words of Paul the blessed apostle who gives meaning and strength to our perseverance in hope and faith, when he says: 'We brought nothing into this world, and it is certain we can take nothing out of it; but if we have food and clothing, we should be content with these. But those who want to be rich fall into temptation and end up trapped by a multitude of senseless and harmful desires that plunge people into ruin and destruction. For the love of money is the root of all kinds of evil, and in their eagerness to be rich some have wandered away from the faith and pierced themselves with many pains.'

Thus it is vital for us who follow Christ to learn not only how to pray, but also from the character of the prayer that Christ has taught us, the sort of people we are aiming to become through our prayer.

Monday after Trinity 15

A Reading from *The Mirror of Charity*
by Aelred of Rievaulx

As I understand it, love is involved in three human acts, namely in the choice of an object to love, in our movement towards that object, and in the enjoyment of it. We make our choices using our reason. We move towards what we want by means of desire and action while our enjoyment comes as the culmination of this process.

We who are endowed with reason have a natural capacity for happiness which is part of our human nature. We were made with it by God, and we are always hungry for it, but we can never find sufficient enjoyment in ourselves. Unfortunately the things which, later on in life, we discover to be insufficient for our enjoyment, we seize upon under the impression that in securing these is to be found our ultimate happiness. Anything will do so long as it is something other than ourselves! This is how we end up placing our happiness in the acquisition of things, or the enjoyment of things, either because we are mistaken, or deceived by the senses, or deficient in faith or intelligence. This is what we choose as the object of our happiness, and set out to attain, because we think it can make us happy. Love, the impulse in our nature of which we have already spoken, makes this choice. Or alternatively, we could say that reason makes this choice by means of that impulse, for love always has reason for its companion. This does not mean that we necessarily love reasonably. It simply means that we have the capacity to distinguish clearly between what we choose and what we reject. Reason can discern the difference between creature and Creator, temporal and eternal, sweet and bitter, pleasant and unpleasant, and love chooses from among these alternatives.

Choice is an act of the soul, but it can also be called an act of love. But although love itself, which is making the choice, is always good, our choices on the contrary can be either good or bad. And in this way one can speak of love also as being either good or bad. We may choose something that is not good for us, either because we have already formed an attraction to it by previous experience, or because we are inexperienced and make a false judgement. The result is unhappiness for us in our love for that particular object. Enjoyment means the use of something that gives pleasure and joy in the using. At the moment when we make our choice, love moves towards the object we have chosen, filling the soul with desire and carrying it towards that object. This movement of desire is also known as love, and if the object of our choice is something that God wishes us to have, then our love is good. If not, it is bad. Finally, when we have achieved the desired object, we can take pleasure in it and enjoy it.

Tuesday after Trinity 15

A Reading from *The Gift of Self*
by Heather Ward

Prayer is primarily something God does in me, it is allowing God to flow through me. My part is to make myself available for this, to become consciously with, and in, the God who is always with, and in, me. Consequently, however much I may feel myself to be the initiator I am, in fact, always responding to a pressure, a hint, an invitation from him. Our ego may desire us to be on equal terms with the Lord, determining the time and place for the meeting, but it is not so. The dethronement of ego begins with this recognition, and continues when we grasp its corollary, that prayer is to make us available to God and not the other way round. Prayer easily becomes need-centred, consolation-centred, experience-centred: we pray for what God does for us, for the strength he gives us, for the satisfaction of feeling with him. All too often we feel that our prayer is totally for God because we have brought all our troubles to him, acknowledging our need, but then praying from within our distress becomes immersion in it. We do not leave our problems with him but continue to chase them round in his presence. Gradually attention has been diverted from God in himself towards our ego, with God as its helper.

Awareness of this tendency leads me to centre all prayer, therefore, in adoration, understood not as one aspect of prayer but as its underpinning and context. Adoration seems to be a word little used and little understood. My understanding of praise is that it tends towards God for what he is, and generally, what he is to, and for, us. Adoration is sheer wonder that God is, and desires simply to let him be. It is an attitude of awe, mixed with longing and with love, in the apprehension of God as loving holiness. It is not the dread-ful awe of the idol worshipper before the fretful and naked power of his deity, but the knowledge of the presence of a Goodness which draws us to itself. The response to this is self-forgetfulness, reduction to insignificance, accompanied by the total inadequacy of our powers of expression, which leads us to silence and prostration, in spirit if not in body. This prostration in spirit is no grovelling but a joyful revelling in the Allness of God. He *is*; nothing else matters because all that is of worth is in him. Adoration, therefore, confirms us in the truth of humility and poverty, opening us to participation in the God who is all, freeing us to delight wholly in him.

Wednesday after Trinity 15

A Reading from a homily of Gregory the Great

When our hearts are reluctant we often have to compel ourselves to pray for our enemies, to pour out prayer for those who are against us. Would that our hearts were filled with love! How frequently we offer a prayer for our enemies, but do it because we are commanded to do so, not out of love for them. We ask the gift of life for them but are afraid that our prayer may be heard. The Judge of our souls considers our hearts rather than our words. Those who do not pray for their enemies out of love are not asking anything for their benefit.

But suppose they have committed a serious offence against us? Suppose they have inflicted losses on those who support us, and have hurt them? Suppose they have persecuted our friends? We might legitimately keep these things in mind if we had no offences of our own to be forgiven.

Jesus, who is our advocate, has composed a prayer for this situation and in this case the One who pleads our case is also our judge. There is a condition he has inserted in the prayer he composed which reads: 'Forgive us our debts, as we also forgive our debtors.' Since our advocate is the One who comes to be our judge, he is listening to the prayer he himself composed for our use. Perhaps we say the words: 'Forgive us our debts, as we also forgive our debtors,' without carrying them out, and thus our words bind us more tightly; or perhaps we omit the condition in our prayer, and then our advocate does not recognise the prayer which he composed for us, and says to himself: 'I know what I taught them. This is not the prayer I gave them.'

What are we to do then, my friends? We are to bestow our love upon our brothers and sisters. We must not allow any malice at all to remain in our hearts. May almighty God have regard for our love of our neighbour, so that he may pardon our iniquities! My dear people, remember what he has taught us: 'Forgive, and you will be forgiven.' People are in debt to us, and we to them. So let us forgive them their debts, so that what we owe may be forgiven us.

Thursday after Trinity 15

A Reading from a treatise *On Prayer* by Origen

It seems appropriate to complete our discussion of prayer by thinking about bodily posture. Certainly there are countless attitudes of the body, but it seems to me that that in which we stretch out our hands and lift our eyes to heaven is to be preferred because it expresses with our body the disposition of the soul during prayer. This would seem to enjoy the warrant of Scripture. Paul tells us that prayer should be offered 'without anger and discord'; and in describing bodily posture, he talks about 'lifting up holy hands'. It would appear that he has taken these words from the psalms in which we also find the words: 'Let my prayer rise as incense before you, and let the lifting up of my hands be as an evening sacrifice.'

This at least should be the way we pray normally when there are no difficulties. But circumstances may lead us to pray sitting down, for example when we have a pain in the legs; or even in bed because of sickness or fever. Similarly, if we are on board ship or if our business does not allow us to withdraw from company to perform our duty in regard to prayer, it is perfectly possible to pray without taking up any particular outward attitude.

With regard to kneeling for prayer, this is essential when we are accusing ourselves of our sins before God and entreating him to heal and absolve us. It symbolises the prostration and humility of which Paul speaks when he writes: 'For this reason I bow my knees before the Father, from whom every family in heaven and on earth is named.' That is spiritual kneeling, so called, because every creature adores God in the name of Jesus and prostrates itself humbly before him. The Apostle seems to be alluding to this when he says: 'At the name of Jesus every knee should bow, in heaven and on earth and under the earth.'

As far as place is concerned, every place is suitable for prayer to God. However, in order to pray undisturbed it is preferable to choose a particular place in one's house (if practicable) and to set it aside as a kind of hallowed spot, and to pray there. The choice of place is important so that not only ourselves, but the place itself, may be worthy of the visitation of God.

Friday after Trinity 15

A Reading from a sermon of Lancelot Andrewes
preached on Good Friday 1604

Comfort is it by which, in the midst of all our sorrows, we are strengthened and made the better able to bear them all out. And who is there, even the poorest creature among us, but in some degree findeth some comfort, or some regard, at somebody's hands? For if that be not left, the state of that party is said to be like the tree, whose leaves and whose fruit are all beaten off quite, and itself left bare and naked both of the one and of the other.

And such was our Saviour's case in these his sorrows this day; and that so, as what is left the meanest of the sons of men, was not left him: not a leaf. Not a leaf! Leaves I may well call all human comforts and regards, whereof he was then left clean desolate. His own, they among whom he had gone about all his life-long, healing them, teaching them, feeding them, doing them all the good he could, it is they that cry, 'Not him, no, but Barabbas rather! Away with him, his blood be upon us and our children!' It is they that in the midst of his sorrows shake their head at him and cry, 'Ah thou wretch'; they that in his most disconsolate estate and cry 'Eli, Eli', in most barbarous manner deride him, and say, 'Stay, and you shall see Elias come presently and take him down.' And this was their regard.

But these were but withered leaves. They that on earth were nearest to him of all, the greenest leaves and likest to hang on and to give him some shade, even of them some bought and sold him, others denied and forswore him, but all fell away and forsook him. Not a leaf left.

But leaves are but leaves, and so are all earthly stays. The fruit then, the true fruit of the vine indeed, the true comfort in all heaviness, is 'from above', is divine consolation. But even that was in this his sorrow this day, bereft him too. And that was his most sorrowful complaint of all others: not that his friends upon earth, but that his Father from heaven had forsaken him, that neither heaven nor earth yielded him any regard; but that between the passioned powers of his soul, and whatsoever might any ways refresh him, there was a traverse drawn, and he left in the estate of a weather-beaten tree, all desolate and forlorn. Evident, too evident, by that his most dreadful cry, which at once moved all the powers in heaven and earth, 'My God, my God, why hast thou forsaken me?'

Weigh well that cry, consider it well, and tell me 'if ever there were cry like to that of his'. Never the like cry, and therefore never the like sorrow.

Saturday after Trinity 15

A Reading from a homily of Gregory of Nyssa

Our greatest protection in this life is self-knowledge so that we do not become enslaved to delusion, and end up trying to defend a person who does not exist. This is what happens to those who do not scrutinise themselves. They look at themselves and what they see is strength, beauty, reputation, political power, an abundance of material possessions, status, self-importance, bodily stature, a graceful appearance and so forth; and they think that this is the sum of whom they are. Such persons make very poor guardians of themselves because in their absorption with externals they overlook their inner life and leave it unguarded. How can a person protect what he does not know? The most secure protection for our treasure is to know ourselves: each of us must know ourselves as we are, and learn to distinguish ourselves from what we are not. Otherwise we may end up unconsciously protecting somebody who we are not, and leave our true selves unguarded.

Remember the extent to which the Creator has honoured you above all the rest of creation. The sky has not been created an image of God, nor has the moon, the sun, the beauty of the stars, nor anything else in all creation. You alone have been made the image of the Reality that transcends all understanding, the likeness of beauty, the imprint of true divinity, the recipient of blessedness, the seal of the true light. And when you turn to God you become what he is.

There is nothing so great among other beings that it can be compared with such a vocation. God is able to measure the whole heaven with his span. The earth and the sea are enclosed in the hollow of his hand. And although he is so great and holds all creation in the palm of his hand, you are able to hold him, for he dwells in you and moves within you without constraint, for he has said, 'I will live and move among them.'

Trinity 16

A Reading from *Eyes to See, Ears to Hear*
by David Lonsdale

It is not always recognised that discernment lies at the heart of Christian spirituality. Trying to be a Christian means learning how to respond with love to God, to people and to circumstances. It means searching for ways of living out the two great gospel commandments of loving God and our neighbour, while recognising the imperfection of our attempts. It also means searching honestly for the most authentic truth; not just the knowledge that can be learned but makes little difference to how we live, but also the deeper gospel truth that makes little sense in fact until it becomes the truth which governs our lives.

Sometimes people talk about the will of God or the plan of God as if it were a large, immensely complex, ever-changing, living blueprint of what God 'wants' to happen in the world. According to this model, finding the will of God means something like getting in touch with that small corner of the immense celestial blueprint that concerns us, and getting to know 'what God wants us to do', so that we can comply and thus 'do the will of God'. Of course, that short description is a caricature to some extent, but it contains enough truth about the model that many people seem to use in thinking and talking about the will of God.

And unfortunately it is a powerful cause of anxiety to many good Christians who spend much time and effort trying to 'find out' God's will according to this model, and who become very distressed and anxious when, not surprisingly, they do not succeed. There are many reasons why this 'management blueprint' model is unsatisfactory, but the principal one is the fact that it constricts our freedom so much. The scope of our freedom is reduced to choosing to fit in, whether we like it or not, with what God has 'planned for us' – once we think we know what that is. And that is very little freedom indeed.

A more satisfactory understanding of the will of God in connection with discernment of spirits gives greater value to our precious gift of freedom. God's will for us is that we should learn to respond in freedom to God's love for us, and to give shape to our individual and common lives in freedom by the choices that we make. In Scripture, tradition, the Church, our own consciences and powers of judgement and in many other gifts, God has given us aids to the responsible exercise of our freedom. God's will is that we should exercise our freedom responsibly and well by choosing what honestly seems the best course of action in a given set of circumstances, using all the relevant aids that we have been given for that purpose. There is a sense in which we create, in terms of concrete action in given circumstances, the will of God in this exercise of freedom. There is no blueprint in God's mind with which we have to comply. Discernment of spirits, within a living relationship with God, is one of the gifts that we have been given to help us to exercise our freedom in the choices that we make and so come to 'find the will of God' for us.

Monday after Trinity 16

A Reading from a treatise *On the Trinity*
by Augustine

No one should say: 'I do not know what I love.' If people love their brothers and sisters, then they will love the love that is God. For we know the love with which we love better than the brother or sister who is the object of our love. Thus we can already know God better than we know our brother or sister. We can know God more clearly because he is more clearly present, more deeply within us and therefore more sure. Embrace the love of God, and by love embrace God. Love itself brings together into a common bond of holiness all good angels and all servants of God, and joins us to them and to each other and all of us to God.

In proportion as our inflated egos are healed of their pride, we become more full of love. And with what is a person full who is full of love, if not with God? But you will say: 'I can see love, and as far as I am able, I can conceive of it in my mind; I believe the Scripture when it says that "God is love; and those who abide in love abide in God, and God abides in them"; but when I see that, I still do not see the Trinity.' My point is precisely that: you do see the Trinity if you see love.

We begin with that which is nearest to us, namely, our brother or sister. Observe how highly the apostle John commends mutual love: 'Whoever loves a brother or sister lives in the light, and in such a person there is no cause for stumbling.' It is manifestly clear that John makes the perfection of righteousness consist in the love of our brothers and sisters; for a person is certainly perfect in whom there is no occasion for stumbling. And yet the apostle seems to have passed over the love of God in silence, something he would never have done if he had not intended God to be understood in the mutuality of love itself. Indeed, in the same epistle he says: 'Beloved, let us love one another because love is from God; everyone who loves is born of God and knows God.' This passage declares succinctly and plainly that such mutuality of love is not only from God, but also is God.

When, therefore, we love our brothers and sisters out of love, we are loving our brothers and sisters out of God. Such love should claim our priority. Moreover, the two commandments cannot exist without each other. Since God is love, a person who loves love, is certainly loving God; and we must needs love love if we are to love our brothers and sisters truly. Hence a little later, John says: 'Those who do not love the brother or sister whom they have seen, cannot love God whom they have not seen.' In other words, the reason why a person cannot see God is because he does not love his brothers and sisters.

So let us stop worrying about how much love we ought to spend on our neighbour and how much on God. The answer is incomparably more on God than on ourselves, and on our sisters and brothers as much as on ourselves. But in reality, the more we love God, the more we love ourselves. We are loving God and our neighbour out of the one and same love.

Tuesday after Trinity 16

A Reading from *The Living Flame of Love*
by John of the Cross

Spiritual directors should reflect that they themselves are not the chief agent, guide, and mover of souls, but that the principal guide is always the Holy Spirit who is never neglectful of souls. Spiritual directors are merely instruments for directing souls to perfection through faith and the law of God, according to the spirit God is giving each of them.

Thus the director's whole concern should not be to accommodate souls to their own method and ideals, but rather to point out to a person the markers in the road along which God seems to be leading them, and if that person does not yet know the road, leave them in peace and do not bother them. A director should always work in harmony with the way God is leading a person, striving to lead them into a yet more profound solitude, tranquillity, and freedom of spirit. A director should give a person space so that when God leads them into this interior solitude they are free from the constraints of spiritual and bodily senses which might lead them to clutch at some object, be it in their external world or within. Do not allow them to become anxious or despondent as if nothing is happening. Even when the soul is not consciously doing anything, God is still working.

Directors should strive to disencumber the soul and set it in a state of repose so that it may not be dependent on any particular knowledge, be it earthly or heavenly, or have need for some satisfaction or pleasure, or indeed anything else. In this way the soul will be empty through the constant negation of every creature, and placed in spiritual poverty. This is what the soul must do of itself, as the Son of God counsels: 'Those who do not renounce all that they possess cannot be my disciples.' This admonition should be understood to apply to the renunciation not only of material and temporal things, but also to the surrender of spiritual things. It is this spiritual poverty which the Son of God describes as blessed.

For when the soul frees itself of all things and attains to emptiness and freedom concerning them, which is what it can do of itself, it is impossible that God will fail to do his part by communicating himself to us, at least silently and secretly. It is more impossible for the sun not to shine on clear and uncluttered ground than for God to fail his people. As the sun rises in the morning and shines upon your house so that its light may enter once you open the shutters, so the God who watches over Israel and who neither slumbers nor sleeps, will enter the soul that is empty and fill it with divine blessings.

Wednesday after Trinity 16

A Reading from *New Seeds of Contemplation*
by Thomas Merton

Detachment from things does not mean setting up a contradiction between 'things' and 'God' as if God were another 'thing' and as if his creatures were his rivals. We do not detach ourselves from things in order to attach ourselves to God, but rather we become detached *from ourselves* in order to see and use all things in and for God. This is an entirely new perspective which many sincerely moral and ascetic minds fail utterly to see. There is no evil in anything created by God, nor can anything of his become an obstacle to our union with him. The obstacle is in our 'self', that is to say in the tenacious need to maintain our separate, external, egotistic will. It is when we refer all things to this outward and false 'self' that we alienate ourselves from reality and from God. It is then the false self that is our god, and we love everything for the sake of this self. We use all things, so to speak, for the worship of this idol which is our imaginary self. In so doing we pervert and corrupt things, or rather we turn our relationship to them into a corrupt and sinful relationship. We do not thereby make them evil, but we use them to increase our attachment to our illusory self.

Those who try to escape from this situation by treating the good things of God as if they were evils are only confirming themselves in a terrible illusion. They are like Adam blaming Eve and Eve blaming the serpent in Eden.

The only true joy on earth is to escape from the prison of our own false self, and enter by love into union with the Life who dwells and sings within the essence of every creature and in the core of our own souls. In his love we possess all things and enjoy fruition of them, finding God in them all. And thus as we go about the world, everything we meet and everything we see and hear and touch, far from defiling, purifies us and plants in us something more of contemplation and of heaven.

Thursday after Trinity 16

A Reading from a homily of Basil the Great
preached in a 'time of famine and drought'

Are you poor? There is someone much poorer than you are. You have enough bread for ten days; another has enough for one. As someone good and kind-hearted, make your surplus equal by distributing it to the needy. Do not shrink from giving of the little you have; do not value your own calamity above the common trial. Even if the food supply amounts to one loaf of bread, and the beggar stands at the door, bring the one loaf out of the storeroom and, presenting it to the hands which are lifted up to heaven, offer this merciful and considerate prayer:

'One loaf which you see, O Lord, and the problem is evident; but as for me, I prefer your commandment to myself and I give of the little I have to the starving brother; for you also give to your servant in trouble. I know your great goodness and I also confidently believe in your power, for you do not defer your grace for another time, but disperse your gifts when you wish.'

And if you speak and act in this way, the bread that you should give out of your scarcity would become seed for planting, would bear rich fruit, a pledge of sustenance, a patron of mercy. Say to yourself what the widow of Sidon said in a similar situation – remember well the story – 'As the Lord lives, I have only this in my house to feed my children and myself.' And if you should give out of your state of deprivation you too would have the vessel of oil abounding with grace, the unempty pot of flour. For God's lavish grace on the faithful is exactly like that of the always emptying, never-exhausting, double-giving vessels of oil.

O poor one, lend to the rich God. Believe in the One who is at all times taking up the cause of the afflicted in his own person and supplying grace from his own stores. Trustworthy guarantor, he has vast treasuries all over the earth and sea. In fact, even if you were to demand back the loan in the middle of the ocean, you would be guaranteed to receive the capital with interest. For in his generosity, he loves honour.

Friday after Trinity 16

A Reading from an *Introduction to the Devout Life*
by Francis de Sales

'Judge not, and you will not be judged,' says the Saviour of our souls; 'Condemn not, and you will not be condemned.' Or as the apostle Paul wrote: 'Judge not, but wait for the Lord. He will bring to light things now hidden in darkness, and disclose the secret purposes of the heart.' Rash judgements are most displeasing to God. People's judgements are rash because we are not meant to be one another's judges, and in so acting, we usurp the prerogative of God. Their judgements are rash because so often they proceed from malice, from the impenetrable depths of the human heart.

Indeed, they are not only rash, but impertinent, because each of us should find sufficient employment in sorting ourselves out without having time to judge our neighbours. Certainly, if we wish to avoid future judgement then we should avoid judging our neighbours and concentrate on ourselves. As St Paul says: 'If we judged ourselves truly, we should not be judged.'

We must ask why it is that we make rash judgements. Some of us are naturally bitter and harsh, and then everything and everyone seems the same. Such folk would do well to seek some sound spiritual advice because such bitterness of heart, being so natural to them, is difficult to overcome.

Some judge rashly out of pride: they pull others down because they need to push themselves up. Others view the faults of their neighbours with complacency because it enhances their opinion of themselves as virtuous souls. Many take the liberty of judging others rashly, delighting in the sound of their own voice, opinions and wit. If unhappily, they err in their judgement, it then becomes very difficult to correct people's perspective because of the force and confidence with which opinions have been expressed. Others judge by feeling and prejudice, thinking well of those they like, and ill of those they dislike. Jealousy, fear, ambition and other weaknesses all contribute towards the breeding of suspicion and rash judgements.

So what is the remedy?

Charity is the sovereign remedy for all ills, and of this ill in particular. All things appear yellow to someone afflicted with jaundice: rash judgement is a spiritual jaundice which makes everything appear evil. The cure is to apply love – to your eyes, to your understanding, and to your affections in which your soul is rooted. If your heart is gentle, your judgements will be gentle; if it is loving, so will your judgements be.

Rash judgement leads to contempt, pride and complacency, and many other evils, among which slander stands out. So I beseech you, never speak ill of anyone, either directly or indirectly. All these things are offensive to God.

Saturday after Trinity 16

A Reading from the discourses of Dorotheus of Gaza

God does not allow us to be burdened with anything beyond our power of endurance, and therefore, when difficulties come upon us we do not sin unless we are unwilling to endure a little tribulation or to suffer anything unforeseen. As the Apostle says: 'God is faithful and will not allow us to be tempted beyond what we are able to endure.'

But we are only human. We have no patience and no desire to brace ourselves to accept anything with humility. Therefore we are crushed by our difficulties. The more we run away from temptations, the more they weigh us down and the less are we able to drive them away. Suppose a person for some reason dives into the sea: if he knows the art of swimming, what does he do when a great wave comes along? He ducks under until it goes past and then he goes on swimming unharmed. But if he is determined to set himself against it, the wave will push him away and hurl him back a great distance. And then, when he begins to swim forward and another wave comes upon him, and if again he tries to swim against it, again it will force him back, and he will only succeed in tiring himself out and make no headway. But if he ducks his head and lowers himself under the wave, as I said, no harm will come to him and he will continue to swim as long as he likes. Those who go on working in this way when they are in trouble, putting up with their temptations with patience and humility, will come through unharmed. But if they get distressed and downcast, seeking the reasons for everything, tormenting themselves and being annoyed with themselves instead of helping themselves, they will do themselves harm.

When painful experiences crowd in upon us, we ought not to be disturbed; allowing ourselves to be disturbed by such experiences is sheer ignorance and pride because we are not recognising our own condition and running away from labour. We will make no progress because we have not squarely taken our own measure; we do not persevere in the work we have begun, and want to acquire virtue without effort. For example, why should an emotional person find it strange to be disturbed by his emotions? Why should he be overwhelmed if he sometimes gives way to them? If you have them inside yourself why are you disturbed when they break out? You have their seeds in you and yet you ask, why do they spring up and trouble me?

In short, it is better to have patience with ourselves and to go on struggling and to beg for God's help.

Trinity 17

A Reading from *The Scale of Perfection* by Walter Hilton

Just as a true pilgrim going to Jerusalem leaves behind him house and land, wife and children, and makes himself poor and bare of all that he has in order to travel light and without hindrance, so if you want to be a spiritual pilgrim you are to make yourself naked of all that you have – both good works and bad – and throw them all behind you; and thus become so poor in your own feeling that there can be no deed of your own that you want to lean upon for rest, but you are always desiring more grace of love, and always seeking the spiritual presence of Jesus. If you do so, you shall then see in your heart, wholly and fully, your desire to be at Jerusalem, and in no other place but there; and that is, you shall see in your heart, wholly and fully, your will to have nothing but the love of Jesus and the spiritual sight of him, as far as he wishes to show himself. It is for that alone you are made and redeemed, and that is your beginning and your end, your joy and your glory.

Therefore, whatsoever you have, however rich you may be in other works of body and spirit, unless you have that, and know and feel that you have it, consider that you have nothing at all. Print this statement well on the intention of your heart, and hold firmly to it, and it will save you from all the perils of your journey, so that you will never perish. It shall save you from thieves and robbers (which is what I call unclean spirits), so that though they strip you and beat you with diverse temptations, your life shall always be saved; and in brief if you guard it as I shall tell you, you shall within a short time escape all perils and come to the city of Jerusalem.

Now that you are on the road and know the name of the place you are bound for, begin to go forward on your journey.

Monday after Trinity 17

A Reading from the Letter of Ignatius of Antioch to the Church in Philadelphia

Your bishop's office, which serves the whole community, was never secured by his own efforts, as I know very well, nor by any other human agency, still less in any spirit of self-glorification; but it was conferred upon him by the love of God the Father and the Lord Jesus Christ. I am deeply impressed by his self-effacing nature; his reserve is more effectual than the empty chatter of others. He is as utterly in tune with the commandments as a harp with its strings. I call down blessings on a mind whose sentiments are so turned to God, for I can vouch for his perfection, his stability and calm, in which he imitates the gentleness of the living God.

As children of the light of truth, therefore, see that you hold aloof from all disunion and misguided teaching; and where your bishop is, there follow him as his flock. There are plausible wolves in plenty seeking to entrap the runners in God's race with their various allurements; but so long as there is solidarity among you, they will find no room.

Everyone who belongs to God and Jesus Christ stands by his bishop. As for the rest, if they repent and come back into the unity of the Church, they too shall belong to God, and so bring their lives into conformity with Jesus Christ. But make no mistake, brothers and sisters; the adherents of a schismatic teacher can never inherit the kingdom of God. Those who indulge in teachings alien to the Christian way must know that they forfeit all part in the Lord's passion.

Make certain, therefore, that you all observe one common eucharist; for there is but one body of our Lord Jesus Christ, and but one cup of union with his blood, and one single altar of sacrifice – even as also there is but one bishop, with his presbyters and deacons, who are his fellow servants. This will ensure that all your doings are in full accord with the will of God.

I overflow in love for you all, and I am only too happy to provide for your security like this – though it is not so much I as

Jesus Christ. It is for his sake that I am in chains; though this privilege only increases my fears, since I am still far from perfection. Nevertheless, your prayers will set the seal on my progress to God, and help me to the inheritance promised for me by the merciful God. I cling for refuge to the gospel message as though to the incarnate Christ, and I appeal to the true ministry of the Church through the apostles.

Tuesday after Trinity 17

A Reading from a homily of Gregory the Great

Our Lord in the gospel says: 'By your patience you will gain possession of your lives.' Patience is the root and guardian of all the virtues. We gain possession of our lives by patience, since when we learn to govern ourselves, we begin to gain possession of the very thing we are.

True patience consists in bearing calmly the evils that others do to us, and in not being consumed by resentment against those who inflict them. On the other hand, those who only appear to bear the evils done them by their neighbours, who suffer them in silence but inwardly are looking for an opportunity for revenge, are not practising patience, but only a charade.

Paul writes that 'love is patient and kind.' It is patient in bearing the evils done to us by others, and it is kind in even loving those it bears with. Our Lord himself commands us: 'Love your enemies, do good to those who hate you; pray for those who persecute you and speak all kind of calumny against you.' Virtue in the sight of our contemporaries is to bear with those who oppose us, but virtue in the sight of God is to love them. This is the only sacrifice acceptable to God.

Often we appear to be patient only because we are unable to repay the evils we suffer from others. As I have said, those who do not pay back evil only because they cannot do so are not truly patient. As Christians, we should not be concerned with the appearance of patience, but with a patience that is rooted in the heart.

Wednesday after Trinity 17

A Reading from *The Country Parson* by George Herbert

The Country Parson being to administer the sacraments, is at a stand with himself, how or what behaviour to assume for so holy things. Especially at Communion times he is in a great confusion, as being not only to receive God, but to break and administer him. Neither finds he any issue in this, but to throw himself down at the throne of grace, saying 'Lord, thou knowest what thou didst when thou appointedst it to be done thus; therefore do thou fulfill what thou didst appoint; for thou art not only the feast, but the way to it.'

At Baptism, being himself in white, he requires the presence of all, and baptizeth not willingly, but on Sundays, or great days. He admits no vain or idle names, but such as are usual and accustomed. He says that prayer with great devotion, where God is thanked for calling us to the knowledge of his grace, baptism being a blessing, that the world hath not the like. He willingly and cheerfully crosseth the child, and thinketh the ceremony not only innocent, but reverend. He instructeth godfathers and godmothers, that it is no complemental or light thing to sustain that place, but a great honour, and no less burden, as being done both in the presence of God and his saints, and by way of undertaking for a Christian soul. He adviseth all to call to mind their baptism often; for if wise men have thought it the best way of preserving a state to reduce it to its principles by which it grew great; certainly, it is the safest course for Christians also to meditate on their baptism often (being the first step into their great and glorious calling) and upon what terms and with what vows they were baptized.

At the times of the Holy Communion, he first takes order with the churchwardens, that the elements be of the best, not cheap, or coarse, much less ill-tasted, or unwholesome. Secondly, he considers and looks into the ignorance, or carelessness of his flock, and accordingly applies himself with catechizings and lively exhortations, not on the Sunday of the Communion only (for then it is too late) but the Sunday or Sundays before the Communion, or on the eves of all those days. If there be any, who having not received yet, are to enter into this great work, he takes the pains with them, that he may lay the foundation of future blessings.

The time of everyone's first receiving is not so much by years, as much by understanding; particularly, the rule may be this: When anyone can distinguish the sacramental from common bread, knowing the institution and the difference, he ought to receive of what age soever. Children and youths are usually deferred too long, under pretence of devotion to the Sacrament, but it is for want of instruction; their understandings being ripe enough for ill things, and why not then for better? But parents and masters should make haste in this, as to a great purchase for their children and servants; which while they defer, both sides suffer, the one in wanting many excitings of grace; the other in being worse served and obeyed.

Thirdly, for the manner of receiving, as the parson useth all reverence himself, so he administers to none but to the reverent. The Feast indeed requires sitting because it is a feast; but man's unpreparedness asks kneeling. He that comes to the Sacrament hath the confidence of a guest, and he that kneels, confesseth himself an unworthy one, and therefore differs from other feasters.

Thursday after Trinity 17

A Reading from the *Conferences* of John Cassian

There will be accomplished in us what our Saviour prayed for when, speaking to the Father about his disciples, he said: 'I pray that they may be one, as you Father are in me and I in you, and that they may be one in us.' On that day the perfect love with which 'God first loved us' will come into our hearts in fulfilment of this prayer of our Lord. And this will be the sign of its accomplishment: God will be our love and our longing, God will be all we want and all we strive for, all we think about, all we talk about, our very breath. That union of Father and Son, of Son and Father, will fill our senses and our minds. As God loves us with a love that is true and pure, a love which is unbreakable, so we too will be united to him in an unshakeable love to the point where we shall be breathing and thinking and speaking only 'God'.

And so we shall arrive at the goal for which we have yearned and which the Lord desires for us in this prayer of his: 'That they may be one even as we are one, I in them and you in me, that they may be perfectly one.' 'Father, I desire that they also whom you have given me may be with me where I am.'

Such should be our aim: to achieve already in this life, this breathing in unity with God which is nothing less than a foretaste of the life and glory of heaven. This is the goal of perfection, to remove the soul from all bodily preoccupation so that it rises each day to the things of the spirit until all its living and willing becomes one unending prayer.

Friday after Trinity 17

A Reading from *The Cost of Discipleship*
by Dietrich Bonhoeffer

To endure the cross is not a tragedy; it is the suffering which is the fruit of an exclusive allegiance to Jesus Christ. When it comes, it is not an accident, but a necessity. It is not the sort of suffering which is inseparable from this mortal life, but the suffering which is an essential part of the specifically Christian life. It is not suffering *per se* but suffering-and-rejection, and not rejection for any cause or conviction of our own, but rejection for the sake of Christ. If our Christianity has ceased to be serious about discipleship, if we have watered down the gospel into emotional uplift which makes no costly demands and which fails to distinguish between natural and Christian existence, then we cannot help regarding the cross as an ordinary everyday calamity, as one of the trials and tribulations of life. We have then forgotten that the cross means rejection and shame as well as suffering.

The Psalmist was lamenting that he was despised and rejected by the people, and that is an essential quality of the suffering of the cross. But this notion has ceased to be intelligible to a Christianity which can no longer see any difference between an ordinary human life and a life committed to Christ. The cross means sharing the suffering of Christ to the last and to the fullest. Only a person thus totally committed in discipleship can experience the meaning of the cross. The cross is there, right from the beginning, we have only got to pick it up; there is no need for us to go out and look for a cross for ourselves, no need for us deliberately to run after suffering. Jesus says that every Christian has his own cross waiting for him, a cross destined and appointed by God. Each of us must endure our allotted share of suffering and rejection.

The cross is laid on every Christian. The first Christ-suffering which each of us must experience is the call to abandon the attachment of this world. It is that dying of our old selves which is the result of our encounter with Christ. As we embark upon discipleship we surrender ourselves to Christ in union with his death – we give over our lives to death. Thus it begins; the cross is not the terrible end to an otherwise God-fearing and happy life, but it meets us at the beginning of our communion with Christ. When Christ calls us, he bids us come and die.

Saturday after Trinity 17

A Reading from a treatise *Against the Pagans*
by Athanasius of Alexandria

By his own wisdom and Word, who is our Lord and Saviour Christ, the all-holy Father (whose excellence far exceeds that of any creature) like a skilful pilot guides to safety all creation, regulating and keeping it in being, as he judges right. It is proper that creation should exist as he has made it and as we see it happening, because this is his will, which no one would deny. For if the movement of the universe were irrational, and the world rolled on in random fashion, one would be justified in disbelieving what we say. But if the world is founded on reason, wisdom and science, and is filled with orderly beauty, then it must owe its origin and order to none other than the Word of God.

He is God, the living and creative God of the universe, the Word of the good God, who is God in his own right. The Word is different from all created things: he is the unique Word belonging only to the good Father. This is the Word that created this whole world and enlightens it by his loving wisdom. He who is the good Word of the good Father produced the order in all creation, joining opposites together, and forming from them one harmonious sound. He is God, one and only-begotten, who proceeds in goodness from the Father as from the fountain of goodness, and gives order, direction and unity to creation.

By his eternal Word the Father created all things and implanted a nature in his creatures. He did not want to see them tossed about at the mercy of their own natures, and so be reduced to nothingness. But in his goodness he governs and sustains the whole of nature by his Word (who is himself also God), so that under the guidance, providence and ordering of that Word, the whole of nature might remain stable and coherent in his light. Nature was to share in the Father's Word, whose reality is true, and be helped by him to exist, for without him it would cease to be. For unless the Word, who is the very 'image of the invisible God, the firstborn of all creation', kept it in existence it could not exist. For whatever exists, whether visible or invisible, remains in existence through him and in him, and he is also the head of the Church, as we are taught by the ministers of truth in their sacred writings.

The almighty and most holy Word of the Father pervades the whole of reality, everywhere unfolding his power and shining on all things visible and invisible. He sustains it all and binds it together in himself. He leaves nothing devoid of his power but gives life and keeps it in being throughout all of creation and in each individual creature.

Trinity 18

A Reading from the *Catechetical Lectures*
of Cyril of Jerusalem

It is not alone among us, who are stamped with the name of Christ, that the dignity of faith is great. All the business of the world, even of those who are outside the Church, is accomplished by faith.

By faith, marriage joins together persons who are strangers to one another; the spouses, though they were formerly strangers, bestow their bodies and material possessions on one another because of their faith in their marriage contract. By faith, agriculture is sustained; for a farmer endures the labour involved only because he believes that he will reap a harvest. By faith, seafarers entrust themselves to a tiny wooden vessel and exchange dry land for the erratic movement of the waves; they surrender themselves to uncertain hopes and take with them a faith that is surer than any anchor.

In other words, most human affairs depend on faith; and this holds good not only among us, but also, as I have already mentioned, among those who are outside the fold. Although they do not accept the Scriptures but advance certain doctrines of their own, they nonetheless receive such doctrines in faith.

Faith is the eye that enlightens every conscience and gives understanding; for the Prophet says: 'Unless your faith is firm, you shall not understand.' Faith closes the mouths of lions, according to Daniel; for Scripture says of him: 'Daniel was removed from the den, unhurt because he trusted in his God.'

Is anything more terrible than the devil? Yet, even against the devil, all we have is the armour of faith, a spiritual shield against an invisible enemy. For Satan lets fly manifold arrows, and shoots in the dark at those who are not vigilant. However, although the enemy remains invisible, we have our faith as a strong protection, according to the saying of the Apostle: 'In all circumstances hold faith up before you as your shield; it will help you extinguish the fiery darts of the evil one.'

Monday after Trinity 18

A Reading from a commentary on the psalms
by Augustine

My brothers and sisters, I beg you above all else to show charity not only towards one another, but also to those who are outside our communion whether they be pagans who do not yet know Christ, or Christians separated from us, those who profess their faith in the head Jesus Christ while separated from the body. Let us grieve for them, my friends, as though they were our own brothers and sisters. For that is what they are, whether they like it or not. They will only cease to be our brothers and sisters when they cease to say 'Our Father'.

They claim no longer to be in fellowship with us and want to rebaptise us, saying that we do not possess what only they can truly confer. They ridicule our baptism and reject us as their brothers and sisters. But why did the prophet in Scripture tell us: 'Say to them: You are our brothers,' if not because we recognise in them what we ourselves refuse to repeat. They, by not recognising our baptism, deny that we are Christians; but we, by not repeating theirs, and acknowledging it as valid as our own, are saying to them: 'You are our sisters and brothers.'

They may say to us: 'Why do you seek us out? Why do you want us?' And we will answer: 'Because you are our brothers and sisters.' They may say: 'Go away! We have nothing in common with you.' But we shall reply that we absolutely do have something in common: we profess one Christ; thus we ought to be united in one body under one head.

I therefore beg you, my brothers and sisters, through the very depth of that love by whose milk we are all nourished and by whose bread we are fortified; I beg you through our Lord Jesus Christ and his gentleness: it is time that we show them great charity and overflowing mercy in praying to God for them that God may finally bring them to their senses, so that they turn and see that they have nothing at all to say against the truth. Nothing is left to them except the weakness of animosity which is all the weaker the more strength it claims for itself. I appeal to you, then, on behalf of the weak, on behalf of those who reason according to this world, on behalf of those who are crude and carnal, on behalf of those who are nevertheless our brothers and sisters. They celebrate the same sacraments even though they refuse to celebrate them with us. They respond with the same 'Amen' which, even though they do not say it together with us, yet it is the same. So pour out the depth of your love to God on their behalf.

Tuesday after Trinity 18

A Reading from *Revelations of Divine Love*
by Julian of Norwich

Our Lord Christ might die no more, but that does not stop him working, for he needs to feed us. It is an obligation of his dear, motherly, love. The human mother will suckle her child with her own milk, but our beloved Mother, Jesus, feeds us with himself, and, with the most tender courtesy, does it by means of the Blessed Sacrament, the precious food of all true life. And he keeps us going through his mercy and grace by all the sacraments. This is what he meant when he said, 'It is I whom Holy Church preaches and teaches.' In other words, 'All the health and life of the sacraments, all the virtue and grace of my word, all the goodness laid up for you in Holy Church – it is I.'

The human mother may put her child tenderly to her breast, but our tender Mother Jesus simply leads us into his blessed breast through his open side, and there gives us a glimpse of the Godhead and heavenly joy – the inner certainty of eternal bliss.

This fine and lovely word *Mother* is so sweet and so much its own that it cannot properly be used of any but him, and of her who is his own true Mother – and ours. In essence *motherhood* means love and kindness, wisdom, knowledge, goodness. Though in comparison with our spiritual birth our physical birth is a small, unimportant, straightforward sort of thing, it still remains that it is only through his working that it can be done at all by his creatures. A kind, loving mother who understands and knows the needs of her child will look after it tenderly just because it is the nature of a mother to do so. As the child grows older she changes her methods – but not her love. Older still, she allows the child to be punished so that its faults are corrected and its virtues and graces developed.

This way of doing things, with much else that is right and good, is our Lord at work in those who are doing them. Thus he is our Mother in nature, working by his grace in our lower part, for the sake of the higher. It is his will that we should know this, for he wants all our love to be fastened on himself. Like this I could see our indebtedness, under God, to fatherhood and motherhood – whether it be human or divine – is fully met in truly loving God. And this blessed love Christ himself produces in us.

Wednesday after Trinity 18

A Reading from the *Instruction* of Vincent of Lérins

Over the years I have made it my business to inquire of a number of people who are outstanding both in holiness and in expounding Christian doctrine, how I might discern criteria and, as it were, formulate a general and guiding principle for distinguishing the true Catholic Faith from degraded falsehoods. The answer that I have received is invariably to the effect that if anyone wants to detect the deceits of heretics that arise and to avoid their snares and to keep healthy and sound in their belief, we ought, with the Lord's help, to strengthen our faith in a twofold manner: first, by the authority of God's law; and secondly, by the tradition of the Catholic Church.

It may be that someone will ask: 'Since the canon of Scripture is complete, and is in itself abundantly sufficient, what is the point of joining to it the interpretation of the Church?' The answer is that because of the very complexity of Scripture not everyone places the same interpretation upon it. The statements of the same writer are explained by different people in different ways; so much so, in fact, that it seems almost possible to extract from it as many opinions as there are people! Therefore, in view of the intricacies of error, which is so multiform, there is great need to formulate a rule for the exposition of the prophets and apostles in accordance with the standard of the interpretation of the Church Catholic, as follows:

Now in the Catholic Church itself we take the greatest care to hold 'that which has been believed everywhere, always and by everybody'. That is truly and properly 'Catholic', as is indicated by the very force and meaning of the word, which comprehends everything almost universally. We shall maintain this rule if we apply the criteria of universality, antiquity, and consent. We shall maintain universality if we acknowledge the one Christian faith to be true which the whole Church throughout the world confesses; antiquity, if we do not depart from the norms of interpretation proclaimed by our forebears; and consent, if in antiquity itself we follow the definitions and opinions of all (or certainly the vast majority) of bishops and teachers of the faith.

Thursday after Trinity 18

A Reading from *Centuries of Meditations*
by Thomas Traherne

You never know yourself till you know more than your body. The image of God was not seated in the features of your face, but in the lineaments of your soul.

Your enjoyment of the world is never right till you so esteem it, that everything in it, is more your treasure than a king's exchequer full of gold and silver. And that exchequer yours also in its place and service. Can you take too much joy in your Father's works? He is himself in everything. Some things are little on the outside, and rough and common, but I remember the time when the dust of the streets were as pleasing as gold to my infant eyes, and now they are more precious to the eye of reason.

Your enjoyment of the world is never right till every morning you awake in heaven; see yourself in your Father's palace; and look upon the skies, the earth, and the air as celestial joys having such a reverend esteem of all as if you were among the angels. The bride of a monarch in her husband's chamber hath no such causes of delight as you.

You never enjoy the world aright till the sea itself floweth in your veins, till you are clothed with the heavens, and crowned with the stars, and perceive yourself to be the sole heir of the whole world, and more than so, because men are in it who are every one sole heirs as well as you. Till you can sing and rejoice and delight in God, as misers do in gold, and kings in sceptres, you never enjoy the world.

Till your spirit filleth the whole world, and the stars are your jewels; till you are as familiar with the ways of God in all ages as with your walk and table; till you are intimately acquainted with that shady nothing out of which the world was made; till you love men so as to desire their happiness with a thirst equal to the zeal of your own; till you delight in God for being good to all: you never enjoy the world.

Friday after Trinity 18

A Reading from a treatise by Baldwin,
Archbishop of Canterbury

Death is strong, for it can rob us of the gift of life. Love too is strong, for it can restore us to a better life.

Death is strong, for it can strip us of this robe of flesh. Love too is strong, for it can take death's spoils away and give them back to us.

Death is strong, for no one can withstand it. Love too is strong, for it can conquer death itself, soothe its sting, calm its violence, and bring its victory to naught. The time will come when death is reviled and taunted: 'O death, where is your sting? O death, where is your victory?'

Love is as strong as death because Christ's love is the very death of death. Hence it is said: 'I will be your death, O death! I will be your sting, O hell!' Our love for Christ is also as strong as death, because it is itself a kind of death: destroying the old life, rooting out vice, and laying aside dead works.

Our love for Christ is a return, though very unequal, for his love of us, and it is a likeness modelled on his. For 'he first loved us' and, through the example of love he gave us, he became a seal upon us by which we are made like him. We lay aside the likeness of the earthly person and put on the likeness of the heavenly person; we love him as he has loved us. For in this matter 'he has left us an example so that we might follow in his steps.'

That is why he says: 'Set me as a seal upon your heart.' It is as if he were saying: 'Love me as I love you. Keep me in your mind and memory, in your desires and yearnings, in your groans and sobs. Remember the kind of being I made you; how far I set you above other creatures; the dignity I conferred upon you; the glory and honour with which I crowned you; how I made you only a little less than the angels and set all things under your feet. Remember not only how much I have done for you but all the hardship and shame I have suffered for you. Yet look and see: Do you not wrong me? Do you not fail to love me? Who loves you as I do? Who created and redeemed you but I?'

Lord, take away my heart of stone, a heart so bitter and uncircumcised, and give me a new heart, a heart of flesh, a pure heart. You cleanse the heart and love the clean heart. Take possession of my heart and dwell in it, contain it and fill it, you who are higher than the heights of my spirit and closer to me than my innermost self! You are the pattern of all beauty and the seal of all holiness. Set the seal of your likeness upon my heart! In your mercy set your seal upon my heart, O God of my heart, O God who is my portion for ever!

Saturday after Trinity 18

A Reading from *Abandonment to Divine Providence*
by Jean-Pierre de Caussade

Since we know that the activity of God embraces everything, directs everything, indeed does everything (apart from sin) faith has the duty of adoring, loving and welcoming it in everything. We should do so full of joy and confidence, rising in everything above appearances, the very obscurity of which provokes the triumph of faith. This is the way to honour God and to treat him as God.

To live by faith is then to live joyfully, to live with assurance, untroubled by doubts, confident in what we have to do and suffer at each moment by the will of God. We should realise that it is in order to animate and sustain this life of faith that God permits the soul to be overwhelmed and carried away on the tumultuous waters of so many pains, troubles, embarrassments, weaknesses and setbacks, for faith is needed to find God in all these things. The divine life presents itself at every moment in an unknown but very certain manner under such appearances as physical death, torments in the soul, ruin in temporal affairs. In all this faith finds its nourishment and support. Faith cuts through these appearances and grasps the hand of God who keeps us alive. A faithful soul should walk on in confidence, where there is no prospect of sin, taking all these things as the various disguises of God, whose intimate presence at once alarms and reassures its faculties.

Indeed, the great God who consoles the humble gives the soul in the midst of our greatest desolations an intimate assurance that we have nothing to fear provided we allow him to act and abandon ourselves completely to him. In the midst of our affliction at the loss of the Beloved, something tells us that it is in possession of him. We are troubled and upset, and yet in the deep places of our heart there is a sort of fundamental weight which keeps us steadfastly rooted in God. As Jacob once said: 'Truly, God is in this place and I did not know it.'

Trinity 19

A Reading from *New Seeds of Contemplation*
by Thomas Merton

A humble man is not disturbed by praise. Since he is no longer concerned with himself, and since he knows where the good that is in him comes from, he does not refuse praise, because it belongs to the God he loves, and in receiving it he keeps nothing for himself but gives it all, with great joy to his God.

A man who is not humble cannot accept praise gracefully. He knows what he ought to do about it. He knows that the praise belongs to God and not to himself but he passes it on to God so clumsily that he trips himself up and draws attention to himself by his own awkwardness.

One who has not yet learned humility becomes upset and disturbed by praise. He may even lose his patience when people praise him; he is irritated by the sense of his own unworthiness. And if he does not make a fuss about it, at least the things that have been said about him haunt him and obsess his mind. They torment him wherever he goes.

At the other extreme is the man who has no humility at all and who devours praise, if he gets any, the way a dog gobbles a chunk of meat. But the humble man receives praise the way a clean window takes the light of the sun. The truer and more intense the light is, the less you see of the glass.

There is danger that Christians will go to such elaborate efforts to be humble, with the humility they have learned from a book, that they will make true humility impossible. How can you be humble if you are always paying attention to yourself? True humility excludes self-consciousness, but false humility intensifies our awareness of ourselves to such a point that we are crippled, and can no longer make any movement or perform any action without putting to work a whole complex mechanism of apologies and formulas of self-accusation.

If you were truly humble you would not bother about yourself at all. Why should you? You would only be concerned with God and with his will and with the objective order of things and values as they are, and not as your selfishness wants them to be. Consequently you would have no more illusions to defend. Your movement would be free. You would not need to be hampered with excuses which are really only framed to defend you against the accusation of pride – as if your humility depended on what other people thought of you!

A humble man can do great things with an uncommon perfection because he is no longer concerned about incidentals, like his own interests and his own reputation, and therefore he no longer needs to waste his efforts in defending them.

For a humble man is not afraid of failure. In fact, he is not afraid of anything, even of himself, since perfect humility implies perfect confidence in the power of God, before whom no other power has any meaning, and for whom there is no such thing as an obstacle. Humility is the surest sign of strength.

Monday after Trinity 19

A Reading from *A Serious Call to a Devout and Holy Life*
by William Law

God Almighty has entrusted us with the use of reason, and we use it to the disorder and corruption of our nature. We reason ourselves into all kinds of folly and misery, and make our lives the sport of foolish and extravagant passions, seeking after imaginary happiness in all kinds of shapes, creating to ourselves a thousand wants, amusing our hearts with false hopes and fears, using the world worse than irrational animals, envying, vexing, and tormenting one another with restless passions and unreasonable contentions.

Let any man but look back upon his own life and see what use he has made of his reason, how little he has consulted it, and how less he has followed it. What foolish passions, what vain thoughts, what needless labours, what extravagant projects, have taken up the greatest part of his life. How foolish he has been in his words and conversation, how seldom he has done well with judgement, and how often he has been kept from doing ill by accident; how seldom he has been able to please himself, and how often he has displeased others; how often he has changed his counsels, hated what he loved and loved what he hated; how often he has been enraged and transported at trifles, pleased and displeased with the very same things, and constantly changing from one vanity to another. Let a man but take this view of his own life, and he will see reason enough to confess that pride was not made for man.

Let him but consider that if the world knew all that of him which he knows of himself, if they saw what vanity and passions govern his inside and what secret tempers sully and corrupt his best actions, he would have no more pretence to be honoured and admired for his goodness and wisdom than a rotten and distempered body to be loved and admired for its beauty and comeliness.

This is so true and so known to the hearts of almost all people that nothing would appear more dreadful to them than to have their hearts fully discovered to the eyes of all beholders.

And perhaps there are very few people in the world who would not rather choose to die than to have all their secret follies, the errors of their judgements, the vanity of their minds, the falseness of their pretences, the frequency of their vain and disorderly passions, their uneasiness, hatreds, envies, and vexations made known unto the world.

Thus deep is the foundation of humility laid in these deplorable circumstances of our condition, which show that it is as great an offence against truth and the reason of things for a man in this state of things to lay claim to any degree of glory as to pretend to the honour of creating himself.

Tuesday after Trinity 19

A Reading from the *Meditations* of William of St Thierry

There is in me, O Lord, so vast and dense a mass of misery, that I can neither analyse it into its component parts, nor get a view of the huge thing in its entirety. The fog of it enwraps me now, as it is wont to do, shrouding the sight of you, O Lord my God, to whom I long to speak, dulling my ears against your voice that I desire to hear. Always it happens thus; my own house, my own conscience, casts me out. Is this the meaning of the words: 'Let the wicked be taken away, that he see not the glory of God'? And when, with mental vision thus obscured, I try to grope somehow toward my goal, my ardent longing wearies and grows shattered in the quest, and from your heights I fall back to my depths. I fall from you into myself, and from myself fall below myself. For, when the motive power of my effort is exhausted, I find myself, like some poor thing of dust, cast from the surface of the earth to be the plaything of the winds, a prey to phantom notions, impulses, and longings as many as the faces of mankind, the minutes in the hours, and the ins and outs of circumstances and events. So, while the face of your goodness is always bent on me to work my good, the face of my misery, bowed ever down to the dull earth, is so enshrouded in the fog of its own blindness that it does not know how to reach your presence. Indeed it cannot do so, save insofar as it can never be hidden from the face of your truth, that sees through everything, whatever its condition.

When all fog is dispelled I can look with healthier eyes on you, O Light of truth. All other things excluded, I can shut myself away with you, O Truth, alone. Making the secret place of your face my hiding-place, I speak to you more intimately and in more homely fashion; throwing open to you all the dark corners of my conscience. Shedding the garment of skin that you made for Adam to cover his disgrace and shame, I show myself to you as naked as when you made me, and I say: Lord, here I am, not as you made me, but as I have made myself to be by my apostasy from you. Behold my wounds, new and old. I hide nothing. I expose everything, both your benefits conferred on me and my own bad actions.

I stand before you in faith, O God. I go forward in hope. Poor and a beggar, I supplicate your love. O Love, O Fire, O Charity, come into us! Be you our leader and our light, the fire that consumes and burns in the repentant sinner, be you our paraclete, our comforter, our advocate and helper in all things for which we pray. Show us what we believe. Grant that for which we hope. And make our face like to the face of God.

Wednesday after Trinity 19

A Reading from the treatise *Pastoral Care*
by Gregory the Great

It often occurs when a sermon has been delivered well and with a powerful message, that afterwards the mind of the preacher is elated with a sense of joy at his own performance. In such circumstances, take great care to examine yourself rigorously, lest in restoring others to health by healing their inner wounds, you disregard your own inner well-being, and foster the cancer of pride. While helping your neighbour, never neglect to examine yourself; never raise up others, but fall yourself.

In many cases, the very greatness of a preacher's virtue can be the occasion of his downfall because he has felt over-confident in his own ability, and has perished through negligence. Indeed, in the struggle of virtue against vice, the mind can sometimes flatter itself. It is almost as if it becomes exhilarated by the contest with the result that the soul ceases to be cautious or circumspect, and puts its confidence in its own ability to perform well. It is at this juncture that the cunning Seducer infiltrates himself, enumerating to the soul a catalogue of our successes, enlarging the ego with conceited thoughts about superiority over others.

This is why it is so important that when a wealth of virtues flatter us, we should turn the eye of our soul to gaze upon our weaknesses, and that for our own good, we should constantly stand in humility before God. We should attend not to the good we have done, but to the good we have failed to do, so that while the heart becomes contrite in recollecting its frailty, it may be the more solidly established in the eyes of the Author of humility. For although almighty God will bring to perfection in large measure the minds of those whose task it is to lead, he will always leave them in some sense unfinished in order that, when they are resplendent in their marvellous achievements, they may still grieve their imperfections; and because they constantly have to struggle over trivial things that plague them, they will not be tempted to over-estimate themselves when confronted by major things. If they cannot overcome the little things of life that afflict them, they will be less likely to pride themselves on the great things they may accomplish.

Thursday after Trinity 19

A Reading from a sermon of Peter Chrysologus,
Bishop of Ravenna

When a doctor persuades a sick person to take some bitter medicine, he does so by making coaxing requests. There is no point in compulsion. The doctor knows that if the sick person spits out the medicine, however health-giving the remedy might be, it will be out of weakness rather than choice. We tend to reject the very things that will help us. A parent encourages their child to exercise personal discipline, but that will only succeed by love, not by force. A parent knows that harsh discipline will engender only rebellion in the young.

So, if a sick person needs to be coaxed by gentle requests towards health, and if the disposition of the adolescent needs to be coaxed to the exercise of prudence, it should not come as a shock to hear the apostle Paul writing as both a doctor and parent to the Church in Rome in a similar vein: 'I appeal to you by the mercy of God.' Is he not trying to entice human souls which have been wounded by bodily disease to accept divine medicine?

But Paul is introducing a new quality of appeal. He could have exhorted the people through God's might, or majesty, or glory; but he chose instead God's mercy. Why? Because it was through mercy alone that Paul himself had escaped from his criminal state as persecutor, and secured the dignity of his great apostolate. He himself tells us this when he was writing to Timothy: 'Formerly, I was a blasphemer, a persecutor and a bitter adversary; but I obtained the mercy of God.' And a little later he says: 'This saying is true and worthy of full acceptance, that Christ Jesus came into the world to save sinners, of whom I am the chief. But I obtained mercy to be an example to those who shall believe in him and so attain eternal life.'

'I appeal to you by the mercy of God.' Paul makes a request, or rather God makes a request to us through Paul, because he wants to be loved rather than feared. God makes a request, because he does not want to be so much the Lord as a father. God makes a request in his mercy, rather than punish in his severity.

Friday after Trinity 19

A Reading from *The Dialogue of Comfort against Tribulation* by Thomas More

May we not always pray for the taking away from us of every kind of temptation. For if a man should in every sickness pray for his health again, when should he show himself content to die and to depart unto God? And that mind must a man have, you know, or else it will not be well with him. It is a tribulation to good men to feel in themselves the conflict of the flesh against the soul and the rebellion of sensuality against the rule and governance of reason – the relics that remain in mankind of old original sin, of which St Paul so sore complaineth in his Epistle to the Romans. And yet may we not pray, while we stand in this life, to have this kind of tribulation utterly taken from us. For it is left us by God's ordinance to strive against it and fight with it, and by reason and grace to master it and use it for the matter of our merit.

For the salvation of our soul may we boldly pray. For grace may we boldly pray, for faith, for hope, and for charity, and for every such virtue as shall serve us toward heaven. But as for all the other things in which is contained the matter of every kind of tribulation, we may never well make prayers so precisely but that we must express or imply a condition therein – that is, that if God see the contrary better for us, we refer it wholly to his will. And if that be so, we pray that God, instead of taking away our grief, may send us of his goodness either spiritual comfort to take it gladly, or at least strength to bear it patiently.

Saturday after Trinity 19

A Reading from *Holy Dying* by Jeremy Taylor

By a daily examination of our actions we shall the easier cure a great sin, and prevent its arrival to become habitual. For to examine we suppose to be a relative duty, and instrumental to something else. We examine ourselves, that we may find out our failings and cure them; and therefore if we use our remedy when the wound is fresh and bleeding, we shall find the cure more certain and less painful. For so a taper, when its crown of flame is newly blown off, retains a nature so akin to light, that it will with greediness rekindle and snatch a ray from the neighbour fire. So is the soul of man when it is newly fallen into sin; although God be angry with it, and the state of God's favour and its own graciousness is interrupted, yet the habit is not naturally changed: and still God leaves some roots of virtue standing, and the man is modest, or apt to be made ashamed, and he is not grown a bold sinner; but if he sleeps on it, and returns again to the same sin, and by degrees grows in love with it, and gets the custom, and the strangeness of it is taken away, then it is his master, and is swelled into a heap, and is abetted by use, and corroborated by newly-entertained principles, and is insinuated into his nature, and hath possessed his affections, and tainted the will and the understanding. And by this time a man is in the state of a decaying merchant, his accounts are so great, and so intricate, and so much in arrear, that to examine it will be but to represent the particulars of his calamity: therefore they think it better to pull the napkin before their eyes, than to stare upon the circumstances of their death.

A daily or frequent examination of the parts of our life will interrupt the proceedings and hinder the journey of little sins into a heap. For many days do not pass the best persons in which they have not many idle words or vainer thoughts to sully the fair whiteness of their souls, some indiscreet passions or trifling purposes, some impertinent discontents or unhandsome usages of their own persons or their dearest relatives. And though God is not extreme to mark what is done amiss, and therefore puts these upon the accounts of his mercy, and the title of the cross; yet in two cases these little sins combine and cluster; and we know that grapes were once in so great a bunch, that one cluster was the load of two men; that is, first: when either we are in love with small sins; or second: when they proceed from a careless and incurious spirit into frequency and continuance.

Trinity 20

A Reading from the *Instructions* of Columbanus
on 'Christ the Fount of Life'

Listen to my words. You are going to hear something that must be said. You slake your soul's thirst with drafts of the divine fountain. I now wish to speak of this. Revive yourself, but do not quench your thirst. Drink, I say, but do not entirely quench your thirst, for the fountain of life, the fountain of love calls us to him and says: 'Whoever thirsts, let them come to me and drink.'

Understand well what you drink. Jeremiah the prophet would tell us; the fountain of life would himself tell us: 'For they have abandoned me, the fountain of living water, says the Lord.' The Lord himself, our God Jesus Christ, is the fountain of life, and accordingly he invites us to himself as to a fountain, that we may drink. Whoever loves him, drinks him. You drink who are filled with the Word of God. You drink who love him fully and really desire him. You drink who are on fire with the love of wisdom.

Consider the source of the fountain; bread comes down to us from the same place since the same one is the bread and the fountain, the only-begotten Son, our God, Christ the Lord, for whom we should always hunger. We may even eat him out of love for him, and devour him out of desire, longing for him eagerly. Let us drink from him, as from a fountain, with an abundance of love. May we drink him with the fullness of desire, and may we take pleasure in his sweetness and savour.

For the Lord is sweet and gracious; rightly then let us eat and drink of him yet remain ever hungry and thirsty, since he is our food and drink, but can never be wholly eaten and consumed. Though he may be eaten, he is never consumed; one can drink of him and he is not diminished because our bread is eternal and our fountain is sweet and everlasting. Hence the prophet says: 'You who thirst, come to the fountain.' He is the fountain for those who are thirsty but are never fully satisfied. Therefore he calls to himself the hungry whom he raised to a blessed condition elsewhere. They were never satisfied in drinking; the more they drank, the greater their thirst.

It is right that we must always long for, seek and love the Word of God on high, the fountain of wisdom. According to the Apostle's words 'all the hidden treasures of wisdom and knowledge are in him,' and he calls the thirsty to drink.

If you thirst, drink of the fountain of life; if you are hungry, eat the bread of life. Blessed are they who hunger for this bread and thirst for this fountain, for in so doing they will desire ever more to eat and drink. For what they eat and drink is exceedingly sweet and their thirst and appetite for more is never satisfied. Though it is ever tasted it is ever more desired. Hence the prophet-king says: 'O taste and see how sweet, how gracious the Lord is.'

Monday after Trinity 20

A Reading from a sermon entitled *Catholic Spirit*
by John Wesley

A man of a catholic spirit is one who gives his hand to all whose hearts are right with his heart: one who knows how to value, and praise God, for all the advantages he enjoys, with regard to the knowledge of the things of God, the true scriptural manner of worshipping him, and, above all, his union with a congregation fearing God and working righteousness: one who, retaining these blessings with the strictest care, keeping them as the apple of his eye, at the same time loves, – as friends, as brethren in the Lord, as members of Christ and children of God, as joint-partakers now of the present kingdom of God, and fellow-heirs of his eternal kingdom – all, of whatever opinion, or worship, or congregation, who believe in the Lord Jesus Christ; who love God and man; who, rejoicing to please and fearing to offend God, are careful to abstain from evil, and zealous of good works. He is the man of truly catholic spirit, who bears all these continually upon his heart; who, having an unspeakable tenderness for their persons, and longing for their welfare, does not cease to commend them to God in prayer, as well as to plead their cause before men; who speaks comfortably to them, and labours, by all his words, to strengthen their hands in God. He assists them to the uttermost of his power in all things, spiritual and temporal. He is ready 'to spend and be spent for them'; yea, to lay down his life for their sake.

Thou, O man of God, think on these things! If thou art already in this way, go on. If thou hast heretofore mistook the path, bless God who hath brought thee back! And now run the race which is set before thee, in the royal way of universal love. Take heed, lest thou be either wavering in thy judgement, or straitened in thy bowels. But keep an even pace, rooted in the faith once delivered to the saints, and grounded in love, in true catholic love, till thou art swallowed up in love for ever and ever!

Tuesday after Trinity 20

A Reading from the homilies of John Chrysostom

'Marriage is a mystery,' says Paul, 'and I understand it in relation to Christ and his Church.' It is a mystery, and the mystery consists in this: the two spouses are united and the two become one. As at the incarnation at the entrance of the Word into the created order there was no ceremony or noise, but great silence, a quiet tranquillity; in the same way, two people come together and are united not in a lifeless image, not even in an image drawn from this world, but in the image of God himself. They form one body. What a mystery of love!

There is no human relationship so intimate as that between husband and wife, if they are united as they should be. It is why Paul spent so much effort in speaking of this subject and why he says: 'Wives, be subject to your husbands as you are to the Lord.' From these words of Paul you sense how absolute should be a wife's subjection to her husband. But now listen to what Paul also requires of husbands, for he employs an identical argument: 'Husbands, love your wives as Christ loved the Church.' You see the measure of obedience that is asked; hear also how much love is required. You husbands want your wives to obey you as the Church obeys Christ? Then you must care for them as much as Christ cares for the Church. Should it be necessary for you to die for your wife, to be cut into ten thousand pieces, to endure and undergo any suffering whatever, you should never refuse. And even if you were to suffer, you would still have done nothing when compared with what Christ has done for you. Indeed, you would be doing things for someone to whom you are already united, whereas Christ did them for us in the face of our opposition and hatred of him; we abused him, we spat at him, and finally rejected him. He used no threats or violence; he never resorted to humiliation or fear; but with unwearying tenderness, Christ wooed his Church in love. You too, must behave towards your wives in the same way. Even if you perceive that your wife despises you, even if she rejects and humiliates you, you can bring her back to you if you cherish her, if you care for her, if you are tender to her, if you love her.

Nothing is stronger than bonds of love, particularly between husband and wife. By resorting to intimidation you might succeed in keeping a domestic servant attached to you; but in all probability the servant will leave you and run away. But the companion of your life, the mother of your children, the ground of your joy, ought she be tied to you by threats and fear? Surely, by love and cherishing? What sort of union would it be where the wife was petrified of her husband? And what pleasure could her husband find in tyrannising her as if she were a slave instead of respecting her as a free woman?

Two souls united in love should have nothing to fear either in the present or the future. For where there is harmony, peace and mutuality of love, then husband and wife already possess everything that is good.

Wednesday after Trinity 20

A Reading from a commentary on the psalms
by Ambrose of Milan

What is more pleasing than a psalm? David expresses it well: 'Praise the Lord, for a song of praise is good: let there be praise of our God with gladness and grace.' Yes, a psalm is a blessing on the lips of the people, a hymn in praise of God, the assembly's homage, a general acclamation, a word that speaks for all, the voice of the Church, a confession of faith in song. It is the voice of complete assent, the joy of freedom, a cry of happiness, the echo of gladness. It soothes the temper, distracts from care, lightens the burden of sorrow. It is a source of security at night, a lesson in wisdom by day. It is a shield when we are afraid, a celebration of holiness, a vision of serenity, a promise of peace and harmony. It is like a lyre, evoking harmony from a blend of notes. Day begins to the music of a psalm. Day closes to the echo of a psalm.

In a psalm, instruction vies with beauty. We sing for pleasure. We learn for our profit. What experience is not covered by a reading of the psalms? I come across the words: 'A song for the beloved', and I am aflame with desire for God's love. I go through God's revelation in all its beauty, the intimations of resurrection, the gifts of his promise. I learn to avoid sin. I see my mistake in feeling ashamed of repentance for my sins.

What is a psalm but a musical instrument to give expression to all the virtues? The psalmist of old used it, with the aid of the Holy Spirit, to make earth re-echo the music of heaven. The psalmist used the dead gut of strings to create harmony from a variety of notes, in order to send up to heaven the song of God's praise. In doing so the psalmist taught us that we must first die to sin, and then create in our lives on earth a harmony through virtuous deeds, if the grace of our devotion is to reach up to the Lord.

David thus taught us that we must sing an interior song of praise, like St Paul, who tells us: 'I shall pray in spirit, and also with understanding; I shall sing in spirit, and also with understanding.' We must fashion our lives and shape our actions in the light of the things that are above. We must not allow pleasure to awaken bodily passions, which weigh our soul down instead of freeing it. The holy prophet told us that his songs of praise were to celebrate the freeing of the soul, when he said: 'I shall sing to you on the lyre, O Holy One of Israel; my lips shall rejoice when I have sung to you, and my soul also, which you have set free.'

Thursday after Trinity 20

A Reading from a treatise *On Spiritual Friendship*
by Aelred of Rievaulx

When God created man, in order to commend more highly the good of society, he said: 'It is not good for man to be alone: let us make him a helper like unto himself.' It was from no similar, nor even from the same, material that divine might formed this help-mate, but as a clearer inspiration to charity and friendship he produced the woman from the very substance of the man. How beautiful it is that the second human being was taken from the side of the first, so that nature might teach that human beings are equal and, as it were, collateral, and that there is in human affairs neither a superior nor an inferior, a characteristic of true friendship.

Hence, nature from the very beginning implanted the desire for friendship and charity in the human heart, a desire which an inner sense of affection soon increased with a taste of sweetness. But after the fall of the first man, when with the cooling of charity concupiscence made secret inroads and caused private good to take precedence over the common weal, it corrupted the splendour of friendship and charity through avarice and envy, introducing contentions, jealous rivalries, hates and suspicions because the morals of mankind had been corrupted.

From that time the good distinguished between charity and friendship, observing that love ought to be extended even to the hostile and perverse, while no union of will and ideas can exist between the good and wicked. And so friendship, which, like charity, was first preserved among all by all, remained according to the natural law among the few good. They saw the sacred laws of faith and society violated by many and bound themselves together by a closer bond of love and friendship. In the midst of the evils which they saw and felt, they rested in the joy of mutual charity.

But in those in whom wickedness obliterated every feeling of virtue, reason, which could not be extinguished in them, left the inclination toward friendship and society, so that without companionship riches could hold no charm for the greedy, nor glory for the ambitious, nor pleasure for the sensuous. There are compacts – even sworn bonds – of union among the wicked which ought to be abhorred. These, clothed with the beautiful name of friendship, ought to have been distinguished from true friendship by law and precept, so that when true friendship was sought, one might not incautiously be ensnared among those other friendships because of some slight resemblance.

This friendship, which nature has brought into being and practice has strengthened, has by the power of law been regulated. It is evident, then, that friendship is natural, like virtue, wisdom, and the like, which should be sought after and preserved for their own sake as natural goods. Everyone that possesses them makes good use of them, and no one entirely abuses them.

Friday after Trinity 20

A Reading from *Befriending our Desires*
by Philip Sheldrake

'God is friendship. What is true of charity, I surely do not hesitate to grant to friendship, since "he that abides in friendship, abides in God, and God in him." ' These words of Aelred, the twelfth-century Yorkshire Cistercian, in his wonderful book on friendship, remind us that it is important not to reduce our understanding of sexuality to genital activity, as if this one area provides the total meaning of love and intimacy. Sexuality, in its broadest sense, covers our whole experience of embodiment. Affective sexuality involves a huge area of feelings and emotions that move us towards other people. And this is true of all kinds of relationships, including those of single people. It is, if you like, what enables all of us to express tenderness, closeness, compassion and openness to touch. It follows that intimacy is not something reserved to certain categories of people (that is, the married) and not to others. Single people, including those committed for various reasons to celibacy, are equally called to intimacy with other human beings.

The call to intimacy that we all experience at different points in our lives is an invitation to take risks. For all human love can come to an end, may deceive, is partial, is not totally and finally reliable. Yet our capacity and need for intimacy is a call to find within this risk of human loving the love of God that is total, constant and faithful. Deep human friendship is a powerful contribution, arguably the most powerful, to a loving union with God. The call to intimacy also involves a realisation that however much two people love each other they will never possess or own each other nor will they ever fully know each other. There is always an area of inalienable strangeness in the other person. There is, therefore, for ever the possibility of greater depth, of 'more', in all relationships.

Whether we are single or in a committed, exclusive relationship, the Christian insights about *eros* love and *agape* love remind us that to become complete we are all called to seek the eventual integration of particular and universal love. Only within our experiences of intimacy with other people, whether genital or not, may we learn a way of being fully present both to ourselves and to others rather than being superficial and remote in our emotional lives. The risk of intimacy, rather than the apparent security of emotional detachment, reveals the truth of ourselves, teaches us about availability, educates us in truthful self-disclosure and of all human experiences is the one most likely to provoke real change in us.

Saturday after Trinity 20

A Reading from a commentary on St John's Gospel
by Augustine

The Lord, the teacher of love, has come full of love in his own person 'with summary judgement on the world', and has taught us that the law and the prophets may be summed up in two great commandments of love.

Always and at all times, reflect on them: 'to love God, with all your heart, and with all your soul, and with all your mind; and your neighbour as yourself'. Constantly ponder them, meditate upon them and remember them for they must be practised and fulfilled. Note that the love of God comes first in the order of command, but the love of neighbour comes first in the order of action. The person who would teach you this love in two commandments would not commend to you first your neighbour and then God, but first God and then your neighbour. But because you do not as yet see God, by loving your neighbour you will gain sight of God because in so doing you are purifying your eye for the vision of God. John says this plainly: 'Those who do not love the brother or sister whom they have seen, cannot love God whom they have not seen.'

The same is said to you: Love God. So if you say to me: 'Show me the one whom I am to love,' what can I reply except what John himself said: 'No one has ever seen God'? But in saying this, do not think that seeing God is altogether impossible for you; for John also states: 'God is love, and those who dwell in love are dwelling in God.' Love your neighbour, therefore, and discern the source of that love within you; and in so doing you will see God.

So then, begin by loving your neighbour: 'Share your bread with the hungry, and bring the homeless poor into your own house; when you see the naked, cover them, and do not hide yourself from your own flesh.' In doing this what will happen? 'Your light will break forth like the dawn.' Your light is your God; to you he is 'morning light', because after the night of this present world he will come to you: God, who neither rises nor sets; God, who always abides.

Remember too what is said by the apostle Paul: 'Bear one another's burdens, and so fulfil the law of Christ.' The law of Christ is charity; and charity is not fulfilled unless we bear one another's burdens. When you were weak, your neighbour carried you. Now you are strong carry your neighbour. In so doing, you will make up what is lacking in you. In loving your neighbour and being concerned about your neighbour, you are on a journey. And where are you travelling if not to the Lord God, the God whom it is our duty to love with all our heart, with all our soul, and with all our mind? We may not yet have reached his presence, but we do have our neighbour with us. So then, support this companion of your pilgrimage that you may come to the One with whom you long to dwell.

Trinity 21

A Reading from *Revelations of Divine Love*
by Julian of Norwich

It is God's will that we see and enjoy everything in love. And it is in our ignorance of this that we are most blind. Some of us believe that God is almighty, and *may* do everything; and that he is all wise, and *can* do everything; but that he is all love, and *will* do everything – there we draw back. And as I see it, this ignorance is the greatest of all hindrances to God's lovers.

When we begin to hate sin, and to mend our ways under the direction of Holy Church, there still remains within us a dread that holds us back, because we look at ourselves and the sins we have already committed. For some of us it is because we sin every day. We do not keep our promises, or the cleansing our Lord has bestowed upon us, but fall so often into wretchedness shameful to behold. And the sight of this makes us so sorry and despondent that we can scarcely find any comfort. This dread we sometimes mistake for humility, but this is to be horribly blind and weak. We cannot despise it as we do any other sin that we know, for it comes from the enemy, and is opposed to truth. It is the will of God that of all the qualities of the blessed Trinity that we should be most sure of and delighted with, is love. Love makes might and wisdom come down to our level. For just as by his courtesy God forgives our sin when we repent, so he wills that we forgive our sin too, and as a consequence, our foolish dependency and doubting fears.

Monday after Trinity 21

A Reading from a sermon of Augustine

'If by the Spirit you put to death the deeds of the flesh you shall live.' This is our task in life – by the Spirit to put to death the deeds of the flesh, each day to strike them down, reduce them, bridle them, destroy them.

Those who are progressing in the faith find themselves no longer attracted by a whole variety of things which once ensnared them. When something used to attract them and they did not give way to it, it was being put to death; and if it no longer attracts them, it has finally been put to death. Trample on the dead and turn to the living; trample on the fallen, do battle with those still fighting. One attraction is dead, but another is still alive. This is our task, this is our warfare. As we do battle in this contest, we have God to watch over us; as we toil in this contest, we entreat him to help us. For if he did not himself help us, we would be unable – I do not say to win – but even to fight.

You were on the point of saying: 'My will can do that, my free-will can achieve that.' What will? What free-will? Unless God rules, you fall; unless he lifts you up, you are on the floor. How can any of this be achieved by your spirit when the words of the Apostle are: 'For all who are directed by the Spirit of God are children of God.' You want to direct yourself in putting to death the deeds of the flesh. What is the use of not being an Epicurean or a Stoic? Whatever you are you will not be numbered among the children of God.

Someone else will say to me: 'So we are directed and do not direct ourselves; we are acted on and do not act ourselves.' My reply is: You both direct and are directed; you act and are acted on; you direct your life well when you are directed by that which is good. For the Spirit of God who acts on you is helping you in your acting. The very word 'helper' shows that you are yourself an agent. Realise what you are praying for and realise what you are confessing when you say to God: 'Be my helper; do not forsake me.' You call God 'helper' but no one can be helped, if he is not prepared to help himself. 'All who are directed by the Spirit of God are children of God' – directed not by the letter but by the Spirit, not by the law with its injunctions, threats and promises but by the Spirit with his encouragement, enlightenment and help. As the Apostle concludes: 'We know that God works all things together for good for those who love him.'

Tuesday after Trinity 21

A Reading from *The Cloud of Unknowing*

See to it that there is nothing at work in your mind or will but only God. Try to suppress all knowledge and feeling of anything less than God, and trample it down deep under the cloud of forgetting. You must understand that in this business you are to forget not only all other things than yourself (and their doings – and your own!) but to forget also yourself, and even the things you have done for the sake of God. For it is the way of the perfect lover not only to love what he loves more than himself, but also in some sort to hate himself for the sake of what he loves.

So you are to do with yourself. You must loathe and tire of all that goes on in your mind and your will unless it is God. For otherwise surely whatever it is is between you and God. No wonder you loathe and hate thinking about yourself when you always feel your sin to be a filthy and nauseating lump – you do not particularise – between you and God, and that that lump is yourself. For you are to think of it as being identified with yourself: inseparable from you.

So crush all knowledge and experience of all forms of created things, and of yourself above all. For it is on your own self-knowledge and experience that the knowledge and experience of everything else depend. Alongside this self-regard everything else is quickly forgotten. For if you will take the trouble to test it, you will find that when all other things and activities have been forgotten (even your own) there still remains between you and God the stark awareness of your own existence. And this awareness, too, must go, before you experience contemplation in its perfection.

Wednesday after Trinity 21

A Reading from a homily of Gregory of Nyssa
'On the Love of the Poor'

Never despise homeless people who are stretched out on the ground as if they merit no respect. Ask who they are and discover their worth. They bear the image of our Saviour. The Lord in his goodness has given them his own image in order that his image might cause the hard-hearted to blush with shame, those who hate the poor, just as travellers who are attacked by thieves present immediately the images of their king so that the credit of the authority will reduce the brigands to better sentiments. Thus, too are the poor the stewards of our hope, the guardians of royalty, who open the door to the just and close it again to the wicked and egotistical. Terrible accusers, vehement prosecutors, although they always judge in silence! For the Judge listens to them and their self-sacrifice, and what we squander cries out to God who fathoms the heart, in a voice clearer than the herald's trumpet.

These are the ones who have prompted God to formidable judgement, for whose sake you have often heard the lesson. In that lesson I envision the Son of Man descend from the sky and walking in the air as one walks on earth. Thousands of angels escort him. Then the thrones of glory appear in the sky and all they who had grown up under the sun and breathed terrestrial air, are separated into two camps, waiting at the foot of the tribunal. One are called 'sheep' and are placed to live on the right. I know that the camp on the left is designated 'goats'. The savage heart of this species merits it this name. The Judge interrogates the accused and I listened to their answers. Each received its due penalty: the species who were true to life won the kingdom. Egoists and the wicked were sent to punishment by fire, and for all of eternity.

The Scripture tells this account with such care, and our court of justice has been painted so precisely, to convince us of the advantages of good works. For it is this divine charity which preserves our life, mother of those who are poor, adviser of the rich, nurse of the little one, presbyter of the aged, treasure of those in need, universal haven of the unhappy, who defends and consoles all ages and all sorrows. As in the useless competitions of the circus, the leader proclaims his love of honour by the sound of a trumpet and announces the prizes to all the competitors, good deeds summon together those who have fallen on hard times and who are in critical circumstances not to honourably reward them with calamity, but to heal their difficulties. Virtue better than all feats of prowess!

Charity lives in the intimacy of God and it is God who by his hands shaped the first works of love and philanthropy in creating everything that is. For God is the first and foremost lover of good deeds who nourishes the starving, waters the thirsty, and clothes those who are naked.

Thursday after Trinity 21

A Reading from *The Go-Between God*
by John V. Taylor

The prayer of stillness is that which most naturally deepens our communion with the Father and reproduces in us the abba-relationship that Jesus knew. But the same manner of praying can make Jesus himself more real to us; it is a form of intercession also whereby other people are held in our loving regard and sympathy. It can make us more profoundly aware of the crying needs of mankind and the mysterious bond between ourselves and the physical world.

This richness should make it impossible for us to disregard the many who can find their God only by the same gradual progression as the disciples, first knowing Jesus as a man who draws them humanly and commands their allegiance as no other being has ever done, who becomes the point of reference by which they set their standards and make their decisions, into whose presence they want to bring their perplexity and pain, whom in fact they begin to treat as God long before they have formulated theologically their convictions about him. If this was legitimate for the fishermen of Galilee – or, rather, if it was illegitimate yet necessary, for them – may it not be permitted to secular men and women to treat the man Jesus as their God even before they can admit that there is any meaning in the word 'divine'?

It does not matter whether the Christ who fills our vision is the historical Jesus, or the living Saviour, or the Christ of the Body and the Blood, or the Logos and Lord of the universe, or the master and meaning of history, or the Christ in my neighbour and in his poor. These are only aspects of his being. In whatever aspect it is most real to us, what matters is that we adore him. For, loving him whom we think we know, we are drawn to that Lord Jesus who transcends our knowing. But all too often we have lost him amid our enthusiasms. What dominates our mind is not the figure of Jesus of Nazareth but our New Testament studies, not the living Saviour but the doctrines of salvation, not Christ in the neighbour but the civil rights movement.

This is not a plea for pietism but for adoration. The Jesus of history, whensoever we discern him, is not a topic of debate but a master and brother to be loved and followed. Christ in his poor is neither a case nor a cause, but a mystery before whom we bow even while we serve. Whatever way of knowing him is valid for us – and it may be simply as the one whose 'give ye them to eat' sends us into the fight for a new world order – we must be in love with him, not with ourselves or our schemes. We must find time to let our minds dwell on him. The beauty of holiness in the midst of this revolutionary world belongs to those who set the Lord always before their eyes. *Venite adoremus!*

Friday after Trinity 21

A Reading from a treatise *On the Love of God*
by Bernard of Clairvaux

Daily in church we hear that saying of our Lord concerning the memorial of his passion: 'Those who eat my flesh and drink my blood have eternal life.' This should be understood as meaning, those who call my death to mind and after my example mortify their bodies have eternal life, for if you suffer with me, you shall also reign with me.

However, even to this day, there are many who refuse to attend to his voice when he speaks thus, who turn away from him, saying by their lives if not their words: 'This is a hard saying, who can hear it?' That is why this generation, whose heart is not set true, whose spirit does not cleave to God alone, but prefers to hope in false riches, cannot abide the gospel of the cross and finds the memory of the passion tiresome.

How will such folk endure the sentence of the Judge: 'Go from me, you cursed ones, into the eternal fire which is prepared for the devil and his angels'? Like a great boulder, this judgement will crush to powder those on whom it falls. But 'the generation of the righteous shall be blessed,' who, like the apostle Paul 'whether present or absent' endeavour to be pleasing to God. Their sentence from the Judge will be: 'Come, you blessed of my Father,' and so on. And on that day the generation that did not set its heart aright will find (too late) just how easy by comparison with what they now suffer is the yoke of Christ, how light is his burden, which earlier on in their lives they deemed too heavy for their proud necks to shoulder.

O wretched slaves of Mammon, you cannot glory in the cross of our Lord Jesus Christ and at the same time hope in earthly riches; you cannot seek for gold *and* prove how gracious the Lord is. One day you will find God very frightening because the thought of him has never been your joy.

Saturday after Trinity 21

A Reading from the *Confessions* of Augustine

O Lord God, grant us peace, for all that we have is your gift. Grant us the peace of repose, the peace of the sabbath, the peace which has no evening. For this entire order in all its beauty will complete its course and pass away. All things have been allotted their morning and their evening.

But the seventh day is without evening and the sun shall not set upon it. You have sanctified it and willed that it should last for ever. Although your eternal repose was unbroken by the act of creation, nevertheless, after all your works were done and you had seen that they were very good, you rested on the seventh day. In your book we read this as a forecast that when our work in this life is done, we too shall rest in you in the sabbath of eternal life, though our works are very good only because you have given us the grace to perform them.

In that eternal sabbath you will rest in us, just as now you work in us. The rest that we shall enjoy will be yours, just as the work that we now do is your work done through us. But you, Lord, are always working and always at rest. It is not in time that you see, it is not in time that you move, it is not in time that you rest: yet you make what we see in time; you make time itself and the repose which comes when time ceases.

As for ourselves, we see the things you have made because they are. They are because you see them. We see outwardly that they are, and inwardly that they are good.

But you, O God, who are one and good, have never ceased to do good. By the gift of your grace some of the works that we do are good, though they are not everlasting. After them we hope that we shall find rest, when you admit us to the great holiness of your presence. But you are Goodness itself and need no good besides yourself. You are for ever at rest, because you are your own repose.

Last Sunday after Trinity

A Reading from a scriptural commentary of
Ephrem of Syria

Lord, who can comprehend even one of your words? We lose more of it than we grasp, like those who drink from a living spring. For God's word offers different facets according to the capacity of the listener, and the Lord has portrayed his message in many colours, so that whoever gazes upon it can see in it what suits. Within it God has buried manifold treasures, so that each of us might grow rich in seeking them out.

The word of God is a tree of life that offers us blessed fruit from each of its branches. It is like that rock which was struck open in the wilderness, from which all were offered spiritual drink. As the Apostle says: 'They ate spiritual food and they drank spiritual drink.'

And so whenever you discover some part of the treasure, you should not think that you have exhausted God's word. Instead you should feel that this is all that you were able to find of the wealth contained in it. Nor should you say that the word is weak and sterile or look down on it simply because this portion was all that you happened to find. But precisely because you could not capture it all you should give thanks for its riches.

Be glad then that you are overwhelmed, and do not be saddened because the word of God has overcome you. A thirsty person is happy when drinking, and is not depressed because of being unable to exhaust the spring. So let this spring quench your thirst, and not your thirst the spring. For if you can satisfy your thirst without exhausting the spring, then when you thirst again you can drink from it once more; but if when your thirst is sated the spring is also dried up, then your victory would turn to your own harm.

Be thankful then for what you have received, and do not be saddened at all that such an abundance still remains. What you have received and attained is your present share, while what is left will be your heritage. For what you could not take at one time because of your weakness, you will be able to grasp at another if you only persevere. So do not foolishly try to drain in one draught what cannot be consumed all at once, and do not cease out of faint-heartedness from what you will be able to absorb as time goes on.

Any of the following readings may be preferred if today is observed as BIBLE SUNDAY

Bible Sunday

A Reading from the *Confessions* of Augustine

From a hidden depth a profound self-examination had dredged up a heap of my misery, and set it 'in the sight of my heart'. I felt my past to have a grip on me, and in my misery I kept crying: 'How long, how long shall I go on saying, "tomorrow, tomorrow"? Why not now? Why not make an end of my impure life at this moment?'

I was asking myself these questions all the while I sat under the fig tree in the garden, weeping with the most bitter sorrow in my heart, when all at once I heard the voice of a child from a nearby house chanting a song. Whether it was the voice of a boy or a girl I cannot say, but again and again it repeated the refrain: 'Pick it up and read, pick it up and read.' At this I looked up, wondering whether this was a kind of game in which children chant words like these, but I could not remember from my childhood ever hearing them. I stemmed my flood of tears and stood up, telling myself that this could only be a divine command to open my book of Scripture and read the first passage on which my eyes should fall. For I had heard the story of Antony, and I remembered how he had happened to go into a church while the gospel was being read and had taken it as an admonition addressed to himself when he heard the words: 'Go, sell all that you have; give to the poor, and you shall have treasure in heaven; and come, follow me.' By this divine pronouncement he had at once been converted to you.

So I hurried back to the place where Alypius was sitting, for when I stood up to move away I had put down the book containing Paul's Epistles. I seized it and opened it, and in silence I read the first passage on which my eyes fell: 'Let us not live in revelling and drunkenness, not in eroticism and indecency, not in quarrels and rivalry, but rather put on the Lord Jesus Christ, and make no provision for the flesh and its appetites.' I had no wish to read more and no need to do so. For in an instant, as I came to the end of the sentence, it was as though the light of confidence flooded into my heart and all the darkness of doubt was dispelled.

alternative reading

A Reading from *The Book of Maxims* of Isidore of Seville

If we want to be always in God's company, we must pray regularly and read regularly. When we pray, we talk to God; when we read, God talks to us.

All spiritual growth comes from reading and reflection. By reading we learn what we did not know; by reflection we retain what we have learned.

Reading the holy Scriptures confers two benefits. It trains the mind to understand them; it turns our attention from the follies of the world and leads us to the love of God.

Two kinds of study are called for here. We must first learn how the Scriptures are to be understood, and then see how to expound them with profit and in a manner worthy of them. We must first be eager to understand what we are reading before we are fit to proclaim what we have learned.

Conscientious readers will be more concerned to carry out what they have read than merely to acquire knowledge of it. For it is a less serious fault to be ignorant of an objective than it is to fail to carry out what we do know. In reading we aim at knowing, but we must put into practice what we have learned in our course of study.

No one can understand holy Scripture without constant reading, according to the words: 'Love her and she will exalt you. Embrace her and she will glorify you.'

The more you devote yourself to a study of the sacred utterances, the richer will be your understanding of them, just as the more the soil is tilled, the richer the harvest.

Some people have great mental powers but cannot be bothered with reading; what reading could have taught them is devalued by their neglect. Others have a desire to know but are hampered by their slow mental processes; yet application to reading will teach them things which the clever fail to learn through laziness.

Those who are slow to grasp things but who really try hard are rewarded; equally those who do not cultivate their God-given intellectual ability are condemned for despising their gifts and sinning by sloth.

Learning unsupported by grace may get into our ears, but it never reaches the heart. It makes a great noise outside but serves no inner purpose. But when God's grace touches our innermost minds to bring understanding, his word which has been received by the ear sinks deep into the heart.

alternative reading

A Reading from a letter of Guigo V,
Prior of La Grande Chartreuse,
to the brethren of the Mount of God

If, when you are reading, you are genuinely seeking God, then anything you read will promote your good, and your mind will grasp and submit the meaning of your reading to the service of Christ.

However, it is important that you spend certain periods of time in the systematic reading of Scripture. For if you read now here, now there, the various things that chance and circumstance cause you to stumble across, it will not consolidate your learning, but make you unstable in spirit. For it is easy to take such reading in, and easier still to forget it. You should also pause over certain authors and allow yourself to become accustomed to their style. For it is important to read the Scriptures in the same spirit in which they were written, because only in that spirit are they to be understood. You will never reach an understanding of Paul until, by close attention to reading his letters and the application of careful reflection, you imbibe his spirit. You will never arrive at an understanding of David until by actual experience you realise what the psalms are all about. And so it is with the rest of Scripture. In every portion of Scripture, real attention is as different from superficial reading as friendship is from entertainment, or the love of a friend from a casual greeting.

A Reading from the preface from
'The Translators to the Reader', in the first edition of the
Authorized Version of the Bible 1611

The Scripture saith not in vain, 'Them that honour me, I will honour.' Neither was it a vain word that Eusebius delivered long ago, that piety towards God was the weapon and the only weapon that both preserved the Emperor Constantine's person, and avenged him of his enemies. But now what piety without truth? What truth (what saving truth) without the word of God? What word of God (whereof we may be sure) without the Scriptures?

The Scriptures we are commanded to search. They are commended that search and study them. They are reproved that were unskilful in them, or slow to believe them. They can make us wise unto salvation. If we be ignorant, they will instruct us; if out of the way, they will bring us home; if out of order, they will reform us; if in heaviness, comfort us; if dull, quicken us; if cold, inflame us. 'Take up and read, take up and read' the Scriptures (for unto them was the direction), it was said unto St Augustine by a supernatural voice. 'Whatsoever is in the Scriptures, believe me,' said the same St Augustine, 'is high and divine; there is verily truth, and a doctrine most fit for the refreshing and renewing of men's minds, and truly so tempered, that everyone may draw from thence, that which is sufficient for him, if he come to draw with a devout and pious mind as true religion requireth.' Thus St Augustine and St Jerome, 'Love the Scriptures, and wisdom will love thee.'

alternative reading

A Reading from *Abandonment to Divine Providence*
by Jean-Pierre de Caussade

Holy Scripture is the language of a mysterious God; the events of history are the obscure sayings of this same God, so hidden and so unknown. They are dark drops of a great sea, a sea of darkness and shadows. Every drop and every movement of water bear the traces of its source. The fall of the angels, the fall of Adam, the impiety and idolatry of humankind before and after the flood in the lifetime of the patriarchs, who knew and related to their children the story of the creation and of the then still recent preservation of the world: here are some of the mysterious accounts in holy Scripture.

Then we have the story of a mere handful of men and women who were preserved from idolatry until the coming of the Messiah, in spite of the general loss of faith throughout the world. Impiety always reigned and dominated; and the little band of defenders of truth were always persecuted and ill-treated the way Jesus Christ was treated. And then there are the plagues described in the Revelation of John! How are we to understand these words of God? Is this what God has revealed? And are the effects of these terrible mysteries which last until the end of the world also the living word which teaches us the wisdom, the power, and the goodness of God? The events that form the history of the world express these divine attributes. All things teach this truth. But alas, we do not see it; though we must believe it is so.

You speak, Lord, to all people in general by the great events of history. Revolutions are but the tides of your providence which stir up storms and tempests in the minds of those who question your ways. You speak in particular to individuals in the events which happen to them from moment to moment. But instead of hearing your voice, instead of respecting the mysterious obscurity of your word, they see nothing but the movements of matter, blind chance and fortune. They find objections to everything; they wish to add to and subtract from your word; they wish to reform it.

They respect the holy Scriptures. 'This is the word of God,' they say, 'and everything contained in them is holy and true.' The less they understand its meaning the more they venerate it; they glorify and justly adore the depths of the wisdom of God. But when God speaks to us at every moment, not with the words written with paper and ink but by what we suffer and do from moment to moment in our life, does this not deserve our equal attention? Why in this do you not similarly respect the truth and the goodness of God? Nothing pleases you, you criticise everything that happens to you. Do you not see that you are measuring by the standard of the senses and the reason what can only be measured by faith? We read with the eyes of faith the word of God in the Scriptures, and we are greatly in the wrong if we read with different eyes the word of God in the daily events which shape our lives.

Monday after Trinity 22

A Reading from the Letter of Ignatius of Antioch
to the Church in Magnesia

When I heard of the disciplined way of life your Christian love has taught you, it gave me so much pleasure that I decided to address a few words to you in the faith of Jesus Christ. As I go about in these chains, invested with a title worthy of a god, I sing songs of praise to the Churches; and I pray for their corporate as well as their spiritual unity, for both of these are the gifts of Jesus Christ, our never-failing Life.

Let me urge on you the importance of doing everything in harmony with God. Let the bishop preside in the place of God, and his presbyters in place of the council of the apostles, and let my special friends the deacons be entrusted with the service of Jesus Christ, who was with the Father from all eternity and who in these last days has been made manifest.

Everyone should observe the closest conformity with God. Respect one another; never allow your attitude to a neighbour be coloured by worldly opinions, but simply love each other consistently in the spirit of Jesus Christ. Allow nothing whatever to exist among you that could give rise to division; maintain absolute unity with your bishop and those who preside over you, as an example to others and a lesson in the avoidance of corruption.

In the same way as the Lord was wholly one with the Father, and never acted independently of him, either in person or through the apostles, so you yourselves must never act independently of your bishop and presbyters. On no account persuade yourselves that it is right and proper to follow your own private judgement. Let there be a united act of prayer in which everybody participates; one united supplication, one mind, one hope, in love and innocent joyfulness. As though you were approaching the one temple of God and the only altar, hasten together to the one and only Jesus Christ who came down from the one and only Father, is eternally with that One, and to that One is now returned.

Never allow yourselves to be led astray by spurious teaching and fables. Nothing of any use can be got from them. If we are still living in the practice of Judaism, it is an admission that we have failed to receive the gift of grace. Even the lives of their divinely inspired prophets resonated with Jesus Christ. Indeed, the only reason they were persecuted is that they were inspired by his grace, so that they might convince future unbelievers of the existence of the one and only God, who has revealed himself in his Son Jesus Christ, his Word proceeding from silence, who in all that he was and did was well-pleasing to the One who sent him.

We have seen how former adherents of the ancient customs have since come to a new hope. They have given up keeping the Sabbath, and now order their lives by the Lord's Day instead – the day when life first dawned for us, thanks to him and his death. That death, though some deny it, is the very mystery which has moved us to become believers, and for this reason we too suffer that we may prove ourselves disciples of Jesus Christ, our only teacher. If this be so, how can we live without him, when even the prophets of old were themselves his disciples in spirit, and looked forward to him as their teacher? Indeed, that was the very reason why he for whom they waited, came to visit them, and raised them from the dead.

Tuesday after Trinity 22

A Reading from *Life Together* by Dietrich Bonhoeffer

Many people seek fellowship because they are afraid to be alone. Because they cannot stand loneliness, they are driven to seek the company of other people. There are Christians, too, who cannot endure being alone, who have had some bad experiences with themselves, who hope they will gain some help in association with others. They are generally disappointed. Then they blame the fellowship for what is really their own fault. The Christian community is not a spiritual sanatorium. The person who comes into a fellowship because he is running away from himself is misusing it for the sake of diversion, no matter how spiritual this diversion may appear. He is really not seeking community at all, but only distraction which will allow him to forget his loneliness for a brief time, the very alienation that creates the deadly isolation of man. The disintegration of communication and all genuine experience, and finally resignation and spiritual death are the result of such attempts to find a cure.

Let those who cannot be alone beware of community. You will only do harm to yourself and to the community. Alone you stood before God when he called you; alone you had to answer that call; alone you had to struggle and pray; and alone you will die and give an account to God. You cannot escape from yourself; for God has singled you out. If you refuse to be alone you are rejecting Christ's call to you, and you can have no part in the community of those who are called.

But the reverse is also true: let those who are not in community beware of being alone. Into the community you were called, the call was not meant for you alone; in the community of the called you bear your cross, you struggle, you pray.

Only as we are within the fellowship can we be alone, and only he that is alone can live in the fellowship. Only in the fellowship do we learn to be rightly alone and only in aloneness do we learn to live rightly in fellowship.

Wednesday after Trinity 22

A Reading from a sermon of Caesarius of Arles

'Blessed are the merciful for they shall obtain mercy.' Sweet is the name of mercy, dear friends; and if the name is sweet, how much more so the reality! Yet though everyone wants to receive it, sadly not everyone lives in such a way as to merit it. Everyone wants to receive mercy: few are ready to show it to others.

What incredible effrontery to want to receive something one constantly refuses to give! You must show mercy in this life if you hope to receive it in the next. And so, dear friends, since we all wish for mercy, let us make her our patroness in this age that she may free us in the life to come. There is mercy in heaven, but we attain it through the exercise of mercy on earth. This is what Scripture says: 'O Lord, your mercy is in heaven.'

There are two kinds of mercy then, mercy on earth and mercy in heaven, one human, the other divine. What is human mercy like? It makes you concerned for the misery in which the poor live. What is divine mercy like? It forgives sinners. Whatever generosity human mercy shows during our life on earth divine mercy repays when we reach our heavenly country. In this world God is cold and hungry in the person of the poor, as he himself said: 'As you did it to one of the least of these my brothers and sisters, you did it to me.' God who is pleased to give from heaven, desires to receive on earth.

What sort of people are we if we want to take what God gives, but refuse to give when he asks? When a poor person is hungry, Christ is in need, as he said himself: 'I was hungry and you gave me no food.' Take care not to despise the misery of the poor, if you would hope, without fear, to have your sins forgiven. Beloved,

Christ is now hungry, he is hungry and thirsty in his poor; and what he receives on earth he returns in heaven.

So I put you this question: what is it you want, what is it you are looking for, when you come to church? What indeed if not mercy? Then show mercy here on earth, and you will receive mercy in heaven. A poor person is begging from you, and you are begging from God. The beggar asks for a scrap to eat, you ask for eternal life. Give to the beggar, so that you may deserve to receive from Christ. Listen to his words: 'Give and it shall be given you.' I say again, what effrontery for you to want to receive what you refuse to give! And so when you come to church give whatever alms you can to the poor in proportion to your means.

Thursday after Trinity 22

A Reading from *Mens Creatrix* by William Temple

By power and by love God would deliver us from pride, which is the one poison of the soul, and bring us into union with himself. This union, however, means something more than the divine control of our conscious wills and affections. In such union our whole nature becomes receptive, and deep in the subconscious nature divinely given thoughts are planted, even as in the same depths of the selfish nature other evil spirits, human or diabolic, plant the thoughts of which it is receptive.

All living thought, or almost all, is subconscious. We hardly ever know the origin of those thoughts which we call our own, as distinct from those which others have given to us by speech or writing. Probably it is by suggesting thoughts to the subconscious minds of his servants that God most normally directs the course of history, even as by similar suggestion the evil powers try to thwart his purpose. Probably the good seed and the bad are sown by the sowers in all hearts; but only those grow to conscious thoughts or plans of action which have found congenial soil. But the evil device, as we have seen, always leads to its own defeat and the greater exaltation of good, while the good will possesses the one supreme and lasting joy of union with the eternal God.

At every moment God is controlling the results of human choice and turning them to the fulfilment of his own purpose; but the choice is human and the wrong choice is an evil thing. But if the whole of history is indeed an ordered system such as the intellect demands for the satisfaction of its ideal of coherence, we are led of necessity to believe in an eternal knowledge to which the whole process, endless though it may possibly be, is present in a single apprehension. For the omniscient mind every episode is grasped as an element in that glorious whole of which it is a constituent part. Everlastingly in the life of God death is swallowed up in victory. It is in the absolute perfection of that eternal experience, in which the whole process of time is grasped in a single apprehension, that the ultimate ground of all that happens in history is to be found. To those who have seen in the life and death and resurrection of Christ the manifestation of the eternal omnipotence, this experience can already be in a small measure shared through faith.

Friday after Trinity 22

A Reading from the writings on prayer
of Theophan the Recluse

What shall we say of this divine prayer, in invocation of the Saviour: 'Lord Jesus Christ, Son of God, have mercy upon me'? It is a prayer like any other. There is nothing special about it in itself, but it receives all its power from the state of mind in which it is made.

The various methods described by the Fathers (sitting down, making prostrations, and the other techniques used when performing this prayer) are not suitable for everyone: indeed without a personal director they are actually dangerous. It is better not to try them. There is just one method which is obligatory for all: to stand with the attention in the heart. All other things are beside the point, and do not lead to the crux of the matter.

It is said of the fruit of this prayer, that there is nothing higher in the world. This is wrong. As if it were some talisman! Nothing in the words of the prayer and their uttering can alone bring forth its fruit. All fruit can be received without this prayer, and even without any oral prayer, but merely by directing the mind and heart towards God.

The essence of the whole thing is to be established in the remembrance of God, and to walk in his presence. You can say to anyone: 'Follow whatever methods you like – recite the Jesus Prayer, perform bows and prostrations, go to church: do what you wish, only strive to be always in constant remembrance of God.' I remember meeting a man in Kiev who said: 'I did not use any methods at all, I did not know the Jesus Prayer, yet by God's mercy I walk always in his presence. But how this has come to pass, I myself do not know. God gave!'

It is most important to realise that prayer is always God-given: otherwise we may confuse the gift of grace with some achievement of our own.

People say: attain the Jesus Prayer, for that is inner prayer. This is not correct. The Jesus Prayer is a good means to arrive at inner prayer, but in itself it is not inner but outer prayer. Those who attain the habit of the Jesus Prayer do very well. But if they stop only at this and go no further, they stop half way.

Even though we are reciting the Jesus Prayer, it is still necessary for us to keep the thought of God: otherwise the prayer is dry food. It is good that the name of Jesus should cleave to your tongue. But with this it is still possible not to remember God at all and even to harbour thoughts which are opposed to him. Consequently, everything depends on conscious and free turning to God, and on a balanced effort to hold oneself in this.

Saturday after Trinity 22

A Reading from *Moral Reflection on the Book of Job*
by Gregory the Great

The elect of God are on a journey from the darkness of night to the full light of eternity. In this process the Church finds herself led from the night of infidelity to the light of faith, and opened gradually by God to the splendour of his heavenly brightness, in the same way that the dawn yields to the day after the darkness of the night. The Song of Songs says aptly: 'Who is this who moves forward like the advancing dawn?' Holy Church, inasmuch as she keeps searching for the rewards of eternal life, has been called the dawn. When she turns her back on the darkness of sins, she begins to shine with the light of righteousness.

This reference to the dawn in Scripture conjures up a still more subtle consideration. Although dawn intimates that the night is over, it does not yet proclaim the arrival of the full light of day. While it dispels the darkness and welcomes the light, it holds both of them in tension, the one mixed with the other, as it were. Are not all of us who follow the truth in this life daybreak and dawn? While we do some things which already belong to the light, we are not yet free from the remnants of darkness. In Scripture the

Psalmist says to God: 'No one living can be justified in your sight.' Scripture also says: 'In many ways all of us give offence.'

When Paul writes that 'the night is passed,' it is interesting to note that he does not add, 'the day is come,' but rather, 'the day is at hand.' Since he argues that after the night has passed, the day has not yet fully come but is rather at hand, he shows that the period before full daylight and after darkness is without doubt the period of dawn, and that he sees himself as living in that period.

It will be fully day for the Church of the elect when she is no longer darkened by the shadow of sin. It will be fully day for her when she shines with the perfect brilliance of interior light. This dawn reaches after the brightness of eternal day, that perfect clearness of eternal vision. When the dawn has been brought to that fulfilment, the Church will retain nothing belonging to the darkness of night. In the words of the Psalmist: 'My soul thirsts for the living God; when shall I come and see the face of God?' Does he not refer to the effort made by the dawn to reach this place of consummation? Paul himself was hastening to such a place when he wrote that he wished to die and to be with Christ. He expressed the same idea when he said: 'For me to live is Christ, and to die is gain.'

Dedication Festival

A Reading from a homily of Origen
on the Book of Joshua

All of us who believe in Christ Jesus are said to be living stones, according to the words of Scripture: 'Like living stones, let yourselves be built into a spiritual house, to be a holy priesthood, to offer spiritual sacrifices acceptable to God through Jesus Christ.'

When we look at the construction of earthly buildings, we can see how the largest and strongest stones are always set in the foundations, so that the weight of the whole building can rest securely on them. In the same way you should understand how some of the living stones referred to by Scripture have become the foundations of a spiritual building. And who are those foundation stones? The apostles and the prophets. This is what Paul himself declares in his teaching: 'You are built upon the foundation of the apostles and prophets, Christ Jesus himself being the cornerstone.'

You should learn that Christ himself is also the foundation of the building we are describing, so that you may more eagerly prepare yourselves for the construction, and be found to be one of those stones strong enough to be laid close to the foundation. For these are the words of Paul the Apostle, 'No other foundation can anyone lay than that which is laid, namely Christ Jesus.' Blessed are those, therefore, who will be found to have constructed sacred and religious buildings upon such a glorious foundation!

But in this building of the Church there must also be an altar. From this I conclude that those of you who are ready and prepared to give up your time to prayer, to offer petitions and sacrifices of supplication to God day and night, such people I say will be the living stones out of which Jesus will build his altar.

Reflect upon the praise that is lavished upon these stones of the altar. 'Moses the lawgiver', Joshua said, 'ordered that an altar be built out of unhewn stones, untouched by a chisel.' Who now are these unhewn stones? Perhaps these unhewn, undefiled stones could be said to be the holy apostles, who together make one altar by reason of their harmony and unity. For Scripture tells that, as the apostles prayed together with one accord they opened their mouths and said, 'You, Lord, know the hearts of all.'

These then, who were able to pray with one mind, with one voice and in one spirit, are perhaps worthy of being employed together to form an altar upon which Jesus may offer his sacrifice to the Father.

But let us too strive to be of one mind among ourselves, and to speak with one heart and voice. Let us never act out of anger or vainglory, but united in belief and purpose, let us hope that God may find us stones fit for his altar.

alternative reading

A Reading from a sermon of Augustine

We are gathered together to celebrate the dedication of a house of prayer. This is our house of prayer, but we too are a house of God. If we are a house of God, its construction goes on in time so that it may be dedicated at the end of time. The house, in its construction, involved hard work, while its dedication is an occasion for rejoicing.

What was done when this church was being built is similar to what is done when believers are built up into Christ. When they first come to believe they are like timber and stone taken from woods and mountains. In their instruction, baptism and formation they are, so to speak, shaped, levelled and smoothed by the hands of carpenters and craftsmen.

But Christians do not make a house of God until they are one in charity. The timber and stone must fit together in an orderly plan, must be joined in perfect harmony, must give each other the support of love, or no one would enter the building. When you see the stones and beams of a building holding together securely, you enter the building with an easy mind; you are not afraid of it falling down around you in ruins.

Christ the Lord wants to come in to us and dwell in us. Like a good builder he says: 'A new commandment I give you: love one another.' He says: 'I give you a commandment.' He means: Before, you were not engaged in building a house for me, but you lay in ruins. Therefore, to be raised up from your former state of ruin you must love one another.

Remember that this house is still in the process of being built in the whole world: this is the promise of prophecy. When God's house was being built after the Exile, it was prophesied, in the words of a psalm: 'Sing a new song to the Lord; sing to the Lord, all the earth.' For 'new song' our Lord speaks of 'a new commandment'. A new song implies a new inspiration of love. To sing is a sign of love. The singer of this new song is full of the warmth of God's love.

The work we see complete in this building is physical; it should find its spiritual counterpart in your hearts. We see here the finished product of stone and wood; so too your lives should reveal the handiwork of God's grace.

Let us then offer our thanksgiving above all to the Lord our God, from whom every best and perfect gift comes. Let us praise his goodness with our whole heart. He it was who inspired in his faithful people the will to build this house of prayer; he stirred up their desire and gave them his help. He awakened enthusiasm among those who were at first unconvinced, and guided to a successful conclusion the efforts of people of goodwill. So God, 'who gives to those of goodwill both the desire and the accomplishment' of the things that belong to him, is the one who began this work, and the one who has brought it to completion.

alternative reading

A Reading from *The Country Parson* by George Herbert

The Country Parson hath a special care of his church that all things there be decent and befitting his Name by which it is called. Therefore first he takes order that all things be in good repair; as walls plastered, windows glazed, floor paved, seats whole, firm and uniform, especially that the pulpit, and desk, and communion table and font be as they ought, for those great duties that are performed in them.

Secondly, that the church be swept and kept clean without dust or cobwebs, and at great festivals strawed and stuck with boughs and perfumed with incense.

Thirdly, that there be fit and proper texts of Scripture everywhere painted, and that all the painting be grave and reverend, not with light colours or foolish antics.

Fourthly, that all the books appointed by authority be there, and those not torn or fouled, but whole and clean and well bound; and that there be a fitting and sightly communion cloth of fine linen, with an handsome and seemly carpet of good and costly stuff or cloth, and all kept sweet and clean in a strong and decent chest with a chalice and cover, and a stoop or flagon; and a basin for alms and offerings, besides which he hath a poor-man's box conveniently sited to receive the charity of well-minded people, and to lay up treasure for the sick and needy.

And all this he doth, not as out of necessity, or as putting a holiness in the things, but as desiring to keep the middle way between superstition and slovenliness.

ORDINARY TIME
BEFORE ADVENT

When has a time existed when God has not reigned? The
kingdom of God is rooted in us through the blood of
Christ's passion, and we have the privilege of being its first
subjects. We pray, therefore, that we may reign with
Christ, sharing in his sovereignty, as he has promised.

Cyprian of Carthage

During the period of **Ordinary Time** between All Saints' Day and Advent Sunday the Church reflects upon the reign of Christ in earth and heaven. Historically, the season of Advent has been of variable length. Thus the designation of these four weeks before Advent as a liturgical season with its own distinctive emphases is not the innovation it may appear. In part it is a concomitant of the relentless encroachment of Christmas upon the proper observance of Advent; in part it is simply a recognition of the 'feel' of November with its various 'remembrances', personal and national.

The section begins with readings for **All Saints' Sunday** – if this is observed in preference to the Fourth Sunday before Advent. Additional readings may be found under **All Saints' Day** in the companion volume *Celebrating the Saints,* pp.399-404. Readings for the **Fourth Sunday before Advent**, and for the rest of the season, then follow.

Many of the eschatological themes of Advent are pre-echoed in the readings. They include reflections upon the nature of sanctity, heaven and hell, mortality, judgement, the kingdom of God and the beatific vision. The readings reflect the liturgical movement from All Saints' Day to Advent in which the theme of kingship provides the thread which weaves and binds the season together. This comes naturally into focus on the last Sunday of the Year with a celebration of **Christ the King.**

Special readings suitable for **Remembrance Sunday** are printed separately at the conclusion of the section. If desired, these may be supplemented by those offered for the **Commemoration of the Faithful Departed** (All Souls' Day) to be found in *Celebrating the Saints,* pp.404-8.

All Saints' Sunday

A Reading from the Letter of Clement of Rome
to the Church in Corinth

My dear friends, it is the example of the righteous that we must make our own. It is written: 'Seek the company of the saints, for those who seek their company shall be sanctified.' There is also another passage in Scripture which states: 'With the innocent you will be innocent, and with the chosen you will also be chosen; likewise with the perverse you will deal perversely.' So let us take the innocent and the just as our companions; for they are God's chosen ones.

Why is there all this quarrelling and bad feeling, divisions and even war among you? Have we not all the same God, and the same Christ? Do we not possess the same Spirit of grace which was given to us? Have we not the same calling in Christ? Then why do we tear apart and divide the body of Christ? Why do we revolt against our own body? Why do we reach such a pitch of insanity that we forget that we are members one of another? Do not forget the words of Jesus our Lord: 'Woe to that person; it would be better for such a person never to have been born rather than to upset one of my chosen ones. Indeed it would be better for such a person to have a great millstone round the neck and be drowned in the sea rather than lead astray one of my chosen ones.' Your disunity has led many astray, has made many doubt, has made many despair, and has brought grief upon us all. And still your rebellion continues.

Read again the letter of blessed Paul the apostle. What did he write to you at the beginning of his ministry? Even then you had developed factions. So Paul, inspired by the Holy Spirit, wrote to you concerning himself and Cephas and Apollos. Perhaps that division was less culpable because you were supporting apostles of high reputation and a person approved by them.

We should put an end to this division immediately. Let us fall down before our Master and implore his mercy with our tears. Then he will be reconciled to us and restore us to the practice of loving one another as befits us who are Christians. For this is indeed the gate of righteousness that leads to life, as it is written: 'Open to me the gates of righteousness. When I have entered there, I shall praise the Lord. This is the gate of the Lord; the righteous shall enter through it.'

There are many gates which stand open before you, but the gate of righteousness is the gateway of Christ. All who enter through this gate are blessed, pursuing their way in holiness and righteousness, performing all their tasks without discord. A Christian may be faithful, may have the power to utter hidden mysteries, may be discriminating in the evaluation of what is said, and pure in actions. But the greater a person seems to be, the more humbly they ought to act, and the more zealous for the common good they should be rather than for their own self-interest.

alternative reading

A Reading from a hymn by Thomas Ken

All praise to thee, in light array'd
Who light thy dwelling-place hast made:
A boundless ocean of bright beams
From thy all-glorious Godhead streams.

Bless'd angels, while we silent lie,
You hallelujahs sing on high;
You joyful hymn the Ever-blest
Before the throne, and never rest.

I with your choir celestial join
In off'ring up a hymn divine;
With you in heaven I hope to dwell,
And bid the night and world farewell.

My soul, when I shake off this dust,
Lord, in thy arms I will entrust;
O make me thy peculiar care,
Some mansion for my soul prepare.

O may I always ready stand,
With my lamp burning in my hand!
May I in sight of heaven rejoice,
Whene'er I hear the bridegroom's voice.

Shine on me, Lord, new life impart,
Fresh ardours kindle in my heart;
One ray of thy all-quick'ning light
Dispels the sloth and clouds of night.

Praise God, from whom all blessings flow,
Praise him, all creatures here below;
Praise him above, ye heav'nly host,
Praise Father, Son, and Holy Ghost.

Fourth Sunday before Advent

A Reading from a treatise on the Creed
by Thomas Aquinas

It is fitting that the end of all our desires, namely eternal life, coincides with the words at the end of the creed: 'Life everlasting. Amen.'

The first point about eternal life is that humanity is united with God. For God himself is the reward and end of all our labours: 'I am your protector and your supreme reward.' This union consists in seeing God perfectly: 'At present we are looking at a confused reflection in a mirror, but then we shall see face to face.'

Next it consists in perfect praise, according to the words of the prophet: 'Joy and happiness will be found in it, thanksgiving and words of praise.'

It also consists in the complete satisfaction of desire, for there the blessed will be given more than they wanted or hoped for. The reason is that in this life no one can fulfil their longings, nor can any creature satisfy human desire. Only God satisfies, he infinitely exceeds all other pleasures. That is why we can rest in nothing but God. As Augustine says: 'You have made us for yourself, Lord, and our hearts are restless until they rest in you.'

Since in their heavenly home the saints will possess God completely, obviously their longing will be satisfied, and their glory will be even greater. That is why the Lord says: 'Enter into the joy of your Lord.' Augustine adds: 'The fullness of joy will not enter into those who rejoice, but those who rejoice will enter into joy. I shall be satisfied when your glory is seen.'

Whatever is delightful is there in superabundance. If delights are sought, there is supreme and most perfect delight. It is said of

God, the supreme good: 'Boundless delights are in your right hand.'

Again, eternal life consists of the joyous community of all the blessed, a community of supreme delight, since everyone will share all that is good with all the blessed. Everyone will love everyone else as they love themselves, and therefore will rejoice in another's good as in their own. So it follows that the happiness and joy of each grows in proportion to the joy of all.

Monday after 4 before Advent

A Reading from a homily of Gregory of Nyssa

Those who see God possess in this act of seeing everything that is good: eternal life, eternal incorruption, unfailing bliss. With these things we shall experience the joy of the eternal kingdom in which happiness is secure; we shall see the true light and hear the delightful voice of the Spirit; we shall exult unceasingly in all that is good in the inaccessible glory of God. This is the magnificent consummation of our hope held out to us by the promise of Christ: 'Blessed are the pure in heart, for they shall see God.'

However, since this seeing is dependent upon our purity of heart, my mind grows dizzy lest it should prove impossible to achieve because what is required of us exceeds our capacity. What do we gain from knowing that we can see God if at the same time we also know that the mind will always find it impossible to do so? It would be just as if someone said that it is blessed to be in heaven because only then can we contemplate what cannot be seen in this life. On the other hand, what if Jesus' words were also pointing out to us the means by which we journey to heaven? Surely it would be valuable for people to know how blessed it is to be there? But then again, as long as the ascent is still declared to be impossible, what is the use of knowing about the bliss of heaven? It only serves to depress those who have learnt about it to realise the things of which they are to be deprived because the ascent is not feasible.

But why should the Lord command something that vastly exceeds our nature and the limits of our power? Surely this is wrong reasoning! God does not instruct those without wings to become birds, nor does he demand those creatures who dwell on the earth to live in the water. The law is adapted to suit the capacities of each in every aspect of life: God never enforces anything contrary to its nature. So we also should realise that nothing is being set forth in this beatitude that outstrips hope. We shall see God.

Tuesday after 4 before Advent

A Reading from *A Serious Call to a Devout and Holy Life* by William Law

If you consider devotion only as a time of so much prayer, you may perhaps perform it though you live in this daily indulgence. But if you consider it as a state of the heart, as a lively fervour of the soul that is deeply affected with a sense of its own misery and infirmities and desiring the Spirit of God more than all things in the world, you will find that the spirit of indulgence and the spirit of prayer cannot subsist together. Mortification of all kinds is the very life and soul of piety, but he that has not so small a degree of it as to be able to be early at his prayers can have no reason to think that he has taken up his cross and is following Christ.

When you read the Scriptures, you see a religion that is all life and spirit and joy in God, that supposes our souls risen from earthly desires and bodily indulgences to prepare for another body, another world, and other enjoyments. You see Christians represented as temples of the Holy Ghost, as children of the day, as candidates for an eternal crown, as watchful virgins that have their lamps always burning in expectation of the bridegroom. But can he be thought to have this joy in God, this care of eternity, this watchful spirit, who has not zeal enough to rise to his prayers?

When you look into the writings and lives of the first Christians, you see the same spirit that you see in the Scriptures. All is reality, life, and action. Watching and prayers, self-denial and mortification, was the common business of their lives. From that time to this, there has been no person like them eminent for piety who has not like them been eminent for self-denial and mortification. This is the only royal way that leads to a kingdom.

Wednesday after 4 before Advent

A Reading from *Abandonment to Divine Providence*
by Jean-Pierre de Caussade

God wishes to dwell in us in poverty and without the obvious accessories of holiness which can cause people to be admired. This is because he wishes to be alone the food of our hearts, the sole object of our desiring. We are so weak that if the splendour of austerity, zeal, almsgiving or poverty were to shine out in us, we would take pride in it. Instead, in our way of following Christ, there is nothing but what seems unattractive, and by this means God is able to become the sole means of us achieving holiness, the whole of our support. Meanwhile the world despises us and leaves us to enjoy our treasure in peace.

God wishes to be the sole principle of our sanctity, and for that reason all that depends on us is our active fidelity which is very trifling. Indeed, in God's sight there can be nothing great in us – with one exception: our total receptivity to his will. God knows how to make us holy, so let us stop worrying about it and leave the business of it to God. All depends on the special protection and operation of providence; our sanctification will occur unknown to us and through those very things which we dislike most and expect least.

Let us walk peacefully, then, in the small duties of our life, in active fidelity, without aspiring to great things, for God will not give himself to us for the sake of any exaggerated effort that we make in this matter. We will become saints through the grace of God and by his special providence. He knows the eminence to which he will raise us; let us leave it to him to do as he pleases. Without forming false ideas and vain systems of spirituality, let us be content to love God without ceasing, walking in simplicity along the road which he has traced for us, a road where everything seems so insignificant to our eyes and to those of the world.

Thursday after 4 before Advent

A Reading from *Centuries of Meditations*
by Thomas Traherne

The best of all possible ends is the glory of God, but happiness was what I thirsted after. And yet I did not err, for the glory of God is to make us happy which can never be done but by giving us most excellent natures and satisfying those natures: by creating all treasures of infinite value, and giving them to us in an infinite manner: to wit, both in the best that to omnipotence was possible. This led me to enquire whether all things were excellent, and of perfect value, and whether they were mine in propriety.

It is the glory of God to give all things to us in the best of all possible manners. To study things therefore under the double notion of interest and treasure, is to study all things in the best of all possible manners. Because in studying so we enquire after God's glory, and our own happiness. And indeed enter into the way that leadeth to all contentments, joys, and satisfactions; to all praises, triumphs and thanksgivings; to all virtues, beauties, adorations and graces; to all dominion, exaltation, wisdom and glory; to all holiness, union and communication with God; to all patience and courage and blessedness which it is impossible to meet any other way. So that to study objects for ostentation, vain knowledge or curiosity is fruitless impertinence, though God himself and angels be the object. But to study that which will oblige us to love him, and feed us with nobility and goodness toward men, that is blessed. And so is it to study that which will lead us to the temple of wisdom, and seat us in the throne of glory.

Friday after 4 before Advent

A Reading from *The Mirror of Charity*
by Aelred of Rievaulx

In heaven there is nothing except true and eternal love, an eternity spent in the delight of love and in the enjoyment of truth, in the beholding of the eternal, true and most loveable Trinity. In heaven alone is the rest and peace of happiness perfectly possessed. Why then do we rush around all over the place, driven by anxiety? Why are we so absorbed in trivia? Whatever we seek and wherever we seek it, ultimately it can be found in God alone. Excellence, knowledge, riches, delight – all are to be found in heaven, and only there, in their perfection.

Does this world's pit of death and miry clay yield true excellence? Can there be perfect knowledge when we live under the shadow of death? What real delight can be found in this howling wilderness, this barren desert? There is no excellence in this world that is immune to fear, no knowledge in a person who does not know himself, no delight in earthly things that will not ultimately render us like a horse or mule. If your pleasure is in the pursuit of glory or riches, remember you can take nothing with you when death claims you, nor will your earthly glory have any power in the land of the dead. True excellence is to be found only where ambition can yearn for nothing higher, true knowledge only where nothing escapes its grasp, true delight only where nothing can ever vitiate the pleasure, true riches only where the possession of them can never be exhausted.

It was a sad day when we ran away from you, O Lord. Our exile drags on, and we yearn to know when we will come and see your face. O that we had the wings of a dove, so that we could fly away to you and in you find our rest! Meanwhile, Lord Jesus, I beg you to allow my soul to grow wings in the nest of your teaching. May my soul embrace you who was crucified for me, and drink the life-giving draught of your precious blood. May the thought of you and your passion dominate my memory so that the fog of forgetfulness does not obscure you. Until I come before your face I will shun all knowledge except that of my crucified Lord, lest the untruth of error undermine the foundations of my faith. May all my love be directed to you, lest its energy be frittered away in useless desires.

Saturday after 4 before Advent

A Reading from an essay entitled 'The Weight of Glory'
by C. S. Lewis

We do not want merely to *see* beauty. We want something else which can hardly be put into words – to be united with the beauty we see, to pass into it, to receive it into ourselves, to bathe in it, to become part of it. That is why we have peopled air and earth and water with gods and goddesses and nymphs and elves – that, though we cannot, yet these projections can, enjoy themselves that beauty, grace and power of which nature is the image.

For if we take the imagery of Scripture seriously, if we believe that God will one day give us the morning star and cause us to put on the splendour of the sun, then we may surmise that both the ancient myths and the modern poetry, so false as history, may be very near the truth as prophecy. At present we are on the outside of the world, the wrong side of the door. We discern the freshness and purity of morning, but they do not make us fresh and pure. We cannot mingle with the splendours we see. But all the leaves of the New Testament are rustling with the rumour that it will not always be so. Someday, God willing, we shall get in. When human souls have become perfect in voluntary obedience as the inanimate creation is in its lifeless obedience, they will put on its glory, or, rather, that greater glory of which nature is only the first sketch. We are summoned to pass in through nature, beyond her, into that splendour which she fitfully reflects.

Third Sunday before Advent

A Reading from the Letter of Clement of Rome
to the Church in Corinth

Let those who claim to be filled by the love of Christ keep his commandments. Who can express the binding power of the love of God? Who can find words for the splendour of its beauty? Nobody can describe the heights to which it lifts us. Love binds us fast to God; it cancels innumerable sins, it has no limits to its endurance, and bears everything patiently. Love is neither servile nor arrogant. It does not provoke divisions or form cliques, but always acts in harmony with others. It was by love that all God's chosen saints have been sanctified; without love, it is impossible to please God. It was in love that the Lord drew us to himself; because he loved us and it was God's will, our Lord Jesus Christ gave his life's blood for us – he gave his body for our body, his soul for our soul.

See then, my dear friends, what a great and wonderful thing love is, and how inexpressible its perfection. Who are worthy to possess it unless God makes them so? To him therefore we must turn, begging of his mercy that there may be found in us a love free from human partiality and beyond reproach. Every generation from Adam's time to ours has passed away; but those who by God's grace were made perfect in love have a dwelling now among the saints, and when at last Christ's kingdom of love appears, they will be revealed. For as Scripture says: 'Take shelter in your rooms for a little while until my rage subsides. Then I will remember the good days, and will raise you from your graves.'

Happy are we, my friends, if love enables us to live in harmony and in the observance of God's commandments, for then it will also gain for us the forgiveness of our sins. Scripture says: 'Blessed are those whose iniquities are pardoned, whose sins are forgiven. Blessed are they', it says, 'to whom the Lord imputes no blame, on whose lips there is found no guile.' This is the blessing given those whom God has chosen through Jesus Christ our Lord. To him be glory for ever and ever.

Monday after 3 before Advent

A Reading from *The Power and Meaning of Love*
by Thomas Merton

The history of the Church is a confusion of successes and apparent failures of Christianity. It is in fact an ever-repeated series of attempts to begin constructing the kingdom of God on earth. This is not surprising, nor is it something Christ himself failed to foresee. The parable of the wheat and the tares shows clearly that he had this in mind, and that it accords with his Father's plan.

The kingdom of God is not the kingdom of those who merely preach a doctrine or follow certain religious practices: it is the kingdom of those who love. To build the kingdom of God is to build a society that is based entirely on freedom and love. It is to build a society which is founded on respect for the individual person, since only persons are capable of love.

One cannot help getting the impression that this is not sufficiently well understood in our day. Love is a word that has been emptied of content by our materialistic society. In our world 'love' is reduced to infatuation. Genuine love cannot be taken for granted. We Christians, however, seem to do. We seem to feel that 'we love one another' and that we know very well what love is. We tend to act as if things were so regulated by love in our household that we could safely forget about it and go out to preach to others. Hence we are not worried about love, so much as doctrine. At all costs we want to get everyone to agree with us, and to accept our beliefs.

In this way we tend to become proselytisers rather than apostles. That is to say that we are looking for 'members' who, by their numbers and their material support will bolster up our own faith and give us more confidence in the doctrine that we preach.

The true apostle, however, is not preaching a doctrine or leading a movement or recruiting for an organisation: he is preaching Christ, because he loves others and knows that thus he can bring them happiness, and give meaning to their lives. The proselytiser is selling his doctrine because he needs proselytes. The apostle is preaching Christ because people need the mercy of God and because only in the love of Christ can they find happiness.

Tuesday after 3 before Advent

A Reading from a sermon of Augustine

Let us sing 'Alleluia' here and now in this life, even though we are oppressed by various worries, so that we may sing it one day in the world to come when we are set free from all anxiety. Why is it that we worry so much in this life? I suppose it is hardly surprising that we should worry when I read in the Scriptures: 'Are not the days of our life full of trouble?' Are you surprised that I am worried when I hear the words: 'Watch and pray that you enter not into temptation'? Are you surprised that I am worried when in the face of so many temptations and troubles the Lord's Prayer orders us to pray: 'Forgive us our debts as we also forgive our debtors'? Every day we pray and every day we sin.

But how happy will be our shout of 'Alleluia' as we enter heaven, how carefree, how secure from any assault, where no enemy lurks and no friend dies. There praise is offered to God, and here also; but here it is offered by anxious people, there by those who have been freed from all anxiety; here by those who must die, there by those who will live for ever. Here praise is offered in hope, there by those who enjoy the reality; here by pilgrims in transit, there by those who have reached their homeland.

So my dear friends, let us sing 'Alleluia', albeit not yet in the enjoyment of our heavenly rest, but in order to sweeten our toil in this life. Let us sing as travellers sing on a journey in order to help them keep on walking. Lighten your toil by singing and never be idle. Sing and keep on walking. And what do I mean by walking? I mean press on from good to better in this life. The apostle Paul says that there will be those who go from bad to worse; but if you persevere, you will indeed keep on walking. Advance in virtue, in true faith and in right conduct. Sing up – and keep on walking!

Wednesday after 3 before Advent

A Reading from a homily on the Book of Ecclesiastes
by Gregory of Nyssa

'There is a time to be born and a time to die.' The fact that there is a natural link between birth and death is expressed very clearly in this text of Scripture. Death invariably follows birth, and everyone who is born comes at last to the grave.

'There is a time to be born and a time to die.' God grant that mine may be a timely birth and a timely death! Of course, no one imagines that the Speaker regards as acts of virtue our natural birth and death, in neither of which our own will plays any part. A woman does not give birth because she chooses to do so, neither does anyone die as a result of one's own decision. Obviously, there is neither virtue nor vice in anything that lies beyond our control. So we must consider what is meant by a timely birth and a timely death.

It seems to me that the birth referred to here is our salvation, as is suggested by the prophet Isaiah. This reaches its full term and is not stillborn when, having been conceived by the fear of God, the soul's own birth-pangs bring it to the light of day. We are in a sense our own parents, and we give birth to ourselves by our own free choice of what is good. Such a choice becomes possible for us when we have received God into ourselves and have become children of God, children of the Most High. On the other hand, if what the Apostle calls 'the form of Christ' has not been produced in us, we abort ourselves. The child of God must reach maturity.

Now if the meaning of a timely birth is clear, so also is the meaning of a timely death. For St Paul every moment was a time to die, as he proclaims in his letters: 'I swear by the pride I take in you that I face death every day.' Elsewhere he says, 'For your sake we are put to death daily' and 'we felt like those condemned to death.' How Paul died daily is perfectly obvious. He never gave himself up to a sinful life but kept his body under constant control. He carried death with him, Christ's death, wherever he went. He was always being crucified with Christ. It was not his own life he lived; it was Christ who lived in him. This surely was a timely death – a death whose end was true life.

'I put to death and I shall give life,' God says, teaching us that death to sin and life in the Spirit is his gift, and promising that whatever he puts to death he will restore to life again.

Thursday after 3 before Advent

A Reading from a meditation of John Donne

Now this bell, tolling softly for another, says to me,
'Thou must die.'

Perchance he for whom this bell tolls may be so ill, as that he knows not it tolls for him; and perchance I may think myself so much better than I am, as that they who are about me and see my state may have caused it to toll for me, and I know not that.

The Church is Catholic, universal; so are all her actions. All that she does, belongs to all. When she baptizes a child, that action concerns me; for that child is thereby connected to that Head which is my Head, too, and engrafted into that Body whereof I am a member. And when she buries a man, that action concerns me. All mankind is of one Author, and is one volume. When one man dies, one chapter is not torn out of the book, but translated into a better language; and every chapter must be so translated. God employs several translators: some pieces are translated by age, some by sickness, some by war, some by justice. But God's hand is in every translation; and his hand shall bind up all our scattered leaves again, for that library where every book shall lie open to one another. As therefore the bell that rings to a sermon calls not upon the preacher only, but upon the congregation to come; so this bell calls us all – but how much the more me who am brought so near the door by this sickness.

There was a contention so far as a suit (in which both piety and dignity, religion and estimation were mingled), which of the religious orders should ring to prayers first in the morning; and it was determined that they should ring first that rose earliest. If we understand aright the dignity of this bell that tolls for our evening prayer, we would be glad to make it ours by rising early, in that application, that it might be ours as well as his whose indeed it is. The bell doth toll for him that thinks it doth; and though it intermit again, yet from that minute that that occasion wrought upon him, he is united to God. Who casts not up his eye to the sun when it rises? But who takes off his eye from a comet, when that breaks out? Who bends not his ear to any bell which upon any occasion rings? But who can remove it from that bell which is passing a piece of himself out of this world?

No man is an island, entire of itself; every man is a piece of the continent, a part of the main. If a clod be washed away by the sea, Europe is the less, as well as if a promontory were, as well as if a manor of thy friends or of thine own were. Any man's death diminishes me, because I am involved in mankind. And therefore never send to know for whom the bell tolls; it tolls for thee.

Neither can we call this a begging of misery or a borrowing of misery, as though we were not miserable enough of ourselves, but must fetch in more from the next house, in taking upon us the misery of our neighbours. Truly it were an excusable covetousness if we did; for affliction is a treasure, and scarce any man hath enough of it. No man hath affliction enough that is not matured and ripened by it, and made fit for God by that affliction. If a man carry treasure in bullion or in a wedge of gold, and have none coined into current monies, his treasure will not defray him as he travels. Tribulation is treasure in the nature of it, but it is not current money in the use of it, except we get nearer and nearer our home, heaven, by it. Another man may be sick, too, and sick to death; and this affliction may lie in his bowels as gold in a mine and be of no use to him. But this bell that tells me of his affliction digs out and applies that gold to me, if by this consideration of another's danger I take mine own into contemplation, and so secure myself by making my recourse to my God, who is our only security.

Friday after 3 before Advent

A Reading from the *Meditations* of Richard Challoner

Consider that death is the passage from time to eternity. If we die well, it will be well with us for all eternity; but if we die ill, it will be ill with us for endless ages; so that upon this one moment of death depends a long eternity. But when shall this moment come? When shall we die? Shall it be this night or tomorrow? Shall it be a week, a month, a year hence? Oh, of all this we know nothing at all, only that it will be when we least look for it. For our Lord has assured us, that he will come like a thief in the night; that is when we least think on it. And therefore he tells us we must always watch, and always be ready, for if we are surprised and die in our sins we are lost for ever.

Consider, secondly, that we are not only wholly ignorant of the time of our death, but also of all other circumstances relating to it.

We neither know the place where we shall die, nor the manner how we shall die; nor whether our death will be violent or natural, by fever or consumption, gentle or sharp, of quick despatch, or more lingering, at home or abroad, whether our last illness will deprive us of our senses or no; whether we shall have the assistance of our ghostly father, and the helps of the sacraments; what dispositions our souls will then be in; or what ability we shall then have to make proper use of those last moments upon which our all depends for eternity. Alas! all these things are quite hidden from us; no wit, no learning, no wisdom upon earth can help any man to the knowledge of any one of these things. O let this dreadful uncertainty of all the particulars that relate to our death determine us to live always in the expectation and preparation for death; that we may not have that great work to do at a time when we shall have no convenience or ability to do it.

Consider, thirdly, that death being so certain, and the time and manner of it uncertain, it would be no small satisfaction to a poor sinner if he could die more than once; that so, if he had the misfortune once to do ill, he might repair the fault, by taking more care a second time. But alas! we can die but once, and when once we have set our foot within the gates of eternity, there is no coming back, and if it be a miserable eternity into which we have stepped, there is no redemption; we pass from death to a second death, to the very extremity of misery, without end or remedy. O how hard it is to do that well which we can do but once, and can never try or practise beforehand! O my soul, see then thou take care to study well this important lesson by a continual preparation for death.

Conclude to make it the great business of thy life to learn to die well. Remember there is no security against an evil death but a good life; everything else leaves thee exposed to dreadful uncertainties.

Saturday after 3 before Advent

A Reading from the *Meditations* of
William of St Thierry

Your heavenly stars do not shine for me, Lord; the sun is darkened and the moon gives no light. In psalms and hymns and spiritual songs I hear your mighty acts proclaimed; out of your Gospels your words and deeds shine forth at me, and the example of your servants strikes unceasingly upon my eyes and ears. Your promises in Scripture, the promises your Truth has made, obtruding themselves without ceasing upon my sight and battering my deafness with their din, shake me with fears and taunt me. But long persistence in bad ways, along with very great insensibility of mind, has hardened me. I have learned to sleep with the sunshine full on my face, and have grown used to it. I have become accustomed to not seeing what takes place before my eyes and, dead at heart as I am, though I am set in the midst of the sea, I have ceased to hear the roaring of its waves and the thunder of the sky.

How long, O Lord, how long? How long will you defer to rend the heavens and come down? How long will you delay to fulfil your wrath upon me, and so to shatter my dullness that I may be no longer what I am, but may know that it is you who rules Jacob and the utmost bounds of earth, and so be turned, at least at eventide, and hunger like a dog that runs about your city – your city of which a portion sojourns still on earth but the greater part rejoices already in heaven – so that maybe I may find some who will receive my fainting soul into their habitation, my soul that has no couch of her own on which to lay her head?

Sometimes indeed I hear your Spirit's voice, and, though it is no more than as the whistling of a gentle air that passes me, I understand the message: 'Come unto him and be enlightened.' I hear, and I am shaken. Arising as from sleep and shaking off my lethargy, a certain wonder fills me. I open my mouth and I draw in my breath; I stretch my spiritual muscles and rouse them from their sloth. I turn my back on the shades of night in which my conscience lies and come forth to the Sun of Righteousness who is rising now for me. But I am drowsy still, and the eyes of my reason are dazzled when I try to look at him. For they are used to darkness and unaccustomed to the light; and, while both pupils and eyelids tremble and blink at the unwonted brightness, as best I can I wipe the rheum of my long sleep from them with the hand of exercise. If by your gift I find a fount of tears such as is wont to spring up speedily in lowly ground and in the valleys of a contrite soul, I wash the hands with which I work and the face I lift in prayer.

Then, as the falcon spreads his wings towards the south to make his feathers grow, I stretch out my two hands to you, O Lord. My soul is as waterless ground in your sight; and as desert land, unwatered and untrodden, I appear before you in your holy place, that I may see your power and your glory.

Second Sunday before Advent

A Reading from *Revelations of Divine Love*
by Julian of Norwich

God will not have perfect pleasure in us until we find our perfect pleasure in him, seeing his beautiful and blessed face in truth. This is why we have been born, and what we achieve by grace. This is how I saw that sin is only mortal for a short while in those who are blessed with eternal life.

The more clearly the soul sees the blessed face by grace and love, the more it longs to see it in its fullness. Notwithstanding that our Lord God lives in us, and is here with us; notwithstanding that he clasps and enfolds us in his tender love, never to leave us; notwithstanding that he is nearer to us than tongue and heart can think or tell, the fact remains that we shall never cease from sighs, complaints, or tears – or longing – till we see clearly his blessed face. In that precious, blessed sight, no grief can live, no blessing fail.

In this I saw reason for cheer, and reason for sighing; cheer in that our Lord and Maker is so near us; he is in us, and we are in him, completely safe through his great goodness; sighing in that we are so spiritually blind and weighed down by our mortal flesh and murky sin that we cannot clearly see our Lord's blessed face. No, and because of this murkiness we have difficulty in believing and trusting his great love and our complete safety. And therefore I say that we never cease from sighs or tears.

Tears do not mean physical tears of the eye only, but also the inner weeping of the spirit. For the natural desire of the soul is so vast and immeasurable that were it to be given for our comfort and solace all the finest that God has made in heaven and earth, but could not see the beautiful and blessed face of himself, our sighs and spiritual tears and painful longing would never cease until we saw the blessed countenance of our Maker. On the other hand, were we to be in the utmost pain that tongue and heart can think or tell, if then we could see his blessed face, none of this pain would distress us. So it is that the Beatific Vision is the end of every pain to the loving soul, and the fulfilment of every joy and blessing.

Monday after 2 before Advent

A Reading from *Love's Endeavour, Love's Expense*
by W. H. Vanstone

The imagery of popular devotion suggests a divine supremacy over the universe – a supremacy such that whatever may be predicated of the universe in terms of glory, majesty or power may be predicated to a yet higher degree of God. Supremacy is not the relationship of the artist to the work of art, nor of the lover to the object of his love. That God should be superior, in every or any respect, to an inferior universe is a quite illegitimate deduction from the doctrine of creation. It is also a deduction which endangers the integrity of religion. For it tends to reduce religion to the prudent recognition of divine supremacy; to suggest that God is to be respected for the superiority of his powers and resources to any challenge or comparison that might be offered; and to make the inferiority of the creature sufficient reason for reverence and worship on the part of the creature. Respect on the part of an inferior may be dictated by prudence: but it can hardly be justified by moral sensitivity. Superiority as such confers no moral right to respect: in particular, superiority of power confers no such right.

The contemporary age has seen more clearly than precursors the moral ambiguity of power. Through the possession and exercise of ever-increasing power in his own hands, man has discovered the distinction between power and worth, and the irrelevance of the one to the other. The argument that one who is great in power should therefore be respected is seen to involve a *non sequitur*; and, psychologically, the display of power has become an obstacle rather than an assistance to respect. Power is seen as involving privilege rather than worth: why should the possession of privilege carry a further entitlement to respect? So religious imagery which displays and celebrates the supremacy of divine power neither convinces the head nor moves the heart. It is relevant only to those to whom the practice of religion is a rule of prudence. If the work of God in creation is the work of love, then truth demands an imagery which will do justice to the limitless self-giving which is among the marks of authentic love: and the imagery which the head demands may have a new power of appeal to the moral sensitivity of the heart.

If the creation is the work of love, then its shape cannot be predetermined by the Creator, nor its triumph foreknown: it is the realisation of vision, but of vision which is discovered only through its own realisation: and faith in its triumph is neither more nor less than faith in the Creator himself – faith that he will not cease from his handiwork nor abandon the object of his love. The creation is 'safe' not because it moves by programme towards a predetermined goal but because the same loving creativity is ever exercised upon it.

Tuesday after 2 before Advent

A reading from the treatise *The City of God*
by Augustine

I speak of the glorious city of God, both as it exists in this world of time, a stranger among the ungodly, living by faith, and as it stands in the secure perspective of eternity. This security it now awaits in steadfast patience, until 'justice returns to judgement', but it is to attain it hereafter in virtue of its ascendancy over its enemies, when the final victory is won and peace is established.

I am aware how difficult it is to convince the proud of the power and excellence of humility, an excellence which makes it soar above all the summits of this world, which sway in their temporal instability, overtaking them all with an eminence not arrogated by human pride, but granted by divine grace. For the King and Founder of this city has revealed in the Scriptures of his people the following statement of the divine law: 'God resists the proud, but gives grace to the humble.' This is the prerogative of God; but the human spirit in its arrogance and swelling pride has claimed it as its own.

It is evident that the two cities of which I speak were created by two kinds of love: the earthly city was created by self-love reaching the point of contempt for God, the heavenly city by the love of God carried as far as contempt for self. In fact, whereas the earthly city glories in itself, the heavenly city glories only in its Lord. The former looks for the glory bestowed by mere mortals, the latter finds its highest glory in God, the witness of a good conscience. The earthly city lifts up its head in its own glory, the heavenly city says to its God: 'You are my glory and the lifter up of my head.' In the former, the lust for power controls its functionaries and determines the fate of the nations it subjugates; in the other both those put in authority and those under them serve one another in love, the rulers by their counsel, the citizens by their obedience. The one city loves its own strength shown in its powerful leaders, the other says to its God, 'I will love you, my Lord, my strength.'

In the heavenly city there will be freedom of will. There that precept from the psalms will find fulfilment: 'Be still and know that I am God.' That will truly be the greatest of Sabbaths; a Sabbath that has no evening, the Sabbath that the Lord approved at the beginning of creation. There we shall have leisure to be still, and we shall see that he is God. It will be an eighth day, as it were, which is to last for ever, a day consecrated by the resurrection of Christ, foreshadowing the eternal rest not only of the spirit but of the body also. There we shall be still and see; we shall see and we shall love; we shall love and we shall praise. Behold what will be, in the end without end!

Wednesday after 2 before Advent

A Reading from *Le Milieu Divin*
by Pierre Teilhard de Chardin

It was a joy to me, O God, in the midst of the struggle, to feel that in developing myself I was increasing the hold that you have upon me; it was a joy to me, too, under the inward thrust of life or amid the favourable play of events, to abandon myself to your providence. Now that I have found the joy of utilising all forms of growth to make you, or to let you, grow in me, grant that I may willingly consent to this last phase of communion in the course of which I shall possess you by diminishing in you.

After having perceived you as he who is 'a greater myself', grant, when my hour comes, that I may recognise you under the species of each alien or hostile force that seems bent upon destroying or uprooting me. When the signs of age begin to mark my body (and still more when they touch my mind); when the ill that is to diminish me or carry me off strikes from without or is born within me; when the painful moment comes in which I suddenly awaken to the fact I am losing hold of myself and am absolutely passive within the hands of the great unknown forces that have formed me; in all those dark moments, O God, grant that I may understand that it is you (provided only my faith is strong enough) who are painfully parting the fibres of my being in order to penetrate to the very marrow of my substance and bear me away within yourself.

The more deeply and incurably the evil is encrusted in my flesh, the more it will be you that I am harbouring – you as a loving, active principle of purification and detachment. Vouchsafe, therefore, something more precious still than the grace for which all the faithful pray. It is not enough that I shall die while communicating. Teach me to treat my death as an act of communion.

Thursday after 2 before Advent

A Reading from *A Rule of Life for a Recluse*
by Aelred of Rievaulx

What the kingdom of God will be like we cannot even think, let alone say or write. But this I know, that nothing at all will be missing that you would wish to be there, and nothing will be there that you would not wish to be. So there will be no mourning, no weeping or pain, no fear, no sadness, no discord, no envy, no tribulation, no temptation, no variable weather, no overcast skies, no suspicion, no ambition, no adulation, no detraction, no sickness, no old age, no death, no poverty, no darkness, no need to eat, drink or sleep, no tiredness, no weakness.

What good then will be lacking? Where there is no mourning or weeping or pain or sadness, what can there be but perfect joy? Where there is no tribulation or temptation, no variable weather or overcast skies, no excessive heat or harsh winter, what can there be but perfect balance in all things and complete tranquillity of mind and body? Where there is nothing to fear, what can there be but total security? Where there is no discord, no envy, no suspicion or ambition, no adulation or detraction, what can there be but supreme and true love? Where there is no poverty and no covetousness, what can there be but abundance of all good things? Where there is no deformity, what can there be but true beauty? Where there is no toil or weakness, what will there be but utter rest and strength? Where there is nothing heavy or burdensome, what is there but the greatest ease? Where there is no prospect of old age, no fear of disease, what can there be but true health? Where there is neither night nor darkness, what will there be but perfect light? Where all death and mortality have been swallowed up, what will there be but eternal life?

What is there further for us to seek? To be sure, what surpasses all these things, that is the sight, the knowledge and the love of the

Creator. He will be seen in himself, he will be seen in all his creatures, ruling everything without anxiety, upholding everything without toil, giving himself and, so to speak, distributing himself to one and all according to their capacity without any lessening or division of himself. That loveable face, so longed for, upon which the angels yearn to gaze, will be seen. Who can say anything of its beauty, of its light, of its sweetness? The Father will be seen in the Son, the Son in the Father, and the Holy Spirit in both. He will be seen not as a confused reflection in a mirror, but face to face. For God will be seen as he is, fulfilling that promise which tells us: 'Those who love me will be loved by my Father, and I will love them and show myself to them.' From this vision will proceed that knowledge of which our Lord says: 'This is eternal life, that they should know you the one God, and him whom you sent.'

Friday after 2 before Advent

A Reading from a *Catechetical Oration*
of Gregory of Nyssa

The human body is subject to all kinds of illness. Some diseases are relatively easy to treat, others less so. In the case of resistant disease it is sometimes necessary to have recourse to surgery, cauterization, or unpleasant medicine. We are told something of the same sort about the judgement in the next world and the healing of our soul's infirmities.

If we are superficial people, the prospect of judgement will be experienced as threat: it will be viewed as a process of severe correction, with the result that sheer fear of painful expiation for our sins will prompt us to flee from wrongdoing, and we will become wiser people. On the other hand, the faith of deeper minds will view the prospect of God's judgement as a process of healing, a therapy applied by God in such a way as to restore the being he has created to its original state of grace.

Clearly, it is impossible when doctors remove boils and warts from the surface of the body, either by surgery or cauterization, not to inflict pain on their patients; but their intention in making the incision is not to cause pain, but to bring healing. It is the same when God is confronted with the blemishes that have formed on our soul. At the judgement they will indeed be cut out and removed, but the action will be performed by the ineffable wisdom and power of the One who is, as the gospel proclaims, the physician of the sick.

Saturday after 2 before Advent

A Reading from a treatise *On the Lord's Prayer*
by Cyprian of Carthage

We pray 'Your kingdom come.' In this petition we are asking that the kingdom of God may be made present to us, just as we have already prayed that God's name may be made holy in us. For when has a time existed when God has not reigned? What has already existed with God can never cease to exist any more than it can be said to have had a beginning. It is for the coming of our kingdom, the kingdom that has been promised to us, that we are praying. That kingdom was rooted in us through the blood of Christ's passion. We have the privilege of being its first subjects, and we pray that we may reign with Christ, sharing in his sovereignty, as he has promised: 'Come, you blessed of my Father, inherit the kingdom that has been in preparation for you since the beginning of the world.'

My dear brothers and sisters, it may be that Christ himself is the kingdom of God, he whom we desire each day to come, whose coming we crave to be accomplished. Since he is himself our resurrection because in him we rise again, so too he can be understood as the kingdom of God because it is in Christ that we are to reign. We do well to seek the kingdom of God, that is the kingdom of heaven, because there is also an earthly kingdom that beckons to us. Those who have renounced the world have already transcended its glitter and power. It is why in dedicating ourselves to God and to Christ, our desire should be not for earthly kingdoms, but heavenly. There is need for constant prayer and petition lest we fall away.

Sunday next before Advent

Christ the King

A Reading from a treatise *On the Consummation of the World* attributed to Hippolytus of Rome

In the holy gospel we are told that the Son of Man will gather together all nations; and that 'He will separate people one from another, as a shepherd separates sheep from goats. The sheep he will place at his right hand, the goats at his left. Then he will say to those at his right: Come, you blessed of my Father, inherit the kingdom that has been prepared for you from the foundation of the world.' Come, you lovers of the poor and strangers. Come, you who fostered my love, for I am Love. Come, you who shared peace, for I am Peace.

Come, you blessed of my Father, inherit the kingdom prepared for you who did not make an idol of wealth, who gave alms to the poor, help to orphans and widows, drink to the thirsty, and food to the hungry. Come, you who welcomed strangers, clothed the naked, visited the sick, comforted prisoners, helped the blind. Come, you who maintained your seal of faith unblemished, who were quick to assemble in the churches, who listened to my Scriptures, who attended to my words, observed my law day and night, and like good soldiers shared in my suffering because you wanted to please me, your heavenly King. 'Come, inherit the kingdom prepared for you from the foundation of the world.' Behold, my kingdom is ready, the gates of paradise stand open, my immortality is displayed in all its beauty.

Then, astonished at so magnificent a spectacle, at being called friends by him whom the angelic hosts are unable to behold entirely, the righteous will reply: 'Lord, when did we see you hungry and feed you? When did we see you thirsty and give you drink? When did we see you, whom we hold in awe, naked and clothe you? When did we see you, the immortal One, a stranger and welcome you? When did we see you, lover of our race, sick or in prison and come to visit you? You are eternal without beginning like the Father, and co-eternal with the Spirit. You are the One who created all things out of nothing; you are the King of angels; you make the depths tremble; you are clothed in light as in a garment; you are our Creator who fashioned us from the earth; you are the ruler of the invisible world. The whole earth flies from your presence. How could we possibly have received your kingly presence, your royal majesty, as our guest?'

Then the King of Kings shall say to them in reply: 'Inasmuch as you did this to one of the least of these my brothers and sisters, you did it to me.' Inasmuch as you received, clothed, fed, and gave drink to those members of my body about whom I have spoken, that is, the poor, then you did it to me. So come, enter 'the kingdom prepared for you from the foundation of the world'; enjoy for eternity the gifts of my heavenly Father, and of the most holy and life-giving Spirit. What tongue can indeed describe those blessings? For as Scripture says: 'Eye has not seen, nor ear heard, nor has the human heart conceived what God has prepared for those who love him.'

alternative reading

A Reading from a letter of Anselm to Hugh the Recluse

Those who will have the grace to reign in the kingdom of heaven will see the realisation of everything that they desire in heaven and on earth, and nothing that they do not want will be realised in heaven or on earth. The love which will unite God with those who will live there, and the latter among themselves, will be such that all will love one another as themselves, and all will love God more than themselves.

Hence, no one will have any other desire there than what God wills; and the desire of one will be the desire of all; and the desire of all and of each one will also be the desire of God. All together, and as one single person, will be one sole ruler with God, for all will desire one single thing and their desire will be realised. This is the good that, from the heights of heaven, God declares he will put on sale.

If someone asks at what price, here is the response: the one who offers a kingdom in heaven has no need of earthly money. No one can give God what already belongs to him, since everything that exists is his. Yet God does not give such a great thing unless one attaches value to it; he does not give it to one who does not appreciate it. For no one gives a prized possession to someone who attaches no value to it. Hence, although God has no need of your goods, he will not give you such a great thing as long as you disdain to love it: he requires only love, but without it nothing obliges him to give. Love, then, and you will receive the kingdom. Love, and you will possess it.

And since to reign in heaven is nothing other than to adhere to God and all the saints, through love, in a single will, to the point that all together exercise only one power, love God more than yourself and you will already begin to have what you wish to possess perfectly in heaven. Put yourself at peace with God and with others – if the latter do not separate themselves from God – and you will already begin to reign with God and all the saints. For to the extent that you now conform to the will of God and to that of the others, God and all the saints will concur with your will. Hence, if you want to rule in heaven, love God and others as you should, and you will merit to be what you desire.

However, you will not be able to possess it to perfection unless you empty your heart of every other love. This is why those who fill their hearts with love for God and their neighbour have no other will than that of God – or that of another. provided it is not contrary to God. That is why they are faithful in praying as well as in carrying on a dialogue in their minds with heaven; for it is pleasing to them to desire God and to speak of someone whom they love, to hear that one spoken about, and to think of the beloved. It is also why they rejoice with those who are joyful, weep with those who are in pain, have compassion on the suffering, and give to the poor; for they love others as themselves.

alternative reading

A Reading from *Mens Creatrix* by William Temple

It is out of the uttermost gloom (of 'My God, my God, why hast thou forsaken me?') that the light breaks. The light does not merely shine upon the gloom and so dispel it; it is the gloom itself transformed into light. For that same crucifixion of the Lord which was, and for ever is, the utmost effort of evil, is itself the means by which God conquers evil and unites us to himself in the redeeming love there manifested. Judas and Caiaphas and Pilate have set themselves in their several ways to oppose and to crush the purpose of Christ, and yet despite themselves they became ministers. They sent Christ to the cross; by the cross he completed his atoning work; from the cross he reigns over mankind. God in Christ has not merely defeated evil, but has made it the occasion of his own supreme glory.

Never was conquest so complete; never was triumph so stupendous. The completeness of the victory is due to the completeness of the evil over which it was won. It is the very darkness which enshrouds the cross that makes so glorious the light proceeding from it. Had there been no despair, no sense of desolation and defeat, but merely the onward march of irresistible power to the achievement of its end, evil might have been beaten, but not bound in captivity to love for ever. God in Christ endured defeat, and out of the very stuff of defeat he wrought his victory and his achievement.

alternative reading

A Reading from a poem by R. S. Thomas

The Kingdom

It's a long way off but inside it

There are quite different things going on:

Festivals at which the poor man

Is king and the consumptive is

Healed; mirrors in which the blind look

At themselves and love looks at them

Back; and industry is for mending

The bent bones and the minds fractured

By life. It's a long way off, but to get

There takes no time and admission

Is free, if you will purge yourself

Of desire, and present yourself with

Your need only and the simple offering

Of your faith, green as a leaf.

Monday before Advent Sunday

A Reading from a scriptural commentary
of Ephrem of Syria

Christ said: 'About that hour no one knows, neither the angels nor the Son. It is not for you to know times or moments.' He has kept these things hidden so that we may keep watch, each of us thinking that he will come in our own day. If he had revealed the time of his coming, his coming would have lost its savour: it would no longer be an object of yearning for the nations and the age in which it will be revealed. He promised that he would come but did not say when he would come, and so all generations and ages await him eagerly.

Though the Lord has established the signs of his coming, the time of their fulfilment has not been plainly revealed. These signs have come and gone with a multiplicity of change; more than that, they are still present. His final coming is like his first. As holy persons and prophets waited for him, thinking that he would reveal himself in their own day, so today each of the faithful longs to welcome him in our own day, because Christ has not made plain the day of his coming.

He has not made it plain for this reason especially, that no one may think that he whose power and dominion rule all numbers and times is ruled by fate and time. He described the signs of his coming; how could what he has himself decided be hidden from him? Therefore, he used these words to increase respect for the signs of his coming, so that from that day forward all generations and ages might think that he would come again in their own day.

Keep watch; when the body is asleep nature takes control of us, and what is done is not done by our will but by force, by the impulse of nature. When deep listlessness takes possession of the soul, for example, faintheartedness or melancholy, the enemy overpowers it and makes it do what it does not will. The force of nature, the enemy of the soul, is in control. When the Lord commanded us to be vigilant, he meant vigilance in both parts of ourselves: in the body, against the tendency to sleep, in the soul, against lethargy and timidity.

Tuesday before Advent Sunday

A Reading from a commentary on the psalms by Augustine

God established a time for making his promises and a time for their fulfilment. The time for making his promises extended from the prophets to John the Baptist; and the time for fulfilling his promises, from John the Baptist to the end of the ages. God, who is faithful, has made himself our debtor, not by receiving anything but by promising such great things.

It was a very small thing to make promises, so he even wished to bind himself in writing, as it were giving us a contract of his promises; in order that when he should begin to carry out his promises we would be able to discern in the Scriptures the order for the fulfilment of the promises.

He promised eternal salvation, everlasting happiness with the angels, an unfading inheritance, endless glory, the joyful vision of his face, his holy dwelling in heaven, and after our resurrection from the dead the assurance of no further fear of death. This is (so to speak) his final promise toward which all our intentions should be focused; for when we have reached it, we shall require nothing more nor demand anything further.

Furthermore, our Lord also manifested in his promises and prophecies the way in which we would arrive at our final goal. He promised humans divinity, mortals immortality, sinners justification, the poor a rising to glory. Whatever he promised, he promised to those who were unworthy, so that it was not a case of a reward being promised to workers but of grace being given as a gift as its name indicates.

Hence, even those who live justly, insofar as men and women can live justly, do so not through human merits but through grace. No one lives justly unless that person has been justified, that is, been made just, and one is made just by him who can never be unjust. As a lamp cannot light itself, so the human soul does not enlighten us, but rather calls out to God: 'O Lord, give light to my lamp.'

But, my beloved, because God's promises seemed impossible to us – equality with the angels in exchange for mortality, corruption, poverty, weakness, dust and ashes – God not only made a written contract with us to win our belief, but also established a mediator of his good faith: not a prince or angel or archangel, but his only Son. He wanted, through his Son, to show and give us the way he would lead us to the goal he has promised.

It was not enough for God to make his Son our guide to the way; he made him the way itself, that we might travel with him as leader, and by him as the way.

Therefore, the only Son of God was to come to us, to become human, and in our nature to be born as one of us, to die, to rise again, to ascend into heaven, to sit at the right hand of the Father and to fulfil his promises among the nations; and after that to come again, to exact now what he asked for before, to separate those deserving his anger from those deserving his mercy, to execute his threats against the wicked, and to reward the just as he had promised.

All this had to be prophesied, foretold, and promised as an event in the future so that it would not inspire fear by coming suddenly but would be believed in and expected.

Wednesday before Advent Sunday

A Reading from the *Confessions* of Augustine

Lord, may I know you, who know me, that 'I may know even as I am also known'. O power of my soul, enter into it and fit it for yourself, so that you may have and hold it 'without spot or blemish'. This is my hope, this is my prayer, and in this hope I am placing my delight when my delight is focused truly. But as to the other pleasures of this life, regret at their loss should be in inverse proportion to the extent to which we weep for losing them. The less we weep for them, the more we ought to be weeping. 'Behold, you have loved the truth,' for he who 'does the truth comes to the light'. This I desire to do, in my heart before you in confession, and before many witnesses through my writing.

Indeed, Lord, to your eyes, the abyss of human consciousness is exposed. What could be hidden within me, even if I were unwilling to confess it to you? I would be hiding you from myself, not myself from you. Now, however, my groaning is witness that I am displeased with myself. You are radiant and I delight in you, and you have become such an object of love and longing that I am ashamed of myself and reject myself. You are my choice, and only by your gift can I please either you or myself.

Before you, then, Lord, whatever I am is laid open, and I have already spoken of the benefit I derive from making confession to you. I am not doing this merely by physical words and sounds, but by words uttered in my soul and the cry from my mind, which is known to your ear. When I am evil, making confession to you means being displeased with myself. When I am good, making confession involves claiming no credit for myself, for you, Lord, 'confer blessing on the righteous' but only after you have first 'justified the ungodly'. Therefore, my God, my confession before you is made both in silence and not in silence. It is silent in that it has no audible sound; but in love it cries aloud.

You, Lord, are my judge, for even if 'no man knows the being of a man except the spirit of man which is in him,' yet there is something of the human person which is unknown even to the 'spirit of man which is in him'. But you, Lord, know everything about us; for you made humanity. Although in your sight I may despise myself and estimate myself to be dust and ashes, I nevertheless know something of you which I do not know about myself. Without question 'we see now through a mirror darkly,' not yet 'face to face'. For this reason, as long as I am a pilgrim absent from you, I am more present to myself than to you. Yet I know that you cannot be in any way subjected to violence, whereas I do not know which temptations I can resist and which I cannot. There is hope because 'you are faithful and do not allow us to be tempted beyond what we can bear, but with the temptation make also a way of escape so that we can bear it.'

Accordingly, let me confess what I know of myself. Let me confess too what I do not know of myself. For what I know of myself I know because you grant me light, and what I do not know of myself, I do not know until such time as my darkness becomes 'like noonday' before your face.

Thursday before Advent Sunday

A Reading from a treatise *On Prayer* by Origen

According to the words of our Lord and Saviour, the kingdom of God does not come in such a way for all to see. No one will say: 'Behold, here it is!' or 'Behold, there it is!' because the kingdom of God is within us. Indeed, the word of God is very near, in our mouth and in our heart. Thus it is clear that one who prays for the coming of God's kingdom prays rightly to have it within, that there it may grow and flourish and reach its full potential. For God reigns in each of his holy ones. Anyone who is holy obeys the spiritual laws of God, and God dwells in that person as in a well-governed city. The Father is present within him, and Christ reigns with the Father in the mature soul as it says in Scripture: 'We shall come to him and make our home with him.'

Thus the kingdom of God within us, as we continue to make progress, will reach its full potential when the Apostle's words are fulfilled, and Christ, having subjected all his enemies to himself, will hand over his 'kingdom to God the Father, that God may be all in all'. Therefore, let us pray unceasingly with that disposition of soul which the Word may make divine, saying to our Father who is in heaven: 'Hallowed be your name; your kingdom come.'

Note this too about the kingdom of God. There is no partnership between justice and iniquity, no compromise between light and darkness, no commerce between Christ and Belial. The kingdom of God cannot co-exist with the reign of sin.

Therefore, if we wish God to reign in us, in no way 'should sin reign in our mortal body'. Rather we should put to death what is base in us and bear fruit in the Spirit. There should be in us a kind of spiritual paradise where God may walk and be our sole ruler with his Christ. In us the Lord will sit at the right hand of that spiritual power which we wish to receive. And he will sit there until all the enemies which rage within us become his footstool, and every principality, power and authority in us is cast out.

All this can happen in each one of us, and the last enemy, death, can be destroyed; then Christ will say in us: 'O death, where is your sting? O hell, where is your victory?' Now therefore, let what is perishable in us clothe itself in holiness and imperishability. Let what is mortal be clothed, now that death has been conquered, so that God will reign in us, and we shall enjoy even now the blessings of rebirth and resurrection.

Friday before Advent Sunday

A Reading from *The Glory of God and the Transfiguration of Christ* by Michael Ramsey

The idea of the 'last things' has often been presented in terms of the destiny of the individual: 'what happens to me when I die?' But the Christian doctrine sees the destiny of the individual as one part of the pattern of the divine design for mankind and for all creation. God, who created the world for his glory, will glorify his creatures and lead them to glorify him. The end is a new creation, forged from out of the broken pieces of a fallen creation, filled with glory and giving glory to its Maker.

The crown of God's creation is man, made in the Creator's own image and possessing an affinity to him in virtue of which he may come to know him, to obey him, to love him and in the end to see him. The service of God in the reflection of God's holiness and love is subsumed in the worship of God: and both the worship and the service are subsumed finally in the seeing of God as he is. The seeing of God amid the shadows of history in the incarnate life of the Son is far less than the seeing of God which will be 'face to face' and 'as he is'. And this perfect seeing awaits the transformation of mankind into the image of Christ and their being made 'like him'.

Besides our affinity to the Creator in whose image we are made and whose vision we strive to attain, man has his place in relation to the rest of creation. He is set to rule over it as God's viceregent, 'crowned with glory and honour' and with all things put in subjection under his feet; and in his worship of God he is the spokesman of all created things. The mystery of evil afflicts not man alone, but all creation too. The sufferings of men and women at this present time, the bondage of corruption in nature, the fact that we see not yet all things made subject to us, all betoken the frustration of the divine design by the fall. But by the cross and resurrection of Christ the inauguration of a new creation has begun, and this new creation will include both mankind brought to sonship and to glory, and nature renewed in union with humanity in the worship and praise of God. The Christian hope is therefore far more than the salvaging of human souls into a spiritual salvation: it is the re-creation of the world, through the power of the resurrection of Christ.

Thus the hope of the beatific vision is crossed by the hope of the vindication of the divine design not only in us but in all things. And the hope of the resurrection of the body, when the body of our low estate is transformed into the body of Christ's glory, is the reminder of our kinship with the created world which the God of glory will redeem in a new world wherein the old is not lost but fulfilled.

Saturday before Advent Sunday

A Reading from *Revelations of Divine Love*
by Julian of Norwich

On one occasion the good Lord said 'All shall be well.' On another, 'You will see for yourself that all manner of thing shall be well.' In these two sayings the soul discerns various meanings.

One is that God wants us to know that not only does he care for great and noble things, but equally for little and small, lowly and simple things as well. This is his meaning: 'All shall be well.' We are to know that the least will not be forgotten.

Another is this: we see deeds done that are so evil, and injuries inflicted that are so great, that it seems to us quite impossible that any good can come of them. As we consider these, sorrowfully and mournfully, we cannot relax in the blessed contemplation of God as we ought. This is caused by the fact that our reason is now so blind, base, and ignorant that we are unable to know that supreme and marvellous wisdom, might, and goodness which belong to the blessed Trinity. This is the meaning of his word, 'You will see for yourself that all manner of thing shall be well.' It is as if he were saying, 'Be careful now to believe and trust, and in the end you will see it all in its fullness and joy.'

So from those same six words 'I shall make all things well,' I gain great comfort with regard to all the works that God has still to do. There still remains a deed which the blessed Trinity will do at the last day – at least so I see it – yet when and how it will be done is unknown to all God's creatures under Christ, and will remain so until it takes place. The reason why he wants us to know about this deed is that he would have us more at ease in our minds and more at peace in our love, and not be concerned with those storms and stresses that stop us from truly enjoying him.

This great deed, ordained by the Lord God from before time, and treasured and hid within his blessed heart, is known only to himself. By it he will make everything to turn out well. For just as the blessed Trinity made everything out of nothing, in the same way shall he make all that is wrong to turn out for the best.

Remembrance Sunday

A Reading from a hymn of Prudentius

The Burial of the Dead

Take him, earth, for cherishing,
To thy tender breast receive him.
Body of a man I bring thee,
Noble even in its ruin.

Once was this a spirit's dwelling,
By the breath of God created.
High the heart that here was beating,
Christ the prince of all its living.

Guard him well, the dead I give thee,
Not unmindful of his creature
Shall he ask it: He who made it
Symbol of his mystery.

Come the hour God hath appointed
To fulfil the hope of men,
Then must thou, in very fashion,
What I give, return again.

Not though ancient time decaying
Wear away these bones to sand,
Ashes that a man might measure
In the hollow of his hand:

Not through wandering winds and idle,
Drifting through the empty sky,
Scatter dust was nerve and sinew,
Is it given man to die.

Once again the shining road
Leads to ample paradise;
Open are the woods again
That the serpent lost for men.

Take, O take him, mighty Leader,
Take again thy servant's soul,
To the house from which he wandered
Exiled, erring, long ago.

But for us, heap earth about him,
Earth with leaves and violets strewn,
Grave his name, and pour the fragment
Balm upon the icy stone.

By the breath of God created
Christ the prince of all its living
Take, O take him,
Take him, earth, for cherishing.

alternative reading

A Reading from a poem by Wilfred Owen

Strange Meeting

It seemed that out of battle I escaped
Down some profound dull tunnel, long since scooped
Through granites which titanic wars had groined.
Yet also there encumbered sleepers groaned,
Too fast in thought or death to be bestirred.
Then, as I probed them, one sprang up, and stared
With piteous recognition in fixed eyes,
Lifting distressful hands as if to bless.
And by his smile, I knew that sullen hall,
By his dead smile I knew we stood in hell.
With a thousand pains that vision's face was grained;
Yet no blood reached there from the upper ground,
And no guns thumped, or down the flues made moan.
'Strange friend,' I said, 'here is no cause to mourn.'
'None,' said that other, 'save the undone years,
The hopelessness. Whatever hope is yours,
Was my life also; I went hunting wild
After the wildest beauty in the world,
Which lies not calm in eyes, or braided hair,
But mocks the steady running of the hour,

And if it grieves, grieves richlier than here.
For of my glee might many men have laughed,
And of my weeping something had been left,
Which must die now. I mean the truth untold,
The pity of war, the pity war distilled.
Now men will go content with what we spoiled,
Or, discontent, boil bloody, and be spilled.
They will be swift with swiftness of the tigress.
None will break ranks, though nations trek from progress.
Courage was mine, and I had mystery,
Wisdom was mine, and I had mastery:
To miss the march of this retreating world
Into vain citadels that are not walled.
Then, when much blood had clogged their chariot-wheels,
I would go up and wash them from street wells,
Even with truths that lie too deep for taint.
I would have poured my spirit without stint
But not through wounds; not on the cess of war.
Foreheads of men have bled where no wounds were.
I am the enemy you killed, my friend.
I knew you in this dark: for so you frowned
Yesterday through me as you jabbed and killed.
I parried; but my hands were loath and cold.
Let us sleep now...'

alternative reading

A Reading from a sermon preached in All Souls' College,
Oxford, shortly after the end of the Second World War,
by Austin Farrer

'May they rest in peace, and may light perpetual shine upon them'
– those millions among whom our friends are lost, those millions
for whom we cannot choose but pray; because prayer is a sharing
in the love of the heart of God, and the love of God is earnestly set
towards the salvation of his spiritual creatures, by, through and out
of the fire that purifies them.
    The arithmetic of death perplexes our brains. What can we do
but throw ourselves upon the infinity of God? It is only to a finite
mind that number is an obstacle, or multiplicity a distraction. Our
mind is like a box of limited content, out of which one thing must

be emptied before another can find a place. The universe of creatures is queuing for a turn of our attention, and no appreciable part of the queue will ever get a turn. But no queue forms before the throne of everlasting mercy, because the nature of an infinite mind is to be simply aware of everything that is.

Everything is simply present to an infinite mind, because it exists; or rather, exists because it is present to that making mind. And though by some process of averaging and calculation I should compute the grains of sand, it would be like the arithmetic of the departed souls, an empty sum; I could not tell them as they are told in the infinity of God's counsels, each one separately present as what it is, and simply because it is.

The thought God gives to any of his creatures is not measured by the attention he can spare, but by the object for consideration they can supply. God is not divided; it is God, not a part of God, who applies himself to the falling sparrow, and to the crucified Lord. But there is more in the beloved Son than in the sparrow, to be observed and loved and saved by God. So every soul that has passed out of this visible world, as well as every soul remaining within it, is caught and held in the unwavering beam of divine care. And we may comfort ourselves for our own inability to tell the grains of sand, or to reckon the thousands of millions of the departed.

And yet we cannot altogether escape so; for our religion is not a simple relation of every soul separately to God, it is a mystical body in which we are all members one of another. And in this mystical body it does not suffice that every soul should be embraced by the thoughts of God; it has also to be that every soul should, in its thought, embrace the other souls. For apart from this mutual embracing, it would be unintelligible why we should pray at all, either for the living or for the departed. Such prayer is nothing but the exercising of our membership in the body of Christ. God is not content to care for us each severally, unless he can also, by his Holy Spirit in each one of us, care through and in us for all the rest. Every one of us is to be a focus of that divine life of which the attractive power holds the body together in one.

So even in the darkness and blindness of our present existence, our thought ranges abroad and spreads out towards the confines of the mystical Christ, remembering the whole Church of Christ, as well militant on earth as triumphant in heaven; invoking angels, archangels and all the spiritual host.

ABBREVIATIONS

CCSL   *Corpus Christianorum: Series Latina*, Turnhout, Belgium, 1953- .

CSEL   *Corpus Scriptorum Ecclesiasticorum Latinorum*, Vienna, 1866- .

ET   English translation

ICEL   *The Roman Catholic Liturgy of the Hours*, 1974, American edition; ET of non-biblical readings by the International Commission for English in the Liturgy.

LACT   Library of Anglo-Catholic Theology, Oxford, 1841-.

Loeb   The Loeb Classical Library, Cambridge, Massachusetts & London, 1923-.

NPNF   The Nicene and Post-Nicene Library of the Fathers, series 1 & 2, general editors Schaff and Wace, New York, 1887-92; Oxford, 1890-1900; reprinted Grand Rapids, Michigan, 1983- .

PG   *Patrologiae cursus completus: Series Graeca*, 161 vols, ed. J. P. Migne, Paris, 1857-66.

PL   *Patrologiae cursus completus: Series Latina*, 221 vols, ed. J. P. Migne, Paris, 1844-64.

SC   *Sources Chrétiennes*, Paris, 1940 - .

NOTES AND SOURCES

The figure in **BOLD** on the left indicates the page number in the anthology. Where no source for an ET is cited, the English version is that of the author. If this has been based on an existing (often nineteenth-century) translation, this is acknowledged in the notes.

ADVENT

Advent 1

3 Cyril of Jerusalem, *Catechesis* 15, 1-3; PG 33, cols 870-4; ET by ICEL.

4 Bernard of Clairvaux, *Sermon 5 'On Advent'*, 1-3; PL 183, cols 50-1.

5 Joseph Addison, 'When rising from the bed of death'.

6 Rowan Williams, 'Advent Calendar', *After Silent Centuries*, Oxford, 1996.

7 Pierre Teilhard de Chardin, *Le Milieu Divin*, 1957, Paris; ET © Collins & Sons, London, 1960, pp.147-9.

8 John Henry Newman, *Plain and Parochial Sermons*, London, 1939 edition, vol. 4, p.378.

9 Clement of Rome, *Letter to the Corinthians*, 59-61 (abridged); Loeb 24, *Apostolic Fathers I*; ET based on Kirsopp Lake, London, 1912, pp.111-17.

10 William Law, *The Spirit of Love*, I.

11 Augustine, *Commentary on Psalm 95 (Hebrew Ps. 96)*, 14,15; CCSL 39, pp.1351-3; ET by ICEL (abridged).

12 Columbanus, *Instructions* 12, 2-3; *Sancti Columbani Opera (Scriptores Latini Hiberniae)*, Dublin, 1957, pp.112-14; ET by ICEL.

Advent 2

13 Anonymous, *Letter to Diognetus*, 7-9; SC 33, pp.66-74; ET by ICEL. NB This short anonymous treatise was probably written in Egypt around 200, and was dedicated to a cultured pagan called Diognetus, otherwise unknown. The text gives a remarkable insight into Christian life in a hostile pagan society.

15 Origen, *Homily 21 'On St Luke's Gospel'*; PG 13, cols 1855-6; ET by ICEL.

16 Bernard of Clairvaux, *Sermon 1 'On Advent'*, 7-8; PL 183, cols 38-9.

17 Augustine, *Commentary on Psalm 109 (Hebrew Ps. 110)*, 1-3; CSCL 40, pp.1601-3; ET by ICEL.

18 Cyprian, *On the Value of Patience*, 13, 15; CSEL 3 (i), pp.406-8; ET by ICEL.

19 Anselm, *Proslogion*, I, 15-54, 100-140; *The Prayers and Meditations of St Anselm with the Proslogion*, ET by Benedicta Ward SLG, London, 1973, pp. 239-43.

21 Eusebius of Caesarea, *Commentary on Isaiah*, 40; PG 24, cols 366-7; ET by ICEL.

Advent 3
22 Augustine, *Sermon* 293, 3; PL 38, cols 1328-9; ET by ICEL.
23 Irenaeus, *Against Heresies,* III, 20, 2-3; SC 34, pp.388-95; ET based on NPNF vol. I, pp.547-8.
24 Augustine, *Treatise 35 on St John's Gospel,* 8-9; CCSL 36, pp.321-2; ET by ICEL.
25 Maria Boulding, *The Coming of God,* London, 2nd edition 1994, pp.146-7.
26 A. G. Hebert, *The Throne of David,* London, 1941, pp.240-1.
27 Richard Challoner, *Meditations for Every Day of the Year,* 1767; Westminster edition of 1915, pp.810-12 (abridged).
28 Augustine, *The City of God,* XVII, 10; CCSL 48, p.574; ET by ICEL.
Advent 4
30 Irenaeus, *Against Heresies,* V, 19, 1; 20, 2; 21, 1; SC 153, pp.248-50, 260-4; ET based on NPNF vol. I, pp.547-8.
Eight Days of Prayer before Christmas
31 Sebastian Moore and Kevin Maguire, *The Experience of Prayer,* London, 1969, pp.84-5.
32 Leo the Great, *Letter* 31, 2-3; PL 54, cols 235-7.
33 Hippolytus, *The Refutation of all Heresies,* 10, 33; PG 16, cols 3452-3.
34 Clement of Rome, *Letter to the Corinthians,* 29-33 (abridged); Loeb 24, *Apostolic Fathers I*; ET based on Kirsopp Lake, London, 1912, pp.59-65.
36 Bernard of Clairvaux, *Sermon 4 'In Praise of the Blessed Virgin Mary',* 8-9; PL 183, cols 83-5.
37 Ambrose, *Commentary on St Luke's Gospel,* 2, 19, 22-3, 26-7; CCSL 14, pp.39-42; ET by ICEL.
39 Bede, *Commentary on St Luke's Gospel,* 1, 46-55; CCSL 120, pp.37-9; ET by ICEL.
40 Austin Farrer, *Said or Sung,* London, 1960, pp.34-5.
41 Augustine, *Sermon* 185; PL 38, cols 997-9.

CHRISTMAS

45 Julian of Vezelay, *Sermon 1 'On the Nativity';* SC 192, pp.45, 52, 60. NB The text of Scripture Julian refers to is Wisdom 18:14 which formed the medieval Latin introit at Christmas.
46 Gregory of Nazianzus, *Oration 38 'For Christmas'*; PG 36, cols 311-14.
47 Irenaeus, *Against Heresies,* IV, 38, 1; SC 100, p.946; ET based on NPNF vol. I, p.521
48 Leo the Great, *Sermon 1 'On the Nativity',* 1-3; PL 54, cols 190-3; ET based on NPNF vol. XII, pp.128-9.
49 Robert Southwell, 'The Nativity of Christ'.
50 Hilary of Poitiers, *On the Trinity,* II, 25; CCSL 62A, p.61; ET based on NPNF vol. IX, p.59.

50 Ephrem of Syria, *Hymns 'On the Nativity '* 11, 6-8; ET by Sebastian Brock, *The Luminous Eye: The Spiritual World Vision of St Ephrem the Syrian,* Spencer, Massachusetts, 1985, p.25.

51 Mark Frank, *Sermon 6; Sermons by Dr Mark Frank,* LACT, Oxford, 1849; vol. 1, pp.80-91 (abridged).

52 John Henry Newman, *Sermon 15,* 1-3; *University Sermons 1826-1843,* reprinted London, 1970, pp.312-14.

53 Basil the Great, *Homily 2 'On the Nativity',* 6; PG 31, cols 1459-62, 1471-4; ET by ICEL.

55 Proclus, *Oration 1 'In Praise of St Mary',* PG 65, 1-2; cols 681-4.

56 William of St Thierry, *On Contemplating God,* 9; ET by Penelope Lawson CSMV; *The Works of William of St Thierry I,* Spencer, Massachusetts, 1971, p.38.

57 Mark Frank, *Sermon 17; Sermons by Dr Mark Frank,* LACT, Oxford, 1849; vol. 1, pp.258-72 (abridged).

58 Augustine, *Sermon,* 194, 3-4; PL38; cols 1016-17.

59 Athanasius, *Letter to Epictetus,* 5-9; PG 26, cols 1062-6.

60 Bernard of Clairvaux, *Sermon 1 'On the Nativity',* 2-4; PL 183, cols 115-17.

61 Gregory of Nyssa, *Catechetical Orations,* 25; PG 45, cols 65-8.

Sundays of Christmas

62 Evelyn Underhill, *The Light of Christ,* London, 1944.

63 Augustine, *Sermon 13 'On the Seasons';* PL 39, cols 1097-8; ET by ICEL.

EPIPHANY

67 Peter Chrysologus, *Sermon* 160; PL 52, cols 620-2; ET by ICEL.

68 Ephrem of Syria, *Hymns 'On the Nativity',* 23, 1, 3, 10; ET by Kathleen E. McVey, *Ephrem the Syrian,* New York & Mahwah, New Jersey, 1989, pp.187-9.

69 Lancelot Andrewes, *Sermon 14; The Works of Bishop Lancelot Andrewes,* LACT, Oxford, 1841, vol. 1, pp.238-49 (abridged).

70 Bernard of Clairvaux, *Sermon I 'On the Epiphany',* 1-2; PL 133, cols 141-3; ET by ICEL, pp.34-5.

71 Leo the Great, *Sermon 6 'On the Epiphany',* 1; PL 54, cols 235-7; ET based on NPNF vol. XII, p.150.

72 Athanasius, *On the Incarnation,* 10, 14; PG 25, cols 111-14, 119; ET by ICEL (adapted).

73 Irenaeus, *Against Heresies,* IV, 6, 3-7; SC 100, pp.442, 446, 448-54; ET based on NPNF vol. I, pp. 547-8.

74 John of the Cross, *The Ascent of Mount Carmel,* II, 22, 2-5.

75 Leo the Great, *Sermon 3 'On the Epiphany',* 1-3, 5; PL 54, cols 240-4; ET based on NPNF vol. XII, pp.145-7.

Epiphany 1 - The Baptism of Christ
77   Gregory of Nazianzus, *Oration* 39, 14-16, 20; PG 36, cols 350-1, 354, 358-9; ET by ICEL.
78   Proclus, *Oration 7 'On the Holy Theophany'*, 1-3; PG 65, cols 758-60.
79   Columbanus, *Instructions,* 11, 1-2; *Sancti Columbani Opera (Scriptores Latini Hiberniae),* Dublin 1957, pp.106-7.
80   Gregory of Nazianzus, *Oration 14 'On the Love of the Poor'*, 23-5; PG 35, cols 887-90; ET by ICEL.
81   Athanasius, *Against the Pagans,* 42-3; PG 25, cols 83-7; ET by ICEL.
82   Cyprian, *On the Lord's Prayer*, 1-3; CSEL 3 (i), pp.267-8.
83   Cyril of Alexandria, *Commentary on St Paul's Letter to the Romans*, 15, 7; PG 74, cols 854-5; ET by ICEL.
84   Augustine, *Commentary on Psalm 85 (Hebrew Ps. 86)*, 1; CCSL 39, pp.1176-7; ET by ICEL.
Epiphany 2
85   Dietrich Bonhoeffer, *The Cost of Discipleship,* 1937; ET by R. H. Fuller, London, 1959, pp.48-9.
87   Ephrem of Syria, *Hymn 14 'On Faith'*, 1-5; ET by Sebastian Brock, *The Luminous Eye: The Spiritual World Vision of St Ephrem the Syrian,* Spencer, Massachusetts, 1985, pp.124-5.
87   Evelyn Underhill, *The Light of Christ,* London, 1944.
88   Clement of Rome, *Letter to the Corinthians,* 31-35; Loeb 24, *Apostolic Fathers I*; ET based on Kirsopp Lake, London, 1912, pp.61-9.
89   Cyprian, *On the Lord's Prayer*, 8-9; 11; CSEL 3 (i), pp.271-2, 274.
90   Thomas Traherne, *Centuries of Meditations,* IV, 90-1.
91   William of St Thierry, *On Contemplating God,* 9; ET by Penelope Lawson CSMV; *The Works of William of St Thierry I,* Spencer, Massachusetts, 1971, pp.40-2.
92   Gregory of Nyssa, *Homily 5 'On Ecclesiastes'*; PG 44, cols 683-6; ET by ICEL.
Epiphany 3
93   Kenneth Kirk, *The Vision of God*, Oxford, 1931; abridged edition 1934, pp.44-6.
95   Ambrose, *Commentary on Psalm 118 (Hebrew Ps.119),* 12, 13-14; CSEL 62, pp.258-9; ET by ICEL.
96   Walter Hilton, *The Scale of Perfection,* I, 90-1; ET by John Clark & Rosemary Dorward, New York & Mahwah, New Jersey, 1991, pp.159-60.
97   Clement of Alexandria, *The Teacher,* 1, 5; PG 8, cols 267-70, 274.
98   William Law, *A Serious Call to a Devout and Holy Life,* 20.
99   John V. Taylor, *The Go-Between God,* London, 1973, pp.134-5.
100   Peter Chrysologus, *Sermon* 147; PL 52, cols 594-5.
Epiphany 4
102   Leo the Great, *Sermon 7 'On the Nativity'*, 2, 6; PL 54, cols 217-18, 220-1; ET based on NPNF vol. XII, pp.139-41.
103   Mechtild of Magdeburg, *Revelations: The Flowing Light of the Godhead,* I, 39-43; ET based on Lucy Menzies, London, 1953, pp.19-20.
104   Jean-Pierre de Caussade, *Abandonment to Divine Providence* I, 5.
105   Aelred of Rievaulx, *The Mirror of Charity,* I, 7; PL 195, cols 511-12.

Notes & Sources   *531*

106 Thomas Merton, *The Power and Meaning of Love,* London, 1976, p.17.

107 Gregory the Great, *Homily 4 'On the Gospels',* 2-3; PL 76; cols 1090-2.

108 Basil the Great, *The Longer Rules for Monks,* 2, 2-4; PG 31, cols 914-15.

Candlemas

110 Sophronius, *Sermon 3 'On the Presentation of Christ in the Temple',* 6-7; PG 87, cols 3291-3.

111 Ephrem of Syria, *Hymns 'On the Nativity',* 6: 12-16; ET by Kathleen E. McVey, New York & Mahwah, New Jersey, 1989, pp.112-13.

112 Guerric of Igny, *Sermon 1 'On the Presentation of Christ in the Temple',* 2, 3, 5; PL 185, cols 64-7.

ORDINARY TIME BEFORE LENT

5 before Lent

117 John Chrysostom, *Homily 15 'On St Matthew's Gospel',* 6, 7; PG 57, cols 231-2; ET by ICEL.

118 Julian of Norwich, *Revelations of Divine Love,* 39; ed. Clifton Wolters, London, 1966, pp.120-1 (abridged).

119 Basil the Great, *Homily 7 'Against the Rich',* 3; ET by Susan R. Holman, *The body of the poor in fourth century Cappadocia: Seven Sermons on Hunger, Sickness and Penury,* Brown University, 1998, appendix, pp.281-2.

120 Francis de Sales, *Introduction to the Devout Life,* III, 4-5.

120 Richard Hooker, *The Laws of Ecclesiastical Polity,* I, xi, 5-6 (abridged).

121 Clement of Alexandria, *The Teacher,* 1, 7; PG 8, cols 315-18.

122 Jeremy Taylor, *Holy Living,* III, 6.

4 before Lent

123 Augustine, *Confessions,* X, xxv (36) - xxviii (39); CSEL 33, pp.254-5.

124 Thomas Ken, *An Exposition of the Church Catechism;* ed. W. Benham, London, 1881, p.144-6.

125 *The Cloud of Unknowing;* ET by Clifton Wolters, London, 1971, pp.98-9.

126 Gregory of Nyssa, *The Life of Moses,* II, 287-90; SC 1, pp.300-4.

127 Dietrich Bonhoeffer, *Life Together;* ET from the fifth edition (1949) by John W. Doberstein, London, 1954; pp.86-9 (abridged).

128 Augustine, *Enchiridion,* 22; PL 40; cols 243-4.

129 Gregory the Great, *Pastoral Care,* II, 5; PL 77, cols 32-4.
NB It is likely that in this book Gregory intended to provide secular clergy with a spiritual counterpart to the *Rule of St Benedict*. Throughout he uses the term *rector* which is more correctly translated in English as 'ruler' but which has been rendered here by the less hierarchical term 'leader'. Gregory was writing primarily for the episcopate, but the term *rector* could and did include 'secular' as well as ecclesiastical leaders.

3 before Lent

130 Cyprian, *On the Lord's Prayer,* 14-15; CSEL 3 (i), pp.277-8.

131　Dorotheus of Gaza, *Discourse V 'On the Need for Consultation'*; PG 88; ET of Greek text by Eric Wheeler, *Dorotheos of Gaza: Discourses and Sayings,* Kalamazoo, Michigan, 1977, pp.122-3.

132　Mechtild of Magdeburg, *Revelations: The Flowing Light of the Godhead,* V, 30; ET based on Lucy Menzies, London, 1953, pp.102-3.

133　Walter Hilton, *The Scale of Perfection,* I, 12; ET by John Clark & Rosemary Dorward, New York & Mahwah, New Jersey, 1991, p.86.

134　Basil the Great, *Letter* 2, 3; Loeb (4 vols), ed. Roy Deferrari, 1926; ET based on Deferrari, vol. 1, pp.11-12.

135　Aelred of Rievaulx, *On Spiritual Friendship,* III, 54-59; ET by Mary Eugenia Laker SSND, Kalamazoo, Michigan, 1977, p.104.

136　Augustine, *Commentary on Psalm 58 (Hebrew Ps. 59),* I, 7; CCSL 39, pp.733-4.

2 before Lent

137　Julian of Norwich, *Revelations of Divine Love,* 5; ET by Clifton Wolters, London, 1966, pp.67-8.

138　Jean-Pierre de Caussade, *Abandonment to Divine Providence,* II, 3.

139　Caesarius of Arles, *Sermon* 75, 2-3; CCSL 103, pp.314-15.

140　Dietrich Bonhoeffer, *The Cost of Discipleship,* 1937; ET by R. H. Fuller, London, 1959, pp.35-6.

141　John of the Cross, *The Dark Night of the Soul,* II, 7, 1-3.

142　Julian of Norwich, *Revelations of Divine Love,* 56; ET by Clifton Wolters, London, 1966, p.161.

143　Thomas Merton, *New Seeds of Contemplation,* New York, 1961; London, 1962 & 1972; new Anglicized edition, Tunbridge Wells, 1999; quotation from 1972 edition, pp. 62-3; © Abbey of Our Lady of Gethsemani.

Sunday next before Lent

143　Origen, *Homily 1 'On Genesis',* 5-7; SC 7, pp.70-3; ET by ICEL.

145　*from* Mattins, 'The Sunday of Forgiveness'; *The Lenten Triodion;* ET by Mother Mary and Archimandrite Kallistos Ware, London, 1978, p.175.

145　William of St Thierry, *Meditation* I, 3; ET by Penelope Lawson CSMV; *The Works of William of St Thierry, I,* Spencer, Massachusetts, 1971, p.90.

146　John Chrysostom, *Homily 'On the Devil the Tempter'* 2, 6; PG 49, cols 263-4; ET by ICEL.

LENT

Ash Wednesday

151　Clement of Rome, *Letter to the Corinthians,* 7-9, 13, 15; Loeb 24, *Apostolic Fathers I*; ET based on Kirsopp Lake, London, 1912, pp.19-33.

152　John Donne, *Sermon* 107, *Works,* vol. IV, London, 1839, pp.459-60.

153　Robert Herrick, 'To keep a True Lent'.

154　Martin Smith, *A Season of the Spirit,* London & Boston, 1991, pp.5-6.

155　Jerome, *Commentary on Joel;* PL 25, cols 967-8.

156　Peter Chrysologus, *Sermon* 43, PL 52, cols 320-2; ET by ICEL.

157   John Chrysostom, *Homily 3 'On the Second Letter to Timothy'*, 3; PG 62, cols 616-17.

Lent 1

158   Leo the Great, *Sermon 2 'For Lent'*, 1-5; PL 54, cols 268-71; ET based on NPNF vol. XII, pp.154-6.

159   Harry Williams, *True Wilderness*, London, 1965, pp.29-34 (abridged).

161   *The Wisdom of the Desert Fathers (The Anonymous Series)*; ET by Benedicta Ward SLG, Oxford, 1975, pp.29, 39, 40.

161   Augustine, *Sermon* 19, 2-3; CCSL 41, pp.252-4.

162.   Cyprian, *On the Lord's Prayer*, 25-7; CSEL 3 (i), pp.285-7.

163   Julian of Norwich, *Revelations of Divine Love*, 39, 40; ET by Clifton Wolters, London, 1966, pp.121-2.

164   Maria Boulding, *The Coming of God*, London, 2nd edition, 1994, pp.36-8.

164   Kenneth Kirk, *The Vision of God*, Oxford, 1931; abridged edition 1934, pp.5-9 (abridged).

Lent 2

166   Leo the Great, *Sermon 10 'For Lent'*, 2-5; PL 54, cols 299-301.

168   George Herbert, 'Discipline'.

169   William Law, *A Serious Call to a Devout and Holy Life*, 14.

170   Cyril of Jerusalem, *Catechesis* 1, 2-3, 5-6; PG 33, cols 371, 375-8; ET by ICEL.

171   Baldwin of Canterbury, *Treatise* 6; PL 204, cols 466-7; ET by ICEL.

172   Maximus of Turin, *Homily 'For Lent'*, 44, 8; PL 57, cols 135-6.

172   John Cassian, *Conferences*, X, 10; SC 54, pp.85-6.

173   Lancelot Andrewes, *Sermon 4*; *The Works of Bishop Lancelot Andrewes*, LACT, Oxford, 1841, vol. 1, pp.356-9 (abridged).

Lent 3

174   Augustine, *Sermon* 256, 1; PL 38, cols 1190-1.

175   Ambrose, *On the Six Days of Creation*, 1, 31-2; CSEL 32, pp.29-33.

176   Caesarius of Arles, *Sermon 'On Fraternal Harmony'*, 1-2; PLS 4, cols 446-7; ET by ICEL.

177   Theophilus of Antioch, *To Autolycus*, I, 2, 7; PG 6, cols 1026-7, 1035; ET by ICEL (modified).

178   C. J. Jung, *Modern Man in Search of a Soul*, 1933; ET by W. S. Dell & Cary F. Baynes, London, 1984, pp.271-2.

180   Proclus, *Oration 1 'In Praise of St Mary'*, 5-6; PG 65, cols 686-8.

181   Gregory of Nazianzus, *Oration* 14, 38, 40; PG 35, cols 907, 910.

Lent 4

182   Aelred of Rievaulx, *Pastoral Prayer*, 5; ET by Penelope Lawson CSMV; *The Works of Aelred of Rievaulx I*, Spencer, Massachusetts, 1971, pp.110-11.

183   Augustine, *Sermon* 25, 7-8; PL 46, cols 937-8; ET by ICEL.

184   Julian of Norwich, *Revelations of Divine Love*, 79; ET by Clifton Wolters, London, 1966, pp.202-4.

185   Augustine, *Sermon* 96, 1; PL 38; cols 585-9.

186   Origen, *Homily 8 'On Genesis'*, 6, 8, 9; PG 12, cols 206-9; ET by ICEL.

187   Gregory the Great, *Moral Reflections on the Book of Job*, 13, 21-23; PL 75, cols 1028-9.

189 Isaac of Nineveh, *Ascetical Treatises,* 2; ET based on A. K. Wensinck, *The Mystical Treatises of Isaac of Nineveh,* Amsterdam, 1923.
NB Some scholars now ascribe this prayer not to Isaac of Nineveh, but to another Syrian theologian of the eighth century, John of Dalyatha.

190 Rowan Williams, *Resurrection,* London, 1982, pp.11-15 (abridged).

Lent 5

191 Cyril of Jerusalem, *Catechesis* XIII, 1, 3, 6, 23; PG 33, cols 771-4, 779, 802; ET by ICEL.

192 John Chrysostom, *Homily 'On the burial place and the cross',* 2; PG 49, cols 409-10.

194 William Law, *A Serious Call to a Devout and Holy Life,* 16.

195 Theodoret of Cyr, *On the Incarnation of the Lord,* 26, 28; PG 83.

196 Theodore of Studios, *Oration 'In Adoration of the Cross';* PG 99, cols 691-5, 698-70; ET by ICEL.

197 Catherine of Siena, *The Dialogue,* 22, 25; ET by Suzanne Noffke OP, New York & Mahwah, New Jersey, 1980, pp.59, 63.

198 Gregory of Nazianzus, *Oration 45,* 23-24; PG 36, cols 654-5; ET by ICEL.

HOLY WEEK

Palm Sunday

203 Andrew of Crete, *Oration 9 'For Palm Sunday';* PG 97 cols 990-4; ET by ICEL.

204 Gregory of Nazianzus, *Oration 45 'For Easter',* 22, 28, 29; PG 36, cols 653, 661, 664.

204 *The Lenten Triodion;* ET by Mother Mary and Archimandrite Kallistos Ware, London, 1978, pp.497, 499.

205 R. S. Thomas, 'The Coming', *H'm,* London, 1972, p.35.

205 John Chrysostom, *Homily 1 'On the Cross and the Thief',* 1; PG 49, cols 399-401; ET by ICEL.

207 Basil the Great, *On the Holy Spirit,* 15, 35; PG 32, cols 127-30; ET by ICEL.

208 Julian of Norwich, *Revelations of Divine Love,* 22; ET by Clifton Walters, London, 1966, pp.96-7.

209 Cyril of Jerusalem, *Mystagogical Catechesis,* 4; SC 126, pp.134-5.

210 Augustine, *Commentary on St John's Gospel,* 65, 1-3; CCSL 36, pp.490-2; ET by ICEL.

211 Ephrem of Syria, *Hymn 3 'On the Crucifixion',* 9-10; ET by Sebastian Brock, *The Luminous Eye: The Spiritual World Vision of St Ephrem the Syrian,* Spencer, Massachusetts, 1985, p.102.

212 Aelred of Rievaulx, *A Rule of Life for a Recluse,* 31; ET by Mary Paul Macpherson OCSO; *The Works of Aelred of Rievaulx I,* Spencer, Massachusetts, 1971, p.98.

213 Leo the Great, *Sermon 15 'On the Passion',* 3; PL 54, cols 366-7.

213 Augustine, *Sermon* Guelfer 3.

Notes & Sources *535*

215 Bonaventure, *The Tree of Life*, 28; ET by Ewert Cousins, New York & Mahwah, New Jersey, 1978, pp.152-3.
216 Lancelot Andrewes, *Sermon 3 'On the Passion'; The Works of Bishop Lancelot Andrewes*, LACT, Oxford, 1841, vol. 2, pp.170-1.
217 George Herbert, 'The Agony'.
218 Helen Waddell, *Peter Abelard*, London, 1933, pp.268-70 (abridged).
220 Ephrem of Syria, *Homily 'On our Lord'*, 3-4, 9; ET by ICEL.
221 *Odes of Solomon*, 42; ET by J. R. Harris & A. Mingana (2 vols), Manchester, 1916, pp.403-5.
    NB These hymns which date from the early part of the second century were written in Greek for the Syriac Church. The attribution to Solomon was a common procedure in Jewish and Jewish-Christian circles, ascribing texts to famous ancient authors.

EASTER

225 John Chrysostom, *Paschal Homily*; PG 59, cols 721-4.
226 Lancelot Andrewes, *Sermon 14 'On the Resurrection'; The Works of Bishop Lancelot Andrewes*, LACT, Oxford, 1841, vol. 3, pp.14-17, 21 (abridged).
227 Edmund Spenser, 'Easter'.
228 George Herbert, 'Easter'.
229 Melito of Sardis, *Paschal Homily*, 2-7; SC 123, pp.60-4, 120, 122.
230 Augustine, *Commentary on Psalm 148*, 1-2; CCSL 40, pp.2165-6; ET by ICEL.
231 Rowan Williams, *Resurrection*, London, 1982, pp.96-7.
232 Cyril of Jerusalem, *Mystagogical Catechesis*, 2, 4-6; SC 126, pp.110-15; ET by ICEL.
233 Ambrose, *Treatise on Flight from the World*, 6, 36; 7, 44; 8, 45; 9, 52; CSEL 32, pp.192, 198-9, 204; ET by ICEL.
235 H. A. Williams, *True Resurrection*, London, 1972, p.33.
Easter 2
236 Augustine, *Sermon 8 'For the Octave of Easter'*, 1, 4; PL 46, cols 838, 841; ET by ICEL.
237 Gregory the Great, *Homily 26 'On the Gospels'*, 7-9; PL 76, cols 1201-2.
238 Clement of Rome, *Letter to the Corinthians*, 24, 27-9; Loeb 24, *Apostolic Fathers I;* ET based on Kirsopp Lake, London, 1912, pp.51-7.
239 Augustine, *Commentary on St John's Gospel*, 84, 1-2; CCSL 36, pp.536-8; ET by ICEL.
240 Anonymous, *Treatise on Easter*, 49-51, 61-2; SC 27, pp.175-91.
241 A. M. Ramsey, *The Resurrection of Christ*, London, 1961, pp.11-12.
242 Mark Frank, *Sermon 36; Sermons by Dr Mark Frank*, LACT, Oxford, 1849, vol. 2; pp.127-45 (abridged).
243 Augustine, *Commentary on St John's Gospel*, 124, 5, 7; CCSL 36, pp.685-6; ET by ICEL.

Easter 3
244 Gregory the Great, *Homily* 23; PL 76, cols 1182-3; ET by ICEL.
245 Rowan Williams, *Resurrection,* London, 1982, pp.82-4.
247 Lancelot Andrewes, *Sermon 16 'On the Resurrection'; The Works of Bishop Lancelot Andrewes,* LACT, Oxford, 1841, vol. 3, p.44.
248 Baldwin of Canterbury, *Treatise* 6; PL 204, cols 451-3; ET by ICEL.
249 Dietrich Bonhoeffer, *The Cost of Discipleship,* 1937; ET by R. H. Fuller, London, 1959, pp.206-7.
250 Columbanus, *Instructions 13, 'On Christ the Fount of Life',* 2-3; *Sancti Columbani Opera (Scriptores Latini Hiberniae),* Dublin, 1957, pp.118-120; ET by ICEL.
251 Ambrose, *Second Oration upon the death of his brother Satyrus,* 77-81; CSEL 73, pp.291-4; ET by ICEL.
252 Basil the Great, *On the Holy Spirit,* 15, 35-6; PG 32, cols 131-3.
Easter 4
253 Gregory the Great, *Homily 14 'On the Gospels',* 3-6; PL 76; cols 1128-30.
254 Ambrose, *Treatise on Isaac or the Soul,* 8, 74-77; CSEL 32, 1, pp.693-5; ET by ICEL.
255 Maria Boulding, *Gateway to Hope,* London, 1985, pp.109-10.
256 Justin Martyr, *First Apology,* 61: PG 6, cols 419-22.
257 Gregory of Nyssa, *Catechetical Oration,* 25, 32; PG 45, cols 65-8, 80-4.
258 Ambrose, *On Death as a Blessing,* 3, 9; 4, 15; CSEL 32, pp.710, 716-17; ET by ICEL.
259 Leo the Great, *Sermon 1 'On the Ascension',* 2, 4; PL 54, cols 395-6.
Easter 5
260 Cyril of Alexandria, *Commentary on St John's Gospel,* 10, 2; PG 74, cols 331-4; ET by ICEL.
261 Thomas Traherne, *Centuries of Meditations,* II, 95, 97.
262 Bernard of Clairvaux, *On the Love of God,* 3; PL 182, cols 978-9.
263 Augustine, *Sermon* 34, 1-3, 5-6; CCSL 41, pp.424-6.
264 Aelred of Rievaulx, *The Mirror of Charity,* II, 14; PL 195, cols 558-9.
265 Thomas Merton, *The Power and Meaning of Love,* London, 1976, pp.142-3.
266 Augustine, *Commentary on St John's Gospel,* 26, 4-6; CCSL 36; pp. 261-3.
267 A. M. Ramsey, *The Resurrection of Christ,* London, 1961, pp.102-3.
Easter 6
268 Leo the Great, *Sermon* 72; PL 54, cols 390-2; ET by ICEL.
270 Cyril of Alexandria, *Commentary on St Paul's Second Letter to the Corinthians* V, 5-6, 2; PG 74, cols 942-3; ET by ICEL.
271 Dietrich Bonhoeffer, *Letters and Papers from Prison*; 3rd English edition by Reginald Fuller, Frank Clarke, John Bowden and others, London, 1970, pp.336-7.
272 Gregory of Nyssa, *Oration 1 'On the Resurrection'; PG* 46, cols 603, 606, 626-7; ET by ICEL.
Ascension Day
273 Leo the Great, *Sermon 2 'On the Ascension',* 1-4; PL 54, cols 397-9; ET by ICEL.
274 Cyril of Alexandria, *Commentary on St John's Gospel,* 9; PG 74, cols 182-3.

Notes & Sources

275 Augustine, *Sermon 'On the Ascension';* PLS 2, cols 494-5; ET by ICEL.
276 George Herbert, 'Praise (II)'.
277 Cyril of Alexandria, *Commentary on St John's Gospel,* 10; PG 74, col. 434; ET by ICEL.
278 Cyprian, *On the Lord's Prayer*, 11; CSEL 3 (i), pp.274-5.
Easter 7
278 Gregory of Nyssa, *Homily 'On the Song of Songs'*, 15; Jaeger VI, pp.466-8; ET adapted from ICEL.
279 John V. Taylor, *The Go-Between God,* London, 1973, pp.226-7.
280 Bede, *Homily 12 'For the Vigil of Pentecost'*; PL 94, cols 196-7; ET by ICEL.
281 William of St Thierry, *The Mirror of Faith*; PL 180, col. 384.
282 Cyril of Jerusalem, *Catechesis* 16, 1, 11-12, 16; PG 33, cols 931-5, 939-42; ET by ICEL.
283 Cyril of Alexandria, *Commentary on St John's Gospel,* 5, 2; PG 73, cols 751-4; ET by ICEL.
285 Basil the Great, *On the Holy Spirit,* 9, 22-3; PG 32, cols 107-10.
Pentecost
287 Irenaeus, *Against Heresies,* III, 17, 1-3; SC 34, pp.302-6; ET by ICEL.
288 Leo the Great, *Sermon 1 'On Pentecost'*, 2; PL 54, cols 404-5.
289 Richard Challoner, *Meditations for Every Day in the Year,* 1767; Whitsunday; Westminster edition of 1915, pp.351-2
289 John V. Taylor, *The Go-Between God,* London, 1973, pp.133-4.
290 Joyce Rupp, *The Star in my Heart,* Sandiego, 1990, p.61.

ORDINARY TIME AFTER PENTECOST

295 Simon Tugwell OP, *Ways of Imperfection,* London, 1984, pp.1-2.
296 Isaac of Nineveh, *Ascetical Treatises,* 85; ET based on A. K. Wensinck, *The Mystical Treatises of Isaac of Nineveh,* Amsterdam, 1923.
296 Dietrich Bonhoeffer, *Life Together;* ET from the fifth edition (1949) by John W. Doberstein, London, 1954; pp.15-16 (abridged).
297 William of St Thierry, *Meditations* 4, 3, 12; ET by Penelope Lawson CSMV; *The Works of William of St Thierry I*, Spencer, Massachusetts, 1971, pp.111, 117.
298 B. F. Westcott, *Words of Faith and Hope,* London 1902, pp.109-13 (abridged).
299 John Chrysostom, *Homily 6 'On Prayer'*; PG 64, cols 462-3, 466; ET by ICEL.
Trinity Sunday
301 Athanasius, *First Letter to Serapion,* 28-30; PG 26, cols 594-5, 599; ET by ICEL.
302 Hilary of Poitiers, *On the Trinity,* II, 1, 31, 33, 35; CCSL 62A, pp.67-72; ET based on NPNF vol. IX, pp.52, 61.

303 Columbanus, *Instructions* 1, 3-5; *Sancti Columbani Opera (Scriptores Latini Hiberniae),* Dublin, 1957, pp.62-6; ET by ICEL.

304 W. H. Vanstone, *Love's Endeavour, Love's Expense,* London, 1977, pp.68-9.

305 Justin, *First Apology,* 66-7: PG 6, cols 427-31.

307 Catherine of Siena, *The Dialogue,* 134; ET by Suzanne Noffke OP, New York & Mahwah, New Jersey, 1980, pp.273-4.

308 Clement of Rome, *Letter to the Corinthians,* 19; Loeb 24, *Apostolic Fathers I;* ET based on Kirsopp Lake, London, 1912, pp.71-3.

Corpus Christi

309 Hilary of Poitiers, *On the Trinity* VIII, 13-16; CCSL 62B, pp.35-8; ET by ICEL.

310 Augustine, *Sermon* 272; PL 38, cols 1246-8.

311 Gregory Dix, *The Shape of the Liturgy,* London, 1945, p.744.

312 Margaret Saunders, *Corpus Christi* (previously unpublished).

313 *Thesaurus Palaeohibernicus,* eds W. Stokes & J. Strachan, vol. II, Cambridge, 1903, pp.354-8; ET by Oliver Davies, *Celtic Christian Spirituality,* eds Oliver Davies & Fiona Bowie, London, 1995, pp.41-3 (omitting stanza at bottom of p.42).
Note: 'St Patrick's Breastplate', also known as 'The Deer's Cry', dates in its present form from the eighth century, but has long been attributed to Patrick. It is a classic example of a Celtic 'breastplate' prayer invoking the Holy Trinity's protection on body and soul.

315 Gregory of Nyssa, *Homily 6 'On the Beatitudes';* PG 44, cols 1269-72.

Trinity 1

316 Thomas Traherne, *Centuries of Meditations,* I, 51-3.

317 Basil the Great, *Concerning Faith,* 3; PG 30; cols 831-3.

318 Thomas à Kempis, *The Imitation of Christ,* 2, 2-3; ET by ICEL.

319 Thomas Merton, *The Power and Meaning of Love,* London, 1976, pp.6-8.

320 William of St Thierry, *Meditation* 3, 4; ET by Penelope Lawson CSMV; *The Works of William of St Thierry,* vol. 1, Spencer, Massachusetts, 1971, pp.103-4.

321 Origen, *On Prayer,* 10, 2 -11, 2 (abridged); PG 11, col. 448.

322 Dietrich Bonhoeffer, *The Cost of Discipleship,* 1937; ET by R.H. Fuller, London, 1959, p.170.

Trinity 2

323 Gregory of Nazianzus, *Oration 14,* 5-8: PG 35, cols 864-8; ET by ICEL (adapted).

324 Francis de Sales, *Introduction to the Devout Life,* III, 3.

325 Gregory the Great, *Homily 19 'On the Gospels',* 5-7; PL 76, cols 1157-8.

326 Gregory of Nyssa, *Catechetical Oration,* 5; PG 45, cols 20-5.

327 Gertrude of Helfta, *The Herald of Divine Love,* II, 3; ET by Margaret Winkworth, New York & Mahwah, New Jersey, 1993, pp.97-9 (abridged).

328 Jean-Pierre de Caussade, *Abandonment to Divine Providence* VI, 3.

329 Bernard of Clairvaux, *On the Love of God,* 1; PL 182, cols 973-5.

Trinity 3

330 W. H. Vanstone, *Love's Endeavour, Love's Expense,* London, 1977, pp.44-5.

331 Dorotheus of Gaza, *Discourse XIII 'On enduring temptation calmly and thankfully'*; PG 88; ET of Greek text by Eric Wheeler, *Dorotheos of Gaza: Discourses and Sayings*, Kalamazoo, Michigan, 1977, pp.192-3.

332 Gregory the Great, *Pastoral Care* II, 7; PL 77, cols 38-9.

333 Basil the Great, *Homily 8 'In time of famine and drought'*; 2, 7; ET by Susan R. Holman, *The body of the poor in fourth century Cappadocia: Seven Sermons on Hunger, Sickness and Penury*, Brown University, 1998, appendix, pp.295, 305-6.

334 John Macmurray, *Reason and Emotion*, London, 1935, pp.40-1, 46-7.

335 John of the Cross, *The Ascent of Mount Carmel*, II, 7, 8-11.

337 George Herbert, *The Country Parson*, XI.

Trinity 4

337 Gregory the Great, *Homily 36 'On the Gospels'*, 11-13; PL 76, cols 1272-4.

338 Ambrose, *Commentary on Psalm 36 (Hebrew Ps.37)*, 65-6; CSEL 64, pp.123-5; ET by ICEL.

340 William Law, *The Spirit of Prayer*.

341 John Cosin, *Sermon 20*; *The Works of Bishop John Cosin, I*, Oxford, 1843, pp.287-9.

342 Gregory of Nazianzus, *Dogmatic Poems*, 29; PG 37, cols 507-8.

343 Simone Weil, *Waiting on God*, Paris, 1942; ET by Emma Craufurd, London, 1951, pp.68-9.

344 Dorotheus of Gaza, *Discourse VI 'On Refusal to Judge our Neighbour'*; PG 88; ET of Greek text by Eric Wheeler, *Dorotheos of Gaza: Discourses and Sayings*, Kalamazoo, Michigan, 1977, pp.135-7.

Trinity 5

345 John Wesley, *Covenant Service: Directions for Renewing our Covenant with God*, IV.

346 John Cassian, *Conferences* X, 11; SC 54, p.92.

347 Cyprian, *On Patience*, 12-13; CSEL 3 (i), pp.404-6.

348 Augustine, *Commentary on St John's Gospel*, 26, 13; CCSL 36, pp.266-7.

349 Philip Sheldrake, *Befriending our Desires*, London, 1994, pp.16-17.

350 Miles Coverdale, *Treatise on Death*, 2, 16; *Remains of Miles Coverdale*, Cambridge, 1846, pp.48-9, 64-5.

351 Ignatius of Antioch, *The Letter to the Magnesians*, 10-14; Loeb 24, *Apostolic Fathers I*; ET based on Kirsopp Lake, London, 1912, pp.206-11.

Trinity 6

352 Augustine, *Treatise 4 'On the First Letter of John'* 6; PL 35, cols 2008-9.

353 Hugh Latimer, *Sermon VI Upon the Lord's Prayer*; *Sermons of Hugh Latimer*, ed. George Corrie, Cambridge, 1844, pp.415-17 (abridged).

354 Bernard of Clairvaux, *On the Song of Songs*, 33, ii; PL 183, cols 931-2.

355 Thomas Merton, *New Seeds of Contemplation*, NewYork, 1961; London, 1962 & 1972; new Anglicized edition, Tunbridge Wells, 1999; quotation from 1972 edition, p.125; © Abbey of Our Lady of Gethsemani.

356 Francis de Sales, *Introduction to the Devout Life*, III, 9.

357 Ambrose, *Commentary on Psalm 1*, 4, 7-8; CSEL 64, pp.4-7; ET by ICEL.

358 *The Art of Prayer*, ed. Igumen of Valamo; ET by E. Kadloubovsky & E. M. Palmer, London, 1966, pp.254-5.

Trinity 7
359 William Law, *The Spirit of Love,* I.
360 John of the Cross, *The Dark Night of the Soul,* I, 1, 2-3; 8, 3.
361 Jean Vanier, *Community and Growth,* London, revised edition 1989, pp.93-4.
362 Cyprian, *On the Lord's Prayer,* 4-6; CSEL 3 (i), pp.268-70.
363 Aelred of Rievaulx, *On Spiritual Friendship,* III, 61-3; ET by Mary Eugenia Laker SSND, Kalamazoo, Michigan, 1977, pp.105-6.
364 Ignatius of Antioch, *The Letter to the Trallians,* 1-3, 8-11; Loeb 24, *Apostolic Fathers I;* ET based on Kirsopp Lake, London, 1912, pp.212-15, 218-23.
365 Gregory the Great, *Pastoral Care,* II, 8; PL 77, cols 42-3.
Trinity 8
367 Hilary of Poitiers, *On the Trinity,* I, 37-38; CCSL 62A, pp.35-7; ET based on NPNF vol. IX, pp.50-1.
368 Bernard of Clairvaux, *On the Love of God,* 7; PL 182, cols 984-6.
369 Clement of Alexandria, *The Teacher* 1, 12; PG 8, cols 367-70.
371 Richard Baxter, *The Reformed Pastor,* I, 3.
372 Augustine, *Letter* 130 'To Proba', viii (15, 17); PL 33, cols 499-500.
372 Gregory of Nyssa, *On Christian Perfection;* PG 46, cols 259-62.
373 Philip Sheldrake, *Befriending our Desires,* London, 1994, pp.39-40.
Trinity 9
374 Aelred of Rievaulx, *The Mirror of Charity,* III, 35; PL 195, cols 608-10.
375 *The Wisdom of the Desert Fathers (The Anonymous Series);* ET by Benedicta Ward SLG, Oxford, 1975, p.28.
376 Augustine, *Commentary on St John's Gospel,* 8, 1; 24, 1; CCSL 36, pp.81-2, 244.
377 Pierre Teilhard de Chardin, *Hymn of the Universe,* 1957, Paris; ET © Collins & Sons, London, 1965, pp.68-70 (abridged).
378 Cyprian, *On the Mortality Rate,* 8, 11-13; CSEL 3 (i), pp.301-5.
379 Peter Chrysologus, *Sermon* 108; PL 52, cols 499-500.
381 Anselm, *Proslogion,* 17, 18; *The Prayers and Meditations of St Anselm,* ET by Benedicta Ward SLG, London, 1973, pp. 258-9.
Trinity 10
381 Tertullian, *On Prayer,* 28-9; CCSL 1, pp.273-4.
383 Bernard of Clairvaux, *On the Song of Songs,* 32; PL 182, cols 945-50.
384 Clement of Rome, *Letter to the Corinthians,* 36-7; Loeb 24, *Apostolic Fathers I;* ET based on Kirsopp Lake, London, 1912, pp.71-3.
385 Francis of Assisi, *Admonitions,* IV & V; ET by Regis Armstrong and Ignatius Brady, New York & Mahwah, New Jersey, 1982, pp.28-9.
386 Thomas Merton, *New Seeds of Contemplation,* New York, 1961; London 1962 & 1972; new Anglicized edition, Tunbridge Wells, 1999; quotation from 1972 edition, pp.1-2; © Abbey of Our Lady of Gethsemani.
387 Caesarius of Arles, *Sermon* 43, 3-4; CCSL 103, p.191.
388 Origen, *Homily 1 'On Genesis'* 4; SC 7, pp.68-9.
Trinity 11
389 Gregory of Nyssa, *Homily 6 'On the Beatitudes';* PG 44, cols 1269-72.

390 Mechtild of Magdeburg, *Revelations: The Flowing Light of the Godhead*, V, 30; ET based on Lucy Menzies, London, 1953, pp.155-6.

391 Dietrich Bonhoeffer, *Life Together;* ET from the fifth edition (1949) by John W. Doberstein, London, 1954; pp.17-18 (abridged).

392 Augustine, *Enchiridion*, 11-14; PL 40; cols 236-7.

393 Julian of Norwich, *Revelations of Divine Love*, 6; ed. Clifton Wolters, London, 1966, pp.69-71 (abridged).

395 Gregory of Nyssa, *The Life of Moses*, II, 162-4; SC 1, pp.210-13.

396 Francis de Sales, *Introduction to the Devout Life*, III, 10.

Trinity 12

397 Cyprian, *On the Lord 's Prayer*, 22-23; CSEL 3 (i), pp.282-4.

398 William Temple, *Mens Creatrix*, London, 1917, pp.362-3 (abridged).

399 Augustine, *Letter* 130, 'To Proba', ix (18); x (19, 20); PL 33, col. 501.

400 John of the Cross, 'A Song of the soul in intimate communication and union with the love of God'; ET by Marjorie Flower OCD, *The Poems of St John of the Cross*, Varroville, Australia.

401 *The Art of Prayer*, ed. Igumen of Valamo; ET by E. Kadloubovsky & E. M. Palmer, London, 1966, pp.52-3.

402 Thomas Traherne, *Centuries of Meditations*, I, 58-60.

403 Gregory of Nyssa, *Homily I 'On the Love of the Poor';* ET by Susan R. Holman, *The body of the poor in fourth century Cappadocia: Seven Sermons on Hunger, Sickness and Penury*, Brown University, 1998, appendix, p.314.

Trinity 13

404 John Chrysostom, *Homily 20 'On the Acts of the Apostles'*, 3-4; PG 60, cols 162-4.

405 John Wesley, *Sermon on the Mount VI.*

406 Dorotheus of Gaza, *Discourse VII 'On Self-Accusation';* PG 88; ET of Greek text based on that by Eric Wheeler, *Dorotheos of Gaza: Discourses and Sayings*, Kalamazoo, Michigan, 1977, pp.140-2 (abridged).

408 Maria Boulding, *The Coming of God*, 2nd edition, London, 1994, pp.36-7.

409 Cyril of Alexandria, *Commentary on St John's Gospel*, 11, 11; PG 74, cols 559-62; ET by ICEL.

410 Augustine, *Commentary on Psalm 32 (Hebrew Psalm 33)*, 1, 7-8; CCSL 38, pp.253-4.

411 Anonymous, *Didache* 9 & 14; Loeb 24, *Apostolic Fathers I;* ET based on Kirsopp Lake, London, 1912, pp.323-31.
NB The *Didache* or *The Teaching of the Twelve Apostles* can be dated to the end of the first century, and probably emerged from Christian communities in Palestine or Syria. It represents a specifically Christian or Judaeo-Christian development of an earlier Jewish catechism. It comprises three sections: the Christian Way, a liturgical section, and the organisation of the Church.

Trinity 14

412 Irenaeus, *Against Heresies*, IV, 20, 4-5; SC 100, pp.634-40; ET by ICEL.

413 Thomas Merton, 'The Philosophy of Solitude', *The Power and Meaning of Love*, London, 1976, pp.58-9.

414   John Climacus, *The Ladder of Divine Ascent*, 24; ET by Colm Luibheid & Norman Russell, New York & Mahwah, New Jersey, 1982, pp.214-15.

415   Philip Sheldrake, *Befriending our Desires*, London, 1994, pp.79-81 (abridged).

416   Augustine, *Commentary on Psalm 121 (Hebrew Ps. 122)*; CCSL 40, pp.1801-13.

417   *The Art of Prayer*, ed. Igumen of Valamo; ET by E. Kadloubovsky & E. M. Palmer, London, 1966, p.232.

417   Bernard of Clairvaux, *The Steps of Humility and Pride*, 3; PL 182, cols 941-3.

Trinity 15

419   Cyprian, *On the Lord 's Prayer*, 18-20; CSEL 3 (i), pp.280-1.

420   Aelred of Rievaulx, *The Mirror of Charity*, III, 8; PL 195, cols 584-5.

421   Heather Ward, *The Gift of Self*, London, 1990, pp.25-6.

422   Gregory the Great, *Homily 27 'On the Gospels'*, 8-9; PL 76, cols 1209-10.

423   Origen, *On Prayer*, 31, 1-4 (abridged); PG 11, cols 549-52.

424   Lancelot Andrewes, *Sermon 2, 'On the Passion'; The Works of Bishop Lancelot Andrewes*, LACT, Oxford, 1841, vol. II, pp.145-6.

425   Gregory of Nyssa, *Homily 2 'On the Song of Songs'*; PG 44, cols 763-5.

Trinity 16

426   David Lonsdale SJ, *Eyes to See, Ears to Hear*, London, 1990, pp.63, 65-6.

427   Augustine, *On the Trinity*, VIII, viii (12); CCSL 50, pp.286-8.

429   John of the Cross, *The Living Flame of Love*, stanza 3, 46.

430   Thomas Merton, *New Seeds of Contemplation*, New York, 1961; London, 1962 & 1972; new Anglicized edition, Tunbridge Wells, 1999; quotation from 1972 edition, pp.17, 20; © Abbey of Our Lady of Gethsemani.

431   Basil the Great, *Homily 8 'In time of famine and drought'*, 6; ET by Susan R. Holman, *The body of the poor in fourth century Cappadocia: Seven Sermons on Hunger, Sickness and Penury*, Brown University, 1998, appendix, p.314.

432   Francis de Sales, *Introduction to the Devout Life*, III, 28-29.

433   Dorotheus of Gaza, *Discourse XIII 'On enduring temptation calmly and thankfully'*; PG 88; ET of Greek text by Eric Wheeler, *Dorotheos of Gaza: Discourses and Sayings*, Kalamazoo, Michigan, 1977, pp.192-3 (adapted).

Trinity 17

434   Walter Hilton, *The Scale of Perfection*, II, 21; ET by John Clark & Rosemary Dorward, New York & Mahwah, New Jersey, 1991, p.229.

435   Ignatius of Antioch, *The Letter to the Philadelphians*, 1-2, 4-5; Loeb 24, *Apostolic Fathers* I; ET based on Kirsopp Lake, London, 1912, pp.238-41, 242-5.

436   Gregory the Great, *Homily 35 'On the Gospels'*, 4-6; PL 1261-3.

437   George Herbert, *The Country Parson*, XXII.

438   John Cassian, *Conferences* X, 7; SC 54, p.81.

439   Dietrich Bonhoeffer, *The Cost of Discipleship*, 1937; ET by R. H. Fuller, London, 1959, pp.78-9.

440   Athanasius, *Against the Pagans*, 40-2; PG 25, cols 79-83; ET by ICEL.

Trinity 18

441   Cyril of Jerusalem, *Catechesis* V, 1, 3-4; PG 33, cols 507-10; ET by ICEL.

Notes & Sources   *543*

442 Augustine, *Commentary on Psalm 32 (Hebrew Psalm 33)*, II, 29; CCSL 38, pp.272-3.
443 Julian of Norwich, *Revelations of Divine Love*, 60; edition Clifton Wolters, London, 1966, pp.170-1.
444 Vincent of Lérins, *Commonitorium* 2-3; critical edition, R. S. Moxon, Cambridge, 1915, pp.7-11.
445 Thomas Traherne, *Centuries of Meditations*, I, 19, 25, 28-30.
446 Baldwin of Canterbury, *Treatise* 10; PL 204, cols 513-14, 516; ET by ICEL.
447 Jean-Pierre de Caussade, *Abandonment to Divine Providence*, VI, 5.
Trinity 19
448 Thomas Merton, *New Seeds of Contemplation*, New York, 1961; London, 1962 & 1972; new Anglicized edition, Tunbridge Wells, 1999; quotation from 1972 edition, pp.17, 20; © Abbey of Our Lady of Gethsemani.
449 William Law, *A Serious Call to a Devout and Holy Life*, 16.
450 William of St Thierry, *Meditation* 9, 1, 5, 12; ET by Penelope Lawson CSMV; *The Works of William of St Thierry, I*, Spencer, Massachusetts, 1971, p.103-4.
451 Gregory the Great, *Pastoral Care*, IV; PL 77, cols 125-6.
452 Peter Chrysologus, *Sermon* 108; PL 52, cols 499-500.
453 Thomas More, *The Dialogue of Comfort against Tribulation*, I, 6.
454 Jeremy Taylor, *Holy Dying*, II, ii, 1-2.
Trinity 20
455 Columbanus, *Instructions* 13, 'On Christ the Fount of Life', 1-2; *Sancti Columbani Opera (Scriptores Latini Hiberniae)*, Dublin, 1957, pp.116-18; ET by ICEL.
456 John Wesley, 'Catholic Spirit'; *Sermons on Several Occasions*, 1750; revised ed. 1787/8; vol. III, p.181ff; see also *The Works of John Wesley*, ed. Frank Baker, Oxford, 1975- .
457 John Chrysostom, *Homily 12 'On the Letter to the Colossians'*, 5; *Homily 20 'On the Letter to the Ephesians'*, 1; *Homily 38 'On Genesis'*, 7.
458 Ambrose, *Commentary on Psalm 1*, 9-12; CSEL 64, pp.7, 9-10; ET by ICEL.
460 Aelred of Rievaulx, *On Spiritual Friendship*, I, 57-61; ET by Mary Eugenia Laker SSND, Kalamazoo, Michigan, 1977, pp.63-4.
461 Philip Sheldrake, *Befriending our Desires*, London, 1994, pp.61-2.
462 Augustine, *Commentary on St John's Gospel*, 17, 7-9; CCSL 36, pp.174-5.
Trinity 21
463 Julian of Norwich, *Revelations of Divine Love*, 73; ET by Clifton Wolters, London, 1966, pp.192-3.
464 Augustine, *Sermon* 156, 9-11; PL 38, cols 854-7.
465 *The Cloud of Unknowing*; ET by Clifton Wolters, London, 1971, pp.102-3.
466 Gregory of Nyssa, *Homily I 'On the Love of the Poor'*; ET by Susan R. Holman, *The body of the poor in fourth century Cappadocia: Seven Sermons on Hunger, Sickness and Penury*, Brown University, 1998, appendix, pp.315-6.
467 John V. Taylor, *The Go-Between God*, London, 1973, pp.226-7.
468 Bernard of Clairvaux, *On the Love of God*, 4; PL 182, cols 980-2.
469 Augustine, *Confessions*, XIII, xxxv, (50) - xxxviii (53); CSEL 33, pp.386-8.

Notes & Sources

Last Sunday after Trinity

470 Ephrem of Syria, *Commentary on the Diatessaron,* 1, 18-19; SC 121, pp.52-3; ET by ICEL.

Bible Sunday

471 Augustine, *Confessions,* VIII, xii, (28, 29); CSEL 33, pp.194-5.

472 Isidore of Seville, *Book of Maxims,* 3, 8-10; PL 83, cols 679-82; ET by ICEL.

473 Guigo of Chartreuse, *Letter* 8, 31; PL 184, cols 327-8.

474 *Authorized Version of the Bible,* 1611, preface.

474 Jean-Pierre de Caussade, *Abandonment to Divine Providence,* II, 4.

476 Ignatius of Antioch, *The Letter to the Magnesians,* 1, 6-9; Loeb 24, *Apostolic Fathers I;* ET based on Kirsopp Lake, London, 1912, pp.196-7, 200-5.

477 Dietrich Bonhoeffer, *Life Together;* ET from the fifth edition (1949) by John W. Doberstein, London, 1954; pp.57-8 (abridged).

478 Caesarius of Arles, *Sermon* 25, 1; CCSL 103, pp.111-12.

479 William Temple, *Mens Creatrix,* London, 1917, pp.363-4.

480 *The Art of Prayer,* ed. Igumen of Valamo; ET by E. Kadloubovsky & E. M. Palmer, London, 1966, pp.95-7.

481 Gregory the Great, *Moral Reflections on Job,* 29, 2-4; PL 76, cols 478-80.

Dedication Festival

483 Origen, *Homily 9 'On Joshua',* 1-2; SC 71, pp.244-6.

484 Augustine, *Sermon* 336, 1, 6; PL 38, cols 1471-5; ET by ICEL.

485 George Herbert, *The Country Parson,* XIII.

ORDINARY TIME BEFORE ADVENT

All Saints' Sunday

489 Clement of Rome, *Letter to the Corinthians,* 46, 48; Loeb 24, *Apostolic Fathers I;* ET based on Kirsopp Lake, London, 1912, pp.87-93.

490 Thomas Ken, 'All praise to thee, in light array'd'.

4 before Advent

491 Thomas Aquinas, *Collation 'On the Creed': Opuscula Theologica 2,* pp.216-17; ET by ICEL.

492 Gregory of Nyssa, *Homily 6 'On the Beatitudes';* PG 44, cols 1267-9.

493 William Law, *A Serious Call to a Devout and Holy Life,* 14.

494 Jean-Pierre de Caussade, *Abandonment to Divine Providence* VI, 3.

495 Thomas Traherne, *Centuries of Meditations,* III, 39, 40.

496 Aelred of Rievaulx, *The Mirror of Charity,* I, 5; PL 195, cols 509-10. C. S. Lewis, 'The Weight of Glory', *Transformation and Other Essays,* London, 1949, p.31.

3 before Advent

497 Clement of Rome, *Letter to the Corinthians,* 49-50; Loeb 24, *Apostolic Fathers I;* ET based on Kirsopp Lake, London, 1912, pp.111-15.

498 Thomas Merton, *The Power and Meaning of Love,* London, 1976, pp.144-5.

499   Augustine, *Sermon* 256, 1, 3; PL 38, cols 1192-3.

500   Gregory of Nyssa, *Homily 6 'On Ecclesiastes';* PG 44, cols 702-3; ET by ICEL.

501   John Donne, *Devotions upon Emergent Occasions, and Several Steps in my Sickness,* meditation 17; *Works,* III, London, 1839, pp.574-5.

502   Richard Challoner, *Meditations for every day in the Year,* 1767; Westminster edition of 1915, pp.450-1

504   William of St Thierry, *Meditations* 2, 4-6; ET by Penelope Lawson CSMV; *The Works of William of St Thierry I,* Spencer, Massachusetts, 1971, pp.97-8.

2 before Advent

505   Julian of Norwich, *Revelations of Divine Love,* 72; ET by Clifton Wolters, London, 1966, pp.190-1.

506   W. H. Vanstone, *Love's Endeavour, Love's Expense,* London, 1977, pp.61-3 (abridged).

507   Augustine, *The City of God,* I Preface, XIV, 28; XXII, 30.

508   Pierre Teilhard de Chardin, *Le Milieu Divin,* 1957, Paris; ET © Collins & Sons, London, 1960, pp.69-70.

509   Aelred of Rievaulx, *A Rule of Life for a Recluse,* 33; ET by Mary Paul Macpherson OCSO in *The Works of Aelred of Rievaulx I,* Spencer, Massachusetts, 1971, pp.100-1.

510   Gregory of Nyssa, *Catechetical Oration,* 8; PG 45, cols 36-7.

511   Cyprian, *On the Lord's Prayer,* 13; CSEL 3 (i), p.275.

Christ the King

512   Hippolytus of Rome (?), *On the Consummation of the World,* 41-3; PG 10, cols 944-5.

513   Anselm of Canterbury, *Letter 112; Opera Omnia,* ed. Schmitt, 3, pp.245-6; ET by ICEL.

514   William Temple, *Mens Creatrix,* London, 1917, p.322-3.

515   R. S. Thomas, 'The Kingdom', *H'm,* London, 1972, p.34.

516   Ephrem of Syria, *Commentary on the Diatessaron,* 18, 15-17; SC 121, pp.325-8; ET by ICEL.

517   Augustine, *Commentary on Psalm 109 (Hebrew Ps. 110),* 1-3; CCSL 40, pp.1601-3; ET by ICEL.

518   Augustine, *Confessions,* X, i-ii (1-2); v (7); CSEL 33, pp.226-7, 230-1.

519   Origen, *On Prayer,* 25; PG 11, cols 495-9.

520   A. M. Ramsey, *The Glory of God and the Transfiguration of Christ,* London, 1949, pp.89-90.

522   Julian of Norwich, *Revelations of Divine Love,* 32; ET by Clifton Wolters, London, 1966, pp.109-10 (modified).

Remembrance Sunday

523   Prudentius, *Hymnus circa Exsequias Defuncti; Liber Cathemerinon,* X; CSEL 61, pp.56-63; ET by Helen Waddell, *Medieval Latin Lyrics,* London, 1929, pp.45-7.

524   Wilfred Owen, 'Strange Meeting', *Collected Poems,* London, 1920, pp.35-6.

525   Austin Farrer, *Said or Sung,* London, 1960, pp.133-4 (abridged).

INDEX OF THEMES

Index of Themes   549

INDEX OF AUTHORS

BIOGRAPHICAL NOTES

The following are biographical sketches of some of the authors
whose writings have been included in this anthology.

Addison, Joseph (1672-1719)
Joseph Addison was a celebrated essayist who enjoyed a distinguished career as a
Member of Parliament. To the Church, he bequeathed a number of magnificent
hymns.

Aelred of Rievaulx (1109-1167)
Aelred was born at Hexham in 1109. His father was a priest and he entered the
Cistercian Order at Rievaulx in about 1133, after spending some years in the court
of King David of Scotland. He became Abbot of Revesby in 1143 and returned to
Rievaulx four years later to become abbot and there to spend the remainder of his
life. He was profoundly influential through his spiritual writings, which he began
at the request of Bernard of Clairvaux, the two having a similar approach to the
spiritual life. He was often called 'The Bernard of the North'. His most famous
works are *The Mirror of Charity* and *On Spiritual Friendship*, the latter of which
was partly based on the writing of Cicero.

Ambrose of Milan (c.334-397)
Born in Trier, Ambrose was of an aristocratic family, and in 374 was made
Governor of northern Italy, with his headquarters in Milan. Whilst trying to bring
peace to the Christian community, with Arianism and orthodoxy each trying to
gain the election of its man as bishop, Ambrose, known and respected by all
though not yet baptized, found himself being urged to accept the role of bishop
himself. He finally accepted and was baptized and consecrated. Ambrose proved
his worth, becoming a teacher and preacher of great renown, promoting the
essential divinity of Christ as being at the centre of Christian faith. He is credited
with being the first person to introduce hymns into Western worship, and wrote
several hymns himself.

Andrew of Crete (c.660-740)
Andrew was a native of Damascus. He was a monk of Jerusalem for many years,
and in around 692 became Archbishop of Gortyna in Crete. He was a celebrated
theologian and hymn-writer. He is said to have been the first writer of the
compositions called 'canons'. His 'Great Canon', a penitential hymn for Lent, is
still sung in the Byzantine liturgy. He was an eloquent preacher and a number of
his sermons have survived.

Andrewes, Lancelot (1555-1626)
After ordination Lancelot Andrewes held several posts before accepting
appointments as Bishop, first of Chichester, then of Ely and finally of Winchester

Biographical Notes 555

in 1619. He was a remarkable and gifted preacher. He was present at the Hampton Court Conference in 1604, which furthered the reform of the Church of England, and he was also a translator of much of the Old Testament of what is known as the 'Authorized Version' of the Bible. His preaching and writings proved highly influential, and his holiness of life and gentle nature endeared him to all.

Anselm (1033-1109)

Anselm was born in Aosta, northern Italy. As a young man, he left home and travelled north, visiting many monasteries and other centres of learning. One such visit was to the abbey of Bec, where he met Lanfranc who advised him to embrace monastic life. Anselm had a powerful and original mind and, during his 34 years at Bec (as monk, prior and finally abbot), he taught many others and wrote many theological, philosophical and devotional works. When Lanfranc died Anselm was made Archbishop of Canterbury and had to subordinate his scholarly work to the needs of the diocese and nation. Twice he endured exile for championing the rights of the Church against the authority of the king but, despite his stubbornness, intellectual rigour, and personal austerity, he was admired by the Norman nobility as well as loved by his monks.

Aquinas, Thomas (c.1225-1274)

Thomas Aquinas has been described as the greatest thinker and teacher of the medieval Church. Born at Rocca Secca, near Aquino, in Italy, he was educated first by the Benedictines at Monte Cassino, and then at the University of Naples. Against his family's wishes, he joined the mendicant Dominican Order of Preachers. His philosophy received its characteristic shape under the influence of the recently recovered metaphysical writings of Aristotle. It is set out in his great *Summa Theologica*. His profound, theological wisdom and capacity to communicate, as well in homilies and hymns as theological treatises, along with his gentleness of spirit in dealing with people, earned him the title 'the Angelic Doctor'. He died in 1274.

Athanasius of Alexandria (295-373)

Athanasius was born of Christian parents and educated at the Catechetical School in Alexandria. He was present at the Council of Nicea as a deacon, accompanying his bishop Alexander, whom he succeeded as Patriarch of Alexandria in 328. Athanasius held firmly to the doctrines of the Church as defined by that Council, and became the leader of those opposed to the teachings of Arianism which denied the divinity of Christ. He was deposed from and restored to his See several times because of his uncompromising faith. In or out of exile, Athanasius continued his writings, ever the proponent of orthodoxy over heterodoxy, and the essential need for the Church to teach the true doctrines of the faith rather than watered-down versions of it. He was a strong believer in asceticism as a means of restoring the divine image in humanity and thus a supporter of monasticism, which was in its nascent state at that time.

Biographical Notes

Augustine of Hippo (354-430)

Augustine was born in North Africa in 354. His career as an orator and rhetorician led him from Carthage to Rome, and from there to Milan where the Imperial court at that time resided. By temperament, he was passionate and sensual, and as a young man he rejected Christianity. Gradually, however, under the influence first of Monica, his mother, and then of Ambrose, Bishop of Milan, Augustine began to look afresh at the Scriptures. He was baptized by Ambrose at the Easter Vigil in 387. Not long after returning to North Africa he was ordained priest, and then became Bishop of Hippo. It is difficult to overestimate the influence of Augustine on the subsequent development of European thought. A huge body of his sermons and writings has been preserved, through all of which runs the theme of the sovereignty of the grace of God.

Baldwin of Canterbury (d. 1190)

A native of Exeter, Baldwin entered the Cistercian monastery at Ford in Devon. He became Bishop of Worcester in 1180, and in 1184, Archbishop of Canterbury. He took part in the Crusade of 1190. He returned very disillusioned at the indiscipline of the Christian troops, and this had a profound effect on the rest of his ministry and preaching.

Basil the Great (c.329-379)

Basil, his brother Gregory of Nyssa, and his friend Gregory of Nazianzus, are known collectively as the Cappadocian Fathers. They were outstanding in their defence of the divinity of Christ, as set forth in the Council of Nicea, against the attacks of Arianism. Basil is sometimes known as the theologian of the Holy Spirit for his powerful treatise on the subject. Near Caesarea he organized a complete city of social service run by monks. The people gave it the name 'Basiliad'. It contained a guest house, a hospice, an orphanage, a hospital, and there were free meals and lodging for the poor. He also developed liturgical life, and the eucharistic liturgy which bears his name continues to be used today in the Orthodox Church. He never had a robust constitution, and died prematurely in his fifties, worn out by hard work.

Baxter, Richard (1615-1691)

Richard Baxter was born in Shropshire. In 1633 he was at the court of Charles I, but was so disgusted with the low moral standards there that he returned home in order to study divinity. He was ordained but after the promulgation of an infamous Oath in 1640, which required obedience to a string of persons ending in the trite phrase 'et cetera', he rejected belief in episcopacy in its current English form, and went as a curate to a poor area of the West Midlands. He opposed the Civil War and played a prominent part in the recall of Charles II, but his continuing dissatisfaction with the way episcopacy was practised led him to decline the See of Hereford. This refusal led him to be debarred from further office in the Church, though he continued to contribute to its life as a prolific hymn-writer. His writings breathe a spirit of deep unaffected piety and moderation, and his book *The Reformed Pastor*, published in 1656, illustrates the great care he took in his pastoral organization.

Biographical Notes   557

Bede (c.670-735)

Bede was born in Northumbria around the year 670. When he was seven years old, his family gave him to the monastery of St Peter and St Paul at Wearmouth. He then moved to Jarrow, where he lived as a monk for the rest of his life. Although it seems he never travelled further than York, his monastery (first under Abbot Bene't Biscop and then Abbot Ceolfrith) was a centre of learning, and Bede studied extensively. He used all the resources available to write the most complete history of Christian England up to the year 729, as well as commentaries on books of the Bible. He was renowned for his monastic fidelity and his love of teaching, and was fondly remembered by his pupils, including his biographer. He died peacefully in 735 and is buried in Durham Cathedral.

Bernard of Clairvaux (1090-1153)

Bernard was born at Fontaines, near Dijon in France. He entered the Benedictine abbey at Cîteaux in 1112, taking with him many of his young companions, some of whom were his own brothers. He was a leader of the reform within Benedictinism at this time, and in 1115 was sent to establish a new monastery at a place he named Clairvaux, or 'Valley of Light'. Though times were hard, he built up the community through his remarkable qualities of leadership. Bernard preached widely and powerfully, and proved himself a theologian of renown. Literally hundreds of houses were founded on the Cîteaux or Cistercian system and Bernard's influence on his own generation and beyond was immense.

Bonaventure (c.1218-1274)

Born at Bagnoreggio in Italy, Bonaventure became a Franciscan Friar in 1243 and his intellectual ability was soon recognized by his Order and by the Church. At the age of thirty-six he was elected Minister General of the Franciscans and virtually re-founded the Order, giving it a stability in training and administration previously unknown. He upheld all the teachings of St Francis except in the founder's attitude to study, since Francis felt the Order should possess no books. He clearly saw, with Francis, that the role of the Friars was to support the Church through its contemporary structures rather than to be an instrument for reform. He also believed that the best conversions came from the good example of those anxious to renew the Church, rather than by haranguing or passing laws.

Bonhoeffer, Dietrich (1906-1945)

Dietrich Bonhoeffer was born into an academic family. Ordained in the Lutheran Church, his theology was influenced by Karl Barth and he became a lecturer: in Spain, the USA and in 1931 back in Berlin. Opposed to Nazism, he was one of the leaders of the Confessing Church, a movement which broke away from the Nazi-dominated Lutherans in 1934. Banned from teaching, and harassed by Hitler's regime, he bravely returned to Germany at the outbreak of war in 1939, despite being on a lecture tour in the United States at the time. His defiant opposition to the Nazis led to his arrest in 1943. His experiences led him to propose a more radical theology in his later writing which was highly influential among post-war theologians. His books on *Ethics* and *The Cost of Discipleship*, together with his little book *Life Together,* continue to be widely read. He was murdered by the Nazi police in Flossenburg concentration camp in 1945.

Caesarius of Arles (*c.*470-543)
Caesarius was born in France. In 489 he entered monastic life at Lérins. So outstanding was he that he was made Archbishop of Arles. He was deeply influenced by the teaching of Augustine on grace, and was a celebrated preacher.

Cassian, John (*c.*360-435)
As a young man Cassian joined a monastery at Bethlehem, but left it soon after to study monasticism in Egypt. Eventually, he seems to have established himself permanently in the West. He wrote two books on monastic life called the *Institutes* and the *Conferences,* out of the material he had gathered during his sojourn in Egypt, which proved highly influential in disseminating the monastic ideal in the Western Church.

Catherine of Siena (1347-1380)
Catherine Benincasa was born the second youngest of twenty-five children. Pious from her earliest years, she overcame family opposition to her vocation and became a Dominican tertiary at the age of eighteen. Nourished by a life of contemplative prayer and mystical experience, she devoted herself to active care for the poor and sick. She became increasingly sought after as an adviser on political as well as religious matters and, in 1376, she journeyed to Avignon as an ambassador to the Pope and influenced his decision to return to Rome. She wrote a *Dialogue* on the spiritual life as well as numerous letters of counsel and direction, which stressed her devotion to the Precious Blood of Jesus.

Challoner, Richard (1691-1781)
Richard Challoner was born in Sussex of Presbyterian parents, but became a Roman Catholic as a boy. At the age of fourteen he was sent to Douai to train for the priesthood. In 1738 he returned to England, and in 1741 was consecrated Roman Catholic Bishop of Debra and coadjutor to the Vicar-Apostolic of the London district. He was author of many influential books among which *Meditations for Every Day of the Year* (published in 1753) enjoyed great popularity.

Chrysologus, Peter (*c.*400-450)
Peter Chrysologus was born in Italy, and became Bishop of Ravenna. He was a faithful pastor, many of whose powerful sermons have been preserved. He was named 'Chrysologus' (Greek meaning 'golden-worded') to make him a Western counterpart of John 'Chrysostom' ('golden-mouthed') in the East.

Chrysostom, John (*c.*347-407)
John was born in Antioch, the third city of the Roman Empire. He was a brilliant preacher which earned him in the sixth century the surname 'Chrysostom', literally 'golden-mouthed'. He is honoured as one of the four Greek Doctors of the Church. Against his wish he was made Patriarch of Constantinople in 398. He set

about reforming the Church and exposing corruption amongst the clergy and in the Imperial administration. 'Mules bear fortunes and Christ dies of hunger at your gate,' he is alleged to have cried out. He fell foul of the Empress Eudoxia, and in spite of the support of Pope Innocent I of Rome, was sent into exile twice, finally dying of exhaustion and starvation in 407.

Clement of Alexandria (c.140-c.220)

Clement was born in Athens of pagan parents. The reasons for his conversion to Christianity are not known. He became head of the Catechetical School in Alexandria in about the year 200. In his teaching he sought to explore the relation between Christian thought and Greek philosophy, and is honoured as Christianity's first religious philosopher. Central to his theology was the doctrine of the *Logos* (Word), who as divine reason is the teacher of the world and its lawgiver. Consequently it is the duty of Christianity to make its own all the religious traditions of humankind, all its philosophical and scientific searchings. His most famous works are *An Exhortation to the Greeks*, *The Teacher* (also known as *The Educator'*), and *Miscellaneous Studies (*literally, 'many-coloured tapestries').

Clement of Rome (d. c.96)

Clement was active as an elder in the Church in Rome towards the end of the first century and was reputed to have been a disciple of the apostles. He wrote a letter to the Corinthians which focused on ministry in the Church and dealt with controversial issues relating to authority and duty. The letter clearly reveals an exercise of authority on the part of one senior presbyter intervening in a conflict in another church, and as such it provides valuable information about the history of the developing Church and its ministry at this time. He seems to have been president of a council of presbyters which governed the Church in Rome and he appears to be writing on their behalf.

Climacus, John (seventh century)

John of Sinai came to be called 'of the ladder' (*klimakos* in Greek) from the name of his principal work. He gave systematic form to three centuries of monastic tradition and ascetic practice.

Columbanus (c.543-615)

Columbanus was a native of Ireland who travelled by way of England to Gaul where he founded a number of monasteries on Celtic lines. A deeply ascetic man, he was driven out of the country because of his outspoken criticisms of the Burgundian court, and eventually settled in northern Italy. A number of his sermons and his monastic *Rule* have survived.

Cosin, John (1594-1672)

John Cosin was born into a wealthy Norfolk family and educated at Cambridge. Following ordination he came under the influence of Archbishop Laud. In 1635 he was elected Master of Peterhouse, Cambridge, whose chapel he reordered according to High Church principles. This attracted the wrath of the Puritans, and during the Commonwealth he was deprived of his fellowship. He went into exile, becoming chaplain to the Anglican Royalists in Paris. Upon the Restoration he was created Bishop of Durham by Charles II, and became a notable apologist for the Anglican settlement.

Coverdale, Miles (1488-1568)

Miles Coverdale was an Augustinian friar in Cambridge where, under the influence of his prior, Robert Barnes, he became an enthusiast for religious reform. His preaching led him to exile on the Continent where he produced the first complete English Bible based on Tyndale and other sources. His translation of the Psalter was included by Cranmer in the *Book of Common Prayer*. He became Bishop of Exeter during the reign of Edward VI, was exiled under Queen Mary, and returned to England upon the accession of Elizabeth I.

Cyprian of Carthage (c.200-258)

Cyprian was a teacher of rhetoric and a lawyer in the city of Carthage before his conversion to Christianity. He gave away his pagan library and set his mind to study the Scriptures and the commentaries that were beginning to proliferate. He became a priest and then, in 248, was elected Bishop of Carthage. He showed compassion to returning apostates, whilst always insisting on the need for discipline and unity in the Church. This may be seen, for example, in his famous treatise *On the Unity of the Church*. During the persecution of Valerian, the Christian clergy were required to participate in pagan worship; Cyprian refused and was first exiled and then condemned to death.

Cyril of Alexandria (d. 444)

Cyril was born in Alexandria and is first heard of as a young priest. He succeeded his uncle as Patriarch in the year 412 and began his great defence of the orthodox doctrines of God the Holy Trinity, and of the Incarnate Christ as a unique, single Person, at once God and human. His chief opponent was Nestorius, the Patriarch of Constantinople, who appears to have taught that there were two separate Persons co-existing in the Incarnate Christ, the one divine and the other human. The Nestorian Party thus rejected the description of Mary as *Theotokos*, 'the God-bearer', and also rejected the papal ruling that they comply with Cyril's doctrinal position that the union between divinity and humanity in Christ was total and real. The Council of Ephesus was convened in the year 431 to rule on the matter and eventually gave its full support to Cyril, making the term *Theotokos* the touchstone of Christian orthodoxy. Cyril's writings reflect his outstanding qualities as a theologian. They are marked by precision in exposition, accuracy in thought and skill in reasoning.

Cyril of Jerusalem (c.315-386)

Cyril was born probably in Caesarea. He became Bishop of Jerusalem when he was about thirty-four years old. There he nurtured both the resident Christian population and the many pilgrims who, with the end of the era of persecution, were beginning to make their way from all over Christendom to the places associated with Christ. Cyril taught the faith in line with the orthodoxy of the

Council of Nicea and the credal statement that became associated with it. Though he found difficulty with the word in that creed which described Jesus as being 'of one substance with the Father', nevertheless he took the side of the Nicene Party against the Arians, who denied the divinity of Christ. His teaching through his *Catechetical Lectures*, intended for those preparing for baptism, shows him to have been profoundly orthodox in theology. His liturgical innovations to celebrate the observance of Holy Week and Easter are the foundation of Christian practices to this day.

de Caussade, Jean-Pierre (1675-1751)

De Caussade joined the Jesuits in 1693 and became a celebrated preacher and spiritual director. His extensive correspondence with the Sisters of the Visitation at Nancy over the years is a leading source of his teaching. His letters of direction were translated into English under the title *Abandonment to Divine Providence*.

de Sales, Francis (1567-1622)

Francis de Sales was born in 1567 in the castle at Sales in Savoy. He was educated in Paris and Padua, first as a legal advocate, and then as a priest. His preaching against Calvinism began in 1593 to win back the Chablais to Roman Catholicism. In 1599 he was appointed Bishop-Coadjutor of Geneva, and moved to Annecy from which he administered the diocese when he became the Diocesan in 1602. It was not until 1799 that Roman Catholic worship was officially sanctioned again in the city. In his preaching and writings, particularly his book *Introduction to the Devout Life*, he concentrated on putting prayer and meditation within the reach of all Christians.

Donne, John (1571-1631)

John Donne was brought up as a Roman Catholic. He was a great-great nephew of Thomas More, although this seems to have had little influence on him, and was extremely sceptical about all religion. He went up to Oxford when he was fourteen, studied further at Cambridge and perhaps on the Continent, and eventually discovered his Christian faith in the Church of England. After much heart-searching, he accepted ordination and later the post of Dean of St Paul's Cathedral. Much of his cynicism dissolved and he became a strong advocate for the discerning of Christian vocation, and in particular affirming his own vocation as a priest, loving and loved by the crucified Christ. He was acclaimed for his sermons and poetry.

Dorotheus of Gaza (sixth century)

Abba Dorotheus (or Dorotheos) spent his youth in diligent study in Gaza. Under the influence of the great monastic teachers Barsanuphius and John, he entered the monastery of Abba Serid. In later life he became abbot of a nearby monastery, and it is to this period that his ascetical discourses or 'instructions' belong. He had a very high regard for humility which he saw as the cement of all other virtues.

Ephrem of Syria (c.306-373)

Born of Christian parents around 306, Ephrem was baptized as a young man and then ordained deacon. His early years were spent as a teacher in Nisibis in Mesopotamia until the city fell under Persian occupation in 363. Fleeing from his home, he settled in Edessa (Urfa in south-east Turkey) where he established a school of theology. Best known for his Syriac poetry, Ephrem is acclaimed as the greatest poet of the early Christian centuries, described by his contemporaries as the 'Harp of the Spirit'. His hymns, still used today, have found a place in liturgical traditions outside the East Syrian Church. He died in Edessa ministering to victims of the plague.

Eusebius of Caesarea (c.260-c.340)

Eusebius is sometimes known as the 'Father of Church History'. In 315 he became Bishop of Caesarea. In addition to his many historical writings, Eusebius wrote a number of apologetic works defending Christianity.

Francis of Assisi (1181-1226)

Francis was baptized Giovanni, but given the name Francesco by his father, a cloth merchant who traded in France and had married a French wife. There was an expectation that he would eventually take over his father's business but Francis had a rebellious youth and a difficult relationship with his father. After suffering the ignomy of imprisonment following capture whilst at war with Perugia, he returned a changed man. He took to caring for disused churches and for the poor, particularly those suffering from leprosy. Whilst praying in the semi-derelict church of St Damian, he distinctly heard the words: 'Go and repair my church, which you see is falling down.' Others joined him and he prepared a simple, gospel-based Rule for them all to live by. As the Order grew, it witnessed to Christ through preaching the gospel of repentance, emphasizing the poverty of Christ as an example for his followers. Two years before his death, his life being so closely linked with that of his crucified Saviour, he received the Stigmata, the marks of the wounds of Christ, on his body.

Frank, Mark (c.1612-1664)

Mark Frank was born in Buckinghamshire, and went up to Pembroke Hall (College), Cambridge in 1627, becoming a Fellow in 1634. He was a friend of Nicholas Ferrar at Little Gidding, and possibly, therefore, of Ferrar's other close friend, George Herbert. He was primarily a scholar and preacher who enjoyed the patronage of Charles I. Stylistically, Frank was influenced by Andrewes, but he is more accessible. In his preaching he stands mid-way between the elegant, highly-wrought sermons of Andrewes, and the plain moralistic preaching that came later. His *Course of Sermons* was published in 1642. In 1644, because of his Royalist and Arminian sympathies, he was ejected by the Parliamentary visitors from his fellowship and had to leave Cambridge. On the restoration of the monarchy, he was reinstated, and in 1662 elected Master of Pembroke. He was at the same time Chaplain to Archbishop Sheldon.

Gertrude of Helfta (1256-*c*.1302)

Gertrude was born in 1256. At the age of five she was given by her parents to be brought up by the Benedictine nuns of Helfta in Thuringia. She was a gifted child and received a good education at their hands. At the age of twenty-five she experienced a profound conversion in consequence of a vision of Christ, and for the rest of her life she led a life of contemplation. Of the so-called *Revelations of Gertrude*, only *The Herald of Divine Love* is genuinely hers, written partly from her notes or dictation, and partly by herself. She is sometimes called 'Gertrude the Great' to distinguish her from Gertrude of Hackeborn who was Abbess of Helfta when she was brought there as a child. Gertrude was one of the first exponents of devotion to the Sacred Heart.

Gregory of Nazianzus (329-389)

Gregory was one of the three great Cappadocian Fathers, a highly cultured man, and a life-long friend of St Basil. Desiring the contemplative life, Gregory became a monk, but somewhat against his will, was ordained, and eventually became a bishop. In 379 he was summoned to Constantinople to help in the controversy following the Council of Nicea. His five *Theological Orations* were widely acclaimed and earned him the title 'The Theologian'. Much of his writing is a celebration of the doctrine of the Trinity. Towards the end of his life he resigned his See, withdrew to live on a family estate, and wrote poetry. His most famous poem is an autobiographical song, a dialogue between the soul and God.

Gregory of Nyssa (*c*.330-394)

Gregory of Nyssa was born at Caesarea in what is now Turkey, the child of an aristocratic Christian family. Unlike his elder brother Basil, he was academically undistinguished, but ultimately proved to be the most original of the group of the theologians known as the Cappadocian Fathers. He was introduced to the spiritual life by his elder sister Macrina who exercised a formative influence upon him, and with whom he maintained close bonds of friendship throughout his life. It was she who, after the death of their father, converted the household into a sort of monastery on one of the family estates. Gregory married a deeply spiritual woman, Theosebia, and at first refused ordination, choosing to pursue a secular career. He was ordained only later in life, and in 372 was chosen to be Bishop of Nyssa. In the year 379 both his brother Basil and his sister Macrina died, and this deeply affected him; but out of this darkness emerged a profound spirituality. For Gregory, God is met not as an object to be understood, but as a mystery to be loved.

Gregory the Great (540-604)

Gregory was the son of a Roman senator. As a young man he pursued a governmental career, and in 573 was made Prefect of the city of Rome. Following the death of his father, however, he resigned his office, sold his inheritance, and became a monk. In 579 he was sent by the Pope to Constantinople to be his representative to the Patriarch. He returned to Rome in 586, and was himself elected Pope in 590. At a time of political turmoil, Gregory proved an astute administrator and diplomat, securing peace with the Lombards. His sermons and writings were pastorally oriented, as seen for example in his treatise on Christian leadership entitled *Pastoral Care*. His spirituality was animated by a dynamic of love and desire for God. Indeed, he is sometimes called the 'Doctor of desire'. For Gregory, desire was a metaphor for the journey into God.

Guerric of Igny (c.1070-1157)

Little is known of Guerric's early life. He seems to have lived a life of prayer and study at or near the cathedral of Tournai. At some point he became a Cistercian novice, and in 1138 was made Abbot of Igny, near Rheims. A number of his sermons have survived.

Herbert, George (1593-1633)

Born into the aristocratic Pembroke family, George Herbert went up to Cambridge in 1614, eventually becoming a Fellow of Trinity College. At the age of twenty-five, he became Public Orator in the University and then a Member of Parliament, apparently destined for a life at court. To everyone's surprise, he decided to be ordained and, after spending a time with his friend Nicholas Ferrar at Little Gidding, he was made deacon in 1626. He married in 1629, was priested in 1630 and given the cure of souls of the parish of Bemerton, near Salisbury, where he spent the rest of his short life. He wrote prolifically, his hymns still being popular throughout the English-speaking world. His treatise *The Country Parson* on the priestly life, and his poetry earned Herbert a leading place in English literature.

Herrick, Robert (1591-1674)

Robert Herrick was the son of a London goldsmith. At the comparatively late age of twenty-two, he went up to Cambridge, and was subsequently ordained. His only volume of verse was published in 1648.

Hilary of Poitiers (315-367)

Hilary was born at Poitiers. His family, though pagan, gave him an excellent education and he was proficient in Latin and Greek. After extensive personal study, he was baptized at the age of thirty. He was elected bishop of the city in 350 and immediately became caught up in the Arian controversy, himself asserting that mortals of this world were created to practise moral virtues, thus reflecting the One in whose image they are made, the eternal and creative first cause, God; and that Jesus Christ, the incarnate Son of God, is of one substance with the Father. His outstanding treatise *On the Trinity* led to his title of the 'Athanasius of the West'.

Hilton, Walter (1343-1396)

Walter Hilton studied Canon Law at Cambridge, but after a period as a hermit, joined the community of Augustinian Canons at Thurgarton in Nottinghamshire in about 1386. Highly regarded in his lifetime as a spiritual guide, he wrote in both Latin and English and translated several Latin devotional works. Controversy with Enthusiasts and with the Lollard movement gave a sharper definition to his exposition of the aims, methods and disciplines of traditional spirituality. Amongst his major works, *The Scale of Perfection* (Book Two) declares that contemplation, understood in a profoundly Trinitarian context as awareness of grace and sensitivity to the Spirit, may and should be sought by all serious Christians.

Hippolytus of Rome (*c*.170-*c*.236)

A leading theologian of the third century, Hippolytus wrote in Greek at a time when Latin was coming to prevail in the Christian community at Rome. His *Apostolic Tradition* was a code of regulations and discipline in the Church which includes eucharistic prayers which are the oldest known in the Roman Church. Theologically and socially, he was very conservative.

Hooker, Richard (*c*.1554-1600)

In his formative years, Richard Hooker came under the influence of John Jewel, Bishop of Salisbury, and through that influence went up to Corpus Christi College, Oxford, where he became a Fellow. He was ordained and then married, becoming a parish priest and, in 1585, Master of the Temple in London. Richard became one of the strongest advocates of the position of the Church of England and defended its 'middle way' between puritanism and papalism. His greatest work was *Of the Laws of Ecclesiastical Polity* which he wrote as the result of engaging in controversial debates. He showed Anglicanism as rooted firmly in Scripture as well as tradition, affirming its continuity with the pre-Reformation *Ecclesia Anglicana*, but now both catholic and reformed. Richard became a parish priest again near Canterbury and died there in the year 1600.

Ignatius of Antioch (*c*.35-*c*.107)

Ignatius was born probably in Syria and was either the second or third Bishop of Antioch, the third largest city in the Roman Empire. Nothing is known of his life bar his final journey under armed escort to Rome, where he was martyred in about the year 107. In the course of this journey, he met Polycarp in Smyrna, and wrote a number of letters to various Christian congregations which are among the greatest treasures of the primitive Church. In the face of persecution he appealed to his fellow Christians to maintain unity with their bishop at all costs. His letters reveal his passionate commitment to Christ, and how he longed 'to imitate the passion of my God'.

Innocent of Moscow (1797-1879)

Innocent was the greatest Russian missionary during the nineteenth century. For a major part of his life he served in eastern Siberia and Alaska, where he preached to the Eskimos and native Indians: he was the first Orthodox bishop to work on the American continent.

Irenaeus (*c*.130-*c*.200)

Irenaeus was probably a native of Smyrna. As a boy, he had heard Polycarp preach, who had in turn been a disciple of the apostle John. Irenaeus is thus one of the important connections between the apostolic Church and the second century. He studied at Rome, and later became a priest at Lyons in Gaul, succeeding as bishop upon the martyrdom of his predecessor in 177. He contended against the mythological, unhistorical beliefs of the Gnostics, giving positive value to the full humanity of the incarnate Christ, and affirmed the public teaching role of the episcopate to combat false doctrine. He is honoured as the first great Catholic theologian, one who drew upon the emerging traditions of East and West.

Isaac of Nineveh (seventh century)

Isaac was one of the greatest spiritual figures of the Eastern Church, his influence spreading in time to India and Russia. He was born on the shores of the Persian Gulf, and as a young man became a monk. At some point betwen 660 and 680 he was consecrated a bishop, but after only five months fled to the mountains to live a life of solitude. His *Ascetical Treatises* display a strong Syriac spirituality, with great emphasis upon the 'heart'.

Isidore of Seville (*c.*560-636)

Little is known of Isidore's early life. Following in the footsteps of his elder brother, he entered monastic life, and during this time read widely. He gained an encyclopaedic knowledge which was freely utilized by later medieval authors. Again following his brother, he became Archbishop of Seville in around 600. He was a distinguished writer, preacher and administrator.

Jerome (*c.*342-420)

Jerome was born on the Adriatic coast of Dalmatia. He studied at Rome, where he was baptized. He tried the life of a monk for a time, but unsuccessfully. Following a dream in which he stood before the judgement seat of God and was condemned for his faith in classics rather than Christ, he learned Hebrew the better to study the Scriptures. This, with his polished skills in rhetoric and mastery of Greek, enabled him to begin his life's work of translating the newly-canonized Bible into Latin which became the standard version for the Western Church for over a thousand years. He eventually settled at Bethlehem, where he founded a monastery and devoted the rest of his life to study.

John of the Cross (1542-1591)

Born to an impoverished noble family near Avila in Spain, Juan de Yepes was brought up by his widowed mother and went to a charity school. He worked as a nurse and received further education from the Jesuits before entering the Carmelite Order when he was twenty-one. Having distinguished himself at Salamanca University, he was ordained in 1567 and met Teresa of Avila soon afterwards. Small of stature, he made a great impression on her and she persuaded him to help with her reform of the Carmelite Order. His labours brought him into conflict with the religious authorities, and he was even imprisoned for a period, yet these experiences prompted some of his finest poetry and mystical writing. In particular, he described the 'dark night' of the soul as it is purified in its approach towards God.

Julian of Norwich (1373-1417)

In 1373, when she was thirty years old and suffering from what was considered to be a terminal illness, a woman of Norwich, whose own name is unrecorded, experienced a series of sixteen visions, which revealed aspects of the love of God. Following her recovery, she spent the next twenty years of her life pondering their meaning and recorded her conclusions in what became the first book written by a woman in English, *Revelations of Divine Love*. At an unknown point in her life, she became an anchoress attached to the church of St Julian in Norwich, and it was by this name of Julian that she came to be known to later generations.

Julian of Vezelay (1080-1160)

Julian was a Benedictine monk who in later life became abbot of his community at Vezelay in France. Some twenty-seven of his sermons have survived which reveal him to have been a man of wide learning, including knowledge of Plato and Greek philosophy.

Justin (c.100-c.165)

Justin was born at the beginning of the second century in Palestine. As a young man he explored many different philosophies before, at the age of thirty, embracing Christianity. He continued to wear the distinctive dress of a professional philosopher, and taught Christianity as a philosophy first at Ephesus, and later at Rome. He became an outstanding apologist for the Christian faith, and is honoured as the first Christian thinker to enter into serious dialogue with the other intellectual disciplines of his day, including Judaism. Justin always sought to reconcile the claims of faith and reason. It was at Rome in about 165 that he and some of his disciples were denounced as Christians, and beheaded. Traditionally, Justin is often surnamed 'Martyr' because of his two-fold witness to Christ, through his apologetic writings and his manner of death.

Ken, Thomas (1637-1711)

Thomas Ken was ordained priest in 1662 and worked first in a poor parish in the diocese of Winchester and then at Winchester College for ten years. He served as chaplain to Charles II for two years and was then consecrated Bishop of Bath and Wells. After the king's death and the accession of the Roman Catholic James II, the new king proposed to rescind the Restoration penal laws, but Thomas and six of his fellow bishops refused to comply with this and were imprisoned. Such was the integrity of Thomas that, when the king abandoned his throne and fled, and the king's Protestant daughter Mary was offered the throne, together with her husband William of Orange, Thomas felt unable in good conscience to forswear his living, anointed monarch. He was deprived of his See, along with many other non-jurors, as they became known. Thomas spent his final twenty years in quiet retirement, having renounced his rights to his bishopric. He wrote many hymns, still much used, and an *Exposition of the Church Catechism.*

Latimer, Hugh (c.1485-1555)

Hugh Latimer was educated at Cambridge, with an articulate and yet homely style of preaching which made him very popular in the university, and he received its commission to preach anywhere in England. He became a close adviser of Henry VIII after the latter's rift with the papacy and was appointed Bishop of Worcester in 1535. He lost the king's favour in 1540 over his refusal to sign Henry's 'Six Articles', designed to prevent the spread of Reformation doctrines, and resigned his See. He returned to favour on the accession of Edward VI but was imprisoned in the Tower of London when Queen Mary ascended the throne in 1553. He refused to recant any of his avowedly reformist views and was burnt at the stake in 1555.

Law, William (1686-1761)

William Law was educated at Emmanuel College, Cambridge and, after ordination as a deacon, became a Fellow of the College in 1711. When George I came to the throne in 1714, William declined to take the Oath of Allegiance, being a member of the Non-Juror party who believed the anointed, but deposed, monarch James II and his heirs should occupy the throne. He lost his fellowship but in 1728 he was made a priest, and in the same year published *A Serious Call to a Devout and Holy Life*, which together with his treatises *The Spirit of Love* and *The Spirit of Prayer,* much influenced such people as Samuel Johnson and John and Charles Wesley. In it he stresses the moral virtues, a personal prayer life and asceticism. He returned to his home town in 1740, where he led a life of devotion, simplicity and caring for the poor.

Leo the Great (d. 461)

Leo the Great became Pope in the year 440 and twice proved his bravery in saving the citizens of Rome from the invading barbarians. He was an eloquent and wise preacher, using simple gospel texts to proclaim the Christian faith, which still read very powerfully today. His administrative skills were unrivalled and he used the resources of the Church for the good of the people. Rather than further confuse Christians by entering into the controversy over the person of Christ, Leo spoke simply of the humility of Christ who was divine and human in his compassion, uniting Biblical images in prayer rather than dividing in debate. His *Tome,* delivered by his legates to the Council of Chalcedon in 451, became a standard of Christological orthodoxy.

Maximus of Turin (d. *c.*408)

Little is known of his life except that he was Bishop of Turin and died in the reign of Theodosius the Younger (408-23). Over one hundred of his sermons survive.

Mechtild of Magdeburg (*c.*1210-1280)

The writings for which Mechtild is known, speak of her experience of the love of God as it was revealed to her. This experience began when she was twelve years old. She responded to it by joining a community of Béguines at the age of about eighteen. After forty years, she moved to the Cistercian convent of Helfta and, in about 1270, completed her writings there. Helfta was a remarkable centre of learning at that time with other outstanding personalities in the community. She wrote with poetic sensitivity in direct and simple language of the exchange of love with God.

Melito of Sardis (d. c.190)

Melito was Bishop of Sardis in Lydia during the second half of the second century and was one of the 'great luminaries' of Christian Asia Minor. He was a prolific writer, but sadly, little of his work survives except his treatise *On the Pasch,* the theme of which is that the new Pasch has been inaugurated by Christ. The work is vibrant with the original meaning of the descent into hell.

More, Thomas (1478-1535)

Born in London in 1478,. Thomas More studied classics and law. His clear honesty and integrity impressed Henry VIII and he appointed Thomas as his Chancellor. He supported the king in his efforts to reform the clergy but disagreed over Henry's disputes with the papacy, caused by the king's desire to annul his marriage to Catherine of Aragon and to find another queen who might provide him with a male heir. Henry could stand no such act of defiance and imprisoned his Chancellor in the hope that he would renege. Thomas refused to take the Oath of the Act of Succession, which declared the king to be the only protector and supreme head of the Church in England, and was executed for treason in 1535, declaring that he died 'the king's good servant but God's first'.

Newman, John Henry (1801-1890)

John Henry Newman's intellectual brilliance saw him appointed to a Fellowship in Oxford at the young age of twenty-one. His Evangelical roots gradually gave way to a more Catholic view of the Church, particularly after liberal trends both in politics and theology appeared to undermine the Church of England's authority. Newman was one of the leaders of the Tractarians who defended the Church and he is associated especially with the idea of Anglicanism as a *via media* or middle way between Roman Catholicism and Protestantism. He continued to make an original and influential contribution to theology after he joined the Roman Catholic Church in 1845. He established an Oratorian community in Birmingham in 1849 and towards the end of his life was made a Cardinal.

Origen (c.185-c.254)

Origen was born in Egypt and became a leading representative of the Alexandrian school of theology. He was the most powerful mind of early Christianity, primarily a Biblical scholar who recognized a three-fold meaning to Scripture: literal, moral and allegorical. He edited the text of the Old Testament in six columns (the *Hexapala*) comparing the Hebrew text with various Greek translations. In his theological treatise *On Principles* he outlines the basic principles of the Christian concept of the world. He was a mystic, and wrote two key ascetical works *On Prayer* and *An Exhortation to Martyrdom,* both of which were read widely. Sadly, the Greek originals of many of his works, including his extensive Biblical commentaries, have been lost. Some are known only now in fragmentary (poor) Latin translation.

Proclus of Constantinople (d. 446)

Proclus was a much acclaimed preacher in Constantinople. He was a key defender of the ascription *Theotokos* (God-bearer) to the Blessed Virgin Mary against

Nestorius and his followers. Eventually in 434 he became Patriarch and was respected for his moderation. The introduction of the *Trisagion* into the liturgy is attributed to him.

Prudentius (348-*c*.410)
Aurelius Clemens Prudentius was Spanish by birth. He was a lawyer by training who after a lifetime of distinguished civil service under the emperor Theodosius, withdrew from court, and at the age of 57 devoted himself exclusively to writing Latin poetry on Christian themes. He was called the Virgil and the Horace of the Christians.

Sophronius of Jerusalem (*c*.560-638)
Sophronius was born in Damascus. He became a monk first of all in Egypt, later near the Jordan, and finally (from 619) in Jerusalem. In 634 he was elected Patriarch of Jerusalem where he was concerned to promulgate the teaching of the Council of Chalcedon about the two natures in Christ. Some of his sermons and poems have survived, many of which reflect the liturgical customs of the Jerusalem Church. Just before he died he witnessed the capture of Jerusalem by the Saracens under Caliph Omar in 637.

Southwell, Robert (*c*.1561-1595)
Robert Southwell was born in Norfolk of a Catholic family, and educated abroad at Douai, Paris, and Rome. He became a Jesuit and returned to England in 1586 as chaplain to the Countess of Arundel. He was arrested in 1592 and executed three years later. His poetry displays a note of intense adoration.

Spenser, Edmund (*c*.1552-1599)
Edmund Spenser was educated at Cambridge. His poetry was highly acclaimed, but in 1579 was sent to Ireland as Secretary to the Lord Deputy. In 1589 he returned to London where he presented to Elizabeth I his poem *The Faerie Queene*. Other poems followed. He died in 1599.

Taylor, Jeremy (1613-1667)
Jeremy Taylor was born and educated in Cambridge. He was ordained in 1633 and, as the Civil War got under way, he became a chaplain with the Royalist forces. He was captured and imprisoned briefly but after his release went to Wales, where the Earl of Carbery gave him refuge. He wrote prolifically whilst there, notably *The Rule and Exercise of Holy Living* in 1650 and of *Holy Dying* the following year. In 1658 he went to Ireland to lecture and two years later was made Bishop of Down and Connor.

Teilhard de Chardin, Pierre (1881-1955)
Marie-Joseph-Pierre Teilhard de Chardin was born and educated in France. He was a Jesuit and a distinguished paleontologist who advocated an evolutionary hypothesis that synthesized modern scientific approaches and traditional Christian theology.

Temple, William (1881-1944)

William Temple was born in Exeter. His father was Bishop of Exeter and later Archbishop of Canterbury. William excelled in academic studies and developed into a philosopher and theologian of significance. After ordination, he quickly made a mark in the Church and at forty became a bishop. Within a decade he was Archbishop of York. He is especially remembered for his ecumenical efforts and also for his concern with social issues, contributing notably to the debate which led to the creation of State welfare provision after the Second World War. He died in 1944, only two years after his translation to the See of Canterbury.

Tertullian (c.160-c.225)

Tertullian was the first major figure in Latin theology. He was born in Carthage of pagan parents, trained as a lawyer, and became a Christian in about 193. It is uncertain whether or not he was ever ordained. He produced a series of significant controversial and apologetic writings. He is particularly noted for his ability to coin new Latin terms to translate the emerging theological vocabulary of the Greek-speaking Eastern Church. He was a man of passionate feeling, full of paradox, with a tendency to extremes. This led him in about 207 to espouse Montanism-a charismatic movement that claimed to be inaugurating the age of the Spirit.

Theodore of Studios (759-826)

Theodore was a leading monastic reformer who in later life became Abbot of Studios at Constantinople. Often in conflict with the Imperial Court over corrupt practices, he was exiled twice. He was a man of austere spirituality and iron will. A number of his spiritual orations have survived.

Theodoret of Cyr (c.393-c.466)

A native of Antioch, Theodoret was educated in its monasteries. In 423 he was consecrated Bishop of Cyr in Syria, and governed his diocese with distinction. He proved an indefatigable defender of the Christian faith, though in his early years, some of his theological teaching was held in question.

Theophan the Recluse (1815-1894)

Theophan the Recluse was known in the world as George Govorov. The son of a parish priest, he was born in central Russia, and followed his father into the priesthood. On graduating he took the habit. Intellectually gifted, he was made professor at the seminary in St Petersburg, and in 1859 was consecrated bishop. His heart, however, was never in diocesan administration, and after only seven years he resigned his See, and retired to a monastery at Vyshen where he remained until his death some twenty-eight years later. He divided his time between prayer and literary work.

Theophilus of Antioch (second century)

Theophilus was Bishop of Antioch in the latter half of the second century, and one of the Christian 'Apologists' – defenders of Christianity who sought to communicate the faith to a hostile pagan society. Of his writings, only his

'Apology', a treatise in three books written to Autolycus, has survived. The idea of men and women made in the image of God is a crucial theme in his writing.

Thomas à Kempis (c.1380-1471)
According to tradition Thomas Hemerken, from Kempen near Cologne, was the author of *The Imitation of Christ*. He joined the Canons Regular and was a much sought after spiritual adviser. His writings – and most notably *The Imitation* – are all pervaded by a strong devotional spirit.

Traherne, Thomas (c.1636-1674)
After studying in Oxford and being a parish priest for ten years, Thomas Traherne became private chaplain to the Lord Keeper of the Seals of Charles II. Thomas was one of the English Metaphysical poets and yet, in his lifetime, only one of his works was ever printed. It was at the beginning of the twentieth century that his poems, until then in manuscript, were published and he took on the mantle of an Anglican Divine. His poetry is probably the most celebratory among his fellow Metaphysical poets, with little mention of sin and suffering and concentrating more on the glory of creation, to the extent that some regard his writings as on the edge of pantheism.

Underhill, Evelyn (1875-1941)
Evelyn Underhill was in her thirties before she began to explore religion. At first, she wrote on the mystics, most notably in her book *Mysticism*, published in 1911. Her spiritual journey brought her in 1921 back to the Church of England, in which she had been baptized and confirmed. From the mid-1920s, she became highly-regarded as a retreat conductor and an influential spiritual director. Of her many books *Worship*, published in 1936, embodied her approach to what she saw as the mystery of faith.

Vincent of Lérins (d. before 450)
Little is known of Vincent's life beyond the fact that he was a monk of the island-monastery of Lérins. His *Commonitorium* was written to provide a guide to the determination of the true Catholic faith. It embodies the famous 'Vincentian Canon'. Despite his emphasis on tradition, Vincent in fact maintained that the final ground for doctrine was Scripture. The authority of the Church was to be invoked only to guarantee the right interpretation of Scripture.

Weil, Simone (1909-1943)
Simone Weil was a French Jewish writer, a social and political activist of international reputation. She was a religious seeker who towards the end of her short life was deeply attracted to Christianity, and wrote sensitively and profoundly about 'waiting on God'.

Wesley, John (1703-1791)
Born at Epworth Rectory in Lincolnshire, John Wesley was the son of an Anglican clergyman and a Puritan mother. He entered Holy Orders and, following a religious experience in 1738, began an itinerant ministry which

Biographical Notes

recognized no parish boundaries. This resulted, after his death, in the development of a world-wide Methodist Church. His spirituality involved an Arminian affirmation of grace, frequent communion and a disciplined corporate search for holiness. His open-air preaching, concern for education and for the poor, liturgical revision, organization of local societies and training of preachers provided a firm basis for Christian growth and mission in England.

Westcott, Brooke Foss (1825-1901)

Born in 1825, Westcott was first ordained and then became a master at Harrow School. Whilst there, he published a series of scholarly works on the Bible, his expertise eventually leading to his election as Regius Professor of Divinity at the University of Cambridge in 1870. With Fenton Hort and J. B. Lightfoot, he led a revival in British Biblical studies and theology. He became influential too in the field of Anglican social thought and was significant in the founding of the Clergy Training School in Cambridge (later renamed Westcott House in his memory). In 1890, he was consecrated Bishop of Durham, where he died in 1901.

William of St Thierry (c.1085-1148)

William was born at Liège. He entered the Benedictine Abbey of Rheims in 1113, and in 1119 or 1120 was elected Abbot of St Thierry nearby. Before his election as abbot, he had already made the acquaintance of Bernard of Clairvaux, and in 1135 he resigned his abbacy and went to join a group of Cistercian monks from Igny. He wrote a number of influential treatises, including several expositions of the Song of Songs. His last years were devoted to a synthesis of his doctrine and experience, known as *The Golden Epistle*.

ACKNOWLEDGEMENTS

A. COPYRIGHT MATERIAL

The Author and Publishers are grateful for permission to reproduce material under copyright. They are grateful in particular for the cooperation of:

The International Committee for English in the Liturgy Inc., (ICEL), for permission to reproduce the English translation of the non-biblical readings from the *Roman Catholic Liturgy of the Hours,* American Edition; © 1974; all rights reserved; adapted with permission; and
The Church Hymnal Corporation of the Episcopal Church of the United States of America, for permission to adopt the modifications in the ICEL texts employed by J. Robert Wright in *Readings for the Daily Office from the Early Church,* New York, 1991 and *They Still Speak,* New York, 1993, to accord with Anglican usage (see Wright, *Readings for the Daily Office from the Early Church,* pp.515-23).

Every effort has been made to trace the copyright owners of material included in this book. The Author and Publishers would be grateful if any omissions or inaccuracies in these acknowledgements could be brought to their attention for correction in any future edition. They are grateful to the following copyright holders:

A & C Black, for an extract from *The Shape of the Liturgy,* by Gregory Dix, 1945.
Addison Wesley Longman, for extracts from *The Vision of God,* by Kenneth Kirk, 1931.
Sr Maria Boulding OSB, for extracts from her book *The Coming of God,* 2nd edition, London, 1994.
Dr Sebastian Brock, for his translations of Ephem of Syria contained in *The Luminous Eye: The Spiritual World Vision of St Ephrem the Syrian,* Kalamazoo, Michigan, 1985. © C.I.I.S. Rome.
Burns & Oates, for extracts from the 1972 edition of *New Seeds of Contemplation,* by Thomas Merton, New York, 1961; London, 1962 & 1972; new Anglicised edition, Tunbridge Wells, 1999; © Abbey of Gethsemani.
Mr D. I. Campell, on behalf of the estate of John Macmurray, for an extract from *Reason and Emotion,* by John Macmurray, London, 1935.

Church House Publishing, for permission to use material translated by the author of this book, first published in *Spiritual Classics from the Early Church*, 1995.

Cistercian Publications Inc., Kalamazoo, Michigan, for extracts from *The Works of Aelred of Rievaulx I*, translated by Penelope Lawson CSMV and Mary Paul Macpherson OCSO, 1971; *The Works of William of St Thierry I*, translated by Penelope Lawson CSMV, 1971; *On Spiritual Friendship*, by Aelred of Rievaulx, translated by Mary Eugenia Laker SSND, 1977; *The Discourses of Dorotheos of Gaza*, translated by Eric Wheeler, 1977.

Constable & Co., for extracts from *Peter Abelard*, by Helen Waddell, 1933; and from *True Wilderness*, by Harry Williams, 1965.

Cowley Publications Inc., for an extract from *A Season of the Spirit*, by Br Martin Smith SSJE, London & Cambridge, Mass., 1991.

Curtis Brown Ltd, acting for the Abbey of Gethsemani and the estate of Thomas Merton, for extracts from the essays of Thomas Merton contained in *The Power and Meaning of Love*, London, 1976; previously published as *Disputed Questions*, New York, 1953.

Darton Longman Todd Ltd, for extracts from *The Experience of Prayer*, by Sebastian Moore and Kevin Macguire, 1969; *Love's Endeavour, Love's Expense*, by W. H. Vanstone, 1977; *Resurrection*, by Rowan Williams, 1982; *Ways of Imperfection*, by Simon Tugwell, 1984; *Community and Growth*, by Jean Vanier, revised edition 1989; *Eyes to See, and Ears to Hear*, by David Lonsdale, 1990; *The Gift of Self*, by Heather Ward, 1994; and from *Befriending our Desires*, by Philip Sheldrake, 1994.

Editions du Seuil and HarperCollins jointly, for extracts from *Le Milieu Divin*, by Teilhard de Chardin, 1957; ET © Collins, London, 1960.

Faber and Faber Ltd, for extracts from *The Throne of David* by Gabriel Hebert, 1941; *The Art of Prayer*, translated by E. Kadloubovsky & E. M. Palmer, 1966; and from *The Lenten Triodion*, translated by Mother Mary & Archimandrite Kalistos Ware, 1978.

Faith Press Ltd, for an extract from *Said or Sung* by Austin Farrer, 1960.

Fount, for an extract from *Gateway to Hope*, by Maria Boulding, 1985.

HarperCollins Publishers Ltd, for an extract from from *Transpositions and other Essays*, by C. S. Lewis, 1949.

Susan R. Holman, for extracts from her translation of some of the homilies of Gregory of Nyssa and Basil the Great, included in the appendix to *The body of the poor in fourth century Cappadocia: Seven Sermons on Hunger, Sickness and Penury*, Brown University, 1998.

Longmans, for an extract from *The Glory of God and the Transfiguration of Christ*, by A. M. Ramsey, 1949.

Lura Media, Sandiego, for a poem by Joyce Rupp in *The Star in my Heart,* 1990.

Macmillan Press Ltd, for two poems from *H'm* by R. S. Thomas, 1972.

Mitchell Beazley Ltd, for an extract from *True Resurrection,* by Harry Williams, 1972.

Mowbray, an imprint of Cassell plc, for extracts from *The Light of Christ* by Evelyn Underhill, 1944.

Paulist Press, Mahwah, New Jersey, for extracts from *Walter Hilton: The Scale of Perfection* translated by John Clark & Rosemary Dorward, 1991; *Bonaventure: The Tree of Life,* translated by Ewert Cousins, 1978; *Catherine of Siena: Dialogue* translated by Suzanne Noffke OP, 1980; *Francis and Clare: The Complete Works,* translated by R. J. Armstrong and Ignatius Brady, 1982; *The Ladder of Divine Ascent,* by John Climacus, translated by Colm Luibheid & Norman Russell, 1982; *Gertrude of Helfta: Herald of Divine Love,* translated by Margaret Winkworth, 1993; *Ephrem of Syria: Hymns,* translated by Kathleen E. McVey, 1989. In the above, all translations are © their translators.

Penguin Books Ltd., for extracts from *The Prayers and Meditations of St Anselm,* translated by Sr Benedicta Ward SLG, 1973; *Revelations of Divine Love* by Julian of Norwich, translated by Clifton Wolters, 1966; and *The Cloud of Unknowing,* translated by Clifton Wolters, 1971.

The Perpetua Press, for a poem by Rowan Williams, 1996.

Routledge, for extracts from Simone Weil, *Waiting on God,* translated by Emma Craufurd, 1951; and *Modern Man in Search of a Soul,* by C. J. Jung, translated by W. S. Dell & Cary F. Baynes, 1984.

Margaret Saunders, for a hitherto unpublished poem.

SCM Press, for extracts from *The Cost of Discipleship,* by Dietrich Bonhoeffer, translated by R. H. Fuller, 1959; *Life Together,* by Dietrich Bonhoeffer, translated from fifth edition (1949) by John W. Doberstein, 1954; *Letters and Papers from Prison*; 3rd English edition by Reginald Fuller, Frank Clarke, John Bowden & others, 1970; and *The Go-Between God,* by John V. Taylor, 1973.

SLG Press, for an extract from *The Wisdom of the Desert Fathers (Anonymous Series),* translated by Sr Benedicta Ward SLG, 1975.

SPCK for an extract from *Celtic Christian Spirituality,* edited by Oliver Davies & Fiona Bowie, 1995.

Varroville Press, Australia, for a translation by Sr Marjorie Flower OCD of a poem by John of the Cross.

B. PERSONAL

Without the support and generosity of friends and benefactors this book would never have got written. It is impossible to mention everybody by name, but particular thanks should be made to the following:

The Master and Fellows of Trinity College, Cambridge; and among them particularly to Dr & Mrs Arnold Browne and Dr & Mrs Alan Weeds for their generous hospitality during the academical year 1988-9; and to Dr Grae Worster for his patience with the Author's modest computing skills;

Canon & Mrs John Bowker, Lady Butler, and the Right Reverend Anthony Russell, and the Right Reverend & Mrs John Dennis, for their generous support;

Ms Sylvia Brand for her friendship and for assisting in the correction of the typescript;

Dr Petà Dunstan, Librarian of the Divinity Faculty, University of Cambridge, for her time and expertise in locating the right reference books;

Ms Margot Edwards for her professional skill in negotiating the intricacies of copyright law and permissions;

Mrs Christine Smith, Publisher at Canterbury Press Norwich, for her enthusiasm for the project;

The American Congregation of The Society of St John the Evangelist for their friendship and support in a time of transition;

Br Tristam Holland SSF for his friendship and collaboration in the project.